THE PAPERS OF ULYSSES S. GRANT

THE PAPERS OF

ULYSSES S. GRANT

Volume 22:
June 1, 1871–January 31, 1872
Edited by John Y. Simon

ASSISTANT EDITORS
William M. Ferraro
Aaron M. Lisec

TEXTUAL EDITOR
Sue E. Dotson

SOUTHERN ILLINOIS UNIVERSITY PRESS

CARBONDALE AND EDWARDSVILLE

Library of Congress Cataloging in Publication Data (Revised)

Grant, Ulysses Simpson, Pres. U.S., 1822–1885.
   The papers of Ulysses S. Grant.

   Prepared under the auspices of the Ulysses S. Grant Association.

   Bibliographical footnotes.
   CONTENTS: v. 1. 1837–1861—v. 2. April–September 1861.—v. 3. October 1, 1861–January 7, 1862.—v. 4. January 8–March 31, 1862.—v. 5. April 1–August 31, 1862.—v. 6. September 1–December 8, 1862.—v. 7. December 9, 1862—March 31, 1863.—v. 8. April 1–July 6, 1863.—v. 9. July 7–December 31, 1863.—v. 10. January 1–May 31, 1864.—v. 11. June 1–August 15, 1864.—v. 12. August 16–November 15, 1864.—v. 13. November 16, 1864–February 20, 1865.—v. 14. February 21–April 30, 1865.—v. 15. May 1–December 31, 1865.—v. 16. 1866.—v. 17. January 1–September 30, 1867.—v. 18. October 1, 1867–June 30, 1868.—v. 19. July 1, 1868–October 31, 1869.—v. 20. November 1, 1869–October 31, 1870.—v. 21. November 1, 1870–May 31, 1871.—v. 22. June 1, 1871–January 31, 1872.

   1. Grant, Ulysses Simpson, Pres. U.S., 1822–1885. 2. United States—History—Civil War, 1861–1865—Campaigns and battles—Sources. 3. United States—Politics and government—1869–1877—Sources. 4. Presidents—United States—Biography. 5. Generals—United States—Biography. I. Simon, John Y., ed. II. Ulysses S. Grant Association.
E660.G756   1967   973.8'2'0924   67-10725
ISBN 0-8093-2198-X (v. 22)

65.00

Contents

Introduction

———

Ulysses S. Grant critically surveyed politics as the time approached for nomination conventions for the next presidential election. Obviously a candidate, Grant skirted the issue and certainly expressed no pleasure at the thought of a second term as president: "Who ever has the place will have a slaves life." Despite eagerly anticipating life after the White House, Grant maintained "a deep interest in the republican party keeping controll of affairs until the results of the war are acquiesced in by all political parties." He expressed scorn for "disorganizers" within the Republican party like U.S. Senator Carl Schurz of Missouri and Horace Greeley, editor of the *New York Tribune*, who disrupted unity and imperiled prospects of electoral success; and Grant harbored special enmity for another critic, U.S. Senator Charles Sumner of Massachusetts: "I feel a greater contempt for him than for any other man in the Senate."

The approaching campaign clearly influenced Grant's public and private actions. Positioning himself as "the President of the whole country, and not as the representative of any party or section" and wielding patronage to heal divisions or to augment strengths, Grant maneuvered for political advantage. Yet factional confrontations and governmental crises, escalating to the point of violence in Louisiana, Arkansas, and New Mexico Territory, defeated Grant's efforts to increase harmony within Republican ranks and to diminish differences among citizens. While he remained committed to friends, his removal of Thomas Murphy as collector of customs in New York City, and Willard Warner as collector of customs in Mobile, showed that Grant could cut his losses when the political price of loyalty became too high.

Grant's support for civil service reform ran counter to his demonstrated willingness to use patronage as a tool.

Nothing in the nation seemed calm or settled. The Ku Klux Klan terrorized locales in virtually every former slave state. Severe outbursts in South Carolina and North Carolina compelled Grant to invoke his extraordinary powers under recent legislation and to order in troops. Clashes between Apaches and settlers in the southwest put advocates of Grant's "humane policy towards the indians" at odds with white residents and Army officers. Grant struggled to find middle ground without noticeable success. When Ely S. Parker resigned as commissioner of Indian Affairs following corruption charges, Grant vouched for his beleaguered friend's "integrity and ability," and reaffirmed his own commitment to a policy that tended "to the civilization of the Indian race." Natural disasters, notably the "terrible scourge" of the Chicago fire, increased burdens.

Unrest within the cabinet posed additional challenges. Grant counted heavily on Secretary of State Hamilton Fish for advice in all areas of foreign policy and especially to conduct the intricate diplomacy connected with the Alabama Claims arbitration. Fish's shrewdness and tact saved Grant from reviving Santo Domingo annexation efforts or exacerbating already troubled relations with Spain over Cuba. Fish also displayed diplomatic deftness in engineering the controversial recall of Russian minister Constantin Catacazy. His intention to withdraw from the cabinet for reasons of health worried Grant. Unable to ascertain a suitable replacement, Grant, to his great relief, convinced Fish to remain in office. Attorney General Amos T. Akerman, on the other hand, fell victim to political pressures. Fearing "the questions that will be asked, and the Speculations that will be indulged in," Grant promptly nominated George H. Williams, former governor of Oregon and United States senator, as Akerman's successor. The change quieted those who believed that Akerman had pursued the Ku Klux Klan overzealously. A jurisdictional feud between Secretary of the Treasury George S. Boutwell and Alfred Pleasonton, commissioner of Internal Revenue, resulted in Pleasonton's messy removal.

Grant secured some respite when he turned from public to private concerns. Though his farm in St. Louis did not make money, he wrote its manager frequently, taking interest in details as minute as spreading manure, constructing a lime kiln, and designing a stable. When General William T. Sherman decided to tour Europe beginning fall 1871, Grant sent along as an aide his oldest son Frederick, recently graduated from West Point and working as a railroad engineer in the Rocky Mountains. Grant wrote with fatherly pride to his sister Mary Grant Cramer in Copenhagen: "You will find him a well grown, and much improved, boy." For his son's spending money, Grant lined up a generous letter of credit with his Philadelphia banker friend Anthony J. Drexel. This indulgence may have stretched Grant's resources because soon afterward he asked Adolph E. Borie, former secretary of the navy and another Philadelphia friend, for a $6,000 loan. Borie complied with the request swiftly and graciously, but Grant must have disliked juggling personal finances.

Other concerns pressed upon Grant. Lacking time but not inclination, he fulfilled an obligation as trustee of the John A. Rawlins estate and guardian of the minor children to suggest new arrangements when Mrs. Rawlins decided to remarry. As 1871 closed, Grant's father, postmaster at Covington, Kentucky, collapsed at the office. Jesse Root Grant rallied but his health remained tenuous. Grant obtained relief from cares during leisurely trips to his seaside cottage at Long Branch, New Jersey, and through visits from friends and relatives.

At no point, however, could Grant fully disengage from political calculation or conflict. A trip through Ohio and the midwest to visit family and childhood acquaintances and another to the Maine border with Canada to celebrate a railroad opening included frequent public appearances and speeches. Newspapers followed his movements carefully and speculated on the meaning of his unusually spare pronouncements. People pinned hopes or hatreds on Grant. Recognizing the unfinished work of his presidency, Grant pressed on with a dogged sense of responsibility.

We are indebted to Timothy Connelly and Michael T. Meier for assistance in searching the National Archives; to Harriet F. Simon for proofreading; and to Andy Gannon, Steve Swearingin, and Monica Tomaszewski, graduate students at Southern Illinois University, for research assistance.

Financial support for the period during which this volume was prepared came from Southern Illinois University, the National Endowment for the Humanities, and the National Historical Publications and Records Commission.

JOHN Y. SIMON

February 1996

Editorial Procedure

―――

1. Editorial Insertions

A. Words or letters in roman type within brackets represent editorial reconstruction of parts of manuscripts torn, mutilated, or illegible.

B. [. . .] or [— — —] within brackets represent lost material which cannot be reconstructed. The number of dots represents the approximate number of lost letters; dashes represent lost words.

C. Words in *italic* type within brackets represent material such as dates which were not part of the original manuscript.

D. Other material crossed out is indicated by ~~cancelled type~~.

E. Material raised in manuscript, as "4th," has been brought in line, as "4th."

2. Symbols Used to Describe Manuscripts

AD	Autograph Document
ADS	Autograph Document Signed
ADf	Autograph Draft
ADfS	Autograph Draft Signed
AES	Autograph Endorsement Signed
AL	Autograph Letter
ALS	Autograph Letter Signed

ANS	Autograph Note Signed
D	Document
DS	Document Signed
Df	Draft
DfS	Draft Signed
ES	Endorsement Signed
LS	Letter Signed

3. Military Terms and Abbreviations

Act.	Acting
Adjt.	Adjutant
AG	Adjutant General
AGO	Adjutant General's Office
Art.	Artillery
Asst.	Assistant
Bvt.	Brevet
Brig.	Brigadier
Capt.	Captain
Cav.	Cavalry
Col.	Colonel
Co.	Company
C.S.A.	Confederate States of America
Dept.	Department
Div.	Division
Gen.	General
Hd. Qrs.	Headquarters
Inf.	Infantry
Lt.	Lieutenant
Maj.	Major
Q. M.	Quartermaster
Regt.	Regiment or regimental
Sgt.	Sergeant
USMA	United States Military Academy, West Point, N.Y.
Vols.	Volunteers

4. Short Titles and Abbreviations

ABPC	*American Book Prices Current* (New York, 1895–)
Badeau	Adam Badeau, *Grant in Peace. From Appomattox to Mount McGregor* (Hartford, Conn., 1887)
CG	*Congressional Globe.* Numbers following represent the Congress, session, and page.
J. G. Cramer	Jesse Grant Cramer, ed., *Letters of Ulysses S. Grant to his Father and his Youngest Sister, 1857–78* (New York and London, 1912)
DAB	*Dictionary of American Biography* (New York, 1928–36)
Foreign Relations	*Papers Relating to the Foreign Relations of the United States* (Washington, 1869–)
Garland	Hamlin Garland, *Ulysses S. Grant: His Life and Character* (New York, 1898)
Julia Grant	John Y. Simon, ed., *The Personal Memoirs of Julia Dent Grant* (New York, 1975)
HED	*House Executive Documents*
HMD	*House Miscellaneous Documents*
HRC	*House Reports of Committees.* Numbers following *HED, HMD,* or *HRC* represent the number of the Congress, the session, and the document.
Ill. AG Report	J. N. Reece, ed., *Report of the Adjutant General of the State of Illinois* (Springfield, 1900)
Johnson, Papers	LeRoy P. Graf and Ralph W. Haskins, eds., *The Papers of Andrew Johnson* (Knoxville, 1967–)
Lewis	Lloyd Lewis, *Captain Sam Grant* (Boston, 1950)
Lincoln, Works	Roy P. Basler, Marion Dolores Pratt, and Lloyd A. Dunlap, eds., *The Collected Works of Abraham Lincoln* (New Brunswick, 1953–55)
Memoirs	*Personal Memoirs of U. S. Grant* (New York, 1885–86)
Nevins, Fish	Allan Nevins, *Hamilton Fish: The Inner History of the Grant Administration* (New York, 1936)
O.R.	*The War of the Rebellion: A Compilation of the Official Records of the Union and Confederate Armies* (Washington, 1880–1901)

O.R. (Navy)   *Official Records of the Union and Confederate Navies in the War of the Rebellion* (Washington, 1894–1927). Roman numerals following *O.R.* or *O.R.* (Navy) represent the series and the volume.

PUSG   John Y. Simon, ed., *The Papers of Ulysses S. Grant* (Carbondale and Edwardsville, 1967–)

Richardson   Albert D. Richardson, *A Personal History of Ulysses S. Grant* (Hartford, Conn., 1868)

SED   *Senate Executive Documents*

SMD   *Senate Miscellaneous Documents*

SRC   *Senate Reports of Committees.* Numbers following *SED, SMD,* or *SRC* represent the number of the Congress, the session, and the document.

USGA Newsletter   *Ulysses S. Grant Association Newsletter*

Young   John Russell Young, *Around the World with General Grant* (New York, 1879)

5. Location Symbols

CLU   University of California at Los Angeles, Los Angeles, Calif.

CoHi   Colorado State Historical Society, Denver, Colo.

CSmH   Henry E. Huntington Library, San Marino, Calif.

CSt   Stanford University, Stanford, Calif.

CtY   Yale University, New Haven, Conn.

CU-B   Bancroft Library, University of California, Berkeley, Calif.

DLC   Library of Congress, Washington, D.C. Numbers following DLC-USG represent the series and volume of military records in the USG papers.

DNA   National Archives, Washington, D.C. Additional numbers identify record groups.

IaHA   Iowa State Department of History and

	Archives, Des Moines, Iowa.
I-ar	Illinois State Archives, Springfield, Ill.
IC	Chicago Public Library, Chicago, Ill.
ICarbS	Southern Illinois University, Carbondale, Ill.
ICHi	Chicago Historical Society, Chicago, Ill.
ICN	Newberry Library, Chicago, Ill.
ICU	University of Chicago, Chicago, Ill.
IHi	Illinois State Historical Library, Springfield, Ill.
In	Indiana State Library, Indianapolis, Ind.
InFtwL	Lincoln National Life Foundation, Fort Wayne, Ind.
InHi	Indiana Historical Society, Indianapolis, Ind.
InNd	University of Notre Dame, Notre Dame, Ind.
InU	Indiana University, Bloomington, Ind.
KHi	Kansas State Historical Society, Topeka, Kan.
MdAN	United States Naval Academy Museum, Annapolis, Md.
MeB	Bowdoin College, Brunswick, Me.
MH	Harvard University, Cambridge, Mass.
MHi	Massachusetts Historical Society, Boston, Mass.
MiD	Detroit Public Library, Detroit, Mich.
MiU-C	William L. Clements Library, University of Michigan, Ann Arbor, Mich.
MoSHi	Missouri Historical Society, St. Louis, Mo.
NHi	New-York Historical Society, New York, N.Y.
NIC	Cornell University, Ithaca, N.Y.
NjP	Princeton University, Princeton, N.J.
NjR	Rutgers University, New Brunswick, N.J.
NN	New York Public Library, New York, N.Y.
NNP	Pierpont Morgan Library, New York, N.Y.
NRU	University of Rochester, Rochester, N.Y.
OClWHi	Western Reserve Historical Society, Cleveland, Ohio.
OFH	Rutherford B. Hayes Library, Fremont, Ohio.
OHi	Ohio Historical Society, Columbus, Ohio.
OrHi	Oregon Historical Society, Portland, Ore.

PCarlA	U.S. Army Military History Institute, Carlisle Barracks, Pa.
PHi	Historical Society of Pennsylvania, Philadelphia, Pa.
PPRF	Rosenbach Foundation, Philadelphia, Pa.
RPB	Brown University, Providence, R.I.
TxHR	Rice University, Houston, Tex.
USG 3	Maj. Gen. Ulysses S. Grant 3rd, Clinton, N.Y.
USMA	United States Military Academy Library, West Point, N.Y.
ViHi	Virginia Historical Society, Richmond, Va.
ViU	University of Virginia, Charlottesville, Va.
WHi	State Historical Society of Wisconsin, Madison, Wis.
Wy-Ar	Wyoming State Archives and Historical Department, Cheyenne, Wyo.
WyU	University of Wyoming, Laramie, Wyo.

Chronology

June 1, 1871–January 31, 1872

⸻

JUNE 1. USG designated George W. Curtis to head a commission to study civil service reforms.

JUNE 1. USG and family left for their summer home at Long Branch.

JUNE 3. USG and Nellie Grant went to New York City to see USG's sister Mary Grant Cramer embark for Europe.

JUNE 5. Interviewed at Long Branch, USG reflected on his decision to leave the army to run for president.

JUNE 6–13. USG and family at West Point. On June 12, Frederick Dent Grant graduated from USMA.

JUNE 15–16. USG at Washington, D.C. On June 16, USG and cabinet discussed a Korean attack on a U.S. naval and diplomatic expedition.

JUNE 17. The U.S. and Great Britain exchanged ratifications of the Treaty of Washington at London. On July 4, USG published the treaty.

JUNE 22. USG and Julia Dent Grant were guests of Abel R. and Virginia Grant Corbin (USG's sister) at Elizabeth, N.J.

JUNE 27. USG attended commencement at Princeton.

JUNE 28–29. USG and Frederick Grant at Washington, D.C. On June 29, USG held a cabinet meeting.

JULY 6. U.S. Senator Roscoe Conkling of N.Y. visited USG at Long Branch.

JULY 13. USG accepted the resignation of Ely S. Parker, commissioner of Indian Affairs.

JULY 14. USG ordered the military to intervene in hostilities between settlers and Apaches.

JULY 17. USG and family toured Fort Hamilton in New York harbor.

JULY 19. USG visited Staatsburg, N.Y., on the Hudson River.

JULY 27. USG went to Philadelphia to see Frederick Grant depart for a civil engineering position in the West.

JULY 30. USG investigated rumors of diseased horses on his St. Louis farm.

AUG. 1–2. At Washington, D.C., USG met the German, Dutch, and Italian ministers.

AUG. 4. USG asked Vice President Schuyler Colfax to replace Secretary of State Hamilton Fish, who wished to resign.

AUG. 8. During a brief visit to Washington, D.C., USG appointed Charles Francis Adams as U.S. arbitrator to the Geneva tribunal, and suspended Alfred Pleasonton, commissioner of Internal Revenue.

AUG. 10. Fish and his wife Julia visited USG at Long Branch.

AUG. 26. Gen. William T. Sherman visited USG at Long Branch.

AUG. 31–SEPT. 1. USG at Washington, D.C.

SEPT. 12–17. USG and family toured Pa. and visited the oil regions.

SEPT. 18–22. After spending two days in Cincinnati, USG visited relatives in Brown and Clermont counties, Ohio.

SEPT. 23. USG visited his father Jesse Root Grant at Covington, Ky.

SEPT. 26. USG traveled to Leavenworth, Kan., for the opening of the Chicago and Southwestern Railroad.

SEPT. 28–29. USG at Galena.

SEPT. 30. USG arrived at Chicago and stayed with his brother Orvil Grant. On Oct. 2, USG and Julia Grant held separate receptions at a Chicago hotel.

OCT. 3. USG visited a home for disabled soldiers at Dayton.

OCT. 4–5. USG at Pittsburgh.

OCT. 6. USG attended the Maryland Agricultural Fair at Frederick, then returned to Washington, D.C.

OCT. 9. USG ordered Lt. Gen. Philip H. Sheridan to aid Chicago fire victims. On Oct. 11, USG donated clothes to the relief effort.

Oct. 12.   USG warned armed bands in S.C. to disperse within five days. On Oct. 17, USG suspended *habeas corpus* in several S.C. counties.

Oct. 13–16.   USG and Julia Grant at Boston. On Oct. 16, USG attended the opening of the new post office.

Oct. 17–21.   USG toured Maine and spoke at ceremonies opening the European and North American Railway.

Oct. 22.   USG and Julia Grant returned to Washington, D.C.

Nov. 4.   USG refused to close federal offices for Nov. 7 elections.

Nov. 6.   USG promised to support federal officials in Utah Territory who had indicted Mormon leaders.

Nov. 10–12.   USG and Julia Grant spent a weekend in New York City with Frederick Grant, who sailed for Europe on Nov. 17.

Nov. 15.   In a letter he never mailed, USG labelled U.S. Senator Charles Sumner of Mass. "unreasonable, cowardly, slanderous, unblushing false."

Nov. 16.   USG borrowed $6000 from Adolph E. Borie.

Nov. 20.   Yielding to political pressure, USG accepted the resignation of Thomas Murphy, collector of customs, New York City. On Dec. 6, USG nominated Chester A. Arthur to replace Murphy.

Nov. 23.   USG met Russian Grand Duke Alexis amid heated controversy over Russian minister Constantin Catacazy.

Nov. 30.   USG and family attended Thanksgiving services.

Dec. 4.   USG submitted his annual message to Congress.

Dec. 13.   Attorney Gen. Amos T. Akerman resigned at USG's request. The next day USG nominated George H. Williams to replace Akerman.

Dec. 15.   The Alabama Claims tribunal first met at Geneva.

Dec. 19.   USG submitted the report of the Civil Service Commission to Congress, and promised to adopt changes by Jan. 1, 1872.

Dec. 20.   Jesse Root Grant suffered a temporary attack of paralysis at Covington, Ky.

Dec. 20.   USG reported to the House on conditions in Cuba.

Jan. 4.   USG ordered an investigation of political turmoil in La.

Jan. 4–7.   USG and Julia Grant visited Philadelphia as weekend guests of Borie.

JAN. 10. USG met black leaders to discuss pending civil rights legislation.

JAN. 12. USG refused to intervene directly in La. affairs.

JAN. 12. Orvil Grant visited USG.

JAN. 15. George and Harriet Pullman arrived for a week as White House guests. Adolph and Elizabeth Borie returned to Philadelphia after a week's visit.

JAN. 20. USG met Cherokee, Creek, and Choctaw leaders.

JAN. 23. USG, Julia Grant, and cabinet members attended the wedding of Secretary of the Navy George M. Robeson and Mary Aulick.

JAN. 26. George W. and Emma Childs returned to Philadelphia after staying at the White House.

JAN. 31. As executor of the John A. Rawlins estate, USG gave instructions after Mary E. Rawlins remarried on Jan. 29.

The Papers of Ulysses S. Grant
June 1, 1871–January 31, 1872

To Amos T. Akerman

LONG BRANCH N. J. JUNE SECD. [*1871*]
A. T. AKERMAN. ATTY. GENL. WASHN.
IT IS REPRESENTED THAT JUDGES MC.KEAN[1] AND
STRICKLAND[2] UTAH ARE INTERESTED IN MINING
CLAIMS SIMILARLY SITUATED AS TO TITLE WITH
OTHER CLAIMS WHICH ARE IN LITIGATION BEFORE
THEM AS JUDGES   IF SO THEY SHOULD RESIGN THEIR
PLACES AND JUDGES BE APPOINTED WHO HAVE NO IN-
TEREST IN DECISION WHICH THEY MAY RENDER.
U. S. GRANT.

Telegram received, DNA, RG 60, Letters from the President. On June 2, 1871, Attorney Gen. Amos T. Akerman wrote to USG. "In pursuance of your telegram of this date Judges, McKean and Strickland of Utah have been informed that if they are interested upon questions in litigation before them, as it has been represented to you, they should not continue in Office, and they have been requested to report the facts" Copy, *ibid.*, Letters Sent to Executive Officers. On June 24, Benjamin H. Bristow, solicitor gen. and act. attorney gen., wrote to USG. "Judges McKean and Strickland have replied to the Attorney General's letters. The answer of Strickland seems to be evasive and unsatisfactory. He does not meet the charges made by Senator Stewart nor refer to the facts disclosed by the records that have been laid before you. Judge McKean says that five or six month ago a man named Appleby, whom he did not know, used his name in locating the Silver Shield Mine. The Judge says that this was without his knowledge, but that he was afterwards offered several thousand dollars for his interest in the mine which he declined to take being told that he would ultimately realize a handsome sum for it. He denies indignantly all charges of improper conduct, but does not refer to the fact that he was the President of the Silver Shield Mine Company, and that on the 27th of March last he signed an agreement of incorporation and subscribed $15.000 stock in said Company. Reading these letters in connection with Senator Stewart's dispatch and the transcript of records filed here by Mr Hillyer matters look badly in Utah. Both Judges, however, request that they may be furnished with copies of the Specific charges against them. There is no authority of law, for directing them to suspend courts. If you desire, I will send or bring these papers to Long Branch by monday morning." Copy, *ibid.* On the same day, USG, Long Branch, telegraphed to Bristow. "I WOULD SEND COPY OF CHARGES TO JUDGES MC.KEAN AND STRICKLING. WILL BE IN WASHINGTON LAST OF NEXT WEEK." Telegram received, *ibid.*, Letters from the President. On June 26, USG spoke to a reporter about

Utah Territory. "'I don't anticipate any particular trouble there. That kind of trouble always prevails where there are people who want offices and can't get them. I suppose there are men outside of Utah similarly afflicted. The charges made against the judiciary of Utah are serious enough; but I don't think they are true. It is stated that, one of the judges has an interest in a silver mine, and that he is using his position as a judge in his own favor. I don't think that that is so; of course if it is so that judge is not the man for the place—he'll have to go. . . . I will not take any steps until I have made a full investigation of the truth or falsity of the charges presented to me. My impression is that the charges are groundless; but I intend to probe the matter, and if any action is necessary—why, I'll act, that's all.'" *New York Herald* (subheading integrated), June 27, 1871. On June 22, U.S. Delegate Jerome B. Chaffee of Colorado Territory and Judge Edgar W. Hillyer of Nev. had visited USG at Long Branch "to urge the appointment of Thomas Fitch as Chief-Justice of Utah. A party favoring the present incumbent also called on the President the same day." *Boston Transcript*, June 24, 1871.

On Dec. 26, 1870, U.S. Representative Thomas Fitch of Nev. had written to USG. "I beseech you to remove Judge Hawley of the Utah Territorial Supreme Court and appoint some lawyer in his stead. I would be glad if you will appoint Mr S A Mann the late Secty of the Territory who is every way competent and deserving, but I earnestly request that Mr Hawley be removed and that some honest competent lawyer from one of the Pacific states who is familiar with mining law and jurisprudence may receive the position   I do not personally know Judge Hawley and the reasons for urging his removal are entirely disconnected with the peculiar social and political conditions of Utah. Rich mines have been discovered and are being worked in Cottonwood Canon and other points in Utah,   Miners—among whom are many of my constituents are flocking in—Litigation of the most important character is inevitable, and it is highly necessary that the bench should be filled with competent men. Judge McKean is I learn an able upright man, & there is no especial fault found with Judge Strickland, but I am informed from the very best authority that Judge Hawley is utterly incompetent and unfit to adjudicate upon the vast interests shortly to be in issue before him   I beg that you will transfer Judge Hawley to some other sphere of usefulness and place a Pacific coast lawyer on the Utah bench   Hon William Haydon ~~of the~~ for many years Judge of the District Court of the Third Judicial District Nevada would I am informed be glad ~~to~~ of the position. Judge Geo D Keeney now of the Tenth Nevada District would I think accept it,   I would be glad of course to have an experienced and able jurist in Judge Hawleys place, but I hope that *he* will be removed, as from my information any change would be for the better" ALS, *ibid.*, Letters Received, Utah. On June 29, 1871, Governor George L. Woods of Utah Territory, Washington, D. C., wrote to Secretary of State Hamilton Fish. "A movement having been made, in Utah Territory, for the purpose of procuring the removal of two of the U. S. District Judges of that Territory upon Charges which I regarded as untrue, and without foundation, acting upon the Judgment of the Federal Officials in Utah as well as upon my own Judgment I came to the Capital, without leave, to see the President and Attorney General in the premises. Under ordinary circumstances I should not violate, in the least, the rule established, but, under the circumstances,— the importance of keeping the Judiciary now there,—~~and~~ [—] the fact that I could not Tel[e]graph for leave of absence with[out] the same being made pu[blic]—a Son-in-law of Brigham Young being Telegraphic Oper[a]tor at Salt Lake City—I thoug[ht] I should be excused for so doi[ng.] Hoping that your assent may be given . . ." ALS, *ibid.*, RG 59, Utah Territorial Papers. On the same day, USG endorsed this letter. "Absence approved." AES, *ibid.*

On June 1, John H. Wickizer, Salt Lake City, wrote to Giles A. Smith, 2nd asst. postmaster gen. "*Personal* . . . Let me have a little private talk with you. about matters in Utah in relation to Courts. Justice is at a stand-still for the want of money to pay Jurors. Many very important, *mine* cases, are at a dead lock for want of a Jury. Congress at its late Session failed to make an appropriation to pay Jurors in Utah. But it is thought here, by legal gentlemen, that if the facts as they really exist here, could be fairly placed before the President, and Atty General of U. S. a mode could be devised by which sufficient funds to pay a Jury here, could be directed from some other or *general* fund, or some mode devised for aid of courts and Justice in Utah If Gov Woods and Chf. Justice J. B. McKean of Utah could have a private interview with President Grant, the Atty General, and Heads of the Departments at Washington, it is thought a mode of relief might be devised for Utah at once—. . ." ALS, *ibid.*, RG 60, Letters from the President. USG endorsed this letter. "Refer to Atty Gn, for his suggestions." AE (undated), *ibid.*

On July 17, F. M. Smith, counsel, Velocipede Mining Co., Salt Lake City, wrote to USG. "The endorsement I made of a letter addressed to you by the Hon Thomas Fitch, Concerning the judicial integrity and ability of J B McKean, Chief Justice of this Territory, I desire to be received in a qualified sense. At the time of said endorsement I had been practicing my profession in the Courts of this Territory for the period of three months, and during said time Chief Justice McKean appeared to perform the duties of his Office impartially. This is the qualified sense in which I wish my endorsement to be received. Of his ability and impartiality in performing the duties of his Office, since the writing of that letter, I have had good reason to withdraw favorable expression of either. In the matter in Controversy between the Silver Shield Mining Company, (of which Judge McKean is President, and party in interest) agst the persons comprising the Velocipede Mining Company, suits now pending in his, McKeans Court, the Conduct of Judge McKean therein, by no means can receive my approbation. The record of his Official acts in said several cases, presented to you for consideration, I know to be a correct copy of the records of the Case now of file in the office of the Clerk of Judge McKeans Court. There several Cases, by reason of the interest of Judge McKean and Associate Justice Strickland therein, and by reason of the refusal of Judge McKean to make such order as will give Associate Justice C M Hawly, jurisdiction, cannot be brought to hearing, and no determination of the Controversy Can be had   The party therefore Constituting the Velocipede Mining Company, are without remidy, and must need Content themselves to have their mining claim despoiled of its mineral wealth by the illegal and unjustifiable act of Judge McKean, and Associate Justice Strickland, and their associates, in jumping, holding possession and working the same." ALS, *ibid.*, Letters Received, Utah.

On Aug. 4, Akerman wrote to USG. "Senator Stewart has filed in this office additional papers upon the subject of the Judges in Utah. I send you herewith a digest of them, supposing that you would not care to peruse the voluminous originals. I do not think that these papers substantially vary the case from what it was at the time of your action upon it several weeks ago. Since that action, papers have been filed remonstrating against the removal of the Judges. Among them was one from Senator Wright, of Iowa, & one from Mr. Poland, of the House of Representatives. Mr. Stewart says that the parties in the litigation in which he is interested have agreed to submit it to arbitration, and therefore he withdraws it from the Courts; but that he is still desirous, upon public grounds, that the Judges should be removed. The best judgment which I can form upon the matter is this: that while it is possible that the Judges have become involved in mining interests to a greater extent than was wise, in view of the amount of litigation affecting such interests, yet there is no evidence of official corruption or partiality—and I think that it would not be a wholesome precedent to remove Judges, (except in a clear case of official demerit,) at the instance of litigants, or their attorneys." Copy, *ibid.*, Letters Sent to Executive Officers. On July 25, Akerman had written to U.S. Senator George G. Wright of Iowa, Des Moines. "Your letter of the 15th instant in relation to the Judges in Utah, has been received. Some weeks ago an effort was made to procure the removal of those Judges, not upon the ground stated by you, but on the ground that they were improperly complicated with interests in litigation before them or with like interests. After some examination, the President became satisfied that no cause for removal existed and accordingly have not been disturbed. I regret that you have thought proper to add you emphatic protest against the removal of those officers for the supposed reason that their adjudication were unpopular, not because I have the slightest difference of opinion with you upon the impropriety of a removal upon any such ground, but because such a protest implies, if not an opininon, at least a suspicion, that such a ground of removal would be intertained here. You entirely mistake the disposition of this Department if you suppose that an application for the removal of a judge for such reason would be received here with the slightest respect" Copy, *ibid.*

1. James B. McKean, born in 1821 in Bennington, Vt., practiced law in N. Y. and served as Saratoga county judge (1854–58). A Republican congressman (1859–63), he also was col., 77th N. Y. (1861–63). On Feb. 15, 1869, Alonzo B. Cornell, Ithaca, N. Y., wrote to USG. "I take great pleasure in saying a word in favor of the appointment of my friend Genl J. B. McKean of this State to some position of responsibility under your administration, General McKeans service in Congress and in the Army of the Republic during its dark days, entitle him to the most favorable consideration, In 1867, he was placed at the head of the Republican State Ticket, which was beaten by the first edition of the great Democratic frauds in this State, the second edition of which placed our State in the humiliating position, of repudiating the savior of our National Government, as a candidate for the Presidency, at the late Election, I feel assured that the appointment of General McKean would give much satisfaction to the Republicans of our State," ALS, *ibid.*, RG 59, Letters of Application and Recommendation. Related papers are *ibid.*

On May 27, 1870, Thomas Marshall, Salt Lake City, wrote to USG. "It is, with extreme reluctance, that I presume to address your Excellency, & recall to your memory the names of my late Father in Law, the Hon James M Hughes now deceased, of Saint Louis Mo, and that of myself; and I do so now merely, as the introduction to a matter of great public interest to all parties residing in this Territory of Utah, and for the purpose of soliciting your personal attention to the contents of my letter. I have just learned through the Telegrams, of your intention to supersede, the Hon C. C. Wilson, Chief Justice of Utah, and beleiving as I do that a thorough understanding on your part, of Judge Wilson's course whilst here, would lead you to sustain him in his position, and thereby retain the services of a valuable and efficient Judge Lawyer and gentleman, I have undertaken to give you such an understanding. When Judge Wilson came here, he found the community divided into cliques and parties Mormons Apostates and Gentiles: Brigham Young controlling almost everything within the Territory, holding an immense Temporal as well as

Spiritual power, & wielding an influence very nigh as supreme as that of the Emperor of the Russias. The Probate Courts filled by Judges, in reality appointed by Brigham Young, exercised concurrent Jurisdiction with the United States Courts, & in fact exceeded them in the extent of their power. The Territorial Marshal, a creature of Brigham Young appointed nominally by the Legislature of Utah, but in reality appointed by the Mormon Church, was the Executive officer of the District Courts, & as such selected both Grand and Petit Juries, & filled the Jury box with men pledged to prevent the execution of the Polygamy law of 1862, and on the action of such Marshal the Courts depended for the service of its every process, the enforcement of its decrees, and the execution of the Laws. For eighteen years, no Federal Judge had met these issues squarely, but had avoided the decision of these two questions, knowing the vast interest taken in them by the Mormon people, and thus, the Federal Laws against Polygamy were allowed to go unenforced and to be and remain a blot and stain on the Statute Book of the United States   Judge Wilson was sent out, & entered upon the discharge of the delicate duties of his office; He did so, quietly yet earnestly, he mixed himself with none of the cliques, was a partisan of no party and of no creed, waged no direct war with Brigham & the Mormons, & showed only such mercy and favor, as the Law gave them, and has already in this District nearly destroyed Brigham's temporal power. At the last term of the District Court, Wilson decided that the Probate Courts had no civil or commercial Jurisdiction, and confined their power solely to legitimate Probate business such as the settlement of Estates of Decedents &c &c   He has also, on quo warranto, ousted the Territorial Marshal and substituted in his place, the United States Marshal, thus placing in the hands of U. S. officers, the entire machinery of the Courts. Your Excellency, will at once observe that these two decisions are vital objects endeavored to be reached by the Legislation, known as the Cullom Bill, now before Congress, and are terrible, if not fatal blows at Mormon rule and Mormon power in Utah. Judge Wilson has done all this with so quiet a manner, without street discussion, and with no direct or harsh reflections on Mormonism when giving his Judicial opinion, that as yet, although greatly affected by his legal conclusions, they have not charged him with any partiality or unfairness on the Bench, and in truth, I have seen nothing that could justify such a charge: His rule of action seems to be so to speak and act at all times, as to disarm even the suspicion of bias or partisanship. Your Excellency, fully understands the necessity for a Judge to inspire and retain the confidence of his constituency, especially of such a people as these in Utah, this Wilson has done to a remarkable extent: He has held his terms regularly and in addition to his two regular terms a year, has held special terms whenever the business of the District required it, and as an evidence of the high esteem of the Bar, I would merely say that today a card was signed by every member of the Bar practising Law in the Courts of Utah, endorsing his Judicial Conduct and requesting his retention, in Office: And I think that in case of the passage of the Cullom Bill, he will be invaluable to the Government, his reputation for fairness, want of bias and eminent Judicial ability, will go far to disarming all resistance here, to the legal enforcement of that Law, and thereby save many lives and the expenditure of monies to the Government. Our firm, Marshall & Carter have at present the largest practice in Utah Territory, and we most earnestly, as a firm, press the request, as I do personally, that your Excellency will reconsider this matter and retain Judge Wilson in his present position   The entire Bar of Salt Lake City request it, and no individuals are so competent to judge the efficiency of a Judge as the Attorneys practising before him, and their request, I sincerely think and hope your Excellency will not wholly disregard, even if you may have forgotten." ALS, *ibid.*, RG 60, Letters Received, Utah. On May 24, USG nominated McKean as chief justice, Utah Territory.

On Feb. 13, 1871, McKean and Cyrus M. Hawley, associate justice, Utah Territory, wrote to USG. "For near twenty years the Mormon leaders packed the Grand and Petit juries of the United States Courts here with their tools and instruments. But within a few months past we have decided against this system, and have decided to recognize only the U. S. Attorney and the U. S. Marshal as the proper officers of our Courts. One of the consequences is that we have already indicted *for capital offences* ten or twelve Mormons—some of them Bishop and other influential men in the Mormon establishment. Another consequence is that the Mormon Territorial Legislature will not appropriate any more funds to pay the expenses of our Courts, nor will the Territorial officials pay for court expenses such funds as are now on hand.—a very small amount. Even our jurors are remaining unpaid; thoug[h] the Marshal has advanced from his own funds considerable sums for other unavoidable ~~ex~~ expenses. The Solicitor of the Department of Justice has decided against the bill that we forwarded for our absolutely necessary expenses, and we are left helpless. The Mormon leaders are rejoicing. They already regard themselves as masters of the situation. I inclose a printed slip from Brigham Young's official organ. Indeed, Sir, some of the witnesses, disaffected Mormons, who have given us valuable evidence, are hunted in the night time by ruffians, and dare not sleep in their own houses. Mr. President, if the Department of Justice does not recede from its ruling; or if congress does not provide for us by legislation or, if in some way we do not get help from Washington, the time is near at hand when we shall be so helpless—so powerle[ss] for good, that perhaps the only honorable thing left for us to do, will be to tender to your Excellency our resignations." LS, *ibid.*, Letters Received from the President. The clippings are *ibid.*

On June 29, U.S. Representative John B. Hawley of Ill., Rock Island, wrote to USG. "I am advised that an effort is being made to Secure the removal of Judge McKean Chief Justice of Utah. It will be remembered by you that Hon Charles C. Wilson Chief Justice of that Territory was removed last year and Judge McKean appointed in his stead. I write you now to express the earnest hope that in Case of the removal of Judge McKean, Judge Wilson may be restored to his place. I have known him for many years intimately having practiced law with him at the Same bar for about ten years. During that time and up to the time of his appointmnt as Chief Justice of Utah he resided in the next County to my own. I bear Cheerful testimony to his integrity and ability. In case of a vacancy as indicated I believe his appointment would be the very best that Could be made. I have ever since his removal been impressed with the Conviction that it occurred under a misapprehension and that it ou[g]ht not to have been made. It would in my judgment be but a Simple act of justice to him in Case of a vacancy to restore him to the position. If re-appointed I am Confident his Course will be Such as to reflect Credit not only upon him but upon the Government from which he receives his appointment   I have the honor to enclose herewith a statement made by the Members of the Bar of Salt Lake at or about the time of the removal of Judge Wilson." ALS, OFH.

On Feb. 5, 1872, Elias Smith and two others, Salt Lake City, telegraphed to USG. "A mass meeting of two thousand citizens of Salt Lake City and County was held here on saturday to select delegates to Constitutional Convention with a view to the admission of Utah to the Union. nineteen delegates Elected. Ten were mormons and nine were prominent gentiles   during the meeting the following resolution was unanimously adopted   Resolved that it is the Candid opinion of this large assembly that Chief Justice James B. McKean in many of his official acts and especially in refusing the bail recently asked for by the deputy U. S. District Attorney J. L. High under instructions from Washington has manifested so unwise and oppressive a spirit and so misused the power of his Office that his judicial Course richly merits Condemnation & his removal from Office is asked for in behalf of justice and equal rights for all before the law" Telegram received (on Feb. 6, at 2:40 A.M.), DNA, RG 60, Letters from the President. Also in Feb., O. C. Pratt, San Francisco, telegraphed to Williams. "Would not it be wise to have McKean of Utah removed   his Course intensifies troubles" Telegram received (on Feb. 6), *ibid.*

On [Feb. 29], A. S. Gould and R. M. Baskin presented to USG a petition "from the people of Utah Territory, expressing their high opinion of Judge McKean as a man and a judicial officer. The President here remarked: 'Sir, the loyal people of Utah can have no higher opinion of Judge McKean than I have.' The President evinced a great interest in the affairs of Utah, and asked many questions in regard to the effect of the late action of the courts upon trade and mining affairs, remarking that it had been suggested to him that the prosecution of leading Mormons for charges of murder and polygamy had a tendency to weaken confidence in the minds of capitalists who wish to invest in Utah, and possibly might lead to a collision." *Washington Chronicle*, March 1, 1872.

On May 26, 1874, USG nominated McKean for a second term. On March 16, 1875, USG nominated Isaac C. Parker as chief justice, Utah Territory. On March 17, George F. Prescott, Tribune Printing Co., Salt Lake City, telegraphed to USG. "The removal of Chief Justice McKean at this time is equivalent to a national recognition of Mormon supremacy in Utah   the man of shiloh vicksburgh & appamatox could not make this unconditional surrender to Brigham Young" Telegram received, DNA, RG 60, Letters Received, Utah. On the same day, Tilford and Hagan *et al.*, Salt Lake City, telegraphed to USG. "As an act of justice to Chief Justice McKean the undersigned members of the Bar ask that action be stayed on his removal until our statement of George E Whitneys outrage on McKean is presented" Telegram received (at 7:00 P.M.), *ibid.* On March 18, U.S. Senators Powell Clayton and Stephen W. Dorsey of Ark. telegraphed to USG. "Mr Parker will accept and the Judiciary Committee will advise his confirmation" Telegram received, *ibid.*, RG 107, Telegrams Collected (Bound). Also on March 18, U.S. Senators Aaron A. Sargent of Calif. and Timothy O. Howe of Wis. telegraphed to USG. "If you withdraw Parker please send in at same time another nominee for Utah" Telegram received, *ibid.* On the same day, USG withdrew Parker's nomination as chief justice, nominated him as judge, Western District, Ark., and named Daniel P. Lowe as chief justice, Utah Territory. A letter recommending Lowe as judge, Western District, Ark., is *ibid.*, RG 60, Records Relating to Appointments. See second letter to John M. Thayer, Dec. 22, 1870; Thomas G. Alexander, "Federal Authority Versus Polygamic Theocracy: James B. McKean and the Mormons, 1870–1875," *Dialogue: A Journal of Mormon Thought*, I, 3 (Autumn, 1966), 85–100; Leonard J. Arrington, ed., "Crusade Against Theocracy: The Reminiscences of Judge Jacob Smith Boreman of Utah, 1872–1877," *Huntington Library Quarterly*, XXIV, 1 (Nov., 1960), 1–45.

2. On March 29, 1869, Thomas J. Drake, Provo, resigned as associate justice, Utah Territory. ALS, DNA, RG 60, Letters Received, State Dept. In an undated letter, U.S. Representative Randolph Strickland of Mich. *et al.* wrote to USG. "The undersigned your Petitioners respectfully request that Mr Obed F Strickland of Salt Lake City Utah Territory may be nominated for the Office of Associate Justice of

the Supreme Court for the Territory of Montana to fill the vacancy now existing there   Mr Strickland is thirty six years of age was admitted to practice in all the Courts of the State of Michigan in 1856, has since practiced in Michigan Montana and Utah is a man of correct habits upright honest and fully competant for the desired position and having resided in Montana and Utah for the last five years it is believed that his appointment will be more acceptable to the Bar of that Territory than that of a man unacquainted there" DS (20 signatures), *ibid.*, Records Relating to Appointments. Related papers are *ibid.* On April 1, USG nominated Obed F. Strickland as associate justice, Utah Territory. On June 7, 1872, Obed Strickland, Provo, wrote to USG. "Private ... If my continuance in office can or will in any manner detrimental effect the comeing campaign. my resignation can be had upon call   Permit me to congratulate you on your unanimous renomination and thanking you for the many kind things said and done by you for me ..." ALS, *ibid.* Strickland's letter of resignation of Jan. 8, 1873, is *ibid.*

On Dec. 20, 1872, U.S. Senator Thomas W. Ferry of Mich. wrote to USG. "I called this morning but found you out of the City. Learning that Judge Strickland now Territorial Judge of the Territory of Utah is soon to resign and lest my application for the appointment of Wm W. Mitchell a Judge in Dakota Territory may not be expedient, I desire that Mr Mitchell a Lawyer of Michn may succeed Judge Strickland ~~also~~ a former resident of that state. May I therefore urgently ask that this Wm W Mitchell be appointed vice Judge Strickland soon to resign as I am informed." ALS, *ibid.* Related papers are *ibid.* On Jan. 8, 1873, USG nominated William W. Mitchell to replace Strickland; this nomination was recalled.

On March 6, U.S. Senators Zachariah Chandler and Thomas W. Ferry of Mich. wrote to USG. "We respectfully recommend Hon. Philip H. Emerson of Michigan, a resident of the city of Battle Creek of the state & now chairman of the Judiciary Committee of that State Senate for the vacant Office of United States associate Juge for the Territory of Utah" LS, NNP. On March 7, USG nominated Philip H. Emerson to replace Strickland.

To James D. Reid

LONG BRANCH, N. J., June 6, 1871.
James D. Reid, Esq., Chairman Morse Telegraph Committee.

DEAR SIR: I am just in receipt of your invitation on behalf of 10,000 telegraphic laborers to be present on Saturday next at the inauguration of the statue in honor of Prof. MORSE. Plans made previous to the receipt of your invitation will prevent my acceptance, but do not prevent my appreciation of the services rendered to science and the wants of commerce, trade and travel by the distinguished man in whose honor you meet. Your obedient servant,

U. S. GRANT.

New York Times, June 11, 1871. James D. Reid, born in 1819 in Edinburgh, Scotland, immigrated to the U.S. (1837), clerked in the Rochester, N. Y., post office, and held a series of positions in telegraph cos. He was a close friend of Samuel F. B. Morse, inventor of the telegraph. On June 10, 1871, elaborate afternoon and evening ceremonies in New York City marked the unveiling of a statue honoring Morse in Central Park. *Ibid.* See *ibid.*, April 29, 1901; Reid, *The Telegraph in America: Its Founders Promoters and Noted Men* (1879; reprinted, New York, 1974), pp. 704–62.

Endorsement

Respectfully refered to the Atty. Gn. who will please carry out the desires of the writer. The Military will be instructed to aid in any arrests called on to make either by the detective[1] named in this Communication, the U. S. Marshal[2] or any of his deputies, the Dist. Atty.[3] or U. S. Commissioner.[4]

U. S. Grant

June 9th /71

AES, DNA, RG 60, Letters from the President. Written on a letter of June 8, 1871, from U.S. Senator John Scott of Pa. to USG. "Mr. Hester, of North Carolina, will bear this to you & explain fully the service, which he believes may be rendered to the country, & the facilities thus afforded to the labors of the Congressional Investigating Committee now in Session in this City. We are satisfied of the character & competency of Mr Hester, & respectfully recommend that such directions in the premises be given to the Attorney General as to make him feel authorized to proceed in the matter, at once. The Attorney General hesitates for want of instructions, & Mr Hester is sent at my instance to communicate with you. There is an appropriation of $50.000, made at the last Session, to aid in prosecuting offences against the criminal laws of the United States. This matter should be put into operation without delay, in order to insure success, & secrecy is indispensable. For this reason I have deemed it best to send Mr. Hester in person, to communicate with you." ALS, *ibid.* On June 7, Joseph G. Hester had testified before the Joint Select Committee to Inquire into the Condition of Affairs in the Late Insurrectionary States. "*Question.* Where do you reside? *Answer.* In Raleigh, North Carolina. . . . I have been living there four years. . . . I was born in the adjoining county of Granville. *Question.* State whether you have been acting there in the capacity of deputy marshal of the United States. *Answer.* I have. . . . *Question.* What name is given to the organization of disguised persons in that part of the State? *Answer.* I have been in the habit of calling them Ku-Klux; some of them say the name is White Brotherhood, and others, Invisible Empire. I have heard different names for them. They themselves say, as the evidence appeared in the trials, that they are not human beings; that they come from the bone-yards at Richmond; that they have been seven years in the bone-yards at Richmond, and have come for vengeance. . . . I think, sir, it is on the increase. From observations and information received from different sources I think they are reorganizing all the time. I think they have changed their *modus ope-*

randi since some of the developments have been made. In fact, I have some evidence of that which I would not like to express here for reasons that it would be best to withhold at present. *Question.* In the part of the State of which you speak, are persons at liberty to express their political sentiments with freedom and immunity from danger? *Answer.* Those with whom I have conversed say they are not; they would be in great danger if they should get up and make a political speech, and express sentiments as republicans.... *Question.* What were the politics of these persons who were whipped? *Answer.* They were republicans. They said they voted for General Grant in the last campaign, and one of them mentioned that when he was being whipped he was told he was whipped because he voted for Grant.... *Question.* Has the passage by Congress of the recent law known as the 'Ku-Klux law' had any effect upon the operations of these persons in disguise in that State? *Answer.* Well, I do not think it has had much, only to encourage it. If anything, they are doing worse in some sections—in sections where they have not been operating much before. Since the passage of the bill I have heard of more occurrences in the western part of the State, where I had not heard of any before. *Question.* What portion of the State do you refer to? *Answer.* Cleveland, Rutherford, and Gaston Counties.... *Question.* What are your political relations? *Answer.* I belong to the republican party. I claim to be a republican.... I have been a republican about a year...." *SRC*, 42-2-41, part 2, pp. 13, 17, 19. See Endorsement, Oct. 14, 1876.

On Dec. 26, 1871, Attorney Gen. Amos T. Akerman wrote to USG. "On the first instant, you referred to me, for investigation, a memorial, endorsed by Governor Caldwell, from certain citizens of North Carolina, complaining that one Allen Bettis had been arrested by U. S. Soldiers and imprisoned at Yorkville, S. C. The memorialists state that Bettis is ready and willing to be tried by his peers in his own State, and claims the right to be tried there. I have made an investigation, and learn that Bettis was arrested upon overwhelming proof of his connection with the Ku Klux Klan in York County, S. C., though his residence is in North Carolina, just over the State line. On the 24th of November, he was turned over to the U. S. Marshal, and by the Marshal taken before a Commissioner, who released him upon his giving bail to appear before the U. S. Circuit Court of South Carolina to answer to any indictment that might be preferred against him for violation of the Enforcement Acts of Congress. As I am advised, there has been no violation of law or justice in the proceedings to which Mr. Bettis has been subjected. His claim to be tried in his own State is utterly inadmissible under the Constitution and laws, the accusation being of an offence perpetrated in another State. I have reported the result of these investigations to Governor Caldwell." Copy, DNA, RG 60, Letters Sent to Executive Officers. A petition of Nov. 11 from J. Jenkins and others, Shelby, N. C., to Governor Tod R. Caldwell of N. C. sought consideration for "Allen Bettis Chairman of the Board of the County Commissioners of Cleavland County ..." DS, *ibid.*, Letters from the President. Caldwell endorsed the petition. "Respectfully referred to the President of the United States for his consideration—directing his attention to the fact that certain Federal officials join in the complaint therein contained—" AES (undated), *ibid.* On Dec. 4, John F. Aydlotte, U.S. commissioner, Shelby, wrote to USG. "I was at Raleigh Recently and had an Interview with Gov Caldwell who Informed me that he had forwarded to you a petition signed by my self & several other federal officers of this County.   the petition was in favor of one Allen Bettis who had been arrested by the US Cavalry from south Carolina I understood the petition simply to ask that ~~the~~ Bettis might be transferd to the District of of North Carolina for Trial. and nothing more and did what I did with that understanding   I do not wish to be Implicated in any manner whatever with

Tying to aid any one from the Due prosecution of the law and for the future be
assured that I will sign no more petitions for any Man that is charged with having
any thing to do with the Ku Klux   Gov Caldwell will write to you on the subject
I hope will satisfy you that in doing what I did was not an Intentional Rong—. . .
P. S. Gov Caldwell requested me to write to you on this subject and also promiced
to write himself—" ALS, *ibid.* On Dec. 5, W. W. Green, postmaster, Shelby, wrote
to USG. "I Learnd through US Commisr J F Aoydlett who has Just Returned from
Raleigh NC where he saw His Excelency Goviner Coldwell who told him he had
Seen petition assigned by Three federal officers of this County and had sent the
petition to You   they was a petition had me by a yong man of this County Young
Mr Bettece to assig for his father Allen Bettece a Citizen of this County who was
in Gail at Yorkville S C to have him Transfered from S C to N C to have his trial
I did not think It was amiss as I done It for the Respect I had for the family and I
want You to forgive me for so doing as I will not do so any more nor I dont belong
to the organization of Ku Klucking and It aint my Intention to Give any such nor
to throug any ofbstickle in the way as of the Republican party in any way and I will
act in future more cautious" ALS, *ibid.* For testimony identifying "Allen Bettis" as
"Allen Pettis," see *SRC,* 42-2-41, part 2, pp. 380–81, 413.

1. On June 15, Orville E. Babcock wrote to Akerman. "The President directs me
to say that he will be pleased to have you employ a detective for Alabama, under like
instructions, and in the same way as one is employed now in North and South Carolina, and to have you consult with Senator Scott as to the selection of the man." LS,
DNA, RG 60, Letters from the President.

On March 19, Secretary of State Hamilton Fish had written in his diary. "*Cabinet*—all present except Robeson . . . Akerman reads a letter from Dist—Attorney in
Alabama of the murder of a Witness in a prosecution against the Ku Klux—& suggesting the employment of the son of the murdered man, (who is a principal witness
in some pending prosecutions) in Washington, until the trial come off at the term to
be held next Autumn—He is to give him some employment" DLC-Hamilton Fish.

On May 2, G. T. F. Boulding, Tuscaloosa, wrote to USG. "Please Take in consideration these few Remarks as this have been the 4th time this Last year that i had an
occation to write to you hopeing not to tax your already and much valud time But
necesesity compels me to write and Let you know how we are treate in this Part of
the country and we appeal to your honor to give us poor people some guarantee for
our Live   we are hunted and shot down as if we were wild. Beast   on Last Saturday
night April 30th the Clique Known as the K. Ks Visited the House of one of our
most guieless Col'd Citizens and Shot him dead after which they Rob'd his house of
about $200 in money and carried off his Gun and Pistol   this is not the only Case
of the kind in the Last ten days But the 3rd or fourth case   we hope as our Lives
Liberty and Property are in Eminent Perilll that you will Do something for us as
soon as Posible   we have Imperilld our Lives to suport you and we look to you to
help us when in distress   this is the time   I have written to several times before
and have not got any answr and cannot tell if you get the Letters or not and Hope
that you will at least write and Let me know if you Recieve this letter   we have
stood By you and are ever Ready to do so with our lives and wish to Be Protected
in our Rights   for A more minute account you will please Refer to the Letter of
Senator Spencer of alabama whos letter have been ~~Recievd~~ written the same Date
of this   in Publishing this Letter if you Should you will please omitt the Name
Signd By Reason of the Danger I am in for I the name was known i would not live

twenty four hours afterward   Pleas answr   I would not Refer to the state orthori-
ties Because I have done so several times without any Reply or action taken   I think
the man Samuels that was shot on Saturday night should be Placed under Bond for
fear he may get well and elope   his Name is Wm Samuels   he may Recover   Senators G. E. Spencer's Letter will give a full detail of the affair   By Request of the
col'd Citizens of this Place" ALS, DNA, RG 94, Letters Received, 1687 1871. Marked
"Please Address E. G. Van lear, Tuscaloosa Ala" On Nov. 3, Elijah Wolsey Peck, Ala.
chief justice, testified before the Joint Select Committee. ". . . I reside in the city of
Tuscaloosa. . . . Last spring there was a colored man attacked in his house about two
miles and a half, or something like three miles, from Tuscaloosa, on the Huntsville
road, northeast of the place. They broke open his house and he fired, and they fired
upon him, and he was shot all to pieces and killed. One of the company was hit by
him, and died some ten days or two weeks afterward. He was a young Mr. Samuel,
who was a clerk in some one of the stores in Tuscaloosa. . . . [H]e was a son of Mr.
Samuel, who, at one time, while he was alive, was clerk of the circuit court of that
county. I cannot say that the young man was living a very reputable life, as I have
always understood that he was living with, and had several children by, a negro
woman; otherwise I do not know of anything that could be said against the young
man. He was in the confederate army and was wounded in the war. *Question.* Were
any of his confederates ever discovered? *Answer.* Well, sir, I have no doubt there
were a good many of them known to a class of people in the town, but I do not
know that I could say that any of them were discovered. I understood that before
he died arrangements had been made that if he did get well he was to be sent out
of the country, for fear of discoveries that he might make; but he died. He was shot
in the breast. They were so close together that the wadding and everything went
into him. *Question.* Do you know what was the imputed offense of the colored man
that was shot? *Answer.* Well, sir, I do not know that he was guilty of any offense
except it was said that he had a white wife; I suppose she was a low woman; I do
not know anything about her, nor do I know anything about him. He was called
Bill Washington, and before he was freed belonged to a gentleman by the name of
Washington, in the county. . . ." *SRC*, 42-2-41, part 10, pp. 1850, 1854.

On June 16, J. F. Files and 33 others, Dublin, Ala., petitioned USG. "all the
undersigned citizens of Fayette county Ala. pray your honor to enforse the late act
of congress in our county in reguard to Ku Klux autrages   they go to our churches
on the Sabbath and disturbe our Sivil courts and they whip or Kill Some one every
Saturday and oft times from five to ten in one night   we know verry near evry man
that belongs to the Klan   they verry often go out in there disguise in day time   we
pray your honor to Send five hundred federal soldiers under some man like general
Butler that will not let them go upon there own Story   We went and arested thirteen and there disguises had them Bound to court and the judge taken no notice of
them dismissed evry case without any trial   our only hope is in your honer   if you
fail to help us we are gone   we have faith in your honor as we was all Soldiers
under general Sherman   help us soon   we are all poore men have to work hard
alday and be on guard all night for fear the Ku Klux will come in on us and now
we make this our only hope of releaf   if we had the power to act with a little help
we could soon put an end to them   there is no way to stop them only to Kill Some
of the leading ones   we Know your honor has the power to help us and we have
faith in geting help   the rebs tell us we cant get help   We leave the case with you
if your honor will not help us please tel us so you can see what want and what we
need   hopeing to here from you soon we remain ever true to the old flag and its

defenders ... this is the ex Soldiers that are living here or trying to live here   we could ad quite a number of citizens on our list if necisary   if there is any thing needed on our part let us know by writing J F Files   We desire all communication to be Sent him at Dublin Fayette county Ala   awaiting your action ... Note—The names to this communication are all original in one handwriting." D, DNA, RG 94, Letters Received, 2327 1871. On the same day, J. Pinckney Whitehead and many others, Dublin, petitioned USG. "Your petitioners respectfully represent that the Condition of Affairs are such in Fayette County Alabama as to render the lives of loyal Citizens wholy insecure   Armed bands styling themselves Ku Klux are Committing Crimes and outrages upon peaceable and law abiding persons   Murders by these ruffians who have long disgraced this County are of common occurrence. The *civil authorities have been overawed and are utterly powerless to execute the laws.* Your petitioners are assured that unless the crimes which have been committed by these ruffians can be put a stop to and the organization itself entirely broken up Civil liberty and personal safety are at an end in Fayette County and life and property and everything else will soon be at the mercy of an organized mob   For such reasons we do most humbly and imploringly appeal for that protection which the Constitution and laws guarantees to every Citizen of the United States ... Please do not give publicity to our names as we are in constant danger of assasination at this time" DS, *ibid.*, 2301 1871. On July 30, 2nd Lt. Horace B. Sarson, 2nd Inf., Montgomery, wrote to 1st Lt. Charles E. Moore, 2nd Inf. "I have the honor to report that in accordance with instructions contained in Special Order No 36 Headquarters Montgomery Ala. July 16 1871, I proceeded to Fayette County Ala. and visited the localities (Fayetteville and Dublin) named in the order, and communicated with persons who were recommended to me as well informed as to the state of affairs there, and also with the signers of the petition handed me for my information, addressed by various citizens of the County, to His Excellency the President of the United States. The result of the investigation thus made, is in my opinion to confirm the statements made in that petition so far as my means of observation extended. The signers of the petition above referred to appear to be small farmers who live mostly in the northern part of the County, and are all (except four) white men, many of whom served in the Union Armies, in those regiments which were raised in Northern Alabama. They seem to be poor, but probably honest and peaceable, and as far as I can judge only desirous to cultivate their small farms, on which the subsistence of their families depends, and to express their political opinions as they please. Differing in political sentiments from other inhabitants of the County, and others adjacent it is not improbable that collisions occur, but brutal crimes appear to have been committed which cannot have the countenance of members of any political party, and their perpretration is exciting in the County as near as I can ascertain the indignation of all right thinking men. . . ." Copy, *ibid.* On Aug. 5, Brig. Gen. Alfred H. Terry, Louisville, endorsed this report and related papers to the AG "with the information that the proper civil Officers will be notified that the required assistance in making arrests will be furnished on requisition. . . ." ES, *ibid.* See *SRC*, 42-2-1, part 8, pp. 559–60.

On June 22, Allen M. Gunn, Gravella, Ala., wrote to USG. "As a private citizen I should not presume to address you again, were it not that I think it the duty of every loyal citizen in the South to furnish, all Specific information, in his possession, to the President of the U States as to the Outrages committed in *his* Vicinity, of which he has a personal knowledge. I am fully Satisfied that hundreds of Outrages are committed on the persons and property of loyal Citizens which are never knon outside of the neighborhood in which perpetrated. I shall State the following facts which occurred to Me in Evergreen on last Monday a week ago—~~and~~ and Merely add that the cause was entirely political. I had been in Evergreen but a short time when I was called to a crowd of Men before the door of a grocery, and as Soon as I got near, one John S Sterns commenced telling the crowd that he had met up with a nephew of mine in Montgomery, who told him that I was a disgrace to the *Gunn Family* Since I had joined the *Radical*-negro party, and that he (my nephew) would never recognize me as his uncle any More. I told Sterns if it was a disgrace to be a Republican, and to be an advocate of the cause and government of the United States, that wherever its Standard was planted and the *Stars* and *Stripes* unfurled to the breezes, I would not only rally around IT Myself, ready to live or die, in its defense, but that I had ten children and would teach them to do the Same. Sterns jumped up with a very large stick in his hand and Struck me Such a blow on the head that it Knocked me down, and in my effort to recover was Knocked down again and beaten until I was insensible as to where I was or what doing. I can prove by John Mosley a respecable citizen of this county, that four or five months ago this Same Sterns threatened to Kill me with a four pound weight if I had *remained* in the *Store* a few *Minutes* longer and Kick me out &c. ~~When~~ he attacked me at that time on the Same Subject of 'being a Radical—I have Said enough, on this point unless I had space to go into all the detailed circumstances connected with the affair. *Another,*—Shortly after the close of the rebellion, United States Soldiers were Stationed Six Miles below Evergreen and one of the men were Sent to Evergreen on Some trifling matter and as Soon as he arrived in Evergreen Some twenty men Surrounded him and one P. D. Page Knocked him down three times with a 4 pound weight Swung in a Shot Sack, and abused him very badly and this was Seen by my wife, and to tell it in her own language 'She Saw it with her own eyes. The officer of the command came up the next day and tried to find out Something about the matter; but all were Silent. My wife would have told him all about it, but we live 8 miles from Evergreen Without comment I merely give a correct Statement of these cases, do not expect any reply, unless you wish . . . NB. Would not an assault, though made in open day light be considered, an act coming under the Ku Klux Bill when committed in Such a locality as ALL would be considered accomplices? I think the *Same* as *done* in *Midnight* darkness. Far be it from Me to endeavor to prejudice the mind of of any man against any *locality* in our country, but I have remained Silent, grinned and endured for the past four years, having a wife and ten children dependant on me for Support, and all the powers of Ku Klux democracy combined against Me to put Me down, for no other reason than that I believe we have a good government, and I intend to Sick to it and support it at the hazard of My ALL;— My fathers *blood* purchased the american constitution, as a faithful and dutiful Son, My blood Shall Seal IT before I yield one inch, in defense of *its honor*; and the *glory* of My *beloved country.* I am not for exciting *Sectional prejudice,* but I believe Democracy is bent on 'rule or ruin,' and I am determined for the future to be at my post; and to cry aloud and Spare not.—I close, but I wish to God I had an opportunity of tell My feelings. Pen and ink fail to communicate,—only exhibit the Skeleton— The life is within. Excuse.—I do not expect an answer, but would willingly hear from you." ALS, DNA, RG 94, Letters Received, 2302 1871.

On Oct. 28, John H. Wager, Huntsville, wrote to USG. "I have the honor to forward the enclosed statement of samuel Horton a victim of these pets of Democracy, and old man, who being driven from his home, poor no depending upon the charity of his friend." ALS, *ibid.,* RG 60, Letters from the President. Enclosed is

Samuel Horton's statement. "... Affiant states that on Monday night the 23rd day of October 1871 he was at Jim Halls on his way to a mill   his son Benjamin C Horton came to him about 10 P. M saying that he had been told by a friend of theirs who had come to the said Benjamin C Hortons saying that he was a friend to both and did not want to see them hurt. That the Klu Klux said they were going to kill the said samuel Horton and William sheppard between that time and saturday night and as for the said Benjamin C Horton they intended to whip him and his wife as long as they could stand it. And for the said samuel Horton not to stay there after that day that on Tuesday night they were be commence   Affiant further declares that he returned to his home on Tuesday morning ~~and~~ his wife and daughters informed affiant that on Last night (Monday) five men came to their house and aroused the said wife and daughters from sleep calling for them to open the door that they were not at this time in disguise, and wanted to look through the house for affiant and his son Benjamin C Horton,   Affiants wife opened the door and these men came into the house searched the room she was in, the loft above and the other parts of the house but would not permit lights to be brought so as to make light, useing abusive ~~language~~ and insulting language to them all the time. This friend of theirs said they inten to have the said Samuel and his son the Benjaman Horton and the said samuel Horton further declares that he was informed by his son Benjamin C Horton was concealed and saw five men dressed in disguise amongst whom he is sure was Shider Copeland That these men went to the house of Mrs sarah E Densinon's and while there the said Benjamin C Horton heard this man shider copeland say that Jim Hall was always meddling where he had no business and he said Hall would 'catch it soon' and as for old Horton and sheppard they both would 'go up before saturday night'   this was communicated at the time the other warning was all this combined and from the treatment to his son and threats given out against ~~the~~ affiant he has his house and now is a wanderer from it fearing he will loose his life if he remans there   That this friend of the said Benjman C Horton said that the Klu Klux gave as a reson for their intend~~ing~~ed actions that the said Parties samuel and the said Benjamin C Horton and the said William sheppard had been giving testimony against them before the Klu Klux committee in Huntsville alabama" Copy, *ibid.* On Oct. 10, Samuel Horton, Huntsville, had testified before a subcommittee of the Joint Select Committee providing additional details on his confrontations with the Ku Klux Klan. *SRC*, 42-2-41, part 9, pp. 729–30, 734–37. On Oct. 11, William Shapard testified concerning Ku Klux Klan intimidation. *Ibid.*, pp. 744–45, 756, 768–69. On Oct. 14, Wager testified. "Please to state your residence and occupation. *Answer.* Huntsville, Alabama; agent and disbursing officer of the Freedmen's Bureau.... I came to Alabama in September, 1865.... I entered the Freedmen's Bureau as a clerk for Colonel Edwin Beecher in May, 1867.... I was stationed at Montgomery until about the last of September, and then I was ordered up to Athens, Alabama.... in February, 1869, I was ordered here, and have been here ever since.... I have kept a kind of a memorandum when anybody came to me. I thought the best way to do, where the outrages were of a very serious nature, was to write their statements out and have them sworn to, either before Judge Douglass, probate judge, or the clerk of the circuit court, and some copies of these I kept and gave to Mr. Lakin, and some copies I forwarded to General Crawford. Most of the valuable testimony I had I transferred to General Crawford's hands, in the shape of affidavits...." *Ibid.*, pp. 926–27. On the same day, Enoch Alldredge testified. "Where do you live? *Answer.* In Blount County, ... I have lived in the county, with the exception of eight months, ever since December, 1816.... I have held a seat in the legislature, or occupied a seat there, twenty-two times in my life, and I have held other little offices under that. . . . I know a man by the name of William Shapard. He is called Shepherd. . . . It is generally understood that Shaphard was a very unreliable man, and one that men would not trust in a court of justice as a witness. *Question.* Do you know a man by the name of Horton?. . . Samuel Horton; an old man? *Answer.* Yes, sir. . . . His character is not as good as the other man's, scarcely. He is thought to be as unreliable as to veracity on oath, or otherwise, as the other could be, and then he stands implicated as meddling with other people's property, slightly. . . . Well, stealing hogs. . . . I never saw the old man do anything wrong; but he is a very unreliable man, I know. . . . *Question.* Did you hear of Horton's son being Ku-Kluxed and whipped?. . . Why was he Ku-Kluxed or whipped? *Answer.* He had married a widow, and he treated the children mighty badly; that was the cause alleged; that is what he told me; that the Ku-Klux told him that it was in consequence of the treatment of these step-children. . . ." *Ibid.,* pp. 984, 986–87.

On Dec. 12, John A. Minnis, U.S. attorney, Montgomery, wrote to USG. "Having recieved from the Department of Justice, some, as I remember two or three communications directed to you, directly, in relation 'Ku Klux' outrages, and although I am constant communication with the Atty Genl, I hope you will not deem it amiss, or improper, that I directly give to you a succinct statement, of a portion, at least, of the true situation. Before my appointment as Dist Atty for the Northern, embracing the Middle, District of Alabama; I was well assured there were 'Ku Klux' organizations in the State under some name or other, and that these organizations were mainly, if not entirely, brought into existence, and so continued and kept up, with a *political* Animus, mainly to control, directly or indirectly, the politics of the Country; I have been, and now am well satisfied that such is the truth; I have frequently so stated publickly, and have so published to the world; and now with a years experience, in office, and constant investigations, I am fully satisfied of the correctness of my positions, and I think when I commence jury trals of some of the cases now under indictment, I shall be able to demonstrate to every unprejudiced mind that I was, and am correct. At the November Term (third monday in November last) of the District Court of the U. S. Northern District in Huntsville Ala, one week only allowed by law; The Grand Jury in Sixteen indictments, presented some seventy men, some of them the very bad cases in the communications addressed to you; These indictments for 'Ku Kluxing.' wWe have an adjourned term at Huntsville, commencing 21st February 1872 (next) when the Grand Jury, not being finally discharged, will resume their labors, and investigations. I exspect at this term to put some of them on trial, as I learn several have already been arrested, in addition to a few I had already bound over from before U S commissioners, some are under bond, a few in Jail, many I think have and will leave the country. In two weeks session at this place commencing 4th Monday in November last (1871) The Grand Jury found, for this offence eleven bills of indictment, embracing about Sixty seven men, one of these a bad case, now in Jail here, others I trust will soon be arrested and some will no doubt flee the Country. To show the animus of this thing, quite a number of Witnesses, and especially Colrd men who had been whipped, said it was by men in disguise, who, sometimes, stated they were from the moon, at other times that they were the spirits of Confederate Soldiers from H-ll; and in both that they had come, and would come again to runn c the d___d Radicals out of the Country, some times simply asked how they had voted and if Republican then whipped them &c. I have examined two white men, amongst the many white men examined, who had belonged to these 'Klans'. One said its objects were to put down the d___d

Radicals and *negroes*, using their language, another speaking of a different 'Klan' said it was to keep the Radicals from voting the negroes. It has never come to my knowledge that any Democrat has been maltreated or even threatened by any of these 'Klans' except in a very few cases, where Democrats, and they are few, have taken a decided Stand against 'Ku Klux' outrages, and in a few cases of that sort, they have received some injury, and have been severely threatened. My late investigations in the Northern and Middle Districts have developed many cases, I had not even heard of before, and and demonstrates, that instead of exageration, as is so often charged, the half has never been told. That these Klans are organized, has been constantly shown by proof that it is impossible for any candid man to doubt: That the organization is a general one, I have not proof so conclusive, but the proof greatly tends to show that it is. If the Act of 31st May 1870, and the Act of April 20th 1871. can be sustained, by the Courts upon a construction that will meet and remedy the evil, and I think they can; then I think a vigorous prosecution in the Courts, so far as Alabama is concerned, can and will put them down. I am sure we have them now demoralized, and upon a routed ~~defeat~~ retreat, and every success brings with it new developments; If this can, as I think it can, be done and we can have free, fair and peaceable elections, I do not think there is a State in the Union more certainly Republican then Alabama. I have no doubt that with such an election last year we would have carried the State by a large and decided Majority, indeed I am satisfied that notwithstanding the intimidation and all the fraudulent voting, that upon a fair honest count Gov Smith was actually elected. It is the opinion of many of the most inteligent Republicans in the State, that if we could have a fair and free election in the State, that it could be carried or nearly so by the white vote. However this may be, I am certain there is a much better feeling towards the Republican party, and its principles in Ala by the white voters, and less proscription from the great body of the people, than herterfore, especially with old Union men in the large white counties. The only danger now in Alabama to the Republican party, at least the greatest, is the internal divisions and wranglings in the party. I do not pretend to say who is right or who, is wrong, or whether to some extent all may not be right and all wrong, unfortunately, with the inception of the party in Alabama, commenced a rivalry, first between Genl Swayne and Judge Busteed, and since continued between Senators Warner and Spencer, and if not caused by, certainly kept up for the sake of Federal patronage: I am certain that notwithstand the intimidations fraudulent voting, fraudulent counting Ku Klux, and all, but for this rivalry, division and bitter hostility among Republicans, we would to day have a Republican Governor, Legislature,—and two Republican Senators. . . ." ALS, DNA, RG 60, Letters from the President. The enclosure is *ibid.* On Oct. 6, Minnis, Huntsville, had testified before the subcommittee. "How long have you lived in the State of Alabama? *Answer.* Since the fall of 1866. . . . I moved from North Carolina to Tennessee in 1838, and lived there in Tennessee until 1866. . . . *Question.* From your knowledge of the tone of public sentiment in the State, do you think a republican can express and advocate his political opinions with freedom and personal safety throughout this State? *Answer.* I think there are some places where he could not; I think there are a great many where he could. . . . When reconstruction first took place, in most portions of the State where I was, it was dangerous to talk about even attempting to educate the negro at all. . . . It is a fact that it is very hard in the best of our counties to convict a white man for any violence done to a colored man, though they do that sometimes; but in cases growing out of anything like a Ku-Klux organization, or men in disguise, I have heard of no convictions in this State as yet. If I have heard of any it has escaped my recollection.... The feature in the fourteenth amendment, disqualifying or rendering men ineligible, was very odious, and I do not know but it has done as much to keep up the irritation as any one thing connected with the whole of the reconstruction. I myself believe that, while it was imposed, I think, for the very best motives, and was well at the time, it ought to have been repealed, or the disabilities removed; and I have thought so for years.... Young men, seeing their fathers disqualified, find it a source of very great irritation, and one that appeals very much to the passions as well as to the reason, if to the reason at all. Take the case of a young man. He says, 'Here is the negro I used to own, eligible to any office; and here is my father, an intelligent man, who is ineligible to any office.' I think it would do a great deal of good to remove such disabilities, and that it could do no possible harm. Aside from that feature in the fourteenth amendment, I think the fifteenth amendment was the most odious of all the reconstruction measures...." *SRC*, 42-2-41, part 8, 527, 532, 552–53, 560–61. On Oct. 20, Minnis, Montgomery, again testified before the subcommittee. *Ibid.*, pp. 562–71.

On March 30, 1872, George A. Clarke, Uniontown, Ala., wrote to USG. "In submitting the enclosed Memorial for your Excellencies consideration I have humbly to ask your pardon for trespassing on your most valuable time. I however hope your Excellency will on the perusal of the facts therein set forth pardon my so doing. Your Excellency is no doubt aware of the difficulty of obtaining employment here in the South. The Public Schools apparently is the only chance I have for employ and no money has been paid over by the Treasury to Teachers since May last nor is it certain when any will be. Trusting your Excellency will please instruct your Secretary to reply at your early convenience and relying on your Excellencies clemency and that it will graciously please you to hearken to the prayer of the enclosed Memorial." ALS, DNA, RG 60, Letters from the President.

On April 6, William H. Chesnutt wrote to USG. "I regret to make this communication to you, but with the hope of getting protection for my[s]elf, and family I am compelled to do so. I have been badly abused by some of the Ku-Klux I have been taken out of my bed and beaten with clubs and my step daughter also because she resented an insult offered to her by one of them, they have broken me nearly up they have nearly got all of my stuff in their hands, some of them wanted my corn and other stuff for to live on, I am not in debt, and if, I have committed any act to justify their brutal acts on me I am not sensible of it, they have told a good many falsehoods to justify their acts on me but I am glad to know that the good citizens of the country who has known me does not believe their falsehoods, I have got a very good place in Tuscaloosa Co. Ala; 12½ miles from Tuscaloosa 280 acres they are a trying to compel me to sell it to them at their own price, I have had to moove my family from off of my place some distance, I have fled from the Ku Klux and am 30 miles off from my family at this time, they have gotten all of my stuff except one waggon load that I mooved with my family, they have left me no chance of trying to help support my family as I have had to flee from them, I had a plenty to support my family on when I was broken up, my life is in danger, I hope you will be pleased to give me and my family protection quickly and send protection to all the Loyal citizens of Tuscaloosa Co. Ala; I have been a resident of Ala; 25 years; I know all the persons that abused me, there has been a great deal of crimes committed in Tuscaloosa Co. I am acquainted with a good many persons who has been abused and some murdered by the Ku-Klux in that county and they go unpunished; I know of several persons whom they have abused and compelled to sell their stuff to them as well as their land because they wanted it, they have abused women and old men; I have always lived a sober steady life with the hopes of laying up something to live on when I got to old and infirm to labor but my hopes is blasted The Honorable E. W. Peck, Judge of the Supreme Co Court of Alabama, he resides in the town of Tuscaloosa, he is acquainted with me, my name is in the General Land Office at Washington D. C., I received my patents for my land from there, and also at the P. O. Department I served as Post Master of Fernvale Tuscaloosa Co. Ala before and since the war; Peter Wheat I am told is a trying to get the office if he has not already got it he is one of the Ku Klux that helped to abuse me and drive me from my home, his father was a rebel soldier and was in the rebel service through out the war, from what I am able to learn there is but one way to secure the full Union vote of the South in the next Presidential election, that is to take up the Ku Klux and punish them for the crimes they have committed and protect the ballot boxes, I do not believe any leniency that the government may show them will ever avail any thing they and the Secession Democrats will always be enemies to the goverment, they are a trying to get all the County, State and United States offices in their hands they can, my Post Office at the present time will be Gordo, Pickens Co. Ala;. . . P. S. If putting the black people in bondage again or paying the secessionist for them will conciliate them it is the only thing that will do it and I doubt very much whether that will conciliate them, I have always been opposed to secession and consequently opposed to the rebellion; I hope your Excellency will be pleased to send the people of Tuscaloosa Co. protection immediately, I dare not return to my family untill I know I can get protection I am sorry to have to make this communication but to save my home and perhaps my life;" ALS, *ibid.*

2. Samuel T. Carrow, born in N. C., served as col., N. C. militia, and defected in 1862. *O.R.*, I, iv, 694–95; *ibid.*, II, ii, 1548. On April 14, 1869, USG nominated Carrow as marshal, N. C. On July 12, 1872, Carrow refuted charges that he maintained "A North Carolina Corruption Fund" to influence elections for USG. *New York Times*, July 13, 1872. See James A. Padgett, ed., "Reconstruction Letters From North Carolina" (Part VI), *North Carolina Historical Review*, XIX, 1 (Jan., 1942), 87.

3. Darius H. Starbuck, born in 1818 in Guilford County, N. C., graduated from Guilford College and began to practice law in 1840. He was a delegate to the secession convention at Raleigh. On Dec. 20, 1865, President Andrew Johnson nominated Starbuck as U.S. attorney, N. C. On Jan. 9, 1869, Governor William W. Holden of N. C. *et al.* had written to [USG]. "We beg leave most respectfully and earnestly to request that the Hon. D. H. Starbuck be re-appointed District Attorney for the State of North-Carolina. Mr. Starbuck has held this office since 1865, and by his learning, diligence and devotion to the interests of the government, has given general satisfaction. We believe the interests of the government and the welfare of society would be subserved by his continuance in the office, while his re-appointment would be a just recognition of the services of an officer who has performed his duties with more than ordinary ability and fidelity." DS (9 signatures), DNA, RG 60, Records Relating to Appointments. On Jan. 21, Judge George W. Brooks, U.S. District Court, N. C., Elizabeth City, wrote to USG. ". . . Mr Starbuck was one of the very small number of citizens of prominence residing in that part of North Carolina, that remained under the controll of the rebels after the first year of the rebellion—who adhered to the Union. Before the rebellion his efforts were against that movement—during the existance of the rebellion his efforts were—directed toward the restoration of the of the authority of the federal governmt—And since the that authority has been restored—he has been an earnest advocate of the reconstruction measurs of Congress—" ALS, *ibid.* About the same time, Judge Thomas Settle, N. C. Supreme Court, Douglas, wrote to [USG]. "Allow me to recommend D. H. Starbuck, as District Attorney for North Carolina. He was appointed to this position, upon the reorganiza-

tion of the Courts in this State; and has discharged its duties to the satisfaction of the good people of the State. He rendered zealous and efficient aid in reconstructing the State upon its present basis. In the general election of April 1868, he was chosen as one of our Superior Court Judges, but declined that position for the place he now occupies. The administration has no warmer friend than Judge Starbuck, and his reappointment would give general satisfaction to our people." ALS (undated), *ibid.* Related papers are *ibid.* On Jan. 17, 1870, USG again nominated Starbuck.

In [*1871*], David L. Bringle *et al.* petitioned USG. "The personal and political friends of William H. Bailey Atty at Law of Salisbury North Carolina, having learned that there is a probability of the office of the U. S. Dist Atty for North Carolina being changed, Would most respectfully recommend the appointment of the above named gentleman for we feel that the intere[s]t of the goverment will be secure in his hands he is a lawyer of first rank son of a distinguished Judge of North Carolina, for his political opinions he has been censured by the Ku Klux party of the State— his appointment will give great satisfaction to your friends in this state" DS (20 signatures), *ibid.* Related papers are *ibid.* No appointment followed. On Dec. 6, 1871, USG nominated Bringle as postmaster, Salisbury.

4. See letter to William W. Belknap, May 13, 1871, note 1.

To Samuel G. Howe

West Point, N. Y.
June 9th 1871

My Dear Dr.

I am just in receipt of your very interesting letter of the 4th inst. forwarded from Washington to this place. I agree with you as to the necessity, and moral obligation, of giving to the people of Santo Domingo all the protection we can against revolutionists, and out side intriguers[1] against the peace and prosperity of that country, until such time as the American people, through their legal representatives, definitely settle the question of holding Samina Bay. That treaty has never been rejected by the Senate and I see no objection to the renewal of it[2] until it is acted upon except the promise to pay, which cannot be complied with, except by an appropriation by Congress. That appropriation cannot be expected unless the treaty is favorably concidered. I will concider this subject when I visit Washington, which will be in the course of next week.

Yours Very Truly
U. S. Grant

Dr. Jas. G. Howe

ALS, deCoppet Collection, NjP. On June 4 and 27, 1871, Samuel G. Howe, Boston and New York City, wrote to USG. "I believe that you can, at this moment, do more than any human being, to avert a civil war which, with all the usual train of blood & misery, impends over a neighboring people. This belief is my apology for addressing you. My advices show that such a war, encouraged by foreign governments & commercial monopolists, impends over Santo Domingo. Whatever may be the merits or demerits of the Baez administration, all who know the history of the Dominican Republic must admit that it has been for years the regular government, *de facto*; & that it has done more to preserve peace & order, than any of its predecessors. The project of that administration (so heartily accepted by the people,) to annex the republic to ours, brought upon it the secret & the open hostilities of those foreign powers which disfavour the growth of our political influence in the West Indian islands, & of those mercantile establishments which dread any change that may disturb the commercial monopoly which they now enjoy. It also stirred up the anger of that party in Haiti which covets the domination of the whole island, even at the price of extermination of all its inhabitants, ~~whether~~ of white ~~or~~ & of mixed blood. All these parties are pressing the Baez Administration to the wall. They subsidize Cabral, & other revolutionists of Santo Domingo, who, though themselves annexationists, prefer to involve their country in bloody strife rather than allow their political rivals to retain power. Being supplied with funds from abroad, they rally about them a few of that class of military vagabonds, engendered in every country which is frequently disturbed by invasions or by civil wars, & who follow the banner of any chief promising pay & booty. Professed revolutionists like Cabral, & bandits like Luperon, can range along the frontiers of the Republic, with a few such followers, & carry on a border ruffian war, sure of a safe retreat over the border into Haiti; just as the Brigands of Greece so long found safe refuge in Turkey. A band, no larger than that of the Forty Thieves, can threaten & disturb a large extent of country, & cause great trouble & expense to any feeble government which defends it. The necessity of this defense has been the main cause of keeping the Baez Administration so wretchedly poor. It cannot support a regular army; & the militia hastily called together when an alarm is given, receive nothing but scanty rations of bread, & vague promises of pay. The civil officers have been unpaid for a long time. I know worthy & accomplished men whose families have been long in an almost starving condition, living on the coursest food, & lacking means to dress so as to be presentable in society in which their culture entitles them to move. The last hope of these men, & of the whole peace party, is that a 'sober second thought' may yet induce our people to lend a favourable ear to the unanimous & earnest prayer of the Dominican people, for annexation. The voice of that prayer has, hitherto, been drowned in the clamour about side-issues; such as, who is legitimate President, Baez or Cabral; and whether the measures of your administration to keep the peace, pending negotiations, were lawful or unlawful; whether annexation would be favourable or unfavourable to the aristocratic & aggressive party in Haiti; and the like. The Dominicans perish while our politicians squabble, & insist that they shall not be saved, except by their prescriptions. It is a curious illustration of party spirit, that while Cabral 'fillibusters' to prevent the President of Santo Domingo from reaping the credit & advantage of Annexation, politicians here fillibuster to prevent the President of the United States from reaping similar supposed advantages. Cabral professed to be an Annexationist; but will not let Baez annex. Some of our politicians profess to desire to *protect* Santo Domingo; but violently oppose the really protective measures of your administration without suggesting any practicable measures of their own. In this way, as I just said, the earnest & unanimous prayer of the Dominican people for annexation, is kept from reaching the ears of our people. Meantime a fearful crisis is at hand. The Treasury is depleted. The general hope & belief, so fondly entertained by the masses, that Annexation would come to give them peace & security, is turning to bitter disappointment & despair. The only thing which feeds hope is the fact that our flag still floats over Samana. If that flag should be struck, there would be a wail of despair from all the peaceful & patriotic inhabitants of the Republic; & a savage shout of joy from malcontents, brigands, & revolutionists, which would be echoed back by that barbarous portion of the Haytians, who covet the possessions & the lives of the whites & mixed breeds of the whole island. The striking of that flag (significant of death to hope of annexation,) would be followed by a revolution, & by the elevation of some faction which would promise to pay. But this would be a small part of the evil. It would be the signal to let slip the dogs of civil war. It would bring in all the brigands & military vagabonds, ever hovering on the Haytian frontier & in the neighboring islands. It would destroy the little settlements of the coloured emigrants from this country. It would repel all other emigrants. It would revive the hopes of the war, party in Haiti, & perhaps renew the bloody invasions so disastrous to both peoples in past times. It would act disastrously upon the so called Negro Republic by crushing out the small party which alone has any republicanism, or any spirit of progress. If I understand aright, we hold Samana in virtue of an article extending the time for ratification of the treaty of 1870, to July 1st 1871. Now, even if the whole project of a treaty was not annulled by the failure of the Senate to ratify it, still, it must expire with this month of June. For the honor of our country, the rent now justly due for our 'use & occupation' of Samana Bay, ought to be paid to the Government of Santo Domingo; & that would enable it to keep the peace. But, if this cannot be, then, for the sake of humanity, I hope that a new treaty may be immediately initiated, in virtue of which our flag may float there for the security of life & property, until our people shall decide for or against Annexation." ALS, NHi. "It was my purpose to seek a personal interview with you this evening and to solicit your attention to the precarious condition of the party of law and order in Sto Domingo. But my health fails. I fear that they will give up in despair unless they receive both material and moral aid immediately. They and their friends here look to you. The Dominican people feel a deep and bitter disappointment at the postponement of annexation. Their only hope is that you will persist in the practical protection which you have thus far extended to them by keeping the peace. It has doubtless occurred to you that the final ratification of the English treaty will make the continuous possession of Samana of greater consequence to our country than ever, since it will prevent us from obtaining coal and supplies from foreign ports in case of war. The ablest persons whom I have consulted agree with me in thinking that unless the Samana treaty is kept alive, the maintenance of our flag there after the 30th of this month will be siezed upon as a pretext for accusations of unwarranted assumption of power. I feel authorized to say that Judge Pierrepont considers it possible so to frame an extension of the time for ratification of the existing Samana treaty as will obviate the objection suggested in your letter of 9th Inst. viz 'excepting the promise to pay which cannot be complied with except by an appropriation by Congress.'" Copy, *ibid.* See *PUSG,* 20, 122–23, 188–89; letter to Buenaventura Báez, Jan. 15, 1871, note 3; Samuel G. Howe, *Letters on the Proposed Annexation of Santo Domingo, in Answer to Certain Charges in the Newspapers* (Boston, 1871).

On April 10, Buenaventura Báez, Santo Domingo, wrote to USG. "Three defeats inflicted upon the rebels in the space of ten days (from the 7th to the 17th of March) the wild enthusiasm of the towns to defend the principles of the Government; the fabulous number of forces which are voluntarily gathering in order to ward off the danger, prove that the Government is supported by the opinion of the great majority of the inhabitants of the country. I have documentary evidence that the Haytians are instigating Cabral and Luperon to appear on the frontiers as a protest against annexation, hoping to deceive the good judgment of the American people by causing them (who are at a distance) to consider these badly disguised Haytian movements as an expression of the will of the Dominican Republic. I do not fear the obstinacy of these adventurers, nor the secret protection of their instigators, provided Your Excellency, understanding the situation of my Government, will continue to protect us by sea against the possible attempts and attacks of Nissage Saget, and will, at the same time, take care to have the necessary pecuniary aid furnished us provisionally, on account of the Treaty of Samaná. Without this aid, it will not be possible for me to prolong so expensive a resistance, without means of subsistence. It was so understood by the honorable members of the Commission, who studied our exceptional condition so attentively while here, admiring the phenomenon of the constancy and self-denial of an entire people living without pay, without presents and without any assistance. I have the honor to repeat to Your Excellency that with the protection of your Government continued as hitherto, and with the means of subsistence alluded to, not only can we quietly await the decision of the Washington Congress, but exterminate the rebels Cabral and Luperon, agents of the selfish policy of Hayti, and even resist Hayti itself on our frontiers. I hope Your Excellency will take the foregoing into consideration, and deign to take the necessary measures in order to insure the success of a plan which has the warmest support of the Dominican people. . . ." LS (in Spanish), DNA, RG 59, Notes from Foreign Legations, Dominican Republic; translation, *ibid.*

On June 16 and 17, Fish recorded in his diary. "The President read a letter addressed to him by Dr S. G. Howe urging renewal of Samana lease, & continuance of protection to San Domingo. Robeson refers to the position of the Navy toward San Domingo, & the orders which have been given—under which (he says) if any power interferes with San Domingo, the Navy will fight. I remark that all obligation, of protection, under the treaty of Annexation is at an end, & suggest that these orders should be revoked—Much sympathy expressed for San Domingo, & discussion whether any money can be given them, 'I have none at disposal of my Department'—Robeson thinks possibly he may find some fifteen or twenty thousand. dollars—Boutwell seems earnest that some be found—President authorises a new lease to be made by treaty, for Samana Bay which may give moral support—protection—I remark that there is no one here authorized to negotiate in behalf of San Domingo—he replies that Fabens is here—to which I reply that it will not answer to negotiate with Fabens—He then says it can be done in San Domingo—" "Mr Boutwell calls early at my House—refers to the discussion in Cabinet yesterday, about the renewal of the lease of Samana— thinks that any renewed measures in that direction might excite criticism, & disturb the political prospects which at present are encouraging—Says he has thought over the idea thrown out by me yesterday, that the acceptance of a lease of Samana would not involve nor authorise a protection of the Govt of San Domingo, & that the renewal of that protection would expose the President to much criticism & censure from all in the Republican Party who wish to find fault with him (he names Greeley as one)   The orders to the Navy are spoken of as exposing the Govt to being involved in active complications, & it is admitted by both, that it is desirable that they be revoked, or considered as expiring with the limitations of time for the exchange of ratifications of the Samana lease treaty—Which by the way, expired long since   The Additional

Article, signed on 7th July 1870 extending the time to 1 July 1871 was not submitted by the President to the Senate in July last—referring yesterday to this fact, the President said 'I think I am responsible for that', to a remark of mine 'that probably it had been overlooked & left in his room in the Capitol' he replied 'I rather think it was left in this room'—" DLC-Hamilton Fish. On Dec. 6, 1870, Joseph W. Fabens had written to Fish. "I have the honor to acknowledge receipt of your letter of 3rd inst. in reply to mine of 2nd in which you state that my letter of credence as Minister Plenipotentiary of the Dominican Republic confered upon me authority to act solely with reference to the pending treaty with that Republic. which treaty was rejected by the Senate. I beg to call to your remembrance the fact that after such rejection. I submitted to you powers as Plenipotentiary to act with reference to the Samana Bay treaty. and signed on the 7th day of July following an additional article. extending the time for ratifying said treaty by the U. S. Senate to July 1st 1871. I have since received full powers. as Minister Plenipotentiary. from the President of the Dominican Republic, to make a new treaty of annexation. which I hope to have the honor to submit to you, on Thursday, 8th instant—The Dominican Government relies upon me to look after its interests generally in this country. . . ." ALS, DNA, RG 59, Notes from Foreign Legations, Dominican Republic.

On July 17, 1871, Báez wrote to USG. "The want of a direct opportunity deprived me of the pleasure of making known to your Excellency the capture of San Juan by the troops of the Government, which took place on the 4th day of June with very considerable losses to the enemy. The Haytians lost in that feat of arms two pieces of artillery which they had sent to Cabral from the town of Mirabalé, one General of five who were to assist the factions, two field officers, a large number of troops killed or wounded, and eight prisoners whom the Consul of the United States in this Republic has seen and examined, one of the prisoners being the son of a Haytian Senator and nephew of one of the Generals who were in the action. The neighboring towns were evacuated by the faction, who, having lost their provisions and munitions of war, part of their armament, and credit for their former partisans, are now without resources. The Haytian soldiers sent to assist Cabral are not volunteer adventurers, but regular troops belonging to organized corps, such as the 10th, the 33d, and other permanent regiments of Mirabalé and other points. The Government of Nissage cannot henceforth deny the material and evident participation which it has voluntarily had in these matters. Time discloses everything! I should much regret if to the warmth with which the propriety of annexation has been dissented from yonder [meaning in the United States] there should succeed an icy indifference on the part of the people, because that would cause to be presaged here a solution contrary to the wishes of the inhabitants in general. It would be sad if after so many efforts and sacrifices, so much time employed in the arrangements connected with that great project, the vanity of one haughty petulant man, and the gratuitous calumnies of the detractors of Your Excellency, should triumph at last, by preventing your country from realizing a beautiful programme of peculiar usefulness, and one of philanthropy in behalf of a brother people not unworthy of its sympathies. . . ." LS (in Spanish), *ibid.*; translation (bracketed material in document), *ibid.*

On Aug. 10 and 22, Fisher W. Ames, commercial agent, Santo Domingo, wrote to Fish. "I have the honor to acknowledge receipt of your despatch of the 28th of June 1871, enclosing my full powers to treat with this Government in reference to the additional articles to the convention of the 29th of November 1869 for the lease of the Bay and Peninsula of Samaná, and also a draft of said additional articles. . . ." "It is my duty to inform you that I have learned unofficially but from a reliable source that the Prussian Government have made propositions to this Government for acquiring the Bay and Peninsula of Samaná and for eventual annexation of the whole Republic, that Prussia shall exercise a protectorate and furnish arms, money &c. . . ." LS, *ibid.*, Consular Despatches, Santo Domingo. On Aug. 22, Báez wrote to USG. "Certain questions now being agitated in this country which render more ample and intimate communication necessary, which could not be done by writing, I have determined to dispatch Mr. Manuel Maria Gautier near Your Excellency. This gentleman is Minister Secretary of State in the Departments of the Interior, of Police and Agriculture, and in charge of the Department of Foreign Relations. He is sent to fulfill near Your Excellency the confidential mission which has been confided to him. I hope that Your Excellency will deign to receive the Envoy, my Minister, with your accustomed kindness, and that you will give full faith and credit to any statements that he may make, both in my name and in that of the Government. . . ." LS (in Spanish), *ibid.*, Notes from Foreign Legations, Dominican Republic; translation, *ibid.*

On Oct. 11, Fish wrote in his diary. "Mr Fisher W Ames M. D. & Col Fabens, call together—Enquiry of Ames what news he has to give me, he replies that he & Fabens have come to speak on the subject of a renewal of the Treaty for a lease of Samana Bay—to negotiate which he says that Fabens has power—They are told with much emphasis that I will not negotiate any treaty, ~~except it~~ with San Domingo except it be done in the most formal, diplomatic manner, & will not recognize Mr Fabens (he being An American Citizen) as the Representative of the Dominica Govt That much of the trouble of the late Treaty arose from the irregularities in the manner of its negotiation—Enquire about the proposed renewal of the Samana lease, sent to Ames for negotiation—He says they refuse to sign it unless the Protection of the US be 'continued'—he & Fabens are told that the Protection long since ceased—that it was intended to last only during the taking of the Vote on the question of Annexation—& that it fell when that was over—Fabens says it was renewed & continued by the article extending the time for Exchange of ratification to which it is replied that that article never went into operation—was never submitted to the Senate—& that 'Protection' can be guaranteed only by Treaty, or Act of Congress. I declare positively that I will not negotiate with Fabens & express the opinion that the whole subject had better be allowed to rest for a year—Ames refers to the visit of Mr St John (British Chargé to Hayti) referred to in a recent dispatch of his—he evidently knew nothing—is very suspicious—& intensely credulous— the suggestion of a British Protectorate, & of the acquisition of Samana by Prussia, come from no authority—only he 'heard Profr Gabb "speak of it," & another person whose name he don't remember'—He wants Salary increased & larger Allowance for rent & Clerk hire! of course!" DLC-Hamilton Fish. See Endorsement, Jan. 3, 1882.

On Oct. 15, Ames, Cincinnati, wrote to Fish. "I have the honor herewith to transmit a communication (from Signor M M Gautier Minister of Exterior Relations of the Dominican Republic) regarding the negotiations—now pending—for the lease of the Bay and Peninsula of Samana" ALS, DNA, RG 59, Consular Despatches, Santo Domingo. The enclosure is a letter of Sept. 27 from Gautier, Santo Domingo, to Ames. LS (in Spanish), *ibid.*; translation, *ibid.* On Oct. 27, Fish wrote in his diary. "I read the letter of M. M. Gautier Minister of For. Affrs of ~~Hayti~~ San Domingo, dated Sept 27, declining to execute the proposed convention for renewal of lease of Samana Bay, £ in which I had inserted the words at the end of the II Article 'And the obligation assumed in the fourth Article shall be conditional upon and subject to the action advice of the Senate or of the Congress of the U. S' He urges reasons against altering the original convention, & wishes simply to renew it—The President very promptly says 'We will then drop the whole matter—and leave the whole question for Congress & the People'—thus, a troublesome, vexatious & unnecessary question, is, as I trust, finally got out of" DLC-Hamilton Fish. See message to Senate, Feb. 28, 1877.

1. On June 1, 1871, Gen. Theophilus James, Samana, had written to USG. "May God add upon you, his evry blessing may he ever Stand by you in evry trying hour may he be à present help to you in time of need may he also bless all the handy works of your hands. I beg that he will pour out all of those blessings upon you for all the good you have done, and are yet doing, for this republic. I have been for some time have wished to mention to his Excellency in person the subject of this letter; but have always found myself unable, from a variety of painful feelings to perform that task, I am therefore compelled to take this mode of communicating what would be culpable in me longer to conceal, viz, I was born heare in Sámañá in the year 1807 under the gouvernement of President Boyer, and after residing à long time in England I returned again in hayti were I occupied public persisions, untill 1867. were S Salnave was elected for years as President of that republic or the republic of hayti; armes being taken up agains his gouvernment the same year I were then brought to occupy the persision of an offercer to help mantain peace, and was shortly afterwards raised to Général of the army where I faught 27 battles the last was the 18th of Decbr 1869. therefore his Excelency can plainly see that I am well posted with all the hiden politics of that part of the republic; I will venture to say that almost two thirds of the people in hayti are in favour annexatin only since the gouvermant of Nesage Saget they are obliged to keep dark and silence, and I being one of the *Salnave* parties can not as yet return, to hayti; there can not be any doubt in you in annexining this Country   Should any thing accour there are men heare as well as myself who are able and willing with Sord in hand march from one end this Island to the other; and I shall further say that I saw a peace in the papers concerning the national debt between hayti France,   the dominnican gouvermant has nothing to do what ever with the debt contracted with hayti and france; otherwise why did hayti alow Spain an emperal gouvermant to purches and take persesion of the Said republic, and nothing could be said—from the haytian gouvermant to pervent them but mad the haytiens pay à large amount of money, for interfeareing with them, ~~who~~ how could this be done if they had so much authority? as it has been said in congress,   no this is only an intrigue but in the *united States* and in hayti; and by a Small potion of dominicans whose eyes are not yet opened; who sill keeps a little confusion in the Country, but it does not amount to much,   Having thus perpared the way for à converstino with you on this subject, I have only to add my warmest thanks for the almost parternal kindness with which you have honnored and bestowed upon us;. . . P. S My Brother Jacob James. the wesleyan Minester heare joins me with Sinceare regards to you and wishes you much prosperity in future life,   Should you think me to have erred in my views, and disaprove of my fowardess towards them; you will nevertheless do me the justice to believe that I am influenced solely by à sense of what appears to be my duty;" ALS, DNA, RG 59, Miscellaneous Letters. On Jan. 29, James and his brother Jacob had testified in favor of annexation before members of the Santo Domingo Commission. *SED*, 42-1-9, 217, 228–31.

On Aug. 3, Ebenezer D. Bassett, U.S. minister, Port-au-Prince, twice wrote to Fish. "*Private No 14* . . . The Government here has recently given prominence in 'Le

Moniteur' to a statement to the effect that Haïtién exiles and refugees had rendez-voused in St. Domingo near Monte Christo for the purpose of raising an insurrection under the connivance and assistance of President Baëz against the Government of President Saget...." "... Soon after the message of President Grant transmitting the Report of the St. Domingo Commissioners to Congress had been forwarded by the Cable *viá* Jamaica to the Government here, a Haïtién force estimated at between one and two thousand men, was quietly collected and as secretly as possible moved out from the valley of the Artibonite to Cabral's headquarters, under command of the Haïtién General M. Benjamin. Near San Juan the army of President Baëz suddenly fell upon and routed the combined forces of Generals Benjamin and Cabral. The Haïtién troops having been pressed into this service against their wishes, fought poorly; they fled in all directions at the first fire, and General Benjamin himself barely escaped with his life. This defeat seems to have disgusted the Haïtién authorities with their friend Cabral, and they are now completing a long cherished plan to supersede him. It has been decided to form under insurgent authority in St. Domingo what they call a *junte gouvernementale*, with Luperon, Cabral, Pimentel and others as chiefs. A meeting is to be held somewhere on the frontiers on the 6th instant to perfect plans to this end.... All these and other proceedings of the Haïtién authorities in this direction are carried on with a guarded caution and with as much secrecy as possible; but they are sufficiently well established to show the bad faith in which the promised neutrality as to the internal affairs of St. Domingo has been observed." LS, DNA, RG 59, Diplomatic Despatches, Haiti. On Aug. 21, Fish submitted both letters to USG. AE, *ibid.* On Sept. 2, Fish endorsed these letters. "Ack—Instruct Minister to be observant of all acts by Haitien Govt or by Representatives of other Powers, tending to embroil Haiti, San Domingo, or to disturb the peace of the latter, to remonstrate earnestly in case of any such acts, & report every thing to this Dept" "Ack—Can the transmission of aid either in money, or in military supplies or in men by the insurgents in San Domingo be traced to the Govt of Haiti?" AE, *ibid.* See message to Senate, Jan. 16, 1871; *Foreign Relations, 1871*, pp. 566–72.

2. On Dec. 12, 1872, Erastus C. Benedict, N. Y. senator, New York City, wrote to USG. "I take the liberty of enclosing to you a Slip from the Independent containing an article on the annexation of Dominica written a year & more ago, but witheld from publication from motives of expediency of temporary character. I now think it well to give a sketchy run over all our annexations, with a view to improving on the whole subject the common mind on the whole subject, as one not looking solely to the acquisition of more public domain but especially to high considerations of public utility. The point which I make on the mode of doing it—joint resolution— I deem very important, the other mode by treaty being more uncertain and less expressive of the public sentiment and less open in the discussion. It seems to me also desirable to accomplish it during this session if practicable—Delays may be dangerous. Political combinations will soon be attempted with a view to the future which may bring unexpected embarrassments." ALS, ICN. The enclosure is *ibid.*

To John Sherman

Long Branch, N. J.
June 14th 1871.

DEAR SENATOR:

Being absent at West Point until last evening, for the last week,[1] your letter of the 5th inst. enclosing one to you from Gen. Sherman is only just received. Under no circumstances would I publish it, and now that the New York Herald has published like statements from him it is particularly unnecessary.—I think his determination never to give up his present position a wise one, for his own comfort, and the public knowing it will relieve him from the suspicion of acting and speaking with reference to the effect his acts and sayings may have upon his chances for political preferment. If he should ever change his mind however no one has a better right than he has to aspire to any thing within the gift of the American people.

Very Truly Yours
U. S. GRANT

HON. J. SHERMAN, U. S. S.

ALS (facsimile), *John Sherman's Recollections of Forty Years . . .* (Chicago and New York, 1895), I, 444–45. On May 18, 1871, Gen. William T. Sherman, Fort Richardson, Tex., wrote to U.S. Senator John Sherman of Ohio. ". . . I see the Herald is out in full blast for me as President. You may say for me, and publish it too, that in no event, and under no circumstances will I ever be a candidate for President or any other Political office, and I mean every word of it. Of course no importance should be attached to a mere newspaper outbreak, but the mere idea that I might have presidential aspirations would make me the object of suspicion, and would taint every honest expression of opinion I might entertain on any matter of fact. I made no speech at all in NewOrleans, but simply in a conversational tone, at a club supper when called on spoke at random of topics that were raised by others, and doubtless said if there were Ku Klux I had seen or heard of none, during my trip south. . . ." ALS, DLC-William T. Sherman. On May 25, Gen. Sherman, Fort Sill, Indian Territory, wrote "To THE EDITOR OF THE HERALD:—I have been skirting the Texas frontier for the past month, and here for the first time I meet files of Eastern papers, by which I see quite an unnecessary muss has been raised by a purported speech made by me at a supper of the Union League Club of New Orleans the night preceding my departure from that city. Whoever reported that as a speech by me committed a breach of propriety, for Governor Warmoth presided, and before I consented to respond to a call I was assured by the president of the society that no reporters were present and that whatever was said would be sacred and confined to the persons present. Now as to politics. I think all my personal friends know my deep-seated antipathy to the subject, yet as you seem not to understand me I hereby state, and mean all that I say, that I NEVER HAVE BEEN AND NEVER WILL BE A CANDIDATE FOR PRESIDENT; THAT IF NOMINATED BY EITHER PARTY I SHOULD PEREMPTORILY DECLINE, AND EVEN IF UNANIMOUSLY ELECTED I SHOULD DECLINE TO SERVE. If you can find language stronger to convey this meaning you are at liberty to use it." *New York Herald*, June 8, 1871.

On June 5, a correspondent asked USG at Long Branch if he were "sorry for promising to be the republican candidate for the presidency?. . . 'I wasn't sorry to be a candidate, but I was very sorry to leave the command of the army. There appeared to be a unanimity in the public mind before the nomination was made that I should be the nominee of the republican party, and it seemed to me that it would be impossible to concentrate on any other candidate. Of course I won't say that any other candidate could not be elected by the republicans, but my acceptance certainly relieved the party from the danger of disagreement and dissension, and made it solid and compact. I consented to give up a life office for a temporary, though a higher one, for good reasons. I believed that if a democratic president was elected there would be little chance for those who fought for the Union. They would certainly have got rid of the office of Commander-in-Chief of the Army, and so shelved me. Believing this I went into the contest in earnest. These were the motives that actuated me. I think they were correct. At least I am not sorry that I acted on them.' 'General Sherman, Mr. President, is named as your successor. Would he take the nomination?' 'Well (after a pause), I don't know. Sherman and I are warm friends, and I am not authorized to speak for him. Of one thing I feel pretty certain, however, and that is, that Sherman won't stand on any platform the democrats will make. . . . No, sir; Sherman can have no affiliation with such men. He is no democrat, and never was. He probably knows very well that if the democracy succeeded, the Southern leaders, who are still hostile to the Union of the States, and, in that view, enemies of the republic, would gain possession of the government and before long annul, so far as they could, the acts of the republican party. That will hardly be permitted, in this century at least.'" *Ibid.* (subheading integrated), June 6, 1871.

On July 8, Gen. Sherman, Washington, D. C., wrote to John Sherman. ". . . I saw General Grant when he was here some days ago, and we talked about that letter sent him, and my published declination of a nomination by either party. I told him plainly that the South would go against him en masse, though he counts on S Carolina, Louisiana & Arkansas, but I repeated my conviction, that all that was vital at the South was against him, and that negros were generally quiescent and could not be relied on as voters, where local questions became mixed up with Political matters I think however he will be re-nominated & reelected, unless by personally doing small things to alienate his party adherents at the North. I will not myself directly or indirectly help either party, though I feel that the Republicans have done all that is possible to alienate me, and the Army Generally. My office has been by law stripped of all the influence & prestige it possessed under Grant, and even in matters of discipline & army control I am neglected, overlooked or snubbed. I have called Genl Grants attention to the fact several times, but got no satisfactory redress—. . ." ALS, DLC-William T. Sherman. On July 16, John Sherman, Mansfield, Ohio, wrote to Gen. Sherman. "Your letter of the 8th is rec'd . . . I will get through with this Canvass and will then be independent of patronage. I never rec'd a courtesy or kindness from Grant & never expect to. I have been his supporter since Shiloh—but owe him nothing—He will be nominated & I hope elected—So will I, & it is better for the

country that in our relative positions we are independent of each other. I hope you &
he will preserve your ancient cordiality for though he seems willing to strip your
office of its powers yet I have no doubt he feels as warm an attachment to you as
from his temperament he can to any one. You have been forbearing to him but lose
nothing by it. . . ." ALS, *ibid.* For additional text, see Rachel Sherman Thorndike, ed.,
The Sherman Letters . . . (New York, 1894), pp. 330–33.

On June 27, 1870, USG had written to Ellen E. Sherman. "As I am under
promise to Father McGuire to attend the Commencement at Georgetown College
on Thursday, I think I will not be able to be present at the Exhibition on Wednesday."
ALS, PCarlA. USG evidently declined an invitation to a student exhibition at the
Academy of the Visitation, Washington, D. C., and did not attend the Georgetown
College commencement. See Ellen E. Sherman to John Sherman, June 29, 1871,
DLC-William T. Sherman; *Washington Evening Star*, June 29, 30, 1870; John Gilmary
Shea, *Memorial of the First Centenary of Georgetown College, D. C. . . .* (New York, 1891),
pp. 228–34. On June 30, Thursday, USG distributed diplomas at the "second annual
Commencement of the National Deaf-Mute College, Dr. GALLAUDET, President." *New
York Times*, July 1, 1870. See *Calendar*, May 1, 1871.

1. On June 6, 1871, USG arrived at West Point, N. Y., along with his father Jesse
Root Grant, Orvil Grant, and Nellie Grant for Frederick Dent Grant's graduation
from USMA. Julia Dent Grant later joined the party. *New York Herald*, June 7, 8, 1871.

On June 10, Isaac F. Quinby, West Point, wrote to Orville E. Babcock. "I take the
liberty of sending you some papers relating to the Custom House at Buffalo and
strongly endorsing Mr Alberger for the Collectorship at that place. The President has
seen some of these papers and he and Mr Alberger have had a long interview about
the politics of the State of New York. I honestly believe that Mr A can do more to
reconcile the differences and bring out the strength of the republican party than any
other man in Western New York, and that his appointment would lead to the most
happy results so far as this State is concerned in reference to the next Presidential
election. I did not think it best to trouble Grant by putting these papers in his hands
at this time & place   Please oblige me by laying them before him when he visits
Washington next week" ALS, DNA, RG 56, Appraiser of Customs Applications. On
April 4, Edwin D. Morgan, New York City, had written to USG. "Mr F. A. Alberger
of Buffalo is a sound Republican, and a good man for collector of Buffalo, if you have
found a necessity for a change   Mr Alberger is energetic. He has been Mayor of
Buffalo, and many years in the common council. He has also held important state
offices. I believe he was one of your most active supporters in 1868, and will be in
1872." ALS, *ibid.* Related papers are *ibid.*

On March 6, William Dorsheimer, U.S. attorney, and E. Carlton Sprague,
Buffalo, had written to USG. "Understanding that a change in the Custom House in
this City is contemplated, we respectfully recommend that *Mr James O. Putnam* be
appointed to the Collectorship. Mr Putnam is one of the most prominent citizens of
Western New York, and is widely known through the State and country. He was,
for many years, a leading member of the Buffalo Bar, and has held many important
executive and legislative positions,—having been a member of the Senate of New
York, and Consul at Havre throughout the administration of Mr Lincoln. We recommend him to you as a gentleman of unblemished character, whose appointment will
be honorable to the public service and to your administration." LS, *ibid.*, Collector
of Customs Applications. On March 10, 1869, U.S. Representative Porter Sheldon of
N. Y. had written to USG. "I take pleasure in recommending to the favorable consid-

eration of your Excellency, the application to mbe made on behalf of the Hon James O. Putnam of Buffalo N. Y. for the Italian Ministry—. . ." ALS, *ibid.*, RG 59, Letters of Application and Recommendation. Related papers are *ibid.* For the Buffalo collectorship, see *PUSG*, 20, 261–64.

To John A. J. Creswell

Long Branch, N. J.
June 20th 1871.

HON. J. A. J. CRESWELL,
POST MASTER GEN.
DEAR SIR:

Recent events prove to me that the postmaster at Pensacola, Fla. F. C. Humphreys,[1] and the postmaster at Warrenton,[2] Fla. Geo. W. Legallais, should both be removed. I do not know that other parties have been recommended for their places but I would suggest that some agt. of the department be directed to look into the matter and suggest names for their places. I would not consult Senator Osborn[3] in the matter.

Your obt. svt.

U. S. GRANT

ALS, Gilder Lehrman Collection, NNP.

On April 10, 1871, Antonio M. Soteldo, Jr., "Special Agent of the Treasury," Pensacola, wrote to USG. "*Personal* . . . My solicitude for the future political success of your administration in the State of Florida, impelled me yesterday to send a brief telegram to Gen Babcock, with reference to the Collectorship of the port of Pensacola, the contents of which he doubtless communicated to your Excellency. In thus taking the liberty of addressing you personally on the several matters set forth below, I am actuated by no other feeling than a desire to deal justly and fairly with a public officer who has been guilty of no crime, unless it be, a faithful and honest performance of his duty to the Government and the Republican party, and whom a corrupt combination of self-styled Republicans have constantly harassed, annoyed, persecuted, slandered and are now endeavouring by misrepresentation and falsehood, to induce you to remove from office. My past services to the party and the proofs I have given of my gratitude for your kindness to me, are, let me hope, sufficient to convince you, that I act in this instance, as I shall ever act so long as I have the honor to possess your confidence, namely, in devoting myself absolutely and unqualifiedly to the furtherance of your interests and that of your administration against all its opponents, within and without the Republican party. In accordance with your desire, as expressed to Mr Lamont and communicated by him to me, I accepted the office I now hold. I was assigned to duty in this State. Shortly after my arrival at Key West, Fla, Colonel Frank N Wicker, the Agent in charge, and myself, started on a tour of inspection, throughout our District. We finally reached this port yesterday and at once proceeded to examine into certain grave charges made against Mr Potter, the Collector of Customs for Pensacola. After a thorough investigation, we both arrived at the conclusion, that Mr Potter had been the victim of an infamous conspiracy, and that his accusers were men of reputation so vile, that we could not believe their statements under oath. The instigator and head centre of Mr Potter's enemies is one George E Wentworth, State Senator and recently United States Marshal. This man has succeeded in gaining the unenviable character of a corruptionist. He proudly boasts of having sold his vote in the state Legislature (for the Littlefield Railroad) for $5000. He also claims to own Senator Osborn whom he familiarly calls Tom Osborn, because, as he asserts, he has laid out $2.000 on him. Senator Osborn, is using his present position and the patronage incident to it, in placing men in office, who will support him for reelection to the Senate in '73. It is asserted by prominent citizens and good Republicans that he proposes to effect the removal of all those who are not friendly to his reelection, whether they be honest Republicans and faithful officers or otherwise. I will inform your Excellency, that I have travelled extensively through Florida and that from private conversation with leading Republicans, I can assure you that Mr Osborn reelection is almost akin to an impossibility. His reputation has never been very good and latterly it has come to light that the sale of $300000 worth of Florida state bonds in 1869 in New York, and the sale of which was obtained through his influence, resulted in a division of the profits resulting from such sale, between the sellers and Mr Osborn. Numerous other charges are made against him of a very serious character, but which I forbear to mention, as they are not authentic. I therefore in conclusion, hope that your Excellency will pause before making any changes in this State on Mr Osborn's recommendation, especially of men whose moral character and personal worth, entitles them to the continued confidence of the administration and the respect of the people. The Republican Party in Florida to-day is far from being united, owing to feuds and dissensions. Should they continue, I very much fear that the Democrats will carry the next elections. Should your Excellency desire it, I will convey some important information, from time to time relative to the character of officials, which you can rely upon as *true*. With respect to Mr Potter, I will just state that he has been identified with the Republican party since its birth and has always borne a high reputation for ability and honesty. He was appointed state assessor of North Carolina by President Lincoln, was a member of the National Republican Convention that nominated your Excellency for the Presidency & was editor of the State paper in Tallahassee until appointed Collector of Customs for this Port. He is not controlled by any combination but discharges his duty and directs his best efforts to secure the continued success of the Republican party in Florida." ALS, DNA, RG 56, Collector of Customs Applications. On March 19, 1869, U.S. Senators Thomas W. Osborn and Abijah Gilbert and U.S. Representative Charles M. Hamilton of Fla. wrote to USG. "We the Senators and Representative from the State of Florida have the honor to request the appointment of George. E. Wentworth of Pensacola Florida—as United States Marshal for the Northern District of Florida. We recommend Mr. Wentworth knowing him well as a prominent Republican—a man of energy, inteligence and integrity. He served with much credit during the war having enlisted as a soldier at the commencement and served to the close being mustered out of service as Colonel. In recommending him for this office we do it beleiving it to be for the best interests of the Country and that the state has no man better fitted to fill the office. We trust the appointment may be made." LS, *ibid.*, RG

60, Records Relating to Appointments. On April 14, USG nominated George E. Wentworth as marshal, Northern District, Fla.; on Dec. 6, 1871, USG nominated Wentworth as postmaster, Pensacola, to replace Frederick C. Humphreys. See Endorsement, Oct. 7, 1872, note 1.

On June 14, 1871, Fla. Representative R. A. Stearns, Pensacola, wrote to USG. "This will be handed you by Rev. A. C. Fisher who has the confidence and respect of a large majority of the Republicans of this county: a majority who elected a republican delegation to the State Legislature last fall against the combined efforts of the bolting Republicans headed by Wentworth & Humphreys and the Democracy—Be so kind as to listen to Mr. Fishers Story and you will confer a great favor upon us—" ALS, DNA, RG 56, Collector of Customs Applications. In July, Richard Gagnet *et al.*, Pensacola, petitioned USG. "The undersigned colored citizens and Republicans of West Florida, respectfully represent to your Excellency that the retention of Hiram Potter Jr as Collector of Customs of this Port will be ruinous to the Republican party, and will give this portion of the State into the hands of the Democracy—Mr Potter has not the confidence or respect of the majority of Republicans here, nor does he exercise any influence outside of the patronage of his office. We also protest against the action and representation of one A: C. Fisher a colored employee of the Custom House, sent on to interview your Excellency as to the removal of Mr Potter, and declare that he is not a voter of our State nor is he a representative man at all of the Republicans of this section. The matter submitted to your Excellency by Mr Fisher and claimed as having been the action of Republicans in Mass Meeting was simply the expression of a secret caucus of Custom House employees and perhaps some dozen outsiders who were deceived as to the purport of their proceedings. We respectfully but earnestly urge the removal of Mr Potter, to the end that our party be re-united" DS, *ibid.*

On April 3, 1869, USG had nominated Hiram Potter, Jr., as collector of customs, Pensacola. On June 23, 1871, U.S. Senator Timothy O. Howe of Wis., Green Bay, wrote to USG. "One of the last Acts of the late Executive Session of the Senate was to Confirm some man to be Collector of Pensacola in place of Hiram Potter Jr. The man was confirmed because you nominated him; But the nomination was a mistake—as I think—Mr. Potter is and always was a sound, reliable republican. That is more than can be said of his successor—Mr. Potter was an honest & efficient officer—There is grave reason to fear you will not find such an officer in his successor. I dont know what the relative influence of the two men in Florida is, but I fancy it wd be difficult to muster a political influence in Florida, worth as much to you or to the republican Cause as the friends of Mr Potter wield in this State—Besides the republican party in Florida is well nigh paralysed by its dessensions: Its factions persecute Each other more than they oppose the Common Enemy. Under such circumstances I should think it wise for the National administration, so far as it could to Command the peace between those factions & not to become a party to their proscriptions—I learn that Mr Potter is now an applicant for the appt of special Treas. Agent—& that there is a vacancy to which he can be appointed—If so I hope he will be appointed   Mr Boutwell told me that Potter was removed because Senator Osborn lived in Pensacola & demanded it. If it is ascertained that Mr Osborne lives in Pensacola, I suppose it will be conceded that he does not live everywhere else. Therefore his hostility to Mr Potter can be no reason for proscribing the latter everywhere. The appointment of Mr Potter will demonstrate to his friends *here* that his removal from the Collectorship indicated not a wish to proscribe him but merely a willingness to remove him from Mr Osbornes door yard" ALS, *ibid.* On July 13, U.S. Senator Matthew H. Carpenter of Wis. endorsed this letter to USG. "I concur in every word Judge Howe has said within. Potter is an excellent man, a sound true republican, and I was very sorry that Osborn insisted upon his removal. I would respectfully suggest that Potter should be retained in the office he now holds, Collector of Pensacola, until next session of congress at all events; as I understand that you have revoked the Commission of Humphrey who was nominated and confirmed for the place." AES, *ibid.* On Aug. 3, [*1871*], A. C. Fisher, Mobile, telegraphed to USG. "A Colored man named Harriod left Pensacola Tuesday for washington it is supposed with bogus papers against Collector Potter there have been no public meetings nor legal petition here as yet please take no notice of him till you hear from me" Telegram received, *ibid.* Related papers are *ibid.* On Feb. 15, 1873, Potter, Tallahassee, wrote to USG requesting reappointment. ALS, *ibid.*

1. A military ordnance storekeeper (1855–61), Humphreys surrendered the Charleston Arsenal on Dec. 31, 1860, and resigned to become maj. of ordnance, C.S. Army (1861–65). See *O.R.*, I, i, 5–9; *ibid.*, III, i, 62; *ibid.*, IV, i, 406–7. On April 12, 1869, USG nominated Humphreys as postmaster, Pensacola; on May 23, 1871, USG nominated Humphreys as collector of customs, Pensacola. On June 20, USG, Long Branch, telegraphed to Secretary of the Treasury George S. Boutwell. "Please suspend appointment of Humphries as Collector of Pensacola, Fla. Send papers by mail." Copy, DNA, RG 56, Telegrams Sent. On June 21, Boutwell telegraphed and wrote to USG. "Commission not issued to Humphries. Been held for enquiry as to responsibility of sureties on bond. Will be held as you direct" Copy, *ibid.* "I replied briefly by telegraph this·morning to your dispatch of last evening concerning the Collector of Customs at Pensacola, Fla. About the time that Mr. Humphreys filed his bond a report came to the Department that the sureties were worthless. An investigation was ordered but no report has yet been received. The commission will be held until I hear from you further. If you decide to allow Mr. Potter to remain it will be well to so inform him, as from our latest intelligence he was preparing to leave July 1. Mr. Potter is a good officer, and the change was made upon the urgent solicitation of Senator Osborne." ALS, OFH. USG endorsed this letter. "Answer that Potter will be retained." AE (undated), *ibid.*

2. USG likely meant Warrington, Escambia County, west of Pensacola, where the postmaster received a salary of $450 in 1871. Probably in Dec., 1871, E. S. Scott wrote to USG. "I have been sent by the republicans of Warrington and Pensacola Florida to request His Excellency to remove four of the civil employees, and Commodore Middleton from the Pensacola Navy Yard as it has now become evident that these men are building up an opposition to the administration which is dangerous to the republicans there as voters, and also as laboring men. I have delivered their petition to the Secretary of the Navy, and he promised to do what he could. Senitors, Osborne and Gilbert and Congressman Walls are in favor of their removal. The republicans have been working hard to unite for the coming campaign, but nothing much can be done if this clique is allowed to exist. Will not His Excellency do what he can to remove them?" ALS (undated), DNA, RG 45, Letters Received from the President. On Dec. 20, USG endorsed this letter. "Refered to the Sec. of the Navy." AES, *ibid.*

3. Born in 1836 in Scotch Plains, N. J., Osborn graduated from Madison University, Hamilton, N. Y. (1860), and practiced law. He rose from capt. to maj., with bvts. as lt. col. and col., 1st N. Y. Art. (1861–66), served as asst. commissioner of the Bureau of Refugees and Freedmen for Fla. (1865–66), eventually settled in Pensacola, and entered the U.S. Senate in 1868. See *PUSG*, 10, 526.

To Horace Capron

Long Branch, N. J.
June 23d 1871

DEAR SIR:

Your place has been tendered to a gentleman from Pa, the editor of an Agricultural College, but his response has not yet been communicated to me. This need not however restrain you longer from any preparation necessary to make for your departure on the very important mission which you have accepted the responsibility of.

If you have not selected all the assistants you propose taking with you to Japan I would suggest to you the name of Jas. R. Wasson,[1] just graduated at West Point. Lt. W. is about 24 years of age; at the age of 16 enlisted as a private and served in that capacity from that time, /63, to the close of the war. At 20, without any schooling after he was 16, he entered West Point and graduated head of his class in almost every branch of studies, and very far ahead in the general average. He is now at my house spending a few days with my son, his class-mate, but is not aware that I am proposing anything for his benefit.

It is my earnest desire that in selecting a sucessor to you in the Agricultural Bureau that I will get some one who will carry out the very satisfactory plans and ideas which you have inaugurated. I look upon the department as a very important one, and full of benefit to the country if wisely administered. But with all its importance it is not equal in value to our country to your new mission. From it I expect to see early evidence of increased Commerce and friendly relations with a hitherto exclusive people, alike beneficial to both.

With great respect,
your obt. svt.
U. S. GRANT

HON. H. CAPRON,
COM. OF AG.

ALS, DLC-Horace Capron. Born in 1804 in Attleboro, Mass., Horace Capron grew up
in N. Y., opened a cotton factory in Laurel, Md. (1836), and undertook farming on an
extensive scale. He went to Tex. as special Indian agent (1852–53), moved to Ill.
(1854), resumed farming with an emphasis on cattle breeding, and served as col., 14th
Ill. (1863–65), being promoted to bvt. brig. gen. On April 9, 1867, President Andrew
Johnson nominated Capron as commissioner of agriculture. On June 29, 1871, a correspondent reported: "General Capron, some two months ago, entered into a contract
with the Japanese Government, through the Commission sent to this country for the
purpose of introducing into Japan the industrial ideas of American civilization. He is
empowered to introduce models of agricultural and industrial machinery, even to the
appliances of railroading. . . . Mr. Capron will receive a salary of $20,000 a year. Profes-
sor Anderson, of the District of Columbia, chemist of the Agricultural Bureau, has
resigned his position, and accepted the offer of the Japanese Government to accompany Mr. Capron as geologist of the expedition. Professor Pool, of Pennsylvania, also
joins the party as geologist and acting special engineer. The President is anxious to
find a worthy successor of General Capron. Hon. Frederick Walts, of Carlisle, Pa., was
yesterday tendered the appointment, but declined it. Hon. Marshal P. Wilder and J. R.
Dodge, Esq., the able statistician of the Department, have also been mentioned in
connection with the post." *Washington Chronicle*, June 29, 1871. See *PUSG*, 19, 31;
letter to Horace Capron, June 28, 1871.

On July 11, Frederick T. Dent wrote to Capron. "When Sheridan met his beaten
demoralized army near Winchester and turned it right about and on to victory, he did
what you have done with the Agricultural Department of the U S   You found it hid
away in the cellar of the Interior Department with a few bags of musty seeds, a few
old musty pamphlets—ashamed of the name it bore, and a disgrace to the great
interest it misrepresented   You took it as Sheridan did his beaten host recruited its
depleted force wheeled into line started it forward—not to one victory alone but to
a succession of them until now its fame and its influence is known and felt from
Maine to Texas from Cape Sable to Fuca's Straits—and far far beyond, for from our
antipodes comes a messenger asking you who have wrought this mighty change to
come to them break down their walls against progress let in upon them the light
of Modern Civilization and bring them into the family of Nations—I feel proud that
the selection has fallen on one of my Countrymen and especially so that it has fallen
on you—the choice is a wise one and they will not be disappointed   To your own
Country and to Japan I predict great results from this Mission—You know it is a
warm friend who writes the little words good bye" ALS, DLC-Horace Capron. Orville E. Babcock also wrote a congratulatory letter to Capron. ALS (undated), *ibid.*

1. On July 3, Secretary of War William W. Belknap wrote to AG Edward D.
Townsend. "Lt. Wasson to have *six* months leave in addition to Cadet leave—Also
permission to draw *four* months pay in advance—& to be ordered to report to Genl.
Schofied. This is by order of the President—" AL (initialed), DNA, RG 94, ACP, 2871
1871. On July 4, USG, Long Branch, telegraphed to Belknap. "Please Send Lt Was-
so[n's] orders to him at west Point without delay" Telegram received, *ibid.* On Dec. 19,
James R. Wasson, 2nd lt., 4th Cav., Washington, D. C., wrote twice to Belknap
applying for a leave of absence and tendering his resignation. ALS, *ibid.* On Dec. 20,
Belknap approved both requests, with Wasson's resignation to take effect on July 1,
1872. AES, *ibid.* See letter to James D. Cameron, Sept. 12, 1876.

To Adolph E. Borie

———

Long Branch, N. J.
June 23d 1871

MY DEAR FRIEND:

Mrs. Grant and myself will expect a visit from you and Mrs.
Borie before we start on our trip to California,[1] and will be pleased
to have you come at any time that best suits your convenience. If
you will set the time however we can invite other friends at such
times as not to interfere. Dont you think you might come early in
July? You can not mention a time when it will inconvenience us in
the least. No other invitation has gone out yet, and we do not propose leaving the Branch for a visit elsewhere this Summer, but once,
and we are not particular as to the time of that visit.

Mrs. Grant & the children join me in love to Mrs. Borie and
yourself.

Truly Yours
U. S. GRANT

HON. A. E. BORIE

ALS, PHi. On Jan. 12, 1871, Thursday, USG telegraphed to Borie. "Sec. Robeson and
myself go to Phila. on Saturday morning" Copy, DLC-USG, II, 5. See letter to George
W. Childs, April 2, 1871, note 5; letter to Adolph E. Borie, Nov. 16, 1871; *Philadelphia
Public Ledger*, Aug. 14, 1871.

1. See letter to George W. Dent, March 27, 1871.

To William Elrod

———

Long Branch, N. J.
June 23d 1871

WM ELROD, ESQ:

As I have not heard from the farm since I was there in Apl. I
presume every thing is right. However I like to hear particulars
occasionally. Have you made any of the proposed improvements

yet? You spoke of mixing lime with manure before putting it upon the ground! That will not do. Lime and manure should not be used at the same time. The lime would releace the Amonia, the most valuable ingredient, from the manure. If you get the lime kiln[1] put about 80 bushels to the acre on all the cleared land as fast as you can and put no manure where you put lime until the latter is all taken up by the soil.

Let me hear all the news from the farm; how many cows, calves, colts &c. I shall probably have to send you two of my horses this fall to work on the farm. They will be fine for that but from injuries are unfit for carriage horses any longer.

You need not sell the three year old grey colt until I see whether Fred.[2] goes where he can take him.

AL (signature clipped), Illinois Historical Survey, University of Illinois, Urbana, Ill.

1. See letter to William Elrod, July 8, 1871.
2. See letter to Frederick Dent Grant, July 30, 1871.

To Hamilton Fish

———

Long Branch, N. J,
June 25th 1871

Dear Governor:

The invitation to attend Columbia College commencement was promptly acknowledged with regrets because I had accepted an invitation previously, for the same date, to attend Princeton commencement.

From Princeton I shall go directly to Washington and spend there two days. I presume as a matter of course that you will want to be in New York at the time your son graduates, and that I will not see you in Washington. I know of nothing special that I want to see you upon except the Apt. of Commissioner to settle Alabama claims, and I presume Mr. Meredith[1] will suit to fill that place.

There is, I understand, to be a meeting within a few days now, of the Commissioners of the Pa Fair of /76?[2] If there are any Coms.

named by Governors of State, who have not yet been commissioned, I wish you would direct that the commissions be ready for my signature on arrival in Washington. You can sign your name in advance.

Very Truly yours

U. S. Grant

Hon. Hamilton Fish,

Sec. of State

ALS, Columbia University, New York, N. Y. On June 17, 1871, Secretary of State Hamilton Fish had written to USG. "*Personal* . . . The enclosed invitation comes under cover to me, from the President of Columbia College, with the earnest request that I urge your attendance at the Commencement—I am very sure that your presence would give great satisfaction and pleasure, not only to the Authorities of the College, but to the young Gentlemen who are about to graduate, (among whom is my youngest son, Stuyvesant) Columbia College is one of the oldest colleges in the Country—the oldest in the State of New York—If you can find it convenient to pass a short time in New York on the 28th I am quite sure that your presence at the Commencement, would gratify a great many people, (& among them, *young men who will remember it*,) very much—" ALS (press), DLC-Hamilton Fish.

On June 24, Fish telegraphed to Horace Porter, Long Branch. "The papers announce a Cabinet meeting next week—Does the President intend to have one— if so, on what day—~~I have to be in New York on Wedn~~" ALS (telegram sent), *ibid.* On June 28, Wednesday, USG telegraphed to Fish. "Please meet me at Long Branch on Friday" Telegram received, *ibid.*

On June 27, USG attended commencement at Princeton College, where President James McCosh introduced him. "Ladies and Gentlemen—This is the fourth occasion on which this college has received a visit from Presidents of the United States. . . . I once spent an evening with him between the period of his election and his inauguration. I had thought, on going to see him, of the saying of the forgotten philosopher, that God had given man two ears and one mouth that he might listen twice and speak once; but I found him unlike European statesmen, who will talk to you of literature, poetry or the drama, but will not say a word on politics. He spoke freely, and he expressed his determination to pay the national debt, to reduce the national expenditure, to do what was possible for the Indians, and above all was determined to have peace. Well, the debt has been reduced so much that it would take Professor Duffield and Professor Alexander all day to compute it, and with the rest of his policy all the world is acquainted. If I may be allowed a word of personal feeling, I would say that the greatest event which has happened in his term of office is the treaty between the two great nations that speak the English tongue—the bulwarks of Protestantism and the Bible. The President of the United States, gentlemen." *New York Herald*, June 28, 1871. USG responded. "Young Gentlemen of Princeton—I did not come here to speak, but to listen. I purpose to follow the maxim you have just heard and to listen with my two ears to what a distinguished graduate of Princeton has to say to you. I am very glad to meet you." *Ibid.* Secretary of War William W. Belknap, an 1852 graduate of Princeton, gave the commencement address. See *PUSG*, 20, 437.

1. Born in 1799, William M. Meredith, a leading Philadelphia lawyer, had served as Secretary of the Treasury under Zachary Taylor (1849–50). On Feb. 28, 1871, U.S. Representative Glenni W. Scofield of Pa. had written to Robert C. Schenck, U.S. minister to Great Britain. "I inclose this letter of Col Worrell recommending that Hon Wm M. Meredith of Phila be invited to advise with the Comrs on the part of the United States." ALS, DNA, RG 59, Letters of Application and Recommendation. On Feb. 27, James Worrall, Harrisburg, had written to Scofield. "I for one am surprised that Mr Meredith was not made *one* of the High Commission—It may have been because his health wd not permit him to go to Washington—But I think he is undoubtedly the ablest advocate in the United States—and I have never yet heard any lawyer of *any party* say otherwise of him than that he was the greatest man in his profession in this Country—This opinion is universal—and unanimous . . ." ALS, *ibid.*

Articles I and II of the Treaty of Washington established an international tribunal of five arbitrators at Geneva to settle claims arising from acts committed by the *Alabama* and other Confederate vessels. The U.S. and Great Britain each selected an arbitrator and an agent to this tribunal, with the remaining three arbitrators chosen by Italy, Switzerland, and Brazil. Article XII created a separate three-member commission—one each from the U.S., Great Britain, and a neutral country—to settle other war-related claims against both countries. Under Article XIII, both countries also appointed an agent to this commission, which met in Washington.

On May 29 and subsequently, Fish had written in his diary. "*President*—I consult him about Arbitrator, & agent before the Tribunal at Geneva, under the Treaty with Gt Britain—I suggest the name of Chas Francis Adams—he does not like it—Caleb Cushing—Beach Lawrence—Wm C Bryant are severally named—Bryant is too old—& is politically opposed to the President—Lawrence a Democrat—he prefers Cushing to either—Would like some one from Pennsa I urge the importance of an able representative—that it requires a peculiar course of study, & of training—that England, Italy, Switzerland, Brazil will send their best men, & we should have one who is equal to the best—that very few men in this Country have given their Attention to the peculiar class of questions involved before this Tribunal—that there are doubtless many of more ability than Adams or Lawrence, but very few who have studied & understand as they do the class of questions to be Considered—He suggests Pierrepont—I had thought of him for the Claims Commission—but had not thought his studies, & professional labor lay in the line required for the Arbitration—that Evarts would be more likely to fill the place, but his political attitude did not entitle him to consideration—He assented cordially to this—saying E. was a man whom he did not entirely admire—He expressed a willingness to secure Morton McMichael—He seems pleased with the idea of Edwards Pierrepont for the Claims Commission—Pratt of Indiana & Morton had recommended some one for one of the positions. Morton told me for the Claims Commission—President says he would place more Confidence in ~~Mortons~~ Pratts' recommendation than in Morton—I suggest Bancroft Davis for the Agent—he receives it very favorably—& I name Beaman, for an associate—he knows nothing of him, but is willing to leave it to me—I ask about Compensation—there is no appropriation unless it be taken from the 'Foreign Intercourse' & there probably, there will have to be a deficiency appropriation—He says they ought to be liberally Compensated—& that there will be no difficulty about appropriation—" "May 31 Wednesday . . . President introduces the subject of the appointments of Arbitrator &c &c under the Treaty with Gt Britain—Boutwell & Creswell strongly oppose Chas Fras Adams—Cresswell 'would prefer Hendricks!'—~~Judge~~ Cresswell asks 'why go out of the Commission?' Judge Hoar—& Williams are spoken of—President seems to incline toward Schenck I tell him that Schenck probably does not wish to remain abroad, as long as will be necessary for the sittings of the Tribunal—in consequence of his engagement with Jay Cookes' Rail Road—that I think there might be an indelicacy in either of the Commrs taking a position which they had aided to create—Edwards Pierrepont is named by the President—It is doubted if he speaks French—& it is questioned whether his reading & studies have been much in the line of international law— Atty Genl names Wm M. Evarts—Prsdt positively objects   Robeson names Wm M. Meredith—& the only question is if his health & age will permit—Prsdt requests me to make enquiry—He decides upon Bancroft Davis as the Agent—& Beaman for Assistant—Boutwell proposes Bemis, for Agent—but Prsdt considers that appointment decided—& authorises me to inform Davis & Beaman   The Senators from Indiana have recommended James S. Frazer, late a Judge of the Supreme Court, for Commissionr under the 12th Art—of the Treaty—The President without deciding to appoint him, for the present, places his name for that position, & Judge Pierrepont, & Govr Bradford of Md for presentation to the Brit—Govt—for the *third* Commissionr." "June 15, Thursdy ... President returned this morning from Long Branch—Cresswell was with him when I went in—Referring to the Arbitrator (to the Tribunal at Geneva, under the Treaty with G. B) he asked what information I obtained as to Mr Meredith, & was told what Mr Boker had told me—also what he had subsequently written—Prsdt remarks that he thinks he is too old, but he has a man who he thinks has most of the qualifications needed—& names O. P. Morton—to which I object most strenuously, saying that I do not think he is in any way competent for the place—Subsequently after Creswell had left the room, I spoke more strongly, referred to his unpopularity with his Colleagues in the Senate, & their want of confidence in him—mentioned what Chandler Carpenter & Conkling & Frelinghuysen had said—alluded to his reputation, for looseness of morals, & that the public had no confidence in him—many persons did not believe him honest— that he does not speak French, & would be entirely without influence on the Board— That the President has much dependent on this Board, ~~that~~ as his treaty would be judged in a large degree by its decision—& that we needed the ablest & most efficient man in the Country, one who had both National & foreign reputation—& therefore it was that I was willing to disregard all questions of politics & appoint Chas Frans Adams—he objects decidedly to Adams—would rather appoint an out- & out democrat—Richd H. Dana's name being mentioned, he says he would much prefer him   He says that Senator Harlan had suggested W. B. Allison as agent under the XII Article (claims) of the British Treaty—Harlan thinks that ~~H~~he will be re-elected to the Senate without much trouble, but that Allison is the only man who is likely to be in his way." DLC-Hamilton Fish. See Speech, April 22, 1871, note 1; letters to Hamilton Fish, July 13, 21, 1871; Nevins, *Fish*, pp. 511–13. On June 29, USG appointed J. C. Bancroft Davis as U.S. agent at Geneva. DS, DLC-J. C. Bancroft Davis.

On May 29, John H. Clifford, New Bedford, Mass., wrote to USG. "Some of my worthiest and most respected townsmen are under the delusion, that from my relations to the Republican party of Massachusetts and to the administration of its choice, I have some influence with the Executive. Notwithstanding all my assurances to the contrary, they urge me to say a word to you in behalf of the appointment of C. C. Beaman Esq as *assistant* counsel for the U. S. in the hearing before the arbitrators at Geneva under the recent Treaty of Washington. . . ." ALS, DNA, RG 59, Letters of Application and Recommendation. On the same day, Edward L. Plumb, New York City, wrote to Orville E. Babcock. "Under the Treaty with England which has been happily ratified by the Senate, there will be appointed, I suppose, a Counsel or Agent on the part of the U. S. to assist the Arbitrator under the Alabama claims, and also, doubtless, one or more Assistant Counsel—As one of the latter, I am sure I only render a service to the President, as well as to the country, in calling his attention to the name of Mr Charles C. Beaman Jr of this City, who has made the subject of the Alabama claims a special study and whose work upon this subject I send to you today—A copy I believe has already been presented to the President— Of this work so high an authority as Mr Cushing has said that it is the best compila- tion we have upon the subject: the English Commissioners, I understand, say it is the worst—. . ." ALS, *ibid.* See *ibid.*, RG 94, Letters Received, 2536 1871. On Dec. 6, USG nominated Charles C. Beaman, Jr., as examiner of claims, State Dept. See Frank Warren Hackett, *Reminiscences of the Geneva Tribunal of Arbitration 1872: The Alabama Claims* (Boston, 1911), pp. 84–86.

On May 25, U.S. Senators Daniel D. Pratt and Oliver P. Morton of Ind. wrote to USG. "Referring to the 12th Article of the Treaty of Washington, providing for the appointment of Commissioners to examine and decide the claims on the part of the corporations, companies and individuals of each government upon the other, we beg leave respectfully to present the name of an eminent citizen of the State of Indiana as a proper person for appointment. We refer to the Hon. *James S. Frazer*, late a Judge of the Supreme Court of the State. In our opinion, he combines in a high degree the qualities desirable in a Commissioner. In the prime of life he has attained a position as a jurist not excelled perhaps by any lawyer of the State. He is cool in judgment, patient in investigation, of unquestioned integrity, and possesses great suavety of manners and a singular faculty of bringing other minds to his conclusions. The people of Indiana have repeatedly given proof of their confidence in Judge Frazer and in our judgment his appointment wld be recognized as exceedingly appropriate" LS, DNA, RG 59, Letters of Application and Recommendation. Related papers, including a letter from Governor Conrad Baker of Ind. and another from Morton, are *ibid.*

On July 15, U.S. Senator James Harlan of Iowa, Mount Pleasant, wrote to USG. "I enclose a letter written by my Colleague, Senator Wright—recommending Ex- Gov. Samuel J. Kirkwood, of this State for Commissioner on the General Claims Commission to settle general claims between the Gov of the U. S. and Great Brittain under the Treaty of Washington. I unite in Senator Wrights strong commendation; and would be greatly pleased and obliged if you can consistently make the appoint- ment." ALS, *ibid.* On July 24, USG endorsed this letter. "Refered to State Dept." AES, *ibid.* On July 29, USG appointed James S. Frazer as commissioner under Article XII. On the same day, USG appointed Robert S. Hale of N. Y. as agent under Article XIII.

On June 27, Richard M. Corwine, White Plains, N. Y., wrote to USG. "Having been ill for some months this Spring, my medical advisers prescribe a European trip. I sail on Saturday the 1st ult. on the Atlantic, accompanied by my wife & 2 sons. I did intend to call on you when you were recently in Washington but you remained so short a time I could not avail myself of that pleasure. I wanted to say to you, what may not be known to you, that for 7 years past I have made the study and practice of International Law a speciality in the discussion of prize, admiralty and other cases, but more especially International law questions that have arisen & are daily arising before the American & Mexican Mixed Commission, where I have quite a large docket. This experience has, to some extent, qualified me to take part in the discussion of similar questions that may arise between my own government & En- gland & other Governments. My object in addressing you this note is to most respectfully ask you to consider whether I can be of any use to the Government while abroad in the consideration of any of the questions now at issue with England or any of the Continental states of Europe. I have not asked any of your friends or mine to bring this subject to your attention but the rather to do it myself, relying upon your personal knowledge of me & my reputation as a lawyer and a citizen. Until Saturday, I can be addressed at the Astor House; after that London, E. C, care Jay Cooke, McClouch & Co" ALS, *ibid.* See *PUSG,* 20, 470–71.

2. See Proclamation, April 29, 1871. The centennial commissioners first met in Philadelphia on March 4, 1872.

To Horace Capron

Washington, D. C. June 28th *186*71

HON. HORACE CAPRON;
COM. OF AGRICULTURE:
DEAR SIR:

Your letter of the 27th inst. tendering your resignation as Commissioner of Agriculture is just received. Appreciating as I do the value of the Dept. over which you have so ably presided for years, to the country at large, I should regret receiving, or accepting, your resignation were it not for the importance attached to the new position which you are called on to fill, and which no doubt will be filled, with credit, and to the inestimable value of the Nation which has secured your services

In the new place, of which you have accepted the responsibilities, I predict results creditable to yourself and to the Nation which has so honored you; as well as the *rapid* advance of commerce between that Nation and all others. Such a result cannot prove otherwise than beneficial to the Worlds interests, leaving out of the account that of Ourselves, as a single Nation.

Your resignation is accepted, from the date proposed by yourself, with anticipations that you will realize all that is expected from your new duties.

With sincere wishes for your future success, I subscribe myself,

Very sincerely,
your obt. svt.
U. S. GRANT

ALS, DLC-Horace Capron. On June 27, 1871, Horace Capron, Washington, D. C., wrote to USG. "In fulfillment of an engagement with representatives of a Foreign Government, the nature and circumstances of which I communicated to you early in May last, it becomes necessary to tender my resignation as Commissioner of Agriculture, to take effect on the first day of August next. In doing this, I desire to express my high appreciation of your confidence and kindness, both officially and personally expressed, and I assure you of their indelible impression upon my mind & heart. I have the satisfaction to leave the Department in efficient working order; its buildings and improvements erected without increasing the very moderate Annual appropriations; its finances unembarrassed, and its current pecuniary obligations without—as heretofore—the necessity for a deficiency appropriation, and with an enlarged fund for the coming fiscal year, yet untouched in the Treasury. The usefulness of the Department has been satisfactorily tested, not only in the exercise of its well known public functions, but in answers to the thousands of personal inquiries, involving every aspect of scientific agriculture, tending to advance the public weal with private welfare of the people at large. Its importance is asserted in decided terms by the industrial authorities official and personal of all quarters of the globe. I scarcely need ask from you a continuation of that intelligent appreciation and fostering care accorded hitherto, which is so essential for the full development and highest utility of this department of the National Government." Copies (3), DLC-Horace Capron; CtY. See letter to Horace Capron, June 23, 1871.

On June 15 and 28, U.S. Senator John Scott of Pa. wrote to U.S. Senator Simon Cameron of Pa. about discussions with USG concerning the appointment of Frederick Watts as commissioner of agriculture. ALS, DLC-Simon Cameron. On June 26, Frederick Watts, president, Cumberland Valley Rail Road Co., Carlisle, Pa., wrote to Scott. "Under the advice of my friends I have concluded to accept the appointment of Commissioner of Agriculture so Kindly offered to me. I may be able to make myself useful, but I can not hope to attain so much on this point as my friends think I will" ALS, DNA, RG 59, Letters of Application and Recommendation. On July 7, Horace Porter, Long Branch, N. J., wrote to J. C. Bancroft Davis, asst. secretary of state. "The President requests that the Commission of Mr. Watts of Penna as Commissioner of Agriculture be sent to him for his signiture, to date from the first of August next   Mr. Hunter has the full name." ALS, *ibid.*, Miscellaneous Letters. On Dec. 6, USG formally nominated Watts. See *New York Times*, July 2, 1871.

On July 3, David A. Brown, president, and A. M. Garland, secretary, Ill. State Agricultural Society, had written to USG. "Since the announcement of the resignation of Hon. Horace Capron, communications have been received at this office from different members of the Illinois State Agricultural Society, requesting us to urge upon your Excellency the appointment of Hon. John P. Reynolds, as Commissioner of Agriculture. After more than ten years of continuous service in our State Society, Mr. Reynolds is, today, among the Agriculturists and stock raisers, the most popular man in the Western States;—while his contributions to the Agricultural literature of the North-west, as well as his exhaustive report as Special Commissioner of Illinois to the Paris Exposition, unmistakably indicate him as the possessor of the comprehensive breadth of information and practical experience necessary to a successful management of the National Department of Agriculture. Hoping the claims of Mr. Reynolds may find favor with you, . . ." LS, DNA, RG 48, Appointment Div., Letters Received. On July 24, Richard J. Oglesby, Decatur, Ill., wrote to USG recommending John P. Reynolds. ALS, *ibid.* See *PUSG*, 15, 303. Letters to USG from A. McLaughlin and W. H. Hornaday, "Eds Weekly Independent," Harvard, Ill., and Judge William Brown, Rockford, urging the appointment of Anson S. Miller as commissioner of agriculture are *ibid.*

Speech

———

[*June 29, 1871*]

BARON: I need not assure you that your relinquishment of your position as the diplomatic representative of your sovereign here will occasion general regret, in which I cordially share. You have been so long accredited to this Government that you have had unusual opportunities of forming acquaintances, not only with our public men, but with others of my countrymen. Many of them have become your personal friends. They will lament that your proposed departure may deprive them of future intercourse with you. Your experience in affairs elsewhere, as well as here, has undoubtedly rendered your suggestions sometimes, especially upon critical occasions, in a high degree useful. I will add that, notwithstanding your absence, your zealous and successful endeavors to strengthen the friendly relations between our respective countries are not likely to be thwarted or counteracted. It shall be my endeavor to do everything which may be in my power toward consolidating them. My best wishes attend you.

Washington Chronicle, June 30, 1871. USG spoke in reply to Baron Gerolt, German minister. "After a residence of more than a quarter of a century in your great country as representative of my august Sovereign, and of so many mutual interests which have been developed during that time between the United States and Prussia, in union with the other States of Germany, it is a great satisfaction to me to leave the mission entrusted to me with the conviction that the friendly relations between the Governments and the people of the two nations have become more and more intimate and durable, to the benefit of the national prosperity as well as to the cause of true liberty and civilization in both countries...." *Ibid.* See Speech, Aug. 1, 1871; Hamilton Fish diary, March 26, April 30, June 1, 27, 1871, DLC-Hamilton Fish.

To Mortimer D. Leggett

—————

Washington, D. C. June 29th *1871*

DEAR GENERAL;

Your note in regard to Mrs Throgmorton, of this date, is just rec'd. Do not keep any one in your bureau for a single day who is not suitable, in all respects, for their place.[1]

Yours Truly
U. S. GRANT

GEN. M. D. LEGGETT,

COM. OF PATENTS,

ALS, University of California, Santa Barbara, Calif. Promoted to maj. gen. (1865) for services during the Atlanta and Savannah campaigns, Mortimer D. Leggett resumed his law practice in Zanesville, Ohio. On Jan. 4, 1871, USG nominated Leggett as commissioner of patents. See *PUSG*, 4, 266; *ibid.*, 6, 161–62, 166–67.

On Nov. 8, 1870, Samuel S. Fisher, commissioner of patents, had written to USG. "I ask permission to renew the tender of my resignation of the office of Commissioner of Patents, made October 24th and temporarily withdrawn at your suggestion. If there be no reason to the contrary, I suggest that the resignation be accepted to take effect at the close of Thursday November 10th inst." LS, DNA, RG 48, Appointment Div., Letters Received. On the same day, USG endorsed this letter. "Resignation accepted to take effect Nov. 10th 1870." AES, *ibid.* Fisher submitted his resignation to USG after a two-hour interview with Secretary of the Interior Columbus Delano. *New York Tribune*, Nov. 9, 1870.

On Oct. 21, U.S. Senator James W. Patterson of N. H., Hanover, had written to USG. "I have heard it intimated that Mr Fisher, Commissioner of Patents, would probably soon tender his resignation. Should that be the case I desire to recommend as his successor, Gen. S. A. Duncan, the present Assistant Commissioner, with whom I have been intimately acquainted for many years, and know to be in every way worthy of the position. He was a student and afterwards a tutor at Dartmouth College, while I was connected with that institution. At the commencement of the war Mr Duncan resigned his position in the College and volunteered in the army, where he served with great credit throughout the war, rising by his merits from an adjutancy to the rank of colonel, and at the close of the war, for gallant and meritorious services, he was bevetted Major General. . . ." LS, DNA, RG 48, Appointment Div., Letters Received. On Nov. 9, U.S. Senator James Harlan of Iowa wrote to USG. "I respectfully recommend the appointment of Gen. Samuel A. Duncan, at present *Assistant* Commissioner of Patents, to the office of Commissioner of Patents. First, because he is a highly educated gentleman, of most excellent natural ability, whose integrity has never been called in question,—who served his country faithfully and efficiently in the Army during the recent war, and who has since firmly stood by the principles for which he fought: Secondly, because he has been thourally trained for the performance of the duties of Commissioner,—having served for a long time as Examiner, and for some time as Assistant Commissioner, making him familiar with all the details of the office: And thirdly, because, in my opinion nothing else would more strongly tend to the improve-ment of the *Civil Service* than the regular promotion of subordinates who are faithful and capable to higher positions of trust." ALS, *ibid.* On Nov. 10, U.S. Senator Aaron H. Cragin of N. H., Lebanon, telegraphed to USG. "I earnestly hope you may find it compatible with good policy to appoint Genl, S, A, Duncan, Commissioner of patents, It would be very gratifying to your friends in this state, I congratulate you on the favorable results of the elections," Telegram received, *ibid.* On Nov. 19, U.S. Senator Hannibal Hamlin of Maine, Bangor, wrote to USG recommending Samuel A. Dun-can. ALS, *ibid.* Related papers are *ibid.* On July 8, USG had nominated Duncan as asst. commissioner of patents. On Nov. 14, J. R. Hayes, Philadelphia, wrote to USG. "I notice by the papers that a Mr *Duncan* will most likely be appointed Comr of Patents, Against this appointment I, as a citizen of Pennsylvania most earnestly *protest,* When, through the vacillation of Mr Johnson the late Executive, a portion of the Republican party become demoralized, and a Mr Foote, the predecessor of Judge Fisher was appointed, by selling his own flesh and blood to Senator Henderson of Mo' who secured said appointment this man *Duncan* was his firm friend—was publicly whipped with a cowhide by a citizen of Washington, for his devotion to him—worked sedulously and unceasingly to have Mr Foote retained at the incoming of your administration and failing in this fawned like a spaniel on the new Comr of Pat's (Judge Fisher) in order to retain his official position—Ask Gen Cameron who I am, and before you appoint *this man* investigate his antecedents, or the truth of that which I state" ALS, *ibid.* On June 3, 1872, Duncan, Washington, D. C., wrote to USG. "An opportunity for entering professional life having presented itself, of such a character that I do not feel at liberty to decline it, I have the honor hereby to tender my resignation of the office of Assistant Commissioner of Patents—. . ." ALS, *ibid.* On the same day, Leggett endorsed this letter. "Respectfully forwarded with acceptance recommended. Gen. Duncan has been a very able and faithful Offi-cer & the loss of his services will be sadly felt by the Office." AES, *ibid.*

On Nov. 5, 1870, U.S. Representative John A. Logan of Ill., Chicago, had written to USG. "*Personal.* . . . I desire to call your attention to the fact that Mr Fisher Comr of Patents may resign his office sometime during this year. and in that event. I ask that you may favorably consider the name of Hon L. L. Bond of this city for that position. he is a man well known here and as a Patent lawyer is well known in Washington City in that Department. . . ." ALS, *ibid.* Related papers are *ibid.* A letter recommending William Blakewell, Pittsburgh, is *ibid.*

1. On April 12 and 15, 1871, Orville E. Babcock wrote to Isabella Fogg, Washing-ton, D. C. "The President directs me to return your paper, and to say that he does not deem it best under the circumstances to over rule the opinion of the Department to order an appointment. The President will have no objection should any of the Depart-ments give you an appointment" "The President directs me to comply with your re-quest and return to you, your letters He directs me to say that as Congress has given you an increased pension—and the head of Departments have declined to appoint you to a Clerkship after a favorable refference of your papers, he does not think it best to over-rule the Departments by ordering an appointment. The President does not intend this decision to be construed as opposing your claim or applications before the Departments." Copies, DLC-USG, II, 1. On March 3, USG had signed a bill increasing Fogg's pension to $30 per month for disabilities incurred while serving as a Civil War nurse. *CG,* 41–3, 1902, 1913, 1942, 1966. See Frank Moore, *Women of the War; Their Heroism and Self-Sacrifice* (Hartford, Conn., 1866), pp. 113–26.

Pardon

To all whom it may concern, these presents shall come greeting—

Whereas on the 13th day of June, 1871, in the Supreme Court of the District of Columbia, holding a criminal term, one C. C. Bowen was convicted of bigamy and sentenced to be imprisoned for two years and to pay two hundred and fifty dollars fine:

And whereas it is represented that he was innocent of any violation of the law; that he acted in good faith, believing his former wife to be dead;[1] and it appears that he rendered good service to the cause of the Union during the rebellion[2] and since its termination, and has endeavored to lead an honest and upright life, and for these reasons eleven of the jurors who found the verdict against him, and many other citizens of the highest consideration and weight, urge his pardon, and United States Attorney Fisher[3] would be gratified by the exercise of Executive clemency:

Now, therefore, be it known, that I, U. S. Grant, President of the United States of America, in consideration of the premises, divers other good and sufficient reasons me thereunto moving, do hereby grant to the said C. C. Bowen a full and unconditional pardon.

In testimony whereof I have hereunto signed my name, and caused the seal of the United States to be affixed.

Done at the city of Washington this first day of July, A. D. 1871, and of the independence of the United States the ninety-fifth.

U. S. GRANT.

Washington Evening Star, July 8, 1871. Born in Providence, R. I., in 1832, Christopher C. Bowen moved to Ga. in 1850 and began to practice law in Charleston, S. C., in 1862. Following service in the C.S. Army and Coast Guard, he joined the Republican Party and served as U.S. Representative from S. C. (1868–71). In Feb., 1871, Bowen stood trial for bigamy; a D. C. jury failed to reach a verdict. *Ibid.*, Feb. 13, 16, 1871. In June, a second jury found Bowen guilty on a separate bigamy charge. *Ibid.*, May 30, June 5, 13, 1871.

On June 26, Susan Petigru Bowen wrote to Gen. William T. Sherman. "I saw the Atty Gen'l, and if I were in my normal condition, I would feel great hope, for he says that the case for his consideration mainly depends upon the *intention* of the act—He bade me say to you that if you would *write* a brief statement to the effect that 'you ~~have~~ were invited by me to give me away, but that owing to the delay caused, as you were told subsequently, to necessary investigations touching a prior marriage of Mr Bowen's, you had after waiting several days, been obliged to leave for the West more than a fortnight before my wedding actually took place,'—it would be a *very* substantial paper in reference to the decision of the case. Will you therefore simply state this, to add to the other evidence before the Attorney General; and you will thereby increase those obligations, the sense of which, with your constant friendship, . . ." ALS, DLC-William T. Sherman.

On July 1, Attorney Gen. Amos T. Akerman wrote to USG. "Since my report to you on the 29th of June last upon the application for pardon in the case of C. C. Bowen, I have learned that his counsel are of opinion that there were errors of law upon his trial, for which a new trial should be granted, and that they intend to have the case reviewed by the Supreme Court of the District of Columbia upon these allegations of error. It is therefore, presumable that if any error was committed upon the trial to the inquiry of Mr. Bowen, it will be corrected by the action of the Supreme Court." Copy, DNA, RG 60, Letters Sent to Executive Officers. On the same day, Mrs. Bowen met with USG at Long Branch to ask for a pardon. *Evening Star*, July 3, 1871. Also on July 1, Akerman again wrote to USG. "In pursuance of the direction in your telegram of this date, I herewith send you the draft of a pardon in the case of C. C. Bowen, together with the report upon the subject which I read to you last Thursday." Copy, DNA, RG 60, Letters Sent to Executive Officers.

1. "Mayor Hall, of New York, has written a letter to President Grant suggesting that before a pardon be extended to ex-Congressman Bowen, he be required to disclose the means by which he, or his counsel, procured a fraudulent decree of divorce from the County Clerk's office in New York City. Mayor Hall says the 'authorities here are desirous of exposing and punishing the fraud which was committed in the interest of Mr. Bowen.'" *Evening Star*, June 27, 1871.

2. Bowen faced recurring accusations in connection with the 1864 murder of a C.S. Army officer near Georgetown, S. C. See *ibid.*, Feb. 11, 1871; E. Culpepper Clark, *Francis Warrington Dawson and the Politics of Restoration: South Carolina, 1874–1889* (University, Ala., 1980), pp. 41–45.

3. Born in 1817 in Del., George P. Fisher had served as U.S. Representative from Del. (1861–63) and D. C. justice (1863–70) before USG nominated him as U.S. attorney, D. C. See *PUSG*, 20, 424–25.

Proclamation

———

Whereas a Treaty, between the United States of America and Her Majesty the Queen of the United Kingdom of Great Britain and Ireland, concerning the settlement of all causes of difference between the two countries, was concluded and signed at Washington by the High Commissioners and Plenipotentiaries of the respective Governments on the eighth day of May last; which Treaty is, word for word, as follows: . . .

And whereas the said Treaty has been duly ratified on both

parts, and the respective ratifications of the same were exchanged in the city of London, on the seventeenth day of June, 1871, by Robert C. Schenck, Envoy Extraordinary and Minister Plenipotentiary of the United States, and Earl Granville, Her Majesty's Principal Secretary of State for Foreign Affairs, on the part of their respective Governments:

Now, therefore, be it known that I, Ulysses S. Grant, President of the United States of America, have caused the said Treaty to be made public, to the end that the same, and every clause and article thereof, may be observed and fulfilled with good faith by the United States and the citizens thereof.

In witness whereof, I have hereunto set my hand and caused the seal of the United States to be affixed.

Done at the City of Washington this fourth day of July, in the year of our Lord one thousand eight hundred and seventy-one, and of the Independence of the United States the ninety-sixth.

U. S. Grant.

Copy (printed), DNA, RG 56, Letters Received; *ibid.*, RG 84, Spain, Treaties. On May 25, 1871, USG had authorized Robert C. Schenck, U.S. minister, London, to sign the ratified treaty with Great Britain. DS, *ibid.*, Great Britain, Instructions.

On June 2, interviewed at Long Branch, USG had discussed press coverage of the Treaty of Washington. "They will grumble, of course: but they won't grumble long. The treaty was fully and ably discussed, and, in my judgment, is the best settlement possible of the outstanding differences between us and Great Britain. There is a good deal of misapprehension on both sides of the water concerning the Treaty of Washington. . . . It is thought by many that it was rushed through and acted upon a whole without proper consideration on the part of both governments. The facts are that every article of the treaty was submitted to me after it was adopted by the Commission and approved by me; and that each article was in the same way submitted to the British Cabinet and approved by the Ministers of the Crown at once. The English Commissioners spent a great deal of money in telegraphing the sections of the treaty. The Queen of England pledged her signature beforehand. I therefore regard the treaty as pratically ratified. There will be pecuniary considerations, of course. . . . Measures will have to be adopted on both sides to carry out the provisions of the treaty. Our House of Representatives will, I feel certain, act patriotically and wisely in the matter. The treaty must be ratified and made a law of both nations—it is necessary—the necessity is immediate. As far as we are concerned we would like to have better terms; but there were two parties to the bargain. If I had it all my own way I think I could make it more favorable to us. (A smile.) The point aimed at was not merely a pecuniary satisfaction for our losses by the Alabama and other cruisers from British ports, but the settlement of an irritating and disturbing question likely any day to bring the two nations into armed conflict. My aim was by this treaty to secure peace through justice, and I believe I have succeeded. No apprehension need be felt as to the course of the

British people. I would regard it as an act of bad faith on their part to reject the treaty after its almost unanimous acceptance by our Senate. The English must surely prefer a fair settlement of our differences with them, for which this treaty provides, than to nurse a cause of war. Settlement or war were the alternatives. (As the President said this he threw away his cigar with a sudden jerk.) The final ratification will be a blessing to both countries. . . ." *New York Herald*, June 3, 1871 (subheadings integrated).

On June 24, Secretary of State Hamilton Fish wrote to Orville E. Babcock. "Will you please telegraph to the President in Cipher, the following— . . . The ratifications of the Treaty with Great Britain were exchanged last Saturday—the ~~Treaty~~ exchanged copy leaves Liverpool to day—British Goverment, still wish it not made public yet—" ALS, OFH.

On July 7, Fish, Garrison, N. Y., wrote to USG. "The newspapers mention your desire to hold a Cabinet meeting next week—the 11th 12th & 14th are named as the day on which you propose to convene it   If so, I shall endeavor to be in Washington, on either day—to day I feel much better than at any time, since I have been here, and hope to be well enough to go, either to Long Branch or to Washington, next week—I expect to take a drive to day, the first time, that I will have been out— Please let me know, either by telegraph, or by letter, of your intention as to the Meeting next week—if it is to be on the 11th a notice by Mail would scarcely reach me in time—The British Treaty being proclaimed, will you not think it adviseable to remove the injunction of Secrecy from the papers &c which were Communicated with the Treaty, to the Senate—The *Protocols* were surreptitiously published—it is desireable therefore to give publicity to the other papers—" ALS (press), DLC-Hamilton Fish. On [*July*] 8, USG telegraphed to Fish. "No truth in the report that I go to Washington next week.   give all the papers relating to the Washington treaty that you think proper to the Public" Telegram received, *ibid.* On the same day, Horace Porter, Long Branch, telegraphed to Fish. "He does not intend to go to Washington for a Month or More" Telegram received, *ibid.*

On July 10, Fish wrote to J. C. Bancroft Davis, asst. secretary of state. "A telegram from the President states that he does not expect to be in Washington, for some time yet—I propose therefore to go to Long Branch, tomorrow afternoon to return possibly Wednesday evnig—otherwise Thursdy Mng   I have yours of 8th—we are countig on the pleasure of a visit from Mrs Davis & you, a week from this" ALS, DLC-J. C. Bancroft Davis. Also on July 10, Fish telegraphed to USG. "Will you be disengaged tomorrow Evening—If so I will go down in the Afternoon" ALS (telegram sent), DLC-Hamilton Fish. On the same day, USG telegraphed to Fish. "Will be at Home to-morrow   will Mrs. Fish be with you?" Telegram received, *ibid.*

Also on July 10, Fish wrote to USG. "A recent severe illness admonishes me of the necessity of relief from the labor & the confinement of official duties—When you did me the honor, something over two years ago, to invite me to a seat in your Cabinet, I accepted it hesitatingly, with a profound sense of gratitude for the confidence you reposed in me—with very earnest misgivings of my ability to meet the duties of the position, and with little expectation of remaining more than a brief period in official life. Your generous confidence and support have greatly lightened the responsibilities and the cares of my office—have sustained me in my humble efforts, and have detained me in public life beyond the period which I had expected— The association & identification with your Administration have been to me the source of great satisfaction & pride, and will be gratefully remembered as long as I shall live—But I feel now the need of rest, & of relief from the severe & confining duties of my office—and I beg leave therefore to tender my resignation of the office of Secretary of State,—to take effect at such time as shall be agreeable to you, and when my successor shall be prepared to enter upon the duties of the office—With renewed assurances of gratitude & of affection, and with earnest wishes for your health, & the continued success of your Administration . . ." ALS, *ibid.* Fish drafted a version of this letter. ADf (initialed), *ibid.* On May 29 and June 15, Fish had written in his diary after talking with USG. "I then mention my desire to retire from office as soon as the business connected with the Treaty is completed, & name the 1st August—He expresses great unwillingness to my withdrawal—says a great many very kind & complimentary things—that he would regret the withdrawal of any member of his Cabinet but (with much emphasis) of none, nearly as much as mine— I urge reasons for my resigning, & he meets them, by admitting that it involves great sacrifice, to me, to remain, but he could not replace me to his own satisfaction, that the Country has entire Confidence &c &c—Delano & Genl Parker come in, & the conversation is interrupted" "I refer to my desire to resign—he remonstrates, & urges me to remain through his term. I assign reasons why I cannot—but say that if I can be absent during the greater part of the time, & during the hot weather, I shall be content to name either 1st of August Septr Octr or even November—but I do not wish to be obliged to bring my wife back here, & wish to make arrangements now in my house accordingly   He says he does not know whom to name—discusses Pierrepont, whose appt he says would not give satisfaction—Morgan he thinks not equal to the place, thinks well of Isaac H Bailey, but he wd not take office—has just gone to Europe, & his name wd not strike the public with confidence—I ask if he has ever thought of transfering some member of his Cabinet?   he says he has—that it has occurred to him that Delano might do—I suggest Robeson—he thinks Robeson would not be as acceptable to the public—Persons are announced, & he remarks, well we will talk it over another time—" *Ibid.* Interviewed at Long Branch on June 2 and 26, USG had denied rumors of Fish's impending resignation. "No, sir. There is not a word of truth in these statements whatever they are. Not a whisper of Mr. Fish's retirement has lately passed me or any of the Cabinet. Mr. Fish will not leave the Cabinet or resign the seals of the State Department with my consent while I am President. He responded unwillingly to my call and entered upon the arduous duties of the Foreign Office with diffidence: he has discharged them well. He has been faithful, patriotic and diligent. I should be grieved if he resigned; but he won't resign." "Well, I think I should have heard something of all that if there was any truth in it. How the political tinkers are to reconstruct the Cabinet, dismiss and appoint officers without my knowledge is more than I can tell. Can you? Mr. Fish is not going to be dismissed; I only hope he will not resign. I should be very sorry if Mr. Fish retired from the Cabinet. I don't think that he intends to retire. I have not heard anything about it." *New York Herald,* June 3, 27, 1871 (subheadings integrated). See letter to Edwards Pierrepont, Dec. 29, 1871.

To Amos T. Akerman

LONG BRANCH NJ. JULY IVTH. [*1871*]
ATTY. GENERAL. WASHN.
PLEASE SEND COMMISSION FOR DIST. ATTY. OF NE-
BRASKA FOR SIGNATURE. IF MORE THAN ONE RECOM-
MENDATION IS IN LEAVE NAME BLANK AND SEND PA-
PERS OTHERWISE APPOINT JAS. . . .NEVILLE.

U. S. GRANT.

Telegram received (ellipses in original), DNA, RG 60, Letters from the President. On
May 23, 1871, Silas A. Strickland, U.S. attorney, Omaha, had telegraphed to U.S. Senator Phineas W. Hitchcock of Neb. "I have this day sent my resignation as US Attorney
to Attorney General. it would please me to have my successor appointed at once."
Telegram received, *ibid.* On the same day, Horace Porter wrote to Attorney Gen.
Amos T. Akerman. "The President request that the nomination of Mr. Girad, recommended by Senator Hitchcock and others be made out to succeed strickland." LS,
ibid. On May 24, USG nominated Leander Gerrard as U.S. attorney, Neb.; Gerrard
declined. On July 5, Akerman wrote to USG. "According to the directions in you
telegram of this date, I send a commission for James Neville, as District Attorney
for Nebraska. The only papers in the office on this subject are these; 1. A letter
from Pat O. Hawes recommending Mr. Neville. 2. A letter from Senator Hitchcock
to yourself recommending Mr. Neville under date of June 20, 1871. 3. A telegram
from Senator Hitchcock to yourself dated June 29, 1871, requesting you to defer
action in the matter until he (Mr. Hitchcock) shall reach Washington." Copy, *ibid.*,
Letters Sent to Executive Officers. On Dec. 6, USG officially nominated James Neville for the position. For Strickland, see second letter to John M. Thayer, Dec. 22,
1870.

To Hamilton Fish

[*July 5, 1871*]

It may be well to speak a friendly word in behalf of Gen Cavado[1]
to the Spanish Minister but no claim can be set up in his favor,
because of Military services or of his being an American Citizen so
long as it is admitted that he was engaged in an act of war against
the Gov't h[ol]ding him in captivity   When may I look for you at
Long Branch?

U. S. GRANT

Telegram received (undated), DLC-Hamilton Fish. On July 5, 1871, Secretary of State Hamilton Fish, Garrison, N. Y., telegraphed to USG. "I have telegraphed and will write to Spanish Minister, in the spirit indicated—Am better, but not yet able to leave home, or to bear any fatigue—Hope to be able to go to Long Branch within a few days" AL (telegram sent—initialed, press), *ibid.* On July 6, USG telegraphed to Fish. "When you come to the Branch. can you not bring Mrs Fish & Edith prepared to spend a few day's with us.   hope you will soon entirely recover your health." Telegram received, *ibid.* On the same day, Fish telegraphed to USG. "Mr Roberts in answer to my telegram about Cavado, telegraphed to me last Evening, that he had transmitted a Message to the Captain General, who, he thought would do for the best in the matter—I am not so well to day,—again confined to my bed." AL (telegram sent—initialed, press), *ibid.*

    1. Born in Cuba in 1831, Frederic F. Cavada moved to Philadelphia with his American mother after his father's death in 1838. Trained as a civil engineer, he served as lt. col., 114th Pa., and wrote *Libby Life: Experiences of a Prisoner of War* ... (1864; reprinted, Lanham, Md., 1985). After serving as consul, Trinidad de Cuba (1866–69), Cavada joined Cuban rebels and rose to command all insurgent forces, employing guerrilla tactics. On July 4, 1871, Charles K. Graham, New York City, telegraphed to Horace Porter, Long Branch. "General Cavada, formerly Lieutenant-Colonel of the One Hundred and Fourteenth Pennsylvania Volunteers, lately Commander-in-Chief of the Cuban army, has been captured by the Spanish authorities. He served under my command during the Rebellion and was a good soldier. His brother was likewise on General Humphrey's staff. Can anything be done to save his life?" O. Wilson Davis, *Sketch of Frederic Fernandez Cavada, a Native of Cuba* (Philadelphia, 1871), pp. 39–40. On July 5, Moses Taylor, New York City, telegraphed to Lt. Col. Stewart Van Vliet, Long Branch. "Enable O. W. Davis to get an interview with the President about General Cavada, late Commander of the Cuban army, who was captured by a Spanish gunboat on Sunday. Davis will come to Long Branch today and see you." *Ibid.*, pp. 42–43. Also on July 5, Oliver Wilson Davis and James P. Lacombe visited Long Branch. "We drove at once to General Grant's cottage, and when we asked to see him, were told that he wished to be excused, as he was about to take a drive with his family. I requested the messenger to say that our business was urgent and involved a matter of life and death. General Grant immediately saw us and I said to him, 'General, our business relates to General Cavada's case.' He replied, 'I have received telegrams from General Meade and other gentlemen on behalf of Cavada, and have already acted in the case.'" *Ibid.*, p. 46. On July 7, a Washington correspondent reported. "Several gentlemen from Philadelphia, for the most part, it is understood, called on Mr. DAVIS, Assistant Secretary of State, yesterday, and sought the intercession of our Government in behalf of the life of the Cuban Gen. CAVADA, who was a Lieutenant-Colonel of a Pennsylvania regiment during the war, and who is now in the hands of the Spanish authorities. It was not urged that our Government could make any efforts for his release other than in the way of friendly intercession, but it was resolved to use such endeavors in his behalf as could be done in the interest of humanity. The representations which were proper to be made to the Spanish authorities were telegraphed to the Consul-General of this Government at Havana, Mr. HALL. He has replied that he has complied with his instructions, but the probabilities of the success of the effort are not stated." *New York Times*, July 8, 1871. Also on July 7, Henry C. Hall, vice consul gen., Havana, wrote to J. C. Bancroft Davis, asst. secretary of state. ". . . I gave Governor Roberts, who was in attendance, a memorandum, as per copy inclosed, which I

doubt not was immediately transmitted to General Valmaseda, now at 'Sanctus Spiritus.' Early this morning, I sent in my communication,—inclosure No 3—to the Political Secretary and have now received his reply a copy and translation of which is also inclosed,   The Secritary states by order of General, Count Valmaseda, that he has no means of communicating promptly with 'Puerto Principe' and beleives that any intervention on his part would arrive too late, as the Department Commanders are instructed to carry out the law, rigourously, ~~the~~ in regard to the insurgent chiefs and especially those who have decreed, and executed, the burning of the most valuable estates. of whom General Cavada has been the most conspicuous. General Cavada, it appears, was brought to Nuevitas on the 30th ulto   the news of his capture was carried thence to Caibarien and received here, by telegraph, on the 3d instant, since when there have been no advices from either Nuevitas or Puerto Principe." ALS, DNA, RG 59, Consular Despatches, Havana. On July 11, Hall again wrote to Davis. ". . . I have now to inform the Department that the papers of this city of today publish an official telegram from the Captain General, Count Valmaseda, who is now at Júcaro, stating that the insurgent General Cavada was executed at Puerto-Principe on the 1st instant. . . ." ALS, *ibid.* See Mary Ruiz de Zárate, *El General Candela: biografía de una guerrilla* (Havana, 1974).

To William Elrod

Long Branch, N. J.
July 8th 1871.

Dear Elrod:

Enclosed I send you $600 00 to pay for lime kiln. In view of the possibility of a rail-road runing up the Gravois, and the almost certainty, if one does, that five acres will be taken from my land where the Gravois road and the rail-road cross each other, it will be well to concider whether a kiln built where I directed would not be taken in by the depot grounds. If so the kiln should be built further up the creek, and on the opposite side. Build a good sized one and where another can be joined to it if desirable hereafter.

Yours Truly
U. S. Grant

P. S. place a stamp on this check before presenting it.

ALS, Dr. John T. Bickmore, Dayton, Ohio. See letter to William Elrod, June 23, 1871. On May 17, 1871, William Elrod, Webster Groves, Mo., wrote to USG. "Inclosed you will find a recommendation from Col Easton to have Mr Baily appointed to a Consulship. I have known Mr Baily Ever since I come to Missouri   he is a good Neighbor and honest—he is a man of limited means and in poor health   he wishes to go across the Ocean for his health you will pleas let me hear from you soone And also state the sise of the lime kiln that you wish to have put up" ALS, DNA, RG 59, Letters of Application and Recommendation. On May 13, Alton R. Easton, assessor of Internal Revenue, St. Louis, wrote to USG. "It will gratify me to have my friend Majr C. C. Bailey, for 20 years a resident of Missouri, appointed to a Consulship— I have known Majr Bailey for 10. years—He was Pay-Master under Mr Lincoln, and afterwards Military and private Secretary to Govr Gamble of this state—He is honest, reliable, and entirely competant to fill the position as Consul,—" ALS, *ibid.* No appointment followed.

To Amos T. Akerman

LONG BRANCH N. J. JULY XITH. [*1871*]
HON. A. T. AKERMAN. ATTY. GENL. WASHN.
NOTIFY CHURCH HOWE[1] THAT HE IS TO CONTINUE AS MARSHALL OF WYOMING IF NECESSARY REAPPOINT HIM.

U. S. GRANT.

Telegram received, DNA, RG 60, Letters Received. On July 5, 1871, U.S. Representative Frank W. Palmer of Iowa, Des Moines, wrote to USG. "I recommend the reinstatement of Howe as Marshal of Wyoming Territory. The gentleman recently appointed having declined, I am satisfied Howe's appointment would be more satisfactory to the people of the Territory than that of any other candidate." ALS, *ibid.*, Records Relating to Appointments. On July 6, U.S. Representative Oakes Ames of Mass., North Easton, wrote to USG. "I hear that there is a vacancy in the office of U. S. Marshall for Wyoming If there is no objection to the reappointment of Church Howe, to the office. it would gratify me much. I understand that Mr Howe has always performed his duties well. and his removal was brot about by misrepresentations to you: If that is the fact. I see no objection to his appointment" ALS, *ibid.* On Dec. 13, Orville E. Babcock wrote to Attorney Gen. Amos T. Akerman. "The President directs me to say that you need not send over a nomination for a Marshal for Wyoming Ter." LS, *ibid.*, Letters Received.

In a document docketed April 1, 1870, E. P. Johnson *et al.* petitioned USG. "We the undersigned members of the Republican Party of the Territory of Wyoming respectfully represent that the interests of the party and people of this Territory imperatively demand the removal from office of Church Howe the present United States marshall for the following reasons *to wit* That during his brief career among us as an officer he has manifested an utter incapacity to *honestly* discharge the duties of his office: in that he draws from the Treasury of the United States money with which to pay jurors and prisoners board and other expenses of the courts in the several Districts but fails to pay the same to those to whom it justly belongs That he receives money from Prisoners of the United States as a compensation for the use of his office in shielding them from the consequences of the violation of the laws of the United States That his corrupt practices are a continual reproach upon the

Administration and party and tend to demoralize the politics of the territory   We therefore appeal to your excellency and earnestly request his removal and the appointment of honest man to the duties of that office in this Territory and your petitioners will ever pray" DS (64 signatures), *ibid.*, Records Relating to Appointments.

In an undated document, W. A. Baker, "Editor Cheyenne 'Leader,'" *et al.* petitioned USG. "We the undersigned citizens of the Territory of Wyoming—irrespect of party predilictions—having the good of our Territory and the proper execution of the laws at heart would most earnestly protest against the removal of Church Howe from the position of United States Marshall for the Territory of Wyoming believeing as we do that his appointment to such office was a creditable one to the administration, and that during his official career the duties of the said office have been most faithfully and efficiently performed by the said Church Howe   Believeing further that the said removal is sought by those not having the love of country or the true—interest of our people and Territory at heart—but rather, urging the said course to & be pursued through personal feeling and petty spite—we do herby-by most earnestly protest against—against the said removal—and respectfully ask that your action in the premises be reconsidered" DS (153 signatures), *ibid.*

On April 5, 1870, U.S. Representative Randolph Strickland of Mich. wrote to USG. "Learning that a change in Office of Marshal for the Territory of Wyoming— I have filed in the Office of the *Atty Genl*—endorsements of Capt Daniel M. Phillips late of *Co A.* 11 *Mich Cav* and with them a request that he may be appointed in case a vacancy Should occur in said Office. Capt Phillips is a first class. man. Has been an Editor. He wrote the first letter published in NewYear in favor of Grant & Colfax. Hoping his case will be made special, . . ." ALS, *ibid.*

On May 6, 1871, Governor John A. Campbell of Wyoming Territory wrote to Babcock. *"Confidential—For the President* . . . I thank you for your letter of the 29th ult., but it was to me a very great surprise. Whatever charges might have been made against me, I never supposed that want of fealty to the Administration could have been included in them; and I pronounce them wholly unqualifiedly and maliciously false—In the first speech that I made after my arrival in the Territory I announced that throughout the war I had to the best of my ability supported the leader of our Armies and that so long as I held office under him in his new position I would continue to support him—and from this I have never wavered. . . . I dislike to make counter-accusations against any officer but it is necessary to a proper understanding of this matter that I state some facts in regard to the U S Marshal   Immediately after his arrival in the Territory Howe announced himself as a candiate for Congress—I was confident that he could not be elected, and would not give him my support. He failed to receive the nomination   Again at the election last Fall he was a candidate   The previous election had demonstrated that there was a Democratic majority of 1400 in the Territory, and I felt that we must select our strongest man in order to insure success—For this reason I used every effort to bring about the nomination and election of Judge Wm T. Jones our present Delegate in Congress— I appeal to the result of that election as my vindication—It was perfectly well understood here that Howe and the small clique that operated with him were the worst disappointed men in the Territory at the triumph of Judge Jones—the Administration candidate   I was particularly anxious for success in the campaign and spent my time and money freely—It was charged that I was one of Gen Grants military appointments and knew nothing of politics or civil affairs, and I was desirous of vindicating the President in appointing me not only to the Democrats but also to the Republican party—and I submit that I succeeded. After the election I received through Congressman Hale the thanks of the Republican Executive Committee Judge Jones' success was the whole head and front of my offending against Howe— Whether the Judge is a friend of the Administration or not can be ascertained by reference to Senator Morton or any person that knows him—I wish to say nothing against Howe except so far as is necessary for my own vindication, but this calumny is in keeping with his whole course since he has been in the Territory—I am surprised that he could make any respectable person that knows him the medium for conveying his slanders to the President—He is the one sole disorganizing element in the Republican party of the Territory, and for this reason all the U S officers present in the Territory with one exception and the Chairman of the Republican Territorial Committee united about a month ago in a letter to the Attorney General requesting his removal—Again I thank you, and wish you to convey to the President my sincere thanks for the confidence he has expressed in your letter—I trust that I am incapable of betraying that confidence—It shall be my endeavor in the future as in the past to see that the Administration suffers no discredit from my connection with it—" ALS, Southern Methodist University, Dallas, Tex.

On May 11, U.S. Delegate William T. Jones of Wyoming Territory wrote to USG. "I respectfully recommend the appointment of Robert H Milroy of Indiana, to the Office of United States Marshal for the territory of Wyoming—Mr Milroy was a Major General of Vol's during the war, is an earnest Republican and a good man." ALS, DNA, RG 60, Washington Territory. On May 15, Horace Porter wrote to Akerman. "The President directs me to say that he will be pleased to have you remove the present U. S. Marshal of Wyoming Ter. and make out a nomination for his successor as soon as you settle upon a good man for the position." LS, *ibid.*, Letters Received. On May 16, U.S. Senator Oliver P. Morton of Ind. wrote to Akerman. "I take great pleasure in recommending for the office of U. S. Marshall for the Territory of Wyoming Gen'l Robert H Milroy of Indiana. General Milroy is a gentleman of high character, was a gallant officer in the late war being promoted to the rank of a Major General, and last year was nominated by the Republican party of Indiana for the office of State Treasurer, but with others on the ticket was defeated— He is in every way qualified to fill the position he seeks and I would consider his appointment a personal favor—" ALS, *ibid.*, Records Relating to Appointments. On May 17, Porter wrote to Akerman. "The President directs me to say that he will be pleased to have you send him a nomination, of Gen. Robt. H. Milroy of Ind. to be U. S. Marshal for Wyoming Territory, to be sent to the Senate to-day." LS, *ibid.*, Letters Received. On May 26, 1869, Robert H. Milroy, Delphi, Ind., had written to USG. "Please consider this *Private* . . . Will you please do an old soldier the favor to read the following yourself—Not being a politician, I have been unable to reach you through politicians. The Senators & Republican representatives in Congress, from this State, all of whom know me personally, promised to obtain for me from you, if possible a lucrative appointment. Relying on this promise, I did not go to Washington, as others did, and was not remembered—It is humiliating to me, to have to apply to you myself & make a statement of my *qualifications* & *merits* for an appointment—A large dependent family, whom my pecuniary misfortunes have reduced to distressing poverty, is the only consideration that impels me to thus trouble you.—As to my *qualifications*—I graduated at the Norwich Military University Vt.; tho' born & raised in this State,—I studied Law & practiced that profession for fifteen years before the war—served one term as circuit judge by appointment of Gov. Jos. A. Wright, & was a member of the Constitutional Convention that framed

the new constitution of this State in 1850, As for my politicle principles, I was
born & raised a Democrat, but left that party before the war, on account of its pro-
slavery,—anti-free-soil proclivities.—I am 52 years old & was never accused of a
dishonorable act, or knowingly wronged a human being out of the value of one
cent.—As for my *merits*, I served in the Mexican war as Capt. of Co. C. of the 1st
Ind. Vol. Inf.—I made the first call for a Vol. Co. for the late War (Feb. 7th 1861) &
had the first Co. ready when Presdt. Lincoln called for Vols. in Apl./61—I was
commissioned as Capt. but was a few days afterwards appointed & commissioned as
Col. of the 9th Ind. Vol. Inf. for the 3 months service.—At the end of that time I
recruited my Regt. to 1049 men, at my own expense, in 20 days, for the three years
service & was ordered back to W. Va. again.—I was appointed Brig. Genl Sept. 3rd
1861. & in the beginning of 1862̶3̶ was promoted to Maj. Genl to rank as such from
Nov. 29th 1862̶ — I was in 21 engagements & served till the latter part of July
1865, when finding that my services were no longer required, I resigned—My usefulness to the country, was to a great extent curtailed & cut short during the war,
by my having, in some way, unfortunately, incured the ill will & hatred of Maj. Genl
Hallock in 1862, soon after he became 'Genl in Chief.'—After I had cut my way out
of Winchester in June 1863, where my little force of 7000 had been surrounded for
two days by Lees' army, then on its march to Gettysburg—& while with my shat-
tered Division & a few Regts. of Pa. Militia, I was in Bedford Co. Pa, skirmishing
with & keeping the Reb. hords from overrunning that portion of the State—I was,
three days before the battle of Gettysburg, placed in arrest by order of Hallock, as
if I had been committing some great crime—No charges were ever prefered against
me, & I have never yet found out why I was placed in arrest. The Court of Inquiry
convened some time afterwards by order of Presdt. Lincoln, at my request, & composed of *Brig. Genls*, of Hallocks own selection, was unable, after a tedious examination of one month, to find any cause for my arrest & I was acquitted of all blame.
But Gen. Hallock would not permit me to have the evidence & proceedings of that
court published—By that cruel & most unjust arrest, I was kept out of command
for 11 months & only then given comd. of the defences of the Nashville & Chatta-
nooga R. R. & stationed at Tullahoma till the close of the war, As an evidence that
my arrest was unjust, every commissioned officer of my Winchester Divs. except 3,
(the 2nd Div. 8th A. C.) signed a petition to Presdt. Lincoln to have me restored to
their Comd. soon after my arrest.—Pardon me for thus mentioning this matter to
you. It is a very painful subject to me, & I do so for the purpose of removing possible
prejudice that an erroneous understanding of it may have left in your mind,—with
the hope that you, in your great power & wisdom, may look into this matter & yet,
to some extent, bring down the hand of justice upon that unworthy bad man, who yet
most unworthily, holds high comd. in the army. As for my pecuniary circumstances, I
had some property—a comfortable home & a lucrative Law Practice at the beginning
of the war, which I left hastily in the hands a young man who had read Law with
me—was considered honest & who I took in as a partner—He was to keep up my
business, but he turned rascal during my absence of over four years, & appropriated
to his own use large sums collected for my clients—burned my books & accounts &
ran away—Finding my self thus deeply involved at the close of the war—with the
hope of retrieving my losses, I was induced to accept the Presidency of an Oil Co.
in Tenn. that had very flattering pecuniary prospects. But after a years effort &
expenditure of $55,000.00 it proved a total failure & left me almost hopelessly in-
volved, & I had to return to my Law practice under depressing circumstances—
having had to sell a large portion of my Law Library to subsist my family—Pardon

the unintended length of this letter. If you can give me an appointment that will *pecuniarily* enable me to get on my feet again—get a home & educate my children, you will do me an immense favor & lift a mountain of depression from my shoulders. The duties of any position to which you may appoint me, would be honestly & faithfully discharged. Should I be permitted to select a position, I would name a foreign mission or a Consulship, such as that to Liverpool or London. But would gladly accept of an Indian superintendency—Territorial Gov. or superv. of Internal Rev. of this State—I frankly admit that the *emoluments* constitute the inducement for my seeking an appointment.—Should you desire to have inquiry made as to my capability &c, I would refer to the Repub. Ind. delagation in Congress—Vice Presdt. Colfax—Gen. W. P. Lasselle & Hon. J. W. Wright Attys. of Washington City, who have known me intimately for many years—Gov. F. P. Stanton also knows me intimately—Secy. Cox also knows me personaly, as I served a short time in his Comd—" ALS, *ibid.*, RG 59, Letters of Application and Recommendation. Related papers are *ibid.*

On July 1, 1871, Milroy, Cheyenne, Wyoming Territory, wrote to USG. "I arrived at this place on the 28th ult. to qulify, and take charge of the office of U. S. Marshal, of this Ter. *provided* I found the emoluments of the office, sufficient to justify me in so doing.... The income of the office for 1870 was increased One Thousand Dollars by pay for taking the census, which of course cannot be relied on for ten years. The salary of the office being only $200.00 and the income thereof, otherwise being wholly dependent on fees, is graduated of course by the number of prosecutions, for violations of U. S. laws. The recent radical amendment of the U. S. revenue laws, and the great reduction, in the number of articles for taxation, has rendered violations of U. S. laws, and consequent prosecutions, much less frequent; so that the whole amount of fees as Marshal of this Ter. *for the last Six months, from all sources*, amounts to but $106.10 and the whole amount of the emoluments of the office for this year, including the salary, cannot exceed $600.00—Having a dependent family and no income, I hope that, under the circumstances, you will pardon me for declining to accept the office of U. S. Marshal of this Ter. which you did me the honor, & favor to tender me. Permit me in declining to accept this office, to state some facts, as I have learned them from leading Republicans, & business men of this place in refference to Maj. Church Howe, the present incumbent of the office, of the U. S. Marshal of this Ter. He is a young Gentleman of *fine talents, excellent culture, good habits, high asperations, and wealth.* His *political aspirations* have induced him to accept, and hold on to the office of U. S. Marshal, as a means of becoming favorably known to the people of the Ter. and his wealth has enabled him to remain in the Ter. with his family, notwithstanding the small income of the office, and being a good Speaker, with popular manners, and having come within two votes of receiving the nomination as Republican candidate for delegate to Cong' at the last election, and only defeated by a combination, that would probably, if viewed from a moral standpoint, appear, any thing but favorable or fair, he has become obnoxious to, & excited the jealousy of, the many other political aspirants of the Ter. and they have combined to crush and drive him out of the Ter. I feel very sure, had your Excellency have known the real facts about this matter, you would not have consented to the removal of Maj Howe, and in my belief, simple justice requires that he should be restored or at least granted a hearing, before he is dismissed from office. I will only add that had I even found the Office of U. S. Marshal of this Ter. highly remunerative, I could not have consented, to be the instrument, *in the hands of a ring*, to crush an honorable opponent, which *they* could not otherwise do, by fair means." ALS, *ibid.*, RG 60, Records Relating to Appointments. For consideration of Milroy as commissioner of Indian Affairs, see letter to George H. Stuart, July 22, 1871.

On July 4, Campbell, Laramie, wrote to Babcock. "Gen'l Milroy came out to the Territory—remained ~~two~~ three days and left refusing to qualify. I saw but little of him as he spent his time while here with the Marshal and his friends. He made an appointment to see me but without filling it left Cheyenne in the night on a cattle train I am informed that Howe has gone to see to see the President to secure a reappointment—I sincerely hope this will not be done, as his retention in office would be the greatest blow that could be given to the Republican party of the Territory—to Judge Jones, our Delegate—to almost all of the Territorial officers and to me personally I would be very glad if Major Frank Wolcott (formerly of Kentucky) present Receiver of the Land Office in Wyoming could receive the appointment, and have so written to Gen Bristow who is I believe at present Acting Attorney General and can vouch for Major Wolcott I am very anxious to make a short visit East this summer—Can you not procure for me a 20 days leave of absence Regards to all friends ... Can it not be arranged with the Republican Executive Committee to give each one of the Territories a vote in the National Convention? I think it would be a good idea" ALS, DNA, RG 60, Records Relating to Appointments. On July 8, Akerman wrote to USG. "Genl Milroy, after visiting Wyoming, has declined the Marshalship of that Terr'y. Church Howe, the former Mars'l., has telegraphed requesting an opportunity to answer the charges before the place is filled. Mr. Taffe M. C. from Nebraska, urges the same There are no recent applications for the office on file. The Chief Justice & the Dis. Att'y. have both written that it is important that the office should be properly ?promptly filled because court is to be held on the 17, inst. I think it the better opinion that in such a case, Howe is legally in office under his old commission and that his acts as Marshal will be good But the authorities leave the question in some doubt, &, therefore, if you are determined upon another appointment, some possible trouble may be escaped by making it promptly I shall be glad to receive directions from you upon the subject." Copy, *ibid.*, Letters Sent to Executive Officers. Howe remained marshal.

On May 18, 1872, Jones wrote to Attorney Gen. George H. Williams urging Howe's removal. LS, *ibid.*, Records Relating to Appointments. On July 22, Brig. Gen. Oliver O. Howard, Colorado City, wrote to Secretary of War William W. Belknap. "I write you this privately for your personal consideration. Governor Campbell, the Governor of Wyoming seems to have procured the removal from the Marshalship of the Territory of Col. Church Howe. Now this, in addition to other acts quite unpopular amongst Republicans, has created a breach in the Republican party that I fear will lose us the Territory. Now General Schofield is the officer who backs Campbell. Campbell seems simply to look out for himself. Republicans who heartily endorse Genl. Grant say that his associations and his actions are altogether opposed to their wishes. Conversing with Senator Hitchcock he said that something ought to be done in Wyoming; that the influence of the Wyoming election, coming so early, would be felt in Nebraska. ~~that~~ Colonel Howe, the removed man, is a friend of Genl. Grants and an active man, &, earnest speaker; his sudden removal, without cause, paralyzes him, so that he can not well do as he intended, go over—into Nebraska and speak for the administration which has struck him a heavy blow—Campbell has always belonged to the Steadman—Fullerton—Andrew Johnson clique, with some dignity of deportment but without much weight. Schofields surroundings have been much of this character. Therefore considering everything, as a true friend to yourself and to the President, I recommend that Governor Campbell, if absolute removal is impracticable or inexpedient, be assigned to some other field of labor. Such citizens as I have seen, and some other republicans have had a consultation and expressed a belief that if Col. Church Howe, whom I remember as one of Genl. Sedgewick's trusted officers, should be appointed as Governor this would satisfy the great major-ity of the people, unify and strengthen the republican party and put in operation an active campaign in the Presidents behalf. Dr. Reed, whom the President will know, will give judicious advise as to the new Governor, if one should be decided upon. A bold stroke, promptly made, will, I think, save us Wyoming and favorably affect Nebraska. . . . P. S. I write you confidentially, but, of course, with the understanding that you will show my letter, if you wish to the President *himself*." LS, *ibid.*, RG 59, Letters of Application and Recommendation. See letter to Edwards Pierrepont, July 3, 1875; Lewis L. Gould, *Wyoming: A Political History, 1868–1896* (New Haven, 1968), pp. 24–39.

On Sept. 23, 1872, Maj. Gen. John M. Schofield, San Francisco, wrote to USG. "Being informed that my old friend and staff officer, Genl J. A. Campbell, now Gover-nor of Wyoming, will be an applicant for a Mission to one of the South American States, I desire to express the hope that you may find it practicable to give him the appointment he desires. You are well aware of the high esteem in which I held Genl Campbell as an officer of the Army, and I believe his Executive administration of Wyoming Territory has been equally creditable to him and to you who appointed him. It would be highly gratifying to know that you are able to show Governor Campbell this mark of your approval of the manner in which he has discharged the duties of his present office." Copy, DLC-John M. Schofield. On March 25, 1873, USG nominated Campbell to another term.

1. Howe, born in 1839 in Princeton, Mass., served with the 6th Mass., became 1st lt. and q. m., 15th Mass., and saw action at Ball's Bluff, the Peninsular campaign, Second Bull Run, and Antietam as a staff officer, earning promotion to bvt. maj. On March 15, 1869, William E. Chandler, Washington, D. C., wrote to USG. "*Maj. Church Howe* of Massachusetts will be an applicant for Marshal of Wyoming territory; and it gives me pleasure in aid of Maj. Howe's application to state what I know of his services to the Republican cause. He was engaged upon the stump during the whole of the Presidential campaign and spoke eloquently and effectively in New Jersey and other contested states. His political service entitles him to friendly consideration from the new administration. Maj Howe's military record is a very honorable one. Enlisting as a private in the famous Massachusetts *Sixth* and serving as a Lieutenant and Cap-tain in the 14th Massachusetts he earned a just reputation for courage and patriotizm. His friends do not hesitate to urge him earnestly for the position he desires." ALS, *ibid.*, RG 60, Records Relating to Appointments. Related papers recommending Howe's appointment as marshal, Mass., are *ibid.* On April 3, USG nominated Howe as marshal, Wyoming Territory.

On March 1, 1869, Nicholas J. O'Brien, Cheyenne, had written to [USG]. "I have the honor to respectfully apply for the appointment of United States Marshall of the Territory of Wyoming, and herewith transmit the enclosed *Resolutions* of the Republi-can Club of Western Dakota, and also the the *Recommendations* of the leading business men, and Republicans of said Territory, in my favor—I further I inclose to Your Excellency the cordial endorsment of the *Delegate* in Congres from said Terr. togather with the *Delegate* in Congres from Colorado, and the recommendation of the *Irish National Republican association* for Nebraska & the Territories, . . ." ALS, *ibid.* The enclosures are *ibid.* On March 22, David Butler and two others, Washington, D. C., wrote to USG. "We respectfully recommend William H. Pierce of Nebraska for the Appointment of marshall of the Territory of Wyoming—Mr Pierce is a Lawyer of decided energy and ability—identified with the improvement of the West, and in every way qualified to discharge the duties of that office." LS, *ibid.* A related paper is *ibid.* On April 3, Marcy H. Randall, Elmira, N. Y., wrote to USG. "I have forwarded to the Atty-Genl. an aplication for the position of U. S. Marshal. for the Territory of Wyoming. I base my claims, upon the following facts. I enlisted as a private in the 12th Ills Infty, and served as Officer and Soldier, for over four years, with credit to my self, and State, and was favorably mentioned in the reports of Genls McArthur A. L. Chetlain, & Major Hugunin. I was wounded at the Battle of Donelson, and *coupled with the exposure*, so diseased my Lungs, that I was *compelled* to start for the mountains as soon as I was dischgd from the Service. I was present, & took part at the *Battles* of Donleson, Shiloah, Seige of Corinth, & battle of Corinth, and several other engagements, of less note.—At the battle of Corinth, I captured the Bearer & Colors of a Texas Regt, after a hand to hand encountre, with one of the Color Guards. I have lived in the Ters of Wyoming Montana & Utah, for over three years: and am well aquainted with the *country*, & *People.* I was the bearer of letters to Secty Cox, Senetor Trumbul, & N. B. Judd M. C. but finding them so over run with aplications & aplicants, I contented myself with forwarding by Mail, from N. Y. City Hopeing that my aplication will be favorably noticed by you, . . ." ALS, *ibid.*

To Columbus Delano

Long Branch N. J.
July 13th 1871

Hon. C. Delano
Sec. of the Int.

Mr. Colier, Sec. of the Board of Indian Peace Commissioners, has told me of the report of Supt. Pope,[1] to the effect that with enlarged powers, and assurances of protection and proper provisions, the wild Indians of New Mexico and Arizona may now be induced to come in to Canada Alamaso.[2] I suggest that enlarged powers be given to Supt Pope to effect so desirable an object, or that Mr Colier be sent with all the necessary powers.

I will direct the War Dept to give all the assistance necessary to carry out the object of Mr Pope, or Mr Colier, as the case may be.

Please call on the Sec of War, or in his absence upon Gen. Sherman, for such orders to the troops, for supplying transportation, provisions, or escorts, as may be needed to carry out the designs of the Indian Bureau in this matter.

Very respectfully
Your obt servt
U. S. GRANT

Copies, DNA, RG 75, Letters Received, New Mexico Superintendency; *ibid.*, RG 94, Letters Received, 2465 1871; DLC-USG, II, 1. On July 21, 1871, Ely S. Parker, commissioner of Indian Affairs, wrote to Secretary of the Interior Columbus Delano. "I have the honor to transmit you herewith a copy of office letter of the 18th of March last to Superintendent Pope, of New Mexico, directing him to send Apache chief Cochise and other prominent Indians of that tribe to this city, for the purpose of conferring with this Department in regard to the condition and welfare of their people. I also forward copies of letters, in reply thereto, from Superintendent Pope, of the dates of April 6, April 21, May 14, and June 28, in which he reports his progress in the search for said Indians and the finding of Cochise, but that he was unable to prevail upon him then to come in, because of his fear of the military and the citizens. I also transmit a copy of a letter from Governor Pile, of New Mexico, dated June 19, 1871, referred to this Department by the Secretary of State. The President having directed that enlarged powers be given to Superintendent Pope, or that Mr. Colyer be sent with the necessary powers to establish friendly relations with and locate the wild Indians of New Mexico and Arizona, I would respectfully suggest, as requested by you in verbal conversation yesterday, that the above letters be taken by Mr. Colyer as his guide of procedure, and that, in addition, he be invested with discretionary powers in the matter, to be used as the circumstances which may develop themselves upon his arrival in those Territories may demand. I suggest that he be authorized to do whatever in his judgment may appear most wise and proper in locating the roving tribes in those Territories on suitable reservations, in bringing them under the supervision of the respective agents, and in arranging issue of the necessary supplies for their wants, as will be for the best interests of the Indians, the Government, and citizens of said Territories." *HED*, 42-2-1, part 5, pp. 493–94. On the same day, Benjamin R. Cowen, act. secretary of the interior, sent instructions to Vincent Colyer, Board of Indian Commissioners. *Ibid.*, p. 493. On July 18, AG Edward D. Townsend had written to Brig. Gen. John Pope, Dept. of the Mo., Fort Leavenworth. "I have the honor to inform you the President directs that so far as your resources will permit, assistance be given in provisions and transportation & military protection, to Mr Vincent Collyer, of the Indian Commission, in endeavoring to collect the wild Indians of New Mexico & Arizona upon a reservation at Cañada Alamosa, and also to such Indians as may be induced to come in both on the way & after arrival at the reservation." Copy, DNA, RG 192, Orders Received. See letter to William W. Belknap, July 14, 1871; *SED*, 42-2-1, part 2, p. 36.

1. Nathaniel Pope, superintendent of Indian Affairs, New Mexico Territory. Born in 1839 in St. Louis, Pope entered the Civil War as capt., commissary of subsistence, and served on the staff of his uncle Maj. Gen. John Pope in Va. as well as under Brig.

Gen. Alfred Sully along the Missouri River. Mustered out as of March 1, 1866, he moved to Fort Benton, Montana Territory, and worked as a merchant and Indian agent. See *PUSG*, 20, 458–59.

On March 11, 1869, U.S. Delegate José Francisco Cháves of New Mexico Territory had written to USG. "I have the honor very respectfully to request the appointment of Tomas Cabeza de Baca of New Mexico as Superintendent of Indian Affairs for that Territory.—Mr. Baca is a native of the Territory, a gentleman of education and of the strictest integrity.—He is very influencial among those people and during the late rebellion exerted all his influence to induce the native portion of the citizens to enlist in favor of the Union.—The office is now vacant, and in view of the fact that at least nine tenths of the citizens of the Territory are of Mexican extraction it would appear but just that at least one of the natives should be appointed to one of the leading offices in the Territory.—He is also very highly endorsed by the Legislature, a large majority of whom are republicans.—" ALS, DNA, RG 48, Appointment Papers, New Mexico Territory. Related papers are *ibid.* On April 16, Charles E. Hovey, Washington, D. C., wrote to USG. *"Elmer Washburn,* of Alton Ill. who served during the war in the 33d Ill. Infty. applied for the office of *Surveyor General* of *New Mexico,* but failed to get it—He would now like to be Superintendent of Indian affairs for New Mexico—No young man has come here from our State with so substantial and cordial a backing, so far as I have heard—The letters of Trumbull, Yates & Morton, and of the State officers of Illinois, are not formal, but real & earnest—Mr Washburn wants to go to New Mexico to live—I know his appointment would be a good one for the Govt & the Indians; and even the Quakers would approve, if they knew him—Will you not take his case into consideration in making this appointment—I learned his worth and ability in the army, where he won his friends—" ALS, *ibid.* On Oct. 15, 1870, Governor William A. Pile of New Mexico Territory wrote to USG. "Genl G. A. Smith during the time he has been in this Territory as Collector of Internal Revenue has been a most faithful and competent officer: he has greatly improved the condition of affairs in connection with the goverment taxes and his office. All his associations have been with the best people of the Territory and he has constantly exercised his influence against the prevailing vices that are the *bane* of this country   I think that his practical good sense devotion to duty and qualities of both *head* and *heart* eminently fit him for the Position of '*Superintendent* of *Indian ₐAffairs*' for this Territory   Genl Smith has acquired much practical knowledge of the Indians and people of this country and I am confident would be able to handle the matter more promptly and efficiently than a new man   If no selection for this office has been made I earnestly recommend his appointment" ALS, *ibid.* Related papers are *ibid.* Papers recommending Lewis J. Blair and James Blake as superintendent of Indian Affairs, New Mexico Territory, are *ibid.*

In March, 1869, T. Rush Spencer, Washington, D. C., had written to USG seeking appointment as superintendent of Indian Affairs, New Mexico Territory. ALS, *ibid.* On March 6, U.S. Senator Roscoe Conkling of N. Y. had written to USG. "Dr Rush Spencer of N. Y. will be presented for an appointment in the Territory of Wyoming, & it gives me pleasure to speak of his fitness & merit. He is a physician of standing, a man of high character and cultivation, and his politics are Republican. Impaired health Constrains a change of climate, and leads him to ask the Surveyor Generalship of Wyoming." ALS, *ibid.* On March 11, Cháves wrote to USG. "I have the honor herewith to enclose a recommendation from all the Republican members of the Territory of New Mexico, asking the appointment of Captain Eldridge W. Little for the office of Surveyor General of the Territory of New Mexico, which office was made vacant by the death of Col. Ben. C. Cutler. His own application together with other recommendations have been already filed with the Hon. Secretary of the Interior. I take great pleasure in this connection to fully and cordially concur in all that is said in favor of Captain Little. His qualifications are, loyalty, strict integrity and eminent capacity, and will be acceptable to the people of the Territory. I most earnestly request his appointment." ALS, *ibid.* Related papers are *ibid.* On April 5, USG nominated Spencer as surveyor gen., New Mexico Territory, and on April 12, Eldridge W. Little as receiver, Santa Fé.

2. On Dec. 23, 1870, Colyer wrote to Townsend. "The President direts me to call on you and see if the War Department cannot promptly issue an order for the Officer Commanding the Department of new mexico, to subsist the Apache Indians of new mexico and south eastern Arizona, now collected, or soon to assemble at Canada Alemosa N. M. and having him keep a correct account of the expense, charge the same to the Indian Bureau. The Indian Department having no fund specially set apart for the purpose of subsisting the apaches and barely sufficent to carry on the current expenses of the Indian agencies of N M & Arizona have, through our Board, with the earnest endorsement of the Secretary of the Interior, applied to Congress for an appropriation of thirty thousand dollars for this special purpose. The House of Representatives passed the bill the day it was sent in, but Congress having adjourned over the holidays, it must await the action of the Senate until 4th of January next. The President says the War department has the power to issue such an order and if the Adujant General of the Army, in the absence of the Secretary of War will draw up the order and send it over to him he, the President will promptly sign it. . . . The acting Commissioner of Indian affairs suggests that inasmuch as a portion of the Apache Indians to be subsisted are the Mescalerros of the Easter side of the Rio Grande the 'Order' had better read that the rations should be issued to the apaches at such places as the Superintendant of Indian affairs of New Mexico may designate." ALS, DNA, RG 94, Letters Received, 196I 1870. On the same day, USG endorsed this letter. "The Indians herein mentioned will be supplied by the Subsistence Department of the Army with such subsistence as can be spared without injury to the service, the cost to be refunded by the Indian Department." ES, *ibid.* Related papers are *ibid.* See *SED,* 41-3-39, 103. On Jan. 23 and 24, 1871, Secretary of War William W. Belknap wrote to Townsend. "The President directs that the Indians referred to in telegram be subsited—temporarily—that one thousand head of cattle be purchased & sent foward from such point as Genl. Augur may determine ~~best~~ & that telegram be sent to that effect to Genl. Augur. Chambers to be notified Also that subsistence be issued to Indians referred to in telegram, ~~Now at Laramie~~ near Laramie.—Capt. T. C. Sullivan now at Sioux City to report to Genl. Augur to take charge of this business." "The President directs that limited issue of ammunition for small game be issued to Indians coming to Laramie—in accordance with recommendation of C. O at Laramie, as contained in telegram from Genl. Augur dated Jan. 11. 71 Also to those coming in at Fetterman" AN (initialed), DNA, RG 94, Letters Received, 113 1871. Related papers are *ibid.*

To Hamilton Fish

Long Branch, N. J.
July 13th 1871

DEAR GOVERNOR:

As I informed Mr. Clews[1] that the foreign disbursments for the Navy would be divided between the house in which he is a Partner, and Jay Cooke, McCullough[2] &c. and now think it better to leave the deposite all with one house, I would suggest that the deposites abroad of the State Dept. be given to Clews & Co. London, instead.

Had I not told Mr. C. of the arrangement that would be made when the appropriation for this fiscal year was drawn upon I should not care what particular American house got the disbursing of this fund, except I should not like McCullough to have anything to do with it.

Respectfully Yours
U. S. GRANT

HON. H. FISH,
SEC. OF STATE

ALS, DLC-Hamilton Fish. On May 16, 1871, Secretary of State Hamilton Fish had written in his diary. "The question of changing the Government Banker in London is brought up—Boutwell favors giving the deposits to Morton, Rose & Co—Robeson has transferred the Navy deposits to Jay Gould & Co (McCullough) late Secy of Treasury) says he ~~pro~~ told H. D. Cooke that if he wd carry the District & then go in to carry Pennsa he would make the transfer that Cooke having done his part, he had order the transfer He is laughed at (pleasantly) for having giving the transfer to McCullough—I object to removing the funds of the State Dept from Barings— that our officers & parties drawing drafts on Barings find them more valuable than on any other House—" *Ibid.* See Henrietta M. Larson, *Jay Cooke: Private Banker* (Cambridge, Mass., 1936), pp. 310–12. On July 15, Fish, Garrison, N. Y., wrote to USG. "I received last Evening your letter directing transfer of the State Department accounts in London, from Baring Bros & Co to Clews—If the transfer is to be made, I wish it could have been to another House—I have however this morning written to Washington to carry out your instructions Enclosed I send a letter from Senator Frelinghuysen in answer to the enquiry I made about Judge Bradleys proficiency in French—From it I fear that the Judge has only that familiarity with French, which is very common with those who have travelled on the Continent, & which enables them to ask for what the are in daily need of, & do some shopping &c But you will be able to judge from what Senator Frelinghuysen says. If you are of opinion, that the Judges fluency & familiarity with French, are not equal to the requirements of the case, it would seem to throw us back, *so far as names have been considered*, to a choice between Messr Adams & Dana—& while both may be open to some political objections, it seems to me that the superior qualifications, of Mr Adams, & his intimate familiarity with all the particulars of the Cruisers &c, indicate him so decidedly as the man most able to render assistance, & give advice & information to our Agent, in the management of the Case, that I cannot refrain from expressing the hope that as between the two gentlemen named; your decision will be in favour of Mr A— Outside of a few politicians I think the Country generally would approve the selection, not only as good in itself, but as exhibiting on your part an elevation above partizanship in matters involving international questions—With him as Arbitrator, should the judgment fall short of popular expectation, it must be admitted that you sent the man of all others most familiar with the Case, and any responsibility for failure to obtain all that the most sanguine may have claimed, will in the public estimation be taken from the Administration—while on the contrary, if the judgment be what we hope, you will have not only the credit of obtaining it, but the additional claim of magnanimity, in having selected an Arbitrator, not politically or personally identified with your Administration—" ALS (press), DLC-Hamilton Fish. See letter to Hamilton Fish, June 25, 1871.

1. Born in 1834 in England, Henry Clews emigrated to N. Y., entered banking, and prospered during the Civil War, rising to prominence in international finance. On April 17, 1872, Clews organized a mass meeting of New York City "merchants, bankers, manufacturers and other business men in favor of the re-election of General Grant." Clews, *Fifty Years in Wall Street* (New York, 1908), p. 316. On the same day, Horace Porter wrote to Clews. "I have received your several interesting letters in regard to the great meeting in New York, and have shown them to the President, who read them with deep interest. I have not written any suggestions, because I know you, being on the ground, could judge so much better of the situation, and the temper of the New York people. You have done a great work, and this evening's success will, I have no doubt, be the reward of your efforts. We shall look anxiously for the reports. What you say is curious about the use of Dix's name and others. Our people are at work in Congress getting up telegrams signed by the Republican members of all the State delegations endorsing the administration of General Grant. I wish we had thought of these sooner, but still we can get them all in time, I hope. I have just come from the House, where I was looking after this matter. Wishing you every success, . . ." *Ibid.*, p. 319. On Nov. 6, Clews, New York City, wrote to USG. "I congratulate you on the glorious result of yesterday, the American people have nobly vindicated both you and themselves by deeds which speak far louder than words—Your dignified silence throughout this most bitter campaign has won for you the hearts of all true and patriotic men, neither last nor least among whom ranks Your devoted friend," ALS, USG 3. Also in 1872, Clews wrote to USG enclosing "a paper signed by leading business men of New York, endorsing his course which had been much criticised by 'irresponsible stump orators.'" William Evarts Benjamin, Catalogue No. 42, March, 1892, p. 7.

2. Former Secretary of the Treasury Hugh McCulloch had become a partner in Jay Cooke's London bank. See *PUSG*, 18, 148; *ibid.*, 19, 315.

To Ely S. Parker

LONG BRANCH, N. J., July 13, 1871.

SIR—Your letter of the 29th of June tendering your resignation as Commissioner of Indian Affairs, to take effect on the 1st day of Augst, 1871. was duly received. Accepting it severs official relations which have existed between us for eight consecutive years, without cause of complaint as to your entire fitness for either of the important places which you have had during that time. Your management of the Indian Bureau has been in entire harmony with my policy, which I hope will tend to the civilization of the Indian race. It has also been able and discreet. In leaving the public service to pursue a more independent course of life, you take with you my sincere wishes for your prosperity and my hearty commendations to all with whom the accidents of life may bring you in business relations for integrity and ability. Very truly yours,

U. S. GRANT.

To General E. S. PARKER, Commissioner Indian Affairs.

New York Herald, July 18, 1871. On June 29, 1871, Ely S. Parker, commissioner of Indian Affairs, had written to USG. "The effect of Congressional legislation, had since I have had the honor to be Commissioner of Indian Affairs, has been to almost wholly divest the Indian Bureau of all its original importance, duties and proper responsibilities. Under present arrangements the Commissioner of Indian Affairs is nearly a supernumerary officer of the government, his principal duties being simply that of a clerk to a Board of Indian Commissioners, operating wholly outside of and and almost independently of the Indian Bureau—I would gladly and willingly do any thing in my power to aid in forwarding and promoting to a successful issue, the Presidents wise and benificent Indian policy, but I cannot in justice to myself longer continue to hold the ambiguous position I now occupy as Commissioner of Indian Affairs. I therefore most respectfully but firmly tender my resignation of said office to take effect on the first day of August 1871 Sincerely thanking you Mr President for the kindness and consideration you have always shown me, . . ." ALS, OFH. See *PUSG,* 19, 191–98.

On Dec. 7, 1870, William Welsh, Philadelphia, wrote an open letter to Secretary of the Interior Columbus Delano charging the Indian Bureau with fraudulent purchase of goods for Indians. *HRC,* 41-3-39, 111–22. On Dec. 12, U.S. Representative Aaron A. Sargent of Calif. introduced a successful resolution calling for an investigation of Welsh's charges. *CG,* 41–3, 67. On Jan. 12, 1871, Parker wrote to Delano. ". . . I desire to express a conviction which has forced itself upon my mind that these gratuitous charges upon the Indian Office is but a determination to carry out certain theories put forth by Mr. Welsh in 1869. It will be recollected that in April, 1869, President Grant appointed Mr. Welsh as one of the Indian commissioners authorized to be appointed under the act of Congress of April 10, 1869. He then claimed that the expenditure of all Indian appropriations was also intended to be placed in the hands of said commission. To this proposition the Hon. J. D. Cox, then Secretary of the Interior, and myself dissented, and in which we were sustained by the President. He then resigned from the commission and has since labored as a voluntary agent, keeping, it seems, a watchful eye upon the transactions of the Indian Office, with a view to detecting irregularties and exposing them, and thereby taking from it the management of the Indian funds. The determination of the President to call in the religious element of the country to aid him in the management of Indian affairs, and the Episcopal Society, of which I understand Mr. Welsh is a prominent member, having had assigned to them most of the Dakota district as their special field of labor, has opened the most plausible pretext to renew the attempt of 1869, at least so far as that society has acquired jurisdiction in Dakota, notwithstanding the Indian Office has maintained the peace and kept the Indians comparatively quiet there and elsewhere. I will not assert that he and his associates or any other religious organiza-tion are not as competent to manage and disburse Indian funds as the Indian Bureau, but there being at present no law authorizeing such a course the Bureau is bound to repel all such attempts. Since the accession of President Grant to the office of Chief Executive of the Nation, the Indian Bureau has been conducted solely and wholly with a view to the maintenance of peace, and the avoidance of expensive and horrible Indian wars, the amelioration of their condition, and their advancement in civilization. I also think it proper to remark, that during the past and preceding year, the communications from Mr. Welsh, relative to Indian affairs, have not always been couched in those terms which might be expected from one not authorized to dictate or control; but as there was a probability that his motive was a desire to promote the welfare of the Indians, his wishes have, as far as the same were practi-cable and not incompatible with existing laws, been complied with." *HRC*, 41-3-39, 125. On Feb. 25, the House Committee on Appropriations issued its report. "... To the mind of the committee, the testimony shows irregularities, neglect, and incompe-tency, and, in some instances, a departure from the express provisions of law for the regulation of Indian expenditures, and in the management of affairs in the Indian Department. But your committee have not found evidence of fraud or corruption on the part of the Indian Commissioner. With much to criticise and condemn, arising partly from a vicious system inherited from the past, and partly from errors of judgment in the construction of statutes passed to insure economy and faithfulness in administration, we have no evidence of any pecuniary or personal advantage sought or derived by the Commissioner, or any one connected with his Bureau.... We think a vigilant supervision by the board of Indian commissioners, with the real supervisory power proposed in the above amendment, would check many evils almost inseparable from the present mode of receipting and paying for goods." *Ibid.*, pp. II, VII. On March 3, USG signed an Indian appropriations act which required the Board of Indian Commissioners to approve payments for supplies purchased by the Indian Bureau. See *CG*, 41–3, 768, 1480, 1926; *U.S. Statutes at Large*, XVI, 568.

On March 6, Simon Van Etten, Washington, D. C., wrote to USG. "You will pleas parden me for taking the liberty to address you, but I feel as though I could advise a plan that would be of great importance to the U. S. and also to the Indians and to do a way with all the milatary and all the Indian Agents and all the Commissi-nors except one at Washington and the necessary Clerks, and in ten years the Indi-ans will all be a Source of revenue to the U. S. Treasury in Stead of drawing out of it. Should you desire to hear me I will take pleasure in doing Sow at your request. drop me a line at the P O Washington D C" ALS, DNA, RG 48, Appointment Div., Letters Received.

On May 1, George H. Stuart, Philadelphia, wrote to USG. "As chairman of the purchasing Committee of Indian Supplies, I have been requested to inquire whether the Commission can be allowed to have the Services of an Army Officer of the Subsistence Dep't., to serve as Inspector of the Subsistence Stores for the Indians— Said stores are to be received by the Commissioners of Indian Affairs, under propos-als, which will be opened May 3rd. This duty of Inspector, we believe to be a very important one, and are of the opinion that the position would be more competently filled by an officer of the Subsistence Dept. than by any other, provided such a one could be spared from other duty. If not inconsistent therefore with the Army regula-tions, we would respectfully suggest Gen'l. Jno. W. Turner, Commissary of Subsis-tence for the position. Knowing Gen'l. Turner to be 'off duty' at present, and being aware of his willingness to undertake this service and also from our knowledge of him, we particularly designate him, and would be pleased, if the exigencies of the Army permitted, to have him detailed to report to the Hon. Commissioner of Indian Affairs. I leave for *New York tomorrow* & should be glad to have an answer by *return mail,* or *telegram early Wednesday morning to my address as under,* . . . *P. S* I am happy to inform you that the competition on Blankets Dry Goods &c was very sharp and instead of *3 or 4 bidders* as formerly we had *92* and the leading articles have been bought in some instances *under,* and *all* at the *lowest* market price for *Cash,*" LS, *ibid.,* RG 92, Consolidated Correspondence, John W. Turner. On May 2, Horace Porter endorsed this letter. "Respectfully referred to the Commissary General of Subsis-tence, in the absence of the Secretary of War, who will telegraph Gen. Turner to report to the Commissioner of Indian Affairs to serve as Inspector of subsistence stores for the Indians. If Gen. Turner is not available, the Com. Gen. of Subsistence will order some competent officer for the duty, at once." ES, *ibid.*

On May 31, USG telegraphed to Stuart. "Your dispatch referred to Sec. of the Interior. Com. Parker's statement will be sent to you." Copy, DLC-USG, II, 5. On June 7, Benjamin R. Cowen, act. secretary of the interior, wrote to USG. "I have the honor to transmit, herewith, communication to this Department, dated the 6th in-stant, from Hon Geo H. Stuart, and, copy of one to him from Nathan Bishop Esq. relative to the transportation of 'Indian Supplies,' for your information in regard to the Subject," Copy, DNA, RG 48, Indian Div., Letters Sent.

In June, Stuart and John V. Farwell, "members of the Indian Commission," met USG "with reference to statements recently published reflecting upon the conduct of the Commission, which they supposed emanated from the Indian Bureau. It is known that the Board and the Commissioner (PARKER) are not in accord on several subjects relating to the management of the finances of the Indian Department." *New York Times,* June 17, 1871. See letter to George H. Stuart, July 22, 1871; William H. Armstrong, *Warrior in Two Camps: Ely S. Parker Union General and Seneca Chief* (Syracuse, 1978), pp. 151–61.

To William W. Belknap

Long Branch, N. J.
July 14th 1871

HON. W. W. BELKNAP,
SEC. OF WAR,
SIR.

A report from Supt. N. Pope, to the Indian Bureau, holds out promise of bringing in the wild indians of New Mexico and Arizona by giving them proper assurances of protection &c.[1] I have directed Sec. Delano to send an agent there to give them such assurances, or to enlarge the powers of Supt. Pope to enable him to do so, and have directed him to call upon you for such orders to the Military as may be necessary to this end.

Please give orders for protection to the agt. and such indians as may come in under any arrangement as he may make with them, for any provisions they may require until they can be bought out of the appropriation for that purpose, and such other proper orders as the Sec. of the Int. may request to enable him to carry out his design of colonizing these indians.

Very respectfully
your obt. svt.
U. S. GRANT

ALS, DNA, RG 94, Letters Received, 2465 1871. On July 18, 1871, Tuesday, a correspondent reported: "George H. Stuart and Vincent Collyer, of the Board of Indian Commissioners, called upon the President at Long Branch, on Friday last, to arrange for the preservation of peace with the Apaches of Arizona and New Mexico, the latest information from that country showing that there is yet hope of effecting this desirable object. The President took a deep interest in the proposal of the Commissioners, and wrote an official order to the Secretary of the Interior and Secretary of War, directing that ample protection should be offered all Apache Indians who might choose to come in." *Philadelphia Public Ledger*, July 19, 1871.

On Jan. 23, Secretary of the Interior Columbus Delano had written to Felix R. Brunot, Pittsburgh. "I have the honor to acknowledge the receipt of your communication, as chairman of the Board of Indian Commissioners, dated the 19th instant, recommending the discontinuance of the Arizona Superintendency. Your views have been laid before His Excellency the President, and I have also conferred with the Commissioner of Indian Affairs, on the subject, The reasons assigned by the Board of Commissioners—though you are entitled to great consideration, and, in the main, are concurred in by the Commissioner of Indn Affairs, as well as myself and the Presi-

dent, In view, however, of what has recently transpired in reference to this Superintendency, to which allusion was made by me, in a recent conversation with you, it
is not deemed best to discontinue this Agency at the present moment, If there are
reasons for declining to discontinue at once, it does not seem to me that these
reasons are likely to require that this Superintendency should be continued for any
considerable length of time," Copy, DNA, RG 48, Indian Div., Letters Sent. On Feb.
2, Gen. William T. Sherman wrote to Maj. Gen. John M. Schofield, Military District
of the Pacific. "Some days ago, when the newspapers contained a notice of recent
Indian Outrages in Arizona, and General Stoneman's proclamation of a relentless
war against the Apaches, the Secretary of War called my attention to the matter
saying that the President wanted all Military Commanders reminded of ~~the modern~~
his policy of moral and religious influences with the savages, ~~as against~~ in preference
to the bloody remedy of war. I showed the Secretary the full instructions which had
been given, more especially to General Sheridan, within whose Division the great
mass of Indians dwell, and as I am not certain that I wrote you to the same effect,
I now enclose you a copy of that letter, so that there may be an uniform policy
throughout the whole country. More recently I received an official copy of General
Stonemans order No 36 of Dec 30, 1870 in which he announces his purpose to
'inaugurate and prosecute a vigorous, persistent and relentless Winter Campaign
against the Pinal and Tonto Branches of the Apache Tribe of Indians.' On the 26 of
January I laid a copy of this order before the Secretary of war, with this endorsmt.
'Respectfully referred to the Secretary of War. The Pinals & Tonto Apaches have
been at war ever since the time we acquired that miserable Land from Mexico They
have no Reservations, and wander from NewMexico to Arizona, killing and Stealing.
If the modern Theory of Indian Civilization is to be practiced among them, now is
the time, and the question is, Shall the troops be withdrawn from Arizona? Shall
they remain passive, whilst those Apaches do their will? or, Shall Gen Stoneman
who is on the spot, and is as full of human sympathy as Mr Colyer himself, do what
his judgmt approves? I cannot reverse his orders unless positively so commanded
by higher authority.' The papers have just been handed back to me by the Secretary,
saying that he had laid them before the President who has no desire to revoke or
qualify Gen Stonemans orders, but he wishes Gen Stoneman to know that his general
policy towards the Savages is to treat them gently and kindly, but ~~not to~~ he does
not wish to circumscribe Gen Stoneman with specific orders that might prevent his
protecting the Mails, and Scattered Settlements as far as he can with the troops on
hand. Please advise Gen Stoneman to be as prudent and cautious as possible—for
there is a sentiment abroad—powerful in its influence, that would sacrifice him, and
his officers & men, on the evidence of an irresponsible newspaper paragraph. Let
the Indian Bureau and their agents, have full control inside their Reservations, and
a chance to tame the wild & roving ones outside, but the military should guard &
protect the mail routes, the settlers on the acknowledged public domain, and at the
mines not on Indian Lands to the best of their ability: and it ~~might~~ would be ~~prudent~~
well for Departmt Commanders, in making their orders, not to use language, which
is sure to be exaggerated & painted in the bloodyiest characters." ALS, *ibid.*, RG 94,
Letters Received, 298 AGO 1871. See *HED*, 42-2-1, part 5, 762–82.

On June 1, Sylvester Mowry wrote to USG. "Will you be pleased to read 'the
enclosed,' and give it such endorsement as you deem fit. I was very desirous of an
interview with you—in reference to Arizona affairs—and especially for reasons
purely personal but I am dangerously sick and forbidden to go out. let me say that
you can in no way so completely serve your own interests on the Pacific slopes as

by putting your strong hand on the Apache Indians. and checking the atrocious nonsense of Commissioner Parker's late recommendations." ALS, DNA, RG 94, Letters Received, 2024 1871. See *PUSG*, 17, 153–55.

On Aug. 22, C. A. Luke, Prescott, Arizona Territory, wrote to USG. "With profound humillity I pen these few lines to you, as the Chief Magistrate of the U. S. to lay before you the condition of the people of Arizona. Before I shall proceed I will state to you, that I am a disinterested party, as to Official position, or any such aspirations, my sole ambition is nothing more nor less than the interest, the developement of this Country, which however is laboring under the greatest immaginable disadvantages. Few men in, or out of this Country can speak with more freedom, as to cause, than I can, having been a resident of this Territory since 1864, during which time I have visited 'on business' four times the eastern States. Therefore my actual and personal experience in and out of this Country, ought to give me some reasonable inside into the causes of the backwardness of this Country. The people of the east do not understand the condition of this Country and the situation of the people at all. This Territory is destined to be of great importance in future to the U. S., the natural Mineral wealth can not fail to bring this now so much neglected Country into the first rank of States in the Union, but how soon this shall be remains to a great extend, yes in fact rests solely with the U. S. Government, which should extend its paternal hand to protect the setlers of this Territory, from a savage and vilenous foe, that continually oppresses us. No words can picture the autrocites of the Indians in this Country, which they continually perpetrate of which the Government can not be ignorant, although their principle knowledge is gleened from official reports, as made from time to time by Officers of the Army, or by other Government Officials, who however are poor judges to make reports, such as any impartial Citizen might or would make. Any Officer or Official will naturely make his report, rather to suit his own advantage, or els shape it with the acknowledged sentiment of politicks of the Country disregarding any thing and everything, that might be of vital interest to the people of this Country, and so, that their own position is not jeopardised. Years ago the principle features of the reports were mainly directed to inform, and convince the world of the barrenness, and utter worthlessnes of this Territory, which time has now in the main dispelled. The main sentiments in later reports has been chiefly directed against the Citizence and Setlers of this Country, as being devoid of principle and destitute of humane feelings, which time will also dispell. The people of this Territory have been stigmatised, as wanting war, no sane men would for a minut entertain such an Idea, this Country is too valuable to allow such reproaches. There are several and numerous tribes of Indians here in this Territory all their destinctive names I cannot mention. Some are classed friendly others friendly inclined, while others are, and have been set down as bad and hostile. This has been their definition by all writers and reporters eccept by Genl Stoneman, who even pronounced the acknowledged bad and hostile Indians, as being inclined to peace. Any reports tending to that end, is nothing less, than gross insult to the living brave, and industrious Setlers, and a positive mockery to the lamented 'murdered' dead. Could you dear Sir, but know the real condition of the Citizence residing and striving to live in this Country, you would proclaim in thunder tones over the heads of all baulkers against us, that the people of Arizona shall and must be protected, which is one of our great fundamental laws of which the American Citizen can boast. All attempts to twart the strong Arm of the Government, is not for the interest of humanity, not for the protection of the 'poor and deluded' Indian, (as the are termed) but a Crime against law and order. We all know and cannot fail to admit, if a men or a set of men, in California, New York or elswhere commits depredations, either robbery or murder, the law hunts them, the robbers are imprisoned, and the murderer is hanged, and what statute gives an Indian that right to rob, and murder, without being persued and punished. Where is that law that provides treaties with robbers and murderers, and are the Indians of this Territory anything less? they are not. even the reported best of them. In 1861 the rebellion broke out, which was promptly met by the U. S. Govt which did not allow one single part of the U. S. to be severed, although it was don at a heavey cost of Treasure, and great sacrifice of lives, but the supremacey of the law and Government was maintained. Later while certain man banded together, committed various depredations in some of the Southern States, the strong arm of the Govt was invoket, and unhesitatingly extended to the law abiding Citizence—I cannot consider the Citizence of Arizona less unworthy, and entitled to the fullest protec-tion. It must in truth be stated, the people of Arizona are good industrious and law abiding Citizence, more so, than proportioned is found in setled and regulated communities. They are hospitable to the stranger, and free and willing to the needy, and any thing said to otherwise is a willful slander. We have suffered and strugled next to indureable, and could some of our Chief opposers in the east be here amongst us, hear the losses inumerated to them by man after man, as sustained by us from the the Indians, a different feeling would at once spring up in our favor. I implore you dear Sir, in the name of this suffering people, to give no heed to pretending peace Commissioneers, for peace with the Indians in this Country is alltogether imposible, until they have thoroughly wiped. They may be cajoled into a peace, under certain stipulation, but will never keep it, hence the danger of them remains. The whole Country rejoiced over the appointment by you of Genl Crook, who will, if sustained deliver this Country from the terrible scourge, that has so long oppressed us. But to do this thoroughly he may yet find it necessary for more troops, which should not be withheld an hour. . . ." ALS, DNA, RG 75, Letters Received, Arizona Superintendency. See letter to William W. Belknap, July 29, 1871.

1. On May 25, Samuel F. Tappan, New York City, wrote to USG. "Again do the representatives of a wronged and persecuted race appeal to you and the country for simple justice, a spot of ground they can call their own and upon which they and their wives and children can be safe from betrayal and massacre. As you answer their reasonable demands the future will answer you and yours. I know that you have done, are doing and, will do, all in your power to secure justice for these unfortunate people, for which we all owe you a lasting debt of gratitude. I know who are the criminals in this matter, where the guilt lies, the responsible parties. It is Congress, and Congress alone. Our Commission called upon that body to wipe out all existing statutes upon Indian affairs and enact an entire new code, to set apart and dedicate forever to the use, and for the benefit, of the Indians, Territorial reservations, to remove the hated ban of outrage and outlawry from the wards of the nation, to pay our national obliga-tions in a way to secure their civilization and citizenship. They have refused to do anything of the kind, but on the contrary have repudiated our treaties and thereby disgraced the legislation of the country. The land speculators, rail-road monopolists in Congress have done this. They heed not the reports and evidence of their own Commissions, the history of the past, your recommendations and protests, and the expressed wish of the country for reform in administering Indian affairs, but rush blindly and madly on, evidently intent upon robbing the Indian of every inch of his land, and forcing the last of his race into the grave by the cowardly and bloody hand

of betrayal and massacre. I am appalled at the collossal magnitude of this contemplated crime against justice and law, and appeal to you, to demand of Congress, such legislation as the exigencies of the public service require, and if they refuse, let the country understand who are the responsible parties. Call them together for this purpose and do all you can to obtain their decided action upon this subject. Unless your wise and humane Indian Policy is made permenant and powerful by incorporation into the law of the land and a simple form of government for the Indian, it must sooner or later prove their destruction, and the recent fate of the Apaches at Camp Grant Arizona, fall upon the remnants of the race, which no one will deplore more than yourself." ALS, DNA, RG 75, Letters Received, Miscellaneous. See *PUSG*, 17, 345; letter to George H. Stuart, July 22, 1871.

On June 7, a correspondent reported a conversation with USG at West Point, N. Y. "I want to see the frontier quiet. I think it can be made quiet without shooting the Indians. . . . Those people . . . who clamor for the destruction of the Indians on the Plains either are interested or know nothing of the condition of affairs in the wild regions where the Indians live. I have lived with the Indians and I know them thoroughly. They can be civilized and made friends of the republic. It takes tact and skill, however, to deal with them. They are shrewd and cunning and won't be shaved out of their rights if they know it. My policy is peace. When I said, 'Let us have peace,' I meant it. I want peace on the Plains as everywhere else. That man was in earnest when he came to see me, and I suppose he wanted to talk of the Camp Grant affair. That attack on the Apaches was murder, purely. . . . They are warlike—that is, the young savages wander off to rob and murder occasionally; but no doubt they have provocation. I will investigate the massacre of the Apaches at Camp Grant and be just to all concerned. The Indian question is not one that the government should be called upon to settle. The citizens of the outlying States and Territories ought to be able to fix that. . . . The Quakers are doing well, have done well, and will do more. Other denom[i]nations of Christians are also laboring with effect among the Indians. They are all laboring for the same end, and I will give them all the support I can. I don't like riding over and shooting these poor savages; I want to conciliate them and make them peaceful citizens. The policy of peace, sir, is much preferable to the policy of war. You can't thrash people so that they will love you, even though they are Indians. You, however, make enemies friends by kindness. Isn't that right?" *New York Herald* (sub-headings integrated), June 8, 1871.

To William W. Smith

———

Long Branch, N. J.
July 18th 1871

DEAR SMITH:

Your dispatch saying that you and Emma cannot pay us a visit because it is too warm to bring the babe is just received. It will do the children good to come. It is delightful here every day and the journey is but one day, a good part of that over the mountains. Mrs. Casey is here now for a week or two, staying at the hotel, and Fred. is still with us but will be leaving in a week or two. If you come now you will see all of them and have a good time beside. Come this week. Telegraph as soon as you receive this whether you can come because we will invite no one else until we hear from you.

Yours Truly
U. S. GRANT

ALS, Washington County Historical Society, Washington, Pa. On [*July*] 18, 1871, USG telegraphed to William W. Smith. "Can you and Emma come Thursday and spend a week with us   we do not go west as proposed" Telegram received, *ibid.*

On July 17, USG had telegraphed to Secretary of the Navy George M. Robeson. "I wish you would come to Long Branch this week or early next,   answer what day," Telegram received, DNA, RG 107, Telegrams Collected (Bound).

To Hamilton Fish

Long Branch, N. J.
July 21st 1871,

DEAR GOVERNOR:

Your letter in regard to the apt. of a Com. to Geneva, to set upon the Alabama Claims, was rec'd, before I started to Staatsburg on Wednesday.[1] I would have answered it then but it was my expectation to stop at Garrison for a few hours on my way home yesterday, and see you in person. I found however that I could not do so, on account of the hours when the trains passed, without putting others to an inconvenience. I will see you before deciding who shall be appointed. I confess to a repugnance to the appointment of an Adams[2] which I would not feel to the apt. of an out-and-out democrat. I have no one in view now, Judge B[3] failing, but hope some name may suggest itself to one of us in a few days.

Yours Truly
U. S. GRANT

HON. H. FISH,
SEC. OF STATE

ALS, DLC-Hamilton Fish. On July 22, 1871, Secretary of State Hamilton Fish, Garrison, N. Y., wrote to USG. "I received yesterday the letter addressed to you by Judge Poland & others, with Genl Porters' endorsement—There is no fund on the State Department which can be applied to the use of the Congressional Committee—Independent of the fact that the 'Secret service fund' is from the appropriation for *Foreign Intercourse,*—the demands upon that fund to meet the expenses of the several Commissions, under the Treaty with Great Britain, are so heavy that the appropriation will, I fear, not be sufficient to meet these payments, (which can alone come from that appropriation) until Congress make other provision for them—I therefore return the letter of the Committee, in hopes that the Treasury may be able to stand their necessities— I have written to Judge Frazer, & Mr Hale and await your decision as to the Arbitrator at Geneva—it is desirable the appointments be made as soon as practicable—I go to Washington on Tuesday or Wednesday & shall probably find much to keep me there until the end of the month—If you can let me know, about the Arbitrator please address me in Washington—Do you contemplate having a Cabinet Meetng next week?" ALS (press), *ibid.*

On June 16, Fish had written in his diary. "Having consulted Boutwell, privately & having his approval of the object, I propose to withdraw on the Presidents Warrant $25.000 from the appropriation for Contingent Expenses of Foreign Intercourse for the Current year (ending 30 June inst.) Baker reports that there are about $75.600 in the Treasury (not drawn) beside a deficiency appropriation of $10.569, and $7.397 in his hands, to the credit of this appropriation—that there will probably be a balance of $ some $25.000 not expended at the end of the fiscal year which will be covered into the Treasury, if not withdrawn on the Presidents Warrant ('Secret service) Warrant') There is no appropriation out of which to pay the several persons who may be appointed or employed under the various Pr provisions of the Treaty with Gt Britain I suggest therefore that this balance of $25.000 be drawn on Presidents Warrant, & used for this purpose—the suggestion is approved & a Warrant drawn accordingly." *Ibid.*

On Monday, July 24, Fish wrote to USG. "I enclose a letter (this day recd) from the Lieut. Governor of NewBrunswick, extending an invitation to yourself & Cabinet to visit that Province—Will you have the goodness to return it to me at Washington, whither I go tomorrow with an intimation of the reply which you desire to be made to it—I received your letter of 21st after I had mailed a letter to you, on the same subject." ALS (press), *ibid.* Also on July 24, USG telegraphed to Fish. "Can I not Meet You in New York on Your way to Washington tomorrow or the day following," Telegram received, *ibid.* On the same day, Fish telegraphed to USG. "I will be in NewYork on Wednesday and meet you at such hour & place as you may name—If agreeable to you, I suggest at my house at Eleven o'clk, but I hold myself at your convenience for any other time or place—Please inform me of your wish" ALS (telegram sent), *ibid.* Again on July 24, USG telegraphed to Fish. "Will you be at home tomorrow. if so I will go to Garrison in first train after two (2) P. M." Telegram received, *ibid.* On the same day, Fish telegraphed to USG. "I will be here tomorrow and glad to see you. The train at three forty five you will find the best after two oclk" ALS (telegram sent), *ibid.* On the same day, USG telegraphed to Fish. "I will meet you at your house in the city on Wednesday at Eleven A. M." Telegram received, *ibid.*

1. July 19.
2. Charles Francis Adams, born in 1807, the son of John Quincy Adams, had

served as U.S. Representative from Mass. (1859–61) and minister to Great Britain (1861–68). For USG's attitude toward the Adams family, see *PUSG*, 20, 318, 321–22. On Aug. 8, USG appointed Charles Francis Adams as U.S. arbitrator at Geneva. See letter to Hamilton Fish, July 13, 1871.

3. Justice Joseph P. Bradley. See letter to Hamilton Fish, July 13, 1871. Born in 1813, Bradley was a prominent New Jersey lawyer when nominated by USG to the U.S. Supreme Court on Feb. 7, 1870. See *PUSG*, 20, 55–57.

To George H. Stuart

Long Branch, N. J.
July 22d 1871.

DEAR SIR:

The recommendation of Mr. Bruno[1] for the place of Com. of Ind. Affairs was duly rec'd. and forwarded to Sec. Delano with the endorsement that I ~~had~~ the apt. would meet with my approbation if he had no other desire in the matter. Sec. D. was absent from Washington at the time, and has remained absent ever since, so that he has not probably heard of the matter yet. He returns, I understand, to-day, and will no doubt send the apt. for my signature next week, unless he had previously thought of some one else whos name he wishes to submit before the question is finally decided.

I will be careful that no one is aptd. Ind. Com. who is not fully in sympathy with a humane policy towards the indians. I will see too that he has the full confidence of the Peace Commissioners.

Wishing you health and happiness I subscribed myself,

your obt. svt.
U. S. GRANT

GEO. H. STUART, ESQ.

ALS, DLC-George H. Stuart. On July 15, 1871, Edward Cromwell, New York City, wrote to USG. "Having been informed confidentially that Gn Parker has resigned his office of Commissioner of Indian Affairs—As one of the Executive Committee of the United States Indian Commission of New York I would respectfully recommend the appointment of Felix R. Brunot of Pittsburg; fully believing him to be a man of incorruptible integrity. and zealous to carry out the present peace policy so happily begun by your administration" ALS, DNA, RG 48, Appointment Div., Letters Received. On July 18, USG endorsed this letter. "Respectfully refered to the Sec. of the Int. If this apt. is well thought of by the Sec. of the Int. I have no objection to it." AES, *ibid.* On

July 19, Edward S. Tobey, Board of Indian Commissioners, Boston, wrote to USG. "I trust that you will allow me to suggest the name of my honored & esteemed associate, Hon Felix R. Brunot as a worthy and suitable successor to Col Parker in the office which he has recently resigned. I am not aware that he would accept the position if offered to him, but I know of no one who more fully possesses the peculiar combination of qualities required to administer the duties of the office with integrity and great efficieny. He is so well known to you personally, that it would appear obtrusive in me to add anything more. I feel confident that the way is fairly open to carry out success-fully your policy in reference to the Indian tribes in spite of the selfish and unprinci-pled opposition which all honest endeavors always are compelled to encounter." ALS, *ibid.* On July 20, William Dorsey, "asst Secretary committe on Indian affairs," Philadel-phia, wrote to USG. "Since the resignation of our friend E S Parker as commissioner of Indian affairs, I have heard Felix R Brunot spoken of as suitable for that position— Should thou be able to obtain his consent to take the office, or the services of some other representative man of the same standing, I believe it would meet the cordial approval of the religious Society of Friends having charge of the Indians in the North-ern Superintendency, and greatly facilitate our efforts on behalf of thy humane & chris-tian Policy—I write unofficially—" ALS, *ibid.* On July 25, Mayor Edward Earle of Worcester, Mass., wrote to USG. "I have heard the name of F. R. Brunot to fill the vacancy occasiond by the resignation of Commissioner Parker was being considered— It seems to me he would give great confidence to all who have the best interests of the Indian at heart" ALS, *ibid.* On July 28, Thomas Wistar, Philadelphia; Benjamin Latham, New York City; William Nicholson, Lawrence, Kan.; and Earle, New York City, wrote to USG. "At a meeting of the Committee of Friends on Indian Affairs, held in this city yesterday, the undersigned were requested to call thy attention to the enclosed copy of a letter of our Secretary, John B. Garrett, addressed to thyself and recommending the appointment of F. R. Brunot to the Commissionership of Indian Affairs, and to say that the sentiments expressed therein, meet the cordial approval of our said Committee—We were also requested to intercede with thee for such inter-vention on thy part as may be right and lawful, to prevent the execution of the sen-tence of death recently passed upon the Kiowa Chiefs Satanta and Big Tree, by a court of the State of Texas. We are prompted to this by the antecedent history of their race, by our opposition to the sacrifice of human life, and by a conviction that the retention of said Chiefs as prisoners will be far more effectual in securing the real objects of punishment, than will be their execution. We apprehend that if they be executed, the Kiowas will be very likely to retaliate and that citizens of the United States will be the sufferers—We regard the delivery of said Chiefs to the authorities of Texas, instead of their retention as Pprisoners of the U. States, as of very questionable propriety and therefore feel the more willing to press the subject upon thy most serious attention— We were furthermore requested to call thy attention to the fact that a large number of settlers, perhaps not less than a thousand, have entered upon the lands within the Indian Territory, west of the present location of the Osages and north of the Arkansas River. It seems to us very important that the treaty stipulations of our Government in relation to the exclusion of white settlers from the Indian Territory, should be faithfully observed. Indeed, we feel that the success of the humane Indian policy, so happily inaugurated by thyself, largely depends, upon the *promptness* with which our Government interferes to prevent the intrusion of unauthorized white settlers upon lands that are sacredly pledged to the occupancy of the Indian—" DS, *ibid.* John B. Garrett's letter of July 19 is *ibid.*

On July 18, U.S. Representative Alfred C. Harmer of Pa., Germantown, wrote to

USG. "I learn from the papers of today that General Parker has resigned his position as Commissioner of Indian affairs,   I am aware of the anxiety. you have felt to have this position filled by a gentleman who would harmonize his administration with the views of the board of Commissioners, and at the same time, conform his work, to that line of policy which you have so wisely initiated for the department of Indian affairs. The object of this note is to say, that I know of no one who would be more suitable to fill the vacancy then Revd Dr Carrow, of Pennsylvania,   My main reasons in favor of his appointment are, 1st That he is a gentleman of great experience, tact, and integrity. 2d That he heartily endorses your Indian policy—and has written several articles for the public press in defence of it. 3rd That he would be able to secure for the Government and its Indian Wards, full justice, and so to cooperate with the board of commissioners as to prevent the friction that has heretofore existed. I will only add that the Doctor can lay before you the strongest recommendations from the Bishops, and Clergy of his own church, the Methodist Episcopal—from the Clergy, and from the most influential men of other churches—and from the most prominent leaders of our party in this State. . . ." ALS, *ibid.* For Goldsmith D. Carrow's unsuccessful applications for other positions, see *Calendar*, March 1, 1871.

On July 25, U.S. Senator Timothy O. Howe of Wis., Green Bay, wrote to USG. "I learn that Genl Parker has resigned—Can you find any where a better successor than in Governor Fairchild? I dont know that he will take the office—But if he will take it & you have not promised it, I really hope you will appoint him—" ALS, DNA, RG 48, Appointment Div., Letters Received. For Lucius S. Fairchild's nomination as consul, Liverpool, see *PUSG*, 19, 426.

On Aug. 2, U.S. Senator Alexander Ramsey of Minn., St. Paul, wrote to USG. "In view of the resignation of Col. Parker as commissioner of Indian Affairs I would respectfully present for the consideration of the President the name of Genl. John B. Sanborn of Minnesota who has had large experience in Indian affairs and whose name was favorably presented by the delegation from this state and by a number of other public men at the time of Gnl. Parkers appointment. I was then given to understand that for a time the President was favorably disposed to the nomination of Gnl. Sanborn—to the strong and favorable recomedatins of Gnl. S., made at the time, and that are now on file, I beg to invite the Presidents attention at this time. Genl. Sherman will bear witness to the fitness of Genl. S. for this place as he was associated with him in important Indian service. This appointmt would be most favorably received in the country at large and especially in the north-west" ALS, DNA, RG 48, Appointment Div., Letters Received. See *PUSG*, 19, 198.

On July 19, Samuel F. Tappan, Manchester, Mass., wrote to USG. "The daily papers inform me of the resignation of General Parker as Commissioner of Indian Affairs and your acceptance of it to take effect on the 1st of August next. While General Parker held that office I was not an applicant or an aspirant for the place, considering him as a representative of an outlawed race, the best illustration of your wise and humane policy, and of your fixed determination to secure justice for the long abused and oppressed red-men. Now Gen Parker having of his own choice retired, I desire the appointment and write to you freely soliciting it, with a view to aid you in carrying out your pacific policy towards the nation's wards and thereby secure the civilization and citizenship of the Indian, and as a consequence the most enduring fame for our country. It is usual in an application for an appointment to accompany it with the endorsement or recommendation of several prominent persons. Unless the confirmation of such a custom is absolutely necessary as a sort of protection to you or the government, I do not care to resort to it, but make my request of you direct." ALS,

DNA, RG 48, Appointment Div., Letters Received. On Aug. 29, U.S. Representative
Benjamin F. Butler of Mass., Boston, wrote to USG. "I see there is a vacancy in the
Indian Commission. I only speak in the public service when I call your attention to
Colonel S. F. Tappan, whom I do not really know as being an applicant for it or not. Mr
Tappan was on the Indian Commission and is known to you to have been an efficient
Commissioner and a friend of your policy of peaceful conciliation of the Indian tribes.
As you know him I need say no more." LS, *ibid.* On Aug. 31, Tappan wrote to USG.
"Mr Brunot having declined the appointment as Commissioner of Indian Affairs, I
respectfully renew my application for that office." ALS, *ibid.* On Sept. 16, Tappan,
Shamburg, Pa., wrote to USG. "Personal . . . I owe you an apology, for so abruptly
leaving you the other day, I wanted to see you, without appearing as a mere 'office
seeker' and so after shaking you by the hand, I hurried on. My application for an
appointment as Commissioner of Indian Affairs, is in your hands. I want that office for
the service connected with it, and facilities afforded its occupant, for an examination
of the historical records of the government upon matters connected with the Indians,
for use hereafter. Therefore I have no hesitancy in asking you for it, and having asked
for it, to leave it entirely with you. As there is no doubt, none whatever, of your reelection, I am confident of the final glorious triumph of your Indian policy, and that,
whether I get the office or not, justice will be done, and a peace-civilizing and chris-
tianizing policy vindicated, as against the absurd and criminal course of outlawry and
outrage so long practiced against the Indians, and the dearest interests of the country.
I am engaged here (Shamburg Venango Co. Penna) for the present, in connection with
the oil business, and this remains my P. O. address." ALS, *ibid.* Letters from Henry T.
Child, Philadelphia, and Howard Crosby, New York City, to USG recommending Tappan are *ibid.*

On Sept. 13 and 21, William Welsh, Philadelphia, wrote to Jacob D. Cox. "Can
you think of a man who would suit the Indian Office President Grant has given practical and written guarantees that no Indian commissioner shall be appointed unless
with the concurrence of the Board and that the office shall be worked in harmony
with it. All that I expected has been accomplished, but as in your own case, with
the loss of personal influence at the White House   Parker was as you know, an
infatuation heightened by a sentiment in favor of an Indian civilizing his brethren.
We are not the weaker with the community, the Press and with Congress, for so
called Reformers are becoming fashionable outside the Ring. The Cincinnati Commercial is still in bondage as you saw lately. How transparent that article was. I
know that you enlightened the editor of the Nation" "Accept my thanks for your
prompt response   I write to my friend J W Andrews to learn, if desirable, the
disposition of his namesake   If Brunot will not yield, we must be ready. I have not
approached the President in any way, after he compelled me to use force against
Parker   I heard that he got Delano to employ Chipman and it is certain that he
rewarded the Defender by making him Secretary of the District   Borie & Stuart are
the power behind the Throne that serves our cause. Cameron would like to have
Indian office patronage under his control   He does not imagine that I know it,
neither does the Secretary who is not quite his own man—I believe President Grant
is as sincere as William Welsh but both have great weaknesses although not quite
in the same direction. I try to keep the Press with us and it is well to have the
Methodists and Quakers strongly on our side   The slip herewith is honestly said
It was Mrs Brunot who sent the letter to me   My regards to Mrs Cox and my
congratulations on the relief from Washington   When you need relief or refresh-
ment by Sunday week I hope you will make me a visit   cracked wheat shall not be
the only diet" ALS, Jacob D. Cox Papers, Oberlin College, Oberlin, Ohio.

On Sept. 30, Mark Hopkins, Williams College, Mass., wrote to USG. "Permit me to commend to your favorable notice as a candidate for Commissioner of Indian Affairs the Rev Henry Fowler of Auburn N. Y. I know Mr. Fowler to be a man of ability, integrity and firmness, and one who would rejoice to carry out your humane policy towards the Indians in such a way as to secure for it the success it deserves, and for which all good people pray." ALS, DNA, RG 48, Appointment Div., Letters Received. On Oct. 3, Isaac F. Quinby, Rochester, N. Y., wrote to USG. "I learn that Prof. Henry Fowler who in former years, filling the chair of political economy, was my colleague in the University of Rochester is about to become an applicant for the office of Commissioner of Indian Affairs Prof. Fowler for many years past has been a most successful and acceptable pastor of a large Church in Auburn N. Y., but is now compelled to resign his pastorate on account of impaired eyesight induced and aggravated by the character of his labors Believing that Prof Fowler by his kind and christian impulses would in the capacity of Commissioner greatly aid you in carrying out your pacific and humane policy in reference to the Indians and that he possesses the honesty, penetration, & determination requisite for the faithful & Satisfactory administration of that Office I unhesitatingly recommend his appointment as one fit to be made." ALS, *ibid.* On the same day, L. A. Ward, Rochester, wrote to USG. "I learn that the friends of Professer Fowler formerly of this City propose to present his name for the position of Comr of Indian Affairs. From an acquaintance of many years standing with Prof F. I most cheerfully and fully concur in the estimate of his character given in Gen. Quimbys letter which this accompanies." ALS, *ibid.* On Oct. 23, Lewis H. Morgan, Rochester, wrote to USG. "If you should choose to appoint Rev Henry W. Fowler of Auburn Commissioner of Indian Affairs, he would bring to the office unimpeachable integrity; the attainments of a Scholar, and the manners of a gentleman. I know of no man who would devote to this important service more faithful attention, and to the cause of the Indian more disinterested zeal than my friend, whom it gives me great pleasure to commend for this appointment I have known Mr Fowler many years, first as a Professor in the University of Rochester, and later as an efficient clergyman, and at one time as a chaplain in the military service of the Country. In these several positions he has acquitted himself successfully" ALS, *ibid.*

On Oct. 18, a correspondent reported from Washington, D. C. "Felix Brunot, one of the Indian Peace Commissioners, whom the President appointed to the vacant Commissionership of Indian Affairs, several weeks ago, arrived here to-day. He persists in his refusal to accept the office. The report is that the President has tendered the office to the Hon. Wm. H. Armstrong of Pennsylvania. Mr. Armstrong was a member of the last Congress, is a leading lawyer of Pennsylvania, and it is doubtful that he will accept. While in Congress he was an active member of the Indian Committee." *New York Tribune*, Oct. 19, 1871.

On Oct. 20, William C. Crooks, Philadelphia, wrote to USG. "In compliance with the desire of many of my friends, I have the honor, to transmit my *name* and offer my *Services*—for your Excellency's acceptance—as Commissioner of *Indian Affairs*. My Service on the *Frontiers* while in the Army afforded opportunities to acquaint myself, in no small degree, with the requirements of that Department and I hope—should your Excellency find it convenient and agreeable to favorably consider my claim—to render entire satisfaction in discharging the onerous duties devolving upon the incumbent of so responsible an office. . . ." ALS, DNA, RG 48, Appointment Div., Letters Received. On April 15, Joseph Leidy, "Professor of Anatomy in the University of Pennsylvania," Philadelphia, had written to USG. "Dr. Wm C. Crooks, late an Acting Assistant Surgeon in the United States Army has informed the Undersigned of his intention to make application for the position of a Medical Purveyor in the Army. The Undersigned hereby certifies that, Dr. Crooks is a regularly educated physician, having graduated in the University of Pennsylvania with the unanimous approbation of its faculty in the Spring of 1866. Besides his Medical education, his subsequent employment in the Army as a Surgeon contributes to fit him for the position he seeks." Copy, *ibid.* On the same day, Daniel G. Brinton, "Office of the Med. Surg. Reporter," wrote to USG. "Having held professional relations for some time with Doctor Wm. C. Crooks, I take pleasure in testifying to histhe standing of that Gentleman in the profession and his general good reputation as one of its members. He has contributed valuable Medical papers to the periodical of which I am Editor and I have no doubt is well qualified for the position he seeks." Copy, *ibid.* Recommendations from John W. Forney, collector of customs, Philadelphia, and others, are *ibid.*

On Oct. 26, U.S. Senator Phineas W. Hitchcock and U.S. Representative John Taffe of Neb., Omaha, wrote to USG. "We most respectfully beg to suggest that we have filed a recommendation with the Secretary of Interior, in favor of Gen. Amasa Cobb, for Commissioner of Indian Affairs. The same action has been taken, as we are informed, by several other senators, and members of Congress.—This is merely to bring the fact to your notice, supposing that a nomination might become necessary during the absence of the Hon. Secretary." LS, *ibid.*

On Oct. 25, Louis DeBarth Kuhn, Reading, Pa., wrote to USG. "If your Excellency will graciously appoint me to the vacant position of 'Commissioner of Indian Affairs,' I will do my best to perform the duty with Honesty and Ability; in the hope, to afford satisfaction and prove worthy of the trust. I respectfully refer to Gen'l Silas Casey USA; to Hon: Jn'o Scott, U. S. Senator from this State, and to Major G. O. Haller, late of the 4th Infantry U. S. Army . . ." ALS, *ibid.* On Oct. 27, Kuhn wrote a similar letter with additional references. ALS, *ibid.* Probably in early Nov., Bishop Matthew Simpson, Philadelphia, wrote to USG. "Will you allow me to suggest to you the name of Dr *Joseph Parrish* of this city—or at present of Media,—as a gentleman, in my opinion, eminently qualified for the office of *Commissioner* of *Indian Affairs.* Dr Parrish is a christian gentleman of Quaker education of an old Phila family, of fine culture, great benevolence of character, & who has given his attention for years to matters of general reform. He was at the head of the institution for feeble minded children, & has labored in behalf of an inebriate asylum. I believe he wd harmonize in all your views, is a man of good administrative ability, of mental resources, & wd command public confidence. I wd most earnestly ask your attention to him, if you have not already made a selection. . . . If you are disposed to inquire as to his fitness, I shd be glad to furnish you the names of eminent men well acquainted with him." ALS (docketed Nov. 6, 1871), *ibid.* On March 25, 1872, Joseph Parrish, Media, Pa., wrote to U.S. Representative Washington Townsend of Pa. "I am about to go to England in compliance with a Summons from the British Parliament, to give evidence concerning inebriate Asylums, & if I can be the bearer of dispatches, or do any service for my country, under instructions from the President, I shall be happy to do so. If I can please advise me. I shall sail somewhere about the middle of April, & will advise you if necessary of the xact time before long." ALS, *ibid.*, RG 59, Letters of Application and Recommendation. On March 27, USG endorsed this letter. "Respectfully refered to the Sec. of State." AES, *ibid.*

On Nov. 9, 1871, Manetho Hilton, St. Louis, wrote to USG. "Desirous of a *private* hearing I presume to have this letter delivered to Your Excellency in person. I trust that I will be pardoned for taking such a liberty. Premising that Your Excellency is familiar with the politics & politicians of Missouri, I infer that I may be remembered. If not, I respectfully recall to your recollection recommendations now on file in the Post Office Dept from Ex-Gov. McClurg C. W. Ford E. W. Fox and others. They were forwarded contrary to my orders, nevertheless I believe the application to which they related was a just one, in the interest of the republican party. But as I did n't make it then, I am not renewing it now. Genl Smith is a good officer. The only wish ever entertained by republicans was that he might be promoted to an office of less political importance to make way for some one of more political influence, in the Post Office here. A judicious change would at least determine the chances in the First Cong. Dist. now doubtful, in favor of the republicans, & that with all proper respect for true ideas of the civil service. But I write now to urge the selection of a Missourian for the vacant Indian Commissionership, if it can be done consistently with the Indian policy of the Executive. . . ." ALS, *ibid.*, RG 48, Appointment Div., Letters Received.

On Nov. 13, Robert H. Milroy, Delphi, Ind., wrote to USG. "I see by the Press that the office of Commissioner of Indian Affairs is still vacant—If you have not filled it when this arives I respectfully tender my services for that position. I have closely watched and much admired your Indian Policy. It is the just policy that my Father attempted to carry out, in spirit on a smaller scale, while Agent for the Miami and Potowattomie tribes many years ago, and will most certainly be successful if *honestly* perseveared in by subordinates. I feel sure I could very materially assist you on *that line*; and that should you honor me with the appointment, you will never have reason to regret it." ALS, *ibid.* For Milroy's nomination as marshal, Wyoming Territory, see telegram to Amos T. Akerman, July 11, 1871.

On Nov. 22, Francis A. Walker, superintendent of the Census, accepted the position of commissioner of Indian Affairs, which had been offered to him in Oct.; he was also designated act. director of the Census. *New York Times*, Nov. 22, 1871. On Dec. 5, USG nominated Walker as commissioner of Indian Affairs. See letter to Ely S. Parker, July 13, 1871; Endorsement, Dec. 7, 1872; James Phinney Munroe, *A Life of Francis Amasa Walker* (New York, 1923), pp. 127–45.

1. Felix R. Brunot, chairman, Board of Indian Commissioners. See *PUSG*, 19, 191, 195–97; Charles L. Slattery, *Felix Reville Brunot* (New York, 1901).

To William W. Belknap

Long Branch, N. J.
July 24th 1871

Hon. W. W. Belknap,
Sec. of War:
Dear Sir:

Please let Maj. G. O. Haller, late of the 4th U. S. Inf.y, an officer who was dismissed by the Sec. of War during the rebellion, by order of the Sec. of War, have access to the charges then made against him, and, so far as proper, have copies of papers on file to make up a defence, which I believe he did at the time of the dismissal, so far as he could learn, from report, the purport of the charges. Please also examine such evidence as may be in the War Dept. relating to the case of Maj. Haller with the view of recommending what action, if any, should be taken in his case at this time.

If the Sec. of War is still absent the General of the Army, or the Adj. Gen. may read this letter and give Maj. Haller an opportunity of filing anything further in his defence, (that may be deduced from reading charges made against him), to be concidered in connection with his case on the return of the Sec. of War.

Very respectfully
your obt. svt.
U. S. Grant

ALS, DNA, RG 94, ACP, H331 CB 1868. See *PUSG*, 1, 236. On Nov. 11, 1867, James F. Shunk, York, Pa., had written to USG. "As counsel and friend of Major Granville O. Haller, formerly of the 7th U. S. Infantry, I desire to present for your consideration the following facts and to solicit at your hands, in behalf of that gallant officer and true-hearted gentleman, the justice which during the excitement of war and the heat of political passion was cruelly denied him. Your personal association with Major Haller in Mexico and your knowledge of his character and career since, render any extended remarks about the *man* superfluous in this place. I shall state in the fewest words possible the wrong done him and the redress asked for him. 1. Major Haller was peremptorily dismissed from the Army on the 25th of July 1863 after active and conspicuous service, in Florida, in Mexico, in Oregon and elsewhere, of nearly twenty four years. 2. The order of dismissal recited as his offence 'disloyal conduct and the utterance of disloyal sentiments.' 3. This order was based solely on the ex-parte statement of one Clark H. Wells, a Lieutenant Commander in the Navy, who averred that on the night of Dec. 16th 1862 while Burnside's army lay before Fredericksburg, Haller, in the presence of Wells and other guests then sharing the hospitalities of his tent, toasted 'a Northern and Southern Confederacy as long as Lincoln should be President.' 4. Of all the persons present on this occasion Wells was the only one who recollected any such toast or the utterance of any sentiment by Major Haller or anybody else at variance with the most exaggerated loyalty. 5. That Wells was indebted to his fancy and not to his memory for this thought surprises nobody who knows him and his history. *He was a lunatic, fresh from the madhouse* when he visited Fredericksburg, and his addled brain was heated to delerium on the evening referred to by draughts of punch. It is not strange, under the circumstances, that he should have 'seen visions and dreamed dreams', but it is marvellous indeed that the wanderings of lunacy should have been treated by the government with the ~~dignity pertaining~~ deference due to hard facts and made the basis of a ruinous judgment against a tried and veteran soldier. 6. Major Haller had no hearing—his trial was conducted within the closed doors of the Bureau of Military Justice—his accuser was the only witness and the first notice that he received that wrong was imputed to him came in the shape of the order of dismissal. He received this startling missive while busy on the Pennsylvania border preparing for its defence against the advancing hosts of Lee. 7. He at once demanded a trial—and, failing to get that, pleaded for a hearing of some kind, not with a view to restoration but that he might leave on the record a vindication of his good name—His appeals were unheeded and ~~on the far shore of Washington territory~~ he has for four long years endured his wrongs in silence and waited for the dawning of a better day when he might assert his cause with a chance of getting justice.... With a firm conviction that your sense of justice will impel you, in view of the monstrous wrong presented by this case, to do what you can, late though it be, to right it, I have only to beg ~~for it~~ a speedy consideration and prompt judgment." ALS, DNA, RG 94, ACP, H331 CB 1868. USG as secretary of war *ad interim* endorsed a subsequent report summarizing the case and Shunk's letter. "In view of the facts stated within I cannot recommend the reinstatement of Maj. G. O. Haller without sworn testimony in his favor to offset sworn statements against him." AES (undated), *ibid.*

On Aug. 12, 1871, Granville O. Haller, York, Pa., wrote to USG. "I take the liberty of transmitting, herewith, a copy of my letter to you of the 3d inst., which I left with the Honl Secretary of War, on the 4th inst., to remit—but which I ascertained had not reached you on the 10th instant. You can imagine better than I can describe how galling the past Eight years have been to me, being unjustly accused and condemned unheard, and find every paper presented by me, to vindicate my character, has been suppressed in the War office. I have full faith in your disposition to do me justice, and I most respectfully urge that the matter be considered at your earliest convenience. *Pere L. Wickes*, Esqre, of York, Penna, a Brother in law of Lieut. Comdr *Wells*, U. S. Navy, (who recognises the injustice done in my case and desires reperation may be made) will cheerfully atte[nd] any Summons or desires on your part in my behalf, and answer any questions which may suggest themselves. Please address communications for me to the care of *Mr. Wickes*, York, Pa, as he will be advised from time to time of my whereabouts until I reach my residence at Coupeville, Whidby Island, Washington Territory." ALS, *ibid.* A letter of Aug. 3 from Haller to USG, discussing the documents in the case, is *ibid.* Related papers are *ibid.* For Haller's early army service with USG, see Charles G. Ellington, *The Trial of U. S. Grant: The Pacific Coast Years 1852–1854* (Glendale, Calif., 1987), p. 169. Haller was appointed col. as of July 1, 1879. See HRC, 45-2-375; SRC, 45-3-860.

To George S. Boutwell

Long Branch, N. J.
July 24th 1871

HON. GEO. S. BOUTWELL
SEC. OF THE TREAS:
DEAR SIR:

The consolidation of the 2d & 3d districts of Ala. if approved by me, was approved without reflection. There is no communication between the two districts by rapid transit except by circuitous routes, through Ga or Miss. They are separated by Mountains through which none but the worst of country roads pass. If the consolidation has not yet been consumated or if the Collector & Assessor to be releived have not yet closed their accounts and ceased to act, I would revoke the order. There is I believe but three Col. districts in Ala. while there are ~~three~~ six Congress districts.

Respectfully, your obt. svt,

U. S. GRANT

ALS (facsimile), USGA. On July 10, 1871, USG had issued orders consolidating revenue collection districts in Va. and Ala. as of Aug. 1. DS, DNA, RG 56, Letters Received; copies, *ibid.*, RG 130, Orders and Proclamations. On July 26, Secretary of the Treasury George S. Boutwell wrote to Alfred Pleasonton, commissioner of Internal Revenue. "By direction of the President the order for consolidating the Second and Third Districts of Alabama is withheld, and the business of the two Districts will go on as though the order had not been made." Copy, *ibid.*, RG 56, Letters Sent. On July 29, Boutwell telegraphed to USG. "Senator Lewis objects to consolidation of first and second Virginia Districts for which order was made to take effect August 1st. The Districts are Eastern Shore and Norfolk and Petersburg District. Shall the order be issued or held for further consideration?" Copy, *ibid.*

On Jan. 9, Horace Porter had written to Pleasonton. "The President directs me to say that he would like you to take measures, with as little delay as practicable, for the consolidation of the revenue districts in New York Brooklyn, Philadelphia and Cincinnati." Copy, DLC-USG, II, 1. On Jan. 23, Orville E. Babcock wrote to Pleasonton. "The President directs me to say that he will be pleased to have you call at the Executive Mansion this morning at 10 o'clock and bring with you your book containing the consolidation of Revenue Districts in the City of New York." Copy, *ibid.*

On March 25, USG had issued an order consolidating the Oakland and San Francisco districts. Copy, DNA, RG 130, Orders and Proclamations. On March 27, USG wrote to Luther H. Cary retaining him as collector of Internal Revenue for the consolidated district. Copy, *ibid.*, RG 56, Letters Sent.

To William W. Belknap

Long Branch, N. J.
July 29th 1871.

GEN. W. W. BELKNAP,
SEC. OF WAR,
SIR;

Enclosed I send you dispatch from V. Colier desiring a change of orders to the Military, directing them to give protection to indians on any reservation where he may place them instead of, as instructions now read, to indians brought in to the reservation of Canada Alimosa. There is no objection to the changed asked that I know of.

Please notify Mr. Colier as requested in the inclosed dispatch.

Respectfully &c.

U. S. GRANT

ALS, DNA, RG 94, Letters Received, 2465 1871. On Aug. 11, 1871, Vincent Colyer, Board of Indian Commissioners, Santa Fé, wrote to Secretary of the Interior Columbus Delano. "Agreeably to the request contained in the letter of authority from the Hon. B. R. Cowin acting Secretary of Interior under date 21 of July that I should from time to time report to the Department my action and progress and the result of my investigations on the condition of Indian Affairs in New Mexico and Arizona. I have the honor to report, That on the day after the receipt of that letter on the arrival of the Hon John D. Lang to take my place in the office in Washington—as member of the Executive Committee of the Board of Indian Commissioners. I left for this place. via New York. where I remained three days to attend a meeting of the Board of Indian Commissioners On my way through Pittsburgh finding that the orders issued from the War Department did not correspond with the authority received from the Department of the Interior, I telegraphed to the President as follows. 'Pittsburgh July 27th 1871 To U. S. GRANT. President U. S.   Long Branch New Jersey   SIR—In your letter of 13th inst to Secretary of War you directed that protection should be given to Indians desiring peace under our care coming in at Cañada Alamosa N. Mexico. Later advices show that they are one hundred fifty miles South west of there. General Parker in his letter to Secretary Interior. suggesting my instructions recommends that I be invested with discretionary powers to do whatever in my judgement may appear most wise and proper in locating the roving tribes of Arizona and New Mexico upon suitable reservations, and the Secretary has so instructed me. In the event of my not being able to get the Indians to Cañada Alamosa would it not be well for you to direct the war Department to enlarge its orders protecting us not only there but, at such other reservations as I may select, in harmony with instructions from the Indian Bureau. A line added to General Townsend's order of the 18th, inst would do it. Please telegraph me early your action, care General Pope Fort Leavenworth Kansas.' On arriving at Leavenworth I received from General Porter, the President's Secretary, a reply that my message had been sent to the Secretary of War and answer sent to me at Leavenworth—which answer was received the following day as follows—'Washington D. C. July 31st 1871. The Secretary of war directs that order of eighteenth Instant for protection to Indians at Cañada Alamosa be extended to include such other reservations as Mr. Colyer may select. signed. E. D. TOWNSEND adjt. General.' On receipt of the above dispatch, on my arrival at Lawrence I telegraphed to you as follows—'Lawrence July 30th, 1871. To HON. COLUMBUS DELANO Secretary of Interior Washington D. C. Agreeably to powers conferred upon me by the President, and communicated in your instructions of, 21st. inst, and to day's supplementary order of War Department of this date to order of Eighteenth inst, I have selected Camp Grant in Arizona Territory as a reservation on the west, where the Apache Indians are to be protected and fed, and beg that the war Department be earnestly requested to retain Leutenant Whitman in charge and that he be instructed to send out Indian runners to notify all peacibly

disposed Apaches to come in and find asylum there. and the order be telegraphed
to Department of the Pacific to forward promptly to Arizona. Please Telegraph
action to morrow at Carson city after that Santa Fé. My plan is to have this reservation at Camp Grant on western border and another which I will select in New
Mexico on eastern border of Apache country, when I get there and invite in, feed
and Pprotect all Apaches who wish to be at peace—The expenses to be paid from
the special appropriation—' On my arrival at Santa Fé I received your reply as
follows. 'To VINCENT COLYER Santa Fé—From Washington D. C. Aug't. 1st 1871.
Rec'd, Aug't. 5th, 1871—11.30. a. m. Your Telegrams received; war department
requested to act as you desire. C. DELANO, Sec'y.' And from the war Department this
reply. 'MR. VINCENT COLYER Santa Fé N. M. From Washington Aug't. 2/71. Rec'd,
Aug't, 6th 1871—9, P. M. Instructions telegraphed for retention of Lt. Whitman
and employment of runners as requested. E. D. TOWNSEND Adj't, Gen'l.' Nathaniel
Pope the Superintendent of Indian affairs for New Mexico, reports that these ~~the~~
Southern Apache Indians continue to come in to Cañada Alamosa. That there are
now over twelve hundred there—the majority well behaved and peaceable who are
being fed. Beef and Corn only being issued to them—with a small amount of calico,
manta; and a few Shirts to cover the extreamely naeked. In so large a crowd it would
be strange if there were not some dishonest ones and there~~re~~fore you will not be
surprised to hear that several thefts of oxen and horses were traced to Indians on
this Reservation. They were promptly detected however by the Indian chiefs who at
once reported them to the agent, O. F. Piper, who delivered up the stolen stock
to their respective owners. See inclosed papers marked, A, B, C, By referring to
communication marked D. being letters from Hon. B. Hudson. Probate Judge of
Grant County N. M. and enclosing series of resolutions passed by the citizens of
Rio Miembres N. M. 19th. July 1871. you will find that the few dishonest acts
referred to in the brief interval of four days from the time these thefts were committed
to the time the Stock was returned to the owners the people had time to Resolve
that: 'The people of Grant Co. n. mexico—organize themselves into a posse and
follow their stock to wherever it may be and take it by force wherever found even
if it be at the Sacrifice of every Indian man woman and child in the tribe. Resolved:
That if opposed by Indians, or their accomplices, be they Indian Agents, Indian
Traders or Army officers, let them be loo~~a~~ked upon as our worst enemies and the
common enemies of New Mexico, and be dealt with accordingly.' And the Hon. R.
Hudson Judge of Probate of Grant County—had time and spirit to write, 'What we
want to know is whether our Stock can be recovered or not, from Indians on your
reservation when fully proved and identified, or if we are to be forever at the mercy
of these thieving murderous Apaches, who have a "House of Refuge" at Alamosa. if
so the sooner we know it the better, because the citizens of this county are determined to put a stop to it, and if they carry out their programme the Camp Grant
massacre will be thrown entirely in the shade and Alamosa will rank next to "Sand
Creek".' See accompanyind do'c. "A." Superintendent Pope—see his letter marked,
"G." enclosed, has asked that troops be placed at Cañada Alamosa, and as I hope to
visit the Indians there early next week, if I find the place suitable I will designate
it as a Reservation and call upon the military to protect it agreeably to your instructions of the 21st, ultimo, and the orders of the war Department of the 18th. Ult."
LS, *ibid.*, RG 75, Letters Received, New Mexico Superintendency; variant copies of
Colyer's telegrams are *ibid.*, RG 94, Letters Received, 2465 1871. See *HED*, 42-2-1,
part 5, pp. 461–62.

On Aug. 18 and 26, Colyer telegraphed to Delano from Cañada Alamosa and
Ojo Caliente, New Mexico Territory. "Arrived here yesterday. Found nearly all the

Indians scattered from the agency from fears of attack threatened by miners at Rio Mine Bres [*Mimbres*] N. M. Hope to gather them in in a few days. Soldiers here." "Examined this valley. Hot springs. Unsuitable for reservation. Start for Tullerosa River today. Our scouts report General Crook enlisting Indians and Mexicans with American soldiers in his war upon Apaches. We find it difficult to secure the confidence of the Indians under such circumstances." Copies (the first marked as received in Washington, D. C., on Sept. 3, 3:48 P.M.), DNA, RG 94, Letters Received, 2465 1871. On Sept. 4, Delano forwarded these telegrams to USG. Copy, *ibid.*, RG 48, Indian Div., Letters Sent. On Sept. 6, Gen. William T. Sherman endorsed copies of these telegrams. "Respectfully submitted to the Secretary of War—If Gen Crook is to conduct the War against the Apaches, he ought not to be interfered with, but on the Contrary should have the largest powers in the Execution of a most difficult task." AES, *ibid.*, RG 94, Letters Received, 2465 1871. On Sept. 22, Sherman wrote to Maj. Gen. John M. Schofield, San Francisco, concerning friction between Colyer and Lt. Col. George Crook. Copy, *ibid.*, Letters Sent. On Oct. 23, Schofield wrote to Sherman on the same subject. ALS, *ibid.*, Letters Received, 2465 1871. On Oct. 10, Crook, Prescott, Arizona Territory, had written to Schofield detailing his problems with Colyer. Copy, *ibid.* On Oct. 20, Colyer, San Francisco, wrote to Schofield defending his actions among the Apaches. Copy, *ibid.*

On Sept. 19, Peter Cooper and three others, New York City, wrote to USG. "Private advices to his friends show that Mr Vincent Colyer is in danger of losing his life at the hands of desperate men who were engaged in the Camp Grant massacre. We have information of a conspiracy formed at Tuscon for his assassination on the part of those who are determined he shall make no report to the President in regard to that massacre. While Mr Colyer does not ask us to make use of this information, we feel bound, as his friends, to acquaint your excellency with the facts and to urge upon you the importance of extending to Mr Colyer all needful assistance at the earliest moment possible" LS, *ibid.*, Letters Received, 2465 1871. On Sept. 21, Secretary of War William W. Belknap wrote to Cooper. "The Prest has referred to me your comn of the 19th inst. in regard to the danger threatening Vincent Collyer, Esq. I enclose copies of instructions heretofore given the Mil'y Com'drs in that section, in relation to Mr Collyer, from which it will be seen that he has only to represent his necessities to the proper Mily officers on the spot, to secure all the protection which it is in their power to give." Df, *ibid.*

On Oct. 11, Henry Van Arman, Sacaton, Arizona Territory, wrote to USG. "haveing left our home in the ledmines two-years ago last my for the west my self and Nephew with the Sad to be the best waggon and team that had crossed the Mo River that Season and $2800 twenty eight hundred Dollars in Cash we brought upon Salt River in this territory about 18 month Since whare we located farms and constructed a canal or ditch about 3 miles in length for the purpose of irrogateing our farms which cost us evry thing we had Save our groing Crop and improvenants which if we could have Saved would made us quite independant but while absent for a few days leaveing my house in care of a neighbor to attend to the Merricopa and Pemi or Pemoi Indians Made a raid aupon my place and Destroid evry thing we had a full Statementment of which we have forworded to the indian department with our affidavits and other testimony now my good President Since doing this we ar told unless we employ a lobby lawyer we will not get any thing in 3 or 4 years and then it will take all we claim to pay him—I am now working for the Indian agent at Gila reservation whare I mit in person Mr Vincent Colier and Stated our Situation to him and he told me he would do all he could for me Since the I have been told by one in authority that he, colier receives thousand of letters that he never reads and will probably neve think of me again   now my Drs I. am 53 years of age have spent all the best part of my life in the mines   you must know about what I am at this time of life and how well I am capasitated to work by the month for my living which this misfortune compels me to do which is terable on me allthough this agent is a verry good Man to work for—now I will close by Saying in gods name help me if you can. and please let me know at your earleyst convenience   Direct to Gila reservation A. T in care of J. H. Stout of whom you can ask any question relative to me you please and he will answer" ALS, *ibid.*, RG 75, Letters Received, Arizona Superintendency.

On Oct. 31, Secretary of State Hamilton Fish wrote in his diary. *"Delano*— mentioned Vincent Collyers movements in the Indian matters—& Peace Commn—& read a letter from him—It appears that he has become something of a nuisance,—& is likely to be removed after Election." DLC-Hamilton Fish. On Nov. 7, Delano wrote to USG. "I have the honor to transmit, herewith, copy of a communication addressed to this Department, by the Hon. Vincent Colyer, one of the Board of Indian Peace Commissioners,—who recently visited Arizona—wherein he states his views in rela- tion to the Apache Indians, and describes certain tracts of country in Arizona and New-Mexico, which, during his recent visit to said Indians, he has selected to be set apart as reservations for their use, as authorized to do by orders issued to him, before visiting the Apaches,   I have the honor to recommend, in pursuance of the understanding arrived at in our conversation—with the Secretary of War, on the 6th inst, that the President issue an order authorizing said tracts of country,— described in Mr Colyers letter—to be regarded as reservations for the settlement of Indians, until it is otherwise ordered,   I have the honor, also, to suggest. that the proper officers of the War Department be directed to inform the various bands of roving Apaches, that they are required to locate upon the reservations, immediately, and, that upon so doing they will be fully protected and provided for by the Govern- ment, so long, as they remain on said reservations, and preserve peaceable relations with the Government, each other, and the White people; and that unless they comply with theis request, they will not be thus provided for and protected,   I suggest that they also be notified that they will not be permitted to send their old men, women and children upon such reservations, and permit their young men and braves to go upon the *War path*. I beg also to request that the proper officers of the War Depart- ment be instructed to notify the White people of Arizona and New Mexico of this determination of the Government to preserve, if possible, peace between the Whites and the Indians, and that neither will be allowed to depredate or trespass upon the other, with impunity; and, that so long and so far, as the Indians comply with these requirements of the Government, and settle upon these reservations before indicated, and conduct themselves peaceably thereafter, they will be protected by the Govern- ment, to the full extent of its power, and no longer,   I beg also to inform you, that it is the intention of this Department to communicate a copy of this letter, to the Sup't's of Indian Affairs, for Arizona, and New-Mexico, and to direct the Sup't of Indian Affairs for Arizona to remove his Headquarters, immediately to the Head- quarters of the Commanding Officer of the Department of Arizona, and to request him to coöperate fully with the officer in charge of the troops, in Arizona, in the execution of the purpose of the Government, as indicated in this request, provided, the views herein expressed, shall have the approbation of the President, and the War Department,   I would further suggest, that the War Department will, for the pres- ent, select some suitable and discreet Oofficer of the Army to act as Indian Agent for any of the reservations in Arizona, which may be occupied by the Indians, under the orders herein contemplated. Such Agents will be superseded by persons hereafter appointed by this Department, at such times as the President may hereafter deem proper," LS, DNA, RG 94, Letters Received, 2465 1871. The enclosures are *ibid.* On Nov. 9, USG endorsed this letter. "Respectfully referred to the Secretary of War— who will take such action as may be necessary to carry out the recommendations of the Secretary of the Interior" ES, *ibid.* See *HED,* 42-2-1, part 5, pp. 508–9.

On Nov. 27, a correspondent reported from Washington, D. C. "Today Delegate McCormick formally presented to the President petitions extensively signed by citizens of all classes, including the Federal and Territorial officers of Arizona from the towns of Tucson, Prescott, Phenix, Florence, Sanford, Wickenburg and Vulture Mine, in that Territory, and one from San Bernardino, Cal., in the following form: '*To His Excellency U. S. Grant, President of the United States:* The undersigned citizens of the Territory of Arizonia, regarding the present anomalous state of affairs concerning the Indian difficulties in the Territory as being in the highest degree unsatisfactory, and perilous to our interests as a community, respectfully represent: That we desire nothing more earnestly than peace with the Apaches; that last Spring many were disheartened by our sufferings and losses from hostile Indians, were preparing to abandon the Territory, where we have labored and waited for years, hoping for the subjugation of the Apaches, when the assignment of Gen. George Crook to the command of this department gave us new hope, and we determined to hold on a little longer, as we believed that the operations inaugurated by the General were calculated to result in a speedy settlement of our troubles; but just as his plans were being successfully put in force we learn that the matter is taken out of his hands and turned over to the Peace Commissioners; that, although we had no confidence in their policy, being satisfied from past experience that no peace treaty to which the Apache is an equal party can be lasting, we were willing to give all the assistance in our power to the Commissioners to aid them in their plans; but, since the arrival of their agent here, we perceive with dismay the most hostile tribes refuse to treat with him, and have continued their murderous and thieving raids as boldly and viciously as ever before; that we are disappointed and discouraged by the policy of the agent in proposing to continue the practice of giving asylum and aid at military posts indiscriminately to all Indians choosing to seek it, as the past has proven that the warriors can thus leave their families in security while they make marauding excursions over the country, and return with the scalps and plunder to the protection of the posts; that we are satisfied that the party having authority to make peace treaties with our Indian enemies should also have power to promptly punish violations of such treaties; and we do further respectfully represent that, if the policy here inaugurated by the agent of the Peace Commission is to be persisted in, the deserted homes of our friends and neighbors, and the graves of those slain by the Apaches, which line every road and travel, and fill every grave-yard in Arizona, warn us that, if we remain here, we must expect a similar fate.' In making the presentation, Mr. McCormick said the petitions were prepared prior to the decision of the Government upon the new programme for the treatment of the Apaches indicated in the recent order of Gen. Schofield, or their language would have been different in some particulars. . . . The President took the petition, and said he hoped the order of Gen. Schofield would satisfy the people of Arizona that the Government intended to deal summarily and vigorously with the Apaches, if, after duly notifying them to go and remain upon the new reservations, where they would be fed and protected, they continued on the war path." *New York Times,* Nov. 28, 1871.

On March 23, 1872, William J. Berry, Prescott, wrote to USG. "Pardon me for

taking the liberty of sending your Excellency the enclosed paper. I am one of your firmest political friends, and I would like to see you always right. Our Indian affairs are in a most deplorable state, and if your Excellency understood them truly, you would not send out 'peace Commissioners' to stifle the operations of Genl Crook. But your Excellency has been imposed upon by the weak and lying Vincent Colyer, please read the enclosed paper, as what it states in regard to Indian matters is true."
ALS, DNA, RG 75, Letters Received, Arizona Superintendency. The enclosed clipping is *ibid.* See letter to John M. Schofield, March 6, 1872; Ralph Hedrick Ogle, *Federal Control of the Western Apaches 1848–1886* (1940; reprinted, Albuquerque, 1970), pp. 89–96.

To Frederick Dent Grant

Long Branch, N. J.
July 30th 1871.

DEAR FRED,

Remember your Mas injunction about Mr. B. She has written you all the news so I will add nothing except to enjoin on you give every energy to perform every thing given to you to do well, and to the entire satisfaction of your employers. By such a course you are sure to succeed! Your rise may seem slow, but it will prove permanent.

Yours Affectionately
U. S. GRANT

ALS, USG 3. On July 27, 1871, USG visited Philadelphia "to see his son Frederick off to the West. Frederick goes out as Civil Engineer on the Pacific Railroad." *Philadelphia Public Ledger,* July 28, 1871. On Aug. 10, Horace Porter, Long Branch, N. J., wrote to Secretary of War William W. Belknap. "I want you to do a good thing for the 'cause,' and a personal favor all round. Tom Scott you know has given every possible evidence of friendship, and with his R. Rs will control Pa. Ohio N. J. &c. He has at the Presidents requests also appointed Fred. to a fine position on the, U. P. R. R. He has never asked anything except to have Elliott appointed Collector of Customs at Phila and in this he was disappointed. He now writes me a *most urgent* letter, begging in the strongest manner that there may be no delay in acting on his plans for elevating his R. R. bridge at Cincinnati which require your approval . . ." ALS, CSmH.
    On Oct. 2, AG Edward D. Townsend telegraphed to 2nd Lt. Frederick Dent Grant, 4th Cav., "Headquarters Engineer Corps, Colorado Central Railroad, via Golden City, Colorado." "Three (3) months extension of leave has been granted you." LS (telegram sent), DNA, RG 107, Telegrams Collected (Bound). See letter to Mary Grant Cramer, Oct. 26, 1871.

To *William Elrod*

———

Long Branch, N. J.
July 30th 1871,

DEAR ELROD:

Three different letters have come to me in the last day or two enclosing the same report of a correspondent relative to the condition of the stock on my farm. The fellow lies unnecessarily in regard to where the stock came from, and how obtained, but I feel distressed at his statement of its condition. Young Hambletonian was foaled mine, from a fast mare which I owned until she died two years ago, and for which I would not have taken $500 00 $5000 00. The "Dutch Belted" cattle I paid a high price for, a price at which if I can sell the progeny will make farming profitable.

Let me know what truth there is in this report.

Yours Truly
U. S. GRANT

ALS, Illinois Historical Survey, University of Illinois, Urbana, Ill. On June 12, 1871, a Washington paper had reported. "The President has lost one of his favorite Hambletonian colts by a disease similar to that which killed one of his blooded mares two years ago. Another colt of the same stock is sick, but is improving, and it is thought will be cured. The disease makes its appearance in the form of a sore, and extends up the back, causing the hair to fall out, and soon kills the horse. Thus far the skill of the veterinary surgeons has been defied in successfully treating this disease. 'Jeff. Davis' and 'Cincinnati' are the only two of the President's horses now here, except the diseased colt, which is kept in a separate building." *Washington Evening Star*, June 12, 1871.

Speech

———

[*Aug. 1, 1871*]

The desire which you express on behalf of the Emperor of Germany for both the preservation and the improvement of the existing relations between our two countries is heartily reciprocated by me. In addition to ties arising from extensive commercial intercourse and from mutual interests, which, in common with other countries, bind the United States with Germany, there is a further bond between them, from the circumstance that many of our best citizens are natives of your country. I welcome you, sir, as the Minister of that country, and will omit nothing which may contribute toward making your abode here agreeable. It is not to be doubted that you deserve my confidence as well as that of the illustrious sovereign whom you represent.

New York Herald, Aug. 2, 1871. USG spoke on Aug. 1, 1871, in response to remarks by Kurd von Schlözer, German minister. "Mr. PRESIDENT—I have received orders to deliver to Your Excellency, the letter whereby His Majesty the Emperor of Germany and the King of Prussia has been pleased to recall from the post, at his own request, Baron Von Gerolt, who has recently resided here in the capacity of Envoy Extraordinary and Minister Plenipotentiary of the North German Union, near the government of the United States. . . ." *Ibid.* On July 27, Secretary of State Hamilton Fish had recorded in his diary. "Mr Schlözer is the same Gentleman who passed through Washington, on his way to Mexico, as Envoy to that Country, some two years since—He then called at the Department—& reminds me of having then met & been presented to me. In the absence of the President he is told that he can enter upon official duties in anticipation of actual presentation to the President   Mr de Westenberg the new Minister from Holland presents a personal letter of introduction from Meredith Read—Is informed that the Presidents absence, & the inability to be presented, will not interfere with his official transaction of business—Is also told that the President having relinquished his intended trip to California, will be here within a couple of weeks, but uncertain at what precise time—that if he will have prepared & furnish me a copy of the remarks he intends to make on his presentation, I will endeavor to arrange his presentation whenever the Prsdt shall arrive—as his stay will be very short—He seems surprised that any address is expected & thinks it not usual in Europe—to which I advance a contrary opinion—He makes numerous enquiries as to questions of etiquette &c—& whether he should wear his uniform on occasion of being presented, &c &c &c" DLC-Hamilton Fish. On Aug. 1, Bernhard de Westenberg, Dutch minister, presented his credentials to USG. *New York Herald*, Aug. 2, 1871. At that time, USG responded. "Mr. Westenberg—I am happy to receive you as the diplomatic representative of your sovereign. It is certain that his disposition is not greater than my own to strengthen the bonds of friendship and good understanding which unite our separate countries. They began at the outset of our career. We have grateful recollections of their origin, and have similar feelings towards the people of the Netherlands, who have uniformly shown a confidence in the people of the United States which, I trust, may never be deemed to have been misplaced. It will be a pleasure to me to do anything which may be in my power towards making your mission agreeable. This is due to you from what we know of your antecedents, which afford warrant that your course will comport with them." *Ibid.*

To Domingo F. Sarmiento

To His Excellency The President of the Argentine Republic.
Great and Good Friend:

Mr. Robert C. Kirk, who has for some time resided near the
Government of the Argentine Republic in the character of Minister
Resident of the United States of America, having expressed a desire
to return to his country, I have acceded to his wish, and he has
accordingly been instructed to take leave of your Excellency. Mr.
Kirk, whose instructions had been to cultivate with your government relations of the closest friendship, has been directed on leaving Buenos Ayres, to convey to your Excellency the assurance of
our desire desire to strengthen and extend the friendly intercourse
now happily subsisting between the two governments and to secure
to the People of both countries a continuance of the benefits resulting from that intercourse. The zeal with which he has fulfilled
his former instructions, leads me to hope that he will execute his
last commission in a manner agreeable to your Excellency.

Written at Washington the second day of August, in the year
of our Lord one thousand eight hundred and seventy-one.

Your Good Friend.

U. S. Grant,

Copy, DNA, RG 84, Miscellaneous Correspondence, Argentina. See *PUSG*, 19, 153–
54. Born in 1821 in Mt. Pleasant, Ohio, Robert C. Kirk studied medicine in Philadelphia and opened a practice in Ill. before returning to Ohio and a business career. Kirk
was elected Ohio state senator in 1856 and lt. governor in 1859. In 1862, Kirk was
appointed minister to Argentina; he resigned in 1866. On March 6, 1869, U.S. Senator
John Sherman of Ohio wrote to USG. "I heartily join with others in urging that Hon
R. C. Kirk be restored to the Mission to Buenos Ayres—He served under Mr Lincoln
at this Mission with very great credit—ability and usefulness gaining the highest
commendations from that Government and our own—and securing the settlement of
claims long deferred—He was turned out by the recent Administration without
cause & upon a false pretext—He is a gentleman of engaging manners—good abilities—long services—and is an active ardent Republican—I have his appointment
much at heart and will be highly gratified at his success" ALS, DNA, RG 59, Letters
of Application and Recommendation. Related papers are *ibid.* On April 12, USG nominated Kirk to the position; on Dec. 6, USG nominated Kirk to serve concurrently as
minister to Uruguay, a post he held until July 6, 1870. For the appointment of John L.
Stevens as minister to Uruguay and Paraguay, see *PUSG*, 20, 144. On May 24, Horace
Porter wrote to Kirk, Buenos Aires. "The President directs me to acknowledge your

letter of the 21st of Feb. last and to convey to you the thanks of Mrs. Grant and himself for your kindness in forwarding the ostrich robe. It has been greatly admired by all who have seen it. The robes sent sometime ago were retained by Mrs. Fish, and in compliance with your request Mrs. Grant will retain the robe above mentioned." Copy, DLC-USG, II, 1.

On June 10, 1871, Kirk wrote to Secretary of the Interior Columbus Delano. "Your letter of April has been received in which you inform me that you have not been able to accomplish my wishes in regard to Paraguay, and thinking I might have acted without due reflection would reconsider my determination. You had not requested the appointment of a successor to this post. You will accept my thanks for your consideration and kindness. I wrote to you by the last mail repeating what I had heretofore said. I now say; if you cannot have me appointed to Brazil, where I know I would be successful, then I would like Portugal, as I see by the papers there is to be a new appointment there. There are many reasons why I would like it, it would give me an opportunity of seeing European life and be a personal gratification to know that Morgan had not held a position superior to myself. Delano every American in this part of S. America feels that the appointment of Stevens was an act of great injustice to me— and I can say to you *confidentially*, that he (has) no influence whatever, and the Americans have no respect for him. I will tell you why when I see you. . . ." Copies, DNA, RG 59, Letters of Application and Recommendation. On Aug. 1, Delano wrote to USG. "A copy of the enclosed is communicated to you and one also to the Secretary of State, fearing that I may not be able to see either of you before I leave for the West. You will observe that Doctor Kirk has decided to leave Buenos Ayres unless his wishes can be gratified in regard to Paraguay. He desires if he leaves Buenos Ayres to be sent to Portugal. I have nothing to add in this case to what I have heretofore said except to express the hope that the Secretary of State will communicate to Doctor Kirk by the steamer to sail on the 23rd instant, your decision and the action of the Secretary of State in the matter." LS, *ibid*. A similar letter of Aug. 1 to Secretary of State Hamilton Fish is *ibid*. On Aug. 2, J. C. Bancroft Davis, asst. secretary of state, wrote to Kirk. "The Secretary of the Interior has communicated to this Department a copy of the letter which you addressed to him under date the 10th of June, last, in which you offer your resignation of the office of Minister Resident to the Argentine Confederation. A copy of the same letter was also communicated by Mr. Delano to the President, who directs me to say that your resignation is accepted. . . ." Copy, *ibid.*, Diplomatic Instructions, Argentina.

On Jan. 13, 1875, USG nominated Kirk as collector of Internal Revenue, 13th District, Ohio; on Nov. 12, USG retained Kirk in the position. On Dec. 3, Kirk, Mt. Vernon, Ohio, wrote to USG. "I see that Genl Badeau has declined the mission to Belgium. I am very grateful for what you have done for me, and know I committed a great mistake, when I resigned my mission at Buenos Ayres! I ask you to give me the mission to Belgium. It is a small matter to you but it is so important me. I know you have a warm heart, and when you can confer happiness you will gladly do it. God knows I have have always discharged my duties faithfully, honestly, and to the credit of my Government. Oh! Mr President, I know the cares and duties which surround you, and dont wish to importune ~~you~~ or annoy you, but I make this my last appeal, and ask you to grant my request. May the good God direct and bless you, . . ." ALS, *ibid.*, Letters of Application and Recommendation. On Dec. 15, Kirk wrote to Fish. "Your note of the 13th inst has been recd. As the mission to Belgium has been filled, cant you give me some other mission   Vacancies often occur, and you cannot confer a greater favor, or give more real happiness, than by granting my request. If important, I could have the support of Sherman, Hays and other leading men of my State...." ALS, *ibid.* On Oct. 9, 1876, John A. J. Creswell and Delano, Mt. Vernon, wrote to USG recommending Kirk as minister to Denmark. LS, *ibid.* No appointment followed.

Endorsement

Respectfully refered to the Atty. Gen. who is authorized to give the Marshal of La.[1] such orders, by telegraph, as may be legally authorized to ~~give~~ secure the protection to free speech and free action asked in the accompanying papers.

U. S. GRANT

AUG. 3D /71

AES, DNA, RG 60, Letters Received, La. Written on a letter of July 29, 1871, from Lt. Governor Oscar J. Dunn of La., New Orleans, to USG. "A Communication signed by the Presidents of the several Ward Clubs (Republican) of this City, and addressed to the Hon. S. B. Packard U. S. Marshal of La., relative to disturbances and violence created by the turbulent and evil minded combinations in this City, has been submitted to me. From personal observation and from reliable information, I am satisfied that the statement of facts in said communication is correct—such combinations exist, such alleged outrages have been, and are being perpetrated, and there is no lawful remedy for this evil available to us, except such as is prayed for from you. We cannot, in the absence of your interposition, exercise our political privileges, except at personal peril, or else by using violence in self protection. I respectfully urge your Excellency to authorize the Marshal to give the protection contemplated, and provided for, in Section 3d of the Enforcement Act, approved April 20th 1871. In addition to signing the aforesaid Communication as the President of the Third Ward Republican Club, I deem this matter of sufficient importance to justify me in addressing you also in my Official Capacity as a State Officer." LS, *ibid.* On July 28, Speaker of the La. House of Representatives George W. Carter, New Orleans, had written to USG. "My attention has been Called to a Communication made this day to the Hon: S. B. Packard, U. S. marshall for Louisiana, and signed by the Presidents of the several Ward clubs of the City of New Orleans. I am satisfied of my own knowledge, as also from entirely reliable information given by parties in the City, that the allegations in said Communication are true; and I would earnestly request, in behalf of the good people of our City & State, that your Excellency instruct & authorize Marshall Packard to give us the protection Contemplated ~~in~~ and provided for in Sec: 3, of enforcment act of April 20th 1871.—" LS, *ibid.* On Aug. 3, Dunn, Mobile, telegraphed to USG, Long Branch. "Information from reliable sources conclusively satisfy me that worst element of new orleans composed of thugs of Know nothing times desperadoes & Rioters of July sixty six & other bad men of city are organized to intimidate & prevent free expression of my people at primary election on monday next   Am further satisfied that police are aiding instead of preventing inauguration of such riotuous proceedings   also learn that Jails & parish prisons will be opened & prisoners released for ~~the~~ purpose of aiding these bad men. monday night a private meeting of citizens was visited by band of such desperadoes accompanied by large squad of police latter coming without solicitation of parties composing meeting & broke said meeting committing unprovoked assaults upon such private citizens so assembled & causing innocent men thus assaulted to be arrested while assaulters were let go free. Similar assaults are daily being committed all over city upon my people by persons heretofore voting against colored people. peace officers of city aiding & abbetting our citizens are denied equal protection of laws for which there is redress from United states authorities only unless united states marshall at new orleans has authority to preserve peace & afford protection. am confidently certain that there will be Riot at primary election on monday next & many of my people will be slaughtered ... If not washin: to be forwarded" Telegram received, *ibid.* On Aug. 5, James F. Casey, collector of customs, New Orleans, Washington, D. C., telegraphed to USG, Long Branch. "Attorney General does not give much encouragement He will consult with Secretary of War and give me his decision at two oclock Every minute of delay the more critical affairs become in our state" ALS (telegram sent), *ibid.*, RG 107, Telegrams Collected (Bound). On the same day, USG telegraphed to Attorney Gen. Amos T. Akerman. "YOU ARE AUTHORISED TO GIVE SUCH INSTRUCTIONS TO THE MARSHAL OF LA AS YOU MAY THINK PROPER AND LEGAL FOR THE PROTECTION OF PUBLIC MEETINGS IN THAT STATE." Telegram received (at 4:45 P.M.), *ibid.*, RG 60, Letters Received.

On Sept. 5, a correspondent reported from Long Branch: "The Warmoth Committee, from Louisiana (twenty in number), arrived here at eleven o'clock A. M. today, the object of their visit being an interview with the President in relation to the recent difficulties in New Orleans, where the Warmoth faction was prevented by the federal authorities from participating in the Convention of the republican party. Carriages were in waiting at the depot, and the delegation were at once driven to the President's cottage, where His Excelency by appointment, received them and ushered them into the reception room, where all the committee's grievances were laid before him. General Campbell read to the President a statement of the views and the wishes of the committee, and presented to him an official copy of the proceedings and the resolutions of the Convention, which suit the committee. The address states 'that the Republican State Central Committee has been managed for the past year or two by Mr. Packard, United states Marshall; Mr. Casey, Collector of Customs, Mr. Lowell, Postmaster of New Orleans; Mr. Joubert, Assessor of Internal Revenue, and the Lieutenant Governor of the State. These gentlemen have all been hostile toward Governor Warmoth, and for nearly two years have waged a fierce contest against him. They desired to control the Convention this summer, and secure a new Central Committee in their own interest and inimical to the Governor, and thus direct the organization of the nominating convention next year. Up to this date there has been no division among the republicans of the State except on State issues. The party was a unit in the support of the national republican party and of the national administration. Governor Warmoth's friends were the hearty and earnest friends of the President.... After considerable conversation in relation to the facts contained iE the address the President requested a copy, which was given him. He then said he would send it to the officers complained of, and have their statement before taking any action in the matter. He remarked also that the address presented a formidable array of charges against the federal officers named therein, he said he had not authorized the use of troops, and that General Reynolds, when he filled the requisition of Marshal Packard, did not know they were to be used at a political convention...."

New York Herald, Sept. 6, 1871. On the same day, Pinckney B. S. Pinchback, New
York City, wrote to Governor Henry C. Warmoth of La. "The committee had an
interview to day with the President, and I think rather stirred him up, and while
many of the committee ~~think~~ are of the opinion that no good will result from it I
am inclined to think otherwise, the position he taken seams to me to be just the one
you or I would have taken under like circumstances   he said you cannot expect me
to act upon such grave charges as you have made against these officers until I have
heard what they had to say in their own defence,   when I have heard from both
parties their statements I will try to adjust matters between you,   he also stated
that if the marshal had appointed the kind of men we accused him of he would be
removed. I am sorry to say it is my impression that the President is biased in their
favor, but when you recollect that for two years these men have been abusing you
to the President and telling him that you are his bitterest enemy, and that you are
opposed to his renomination and that if you are sustained the deligation from Louisiana to the National Convention will be against him it is not surprising that he should
stop to consider or that he is in sympathy with these men who claim to have no
interest in the contest except the reelection of the President. It nesessarily must
take some time to put our case before him in its proper light but that all will come
out right in due time I have no doubt. Our friends must be discreet, give the President time to study this matter,   he cannot be driven,   any attempt to drive him will
surely fail and we have too much at stake in this fight to risk a failure when it can
be avoided   I will leave here to morrow night for Washington, will return to New
York on the 10th Inst   would be pleased to hear from you before I leave for the
west,   If you write direct to New York and if I leave before its arrival it will be
forwarded to me   The colered men on the Committee made a fine appearance and
I am proud of them, they were the observed of all the observers,   Most of the
persons I have talked to on Louisiana matters are with us in this fight, and all have
expressed the opinion that the President would certainly remove those men when
he learned the facts,   If he fails to remove them now that the facts are in his
posession, he will be universally condemned," ALS, Warmoth Papers, Southern Historical Collection, University of North Carolina, Chapel Hill, N. C.

In [*Sept.*], Stephen B. Packard, U.S. marshal, La., wrote at length to USG. "I
have the honor to acknowledge the receipt of the communication referred to me by
your Excellency, embracing certain charges preferred against myself and other Federal officers by Hugh J. Campbell, on behalf of himself and others, acting as a committee under the instructions of an assemblage claiming to represent the republican
party of Louisiana, held in Turner's Hall, New Orleans, August 9, 1871. In reply
thereto I respectfully submit the following statement in vindication of the official
conduct of myself and associates in the matter complained of, and also in justification
of our opposition, and that of the republican party of Louisiana, to Governor H. C.
Warmoth and his faction of official appointees.... In my judgment and that of the
most honored leaders of the republican party of Louisiana, the character and extent
of the outrages perpetrated by Governor Warmoth and his partisans upon many of
the primary clubs in the city and threatened against the convention were so grave
and aggravated as to have justified us in claiming your direct interference under the
third section of the enforcement bill of April 20, 1871. The course pursued by us,
and which we believe we were fully authorized in taking, in obedience to law and
the requirements of our official duty, secured order and safety in the convention; and
all my official actions and utterances have proceeded upon this belief.... On the 9th
of August, Mr. President, I had no personal interest to subserve; no nominations of

State or Federal officers were to be made at the convention. I saw the delegates hunted from their primaries, and denied a place of assemblage. I heard upon one side their pleas for protection, and upon the other the threats against their lives. I felt that the United States Government would not grudge United States citizens an asylum from bloodshed under a United States roof, and I prefer the responsibility of having thrown open to them the door of a vacant United States court-room, rather than to-day to be charged by my brethren with standing upon its threshold in pitiless indifference to their peril. In conclusion, Mr. President, permit me to say that the republican problem in Louisiana is to be mastered chiefly by 85,000 colored men. In their political inexperience, they mistook certain of their pretended friends in 1868. They have seen a demagogue re-establish the old ethics of slavery so far as to enforce a partisan servitude to himself, and, if need be, invoke violence to promote his selfish ends. They now propose to clearly disavow all mischievous men and measures, and husband their confidence from further abuse as a sanction for crime. To this end they have declared in convention that H. C. Warmoth, having shown clearly that he would sacrifice the republican party to advance himself, can no longer be safely followed as a republican leader; having pronounced for a thorough reform in matters of local administration, and addressed themselves to a better solution of the national question in 1872 than their official incumbrances permitted them in 1868. I respectfully submit this statement, with accompanying proofs, as my answer." *HMD*, 42-2-211, 165, 167–73. The appendices are *ibid.*, pp. 173–212. See letter to William W. Belknap, Jan. 15, 1872.

On July 8, 1871, James Longstreet, surveyor of customs, New Orleans, had written to USG. "The unsettled and unsatisfactory condition of our political affairs, is such as to induce me to trespass upon your valuable time, so far as to explain my appreciation of them, and to express the hope that you may make such suggestions as you deem most necessary and wise in their adjustment. I have just returned from a visit to his Excellency Governor Warmoth, at Pass Christian,—where he is rapidly recovering from his severe injuries,—and have had a full understanding with him as to his views and purposes in regard to the politics of this State. He gives me now the assurances ~~that~~ he has often repeated, 'that he will to the utmost of his ability and power, encourage and support the present National Administration, and that he will, in the State Convention, to meet next month, introduce resolutions himself declaring the same and pledging the party of the State to continued support, and to your renomination in the convention of next year.' So earnest and sincere is he in this that he ~~will~~ is ready to give written assurances to this effect in any shape that any one can wish. But aside from these assurances, it is patent to any one, who will exercise unprejudiced judgement, that all of his political interests and aspirations, if he understands and appreciates them, compel him to the course that he indicates; even if feelings did not which of itself should be a sufficient guarantee of his good faith—: So that to my mind he is more certainly bound to you and your administration than are the prominent persons who are now seeking to make an open rupture in the ranks of the party. Beleiving this to be a practicable and just view of this branch of the subject—it seems to me that it would be unwise to take the risk of carrying the state after a break in the party, and the disaffection that must necessarily follow. In fact I may say that I think that it will be impossible to carry the vote of the State without him, and his earnest supporters. He complains that some disaffected parties have mislead Collector Casey to such extent as to induce him to take part against him, and to use the influence of his patronage in supporting their efforts to break down him and his administration, and that they are now united in their efforts and purposes to do so. Whilst he has no doubt of his ability to hold the greater portion of the party, and to overcome these combined efforts against him, he thinks it due to you and to himself that an explanation should be made, and that he should appeal to you to exercise such influence as you may think proper, and necessary, to cause these gentlemen to abandon their violent effort[s] against him, and to extend impartial if not entire support in his struggle for the party and for yourself. There is no doubt, but the Collector is as anxious and earnest in his wishes for your entire success, as any one in the country: but it is my judgment that in giving up the certainty of the State—with the party united— for the problematic chance of a disaffected party—with antagonistic elements—he has made a mistake. And it is singular, that in this alliance he has given his confidence to those who were most prominent in their opposition to him, and at least lukewarm in their support of yourself. With the influence of his patronage in support of the State Administration, the party again becomes a unit. That influence thrown against the State Administration, and in support of the disaffected element, a division will be made which will probably defeat both. I think it important to preserve the harmony of the party in the State for another important reason, i. e. The prestige and influence that unity may give us with the delegates from the other southern States in the Chicago Convention of next year. I have made this statement as frankly and as concisely as possible in order that I may tax your patience as little as possible. Hoping that the statement may give you an insight of the condition of our affairs, and that you may pardon this liberty of an earnest and grateful friend—" LS, Warmoth Papers, Southern Historical Collection.

On Feb. 3, 1872, Henry C. Dibble, New Orleans, testified before the Select Committee to Investigate the Condition of Affairs in the State of Louisiana. "I am judge of the eighth district court for the parish of Orleans; I was appointed March 24, 1870. . . . Q. Did you complain to the President of the action of the Federal officers in connection with this convention?—A. Yes, sir; I made a very emphatic representation to him at Long Branch. . . . He said that the charges against these gentlemen were very extraordinary, and he would investigate them. I have no doubt he did. Q. Were any Federal officers removed in consequence of this proceeding?— A. No, sir; They ought to have been. Q. Do you hold, then, that the approval of the President is fairly to be inferred from his continuing these gentlemen in office?— A. Yes, sir; I think he knew the facts. There is no doubt about that. I saw the President personally at Long Branch before the committee met him, and made arrangements for a meeting between him and the committee. Q. Did the President justify the conduct of the custom-house officials in bringing armed soldiers into the building?—A. He made use of a very curious phrase in regard to that. He wanted to know what objections we had to the troops if we did not intend to do any harm. Q. He then justified the bringing into the custom-house of these United States troops?—A. I do not think he did directly. I think the President has a very poor opinion of the republican party down here, and that he had come to the conclusion that anything was justifiable to overthrow Governor Warmoth. I think that the President's personal dislikes to Governor Warmoth has as much to do with his opposition as anything. If the President had told these gentlemen down here in the custom-house to quit, they would have quit long ago. I think the President is in that way responsible for the division in our party. . . . I think it is his intention to sustain this custom-house wing of the party down here as long as he can safely. That is merely my opinion. I only infer it from the fact that he was fully acquainted with all the circumstances attending the assembling of the convention in the custom-house, and the use made of the United States troops there. He must have known that it was in violation of republican institutions, and I think he must have been of the opinion that almost anything was justifiable in overthrowing Governor War-moth...." *HMD*, 42-2-211, 265–72. For Warmoth's related testimony, see *ibid.*, pp. 357, 387–90.

1. Born in 1839 in Auburn, Maine, Packard studied law, served as lt. and capt., 12th Maine (1861–64), and settled in New Orleans after his discharge. See *PUSG*, 19, 335–36; *HMD*, 42-2-211, 117, 119–20, 123.

On Jan. 28, 1873, Job B. Stockton, Algiers, La., wrote to USG. "Allow me to preface the proposition I am about to make by a statement of fact: I have never been a Delegate to a political Convention, or even a member of a political Committee during my residence of four years in Louisiana, and therefore claim to be as nearly a disinter-ested observer as any one else. There is *one man* whom the people & Republican Party of this state, more than to any one else, owe their success in the past and without his aid, &, I may almost say direction the Republican Party could not have been held together, and could never successfully cope with the desperate & corrupt men opposed to us. That man is no less a person than Col. S. B. Packard U. S. Marshal, and now the Republicans of the state ask your Excellency, to give Mr. Packard a Foreign Mission, which shall be a worthy recognition of the distinguished services he has rendered the Republican cause in Louisiana. I venture the assertion that there is not a single Repub-lican in the State, whose fidelity to the Party is worth notice, who would not willingly sign this request and rejoice at its fullfilment. We do not ask this as a right to the state because she may have no representative at a Foreign Court, but upon the merits of the man himself. No man in the Union has gone before Stephen B. Packard in his devotion to Republican principles, and in his unflinching, unwavering, constant and devoted support of your Administration." ALS, DNA, RG 59, Letters of Application and Recommendation. See Endorsement, Feb. 8, 1871.

To Schuyler Colfax

Private

Long Branch, N. J.
Aug. 4th 1871.

MY DEAR SIR:

I owe an apology for not writing to you soon after coming to this place, as I fully intended to do, to enquire after your health.[1] But hearing through the papers daily of your steady improvement, and knowing your proneness to answer all letters, a task which I did not want to impose, and my own laziness, must be accepted as a full apology. (This is a long sentence to contain so little; is it not?) To be candid, I do not know that I would impose on you a letter now, knowing that it must be answered, only that I am, *just the least*, selfish.—You know that Gov. Fish come into my Cabinet reluctantly; that I have retained him by persistence, against his will, as long as I have. Now he says he must go, and seeing as I do that he is suffering in health, I have not the heart to urge him stronger than has already been done to remain longer than he has consented to; the meeting of Congress in Dec.[2] I have cast about, in my own thoughts, for a man from N. Y. or Pa who would strike the public favorably, and suit me at the same time. Now I have one suggestion, going out of those states, that will suit me exactly, and I believe the public generally, if he will give up a higher for a lower, and harder, position. In plain English will you give up the Vice Presidency to be Sec. of State for the balance of my term of office? That is a question which might have been asked in one sentence. It requires an answer too. In all my heart I hope you will say yes, though I confess the sacrifice you will be making.

I will say to you, confidentially, that I have thought of Andrew White[3] as coming nearest to my own notions of any one in the State of New York. He has filled no public position to bring him prominently before the people. In Pa I have not been able to think of any one. Now I want a short letter from you giving your views about this matter.

Every thing seems to be working favorably for a loyal Administration of the goverment for four years after the 4th of March /73. It is important that we should have such an Administration, though it is not important who the head may be. Who ever has the place will have a slaves life. My only anxiety in the matter is that there shall be entire harmony, and unaniminity, in favor of the choice of the convention which nominates him. Tamany, and the "New departure democracy,"[4] are working to that end. Some who profess to be with us take a course to defeat them. All will be well however I hope, and confidently believe.

Please present my kindest regards to Mrs. Colfax, and Colfax, Jr.[5]

Faithfully yours,
U. S. Grant

Hon. S. Colfax,
Vice President.

ALS, deCoppet Collection, NjP. On Aug. 9, 1871, Vice President Schuyler Colfax, South Bend, Ind., wrote to USG. "CONFIDENTIAL ... I have just received your letter, having returned from Andover O, where Mrs C, & the baby of babies & his nurse will sojourn at her old home, while I ramble for 3 or 4 weeks over Minnesota, whither I start at 5 A. M. tomorrow. My wife is very well & so is the boy who is 'gay & happy,' & a Smiler, & who crows more exultingly when he walks 3 or 4 steps by himself than when you captured 3 or 4 rebel armies. Your letter is a very welcome one to me altho' I cannot accept your kind offer to take the Premier's place in your Admn. It is welcome because it is so substantial an evidence of your confidence & regard which I have striven to deserve by faithful & unswerving friendship, as well as public vindication of your Admn. This has been no more than duty, political & personal, but in my 20 years of public life I have seen so many V. Ps add so pitilessly to the manifold annoyances of their President, & play the role of Absalom so unkindly, that I determined that this term should be an exception in that regard; & it has been a pleasure to me that it has been. Enough on that head. It is with me a matter of conscientious duty to serve out my term as V. P., after millions voted for me for it. They did it, supposing I was the most radical of the two. But they did not realize then, as they have since, your strong fidelity & attachment to Repn principles. It was this idea of conscientious duty that compelled me to decline an offer of $25.000 pr year last winter. And, with 1873, I intend & expect to quit a kind of life which you have realized as well as I has so many thorns in it. I look however to your triumphant reelection, with some good man associated with you. My theory has always been that we owe our victories, half to the excellence of our principles, & half to the blunders & misdeeds of our enemies. Our chief danger next year was that the Dems would hide their real intentions, & go *purring* all over the country to allay the ~~fe~~ just fears of the people—New York City has, unintentionally on their part, unmasked their claws, & shown the Am. people palpably what they are to expect with Dem. leaders in power. They will not forget these revelations by next year; & with unity in our ranks & judicious legislation next winter, a Repn triumph is assured. We must cut down expenses next session sharply, have the estimates reduced all they will bear, & relieve the people of the most excessive & most irritating of the burdens of taxation. But I did not intend to enlarge on this head. As you ask me for my views about Sec of State, let me say I have always insisted that there are not over a dozen men generally alive at once, who are in all respects fitted for it. You made a lucky hit, & got one of them, & I deeply regret that he cannot stay the whole of your term. Were I in your place, my first choice if I went to N. Y. would be Geo Wm Curtis. He has the requisite culture, manners, &c &c besides being a sound & popular Repn. But he gets $10.000 a yr from the Harpers, & I dont suppose he could give that up for office. The public, I think, expect you to appoint Gov. Morton. He has marked ability & many qualifications for the place by his long political & executive service. But he might not desire to leave the Senate. The one you suggest, Mr White, does not in all things strike me as favorably. He has the culture of collegiate life, but he has not had the experience of official life, nor the hold on the public mind that others would have. But if you still think of him, I would suggest writing to Senator Wade at Jefferson, O, & asking his opinion. He was with him for months under circumstances that compelled him to know him quite thoroughly. I doubt whether he would strengthen your Admn. I would incline to Edwards Pierrepont in preference. I have been thinking, while writing, of another name, Mr Frelinghuysen: but that would be impracticable while ~~Rob~~ Mr Robeson remains in the Cabinet, & perhaps he would not be willing to leave the Senate at any rate. There is still another name, Ex Senator

Williams of Oregon. He has some qualifications & lacks others. But he has a strong hold on our best Repn public opinion in the country. I would prefer him for some other position in the Cabinet; but his name is worth considering with the rest. Senator Howe has many qualifications for it; but I think next after Mr Curtis, Williams would strike Reps the most favorably. I shall stop one day at Milwaukee with that veteran freesoiler you met one evening at my house, E. D. Holton, & over Sunday at Winona. I will keep all you have written me *confidential closely*, but will think it over, & shall meet many Reps. If any thing else occurs to me, will write you from Winona. Our people out here were glad when you ended the Pleasonton imbroglio. It had become a running sore & offensive, so that it needed extirpation. The public too began to think his decisions too costly for the Treasury. I have been resting as I have never done before, picking berries & apples, working in the garden, riding out &c, & am now in fine health, better than for years; & am taking better care of it than heretofore. With regards to Mrs Grant & Nellie & all, & also to Gen Porter, . . . My address in Minnesota will be *Winona*; whence my mail will be forwarded." ALS, USG 3. See letter to Schuyler Colfax, Nov. 14, 1871.

1. On May 22, Colfax collapsed in the Senate. He remained in the Capitol where USG visited him on May 24 and 27. On May 31, Colfax left for his home in South Bend. *Washington Chronicle*, May 23, 27, June 1, 1871; *New York Tribune*, May 24, 1871; *Boston Transcript*, May 25, 1871. On June 15, Colfax wrote to Frederick T. Dent. ". . . Every day I am a little less weak than the day before. Quiet & rest, I feel sure will restore my former robust health, except that I realize I am to be 50 hereafter & not 25, & must govern myself accordingly—Mrs C. takes me out driving 2 hours every day & I work in the garden one hour each day, see few visitors, write but few letters, & lead the laziest life possible, an odd thing for me. . . ." ALS, ICarbS.

2. See letter to Edwards Pierrepont, Dec. 29, 1871.

3. See letter to Buenaventura Báez, Jan. 15, 1871, especially note 2.

4. In May, Clement L. Vallandigham had presented a new Democratic platform, accepting the result of the Civil War, promoting reform, and inviting disenchanted Republicans to switch party allegiance. See William B. Hesseltine, *Ulysses S. Grant: Politician* (New York, 1935), pp. 257–60.

5. Colfax's first wife died in 1863. He married Ellen M. Wade, a niece of Benjamin F. Wade, on Nov. 18, 1868. Schuyler Colfax, Jr., born in 1870, was their only child. See *New York Times*, Jan. 14, 1885.

To Zachariah Chandler

Long Branch, N. J.
Aug. 4th 1871.

MY DEAR SENATOR:

I received your very kind letter just as I was starting for Washington the last time. I agree with you that Tamany, and the "New departure democracy"[1] are doing a great deal to produce harmony in the republican ranks, and no doubt to the discomfort of some who think themselves the fathers of the republican party. I will not be personal and mention names, nor will I give theories which may lead you to suspect who is meant. I once said that I believed all men were wiser than any one man and immediately was accused of using personalities towards an old, distinguished and mild Senator who never said an unparlamentary thing in his life, nor used hard words about anyone. I can prove that he never did because he says so.[2]

Seriously, I think we have a very promising chance of securing a loyal Administration of the government for four years from the 4th of March /73. It does not matter who may be the choice of the convention who selects the candidate for that head so long as there is unanimity for him. My best efforts will be given to his support.

Please present Mrs. Grant's and my kindest regards to Mrs. Chandler & Miss Minnie,[3] and accept the same for yourself.

Faithfully yours
U. S. GRANT

HON. Z. CHANDLER, U. S. S.

ALS, DLC-Zachariah Chandler. U.S. Senator Zachariah Chandler of Mich. served as chairman of the Republican National Executive Committee (1868–76). See *PUSG*, 1, 195.

In 1870, Chandler had written to USG concerning the annexation of Santo Domingo. William Evarts Benjamin, Catalogue No. 27, Nov., 1889, p. 5.

On Oct. 27, 1871, Chandler, Detroit, wrote to Secretary of State Hamilton Fish. "Gov Giddings of New Mexico is of the opinion that it is not expedient *at present* to make any changes of the appointees by the Government in that Territory For reasons set forth in a confidential communication to myself. I fully concur with the Gov in that Opinion   There are certain bickerings & heartburnings there, which have caused a disaster politically. Oil & *not* vinegar, is in my judgment the better paliative   Let the Parties wait untill the assembling of Congress, when cooler & perhaps *wiser* counsels may prevail" ALS, DNA, RG 59, Letters of Application and Recommendation.

1. See previous letter, note 4.
2. USG probably alluded to U.S. Senator Charles Sumner of Mass.
3. Chandler's daughter, Mary D. or "Minnie," born in 1848, married U.S. Representative Eugene Hale of Maine on Dec. 20, 1871.

Proclamation

To All Who Shall See These Presents, Greeting:
Know Ye, That by virtue of the authority conferred upon the President by the second section of the Act of Congress approved April 5, 1869, entitled "An Act to amend an Act regulating the tenure of certain civil offices," I do hereby SUSPEND Alfred Pleasonton,[1] *from the office of* Commissioner of Internal Revenue, *until the end of the next session of the Senate; and I hereby* DESIGNATE John W. Douglass,[2] *to perform the duties of such suspended officer in the meantime, he being a suitable person therefor; subject to all provisions of law applicable thereto.*

In Testimony Whereof, I have caused these Letters to be made Patent, and the Seal of the United States to be hereunto affixed.

Given under my hand, at the City of Washington, the Eighth *day of* August, *in the year of our Lord one thousand eight hundred and* Seventy one, *and of the Independence of the United States of America the* Ninety-sixth.

U. S. GRANT.

D (fonts regularized), DNA, RG 59, General Records. On Aug. 8, 1871, Alfred Pleasonton wrote to USG. "In answer to your request, transmitted through General Porter last evening, that I should tender my resignation of the office of Commissioner of Internal Revenue; I can only reply that under ordinary circumstances, nothing would give me greater pleasure than to accede to any request you might make of this kind. But the cause for making this request, was stated by General Porter to be the difference existing between the Secretary of the Treasury, Mr Boutwell, and myself as regards the government and management of the Internal Revenue Bureau. Mr Boutwell claims powers, which under the laws of Congress governing that Bureau are vested solely in the Commissioner. The question is therefore purely a legal one, and the precedents of our Government have been to have such questions, when appealed to the President, referred to the law officer of the Government for his opinion, and upon which the President would base his decision. This course was pursued by Presidents Jackson, Tyler, Pierce, Van Buren and others, and has been the uniform practice of the Government. Knowing these facts and believing this to be the proper way to settle any difference of view as regards the law, which might exist between the Secretary and the Commissioner, I addressed you a communication some time since, making an appeal for your decision of the powers of the Commissioner under the Act of July 20, 1868. This appeal, as I understand it, is not to be entertained, but the subject is to be treated rather as a personal difference between the Secretary and myself. In this connection, it is proper to add, the personal conduct of the Secretary towards myself, has been such as to preclude the tender of my resignation until some opportunity is granted for vindicating my administration of the Internal Revenue Bureau. In justice to the public interests placed under my charge and the importance to the tax payers of a proper solution of these difficulties, I must respectfully decline to tender you my resignation; and trusting it will not be deemed inappropriate, I will again request that your present determination may be reconsidered and an investigation of the matter of difference between the Secretary and my self be referred to the Attorney General for his legal opinion." ALS, *ibid.*, RG 46, Papers Pertaining to Certain Nominations. On the same day, a correspondent reported from Washington, D. C. "This letter was accompanied by a private note from Gen. PLEASONTON, expressive, it is said, of his devotion, friendship and support of the President in the future. Within two hours of the receipt of Gen. PLEASONTON's communication, the President sent to him the notification of suspension, which was delivered by Solicitor BANFIELD and Mr. VANDERBILT, the Appointment Clerk in the Treasury Department. The immediate causes assigned in official quarters for the suspension of Gen. PLEASONTON are that the internal revenue was not collected with efficiency; that Gen. PLEASONTON reversed the rulings of his predecessors in several important particulars, and made decisions, the effect of which was unnecessarily to lessen the public receipts; acting independently of and not consulting with his superior officers as to these and other matters of administration, and that a change was necessary in order that there be harmony in the working of the Treasury Department." *New York Times*, Aug. 9, 1871.

On July 4, 1870, Edwards Pierrepont, U.S. attorney, New York City, had written to U.S. Senator Simon Cameron of Pa. "General Pleasanton will call to see you on Political matters of this City & State   he is well informed discreet and has our entire confidence & that of Gen. Grant" ALS, DLC-Simon Cameron. On Dec. 7, "KAPPA" reported from Washington, D. C. "Gen. Logan yesterday called upon the President for the purpose of protesting against the appointment of Gen. Pleasanton of New York as Commissioner of Internal Revenue. Logan said he came as the representative of the Grand Army of the Republic, and he was prepared to show that Pleasanton had neither personal nor political claims to the place. Upon being asked by the President who he favored, he answered, Douglass. Several gentlemen from Pennsylvania called at the White House today to urge Douglass. They were introduced by General Cameron." *Boston Transcript*, Dec. 7, 1870. See *PUSG*, 20, 298–99; George S. Boutwell, *Reminiscences of Sixty Years in Public Affairs* (New York, 1902), II, 131–33.

On June 17, 1871, Secretary of the Treasury George S. Boutwell wrote to USG. "I enclose a letter from Wm Orton, Esq. which was designed for you and which it is important you should see. The circumstance to which he refers in the first paragraph was my application for copies of telegrams which passed between Thomson and Elmore in Feby. last." ALS, OFH. A copy of the enclosure, a letter of June 15 from William Orton, president, Western Union Telegraph Co., New York City, to Boutwell, disparaging Pleasonton as incompetent and corrupt is *ibid.*

On June 28, Pleasonton, Washington, D. C., wrote at length to USG. "By the favor of your appointment, I have, for some time, held, and sought faithfully to execute, the duties of the office of Commissioner of Internal Revenue. In the discharge of the duties imposed upon me by law, I am sure I have endeavored, with all fidelity, to do what the constitution of the office required at my hands. It is perhaps, natural, that questions should arise respecting the powers actually invested in the Commissioner by law: because in the division of powers between the Secretary of the Treasury and the various Bureaus of that Department of the Executive Government, it is hardly possible that there should not arise more or less conflict of authority in their practical administration. . . . I beg, therefore, that you will for yourself determine the Scope of my authority in connection with that of the Secretary of the

Treasury, so that I may understand how far you deem me to be empowered with authority in respect to all the Administrative processes of collecting Internal Revenue through the Office of the Commissioner. I need not assure you that in submitting this matter, I am governed by no ambition to assume the discharge of duties not assigned to me by the law; but that by your decision I may avoid difficulties, and thus the more effectively administer the great office I hold at your hands." ALS, DNA, RG 46, Papers Pertaining to Certain Nominations. On June 29, a correspondent reported from Washington, D. C. "At the Cabinet meeting to-day nothing whatever was said in reference to the Boutwell-Pleasonton differences, or the alleged conflict of authority.... After the Cabinet meeting this afternoon Commissioner Pleasonton had a long interview with the President, and afterwards proceeded to the office of Secretary Boutwell, where the two had an extended conversation. Although nothing positive concerning it has transpired, the belief is that it had reference to a clearer understanding of their respective duties, as it is known that the President is friendly to both gentlemen and desires that there shall be a harmonious administration of all the business of the departments." *Philadelphia Public Ledger*, June 30, 1871.

On July 15, Boutwell wrote to USG. "I enclose a copy of a communication I have this day made to the Commissioner of Internal Revenue in reference to the claim against the NewYork Central Rail Road Company. As I view the subject the case is now left where and as it should be left; and I see no ground for criticism on the part of any one. Some time may and probably will elapse before a final settlement can be made. The information I receive in regard to affairs in the Internal Revenue Office is not favorable." ALS, OFH. See *SED*, 41-3-9, 46-2-216.

On Aug. 1 and 7, correspondents reported from Washington, D. C. "At noon the President called a special Cabinet meeting which was attended by all the members except Mr. Creswell. The Boutwell-Pleasonton imbroglio occupied most of the session, and while no positive decision was reached the tenor of the debate indicated that Gen. Pleasonton would be removed at no distant day. His successor was not even hinted, but will probably be Deputy Douglass, of Pennsylvania. It is stated the Mr. Boutwell made a speech, showing that the effect of Pleasonton's decisions, since he had been in office, had been to reduce the revenue eight millions of dollars a year." *Louisville Courier-Journal*, Aug. 2, 1871. "Nothing new has transpired to-day relative to the Commissioner of Internal Revenue, except the report that the time of resignation of the office was left to himself, after his interview with the President last Tuesday. As General Pleasonton declines to converse on the subject, the truth of this statement is sustained by the private utterances only of other parties supposed to have knowledge of all the facts. Prominent gentlemen express surprise that the question is not yet definitely settled, as they were led to believe last week that before now the President would have appointed a successor to General Pleasanton, in the person of J. W. Douglass, the First Deputy Commissioner." *Philadelphia Public Ledger*, Aug. 8, 1871.

On Dec. 1, Pleasonton, Washington, D. C., wrote to the Senate. "The undersigned, being the Commissioner of Internal Revenue, by the appointment of the President of the United States and by and with the advice and consent of the Senate, was suspended by the President on the 8th day of August 1871, from exercising the functions of that office. On the 28th of June 1871, previous to this suspension, the undersigned addressed an official letter to the President of the United States, a copy of which is enclosed, ... After its receipt, the President proposed as a solution of the question, in a personal interview with the undersigned, that he should tender his resignation and accept an appointment to a foreign mission. In making this proposition, the President was doubtless actuated by the kindest personal considerations, and the undersigned, who would have been glad to have relieved the President of any embarrassment, consistent with his sense of duty, immediately expressed his willingness to resign his office, but stated at the same time he could not accept any other position so long as the question of law at issue should remain undecided. The President then requested the undersigned, to call upon Secretary Boutwell and in his name ask of the Secretary, to state his points of difference as regarded the Act of Congress, Approved, July 20, 1868, to see if the difference of views between the Department and the Bureau could not be reconciled, and report the result to him. The undersigned presented the request of the President to Secretary Boutwell, who paid no attention to it, but abused the Administration of the Internal Revenue Bureau, and stigmatized it as a failure in the hands of the undersigned. This was denunciation, not an indictment for error, if any existed. The result of this interview was reported to the President, and he was requested to have the questions at issue submitted to his legal adviser for decision; as they effected directly the administration of the laws. To strip the Internal Revenue Bureau of its prestige of nine years growth and complicate its well defined functions, by adding them to an official whose hands are more than full already, is the duty of Congress—not the Secretary of the Treasury. To this request no answer was received; but on the 7th of August 1871, General Horace Porter, Private Secretary of the President, called upon the undersigned and stated, the President desired him to tender his resignation. The reply to this request, dated August 8, 1871, is enclosed,... The President upon receiving this reply, returned it to the undersigned by General Porter, with the request it would be withdrawn, and a letter of resignation tendered, when a complimentary letter accepting it would be returned. The undersigned could not accept a complimentary letter from the President under such circumstances, and communicated through General Porter, to the President, his decision. His suspension followed the same day. It will be seen from this statement that in consequence of the usurpations by the Secretary of the Treasury, of the powers conferred by law upon the Commissioner of Internal Revenue, the latter appealed to the President for his decision and action to enable him execute the law. The President failed to give the Commissioner the proper support in the discharge of his duties, but suspended him from office, thereby countenancing the usurpations of the powers of the Internal Revenue Bureau by the Secretary of the Treasury.... 1. It is claimed that the Secretary of the Treasury usurped the powers conferred upon the Commissioner of Internal Revenue, in Section 49, of Act of July 20, 1868, in giving orders to Supervisor Presbury of the Internal Revenue Bureau, to proceed to Baltimore, Maryland, and investigate certain alleged whiskey frauds. This when the Commissioner had already given the necessary instructions to the proper Internal Revenue Officers to investigate the same, and they were engaged performing that duty. 2. It is claimed the Secretary of the Treasury usurped the powers conferred upon the Commissioner of Internal Revenue, in Section 50, of Act of July 20, 1868, in directing Supervisor Presbury, to employ as detective, Wm P. Wood, of Washington, to aid him in the discovery of frauds on the internal revenue in illicit distillation in Baltimore, Maryland. This without the knowledge or consent of the Commissioner of Internal Revenue, and when he had the proper officers engaged on that duty. The Secretary of the Treasury at the same time authorizing that five thousand dollars should be paid to said Wood for his services. This Wm P. Wood, being the same individual, who publicly charged Secretary Boutwell in a letter dated Aug 12, 1869, with having attempted to bribe him with twenty five thousand dollars, to give certain testimony in the Impeachment trial of President Johnson. 3. It is claimed the Secretary of the Treasury usurped the powers conferred upon the Commissioner of Internal Revenue, in Sections 25 and 26, 67 and 87, of the Act of July 20, 1868, and of Section 52, of Act of July 13. 1866. in revoking the contract for paper for revenue stamps made by said Commissioner. 4. It is claimed the Secretary of the Treasury usurped the powers conferred upon the Commissioner of Internal Revenue by the Act of July 1. 1862. to assess and to collect all internal revenue tax, when he claimed to have appellate jurisdiction over the decision of the Commissioner, and suspended the collection of the tax on the interest certificates issued by the New York Central Railroad Company, amounting to one million one hundred and fifty thousand dollars, after the Commissioner had ordered its collection. 5. It is claimed the Secretary of the Treasury usurped the powers conferred upon the Commissioner of Internal Revenue, when he claimed to have the power to send for persons and papers belonging to the Internal Revenue Bureau office, and did send for the same without the knowledge or consent of said Commissioner. This, when Mr George S. Boutwell, Secretary of the Treasury had unsettled accounts to a large amount before said Bureau, incurred when said Boutwell was Commissioner of Internal Revenue; and which unsettled accounts rendered the said George S. Boutwell an improper and unsuitable person to be empowered to send for persons or papers belonging to the Bureau of Internal Revenue, without the consent of the Commissioner. 6. It is claimed that the appointment of James W. Douglas, as Acting Commissioner on the suspension of the Commissioner, was in violation of Section 16. of the Act of August 6. 1846. The said Douglas having been the Collector of the 19th Internal Revenue District of Pennsylvania, at Erie, when some $29,000 dollars were embezzled from the funds in his charge, in the year 1864; and from that time up to the day of his appointment as Acting Commissioner, he had never properly accounted for the same, and his accounts had never been disposed of or settled by the Accounting Officers of the Treasury. 7. It is claimed by the undersigned, that as Commissioner of Internal Revenue, he reported to the President, the usurpations of Secretary Boutwell, as well as the unsettled state of the said Boutwell's accounts in the Internal Revenue Bureau. He, also, reported to the President the condition of the accounts of James W. Douglas, afterwards appointed Acting Commissioner of Internal Revenue, and requested the President to have such examination made, while the undersigned was in office that he might produce the proper testimony & papers, as would be necessary to establish the above facts. No such examination was made within the knowledge of the undersigned. . . ." ALS, DNA, RG 46, Papers Pertaining to Certain Nominations. On Dec. 8, John W. Douglass wrote to U.S. Senator John Scott of Pa. countering Pleasonton's charges. ALS, *ibid.* See next letter.

1. Born in 1824 in Washington, D. C., Pleasonton, USMA 1844, commanded as capt. the 2nd Cav. march from Utah Territory to Washington, D. C. (1861). Promoted to brig. gen. vols. (1862) and maj. gen. vols. (1863), he fought at Antietam, Fredericksburg, and Chancellorsville, was transfered to Mo. (1864), and resigned as maj. and bvt. maj. gen. (1868). On April 2, 1869, USG nominated Pleasonton as collector of Internal Revenue, 4th District, N. Y.; on March 18, 1870, USG nominated Pleasonton as collector of Internal Revenue, 32nd District, N. Y. See *PUSG*, 13, 199–200; *ibid.,* 15, 577; *ibid.,* 19, 62.

2. Born in 1827 in Philadelphia, Douglass practiced law in Erie and served as collector of Internal Revenue, 19th District, Pa. (1862–69). See *ibid.,* p. 349.

To Gen. William T. Sherman

————

Washington D. C.
Aug. 8th 1871.

DEAR GENERAL:

In case I do not see you to-day to verbally invite you to visit me at Long Branch for a few days, say next week, I will do so by note. Mrs. Grant and myself will both be pleased to have you and it will give you a good chance to coll off.

Yours Truly
U. S. GRANT

GN. W. T. SHERMAN,

ALS, DLC-William T. Sherman. On Aug. 9, 1871, Gen. William T. Sherman, Washington, D. C., wrote to U.S. Senator John Sherman of Ohio. ". . . Yesterday the President came over, avowedly to bring the Pleasanton Matter to a conclusion, and has suspended him—That Pleasanton is honest no one doubts—that he has the same measure of ability now as he had when appointed is true & Grant knew him personally since 1849.—That he construed the Law made by Congress for Rollins as against McCullough, literally is so, and he appealed as a fair man had a right for an Authoritative decision by the Attorney General has been denied him, and there is much in his Case which appeals to that sense of fair dealing which ought not to be disregarded—I have kept entirely aloof from the controversy, because I saw he was to be sacrificed.—I purposely kept away from the White house yesterday, and went down to my house at 2 PM. shortly after which I got a private note from the President saying that if he did not see me, he wanted to prepare me, for an invite by himself & Mrs Grant to visit them at Long Branch. I answered by note, that if I received such invitation I should come of course, but that I had promised Alice the trip to Carlisle &c—Grant promptly responded saying that the time was not material, only he wanted me to visit him there before he came back here about Sept 14. I may therefore visit Long Branch for a few days in All August—I know nothing about the gossip of Fish, Boutwell, & Ackerman leaving the Cabinet, except that the giving up of his house by Fish seems suggestive. All such changes now would be damaging to your Party. . . ." ALS, *ibid.* See following letter.

To Gen. William T. Sherman

————

Washington, D. C. Aug. 8th *1871*

DEAR GENERAL:

Any time while I am at Long Branch will suit me to have you come and pay me a visit there. I do not want to disturb any of your plans, but want you to take a convenient time for going. Any time in the next five weeks will do. I shall not probably leave there before the Tenth of September.[1]

Yours Truly
U. S. Grant

Gn. W. T. Sherman,

ALS, DLC-William T. Sherman. See letter to William T. Sherman, Aug. 18, 1871.

1. See letter to Hamilton Fish, Sept. 19, 1871, note 3.

To Benjamin F. Butler

Washington, D. C. Aug. 8th 1871

Dear Gen:

I am in receipt of your kind letter of the 29th. ult. inviting me to be present at the inauguration of the Miles Standish monument on the 17th inst. and also to spend a day at the camp meeting at Martha's Vinyard. I regret that I am unable to accept your kind invitation as it would give me great pleasure to be present and participate in the inauguration of the monument to commemorate the first American soldier, and I should appreciate very highly a visit to Martha's Vinyard during the camp meeting, but my arrangements as already made for the next few weeks will not permit.

Please accept my sincere thanks for your kind invitation.

I am Gen. Very truly yours
U. S. Grant

Gen. B. F. Butler,
Bay View, Mass.

Copy, DLC-USG, II, 1. Declining an invitation from the Standish Monument Association, USG wrote: "I am heartily with your Association, in sympathy with any movement to honor one who was as prominent in the early history of our country as Myles Standish; but my engagements are such that I regret I am unable to promise to be present at the dedication in August. With many thanks for your kindness in sending me the invitation, . . ." Stephen M. Allen, *Myles Standish, with an Account of the Exercises of Consecration of the Monument Ground on Captain's Hill, Duxbury, Aug. 17, 1871* (Boston, 1871), p. 74. See *New York Times*, Aug. 1, 1871; *Boston Transcript*, July 31, Aug. 17, 18, 1871.

On Oct. 7, 1872, USG wrote to Stephen M. Allen, corresponding secretary, Standish Monument Association, Duxbury, Mass. "I regret my inability to be present to day at the laying of the Corner Stone of the Monument to that Patriot & Soldier, Miles Standish. His name will be green in the history of New England's great men long after the Monument which you are about to erect has crumbled to dust." ALS, DLC-Charles C. Hart. See *Boston Transcript*, Oct. 7, 1872.

Endorsement

Respectfully refered to the Atty. Gen.

Should any information be required as to what I know in regard to the subject within it will be found in the records of the War Dept. of the the time of the occurrence.

My opinion is that Mr. Talbot[1] is not a suitable person for the place which he now holds.

U. S. GRANT

AUG. 11TH /71

AES, DNA, RG 60, Letters from the President. Written on a letter of July 12, 1871, from Thomas H. Talbot, asst. attorney gen., Court of Claims, to USG. "I have the honor to enclose a report of Rear Admiral Walke, U. S. Navy, (just received,) with reference to the seizure of an unfinished steamboat on the Ohio river in October 1861, by your direction, as he states. Please furnish me a statement of all such facts as are within your personal knowledge, as to the *order* for seizure, seizure, and loss, (if lost) and the attending circumstances. If the order for seizure was in writing, please have a copy furnished me. I infer from the report of Admiral Walke, that he delivered the vessel to you. Please return enclosed with your reply." LS, *ibid.* On March 16, 1870, U.S. Senator Daniel D. Pratt of Ind. had introduced a joint resolution authorizing the Court of Claims to hear the claim of William B. Campbell "for the loss of an unfinished steamer, alleged to have been seized in the fall of 1861 by order of General Grant, . . ." *CG*, 41–2, 1985. On June 23, USG signed the joint resolution. See *PUSG*, 3, 56, 388–89; *ibid.*, 18, 599. On Jan. 20, 1873, the Court of Claims awarded Campbell $8,900; he had claimed $32,068.65. *SMD*, 43-1-7, 4.

1. Born in 1823 in Maine, Thomas H. Talbot graduated from Bowdoin College (1846), attended Harvard Law School, practiced law in Portland, served as lt. col., 1st Maine heavy art., and was promoted to bvt. brig. gen. as of March 13, 1865. On Dec. 6, 1869, USG nominated Talbot as asst. attorney gen. On Aug. 14, 1871, Talbot wrote to USG resigning his position. ALS, DNA, RG 60, Letters from the President. On Aug. 18, USG endorsed this letter. "Accepted to take effect at the will of the Atty. Gn." AES, *ibid.*

To Daniel Ammen

Long Branch, N. J

Aug. 11th 1871

DEAR AMMEN;

I can not state exactly the time when I will be in Ohio;[1] but as near as I can fix upon a programme it will be about this: four weeks from Wednesday next I shall start, via the Oil regions of Pa for Washington Pa   There I will remain two or three days and then go to Covington, Ky, direct. It will be probably about the 20th of Sept. when I will want to start for Georgetown. I am glad to hear that Mrs. Ammen and the child have recovered. My family are all very well and enjoy the Sea Shore very much. Buck was much pleased with the idea of accompanying you to the Pacific Coast. I thought however that he had better not go at this time.

Mrs. Grant and the children join me in kindest regards to yourself and family.

Yours Truly

U. S. GRANT

ALS, University of California at Los Angeles, Los Angeles, Calif. On June 21, 1871, Capt. Daniel Ammen, Washington, D. C., had written to USG. "I take the liberty of enclosing all the sections of Naval Laws bearing on the retirement of officers from length of service, also an argument or application in a special case. I have heard it said that admiral *Goldsborough* should have been retired in '67 but as he was not, then he should be continued ten years longer, although he argued that he should be retained until July '71.—Now he thinks his official life should be prolonged.—It seems to me that if he should have been retired in '67 that a further given extension of time does not imply a wrong to him however short that time may be & especially is this the case when he has reached that period which he himself stated as just. He has argued that his being borne on the Navy Register when so young as not to be able to serve had not worked to the prejudice of any one, or to his advantage, yet it was shown that when a very young man he had urged his seniority & obtained an acting appointment which gave him rank and additional pay over an officer who had served years afloat when he was too young to serve at all.—This officer was presumedly the more capable and yet was passed over because Goldsboroughs name had been borne on the Navy Register. He no doubt will say that as those on the active List through a vote of thanks are additional numbers therefore his retention is no harm to any one. If by law the number of Rear admirals is reduced as is certainly probable his retention will certainly prevent Commodore Case reaching the grade of Rear admiral. I doubt not that a great deal of time will be demanded of you to extend to its furthest limit possible under shadow of the law the retirement of the admiral. It does not seem to me malicious that

Navy Men generally do not see why he was proposed for a vote of thanks, nor do they know of any thing he has since done that is especially meritorious, or why he should wish to have another 'Cabinet decision' when he has received what he asked for in this matter on a former occasion. Please present me very kindly to the family." ALS, OFH. See *PUSG*, 19, 478.

1. On July 14, USG had written to Ammen concerning plans to visit Ohio. "I have been compelled to run about so much this Summer however that I have pretty much abandoned the idea of going at all if I carry out the design of visiting the Pacific Coast. . . . I am not surprised that your faith is shaken as to the reliability of all you see in the papers. For some time I have believed everything except what I see in print. No one seems responsible for what types say . . ." *The Collector*, No. 886 (1982), P-651. USG left Long Branch for the West on Tuesday, Sept. 12, 1871.

To Gen. William T. Sherman

Long Branch, N. J.
Aug. 18th 1871.

DEAR GENERAL:

We will be glad to see you at the time designated in your letter of yesterday. Our house is large and any time you choose to come you will find a spare room and a hearty welcom.

Yours Truly
U. S. GRANT

GEN. W. T. SHERMAN,

ALS, DLC-William T. Sherman. On Aug. 26, 1871, Gen. William T. Sherman arrived at Long Branch for a brief visit with USG. *New York Times*, Aug. 27, 1871. See letters to William T. Sherman, Aug. 8, 1871.

To Hamilton Fish

Long Branch, N. J.
Aug. 26th 1871,

MY DEAR GOVERNOR:

I shall go to Washington on Wednesday evening next[1] and re-main until Friday evening. Gen. Porter has written to Sec. Boutwell and Sec. Delano, and to Gn. Babcock to notify the balance of the

Cabinet, that there will be a Cabinet meeting on Friday, the 1st prox.

I agree with you that our interests should be represented at Geneva Conference by the ablest and best Council that can be procured. When we meet, next week, we will fix upon who shall go. I shall defer to you largely in this matter feeling that so much is due to you for the conception and bringing about of a settlement with the English Govt.

My kindest regards to Mrs. Fish and Miss Edith.[2]

Yours Truly

U. S. GRANT

HON. H. FISH,

SEC. OF STATE,

ALS, DLC-Hamilton Fish. On Aug. 25, 1871, Secretary of State Hamilton Fish, Garrison, N. Y., wrote to USG. "Great Britain is making a formidable array for the Geneva Tribunal—Mr Davis is preparing, & has nearly completed, a most able presentation of the Case on our side—It will be submitted to several of the ablest Jurists in the Country, & will probably be ready for submission to yourself, & to the Cabinet, by the middle of the next week. It has been submitted to me, as he has advanced with it—I have no distrust of the case, or of Mr Davis ability to present it before the Tribunal—But when Great Britain is presenting such eminent names, & her public is encouraged by the assurances that the Lord High Chancellor, aided by Lord Tenterden & Mountague Bernard, is preparing her case, that her Lord Chief Justice is to be the Arbitrator on her part, & that Sir Roundell Palmer, unquestionably the ablest Advocate at her Bar, is to be Counsel to present & argue her side, it appears to me, that it will be wise, and a matter of policy, if not a political duty, to have more than one hand at Geneva, to meet the British Jurists, & their great array of *imposing names,*—however competent Mr Davis may be, it would be impolitic to leave him alone to meet the ~~array of~~ imposing array of British names—Should you agree to the propriety of sending some '*Counsel*' (as Great Britain does) in addition to the 'Agent' (a person who prepares the Case,) you will, I trust, allow me to suggest, that he should be some person of very admitted & generally recognized ability & prominence at the Bar—he should have a familiarity with the History of the Case, & it is *very* desirable that he be able to speak, or at least to read, French—Although it is not *essential* that an appointment be made *immediately*, it is desirable, that it be determined soon—I shall go to Washington on Tuesday—Some recently received Despatches from Mr Low represent a serious state of things in the East—and some from Mr Bassett also require serious consideration—so much so that I should be very glad to know that you purposed having a Cabinet meeting within about a week or ten days from now—The Chinese & Corean question may require instructions to the Navy, as well as to the Minister to China—" ALS (press), *ibid.* On Sept. 1, Fish wrote in his diary. "President authorizes me to offer appt of Counsel before the Tribunal at Geneva, to Wm M. Meredith & Caleb Cushing—Prsdt said he would not under any Circumstances appoint Evarts—Judge Hoar was named by myself, but under reservation of objection from the fact of his having been on the Joint Commrs & the Atty Genl named Judge Williams, who is open to the same objection" *Ibid.*

On Aug. 12, Benjamin Moran, secretary of legation, London, had written in his diary. "I got up early this morning and took breakfast with Hon: W. M. Evarts at Hanover House Hotel. He talked in his usual able & natural way; and I am sure that he would accept the post of Solicitor or Legal Adviser to the American Arbitrators if it were tendered him. The announcement made by Lord Granville last evening that Sir Roundell Palmer has been selected for ~~the~~a similar post by this govt. puts him on his mettle. . . ." DLC-Benjamin Moran.

On Oct. 25, Fish wrote to Charles Francis Adams. "I have taken the President's opinion on the questions submitted in your letter of the 15th instant. It is thought that nothing in the nature of instructions would be appropriate in view of the capacity in which you are to act and that no suggestions are needed; this Government having the most entire confidence that your intelligence, familiarity with the questions to be considered, and devotion to the interests and the honor of your country will suggest all that may be proper. The only point on which the President desires to express a wish for your action, is to ensure what your letter indicates as your intention, your presence in Geneva, before the expiration of the six months from the date of exchange of the ratifications of the Treaty,—that period will expire on the 16th of December. In the absence of an appropriation to meet the full expenses of the Arbitrator and Counsel &c. arrangements have been made to advance twenty-five hundred dollars, in coin, to yourself and to each of the Counsel. I will place that sum at your disposal in such manner as you may indicate. Mr. Meredith has declined the appointment of Counsel, which he had accepted, and the appointment has been offerred to mr. William M. Evarts. His answer has not been received, and until officially announced is to be considered as 'confidentially communicated.' It is the President's intention to invite also Mr. Benjamin R. Curtis to act as counsel in the case. He is understood to be at present on his return from Europe, and his arrival to be expected during the next week." Copy, DNA, RG 59, Domestic Letters. On the same day, Fish wrote to William M. Evarts and Benjamin R. Curtis, inviting both to act as counsel, with Caleb Cushing, at Geneva. Copies, *ibid.* On Oct. 27 and subsequently, Fish wrote in his diary. "Wm M Evarts accepts the appointment of Counsel before the Geneva Tribunal—He goes to see the President—& on the way drops in the Street, the printed copy of the 'Case' which I had handed to him—" "Friday Novr 10 . . . I read Mr B. R Curtis letter declining to act as Counsel in Geneva—Several names are mentioned in Connection with it—Richd H Dana—Judge Trumbull, M H. Carpenter—Mr Delano names a Mr Waite of Toledo, who, he says is the equal of any man in the Country as a Lawyer— Chas O'Connor—Edwards Pierrepont—Jere. Black—Mr Steele of Balto—I name Judge Hoar—Boutwell names Wm Whitney   Prsdt thinks well of it (Hoar's appointmt)—says he will not decide until Monday—but authorises me to say to Evarts that Hoar will probably be named" "Novr 14 Tuesday . . . President directs telegram be sent to M R. Wait of Toledo, offering appointment as Counsel before the Tribunal at Geneva—" DLC-Hamilton Fish. See Nevins, *Fish*, pp. 511–13.

1. Aug. 30. On Aug. 23, Secretary of the Navy George M. Robeson wrote to USG. "I herewith enclose copies of Admiral Rodger's despatches with the general accounts of the Corean affair together with a copy of the chart which he sent for its better understanding. The affair in its execution seems to have been very creditable to our people, and, indeed, it seems to have been the only thing left for them after the treach-

ery of the Coreans, and their wanton attack upon us. What we may be called upon to do in the future, and whether alone or in connection with the other great powers, will, of course, be a matter for careful consideration; but I send you all the general information that I have upon the subject. I hope that Mrs Grant, and your family, are well, and rejoicing that you are away from our extremely hot weather, and sickly city, . . . N. B.—If you have intention of coming to Washington please telegraph me. I congratulate you upon the great success in placing our Five per cent. loan. This shows the wisdom of dealing with the real powers, and is a great triumph for yourself, for the administration, and for the country." LS, OFH. On June 16, Fish had written in his diary. "Robeson reads telegram from Admiral Rodgers, from the Corea June 3—informing of attack made by Coreans on the Expedition of the U. S Minister to China, on his way to treat with the Coreans—" DLC-Hamilton Fish. On June 3, Admiral John Rodgers, Borsu Island, Korea, had telegraphed to Robeson. "Our Minister & Corean Envoys exchanged professions of amicable intentions. Coreans made no objections to proposed examination of their waters. . . . where navigation is most perilous batteries manned by several thousand Coreans unmasked and opened heavy fire without warning. . . ." Copy, *ibid.* On Sept. 1, Fish wrote in his diary. "Robeson—read despatches from Admiral Rodgers proposing a plan of military operations against Corea—Prsdt thinks it not necessary to consider at present—" *Ibid.* See Annual Message, Dec. 4, 1871; *HED*, 42-2-1, part 3, pp. 12–13, 275–313; Richard S. Collum, *History of the United States Marine Corps* (Philadelphia, 1890), pp. 190–97.

On Aug. 5, Charles W. LeGendre, consul, Amoy, had written to Orville E. Babcock. ". . . You have heard of Corea. In my Estimation Admiral Rodgers has done very well, ~~he could not have done more~~. . . . We all entertain the hope that such reinforcements & additional instructions as he may requi[re] to accomplish more will be sent to him . . ." ALS, DLC-Charles W. LeGendre. On Sept. 30, Babcock wrote to LeGendre. ". . . The President ha[s] been endorsed unanimously almost. from Me to Cal and from Texas to Minnesota—*Mass* notwithstanding Mr Sumner, *N. Y.* notwithstanding Mr Greely and Mr Fenton, an[d] *Ill* notwithstanding Trumbull Logan & Horace White. It looks now as though the re nomination and reelection of Gen Grant will be an easy thing. Ohio will give a big republican majority this fall. Penn is safe and sound—We stand a good chance to carry N. Y. were it not for the slate quarrels there would be no trouble—The President is away, in Chicago, will be here about the 8th. My family is still away, but will soon be home—about the Corean affair—probably nothing will be done at present, our Navy is too small to do much, so far from home. . . ." ALS, *ibid.*

On Aug. 24, Charles O. Ferris, Vallejo, Calif., wrote to USG. "Understanding from public report, that probabilities exist of hostilites commencing between the United States and the Corean Government, also that the United States are about preparing a Naval expedition to proceed to that country, and in anticipation that a Military force, may also be required I address you in my own behalf, desiring to obtain a commission to raise a Regiment of Volunteer Soldiers in this State, drilled either as Infantry or Cavalry, for the object above named. I am an American by birth—being born in Loudon Co Va and am 43 years of age   Bore arms in the Mexican War, Co G. 2nd U. S. Artillery, was also in the late Rebellion from its commencement to its end, . . ." ALS, DNA, RG 45, Letters Received from the President.

2. Edith Fish was the youngest of eight children. See *New York Times*, Dec. 1, 1873.

To Charles W. Ford

———

Long Branch, N. J.
Aug. 28th 1871

DEAR FORD:

I have written to Elrod directing him to get a proper man to look after the stock, and have sent him Mr. Jame's letter as a hint what should be looked after.[1]

I should like very much to get out to St Louis again this fall but see no chance of doing so. I shall leave here in about two weeks.

Yours Truly
U. S. GRANT

ALS, DLC-USG.

On Aug. 5, 1871, Charles W. Ford, St. Louis, had signed a petition to USG. "We the undersigned take a more than an ordinary interest in the welfare of every former Soldier of this Republic. We do not desire to indulge in any lengthened remarks upon the merits of John Tobin the subject of this appeal. Nor to go into the Stereotyped form of memorials. We say this because we know we are addressing a Soldier. Mr Tobin's long and active services in the regular Cavalry in Texas, New-Mexico, Utah, California, Oregon, and Washington-Territory, which are well known here, entitle him, we firmly believe to the recognition and patronage of the Executive of the Nation. . . . Having said thus much, we ask you Mr President to appoint him to an Indian-agency or to the position of Superintendent of Cemetries, or such other position which you may have in your disposition." DS (9 signatures), DNA, RG 94, Applications for Positions in War Dept. On Oct. 11, John Tobin, St. Louis, wrote to USG on the same subject. ALS, *ibid.*

1. See letter to William Elrod, July 30, 1871.

To James G. Blaine

———

Washington D. C.
Aug. 31st 1871.

DEAR MR. SPEAKER:

Your favor of the 28th inst. was received yesterday just before I started for Washington. I have given Mr. Hamlin, and two other gentlemen who called with him, a reply to the questions contained in your letter. I can reach Bangor on Tuesday evening, the 17th of Oct. and can remain *down East*, low down, until about Friday Morning. I can not however leave the limits of the United States. Some how I am under the impression that there is a Statute, or some provision, against the President leaving the territory of the U. S. However, whether there is or not, I think I will not be the one to establish the precedent of an Executive going beyond the limits of his country.[1]

I anticipate a very pleasant visit to Me. It will be the second time only that it has fallen to my lot to get so far East, and I never got among cleverer people.[2] When I was there before I had not yet become politician, had not arrayed a section and a half against me; and it was too just at the close of a great war in which the ignorant but enthusiastic Maine people, not looking to the New York World and other equally veratiou[s] democratic papers for true light, supposed I had taken a small part. Their ardor being cooled by time, and true light having been forced in in spite of Yankee prejudice in favor of a united country, may make a change now. I will trust myself among them again however, Providence permitting, taking all the chances of having very pleasant recollections dashed.

My kindest regards to Mrs. Blaine[3] and the children whom I hope are all well and enjoying their vacation

Yours Truly

U. S. GRANT

HON. JAS. G. BLAINE,
SPEAKER HOUSE OF REPS

ALS, DLC-Blaine Papers.

On Aug. 5, 1871, Speaker of the House James G. Blaine, Augusta, Maine, had written to USG. "John Holmes Goodenow of this state was appointed Consul Genl at Constantinople by Mr. Lincoln at the beginning of his second term March 1865—I have recently heard that a movement is on foot to induce his removal and the appt of another—I sincerely hope you will not remove Goodenow—He is a most excellent man and one of the best of officers and truest of Republicans—A very large personal interest is felt in his welfare among the best of our Maine people—and yr best friends—Allow him to remain till the first month of your second term and that will give him the eight years which you found so many office holders had enjoyed at your first inauguration—Political matters are looking well in all directions—The Democracy have lost ground fearfully within the last three months—There is some feeling among our own people about the Boutwell Pleasanton affair—I do not mean in the way of taking sides—but disturbed at such a prolonged contention between those who should be in harmony—I think the trouble should not be allowed to continue in its present shape" ALS, DNA, RG 59, Letters of Application and Recommendation. On

Dec. 8, 1875, USG nominated Eugene Schuyler as consul gen., Constantinople, in place of John H. Goodenow.

1. See letter to Hamilton Fish, July 21, 1871; letter to Lemuel A. Wilmot, Sept. 1, 1871.

2. On Oct. 20, 1871, USG spoke in Portland, Maine. "I have a vivid recollection of visiting your city six years ago. This is the second time that I have been in your city, and am much pleased with the reception here, as well as other places I have visited in your State. If I do not come oftener than I have heretofore I shall not make many more visits before I shall be an old man." *Boston Transcript*, Oct. 20, 1871. See *PUSG*, 15, 269–71.

3. On Sept. 2 and Oct. 19, Harriet S. Blaine, Augusta, Maine, wrote to Robert Walker Blaine. ". . . Your Father also had a very friendly and most excellent letter from the President. I had no idea that he would write so good a letter. He wanted to be remembered to you children. . . ." ". . . Father is in Bangor, accompanying the President. I took M. and J'aime and drove as near the depot as I dared Tuesday afternoon. There was a great crowd, and Grant was as miserable as is his wont on such occasions. . . ." Harriet S. Blaine Beale, ed., *Letters of Mrs. James G. Blaine* (New York, 1908), I, 24–25, 48. USG spoke briefly at Augusta on Oct. 17. *New York Times*, Oct. 18, 1871.

To Lemuel A. Wilmot

Washington, D. C. Sep. 1. 1871

DEAR SIR:

I have the honor to acknowledge the receipt of your kind favor of the 25th ult. inviting me to visit New Brunswick on the occasion of the opening of the European and North American Railway in October next.[1]

It would be very gratifying to me to be able to comply with your very kind invitation and would afford me personally great pleasure to be present upon so interesting an occasion, but it has never been the custom for the President to leave the United States during his term of office and I should not like to establish such a precedent. I must beg you to accept my sincere thanks for your kindness.

I have the honor to remain
Very respectfully yours
U. S. GRANT

HON. J. A. WILMOT, LT. GOVERNOR
FREDERICKTON, N. B.

Copy, DLC-USG, II, 1. Lemuel A. Wilmot, born in New Brunswick in 1809, studied at the College of New Brunswick and began to practice law in 1832. He served as New Brunswick attorney gen. (1848–51) and judge of the Supreme Court (1851–68) before becoming the first native-born lt. governor in July, 1868.

1. On Oct. 18, 1871, USG spoke at ceremonies opening the European and North American Railway, connecting Bangor and St. John, New Brunswick. "LADIES AND GENTLEMEN: I congratulate you and the people of the State of Maine and the people of the nation at large upon the occasion which has brought all of us here. It is a matter in which you are particularly interested, and the nation at large, I believe, is almost equally interested with you. I hope that this may prove to you and to us, all that is expected of it in fostering and building up a friendly feeling between us and the people of the same language as ourselves, and who, I think, are equally interested, in the most cordial friendship." *New York Times*, Oct. 19, 1871. On Oct. 19, USG spoke at Vanceboro, Maine, where the tracks crossed into New Brunswick. "FELLOW-CITIZENS AND CITIZENS OF THE BRITISH PROVINCES: It is pleasant for me to be here on this occasion, an occasion which will be celebrated in speeches by persons much more capable than myself of treating the subject. But I will say that it is a pleasure for me to hear and see citizens of the continent belonging to the two nationalities meeting in such friendly communion." *Ibid.*, Oct. 20, 1871. See preceding letter; *SMD*, 39-1-13; *SRC*, 41-1-4; Laura Elizabeth Poor, ed., *The First International Railway and the Colonization of New England: Life and Writings of John Alfred Poor* (New York, 1892).

To Virginia Grant Corbin

Long Branch, N. J.
Sept. 4th 1871

DEAR SISTER:

Julia is delighted at the idea of having you go out to Cincinnati with us, and said she would write to you to-day. I expect she will put it off for several days and then telegraph in a great splutter.— We expect to leave here on Tuesday morning. I will telegraph you however on Monday and let you know the exact day and hour when we will stop.

All send love to you—

Affectionately Yours
U. S. GRANT

MRS. JENNIE G. CORBIN,
ELIZABETH, N. J.

ALS, Berg Collection, NN. On Sept. 7, 1871, Horace Porter, Long Branch, wrote to William W. Smith, Washington, Pa. "The President wishes me to write you and say that he and the family will leave here on Wednesday morning next, stop a day with Coleman at Lebanon, and spend a few days in the oil regions. He will reach your place about Friday or Saturday, and will telegraph you definitely while *en route.* With kindest regards to Mrs. Smith, . . ." ALS, Washington County Historical Society, Washington, Pa. On Tuesday, Sept. 12, USG, Lebanon, Pa., telegraphed to Abel R. Corbin. "Let Jennie take morning train for Harrisburg Via Allentown and our special train Will attach at this place   Check Baggage no further than Harrisburg—" Telegram received, Nellie C. Rothwell, La Jolla, Calif.

To William Elrod

Long Branch, N. J.
Sept. 4th 1871,

DEAR ELROD:

I am just in receipt of your letter enclosing plan of a stable you propose building. You do not acknowledge receipt of check for $500 00 which I sent in my last letter! Nor do you say whether you will want more money to build with, nor how much. The stable is really very much wanted. I want it built if I am not to furnish too much money to build it with. I would change the plan however in one small particular. I would make at least eight box stalls, taking the place of sixteen or eighteen of the stalls, thus reducing the capacity of the stable from forty to thirty-two or thirty horses. More stables will have to be built afterwards, and I hope much better ones as the place pays the expense of them.

In regard to the matter of the purchase you speak of from the Qr. Mrs Dept. I know you do not understand the subject or you never would have made such a proposition. The legal agents sell all property of the United States which ~~have~~ has to be disposed of, and exactly as is provided for by law. No favor is secured to any bidder by any influence whatever. Your informant is mistaken if he thinks so. Sometimes possibly sales may be stopped because of the insufficiency of public bids. Private bids may then, in some cases, be received; but no assurance is given that a bid will be accepted. Write me what such a stable as you propose will cost, and how much money you will expect from me.

Yours Truly
U. S. GRANT

ALS, Dr. John T. Bickmore, Dayton, Ohio.

To Gerrit Smith

Long Branch, N. J., Sept. 4, 1871.

My Dear Sir—Your favor of the 11th of August enclosing me a few copies of an article[1] from your pen, favoring my re-nomination and election to the office of President, was duly received. I have no valid excuse for not acknowledging the receipt of it earlier and thanking you for your good opinion which I prize very much. The fact is I put your letter in my pocket, with many others, to prevent it being mislaid until an opportunity occurred to answer it. It has been there ever since. Please accept my thanks at this late day and overlook my negligence.

With great respect,
Your obedient servant,
U. S. GRANT.

HONORABLE GERRIT SMITH.

Octavius Brooks Frothingham, *Gerrit Smith: A Biography* (New York, 1878), p. 339. Gerrit Smith, born in 1818 in Utica, N. Y., advocated temperance and women's rights, but became best known for opposition to slavery and financial support of John Brown. A founder of the Liberty party, Smith served in Congress as an independent (1853–54), then embraced the Republican party, endorsing the reelection of Abraham Lincoln and the candidacy of USG. On Sept. 13, 1871, Smith, Peterboro, N. Y., wrote to USG. "On my return home after a short absence, I was happy to find myself honored with a letter from you. It is a much esteemed & very welcome letter. The Republican Party saved our nation. But if this Party shall now break up into factions & have a different Presidential candidate for each faction, it will make itself guilty of giving up the nation to destruction. God grant that it may be kept back from such suicidal folly & sin! There are a dozen men in the land, any one of whom would make a good President. But the Republican Party must unite on one of them, or fail. Manifestly, they can unite on no one but yourself—& on yourself I firmly believe they will unite. Please make my very kind regards to Mrs Grant" Copy, Syracuse University, Syracuse, N. Y.   See letter to Gerrit Smith, July 28, 1872.

1. Possibly a broadside printed by Smith in Aug., 1871. "It is but too probable that the republican party will sink down into a low chase with the democratic party after votes. So far from going forward, and making itself more and more a reform party, its murmurings against President Grant and frequent signs of disaffection toward him *reveal its declining appreciation of even those great moral ideas it had already espoused.* For to which of the grand undertakings and precious interests of the republican party, at the time of his election, *has he been found unfaithful?* To not one of them. Identified, therefore, as he is, *with them all, and the most prominent upholder of them all* every one of them is *necessarily disparaged when he is traduced or undervalued.* For the republican party to turn its back upon President Grant is to turn its back upon its honorable past—upon the past of its *better and more patriotic days.* He remains *the same man he was in those days.* He has proved himself to be free from the *accursed spirit of caste, and true to the equal rights of all men*—of the red man and black man as well as the white man. *He has deferred to the popular will, instead of moulding and fostering* a policy of his own. He has proved, with what *entire sincerity* it was that, in entering upon its office, *he expressed his desire* for peace. The late treaty between England and America *in the credit of which he shares so largely*, is the grandest and most auspicious peace measure the world has ever seen. The rapidity with which we are paying our national debt is a high proof *of his wisdom and honesty.* And yet, such a President, no very small share of the republican party—certainly no very small share of its leaders—seem willing to drop! We hear them say that General Grant cannot be re-elected. But if he, who confessedly, did more than any other man to save our country in the perils of war, and *whose great influence in peace has all gone to make that peace more perfect and more blessed*, cannot be made our next President, *what republican can be? Manifestly, either he or the democratic candidate will be our next President;* and if the democratic candidate shall be, and shall represent and be a specimen of the bad, very bad democratic party, what then can save our country from ruin?" Frothingham, *Gerrit Smith*, pp. 327–28. See *ibid.*, pp. 328–34.

To Hamilton Fish

Long Branch, N. J.
Sept. 10th 1871.

MY DEAR GOVERNOR:

I break up here on Tuesday, the 12th inst. but will not return to Washington before the 1st of Oct. Before that time it may be necessary to take some action towards the removal of the Russian Minister[1] if he should not be recalled by his Govt. My judgement is that he should be presented with his *walking papers* by our Govt.

if not recalled. In this matter however I defer entirely to your judgement. I will be in Washington, Pa on Friday next and will remain there until the following Monday. From there I go direct to Covington, Ky. where my address will be for the balanse of next week. After that letters addressed to me either at Chicago or Galena will reach me for a few days, up to my start direct for Washington. If you desire to consult me in this matter you can address as above.

I will not have with me a Secretary, and as I have not the key to the State Dept. Cipher I can not be consulted by telegraph when secrecy is required.

Please present Mrs. Grant's and my kindest regards to Mrs. Fish and family.

Yours Truly

U. S. GRANT

HON. H. FISH,

SEC. OF STATE,

ALS, DLC-Hamilton Fish. On Sept. 15, 1871, Secretary of State Hamilton Fish, Garrison, N. Y., wrote to USG, Covington, Ky. "I enclose a despatch dated 27th August from Mr Curtin, on the subject of Catacazy's recall—At its date he had not received a despatch which was sent him on 18th August, by mail, although he had a telegram from me of same date, which, it seems he did not receive until the 25th   Before I left Washington, (ten days ago,) I telegraphed again to Curtin, but have no answer—I have again telegraphed to him to know if he had received my last telegram—I think it probable that by this time some conclusion has been reached by the Russian Government—of which we should hear very soon—Throughout the whole of this business Mr Curtin seems to have been impressed by what he calls the 'seriousness' of the affair—He sends his telegrams, & confidential letters, by private conveyance to London to be forwarded thence—No doubt, there will be some disappointment among our people, should the visit of the Prince, be abandoned—& there will be an effort to excite feeling against the Administration—& there will also be the effort of other Powers to work up a jealousy, & mistrust between the two Governments— Our people have an exaggerated idea of the friendship of Russia for this Government—like all international friendships, this one is of interest rather than of sentiment or sympathy—but the popular belief that it is real, cannot be mistaken   Russia has used it, (as we have also done) as an element to operate upon other Powers, in negotiating with them—It may still be of some avail, to us, while the Arbitrations of the Alabama question & of the San Juan boundary are pending—and although the peremptory dismissal of a Minister would not afford any just grounds of complaint, it might produce some irritation, which would exhibit itself by arresting the visit of the Prince, of which an effort will be made to take advantage in connection with the pending Arbitrations—If you think these considerations of sufficient importance to postpone the dismissal of the Minister, I would suggest that a telegram be sent to Curtin saying that the Presidents desire to manifest his friendship for the Russian Government, and to receive the visit of the Grand Duke, determines him to endure the continuance of a very obnoxious Minister from that Government until after the visit of the Prince—after which he will be immediately dismissed unless recalled—& that in the mean time the President will not receive ~~him~~ the Minister, except in company with the Prince—A copy of this may be sent to M Catacazy and will, practically, be a dismissal to take effect at a not distant day—& will leave it with the Russian Goverment to decide whether the Prince shall be accompanied by a Minister thus denounced—Should you approve of this suggestion, please telegraph to me, to that effect, and I will immediately forward the telegram and note—or, if you think best to dismiss the Minister, immediately it will be done, unless some new phase is assumed by what may be done in St Petersburgh. We are in the midst of a Cold Season and I have had the Ministers of Austria, Spain, & Italy, on a visit for some days—My wife unites with me in most respectful regards to Mrs Grant—" ALS (press), *ibid.* The next day, Fish added a postcript to this letter. "While writing the foregoing letter, a long cipher telegram from Curtin was received at the Department—they have not been able to decipher it, so as to make out the whole of it— Catacazy has telegraphed to his Goverment of his call upon you, & that 'you had received him amicably & treated him with great courtesy.' Westman (the Vice Chancellor) says that 'the Grand Duke cannot come unless there be a Minister here, & there is not time to appoint another in Catacazy's place'—As far as I can understand the cipher, Westman expresses a wish that Catacazy 'be regarded as Minister until after the Prince's visit'—I will have the telegram repeated, & send you a copy if it be more intelligible—but think the substance is about what I have mentioned— Should you think advisable to allow Catacazy to remain until after the Princes visit, I would suggest to add to the telegram proposed in ~~the~~ my letter, that 'the President can hold no conversation with him—(Catacazy)   Please return the enclosed despatch of Govr Curtin—I have telegraphed to Mr Chew to send you, copies of Curtin's telegrams &c & despatches & beg you will take pains not to allow them to get out. A premature publication would add to the complication of the question—" AL (initialed—press), *ibid.* On Sept. 19, USG, Cincinnati, telegraphed to Fish. "Send such despatch as suggested in your letter of fifteenth in regard to Prussion Mission with any modifications suggested by more recent word from Minister Curtin" Telegram received, *ibid.*

USG had nominated Andrew G. Curtin as minister to Russia on April 12, 1869. On Aug. 27, 1871, Curtin, St. Petersburg, wrote to Fish. ". . . Since my telegram and despatch and private letter of the 7th July Mr. de Westmann has several times asked if I had heard from you and at once complained of the delay. He seemed much annoyed and distressed, and said that 'there was a time for everything; that the Grand Duke will sail on Wednesday and it is impossible to withdraw Mr. Catacazy and appoint a new Minister before his arrival in America. The Grand Duke could not make his visit unless the Empire was represented there by a Minister. I begged him to consider that it was the desire of the President to extend to the Grand Duke such amenities as would be most agreeable to him, and acceptable to the Emperor and people of Russia, but that he desired that the representative of Russia should not be a person obnoxious to him and one who has been in the habit of defaming him;. . . Pardon me, my dear Governor, if I exceed the proprieties of my place when I suggest, that if it is at all possible to tolerate the presence of Mr. Catacazy, the visit of the Grand Duke had better not be interfered with by the demand for the recall of the Minister. It would excite invidious comment in Europe, and it might be hard to explain the reasons to our people who seem to be much excited in anticipation of the event. I could not advise any undignified condescension on the part of the President and his Cabinet, and even in the face of an unpleasant explanation to our people if the conduct of Mr. Catacazy is of such a character as to make his presence intolerable I would not advise against such a responsability. . . . I need not say to you that in Russia the visit of a member of the Imperial family to a nation of such growing power as the United States and especially as free institutions are regarded in Europe as firmly established there—as an event of great political significance, and in the other countries of Europe it will be regarded as evidence of sympathy and friendship of the Governments and people of the two countries. Viewed from such a stand point you can understand how it is that an event so trifling in itself is magnified and realize why the apprehension of failure agitates the Officials here: Although it will be with extreme regret if not distress, yet I am quite sure if I insist upon this presentation of your despatch demanding the recall of the Minister to the Emperor,—the fleet will not cross the Ocean. . . ." LS, DNA, RG 59, Diplomatic Despatches, Russia. Related correspondence is *ibid.* See letter to Hamilton Fish, Sept. 19, 1871.

On July 14, Joseph Harrison, Philadelphia, wrote to USG. "At the suggestion of the Hon. A. E. Borie, who informs me that he has already spoken with you on the subject, I send the enclosed letter. If quite convenient to yourself may I ask the favor of its transmission at the proper time, to the person to whom it is addressed." ALS, DNA, RG 59, Miscellaneous Letters. On June 28, Harrison, an engineer who helped pioneer railroad construction in Russia, had written to Russian minister Constantin de Catacazy offering his Philadelphia mansion for the expected visit of Grand Duke Alexis Aleksandrovich. ALS, *ibid.* On July 17, Adolph E. Borie, Philadelphia, wrote to USG enclosing Harrison's letters. ALS, *ibid.*

1. See *PUSG*, 19, 535–36. On June 16, Fish wrote in his diary. "Catacazys case is brought up—I mention the purport of the Article in NY World of 29 Nov 1870 'Russia & America' and I traced it so as to leave little doubt in my mind that Catacazy had inspired, if not written it—to the Article from the Cincinnati Enquirer, copied into the NY Sun, some time in February last, which 'a gentleman' (Frank Turk—but I do not name him) had shewn me & said that Catacazy had admitted to him having written it—read Turks letter to me of 2d & 12th June—& the proposed draft of a letter to Govr Curtin requesting Catacazs recall—President suggests immediate dismissal—but I object—it is more courteous to the Russian Govt to ask his recall—to which he assents" DLC-Hamilton Fish. See Nevins, *Fish*, pp. 503–11.

To Orville E. Babcock

Long Branch, N. J.
Sept. 10th 1871

My Dear General:

On Tuesday I leave with my family for the West. The Steward,[1] servants and such property as ~~retur~~ returns to Washington start on the same day, or the day following. I wish as soon as you can have every thing in hand you would have the Steward discharged. It is not necessary that reasons should be given.

It will probably be the 1st of Oct. before I will return to Washington. Any thing addressed to me this week, to Washington, Pa and to Covington Ky.[2] for the next week will reach me.

Please present Mrs. Grant's and my kindest compliments to Mrs. Babcock, if She is in Washington. If she is in Chicago we will probably see her before you do.

Yours Truly
U. S. Grant

Gen. O. E. Babcock,
Com. Pub. Buildings.

ALS, Babcock Papers, ICN.

1. Valentine Melah, USG's steward, returned to Washington, D. C., "bringing with him the house servants and the President's horses." *Washington Chronicle*, Sept. 15, 1871. See *PUSG*, 19, 412–13; letter to Frederick T. Dent, Sept. 16, 1871. A "Steward and Waiting Maid" accompanied the Grant family on the western trip. [Titusville, Pa.] *Oil City Derrick*, Sept. 15, 1871. On Jan. 26 and Oct. 30, 1871, Orville E. Babcock wrote to Secretary of War William W. Belknap. "I am directed by the President to say that he will be pleased to have you enlist into the General Service John Henry Whitlow (colored) for duty at the Executive Mansion." "The President directs me to request you to order the discharge from the General Service of John H. Whitlow (colored), to date from the 1st of October; and the muster into the General Service of James B. Haliday to take effect on the 1st of November." Copies, DLC-USG, II, 1. On Oct. 31, Horace Porter wrote to Maj. William Myers, q. m. "John Henry Whitlow (colored) a General Service man, on duty at the Executive Mansion, has been mustered out of the Service, on the 1st of October, and should be cancelled upon your rolls." Copy, *ibid.* John H. Whitlow served as steward until the end of USG's administration. On Jan. 26, Babcock had written to Belknap. "I am directed by the President to say that he will be pleased to have you enlist into the General service, Geo. William Barnes (colored) for duty at the Executive Mansion." Copy, *ibid.* USG had previously

employed George W. (Bill) Barnes as servant. See *Julia Grant*, pp. 133–34; Jesse R. Grant, *In the Days of My Father General Grant* (New York, 1925), pp. 66–67, 210–11.

2. On Sept. 23, 1871, USG arrived in Covington, Ky., from Brown County, Ohio, and visited his father and Amos Shinkle. Local officials and citizens greeted USG that evening at Shinkle's residence. USG spoke following Mayor L. E. Baker of Covington. "MR. MAYOR: Through you I wish to tender my most hearty thanks for the greeting I have received from the citizens of Covington, and particularly am I grateful that it has not been an ovation shown to the Executive, because he was such, by a single political party. It will be my object, so long as I hold the office which I do, to be regarded as the President of the whole people; and there is no reason why the party in the minority should not receive the same protection and enjoy the same privileges as the party in power. I therefore return to you my most hearty thanks for the cordial greeting I have received from the citizens of Covington to-night." *Cincinnati Gazette*, Sept. 25, 1871.

On March 23, 1869, Shinkle, Covington, had telegraphed to Jesse Root Grant, Washington, D. C. "Am informed by H. Curtis that Rankin is appointed Assessor. If so how was it brought about" Telegram received (at 4:00 P.M.), DNA, RG 107, Telegrams Collected (Bound). On April 12, Jesse Grant and Shinkle, Covington, telegraphed to USG. "We would respectfully suggest that appointment of Judge for this District be deferred until receipt of letters this day mailed" Telegram received (at 7:00 P.M.), *ibid.* See *PUSG*, 14, 471.

On April 17, 1871, Jesse Grant wrote to USG. "I have been thinking of writing to you for some time, and there are various subjects on which I will say a little. First I will mention that an effort has been making for some months to create a new, or third party. I have wached its progress with a good deal of silent care & interest. I find it is led & managed largely by persons who have been disappointed in geting appointments. J. D Cox is a very prominant *leader*, what his motives, or what has caused his disaffection I cant learn—But one thing I have suspected—He is not heartily a Republican—I have learned that his Dept was largely filled with Reb Clerks. & attachees   Many think he did not lack much of being a Demt   Herr Hoserack [*Hassaurek*]—a very talented, & highly educated German—like Shurze—as the Constitution prohibits him from ruling the Nation, wants his influence felt in some other way—In '69 he got up a fusion ticket, & with his influence with the German element which holds the balance of power here, he succeeded in carrying. Herr Halstead of the Commershal is laboring for the cause but if it is likely to succeed he will go back on it—Magrue the dismissed Assessor of the Second district, and who went to San Domingo, as bearer of dispaches, as the papers say—He goes into this new party, or the Democratic party, which ever he thinks will be most likely to defeat you—Then there are three or four Judges who all wanted the place Swing got— They are all leaning to the new party—But this oposition will mostly all die out before the next Presidencial election   Gov Denason is said to lean that way—He wanted to be reappointed P. M G. and I always thought he shoud have been appointed—Then Len Harris is with them. The San Domingo Message, & all of your course gives general satisfaction. The appointment of Swing, is a most popular appointment, and one that none takes takes exception to, except perhaps those that wanted it themselves—And now the appointment of Gen Cowen is ano[th]er giving most perfect satisfaction   I have thought a good deal about a suggestion I made to you while in Washington about the full pardon of of John C. Breckinridge, & spoke to a few other prominant men on the subject. All agree it would be a good idea—

He has always been regarded as an honest man, and in Ky has always been popular— The state is hoplessly wrong—But the unasked for pardon of B. would do much to softening down the bad blood I understand that the Sherman influence is with this new party—Dayton & one other of Gen Shermans Staff signed the bill of Inditment against the policy of the Adminitstration And if that party is likely to succeed John Sherman will be with it There is one thing about Senator John that dont tell well for his Republicanism When Johnson was runing the government, through Democratic influence Murphy was appointed Collector. He offered Col Molton $1000 to Engineer him through the Senate. He & John Sherman put him through—I wrote to Sherman that Murphy was an open & avowed Rebble and otherwise an unreliable man, and advised him to prevent the confirmation—He wrote to me a very insulting letter. I put it into the fire, & dont remember the language, but the substance was, 'I know what I am about, you attend to your business & I will attend to mine'— And the result was that the collictions under Nixon which 2½ to 3 millions I have but little faith in the Shermans, or the Ewings—When I was last in Washington a Lady & her husband called on me, the Lady said to see if we were not related, &, if how near—I found her Grand father Isaac Kelly, was my Mothers Brother—He was a man of largely more than common abilaty. I lived with him about one year after my Mothers death—Uncle Isaack wife was of good abilaty, but not equal to himself—But the country was then new & the people unrefined, and they were rough Dimonds—I left the family 64 years ago, & have not seen any of them since except Uncle Isaac about 37 years ago. Dr Poe, who was agt of the Methodist Book concern, & whoes Mother I knew before I left Columbiana County, has often told me that, he taught a high school there, & Uncle Isaacs two sons attended—He says they were the most talented sholars he had—the oldest Daniel, (this Ladies father) studdied Medicine & was quite an eminent Dr—The other went into the Ministry. Mrs Bialy (for that is the Ladies name) says she is now the only one left of the family—I recd a letter from her a few days ago—She says, she has made several efforts to see you, but has never been able to pass GEN DENT—She says she wants to get her son who was with her when she called on me, appointed a Cadet—I will write to her to make another attempt to see you, and if as I suppose is the case, you have filled all your appointments, & there should be any to fail in their examination this young man may fill the vacancy—I will write again to morrow & send Mrs Balies letter—Her husband is a Book keeper in Treasury Dept—All well" ALS, Mrs. Paul E. Ruestow, Jacksonville, Fla. For Philip B. Swing's nomination as judge, Southern District, Ohio, and letters recommending Benjamin R. Cowen, see *PUSG,* 20, 363–64, 468–72. On March 20, William T. Otto had written to USG. "I have the honor to tender my resignation of the office of Assistant Secretary of the Interior." LS, OFH. On April 14, USG nominated Cowen as asst. secretary of the interior.

To Frederick T. Dent

———

Long Branch, N. J.
Sept. 10th 1871

DEAR GENERAL:

The letter of Mr. Belt, or Priest, I forget which, forwarded by you to me was only opened and read last evening. I can not lay my hand on the letter or I would return it. However in regard to the deed which I have for your land it need not prevent the sale for a single day. If the land is sold I will join you in making a deed to your seventy odd acres; or as soon as I return to Washington will quitclaim to you.

The circumstances of the Sheriffs deed to me are these: In /68,[1] while in Galena, I received notice that my farm was to be sold at the Courthouse doore within two days of that time on a judgement obtained against your father by Burnes.[2] I telegraphed Ford at once to pay the money and stop the sale. In as much however as I had paid off one Mortgage before, at an expense of $8000 00,[3] and had entered satisfaction without a sale to me, and as a sale of the property at that time, and record of Trustees Deed, would have secured me from the payment of a debt which was not contracted by myself, and which was fraudulent as against your father, I suppose fFord had the property sold under the execution, and the Sheriff's Deed properly recorded. This being the case I shall have to deed to Dr Sharp[4] & Wrenshall[5] before they can ever give a clear title.

I paid in that transaction, costs and all, about $1500 00   I never however expected to collect any portion of the money from the other owners of the land sold.

Yours Truly
U. S. GRANT

ALS, ICarbS. On Aug. 21, 1871, Henry B. Belt and John G. Priest, real estate agents, St. Louis, had written to Frederick T. Dent. "Mr Pitzman who drew the plat Sent to Mr. Huntington is not in the city and we can not Send copy before his return—We can find property as described assessed in your name—The land as described is assessed in the name of U. S. Grant and has been for two years past—(it may have been

conveyed to him the Assessor so informs us)   If you will Send us the tax receipts as
paid by yourself or Agent Since the assessment of two years ago, we will be pleased
to attend to the payment of taxes &c,   We herewith hand you a copy of the plat of
land Sold by the City of St Louis adjoining yours as indicated   We do not think
your way of laying it out a good one—had it not better conform to the Sale made
by the city of the McKenziee Tract   The Subdivision to be made of your land to
make it Sell can be arranged hereafter—Please advise us as to what we shall do"
LS, *ibid.*

    1. See *PUSG*, 19, 60–61.
    2. Calvin F. Burnes. See *ibid.*, 20, 145–47, 165; letter to William S. Hillyer, [*Jan.,
1873*].
    3. See *PUSG*, 16, 409.
    4. Alexander Sharp, husband of USG's sister-in-law Ellen Dent Sharp.
    5. George Wrenshall Dent, USG's brother-in-law.

To Josephine S. R. Hoey

————

Long Branch, N. J.
Sept. 11th 1871

My Dear Mrs. Hoey:

    I return by the bearer the cow which Mr. Hoey, your kind hus-
band, was kind enough to send me at the begining of the season,
and thank you and him for your many favors. To-morrow we break
up here with many pleasant recollections of Long Branch and the
agreeable acquaintances formed. We shall hope, however to meet
them all, in good health, at their old places, next season. Please
present Mrs. Grant's and my best regards to Mr. Hoey & your
daughter[1] when you write to them next, and say that we shall expect to meet them, and you, in Washington next winter.

With great respect
Your obt. svt.
U. S. Grant.

Copy, International Literary Bureau, NN. See *PUSG*, 20, 259.
    On Jan. 18, 1871, USG had written to "Ministers and Consuls of the United
States." "I take pleasure in introducing to you Messrs. Richard G. Murphy and George
C. Hoey of New York, who are making a tour around the world. I commend these
gentlemen to you and bespeak for them the good offices of all United States officials
residing abroad." Copy, DLC-USG, II, 1. On the same day, Horace Porter wrote to J. C.
Bancroft Davis, asst. secretary of state. "Messrs. Richard G. Murphy and George C.

Hoey purpose going on a trip around the world on board the 'Alaska', which sails next Saturday. I will be obliged to you if you will send to me all necessary papers for them securing passports and I will send them to these gentlemen at New York and be responsible for any requirements which may be necessary. Your early attention will very much oblige ..." LS, DLC-J. C. Bancroft Davis. Richard G. Murphy and George C. Hoey were the eldest sons of USG's friends, Thomas Murphy, collector of customs, New York City, and John Hoey, gen. manager, Adams Express Co. See *New York Times*, Oct. 3, 1883, April 12, 1890, Aug. 10, 1893. On April 18, 1872, USG wrote to John Hoey about appointing his son to the consular service. Charles Hamilton Auction No. 113, July 13, 1978, no. 159.

1. Josephine Hoey. See *New York Times*, June 7, 1905.

To John W. Forney

Lebanon, Pa. Sept. 12th *1871*

COL.

Mr. G. D. Coleman,[1] at whos house I arrived an hour ago, has just handed me your letter of yesterday, urging upon me to accept an invitation to be present at the unveiling of the Monument to Abraham Lincoln,[2] in Fairmount Park, on the 22d inst.—I regret that I cannot be present on so interesting an occasion. Had I known of this event before other arrangements, which can not well be changed, had been made I certainly would have entered into no engagement which would prevent my presence. But I am now on my way, with my family, to visit relations & friends among whom I was raised, and who I left thirty-two years ago, and who have been advised of the time of my coming. I do not see how I can make a change now, but permit me to express, through you, the regret I feel for it.

There are no Patriots, dead or alive, who will be remembered more gratefully for for their loyalty and services to their country than the man whos memory will be comemorated at Fairmount Park, Philadelphia, on the 22d of this September, nor none whom I more honor as a good, as well as a great, man.

I know the occasion will be an interesting one, and one long to be rememberd by those who witness it, and by posterity through the accounts of it which will be published.

With expressions of regret that I am to be debared the duty of being with you on the 22d ~~of~~ inst. and of the kindest regards for the Committee who have invited me, and for yourself, I subscribe myself,

> with great respect,
> your obt. svt.
> U. S. GRANT

COL. J. W. FORNEY,
PHILA PA

ALS (written on stationery of Lebanon Furnaces), Lehigh University, Bethlehem, Pa.

1. Son of an iron manufacturer, G. Dawson Coleman, born in 1825, graduated from the University of Pennsylvania (1843), briefly studied medicine, then entered the iron business (1846), building a furnace at Lebanon, Pa., with his brother, Robert. Coleman raised and equipped the 93rd Pa. Vols. and served in the Pa. legislature (1863–64, 1867–69). See *PUSG*, 20, 453; letter to G. Dawson Coleman, Dec. 31, 1873.
2. See *Philadelphia Inquirer*, Sept. 23, 1871; F. Lauriston Bullard, *Lincoln in Marble and Bronze* (New Brunswick, N. J., 1952), pp. 45–51.

Speech

[*Sept. 14, 1871*]

FELLOW-CITI[Z]ENS: I feel very grateful to you for this kind reception. This is my first visit to the oil regions.[1] I am aware that this section of the country furnished its full share of men and means for the suppression of the rebellion, and your efforts in the discovery and production of petroleum, added materially in supplying the sinews of war, as a medium of foreign exchange, taking the place of cotton. You are aware this is a much longer speech then I usually make. I again return you my thanks.

Titusville Herald, Sept. 15, 1871. Variant text in *Oil City Daily Derrick*, Sept. 15, 1871. USG responded to welcoming remarks at Titusville, Pa. Also on Sept. 14, 1871, USG spoke at Petroleum Center. "I acknowledge the courtesy and enthusiasm of this welcome. I have long wished to visit this section and anticipated much pleasure from the tour; but I was hardly prepared for such a demonstration here. I only regret I have not more time to enjoy your hospitality." *Ibid.* Later the same day, USG spoke at Franklin. "LADIES AND GENTLEMEN—I thank you most heartily for the cordial welcome that I have received here and throughout the oil regions generally, a pleasure which is enhanced by remembering, not alone how promptly Pennsylvania contributed her war quota during the rebellion, but also the importance of her oil products as an element of national wealth and resource during the same period. If I could speak as eloquently as my friend Judge McCalmont, whom I have known for many years, I should have pleasure in talking to you at greater length. As it is, I must content myself with again thanking you." *Venango Citizen*, Sept. 21, 1871.

1. On Aug. 21, Horace Porter, Long Branch, had responded to an invitation. "The President directs me to acknowledge the receipt of your letter of the 4th inst., and to convey to you his thanks for the very kind invitation which you have extended to him, to visit your section of Pennsylvania this season. It is his present intention to be with you about the 15th of September, and during his visit it will afford him great pleasure to examine, personally, the oil producing region of your State." *Ibid.*, Sept. 7, 1871.

To Frederick T. Dent

———

Washington Pa
Sept. 16th 1871,

DEAR DENT:

Say to Gen. Babcock, when he returns, that Mrs. Grant paid the female servants their pay up to the 1st of Sept. Also ask him to get from the Steward his receipts ~~and~~ for moneys paid, and memorandum book so as to avoid paying the . . . I wish you would see Capt. Ammen and secure, if possible, the cook he spoke of some time since. We will return about the second or third of Oct. and will want her then. The Steward has telegraphed me to be allowed to retain his position until I return. I did not answer it however and think he might as well leave now as later. If he chooses to resign however he can do so. We leave to-morrow for Cincinnati. Will . . .

AL (mutilated), Main Street Fine Books & Manuscripts, Galena, Ill. Valentine Melah, "the steward at the President's House, has resigned his position there, with the intention, it is stated, of opening a club house in this city. No successor has yet been selected." *Washington Chronicle*, Sept. 26, 1871.

Speech

———

[*Sept. 19, 1871*]

GENTLEMEN: It is very pleasing to me to meet you on 'Change to-day, and thank you as well as the citizens of Cincinnati generally for the very hearty and generous welcome which I have received here in almost the home of my youth and birth. It has not been my good fortune to visit this city so often in the past quarter of a century as I would like to have done, but the few times I have been able to come here, I have always been kindly received; and I remarked this morning[1] that it was particularly gratifying to me to know that I am received by the citizens of Cincinnati as the people of one nation and not as a single party.[2] In other words, that this welcome has been extended as the citizens of our common country, which I love and hope to be ever prosperous. I believe that such a course is better for all parties on occasions of this character, where political questions have no significance, and better for the party which happens to be ruling at the time. Gentlemen, I thank you.

Cincinnati Gazette, Sept. 20, 1871. USG spoke following John Morrison, vice-president, Cincinnati Chamber of Commerce. USG later held a public reception at the Burnet House, visited the Industrial Exposition, and attended *Rip Van Winkle* at Pike's Opera House with his two younger sons. *Ibid.* On Sept. 20, 1871, USG left Cincinnati to visit relatives in Brown and Clermont counties, Ohio. *Ibid.*, Sept. 21, 1871.

1. On the morning of Sept. 19, following a procession to the Burnet House, Republican Mayor Simon S. Davis of Cincinnati introduced USG as "an old neighbor." USG responded. "Mr. Mayor: It affords me very great pleasure to get back again to the scenes of my youth, among my old neighbors and friends, who were my friends long before I ever dreamed of leaving the peaceful avocations of an Ohio citizen. It is very gratifying to be received by citizens without distinction of party—much more so than to be the mere guest of a party. I thank the citizens of Cincinnati, through you, Mr. Mayor, for the very hearty welcome with which they have honored me." *Ibid.*, Sept. 20, 1871. Realizing that he had spoken too softly to be heard, USG asked Benjamin Eggleston to announce that he had concluded his speech. USG had remarked earlier to Davis about cries from the crowd: "There it is; you never can get half a dozen American citizens together without their wanting a speech." *Ibid.*

2. On Jan. 16, Horace G. Stoms, assessor of Internal Revenue, Cincinnati, had written to USG. "[Strictly private and confidential.]. . . Information comes to me that through the influence of Mr. Jesse R. Grant Messrs. Pullan and Weitzel have been selected as Collector and Assessor of the First and Second Ohio consolidated districts. Mr. Jesse R. Grant has been in favor of my removal for over a year for the following reasons, viz.: Mr. Grant requested of me the reappointment of a removed Gauger (displaced for malfeasance in office), accompanied with a proposition that I sincerely trust that I may never be compelled to disclose to any but yourself. He, Mr. Grant, in conversation with me made use of these words substantially: 'So and so has offered me five hundred dollars if I can get you to recommend his reappointment; he is a rascal, but I will take his money and divide with you.' I declined, hence his opposition. My numerous friends here are curious to know why Mr. Grant, my *supposed* warmest advocate, did not secure for me either the Assessorship or Collectorship of the proposed consolidated districts. I trust when I hear from you I will be enabled to reply that there is no further occasion to interrogate me upon the subject." *Ibid.* (bracketed material in origi-

nal), March 29, 1871. On the same day, William Stoms, Cincinnati, wrote to USG. "[Private and confidential.]. . . In all your eventful career in the army and Presidency, I have ever been your unflinching friend. An imperative duty now demands at my hands the indictment of a letter to you of an extremely painful nature. The newspapers are reporting the discharge of my son, Capt. Horace G. Stoms, from the Assessor's office of the First Ohio District, *through the influence and request of the President's father!* Now, Mr. President, if you knew all the facts in this case, that deed would never have been perpetrated! My son has lost a small office, because of his sterling integrity. A few discreditable people, in this region, finding out that the President's father had a weakness in the love of money, sought his influence with my son to be made Gaugers by bribery. To the everlasting surprise of my son, and myself, the President's father proposed acceptance of these bribes! My son refused, and hence the trouble! To this day, out of pure pity for the infirmity of the President's father, and respect for the President himself, the matter has been kept from publicity. Suffice to say an exposure would dishonor his name, and damage the party following so closely his advice against the troops of friends who had indorsed my son. And now, Mr. President, I am a man of character, and speak to you of that *which I do personally know.* I would be glad of a private interview, but just now that is not possible. What I have written to you is done more in sorrow than in anger. All my son wants is stern justice, and this he has not had. The office he had was of much smaller import than those of the Second District. I mean in salary. The consolidation made an office of which no one was more worthy to fill than he. No mortal knows of my sending you this letter, not even my wife or either of my sons. And all I have to say in conclusion is, to 'Let Justice be done, if the heavens fall.'" *Ibid.* (bracketed material in original). Horace Stoms had resigned as capt., 39th Ohio (1864). On Feb. 13, 1868, President Andrew Johnson nominated Stoms as assessor of Internal Revenue, 1st District, Ohio.

On March 20, 1871, Jesse Root Grant, Covington, Ky., wrote to the editor of the *Cincinnati Gazette.* "If I remain silent, people will think that what the Stomses have said and what reporters have told as being said by me is true. I have to defend myself, as the Republican papers act as though it would be better for the party to let me be buried alive by the Stomses than to offend them. If it would, I can not consent to it. My good name is dearer to me than the success of any party. The cause of my trouble is in having placed confidence in the Stomses. This is the way I came to have any: I was going along Lower Market street, about a month before the Chicago convention met, when a young man came out of a store and said his father wanted to see me. I did not know who his father was. He said Mr. Stoms. I did not know any more than I did before, but followed him in. A very pleasant, smiling little man met me; was glad to see me, said he was Chairman of the Republican committee of Hamilton county, and was going to get elected a delegate to the Chicago convention on purpose to vote for General Grant. He saw me two or three times before the convention, and after the nomination kept coming often, and whenever I was near his store they would run after me to come in. He was very pleasant. He is a talkative, confidential kind of man. Toward the end of February he came and gave me tickets for Miss Grant and myself, and said the railroad company had sent them. I never expected him to get any tickets, or do anything. He went on the same train with us, and did every little thing to make the journey pleasant. On the way he told me all about his son Horace, the Assessor of the First District; what a good soldier he was, and what a good Republican he had always been, although President Johnson did appoint him, and that he was a first rate young man, and very popular. During the journey, and at times when we met before, he told me all about himself—that he was one of the original Republicans, and had always worked hard, and spent a good deal of money for the party, and thought he ought to have General McGroarty's place, the Collector of the Second District. He said if he got that, his son Horace would give up the Assessor's office. After the inauguration, I told the President all about Mr. William Stoms, and how kind he had been, and asked him to appoint him Collector of the Second District. He did not say what he would do. We returned home on the 26th of March. About a week after I saw in the dispatches that the President had decided to appoint somebody else than William Stoms Collector of the Second District, and to turn out Horace from the Assessor's office in the First. Immediately I wrote and made an earnest request that the son of my friend might be retained. I always thought it was this request that caused Horace's retention. But he says now that it was not, but that he is under obligations to his friend Secretary Cox for keeping him in his place. I hope it is so, for it will relieve me of a heavy burden. I called on Horace the first time I went over to Cincinnati after my return from Washington. It was the first week in April, 1869. I think it was the first time I had ever seen him to speak with him. I told him that a person in Covington, who had been a Gauger, wanted me to ask if there was any chance for his getting an appointment as Gauger. He said that he was very glad of the opportunity. This man's name was Pease. He had been very kind and attentive to me, just like Mr. William Stoms, and I came to like him in the same way. A few days afterward I gave Mr. Sackett a note, recommending him for a Gauger. That is all I did in his case. Both Pease and Sackett were appointed without hesitation. A few days afterward, it was about the middle of April, 1869, I told William Stoms, at his store, that several merchants in the bottom had asked me to speak to him about two of the oldest and most experienced Gaugers in the city—Taylor and Weithoff. He said Taylor was a drunkard worth $75,000, and Weithoff was a rascal. I told those who had spoken to me what Mr. Stoms said. Everyone said Weithoff was an industrious, hard working Dutchman, who did his work well and was not a rascal, and that Horace was trying to turn him out because he had not worked to elect his father. One of them, in talking, said that he would give $500 to have Weithoff appointed. I went again to William Stoms' store, and told him all I had heard; that I knew Taylor was not a drunkard, and that every one gave Weithoff a good name; that he ought not to suffer because of what that man said, and that he had better take the $500, and give it to the poor, and try Weithoff, and if he ever did anything wrong to turn him out. I do not believe Wm. Stoms looked upon the remark of the man as an offer to bribe any more than I did. He did not say so, at any rate. His whole talk was to abuse Weithoff, and this made me want to have him appointed more, because it proved what I had been told that he was an obstinate kind of Dutchman, who could not be used by old Billy—this was the name he went by with some of his neighbors that spoke to me—and might blow on some things he was fixing up to make money out of the gauging business for his relatives. I thought, if there was anything in this, I would try and stop it without hurting any one's feelings. It was on this account I talked with the father about it, and did not say anything to the son. What I said was taken so hard that I let the matter drop, and did not think anything more about it, which I surely would if I had been conscious of having done any wrong. . . . This state of good feeling continued to near the close of the year 1869, although something took place in August that disturbed it some. One thing was that I found the gauging business was carried on as I was told Mr. Wm Stoms intended to fix it, and without saying anything to the Stomses about it, I asked Mr. Delano to appoint Mr. Beck Gauger, and the first thing they knew of it was when they got the notice from the department. They did not know exactly how it came about, for they knew that Mr. Beck's services to the government in exposing rascality in Johnson's time was well known there. Another thing was that I showed Wm. Stoms, at his store, a letter I had received from Mr. Delano, and told him Horace ought to do what was asked, and appoint somebody else for his chief clerk. I talked to him like a friend, and told him that his remaining there would only make trouble for them; that there was no use trying to fight public opinion when it was right; that I felt myself that a man who had been convicted of one of the blackest crimes, and who had been kept out of the Penitentiary by the tricks of lawyers, had no business in a public office, where every one had to come to do business, and where his presence was an offense to the many friends of the family he had injured. He was very angry, and cursed and swore awfully. I always thought he was a member of the Methodist Church before that. I did not suppose he harbored any malice because I had talked to him, but it seems from the date of a certificate of Pease, that he publishes, that he did. The thought then likely came up that he could make some use of the conversation about Weithoff in April, but he did not show it, and our meetings continued friendly until a week or two after Wright Clarke came here, I think in December. I called at his store, and told him that Horace had tried to insult me in the manner he had turned Pease off. I told him that Pease and Sackett were the only men that had been appointed at my request, and ought to be treated as well as the others, and not turned out without any hearing or any notice, and told him that Horace ought to do as he would be done by, and think how he would feel if he was treated in that way. As soon as the words were out of my mouth my old friend said with an oath: 'If that is ever tried, somebody else will have to suffer.' Who it was he did not say, and I never knew until, about the 22d of January, 1871, I received a few lines from the President, with two letters inclosed, written to him by Wm. Stoms and Horace Stoms. They shocked me   I would not have cared if they had been sent to anybody else, but it was too bad to send them to my own son without even giving me a chance to deny the charge they made. The ingratitude and perfidy of these two men bewildered me. When talking to persons about them I have given way to my feelings, but the provocation ought to be an apology for any want of discretion. Their wickedness was made worse by the way they took to make their attack upon me appear as if it was to vindicate themselves against what I said. Now I was careful not to say anything about them except to my near friends. About a month after I received the letters one of the city papers had an account of a private conversation with me. It seems I had been deceived by an impostor, who had called to see me to express the pleasure he felt at seeing his old classmate and intimate friend confirmed as Minister to Denmark. He talked familiarly about things connected with my family, and I was much entertained by his talk. If he told his name I have forgotten it, but he lived in Xenia. I believe now that somebody sent him to find out whether I had heard anything of the two letters, and to tell anything I said. Somebody, who was willing to believe such a thief, made a long story out of what he told him, and published it. Every one knows what use the Stomses and their friend Bloss made of it. They tried to drive me to publish their confidential letters, and, when I would not, they did it. Wm. Stoms said he had kept no copy of his, but published what he could recollect of it, and Bloss published Horace's from recollection after hearing it read, as Horace would not let him have the letter itself. I here give the exact copy of the letters to show what good memories Stoms and Bloss have. Horace's letter has the marks of having been copied into a book by the letter press. If what I have said does not prove that the charges in the letters are malicious and false, it is no use for me to say so again:... Before I close I will correct other falsehoods that have been spoken, saying that I have been setting up the offices here. This is all I can remember doing: I wrote a letter recommending Mr. Stephenson for the Custom House, and I tried all I could to get the Postoffice for Fred. Mayer. I do not remember of ever hearing of Weitzel or Pullan, until after they were made Collectors, and I never wanted Shaw for Assessor. All I did about the Supervisor's office was when Wright Clarke sent for me to help him turn out Weitzel and Pullan, and put John Hooker and James Sands in their place. Then I blew up the whole plot that Stoms and Sands and that set had laid to get hold of the revenue offices. I think I did some good then in stopping the whisky and tobacco ring from starting again. I do not remember ever to have said anything about any of the other offices. The only thing about the offices here that I ever *thought* the President did for me, was to leave Stoms in the office Johnson gave him, and he has turned out so bad that I conclude to give no more recommendations. I find good men do not come for them, and mean ones do; one or two of that kind have lately. I think the papers will not make anything by abusing me, now nearly eighty years old, only because I am the President's father, nor that all of them put together can cause him to honor his father and mother less in the future than he has in the past, even as God has commanded him." *Ibid.* Editorials in the *Cincinnati Gazette* on March 29, April 1 and 3, defended Jesse Grant. On April 3, 1869, USG had nominated Richard B. Pullan as collector of Internal Revenue, 2nd District, Ohio, in place of Stephen J. McGroarty. On the same day, USG nominated Lewis Weitzel as collector of Internal Revenue, 1st District, Ohio. On Jan. 30, 1871, USG nominated Weitzel as assessor of Internal Revenue, 1st District, Ohio, following consolidation of the former 1st and 2nd Districts.

On Dec. 20, Jesse Grant, Covington, wrote to USG. "I wrote to you on the 16th & through mistake dated it 9th. You better look that letter through carefully, and note my suggestions. I now write a sort of continuation of the subject—There are in Cin three Rings all professing to be working in & for the Republican party. First there is the Cronicle ring   The Cronicle is the only real Republican paper in Cin. But it is badly weighed down by *Dead* weights. First there is the Hon Ben Egglesto, the most perfectly 'played out' man in the city—Then Jas Fitzgerald, he has not been quite played in—They were the self constituted committee, to take care of you—The Sands I am not acquainted with, but they are not well spoken of. Cal Thomas is the late P. M. And really is of *no* force only to drink beer—These men are a dead weight to the Cronicle   The second Ring profess to be, & really are Union men & Administration Republicans—They hold to the Gazette   I have but little to say of them—The third ring are the New Departures   They are led by J. D. Cox Housreck Gen Noyse, Senetor Young, Halsted &c—They are the most noisy, & most industrious of any, & outside of intrig Cunning & fraud, of the least force—If the Presedencial election were to come off this week you would you would get as large a vote in Cincinnati & in the state as you did before—The Masses are right only sore heads & Demagogues are making a fus to carry a point—That made Noyse Govenor, & they want it to make J. D Cox Senator   Noyse & Young went to Washington to get Pullen removed to make a nice place for Dan Webber, and in some way to cripple the Cronicle   Dan has been one of the noisest of the new Departurists. He has cursed the Administration, & denounced you personally—But I am told he is now a good Grant man   Now I wach this matter & see how it is going—I have nothing to loose or gain, but I feel like leting you know the facts, that you may be on your guard. I think Pullen" AL (incomplete), Mrs. Paul E. Ruestow, Jacksonville, Fla. Ellwood S. Miller, clerk, Covington post office, added a note to this letter. "Mr Grant requests me to say that he considers that Gen'l Garfield is not your friend, and calls attention to the fact that W. E. Davis is on State Central Committee of Ohio and President of Hamilton Co Republican Ex Committee also President of

Chronicle Co—Mr. Sands of Chronicle Co is also on State Central Committee of Ohio—The Chronicle is the only paper that has given you its unqualified support. Mr Grant seemed very anxious to have this added to his letter and sent immediately He could barely articulate" ANS (undated), *ibid.* On Dec. 21, a newspaper reported. "A telegram from Cincinnati last night announced that Jesse R. Grant, father of the President, was stricken with paralysis in the post office at Covington, Ky., yesterday afternoon. He fell to the floor, and remained insensible an hour, but was able to sit up and converse afterwards." *Washington Evening Star,* Dec. 21, 1871. On Jan. 10, 1872, Horace Porter wrote to Postmaster Gen. John A. J. Creswell. "The President will be pleased to have you designate an Agent of your department to take charge of the Post Office at Covington, Ky: during the illness of Mr. Grant." Copy, DLC-USG, II, 1.

On Jan. 18, 1871, Orville E. Babcock had written to Joseph H. Barrett, editor, *Cincinnati Daily Chronicle and Times.* "*Personal* ... The President is in receipt of your letter and directs me to inform you that he has already intimated to the heads of departments that it is his wish to have such advertisements as can be, given to your paper" Copy, *ibid.*

To Hamilton Fish

CINCINNATI, Sept. 19th *1871*

DEAR GOVERNOR;

I have read the copies of dispatches passed between you and Minister Curtain, relative to Mr. Chatecazi, and returned them to the State Dept.[1] The course you recommend is no doubt right, but I feel very much like sending Mr. C. out of the country verry summarily. The idea of his making an interview with me, sought by him self, and when he was notified in advance that the subjet of the charges against him could not be discussed except through the Sec. of State, the ground of proof that he was well received except by the State Dept. is too bad. No Minister of any pride of character would concent to remain at a Capital after just such an interview as Mr. C. had with me. How he is to be received now at any entertainment given to the Prince[2] I do not exactly see. We will settle this however when I go back to Washington, which will be in about two weeks from this time.[3]

Yours Very Truly
U. S. GRANT

HON. H. FISH
SEC. OF STATE

ALS, DLC-Hamilton Fish. USG wrote on stationery of the Burnet House in Cincinnati. On Oct. 7, 1871, Secretary of State Hamilton Fish wrote to Elihu B. Washburne, Paris. "Personal & unofficial ... The President returned last Evening—in good health & spirits—his vacation has been of service, he is looking better than he has been for two years—whether this is owing wholly to relaxation, or how far the result of recent elections, & the prospect of those about to take place contribute, I will not undertake to say—but passing an hour with him last Evening, I could not fail to notice his cheerfulness, & his hopefulness—he thinks we shall have 40.000 majority in Ohio, next week & that the Legislature will surely be Republican—Delano put the majority at 30.000, & 'felt confident' of the Legislature—... I enclose an Article on Catacazy— which I have furnished—his conduct has been atrocious—continual low intrigue, & resort to the newspapers, with calumnious insinuations against the President and other officers of the Government, & against private Citizens—The *immediate* cause for the demand of his recall, was the obtaining evidence that he had furnished an Article to a Democratic paper (he admitted to a friend, ~~from~~ whom I compelled to give me the information in writing, that he had *written* the article) charging the President with a pecuniary interest in the Perkins claim—he has been making this claim his grand 'pièce de rèsistance,' and continually obtruding it in the public prints since his first arrival here—the scandal of his private & domestic life, is terrible—but with that we cannot officially concern ourselves—he is a first-class scamp, & his reputation with his Diplomatic Colleagues is infamous—I believe, that without a solitary exception, they detest & despise him—several of them have expressed their opinions of him to me, & wondered that we 'tolerated' him so long—Westmann, for some time refused to entertain our demand for his recall—talked of its being a 'very serious' thing— that he would not dare mention it to the Emperor—We insisted—& would have dismissed him—then it *was* mentioned to the Emperor, who 'requested that the President would *tolerate* him until after the visit of the Grand Duke'—this was conceded to the request of the Emperor, but had been refused to the request of the Vice Chancellor—but with the declaration that the President would not again receive him, unless when he accompanies the Grand Duke, & on no occasion would hold any conversation with him—After he had been informed by me of the request for his recall, he went to Long Branch, forced himself upon the President, who told him he wd hold no conversation on the subject, & treated him with the greatest possible coldness, he telegraphed however to his Govt that the President had received him with the greatest cordiality & friendship & had addressed him as 'my dear Mr Catacazy' &c—&c—the knowledge of this misrepresentation, inclined the Prsdt very strongly, to dismiss him, but as he had authorised a telegraph to say he would be 'tolerated' for the time it was adhered to, but the actual relation in which he was to stand was defined—I mention these particulars that you may be in possession of the facts, in case the subject be alluded to—He has endeavoured to represent to his Govt that the 'Perkins claim' & his resistance to it, is the cause of his unpopularity in this Country—while in truth, *he alone* has agitated this claim—we have only required that it be *investigated* & have not pressed it—He knows that Gortchacow is determined not to allow the claim, & he tries to minister to the old Chancellor's prejudices & passions—" ALS, DLC-Elihu B. Washburne. See *PUSG*, 19, 535–36.

On Nov. 14, 15, and 17, Fish wrote in his diary. "Question is raised as to Catacazys position—President states that he is only tolerated for the purpose of attending the Grand Duke—that he is not to receive the honours due to a Minister fully accredited—& directs the Secretaries of War & Navy to write to the Officers in Command at NY that no salutes or other honours are to be paid to him unless when he accompan-

ies the Grand Duke—" "In the Evening Genl Gorloff, presents a letter from Catacazy & asks the construction of the concluding sentence in the note of 10th inst. written to Catacazy—this note was written by Mr Hunter, & the sentence is very
unfortunate, it is as follows—that his passports 'will be ~~sent~~ transmitted *when this
Government shall consider the visit of His Imperial Highness the Grand Duke Alexis as concluded'*—He is told that there is no desire to indicate the time when the visit of the
Grand Duke shall be considered as concluded—but that Mr Catacazys sustained in-
trigues & interference, of which daily reports reach us, will probably induce the delivery of the passports immediately after the visit of the Grand Duke to the President—
He thinks it will be unfortunate, & I express regret that necessity compels this Course,
but it is the result of Mr C's conduct—Refer to his note announcing the granting him
'leave of absence' & say its in violation of the understanding that he was to be recalled
that this Govt asked last June the termination of his official relations—had a right to
insist upon it—was delayed—& finally acceded to request of the Emperor to *tolerate*
&c, with the promise that he would be 'recalled' which would *terminate* his relations—
the 'granting of leave of absence' will not terminate, but leaves him still accredited as
Minister—with liberty to return—that C. has boasted that he would go to Russia 'on
leave' & return, when a different or better Administration should be in power here—
that we do not care to have him travelling through the Country in his official capacity,
intriguing against the interests & the policy of the Country, in its relations with other
Powers—He asks if some Compromise could be effected—I ask what he has to propose—he replies that he is not instructed to make any suggestion—to which I answer
that the suggestion coming from him, the proposal should come from him—that I am
ready to hear any proposal he or Catacazy may have to make—He contends that the
'granting of leave' to return to St Petersburgh is only a different mode of recalling
him—which I positively deny, ~~& say that if so that explan~~—he says that it is not
intended that he return to the US. to which I reply that if such is the intention &
purpose of the Russian Govt it was due as a proper respect to this Govt to have made
that explanation either through Mr Curtin, or in some other appropriate way, & not
have left it for C— to send a note, (the purport of which he had already published
through the newspapers) stating that on *his own request* leave of absence was granted
him, instead of his being recalled on the request of this Govt as was promised—" "...
Genl Gorloff calls in the Evening—proposes what he calls a compromise, & to read
certain papers: before he reads these I tell him that I can only listen to them informally,
to which he replies 'certainly—altogether informally'—He then reads extracts from
what he says is a letter from Mr Westmann to Catacazy giving our account of the
interview with Curtin at which the Emperor's request that Catacazy be 'tolerated' was
authorised to be made—the letter (as read by him) gives a different version of the
Emperor's request from that in Curtin's despatch—also my telegram & reply, in which
among other things it is stated, that 'the President will receive him (Catacazy) in company with the Grand Duke' instead of that 'he would not receive him unless when he
accompanies the Grand Duke.'—He then states that C— proposes to withdraw his
note of 2d inst—(announcing that his Govt at his own request had given him leave of
absence after the Princes visit) and to substitute another saying that his Govt had
'instructed him to return' after the Princes visit—and he reads a paper in which Catacazy promises certain things—that he will not make public demonstrations—&c &c
Genl G admits that the notice given by C— in his note of 2d inst—was inconsistent
with what this Govt had the right to expect—He thinks that exaggerated reports
of what C— has done reaches us—that he is beset by Reporters, & if he says nothing
they are angry—if he says any thing they exaggerate or mis represent him   I de-

cline the proposition—We had intended to await the end of the Grand dukes visit—but the notice of 2d Novr was a departure by Russia on her part from the understanding and we were thereby absolved—that C— has continued to violate proprieties—that when we agreed to 'tolerate' him, we had a right to suppose he would observe a proper line of conduct—but he had not—& even within the last week I heard of his intriguing in order to defeat our negociations with G. B. & to embarrass our position before the Tribunal at Geneva, that we should therefore give him his passports as soon as the Grand Duke had called upon the President—He refers to C's promises & guarantees of good behaviour—I reply that unfortunately we cannot place confidence in them—that unless C— is intriguing he is nothing—(he subsequently repeated this remark of mine which he said was just)   I mentioned to him his denial of the letter in the World & the Article in the Cincinnati Enquirer—& his Connection with the 'forged despatches' (as C. calls them)   He professed to be shocked—spoke of the disappointment the People would experience if the visit of the Prince were interrupted—is told that the company of the Minister is not essential, that Prince Arthur, & (I believe) Prince Albert had not been accompanied by their Minister in their journeyings through the Country neither had Prince Napoleon—and assured him that the Prince wd be cordially welcomed wherever he should go, and would be more kindly received without C— than with him   During the conversation Catacazys attempt to make it appear that a social question was connected with his troubles was referred to, and positively denied—explanations given of his personal reception, & of the respect & treatment of Mr C—" DLC-Hamilton Fish.

1. See letter to Hamilton Fish, Sept. 10, 1871. On Dec. 6, Fish wrote to USG. "The Secretary of State, to whom was referred the Resolution of the Senate of the 5th instant, requesting the President to communicate to that Body 'if in his opinion this should not be contrary to the public interest, all official correspondence upon the subject of the retirement of Mr Constantin Catacazy, Envoy Extraordinary and Minister Plenipotentiary of His Majesty the Emperor of Russia, to the United States,' has the honor to lay before the President the correspondence above referred to, and which is specified in the list hereto annexed." LS, DNA, RG 46, Presidential Messages. On the same day, USG wrote to the Senate. "I transmit to the Senate, in answer to their Resolution of the 5th instant, a report from the Secretary of State, with accompanying papers." DS, *ibid.* See *SED*, 42-2-5.

2. Grand Duke Alexis Aleksandrovich, born in 1850, the fourth son of Czar Alexander II, arrived in New York City on Nov. 20, 1871, and visited the White House on Nov. 23 as part of a three-month U.S. tour. On Nov. 23, Orville E. Babcock wrote to members of the cabinet. "The President directs me to inform you that the Prince will be received at the Executive Mansion to-day at one o'clock. The President will be pleased to have you (and Mrs.—) present, and to have you appear in dress coat with black neck tie." Copy, DLC-USG, II, 1. On Nov. 21–24, Fish wrote in his diary. "Late in the evening a telegram was recd from Catacazy announcing that the Grand Duke would leave NY tomorrow, & desire to pay his visit to the President on Thursday if convenient   I took it to the President, & with his approval replied that he would be pleased to receive H. I. H on Thursday at such hour as shall be Convenient, to be agreed upon—Wednesday—Novr 22   Catacazy calls a little past 8 in the Evening, 'by orders of H. I. H. to announce his arrival'   I enquire at what hour tomorrow it will be agreeable to his Highness to call upon the President—he replies at what ever hour the President shall designate—I answer that the President names the

hour which will be most agreeable & convenient to the Prince—He then suggests
One *PM*—... I then ask what will be the order of introduction &c   he replies that
the Prince will introduce himself, inasmuch as he (C) has been informed that the
President will hold no conversation with him—I reply it is true the President will
hold no conversation with you, but he does not prohibit you doing what is appropriate to your official position   it will be better to observe the same Course pursued
when Prince Arthur was here—he & his suite, & the British Minister &c at the
appointed hour, attended at the White House were shewn into the Blue Room—the
President & Cabinet then entered, when Mr Thornton introduced the Prince &c   I
told him he had better pursue the same Course—& introduce the Prince, & confine
himself to the simple introduction—He said he would do so—& that the Prince
would introduce his suite—I observed that I understood there was not to be any
formal speech or address to which he replied 'no—only such Conversation as may
be thought proper between the President & the Duke'   He asked if the Duke would
have the opportunity of seeing Mrs Grant—I replied that I had no doubt if it would
be agreeable to him—... Novr 23—Thursday   See the President—he wishes the
Cabinet to attend in Dress Coats & *black* (?) cravats—at 10 call upon the Grand
Duke—very affable, speaks English fluently, as does also Admiral Possiett—Catacazy is limping, walking with a Cane—(I think) for the purpose of exciting sympathy & inducing questions to him to enable him to be in Conversation with some
persons at the reception   The Duke speaks with uncertainty of his visit to San
Francisco—Queer? is this in consequence of his knowledge of the intended dismissal
of Catacazy—no doubt his Govt is informed of it—Catacazy tells me the G. D
received this morning a Courier from his Father—At One PM the Duke & suite
arrived at the White House   the President & Cabinet, with Porter, Babcock, Dent &
Sharpe entered the Blue Room (where the Prince & suite were) & Catacazy introduced the Duke to the President—the President introduced the Cabinet &c to the
Duke—the Duke then introduced his suite to the President—Catacazy introduced
Admiral Possiett—shortly the President & Duke went into the Red Room (through
which we had passed into the Blue Room) where Mrs Grant & Nellie, Mrs Delano,
Mrs Sharpe, & Mrs Akerman were—the President introduced the Duke—I introduced the other Gentlemen of the suite—after some twenty minutes of conversation,
the Party left—... In the Evening Genl Gorloff calls to return a visit—when about
to leave he enquires if the matter of Catacazy cannot be arranged—I tell him that
we will not consent to let him remain in charge of the legation & travel through
this Country—... Novr 24 ... Genl Gorloff hands me a letter from Catacazy dated
this day saying that is ordered to attend (wait upon) the Grand Duke during his
tour through the U. S. & upon the termination thereof immediately to return to
Russia, & that from to day the management of the affairs of the Legation passes to
H. E. Major General Gorloff—I take the letter to the Cabinet—consult the President who refers the matter to me—I express the opinion that we can regard this
as a practical compliance with our request for Catacazys recall—that we get rid of
further intercourse with him—& avoid the possibility of interrupting the Duke's
progress or any delay by the delivery of passports—that it leaves C. without the
prestige of his official position to intrigue or to calumniate—that Gorloff is a Gentleman, & will possibly be made Chargé—&c   President concurs in this view—In the
Afternoon I see Genl Gorloff at dinner—& tell him that I have written in reply to
Catacazys note that we will receive any official Communications on the affairs of the
Russian Govt from him (Gorloff) and that the delivery of his passports will be
suspended until the close of the ~~visit~~ tour of the Grand Duke, unless a ~~repetition~~

recurrence of the causes which led to the demand of his recall, make an earlier delivery of them necessary—Gorloff remarks 'I thought you would add that last notice'—'certainly—(in reply) it was necessary for even our self respect & protection—& the fact that you expected it, shews that it was necessary'—I added—'if we hear of his intriguing or talking offensively, or inspiring newspaper abuse, the passports will be sent him instantly even if it be to California'—'But, (he replies) he can't help ~~talkin~~ talking to Reporters   they come continually about him & insist upon his telling them things—I was with him, some time since, & a Reporter of the N. Y. Sun, came in & interrogated him—he declined giving any information, & the Reporter said "we have done so much for you, & written so much, that you ought not to refuse us"—It did not seem to occur to Gorloff that this was an admission of one of the charges against Catacazy & that it connected him directly with the most malignant & abusive of the newspaper attacks on the President & other officials . . ." DLC-Hamilton Fish.

On Dec. 9, Catacazy spoke at a banquet for the Grand Duke in Boston. "Gentlemen: If the goddess of diplomacy were to be sculptured I would present her wrapped in a dark robe with a finger on her lip. More than any one else I should adopt that attitude, and wrap myself as close as possible and hold my finger as tight as possible to chain my lips, . . ." *New York Times*, Dec. 11, 1871. See *His Imperial Highness The Grand Duke Alexis in the United States of America During the Winter of 1871–72* (Cambridge, Mass., 1872; reprinted, New York, 1972). On Dec. 21, Fish recorded a conversation with the Turkish minister. "Blacque Bey (alway inquisitive) has seen in the newspapers that Catacazy has been recalled & that Curtin has telegraphed that Danzas is to be Chargé—wishes to know if it be true—Is told that a despatch from Curtin has been recd—somewhat confused, but stating that Catacazy is ordered to quit the Grand Dukes party at St Louis & to return home immediately—that he is no longer Minister—that Danzas is to be Chargé d'Affaires until the arrival of another who will be named & leave Russia speedily" DLC-Hamilton Fish. See Speech, April 30, 1872.

3. USG left Long Branch Sept. 12 and returned to Washington Oct. 6 after a tour that included Pittsburgh, Cincinnati, Chicago, Galena, and Leavenworth.

To Charles W. Ford

Covington Ky.
Sept. 24th 1871,

Dear Ford;

I am in receipt of your letter giving an account of the condition of my stock, or that portion of it which is to be exhibited at the Fair.[1] I regret that I shall not be able to be there. It is probable that the arrival of the Russian Prince will prevent. I certainly should however avail myself of Mr. Blow's[2] kind invitation if I should go.

You say nothing about the promised speed of young Hambletonian? When he was a two year old, and before, he gave great promise. I want to bring Legal Tender to Washington to use as a saddle horse and the two year old gray to work with a Hambletonian, of the same age, I have there. My horses in Washington are fast wearing out. Two have gone by the board and two more are failing.[3] I believe however I will let the colts Winter on the farm particularly as there will be plenty of room there for them. I have authorized Elrod to build a new stable.

Yours Truly

U. S. GRANT

ALS, DLC-USG. On Sept. 29, 1871, 10:20 A.M., USG, Galena, telegraphed to Charles W. Ford. "It will be impossible for me to visit St Louis fair this year as much as I desire to be there—" Telegram received, *ibid.*

　1. For a description of livestock from USG's farm exhibited at the St. Louis Agricultural and Mechanical Fair, see *Missouri Democrat*, Oct. 1, 1871.
　2. Probably Henry T. Blow.
　3. See letter to William Elrod, July 30, 1871.

To Oliver P. Morton

Chicago Ill.

Oct. 2d 1871,

MY DEAR GOVERNOR:

It would have afforded me pleasure to have gone by Indianapolis if I had thought of it in time. It is too late now however because I have notified the Dayton people, who have expressed great anxiety to have me visit the "Soldiers Home" in th[eir] city, that I would be there to-morrow morning; and the Pittsburg people that I would be in their city by the following morning. I would like to see you very much to thank you in person, and congratulate you, for your late efforts, and particularly for your Cincinnati speech.[1]—I was told since my arrival in Chicago that you were going to San Francisco, and that you had probably started. Knew no better until I received your letter in relation to the promotion of Col. McClure.[2]

I do not know what you may think of Col. McC. but my impressions of him are such that it would require a great deal of influence to induce me to promote him where I have discretion in the matter. I looked upon the Col. during the rebellion, as being quite as friendly to the enemies of those supporting the Govt. as to the soldiers engaged in suppressing the rebellion. If I do him injustice I would like to know it.

I hope you will have a very pleasant trip "across the Continent" and return invigorated in health and strength.

Please present Mrs. Grant's and my kindest regards to Mrs. Morton, and receive the assurances of my highest esteem for yourself.

Yours Truly
U. S. GRANT

HON. O. P. MORTON U. S. S.

ALS, Butler University, Indianapolis, Ind. After visiting Leavenworth, Kan., and Galena, USG, accompanied by Julia Dent Grant and their daughter Nellie, arrived in Chicago on Sept. 30, 1871, and stayed at the home of Orvil Grant. On Oct. 2, USG and Julia Dent Grant each held a public reception at the Tremont House. *Chicago Tribune*, Oct. 3, 1871.

1. On Sept. 16, campaigning for Ohio Republicans in Cincinnati, U.S. Senator Oliver P. Morton of Ind. defended the Enforcement Act. On Oct. 6, Morton left for a California vacation. See William Dudley Foulke, *Life of Oliver P. Morton* (1899; reprinted, New York, 1974), II, 202.

2. Presumably Col. Daniel McClure of Ind., USMA 1849, who surrendered to C.S.A. troops in Tex. in 1861, was paroled, served as chief paymaster for Ohio, Mich., Ind., Ill., and Wis. (1862–64) and at New Orleans (1865), and was promoted to col., asst. paymaster gen.

To William Elrod

Chicago Ill.
Oct. 2d 1871

DEAR ELROD:

I should like very much to be in St Louis this week to attend the Fair, but cannot be. I hope however the stock you have entered will mak[e] a good appearance. It is my intention to send two or three of the horses I now have in Washington, now getting a little old, to the farm and take from there Legal Tender for a saddle horse and his half-brother for a buggy horse, to work with one of his own age that I have there. The colt I want to work him with is a sister to "Young Hambletonian and promises more size and speed than he does. Unless Basshaw promises speed therefore I will not want him.

I engaged a thorough bred Alderney bull calf in the East which will be sent out to you this Fall. He will do for service in the Spring. You may then sell or kill the bull you now have. The one Bass Sappington has you may dispose of now in any way you think best. Alderney bulls are so visious when they get old that it is best to dispose of them as soon as they are three years old.

Yours Truly
U. S. GRANT

ALS, Illinois Historical Survey, University of Illinois, Urbana, Ill.

Speech

[*Oct. 3, 1871*]

MR. MAYOR—I have to thank you, and through you the people of Dayton, for the cordial reception extended to me, and to express the gratification that it affords me to visit your city and the Home of Disabled Volunteer Soldiers[1] in your vicinity.

This is a day I shall long remember.

Dayton Journal, Oct. 4, 1871. USG spoke from the balcony of the Beckel House in response to a welcoming address of Democratic Mayor James B. Morrison of Dayton. *Ibid.* On Oct. 3, 1871, 8:30 A.M., USG had arrived in Dayton on a train from Chicago with Julia Dent Grant, and Jesse and Nellie Grant. The party left for Pittsburgh that night following a formal dinner.

1. During the afternoon of Oct. 3, USG, Attorney Gen. Amos T. Akerman, Lewis B. Gunckel, Thomas J. Wood, and others visited the Soldiers' Home. Akerman had come to Dayton on his own initiative from a visit with relatives in Lebanon, Ohio. Gunckel, a manager of the National Homes for Disabled Volunteer Soldiers, spoke: "Mr. PRESIDENT:—The Officers and Veterans of this the Central Branch of the Na-

tional Asylum for disabled volunteer soldiers, have placed upon me the very pleasant duty of giving you a formal welcome, and of extending you the freedom and hospitality of their Home. They bid you welcome as the President of the United States; welcome as the Commander-in-Chief of the Army and Navy, welcome as one of the Board of Managers, ex-Officio, of this and the other branches of the National Asylum, welcome as their dear old Commander, who shared with them the sufferings and dangers of the war, who led them from battle to victory, from Fort Donelson to Appomatox. Seventeen hundred and fifty disabled soldiers unite, cordially and heartily in this welcome. They are not all here to-day. Three hundred are upon Hospital beds and as many more are absent, on furlough visiting relatives and friends. Of those, that are here, nearly 50 are blind, some 200 have lost each a leg, over 150 have lost each an arm, a few have lost both legs, and a few others both arms. . . ." *Ibid.* USG expressed to the veterans "his sincere gratification to meet them. It gratified him to see them so comfortable and happy. They had received their wounds in an honorable cause, and deserved the gratitude of the people. It was true that this was the first time he had visited them, but this was owing to circumstances he could not control. Hereafter he would make it a point to visit them not only at this Home but the others." *Ibid.* USG later told a reporter that he had thought the disabled soldiers "had but the ordinary treatment of men in their condition—barracks and subsistence. But he was gratefully surprised. They had a beautiful home, and, besides, were contented. Their industries occupied their attention, and they were provided with luxuries that many people in other situations might envy." *Ibid.*

On Dec. 11, USG presided over a meeting of national military asylum managers at the White House and "spoke in especially warm terms of the management of the Dayton (Ohio) Asylum." *New York Times*, Dec. 12, 1871. See too *New York Tribune*, Dec. 13, 1871.

On March 27, Orville E. Babcock had written to William Earnshaw. "The President directs me to acknowledge the receipt of your letter—and to say that he would most happily comply with your request, but that one thing after another has been given away, until he is not able to find anything suitable to send you. Mrs: Grant will as early as she can find something and have it forwarded to you. When coming to the Executive Mansion—most of the Presidents articles used in the War—and now in possession of the family were boxed and packed away in storehouses, as soon as they can be overhowled he will send you something. The President request me to communicate his most hearty wishes for the success of you institute and the happiness of those who now suffer from the wounds received in their countries defence. He believes the people of the United States will never forget those herose" Copy, DLC-USG, II, 1. Born in 1828 in Philadelphia, Earnshaw became a Methodist preacher (1853) and served as chaplain, 49th Pa., and as hospital chaplain, U.S. Army. On April 2, 1867, USG endorsed papers advocating Earnshaw as post chaplain, Nashville: "Should there still be a vacancy among the Chaplains I would respectfully concur with the recommendation of Gn. Thomas for the appointment of the Rev. Mr. Wm Earnshaw" AES, DNA, RG 94, ACP, E211 CB 1865. On Sept. 5, Earnshaw was appointed chaplain, National Soldiers' Home, Dayton.

Speech

[*Oct. 4, 1871*]

JUDGE MCCANDLESS.—Sir: Through you allow me to return my hearty thanks to the citizens of Pittsburgh, Allegheny and the surrounding districts for the very hearty welcome I have received. The reception is much more welcome from the fact that it is the welcome of the whole people, without respect to political divisions. I hope the day is not far distant when our citizens will look up to the Executive as the President of the whole country, and not as the representative of any party or section. I know that my stay in this city shall be enjoyable, and I shall take the opportunity of visiting your workshops,[1] which I recognize as a source of wealth not only to the artizan and the city, but to the whole nation. I hope we shall soon see the day when the consumptions of the country will be more largely the productions of our own people.

Pittsburgh Gazette, Oct. 5, 1871. Wilson McCandless boasted of local industries when introducing USG. *Ibid.* Born in 1810 in Pittsburgh, McCandless, a staunch Democrat, was appointed judge, Western District, Pa., in 1859.

On Oct. 1, 1871, Sunday, USG, Chicago, had telegraphed to Joseph M. Gazzam. "Will leave Dayton, Ohio, at seven-thirty on Tuesday night. The train may be stopped to bring it to Pittsburgh at any time." *Pittsburgh Commercial*, Oct. 3, 1871. On Oct. 2, USG telegraphed. "I go to Pittsurgh by the Panhandle Railroad." *Ibid.* On Oct. 4, USG received public greetings at Steubenville, Ohio, and Burgettstown, Pa., before arriving in Pittsburgh shortly after 1:00 P.M. He attended a reception that evening at the Monongahela House. *Pittsburgh Gazette*, Oct. 5, 1871.

1. On Oct. 5, after visiting factories, USG responded to an address welcoming him to Allegheny. "CITIZENS OF ALLEGHENY: It affords me great pleasure to accept the hospitalities of your city, and I am deeply sensible of the honor conferred upon me by this reception. I am greatly pleased with the evidences all around me of the fact that you are a busy, thrifty and prosperous people. In the administration of the affairs of the government, it is my earnest desire to meet the approval of the people of the United States irrespective of party. I tender you my sincere thanks for this flattering reception." *Ibid.*, Oct. 6, 1871. On the same day, USG left Pittsburgh on the 6:00 P.M. train.

To Charles W. Eliot

Washington, D. C. Oct. 8th *1871*

DEAR SIR;

Your favor of the 4th inst. inviting Mrs. Grant or myself, or both, to visit you during our contemplated visit to Boston, the latter part of this week, has only just been reached among the many letters which I found on my return last Friday evening.[1] We both thank you for your kindness but as some members of the Cabinet will accompany us, and as preparations have been made, or engaged, at the St. James Hotel, I think we had better occupy them. I will esteem it a very great favor however if you will allow my son to spend as much time with us, during our stay in Boston, as is consistent with the regulations of the College. Our stay will probably be from Saturday evening until the following Tuesday morning.[2] I am pleased to hear the favorable account you give of my sons progress and of his standing with the professors and his fellow students.

With highest esteem
your obt. svt.
U. S. GRANT

CHAS. W. ELIOT
PRES. HARVARD UNIVERSITY

ALS, MH. Born in 1834 in Boston, Charles W. Eliot graduated Harvard College in 1853 and became its president in 1869.

On Oct. 16, 1871, USG and several cabinet members attended the dedication of a combined Post Office and Treasury building in Boston. On Oct. 11, USG had telegraphed to U.S. Representative Samuel Hooper of Mass. "Would it not be well for the good people of Boston to dispense with the ceremony and expense of a public reception on the occasion of my visit to your city, and appropriate such portion of the funds set apart for that purpose as is deemed advisable for the relief of the sufferers by the Chicago disaster? I am sure such a course would please me." *Boston Transcript*, Oct. 12, 1871.

1. USG returned from a western trip on Oct. 6.
2. USG and party left Washington on Friday night, Oct. 13, and left Boston on Tuesday morning, Oct. 17.

To Lt. Gen. Philip H. Sheridan

Dated Washington DC [*Oct.*] 9 *1871*

To GEN. P. H. SHERIDAN—

In addition to food and clothing you are authorized to draw from any accessible portion of your command camp equipage and everything that in your judgment will relieve sufferings from the great calamity that has befallen the city of Chicago   Render all the aid you can—

U. S. GRANT

Telegram received (on Oct. 10, 1871), DNA, RG 393, Military Div. of the Mo., Letters Received. See letter to John M. Palmer, Nov. 9, 1871. On Oct. 9, 1871, Orville E. Babcock wrote to Secretary of War William W. Belknap that Lt. Gen. Philip H. Sheridan was "empowered to call upon the military officials at St. Louis for farther supplies if he deems it best." Copy, DLC-USG, II, 1.

On Oct. 10, USG telegraphed to Sheridan. "If my Brother or Gen Rucker are burned out offer them my furnished house in Galena for their families as long as they want   if neither want it you may tender the use of it to any one you Choose" Telegram received (on Oct. 11, 1:51 P.M.), DNA, RG 393, Military Div. of the Mo., Letters Received. On Oct. 11, Sheridan telegraphed to USG. "Your brother and family are allright   He has lost his business place but his residence is intact and he himself in good spirits. General Rucker and family saved only the clothing on their persons. I will show them your kind invitation to your house at Galena. The sufferers are being well provided for in the way of shelter and food for the present. In a day or two we will be more perfectly organized; but nearly all those made very poor will have to be cared for during the winter." Copy, *ibid.*, Telegrams Sent.

Also on Oct. 11, William B. Franklin, vice president, Colt's Fire Arms Manufacturing Co., Hartford, wrote to Frederick T. Dent. "I received your letter of the 9 inst, and have sent the model to your address, Washington. D. C. I hope that it will arrive safely. If you are poor enough to own nothing in Chicago, and no Insurance Stock you are a fortunate man. This place suffers to the figure of twenty millions, from loss of insurance and loans based on insurance policies." ALS, ICarbS.

On Oct. 12, George H. Waite, chairman, Cook County Board of Supervisors, Chicago, telegraphed to USG. "I have the honor to call your attention to the following: Resolution which was unanimously adopted by the Board of Supervisors of Cook County at their session this day Viz Whereast the City of Chicago has been devastated by a deluge of fire destroying the public buildings & the business centre of the South Division also three miles in length and one mile in width of the north division & one mile square in the West division consuming hundreds of millions of property therefore Be it Resolved that in view of the terrible unparalled calamity this Board do request the Prest of the US to call a special Session of Congress that such national aid be extended to Cook Co for the Reconstruction of the public buildings as may be done and also to take such other action as the great emergency demands" Telegram received (at 7:20 P.M.), DNA, RG 59, Miscellaneous Letters. On

Oct. 27, Horace Porter wrote to Waite. "The President directs me to acknowledge the receipt of the copy of the resolutions of the Board of Supervisors of Cook County relative to the assumption by Congress of the war debt of Chicago, and say to you that he will submit the matter to Congress at its next session." Copy, DLC-USG, II, 1.

On Nov. 8, Gen. William T. Sherman wrote to Dent. "The Bearer Profr Beleki of Chicago is a total sufferer by the fire & insists on seeing the President. All I know is he is a most worthy man—and if the President could see him for a minute, he might do an act of Kindness" ALS, ICarbS. On the same day, USG wrote to Caspar J. Beleké, Chicago. "Sympathizing with you in the calamity which destroyed your college in Chicago, and from easy circumstances reduced you to poverty, and appreciating the value to the citizens of Chicago, of the institution which you headed and owned, it would afford me pleasure to see such aid extended as will enable you to build it up again." Copy, DLC-USG, II, 1. Beleké, "formerly Professor of the German Language in the University of the City of New York—author of a German Grammar & Reader &c." moved to Chicago about 1864 and in 1871 headed a classical school on the near north side. Unsigned circular, Nov. 15, 1864, Adolphus S. Hubbard Papers, ICHi.

On Nov. 25, 1871, John C. Freeman, "Associate Prof. anc. Languages," University of Chicago, wrote to USG. "The late disaster to this city, which, although sparing our University buildings, has deprived the Professors of their salaries, coupled with the fact that the hostile winters of the lake shore and the labors of the classroom combined render it imperative upon me to seek some more favorable climate leads me to speak to your Excellency upon a subject which has long been in my mind and to ask whether an application for a consulate on the ground of fitness to do credit to the position by scholarship and business capacity—and on the ground that I deserve well of the country on account of military service (in 27th & 168th N. Y. Inf. [1862 & 3]—Capt. 1st N. Y. Vetrn Cavly, 1864,—& A. Inspr Genl of Cavly in Dept. W. Va. 1865) and recommended by the fol. among others; Andrew D White Pres. Cornell University . . . to ask (as I said) whether your Excellency would look with favor on an application based as above." ALS (brackets in original), DNA, RG 59, Letters of Application and Recommendation. No appointment followed.

On Jan. 22, 1872, Professor Carl Hübner, Düsseldorf, wrote to USG. "In consequence of the terrible calamity which has visited the city of Chicago, I have appealed to my friends and colleagues here for contributions of paintings, sketches, drawings and engravings, to be sold at auction in New York for the benefit of our suffering countrymen in Chicago. I have already received a considerable number, from the best artists. The railway company has readily promised free transportation of these works of art from here to Bremen; the North German Lloyd steamship company has also declared its readiness to carry them across the ocean free of charge. My request to Your Excellency is that these articles may be introduced into the port of New York duty-free. If this cannot be done, it would be desirable to have them introduced at lower rates than is customary. The sum to be applied to the relief of the necessities of our suffering countrymen in Chicago would thus be considerably larger, and our object would ~~thus~~ be more satisfactorily attained. Hoping for a favorable reply, . . ." ALS (in German), *ibid.*, RG 56, Letters Received; translation, *ibid.* On Dec. 31, 1871, Hübner had informed the German Relief Society of Chicago that 113 donations were ready for shipment to M. Knoedler's gallery, New York City, for auction, but that Secretary of the Treasury George S. Boutwell had decided against admitting them duty-free. Copy, *ibid.* This donation is not listed in the *Report of the*

Chicago Relief and Aid Society of Disbursement of Contributions for the Sufferers by the Chicago Fire (Chicago, 1874).

When Congress reassembled on Dec. 4, U.S. Senator John A. Logan of Ill. introduced a bill to aid Chicago fire victims. On Jan. 16, 1872, Logan gave the Senate a firsthand account of the fire. "... Can any one having witnessed this sad scene do less than plead for the ruined city?" *CG*, 42–2, 409. On Jan. 24, U.S. Senators Zachariah Chandler and Thomas W. Ferry of Mich. and Matthew H. Carpenter of Wis. argued for aid to victims of fires in their states. *Ibid.*, pp. 548–64. On Feb. 23, USG promised a delegation from Chicago that he would support the relief bill. *Louisville Courier-Journal*, Feb. 24, 1872. On April 5, USG signed an amended relief bill. On March 7, Belknap wrote to USG endorsing a bill to reimburse soldiers for clothing lost in the fire. Copy, DNA, RG 107, Letters Sent, Military Affairs. See *CG*, 42–2, 907, 1560.

Proclamation

[Whereas unlawful combinations and conspiracies have long existed and do still exist in the State of South Carolina, for the purpose of depriving certain portions and classes of the people of that State of the rights, privileges, immunities, and protection named in the Constitution of the United States, and secured by the act of Congress approved April the twentieth, one thousand eight hundred and seventy-one, entitled "An act to enforce the provisions of the fourteenth amendment to the Constitution of the United States;"

And whereas in certain parts of said State—to wit, in the counties of Spartansburgh, York, Marion, Chester, Laurens, Newberry, Fairfield, Lancaster, and Chesterfield—such combinations and conspiracies do so obstruct and hinder the execution of the laws of said State and of the United States as to deprive the people aforesaid of the rights, privileges, immunities, and protection aforesaid, and do oppose and obstruct the laws of the United States and their due execution, and impede and obstruct the due course of justice under the same;

And whereas the constituted authorities of said] State are unable to protect the people aforesaid in such rights within the said counties:

And whereas the combinations and conspiracies aforesaid within the counties aforesaid, are organized and armed and are so numerous and powerful as to be able to defy the constituted authorities of said State and of the United States within the said State, and by reason of said causes the conviction of such offenders and the preservation of the public peace and safety have become impracticable in said counties:

Now, therefore, I, Ulysses S. Grant, President of the United States of America, do hereby command all persons composing the unlawful combinations and conspiracies aforesaid to disperse and to retire peaceably to their homes within five days of the date hereof; and to deliver, either to the Marshal of the United States for the District of South Carolina,[1] or to any of his deputies, or to any military officer of the United States within said counties, all arms, ammunition, uniforms, disguises, and other means and implements, used, kept, possessed or controlled by them for carrying out the unlawful purposes for which the combinations and conspiracies are organized.

In witness whereof I have hereunto set my hand, and caused the seal of the United States to be affixed.

Done at the city of Washington this twelfth day of October, in the year of our Lord one thousand eight hundred and seventy-one, and of the Independence of the United States of America, the ninety-sixth.

U. S. GRANT

DS (bracketed material from a printed copy), DNA, RG 130, Presidential Proclamations; *ibid.*, RG 94, Letters Received, 3668 1871. On Oct. 7, 1871, Attorney Gen. Amos T. Akerman, Carterville, Ga., wrote to Benjamin H. Bristow, solicitor gen. "I saw the President at Dayton last Tuesday and suggested the possible necessity of suspending the *habeas corpus* in certain parts of South Carolina. It was agreed that I should draft a proclamation and send it to you, for use if the occasion should be found to exist. I hope to reach Yorkville next Monday—the 9th and if there appears a necessity for decided steps, I will inform you by telegraph through the War Department which has a cipher understood by the military officers. The ordinary telegraphic language is not safe, for the K. K. have a machine and sometimes tap the wires. I have drafted the warning Proclamation required by the latter part of the fourth section of the act of April 20, 1871. I will follow with a draft of a Proclamation suspending the habeas corpus, at the end of the five days. My suggestion is that this be issued on the 11th If my information is correct, there is not the least reason for forbearing a single day longer than is required for the formalities; and I can verify the correctness of the information in one day at the place. I purpose to stay at Yorkville until action is taken, if the President should conclude to take it. I shall send to him a formal report from Yorkville, if the reports appear true. You and Mr. Hill must take care of the office and the Supreme Court.... P. S. On reflection I think it best to first confer with State officials at Columbia, and hence shall not reach Yorkville until Tuesday. The draft is merely a hint. Perhaps you can prepare a better one. The awkwardness of the statute makes it difficult. I have tried to follow the 3rd and 4th Sections, as closely as possible." ALS, *ibid.*, RG 60, Letters from the President. Enclosed is an undated draft in Akerman's hand, which differed most substantially in the passage corresponding to the second paragraph of the final version. "Whereas In certain parts of said State, to wit, in the Counties of Spartanburg, York, Union and Chester, such combinations [and conspiracies do oppose and] so obstruct ~~and hinder~~ the execution of the laws of said State and of the United States as to deprive the citizens aforesaid of the rights, privileges, immunities and protection aforesaid ~~within the said Counties~~; and the Constituted Authorities of said State are unable to protect the citizens aforesaid in their rights aforesaid within the said Counties;..." ADf (bracketed material in another hand), *ibid.*

On Sept. 1, 1871, U.S. Senator John Scott of Pa. had written to USG. "Since the return of the sub-committee sent to the State of South Carolina by the Joint Committee of Congress appointed 'to inquire into the condition of the late insurrectionary States, so far as regards the execution of the laws and the safety of the lives and property of citizens of the United States,' communications have been forwarded to me from citizens of Spartanburg and York Counties, and from the officer commanding the United States troops at Yorkville, which I consider it my duty to lay before you, with this letter. The Sub-committee visited both these counties, and took testimony in them. That testimony has not all been printed, but with this I forward the testimony of Rev. A. W. Cummings, of Spartanburg, and of Col. Lewis Merrill, relating to York County. That of Dr Cummings shows that, from October last until July, when the committee was there, outrages had been committed upon two hundred and twenty seven citizens whose names are given, two of whom had been murdered. This list does not embrace all the cases that had occurred, and the Deputy Marshal in that county testified, that the actual number largely exceeded this. Some forty or fifty persons were before the committee who proved the outrages committed upon themselves and others by bands of armed men in disguise. The extent of this violence was so great, that leading citizens of that county were informed that if any of the witnesses who testified were interfered with, or if any outrages of a character similar to those proved were again committed, the fact would be reported to the President, that he might consider the propriety of exercising the full extent of the power conferred upon him for the protection of citizens of the United States against such lawlessness. It is due to these citizens to say that they promised to exert their influence to repress disorder, and I have since seen published notices of meetings held for that purpose. Before the committee left, one witness who had been examined, reappeared and testified that he had bought a gun, returned home, and had been visited by armed men in disguise from whom he escaped but who took his gun away and threatened to his family that they would kill him. I forbore to report this case, hoping that the promises of leading citizens would be fulfilled and be effective to stop further violence. On the same day that the committee left Spartanburg the County Court assembled. As an evidence of how far the State law is effective in reaching such offences, I quote ~~an extract~~ from the report of the Grand Jury made under date of 20th July: 'We regret to report that we have heard of a number of outrages having been committed in various portions of the county, but express the hope that the good and influential men in every part of the community will unite their efforts in preventing every infraction of the law, and in assuring to all perfect security in their person and property' This is the notice taken of such a state of affairs as that presented by Dr Cummings' testimony. No man has yet been convicted or punished in that county for any of these offences. Dr Cummings' letter of the 10th inst. shows a number of outrages committed since the Committee left, one of which, as appears by the affidavit of Dr Bates, was of a most brutal character. One of the witnesses before the committee is also stated to be now a refugee in Spartanburg, having been threatened with death. Col Merrill's testimony gives the names of sixty eight victims of violence, in York County, since October last, six of whom were killed; and shows the actual number to have been from three to four hundred. His letter and that of Hon. A. S. Wallace, which I enclose, inform me that, since the Committee left, the Ku-Klux have renewed their deeds of violence and crime in that county, whipping inoffensive men, 'for no other cause than their political opinions and the color of their skin,' and burning a Negro school-house. The state of insecurity was, I am satisfied, as great in Union County as in either of those above named, one witness having testified that the county was in effect under Ku-Klux rule; that no order issued by the Klan would be disregarded. As showing the state of feeling in that county the number and power of the organization, and especially to give the views of those who think it no part of their duty to have such offences as are committed by the Ku-Klux prosecuted, I submit to you the testimony of R. W. Shand Esq, a prominent democratic lawyer of that county. I have no report of any renewal of violence in that county since the visit of the committee. Information has been sent me of occurrences in Chester, Fairfield and Newberry counties which would indicate that the cessation of lawlessness is but temporary. The state of public sentiment in the counties of Spartanburg, Union, Laurens, Newberry, Chester, and York is such that if these outbreaks continue, there is no hope of protection from the local tribunals, and I earnestly invite your Excellency's attention to the testimony submitted with a view to action for the protection of those who have so long suffered without redress. The cruelties that have been inflicted in Spartanburg and York Counties are shocking to humanity, crimes that ought not to go unpunished in any civilized country. The perpetrators are at large and unwhipped of Justice. Although inquiry has been made in their midst and the enormity of their crimes exposed, and the consequences of their repetition foreshadowed, the members of these lawless organizations have again resumed their arms and their midnight raids of brutality and assassination. In these counties of Spartanburg and York crime has run riot with impunity, all warnings have been disregarded and the efforts of the well disposed citizens have proved unavailing. I submit whether the time has not come, in view of these facts, when the people of these counties at least should be informed by proclamation that the limit of endurance has been reached, and that the whole power of the Government will be exercised to protect its citizens in the enjoyment of the rights and privileges guarantied to them by the Constitution. Reluctant as I am to do so, the facts proven before the committee in these counties, the state of feeling witnessed there, the warning given the citizens and in the face of this the speedy reappearance of the same criminal disorders which have been the subjects of investigation, defying the execution of the laws, rendering life insecure, and property of but nominal value, induce me, in justice to the suffering people who have endured so much, in ~~justice~~ mercy even to those whose sympathy with or indifference to these wrongs may arouse a retribution more terrible than they dream of, a retribution I would go to any lawful limit of power to prevent;—all these considerations impel me to call your attention to the facts contained in the testimony, letters, and affidavits submitted, and to ask whether they do not justify such a proclamation, as to these two counties, as is required before the exercise of the power conferred upon you by the 4th Section of the Act of 20th April 1871. As there are outrages reported in other counties, and there is some hesitation among the military officers as to their right to arrest persons found armed and in disguise upon the highways until after called upon by the civil authorities, let me also direct your attention to whether you have not the power of issuing explicit instructions, giving authority, under the third section of that act, to the military to make arrests of persons found in disguise and armed, and to hand them over to the Marshal, directing the Military officer to lodge such information with the United States District Attorney as will enable him to proceed at once and obtain the evidence upon which to prefer indictments." LS, *ibid.* The enclosures are *ibid.* For related testimony by Anson W. Cummings, Robert W. Shand, and Maj. Lewis Merrill, see *SRC,* 42-2-41, part 4, pp. 917–36, 968–1010, part 5, pp. 1463–87. On Aug. 27, U.S. Representative Alexander S. Wallace of S. C., Columbia, had written to Scott. ". . . The U. S. court at Greenville is progressing Slowly and have had two cases up from Spartanburg for K. K. outrages, in which they made a mistrial—. . . It is very difficult to get the court to work with any Sort of energy—. . . The Atty is very well represented but the Marshals office is about as badly managed as you could well conceive—The Marshal and his principle employees are indiferent if not in actual Sympathy with the K. K—. . . You will recollect that I told you that with Johnson in the Marshals office we could not hold the State for the party—. . . Gov Scott appears to be perfectly indifferent—Decisive action on the part of the President would be a matter of humanity—" ALS, *ibid.* On Sept. 1, a correspondent reported on cabinet consideration of Scott's letter to USG. *Philadelphia Public Ledger,* Sept. 2, 1871. On Aug. 31, Scott had discussed the situation in S. C. with USG. *Ibid.,* Sept. 1, 1871. On Sept. 12, Scott, Huntingdon, Pa., wrote to USG. "On the 8th Inst a despatch, dated at Charleston on the 7th, was published in the leading newspapers, stating in effect that a number of the citizens of Spartanburgh, including the United States Commissioner and other Officials, had addressed a letter to me referring to the Statements and Affidavits submitted to you with my letter of the 1st Inst, and declaring that, upon inquiry, they were unable to hear of any outrage having been committed in that County since the Sub-Committee, of which I was Chairman, left it, but that, on the contrary, there was profound peace and quiet in the County. I was glad to learn that there was evenn a probability of my informant having been mistaken, and rested satisfied that your Excellency would delay any further action until this conflict of statement was cleared up. I am, this morning, in receipt of the letter, alluded to in the despatch, and of other communications upon the same subject, all of which I take pleasure in laying before you for your consideration. The aggravated case mentioned in the papers submitted to you as having occurred in Spartanburg County was that of a man named Quinn who was stated to have been brutally whipped in Pacolet township in that County. The letter of Col Gabriel Cannon and another letter of Dr. A. W. Cummings, both reacheding me to-day and herewith submitted, taken together show that the outrage was committed in Union County a short distance from the line of Spartanburgh, while Quinn was there on a visit to his brother-in-law, that Quinn is a citizen of Spartanburgh County, and that one of the persons arrested for the offense is also a citizen of that County. This correction of the former statements would therefore show that instead of violence having been renewed in Spartanburgh County and not in Union, as before stated, it has been renewed in the border of Union, near to Spartanburgh, upon a citizen of Spartanburgh and, in all probability, by citizens of Spartanburgh. The disclosure of what had occurred in the Count~y~ies alluded to, and the state of feeling existing there satisfied at least a ~m~Majority of the Sub-Committee, that if violence was again commenced by disguised men, no remedy exist~ing~ed either in public sentiment or the local tribunals, and it was in that belief that citizens were informed that your attention would be called to any renewal of such offences with a view to a more rigid remedy. It was for the purpose of discharging that duty that I before addressed you, and, in again doing so, I invite your attention to the whole correspondence transmitted with this and ~by~ my former letter. No one will rejoice more than I if, in the Counties affected by these occurrences, the rights and privileges of all citizens can be secured and protected, without resort to the extreme limit of power entrusted to you by the law." LS, DNA, RG 60, Letters Received, Senate.

On Sept. 1, Warren Diver, Montmorenci, Barnwell County, S. C., had written to USG. "I demme my duty to inform you of the State of things here for we are fast drifting into Anarchy. betwen one and two years ago I purchased a Plantation here being assuered that it was a very quiet community and Northern men and money was wanted here and would be kindly received. now I am told plainly that I must leave here or change my Politics or they will kill me as no damed Radical will be tolerated. told so by the leading man of this section no one alledges anything against me but my being a Radical or supporter of your Administration I have not made myself officious in Politics or scarcely mentioned the subject not being a voter until now there are armed Bands of Ruffians roaming through the country with impunity murdering inoffensive People thre has been five murders commited in as many weeks in my vicinty to my knowledge no one Arrested for it. on the 27 of August a Colored man came to me at 2 o.clock at Night for Protection his house having been surrounded by a band of Armed and Masked men he escapeing Almost by a Miracle through a hole in the floor no one alledging anything against him only that he taught a Coloured Sunday School. now for protecting and keeping him 2 or 3 Nights I must leave the country or fight a Night Battle with the odds of about 40 to one. I have called on State Authority for Protection but they are Powerless, and the fact is the entire white People obstruct the execution of the laws in all Possble ways I have been told ~by~ Privately by two Ladies that I might depend on being Assaulted in a short time I am quite neveous and can Scarcely write inteligibly haveing been Stading guard four Nights in succession being the only white man that is a Repulican in this vicinity Mr President is it not time that these ~Butchries~ Butcheries ceased is it ~that~ not time that a heavey hand was laid on these Demons I fear our State Government is not as vigorous as the times require" ALS, *ibid.*, RG 94, Letters Received, 3078 1871. On Sept. 22, Capt. Birney B. Keeler, 18th Inf., Columbia, wrote to the post adjt. concerning his investigation at Montmorenci. ". . . All persons with whom I conversed, including Mr. Diver, averred their belief that the Ku Klux organization does not exist in Barnwell Co. This gentleman in his letter to the President makes many statements which the facts do not justify prominent among which is the one 'no one alleges any thing against me but my being a Radical or supporter of your Administration' Mr. Diver is living publicly with a woman who is not his wife and to this his best friends and neighbors (Northern men and Republicans) attribute solely the hostility, if any, existing against him. He has not been told, as he says, to leave the country but has heard that certain men have said he must do so. The 'five murders' he reports to the President as having been *to his knowledge* committed in his vicinity he declared to me he knew nothing about but had 'heard' of. I could not find any other person who had been *so* unfortunate. For other statements in his letter he makes heavy drafts upon his imagination. In conclusion I am of the opinion that Mr. Diver will shortly be an applicant for an appointment in the Post Office Department and seeks to appear in the character of an ardent but much abused Republican. Hence his letter to the President which induced this investigation." ALS, *ibid.*

On Sept. 8, Javan Bryant, Spartanburg County, S. C., had written to USG. "In view of the great effort which is now being made to avert what is denominated 'the calamity of marshal law' from this County, and in view of the grave results attendant upon the success of such effort, I feel that my duty, as one of the humbles citizens, will not have been performed until I shall have made to your Excellency a faithful statement of the present condition of affairs in this community, as they address themselves to the understanding of those whose only request is the equal protection of the law to all, whose only interest is in the peace and prosperity of the country, and whose only sympathies are with the friends of law and order and the supporters of the present administration. As regards the state of affairs in this County up to July, 1871, you are fully informed by the Congressional Committee who have recently made known the result of their able and impartial investigation of the matter. It only remains for me to state that the spirit of insubordination, intolerance and opposition to the United States government is as rife to-day as when the Committee were here. It is true that the number of outrages has not been as great since the visit of the Committee as it was during a corresponding length of time prior to their visit; but this is easily accounted for by the collapse which the 'Klan' must have sustained from the sudden and startling disclosures which were made to the Committee relative to its operations. A sufficient number, however, have been perpetrated to convince every reasonable mind that the collapse was only temporary, and that the same spirit which animated them before still rankles in their bosoms and only awaits a favorable opportunity to rekindle with increased fervor. For a few weeks immediately succeeding the visit of the Committee, confidence seemed to be partially restored to the loyal men, and they began to idulge the hope that they would be allowed to remain at their homes and pursue their avocations in peace and quietude. But of the scores of persons whose identity were established before the Committee, it is an indisputable fact that not a dozen have been arrested, and *not one has been convicted.* It is a common thing for men to say in the country that they will kill any body who reports them as Ku Klux. Men who have been guilty of the gravest offences against the laws of the United States, and some who have committed the most atrocious murders stalk abroad in open daylight without molestation. It is no uncommon thing for men to boast that when the 'Yankees' leave here then 'we'll have KuKluxing right.' The Democrats have had several public meetings in the County professedly to put down violence and outrage; but they ocupied the time in the most unqualified and bitter denunciation of the KuKlux Law and the U. S. government generall; and would close by advising that we would best put up with it the best we can in order to avoid marshal law. It appears to me that no better evidence of a man's criminal connection with the 'Klan' need be asked than his detestation of the KuKlux law and his mortal dread of military rule. I do but speak the sentiment of every honest republican in the County, when I say that remove the hope of martial law and we would be more completely under the dominion of fear than we have ever been. All eyes are turned to the Executive of the Nation. In him alone are concentrated all our hopes. We look upon the KuKluxKlan as rebellion in its worst form. At Appomattox Court-house the great rebellion was cut off at the ground. In Spartanburg

County it has sprouted out from the stump, and the scions are more poisonous than the parent tree. We humbly pray, Allmighty God, that he who cut it off at Appomattox Court-house may declare martial law in Spartanburg County, and never stack arms until the last root has been extirpated." ALS, *ibid.*, 3215 1871.

On Oct. 13, S. C. Representative Hezekiah H. Hunter, Charleston, wrote to USG. "allow me to thank you for the 'Proclamation' of the 12th inst; in behalf of an outraged and oppressed people of my race and also in behalf of the interests of a common humanity, which acknowledges the Fatherhood of God and the Brotherhood of Man;—And that you have and do, command and demand, that such combinations commonly known and designated as Ku Klux shall cease, in making night hideous with the cries of the poor women and children of the Black and White races, pleading for their own and the lives of their natural protectors;—their Fathers Sons and Husbands;—that *they* may be spared to minister to their varied wants. Mr President May God nerve you with firmness and endow you with wisdom for the multifarious duties of the Office to which He has called you. Are you not our Joshua? Our Moses (President Lincoln) was not allowed to see us safe, secure, in our lives, persons and property in the Southern states. O then Mr President be true in the future as in the past in defending the rights of the poorest of your race in the South as well as protecting the most ignorant of mine whether Republican or Democrat and you will have the prayers and praises of all good men of either race and of the Christians of every race nation and clime;—and what is best of all that peace of conscience which none can impart:—Heed not the voice of traitors among my race; for we have them who will write and speak for the Ku Klux for money or other considerations as against protection; which requires Martial law in the counties of this state named in said Proclamation. I reiterate we have traitors in this city:—Heed them not nor those of your race and mine who are trying to serve Two Masters;—who are on both sides of every question;—with both the parties of this State the Ku Klux ad Republican. Thanking you again Mr President in behalf of the Persecuted Republicans of this State and all the Southern States of your race and mine for this Public manifestation of protecting *all* wherever the Starry Banner Floats;—and praying that your life and health may be precious in the Sight of God—" LS, OFH. See Proclamation, Oct. 17, 1871.

1. On March 12, 1869, Louis E. Johnson, Charleston, had written to USG. "I have the honor to respectfully make application for the appointment of United States Marshall for the Judicial District of South Carolina. . . ." LS, DNA, RG 60, Records Relating to Appointments. Related papers are *ibid.* On March 15, Julius C. Carpenter, Charleston, wrote to USG. "I respectfully apply for the appointment of U. S. Marshal for the District of South Carolina. The reasons therefor given by those who are closely connected with your Excellency, will avail more than any statement made by myself; and I consequently simply refer your Excellency to your Father J. R. Grant Esqr, to Major Genl: Rawlings the Secretary of War; and to Hon: Jas. G. Blaine Speaker of the House of Representatives. Hoping that these Gentlemen may be heard by you before any Appointment is made, . . ." LS, *ibid.* On April 15, USG nominated Johnson, son of Reverdy Johnson and additional paymaster vols. (1861–64), as marshal, S. C.

In March, 1871, U.S. Senator Thomas J. Robertson and U.S. Representatives Wallace, Joseph H. Rainey, Robert C. DeLarge, and Robert B. Elliott of S. C. wrote to USG. "Permit us to present, to you the claims of Mr Robt M. Wallace of our State, and Respectfully, ask his appointment to the Office of Deputy United States Marshall for the Judicial District of South Carolina   Mr Wallace is a native of South Carolina, we know him intimately, he is a *firm unflinching Republican*, affiliateing, and associateing with our party in all its efforts, for perpetuation. Fully in accord with the administration, was one of Seven men who Voted for the call of a Convention to accept and ratify the *Reconstruction Acts* of Congress, . . ." DS, *ibid.* On March 27, Alexander Wallace wrote to Akerman urging Johnson's removal for failing to arrest illegal distillers. ALS, *ibid.* On May 20, John Cessna, Washington, D. C., wrote to USG. "During the last two sessions of Congress, I had very frequent interviews with Hon. A. S. Wallace, of South Carolina, Occupying the same building, as we did, I had opportunities and occasion to examine and hear the correspondence between himself and his son Robert, on political subjects, and in regard to the condition of affairs generally in South Carolina. I take great pleasure in bearing testimony to the loyalty, fidelity and general intelligence of both father and son. I think they have a full understanding and comprehension of the difficulties existing in that State, as well as the remedy required for their correction. I do not wish to interfere with matters outside of my own district, yet as a friend of the Administration, and the Republican Party, I venture to suggest the opinion that the appointment of Mr. Robert Wallace as Marshal of South Carolina would do much to promote the cause of law and order, and the success of the party in that State." ALS, *ibid.* On May 31, USG suspended Johnson and appointed Robert M. Wallace as marshal, S. C. On June 21, Bristow wrote to USG. "General Dent has handed me your telegram to him, of yesterday, in which you direct that the suspension of Marshal Johnson of south Carolina, be removed. In compliance with your directions I have recalled from the State Department the original Executive order suspending Mr. Johnson from the office of Marshal of the United States for the District of South Carolina and designating Robert Wallace to discharge the duties of that office until the end of the next session of the Senate, which is herewith submitted to you, together with the original order notifying Mr. Johnson of his suspension from office. I have the honor to suggest that the enclosed orders should be cancelled by the President and returned to this Department." Copy, *ibid.*, Letters Sent to Executive Officers.

On March 22, David T. Corbin, U.S. attorney, *et al.*, Charleston, had petitioned USG. "Having learned that efforts are being made in Washington to procure the removal from office of Major Louis E. Johnson, United States Marshal, for the District of South Carolina: we, as true Republicans, and earnest supporters of your Excellency's administration, beg leave to enter our protests against the actions of those men, who, to gratify their own personal ambitions, would sacrifice the best interests of the Republican party in this State; and at the same time to pray that your Excellency will continue Major Johnson in the office of United States Marshal for this District, for the following reasons: Major Johnson has been at all times a good, and true Republican, has never voted any other than a Republican ticket, and has always contributed largely of his means to promote the success and welfare of the Republican party; he was the first Military Magistrate and last Provost Judge on the Sea Islands of South Carolina, in which positions he gained, not only the esteem and confidence of his superior officers, Generals Sickles, and Canby, but likewise the affections of that large constituency, and to his judicious management whilst holding the Said positions is due the credit of the almost unanimous Republican vote, which these Islands invariably poll. As the Executive officer of the United States Courts, Major Johnson has at all times Executed the processes issued by such Courts, without fear or favor, and it is on account of his having so faithfully performed this duty, and used his utmost endeavours to fullfil the wishes expressed by your Excellency in your message to Congress in December last; to defend the sanctity of the ballot box, and the right of all citizens to vote, once; that a few Seek for his removal. We know of no one in South Carolina who can show a clearer Republican record than Major L. E. Johnson; and knowing likewise your Excellencys admiration of all good Republicans, who faithfully perform their duty in carrying out the laws of the United States, we feel confident you will grant the prayer of Your Excellency's Humble Servants." DS (10 signatures), *ibid.*, Letters Received, Senate. U.S. Senator Frederick A. Sawyer of S. C. endorsed this petition. "The signers of the within letter are among the very best men in the Republican Party in S. C. and both by knowledge of Mr Johnson and by political sagacity entitled to be heard on the subject in question,   I heartily concur in their suggestions," AES (undated), *ibid.*

On June 5, Sawyer, New York City, wrote to Akerman. "I have seen the President today and the commission of Mr R. M. Wallace as Marshal of South Carolina will not issue till the Prest has examined the papers. I therefore submit the accompanying statement to be filed with the papers in the case. Major Johnson will probably forward some other papers to go on file." ALS, *ibid.*, Records Relating to Appointments. The enclosure is a letter of the same date from Sawyer to USG. "I learn with regret that it has been deemed proper to suspend Maj. L. E. Johnson, U. S. Marshal for South Carolina, and to appoint Mr R. M. Wallace as his successor, and I beg leave to place on record my reasons for this regret. *1.* Major Johnson has been a consistent and zealous Republican from the passage of the Reconstruction acts to this time, . . . *7.* His removal is sought by those who would break down and destroy the influence of that wing of the Republican Party in S. C. which aims at its purification and elevation, and which sees future success for the party only by such purification. Especially does Gov. Scott desire his removal, for he is determined, that, so far as lies in his power, no man who has failed to support his always vacillating, often corrupt course, shall be in office. *8.* Without desiring to include the Congressional delegation in the above-named class, I call attention to the fact that they have put on record no charges which have not been fully met and rebutted. They simply endorse the request of the Hon. A. S. Wallace that Mr Johnson may be removed to make place for his son. *9.* Major Johnson's removal would be taken by the people as a sign that the national administration sympathized with the State administration which has brought upon the party so much disgrace. *This would be a very serious evil.* It would also be regarded as a blow aimed directly at *my friends* and *myself.* . . . I think justice to Major Johnson demands that any charges against him should be filed in the proper department: and when he fails to refute charges of inefficiency, want of integrity or zeal, or party infidelity, I shall not only consent to, but advise his removal." ALS, *ibid.*

On June 10, Johnson, Washington, D. C., wrote to USG. "I have to-day examined the papers on file in the office of the Attorney General. I recognized the fact that it is for you to judge of the propriety of making a change in the office which I have had the honor to hold under your appointment but I must respectfully ask that I may not be removed upon charges made unless those charges are sustained by proper evidence. The substance of the charges lately preferred against me is that I have made deductions from the pay of the deputy-marshals employed to take the census, and that I have issued pay certificates instead of paying money to witnesses, jurors, &c. I am astonished that such charges should have been made. The facts are simply these, and I challenge proof from any source to the contrary. In making my appointments for deputy-marshals I was so anxious to select only Republicans that in many instances I did appoint men who were not competent to discharge their duties. The result was that when the returns of the census came into my office, they were found to be so incorrect that I was compelled to employ clerical force to correct them. I accordingly employed such clerical force as was needed, where no errors were discovered, no charge was made, but where there were errors I charged *precisely what* I *was obliged to pay*, namely, twenty-five cents an hour,—this amount was paid by me and charged to the deputy-marshals. When the work was completed I notified the deputy-marshals of this, and also the Superintendent of the Census. It was a necessary, fair, honest, open transaction on my part, and never in a single instance was one cent deducted except what was actually paid by me for the corrections made. In addition to this I advanced about eight hundred dollars to the census-deputies in order to enable them to obtain food and transportation while engaged in their work. Had I not ~~have~~ taken this action there would have been a complete stoppage of the census. In my anxiety to do my duty I kept my clerical force on the revision of the returns at work every day Sundays included until eleven and some-times twelve o'clock at night for three months. As I have already said I challenge proof to the contrary and I respectfully refer your Excellency to the accompanying correspondence with Gen. Walker, the Superintendent of the Census Bureau. In reply to the second charge of issuing pay certificates to witnesses and jurors I have to say that I issued the pay certificates for the simple reason that I had no money on hand and could not obtain it from Washington, and that I did so at the urgent request of many of the witnesses and jurors, so as to enable them to procure money in advance of its coming from Washington. As soon however as I learned that these certificates were being heavily discounted I obtained from the First National Bank of Charleston upon my own note endorsed by the District Attorney D. T. Corbin sufficient money to meet the liabilities of the Government; and which money I used solely to anticipate the payment by the Government. This I did solely for the purpose of preventing these certificates of indebtedness from being discounted by brokers. Never in any instance have I issued a pay certificate when there were funds on hand, nor have I ever neglected to make my requisitions for funds in due time. The cause of my not being able to procure money at a requisite time was in consequence of the terms of the District and Circuit Court following each other so closely, I was unable to make up the vouchers of my office within ten days from the adjournment of each term, and another ten days was consumed in obtaining the money from Washington. Finally, in answer to the charges made by Gov. Scott, I have to say that not one of these charges has any foundation in fact and I defy him to make good any one of them. . . ." LS, *ibid.* On June 12, Daniel H. Chamberlain, S. C. attorney gen., wrote to USG. "I have been informed that Major Johnson has been suspended from the Office of U. S. Marshal for the District of South Carolina, with the view of appointing a successor. I have also been informed that this action was taken at the urgent solicitation of Governor Scott, and upon general charges of inefficiency, want of party fidelity, &c. &c. I beg to say to Your Excellency that I have a most intimate knowledge of the conduct [of] Major Johnson and I am prepared to assert that not one of these charges is founded upon fact—On the contrary Major Johnson has on all occasions shown himself to be a faithful officer and a faithful Republican—The one great cause of the present attempt to remove him is this: that in the Election last fall gross and outrageous frauds were committed in the election by the conniv-ance and assistance of corrupt Republican Managers and Commissioners of Elec-tion,—frauds which have disgraced our party in South Carolina and before the whole country—Major Johnson in his official character was obliged to execute the laws of Congress against these offenders. The result has been the conviction of many Repub-licans who engaged in the frauds, and the cry of oppression, rebel sympathy, &c.

against Major Johnson—The truth is, and I am ready to stand by the statement, that Major Johnson has been *too* efficient in executing the laws to please those who now seek his removal—The Republican party has a thousand times more to fear from fraud and corruption within itself than from all its political enemies, including the Ku Klux—Nothing but our own abuses can defeat us in 1872, and unless soon checked by a strong hand these *will* ruin us—Now, the removal of Major Johnson at the present time will accomplish nothing but to give comfort to our own corruptionists—In saying this I do not refer to Senator Robertson, or Representative Wallace, or to Mr. R. M. Wallace, but I refer to the hostility to Major Johnson which has caused the charges to which I have referred, to be made—Major Johnson's removal will be a blow at the best interests of our party—a result which I know Your Excellency does not intend," ALS, *ibid.* On June 15, Horace Porter wrote to Bristow. "The President will be pleased to have you call at the Executive Mansion tomorrow morning and bring with you any papers you may have in the case of Mr. Johnson, U. S. marshal of South Carolina." Copy, DLC-USG, II, 1.

On Feb. 17, Governor Robert K. Scott of S. C. had written to USG recommending a diplomatic appointment for Solomon L. Hoge. LS, DNA, RG 59, Letters of Application and Recommendation. On March 28, Chamberlain wrote to USG. "I learn that Hon. S. L. Hoge, of this state, is an applicant for the position of United States Minister to Brazil. I take pleasure in saying that Judge Hoge was always an ardent and faithful Republican in this State and his zeal and labors were held in high esteem by the party as was evidenced by his election to the position of Associate Justice of our Supreme Court and subsequently a member of the 41st Congress. His appointment would give satisfaction to his many friends in this State." ALS, *ibid.* On April 20, Robertson wrote to Secretary of State Hamilton Fish. "I desire to withdraw my name from the papers, endorsing, Judge S. L. Hoge for a Foreign Mission. I am quite sure I did wrong in endorsing him for any position, to be credited to South-Carolina." ALS, *ibid.* Related papers are *ibid.* On Sept. 1, S. C. Senators William B. Nash, Robert Smalls *et al.* petitioned USG. "We the undersigned Republicans, of the State of South Carolina would respectfully recommend and urge the appointment of the Hon. S. SL. Hoge to the position of United States Marshal for this State; Judge Hoge in our opinion will give entire satisfaction to all the leading republicans of the State, and will in our opinion do more to aid in arresting and bringing to justice the Ku Klux than any other man in the State. He is a brave man and competent for the work and a good earnest republican" DS (47 signatures), *ibid.*, RG 60, Records Relating to Appointments. On Sept. 5, Governor Scott favorably endorsed this petition. AES, *ibid.* On Sept. 22, Elliott, Columbia, favorably endorsed this petition to USG. AES, *ibid.* On Oct. 3, Robertson and Alexander Wallace, Columbia, telegraphed to USG. "Should you desire to make a change in the office of marshal for south Carolina Solomon L Hoge is not the choice of a majority of the Republican party. await information" Telegram received (at 10:00 P.M.), *ibid.* On Oct. 4, L. Cass Carpenter, editor, *Daily Union*, Columbia, wrote to USG. "Hon S. L. Hoge, late member of Congress from this state, is an applicant for the position of U. S. Marshal for S. C. He is fully and heartily endorsed for the place he seeks, not only by the leading republicans throughout the state, as individuals, but also by the party, as an organization. Judge Hoge possesses qualifications which, in the judgment of those who know him best, eminently fit him for the Marshalship. He is an uncompromising republican, a foe to the democratic Ku Klux, and we believe will do more to arrest the members of this hellish gang than almost any other man in the state. The party needs the assistance of every friend of republicanism, and the removal of Mr Johnson, and the appointment of Judge Hoge will send a thrill of joy throughout the entire republican ranks of our state, and will carry dismay to the camp of the enemy, now in a great measure supported by the U. S. officials. We earnestly appeal to your Excellency to assist us in strengthening the party, by the appointment of loyal republicans to places of honor and trust." ALS, *ibid.* On Oct. 5, James M. Edmunds, "Union Republican Resident Executive Committee," Washington, D. C., wrote to Orville E. Babcock recommending Hoge's appointment in order to "enable the administration to suppress outrages without a resort to marshall law." ALS, *ibid.*

On Oct. 3, Robertson, Columbia, had written to USG. "I am informed that a petition will be presented to you, by Hon R. B. Elliott, asking the removal of Louis M. Johnson, U. S. Marshall for the district of south-Carolina, and the appointment of Judge S: L. Hoge. Said petition purports to represent the Republican-Party of South-Carolina. In my opinion it only represents a small portion of said party. Should you decide to remove Mr Johnson, I beg to refer you to the application of Robert M. Wallace, now on file in the Attorney-general's office. Mr Wallace is the son of Hon A. S. Wallace, M, C, 4th Dist of So. Ca, And would be the most suitable person in our party, in the state, for the position." ALS, *ibid.* On the same day, Junius S. Mobley, Columbia, wrote to USG. "As a member of the late Convention of the State Central Republican Committee of South Carolina I desire to make a statement in relation to the U. S. Marshal's place for South Carolina. A resolution was introduced in the Convention asking for the removal of Major L. E. Johnson, the present Marshal, which was adopted unanimously—afterwards an amendment to the former resolution was introduced asking for the appointment of S. L. Hoge—when it was put to the House, I heard only one vote in the affirmative and no vote in the negative—The members of the Convention were so desirous of the removal of Johnson that they were willing to endorse any one who could displace him. One speaker Mr. Donaldson said that he had no preference for Mr Hoge but would take him, to get Mr Johnson removed. I would further state that I signed the petition for appointment of Mr. Hoge, after being informed by him that Mr. Wallace whom I had formerly endorsed had withdrawn his claims for the appointment. I still fully endorse the claims of R M Wallace as I was misled into signing the last application. I had the honor to introduce in the Convention a resolution, which was unanimously adopted, 'endorsing President Grant and his administration.'" LS, *ibid.* On Oct. 4, Alexander Wallace, Columbia, wrote to USG. "I forwarded to you by mail on yesterday letters from two members of the State Central Republican Committee and after late convention, which partially explain the manner in which the resolutions endorsing S. L Hoge for the appointment of U. S. Marshal for South Carolina were passed by that Convention. In addition thereto I have the honor to present to you a statement of facts to which I respectfully ask your attention   There was a strong feeling in the Convention to urge the prompt removal of L E Johnson and after resolutions to that effect had been passed a resolution purporting to be an amendment to the first was introduced late in the evening when a majority of the members had retired and was passed before the attention of any one was drawn to it. This meeting of the State Central Committee was called for the purpose of appointing delegates to a National Convention of colored men which meets in this place at an early day but advantage was taken of it to get a recommendation. Mr Hoge knew that an application for the appointment of R. M. Wallace was on file in Washington and was told positively that it had not been withdrawn, yet he and his friends represented to the friends of Wallace that he had withdrawn his application and would endorse Hoge—and in this way secured a number of names to his petition who would not otherwise have signed it. . . ." ALS, *ibid.*

On Oct. 3, Johnson, Spartanburg, via Columbia on Oct. 5, telegraphed to USG.

"In Justice to the late Suffering Republicans of this section of the State as well as myself will You please Suspend action in my case until I have furnished Satisfactorily the duty I am engaged in feeling here is very bitter & knowing it as I do to be a post of danger I object to leaving even for the purpose of reporting to your excellency and bringing with me papers proving that I have done and am doing more in Crushing out the Ku Klux Klan than the entire State Government has done Since its organization See my Communication to Attorney General of Saturday last please reply" Telegram received (at 3:35 P.M.), *ibid.*

On Jan. 26, 1872, Corbin and Chamberlain, Washington, D. C., wrote to USG. "We have the honor to recommend Fredrick Bush of Columbia S. C. for the position of United States Marshal for the District of South Carolina in the place of Louis E. Johnson the present Marshal. Our motive for recommending this change is this; The vast amount of business now devolving upon the Marshal of South Carolina requires an active, energetic and practical business man, and one who will devote himself intelligently and personally to the duties of his office. We feel that Mr. Johnson does not combine all these qualities to as great a degree as the emergency requires. We are personally friendly to Mr. Johnson and regret that our observation compels us, in the interest of public justice, to make this statement. Mr. Bush is a gentleman of large experience in business, of high character, and much experience in the line of duties required in this office. We believe him to be eminently fitted in every way to discharge the duties of the office of United States Marshal in the pressing emergency now existing in South Carolina, and, therefore, most earnestly recommend his appointment. Mr. Bush is a staunch republican and has been since the organization of the party." DS, *ibid.* Rainey and Sawyer favorably endorsed this letter. AES (undated), *ibid.* Related papers are *ibid.*

On Feb. 16, James L. Orr, Anderson, S. C., telegraphed and wrote to USG. "I respectfully recommend Col J P Low for the position of U. S. Marshall for the district of South Carolina he is honest competent and faithful he was a union officer during the War he has all the qualifications requisite to make him a first class marshall and I cheerfully commend his name to your favorable consideration" Telegram received (via Columbia, S. C.), *ibid.* "I respectfully recommend Col J. P. Low for the position of U. S. Marshal for the District of S. C. He has for several years been Chief Engineer of the Blue Ridge RR in this state and has proved himself master of his profession—. . ." ALS, *ibid.*

On Feb. 1, Robert Wallace, Columbia, had written to USG requesting appointment as marshal, S. C. ALS, *ibid.* Attached to this letter was a petition from S. C. Senator Charles W. Montgomery and many others. "The undersigned most respectfully recommend Col. Robt M. Wallace for the appointment of United States Marshal for the State of South Carolina. Col. Wallace is a recognized Republican and will in our judgement discharge the duties of the position with diligence and fidelity, We disire to add that, Mr Frederick Bush who it is alleged is being urged for the position thro certain parties in Washington is not now a resident of this State. and is for just cause obnoxious to Republicans here. and has never been affiliated with the Republican party of South Carolina. but on the contrary he has by his private associations and public declarations openly allied himself with the leaders of the Democratic party." DS, *ibid.* On Feb. 2, Elliott and DeLarge, Columbia, wrote to USG. "We take pleasure in endorsing the application of Col. Wallace for the appointment of United States Marshal, and do most fully and cordially concur in the views expressed by the gentlemen who have herein endorsed Mr. Wallace. We know Col. Wallace as an uncompromising and ardent Republican, a strong and unselfish supporter of Your

Excellency and the National Administration, and in the performance of his duties as Revenue Collector in this State, has done much towards securing from the people, not only respect, but confidence in the National Administration. . . ." LS, *ibid.* On Feb. 8, Cummings, Washington, D. C., wrote to USG. "My home is Spartanburg S. C. —On my way North to seek aid in building two or three plain, cheap churches in my county for our poor, persecuted Republican Methodists of the old M. E. Church of America, spending a day in Washington, I learn that there is a prospect of a change in the office of U. S. Marshall for the State of South Carolina. At this juncture in our affairs in that state it is vastly important that, that office be filled by a man of ability, integrity, energy. The work of arresting and punishing the infamous K. Klux has only been commenced—Our life as a people, and especially as Republicans depends on its prosecution—With Robert M. Wallace Esq. I have long been acquainted, and believing him to be just the man I would most respectfully request his appointment to the Office of United States Marshall for the State of South Carolina." ALS, *ibid.* On Feb. 23, Robertson wrote to USG. "Enclosed please find the endorsement of *Robert M. Wallace,* for *Marshall* of the district of South Carolina, by the entire delegation to the National convention (Republican) to be held at Philadelphia Penn. The within endorsement was this moment received by mail, and I hasten to forward it, for your consideration." ALS, *ibid.* In [Feb. 1872], G. W. Tucker *et al.,* Spartanburg County, petitioned USG. "We the undersigned Citizens of the State and County aforesaid, certify that a few months ago, we petitioned your excellency, to retain Majr L. E. Johnson, as united States Marshal for the District of South Carolina. because we felt that the necessity of arresting the members. of the Ku Klux Klan, in this County was so pressing that we were afraid that a change in Marshals might Cause a delay, that would be disastrous to us; That since sending that petition. we have had Maj. Johnson in our County for Several Months under the pretense of arresting Ku Klux, but that no Case of any importance whatever has been ferited out. by said Johnson; notwithstanding many murders have been committed in this County by the masked villians; and that we are Satisfied that if any man who was competent, and who desired to do So, Could have arrested hundreds of the worst men by this time. We therefore being satisfied that said L. E. Johnson is totally unfit to discharge the duties of the Office of united States Marshal, and being the parties immediately interested in having the Ku Klux brought to Justice Most respectfully petition Your Excellency to remove Said L. E. Johnson from the Office of united states Marshal for the District of South Carolina, and to appoint some man who is competent to discharge the duties of that office." DS (24 signatures), *ibid.* This petition was endorsed: "Hundreds Would Sign if presented" E (undated), *ibid.* On Feb. 26, Johnson, Washington, D. C., wrote a letter of resignation to USG with the request that it take effect on April 19. ALS, *ibid.,* Letters Received, S. C. On Feb. 28, USG nominated Robert Wallace as marshal, S. C.

On Sept. 29, Alonzo J. Ransier, Columbia, wrote to USG. "The State Central Committee of the Republican Party of South Carolina respectfully represent to your Excellency. That the prevalence of disorders in South Carolina the impunity with which violence is committed and outrages perpetrated by the organization known as the Ku Klux Klan the sense of insecurity which obtains with all classes of citizens and the responsibility for the lack of proper zeal and effectiveness in the execution of the laws of the United States in this State, is largely attributable to the indecision, incompetency and un-republican proclivities of the United States Marshal of this District. We charge him with sympathizing with those who are antagonized to the present administration Federal and State; with indisposition to execute the laws of the land in letter and spirit; and countenancing the acts of disloyal men by neglecting to secure their subjection to trial and punishment; with the appointment of corrupt and incompetent assistants; and above all, with a manifest disposition to embarrass and retard the efforts of the Republican Party to reconstruct the government upon the permanent basis of equal justice and rights to all classes and conditions of men. In view of these facts, we earnestly recommend your Excellency to remove him from office forthwith; and at the same time, we take the liberty of suggesting Hon Solomon L Hoge, a true and trusted Republican, an earnest and unfaltering supporter of your administration and of the government of the State, and an intelligent, courageous, and incorruptible man, as a worthy successor to the office." LS, *ibid.*, Records Relating to Appointments. Robert Wallace continued as marshal, S. C.

Proclamation

Whereas by an act of Congress, entitled "An Act to enforce the provisions of the Fourteenth Amendment to the Constitution of the United States, and for other purposes", approved the twentieth day of April, Anno Domini, one thousand eight hundred and seventy-one, power is given to the President of the United States, when, in his judgment, the public safety shall require it, to suspend the privileges of the *writ* of *habeas corpus* in any State or part of a State whenever combinations and conspiracies exist in such State, or part of a State for the purpose of depriving any portion or class of the people of such State of the rights, privileges, immunities, and protection named in the Constitution of the United States, and secured by the act of Congress aforesaid; and whenever such combinations and conspiracies do so obstruct and hinder the execution of the laws of any such State and of the United States, as to deprive the people aforesaid of the rights, privileges, immunities, and protection aforesaid and do oppose and obstruct the laws of the United States, and their due execution, and impede and obstruct the due course of justice under the sam[e; and whenever] such combinations shall be organized and armed and so numerous and powerful, as to be able by violence either to overthrow or to set at defiance the constituted authorities of said State and of the United States within such State; and whenever, by reason of said causes, the conviction of such offenders and the preservation of the public peace shall become in such State or part of a State impracticable.

And Whereas such unlawful combinations and conspiracies for the purposes aforesaid are declared by the act of Congress aforesaid to be rebellion against the Government of the United States:

And whereas by said act of Congress it is provided, that, before the President shall suspend the privileges of the *writ* of *habeas corpus*, he shall first have made proclamation, commanding such insurgents to disperse: *And Whereas* on the twelfth day of the present month of October, the President of the United States did issue his proclamation, reciting therein, among other things, that such combinations and conspiracies did then exist in the counties of Spartansburg, York, Marion,[1] Chester, Laurens, Newberry, Fairfield, Lancaster, and Chesterfield in the State of South Carolina, and commanding thereby all persons composing such unlawful combinations and conspiracies to disperse and retire peaceably to their homes within five days from the date thereof, and to deliver either to the Marshal of the United States for the District of South Carolina, or to any of his deputies, or to any military officer of the United States within said counties, all arms, ammunition, uniforms, disguises, and other means and implements used, kept, possessed or controlled by them for carrying out the unlawful purposes for which the said combinations and conspiracies are organized:

And whereas the insurgents engaged in such unlawful combinations and conspiracies within the counties aforesaid have not dispersed and retired peaceably to their respective homes, and have not delivered to the marshal of the United States, or to any of his deputies, or to any military officer of the United States within said counties, all arms, ammunition, uniforms, disguises, and other means and implements used, kept, possessed, or controlled by them for carrying out the unlawful purposes for which the combinations and conspiracies are organized, as commanded by said proclamation, but do still persist in the unlawful combinations and conspiracies aforesaid.

Now, therefore, I, Ulysses S. Grant, President of the United States of America, by virtue of the authority vested in me by the Constitution of the United States, and the act of Congress aforesaid, do hereby declare that, in my judgment, the public safety especially requires that the privileges of the *writ* of *habeas corpus* be suspended, to the end that such rebellion may be overthrown, and do hereby suspend the privileges of the *writ* of *habeas corpus* within the counties of Spartansburg, York, Marion, Chester, Laurens, Newberry, Fairfield, Lancaster, and Chesterfield in said State of South Carolina in respect to all persons, arrested by the marshal of the United States for the said district of South Carolina, or by any of his deputies, or by any military officer of the United States, or by any soldier or citizen acting under the orders of said marshal, deputy, or such military officer within any one of said counties, charged with any violation of the act of Congress aforesaid during the continuance of such rebellion.

In witness whereof I have hereunto set my hand, and caused the seal of the United States to be affixed.

Done at the city of Washington, this seventeenth day of October, in the year of our Lord, one thousand eight hundred and seventy-one, and of the independence of the United States of America, the ninety-sixth.

U. S. GRANT

DS, DNA, RG 130, Presidential Proclamations. See Proclamation, Oct. 12, 1871. On Oct. 14, 1871, USG, Bridgeport, Conn., telegraphed to Benjamin H. Bristow, solicitor gen. and act. attorney gen. "IF POSSIBLE PREPARE S. C. PROCLAMATION AND MAIL TO ME AT BOSTON TOMORROW EVENING   SEND SPECIAL MESSENGER." Telegram received (at 10:47 A.M.), DNA, RG 60, Letters Received. On the same day, Bristow wrote to USG. "In compliance with your telegram of this morning from Bridgeport, Connecticut, I have prepared a proclamation suspending the privileges of the writ of *habeas corpus* in certain counties in South Carolina, and send it to you by Mr. Sherman, of this office, who will leave the city to-night, and take the first train from New York to Boston. In the preparation of this proclamation, I have pursued as literally as possible the language of the statutes under which it is prepared, following also the language of your proclamation of warning. You will observe that the suspension relates solely to persons arrested for violation of the Act of Congress in question. Without this qualification your proclamation might be deemed a suspension of the writ in ordinary cases arising in the State Courts, and having no relation whatever to violations of this Act. Inasmuch as the Proclamation cannot be issued before next Tuesday, the 17th instant, I have left the date blank, that it may be dated and issued on such day as you may see proper. Mr. Sherman will await your pleasure." Copy, *ibid.*, Letters Sent to Executive Officers. On Oct. 16, Orville E. Babcock, Boston, wrote to Bristow. "The President says date this tomorrow the 17th 1871   All well and very busy. All say they are having a nice time. Porter sends *love*" ALS, DLC-Benjamin H. Bristow. On Oct. 18, Bristow telegraphed to Attorney Gen. Amos T. Akerman, Yorkville, S. C. "Failing to receive any communication from you since the proclamation of warning was issued, I prepared a proclamation suspending the writ of *habeas corpus* in the nine counties in South Carolina named in the first, and by direction of the President it was issued yesterday." Copy, DNA, RG 60, Letters Sent to Executive Officers.

On Oct. 13, USG authorized "Clement Hugh Hill, Assistant Attorney General . . . to perform the duties of the Attorney General at the Seat of Government, during the absence of the Attorney General and Solicitor General, until otherwise ordered." DS, *ibid.*, Letters from the President. On Oct. 16, Akerman, Yorkville, wrote to USG. "In pursuance of your directions, I have come to this place and have made careful inquiry here concerning the unlawful combinations which have been reported as existing in this part of South Carolina. In the counties of Spartanburg, York, Chester, Union, Laurens, Newberry, Fairfield, Lancaster and Chesterfield, there are combinations for the purposes of preventing the free political action of citizens who are friendly to the Constitution and government of the United States and of depriving the emancipated class of the equal protection of the laws. These combinations embrace at least two thirds of the active white men of those counties and have the sympathy and countenance of a majority of the other third. They are connected with similar combinations in other counties and States, and no doubt are part of a grand system of criminal associations ~~extending through~~ pervading most of the Southern States. The members are bound to obedience and secresy by oaths which they are taught to regard as of higher obligation than the lawful oaths taken before civil magistrates. They are organized and armed. They effect their objects by personal violence often extending to murder. They terrify witnesses. They control juries in the State Courts and sometimes in the Courts of the United States. Systematic perjury is one of the means by which prosecutions of the members are defeated. From information given by officers of the State and of the United States and by credible private citizens, I am justified in affirming that the instances of criminal violence perpetrated by these combinations within the last twelve months in the above named counties ~~should~~ could be reckoned by thousands. In consequence of the recent convictions in North Carolina and of the presence of troops, there is now some abatement in their activity. But the organizations and discipline are industriously kept up, with the determination to act with increased energy as soon as the special vigilance which the government is now exercising shall be relaxed. Unless these combinations shall be thoroughly suppressed, no citizen who opposes their political objects will be permitted to live, and no freedman will enjoy essential liberty, in the territory now subject to their sway. They cannot be suppressed by the State law, which necessarily acts through resident officers and jurors. Relief can only come from the power of the United States. It is a common opinion among the oppressed classes here that military tribunals only are adequate to the exigencies of the case. I have not adopted this opinion; and shall not do so, unless there shall be a demonstration of the ~~inefficiency~~ impotency of the civil tribunals after they shall have received all the aid that can be given to them under existing laws. I am not at liberty to suppose that the laws of the United States will not be faithfully administered by the judges, or that the District Attorney or Marshal will come short of his full duty. With due care to select impartial and courageous jurors, ~~who are not connected with the unlawful combinations, there~~ we may hope for righteous verdicts. The most serious difficult~~ies~~y is in insuring safety to witnesses. To obviate this difficulty, I think it necessary that officers should have the power of detaining in custody for a reasonable time such persons as are ~~suspected~~ believed from information that cannot at once be prudently disclosed, to have violated the laws. I therefore recommend that you forthwith issue your proclamation suspending the privileges of the writ of habeas corpus in the counties above named, under the power conferred in the act of April 20, 1871. You have twice, by proclamation, warned these conspirators to desist from their crimes, but they have not obeyed the admonition. They must now be taught that there is some force in the law which they have despised." ALS, Free Library of Philadelphia, Philadelphia, Pa. See William S. McFeely, "Amos T. Akerman: The Lawyer and Racial Justice," in J. Morgan Kousser and James M. McPherson, eds., *Region, Race, and Reconstruction: Essays in Honor of C. Vann Woodward* (New York and Oxford, 1982), pp. 395–415.

On Sept. 11, AG Edward D. Townsend had written to Brig. Gen. Alfred H. Terry, Louisville. "*Confidential.* . . . I am directed by the Secretary of War to inform you that Hon. A. T. Akerman Attorney General of the U. S. contemplates visiting, in about two or three weeks, the districts of South and North Carolina where the Ku Klux outrages have been lately represented as rife, for the purpose of directing in person such legal proceedings as he may judge ~~to be~~ proper—The President desires you to give him every aid and facility in your power in prosecuting his plans, and to cause persons indicated by him to be arrested for the civil authorit~~y~~ies. Although it is conceived tha[t] ample power for this action is conveyed in the order promulgating the President['s] Proclamation; (G. O. no. 48) yet it is deem[ed] essential that there shall be no doubt on the point. I have sent a copy of the new cipher key to Major~~s~~ Merrill at Yorkville So. Ca. and Major C. H. Morgan, 4th Arty Commanding troops in ~~South~~ & North Carolina at Raleigh in order that they may communicate by telegraph in cipher with ~~you~~ Dept. head-quarters, if necessary. ~~Is~~ In the operations to be carried out it may be that a considerable force will be needed by the Attorney General near the boundary between North & South Carolina, and that it or a portion of it, may have to cross the line, without regard to the Departmental Command—For this you will please provide. The Attorney General will go first to his home in Georgia, and will communicate with you in person or by writing, before any steps need be taken by you, except perhaps the gradual concentration of more troops near the scene of action, if such measure be necessary—You will please acknowledge receipt of ~~T~~this communication ~~is to be~~ and regard~~ed~~ it as confidential" ADf (initialed and originally dated Sept. 9), DNA, RG 94, Letters Received, 1612 1871. On the same day, Townsend wrote to Brig. Gen. Irvin McDowell, New York City. "*Confidential* . . . I send you herewith a copy of a letter to Brigdr Genl Terry— In addition to the information therein conveyed, the President directs that ~~you take~~ in order that such steps may be taken as will enable the Attorney General to carry out his plans for arresting some of the principal Ku Klux leaders, should it become necessary for him to operate within the State of No. Ca. ~~and that~~ the troops in the disturbed district of that State, ~~especially near the dividing line between the North & So. Carlo be instructed to give the Attorney General every possible aid.~~ ~~may~~ shall ~~if necessary~~ . . . receive the orders of Brigdr Genl. Terry—as ~~will be~~ indicated in the letter to Major Morgan, of which a copy is herewith enclosed ~~herewith~~—" ADf (initialed), *ibid.* Also on Sept. 11, Townsend wrote to Maj. Charles H. Morgan, Raleigh. "The Hon. A. T. Akerman Attorney Genl. of the U. S. may have occasion to call upon you for assistance in certain contingencies   The President directs that you promptly comply with any request he may make upon you for ~~the~~ military aid ~~of troops~~ during his proposed visit to No. Cara—" ADf (initialed), *ibid.* Related papers are *ibid.*

On Oct. 27, 1871, R. J. Cameron, Washington, D. C., had written to [USG]. "I reached here last night direct from South Carolina & intend calling on you today but I find a letter which calls me to N. York on the early train today—My object in calling on you was to have requested you to send some one in whom you could confide immediately to S Carolina & ascertain precisely the state of things there—as ardent a Republican as I am I fear you have gone too far—a letter in yesterday N. Y Herald will give you a more truthful & concise statement than my limited time will allow me—as strong as we are as a party we cannot afford to weaken it by such acts as are now being committed there. Hence I insist that you send some one ascertain for yourself the truth   you have certainly been deceived by parties who in their eagerness to help the Republican Cause have gone too far,   Read the correspondence in the Herald & act for yourself" ALS, *ibid.*, RG 60, Letters Received.

On Oct. 28, a correspondent reported: "The President is in receipt of advices from South Carolina to the effect that affairs in that State are in a very disorganized condition, showing that the issue of his proclamation at this time was not inopportune. It is also stated that, from present indications, many of the influential leaders in Ku-Kluxism will continue to make confessions. Senator Pool, of the Southern Outrage Committee, had a lengthy interview with the President to-day, when the Ku-Klux disorders were generally talked over. . . ." *Philadelphia Public Ledger*, Oct. 30, 1871.

On Dec. 4, U.S. Senator Francis P. Blair, Jr., of Mo. introduced a resolution requesting USG "to inform the Senate under what provisions of the law of April 20, 1871, if any, and if not under that law, by what authority he has caused the Constitution and laws of the United States, and the constitution and laws of the State of South Carolina, to be set aside and martial law declared and the writ of *habeas corpus* suspended in the counties of Spartanburg, Marion, York, Newberry, Chester, Laurens, Fairfield, Lancaster, and Chesterfield, in the State of South Carolina, whereby the courts and civil authorities are unable to afford protection to the lives, liberties, and rights of the people therein, and all of them left at the mercy of such military subordinates as he has seen or may see fit to place over them. . . ." *CG*, 42–2, 3. On Dec. 5, Blair spoke. ". . . The President states in his message that the testimony taken before the committee on southern affairs amply sustains him in his proclamation of martial law. I do not know how the President got that information. Certainly, he could not have got it by any report from the committee. Nobody was authorized by the committee to make any such report to the President. As a member of the committee, I can give my opinion that the facts elicited by that examination did not justify the proclamation of martial law, and I suspect that I know more about the facts elicited before the committee than the President himself. . . ." *Ibid.*, pp. 13–14. See message to House of Representatives, April 19, 1872, note 1.

On June 17, 1871, Anna R. Orindorf, Van Buren Furnace, Va., had written to USG. "I come to you for sympathy. I am among rebels   I cannot receive justice here through the law   I have tried it   I brought a sick husband here in the mountains for his health from Missouri.   this is my husbands native place   I am formerlly from Ohio   My husband has always been a Union man was in the Northern Army Elnlisted in Cleveland Ohio, and I am strictly Union   this is why we cannot receve justice   I have seen as many as 7 revolvers drawn upon my husband at one time just for claiming our own right about matters. And now these people are haveing their own way and would impoverish my family   I saved money for years and when I came here invested it on a farm   my husband's brother was liveing with us at times and now the rebs want to make it appear that he has an interest in the land and stock   I was on the witness stand 10 hours   this testimony they cast aside my husbands also and retained here say   No one ever saw my ~~my~~ money here untill it was counted out to the man off whom we purchased   I brought this money paid for the farm in government funds on my person in a belt. The man of whom we purchased is know State Treasurer Geo Rye   he was in the United States Navy during the war   he was obliged to leave this county during the war so was my husband   I have never called upon the United States Government for help before I am the mother of two children and I wish to retain this home for my boys, and if the government of the United States do not assist me I must sink   my husband cant work as he could once. I have tried to retain my home for three years   I employed two of the best lawyers in Woodstock but they must go with their party   my husbands brother turned rebel to gain the day. . . ." ALS, DNA, RG 94, Letters Received, 2231 1871.

On July 3, S. N. Millwer, Adairsville, Ga., wrote to USG. "private & confidential . . . as the Executive of this Great Nation I adress you as a private citizen upon a subject of vital Interest to Every friend of the federal Goverment who resides in the south   I do so at the request of a No Republicans of this County   in order that you may understand me clearly I will State My case   I am a Native of this County was forced to leave in 1861 went to Knoxville Tennesse Returned With Gen Sherman and Since the Surrender Settled here again and find it difacult to remain here in peace   I am no office Seeker and all I wish to Know is whether I am to Expect any protection from the Goverment or Not   have I any appeal from Courts held by Ku Klux to Courts in Other States   I Met you in the Lamar House at Knoxville Tennesse in 1864 though you doutless have forgotten me   I Respectfully Refer you to W G Brownlow Horace Maynard R. R. Butler W. B. Stokes" ALS, *ibid.*, 2336 1871.

On July 20, Ira A. Mason, Covington, Ga., wrote to USG. "In conformity with the Laws of the United States, and Proclamaitions hitherto published, by the Supreme U. S. Executive; and having implicit confidence in your integrity, as the Chief Ruler of the U. S. Laws, Peace, and good Order: as also, the protection of all Loyal Citizens, in their Legal rights:—therefore, I am authorised by the Power of the Holy Ghost; to inform you, of the hostile acts, & apparent intentions of the White Citizens, & Kuklux of this place, & its vicinity. I am known as Doctor Ira A. Mason A Native of New York, and always a Loyal Citizen of the United States.—I have been three years in Tennessee, and taught a Public Colored School, in the vicinity of Nashville.—I came here, and have been engaged teaching a Colored School, in the School-House; built & owned by the U. S. Government, and on the same ground, where the rebels caused a School house to be burned about a year since. The White & black rebels, declare that a Colored & black School, shall not be taught more than a month or two. I have been unable to board with any white family; and consequently, have been compelled to stop with a respectable black family, & in the same room, (separate beds,) with the Colored Pastor, of the Colored Methodist Church. This black person with whom I boarded, is the the owner of his house and Lot; and within about 30 rods of Oxford College, where are Students from nearly all parts of Georgia. One night, about 2 O'Clock, a few persons came to the house, & called for me to come out; & when I said that they could not see me at night; they commenced throwing large rocks against the house, threatening to set fire to the house, & finally firing a shot through the window shutter & house; and when I said that I would have U. S. Troops to talk to them; they fired several shots, & departed, while they said that they would return the next night, and if they found me there, they would bring my coffin, and I would live no longer.—The next morning, I wrote a letter to Govenor Bullock, and the Rev. E. B. Davis—who is an Ordained Minister by Bishop Scott, of (I believe Ohio,) the Northern Methodist Church—visited the Govenor, gave him the letter, (in which I made a full description,) & had an interview;

and the Govenor said that he could not send troops, but if they should again interfere with me, that we should shoot them.—A few days after, a Student whose name is Pink Price, grossly abused me, a said that they (meaning the Students,) would hang me; all this in the presence of several colored witnesses. All this occurred about 2 or 3 weeks ago, & the reason that I have not been attacked, is because I have been armed with a Colt's revolver, and my colored friends have had an armed guard to protect me at night.—The Students have had Commencement for 3 days, which Expired yesterday, & many of them have returned home; as it is vacation until September. The Students and their friends gathered within 20 or 30 rods of my boarding house, (I have changed it, & stop near the Schoolhouse,) to consult how they should get me into their power. This has been done 2 days in succession; & last night, several of the Students were seen to carry false faces, & Kuklux caps, late at night.— I expect a riot here within a few days, between the blacks & whites.—Elder Yarborraugh, of the North Methodist Church, stationed here for 20 years; says that a riot & war must soon break out, unless troops are stationed here without delay. I communicate these facts in behalf of the Loyal Colored people Who at present protect me.— A letter cannot reach me only by Express,—We claim protection." ALS, *ibid.*, 2582 1871.

On Sept. 3, Lindsey Hudson, Savannah, wrote to USG. "I want to let you no about the ku kulxs. has come in my house trying to kill me and I shot and killd one man. then I Replyed to the Govenorer of the state Mr Bullock to help me and I want to let you no about him and how he is doing me all, so I will send you his letter and let you no yourself, since I have killd the man I have gone of. I can not stay Home at night. the will come and killd me. do please do somthing for me you is the last man that I can get to help me. the men shot at me five time before I s[— —]d Broke down the door and come in, than I shot and killd one man. I am write and I must write to you about this. I off form Home and can not come over come. Mr Bullock says that I must got to the men in my County but it will not do, for the men will come at night and kill me, please write to me soon as you can and let me no if you will help. . . . the man was kild in Jefferson Co, Ga. . . . the man that I kild Was name Joe Calmond. I have witennesses for ths. Mr Bullock is not doing me write. he no that if I go Back in my County the will kill me" ALS, *ibid.*, 3113 1871. The enclosure is a letter of Aug. 21 from R. H. Atkinson, secretary, to Hudson, Augusta. "In reply to your communication of 20th inst. I am directed by His Excellency the Governor to say, that the proper course for you to pursue is to report your case to the civil authorities; and that your construction of the Proclamation offering rewards for the arrest of Ku Klux is wrong, as no such reward as the one stated in your letter for killing Ku Klux has been offered by the Governor." LS, *ibid.*

On Nov. 20, Ga. Representative Charles Hooks wrote to USG. "With the utmost anxiety I write to ask if something cannot be done to suppress Klu Kluxism in Geo for these Devils incarnate are riding at night whiping Colored people and killing whites, Though I was a member of the Constitutional Convention with Mr Akerman your Attorney Gen, the danger of staying at home was not as great as now, As the enemies of the Government have everything systamatised and their Persecution of union men is most carefully fortified by secreet grips, passwords &c, A number of my friends have been killed and I as a Republican ask you to have it stoped. I am representing the County of Wilkinson where every few weeks these masked Assassins ride as if your arms had never prevailed over this Country, Think of waking up at midnight and looking out of your window and seeing one or two hundred of these mounted men on a raid to kill a neighbor, or whip a colored man who has with you voted for the man of your choice,   Do while we have a vestage of Republicanism left in the Gubernotorial Department, listen to the Calls for help, from Georgia for unlike South Carolina who has been carried Republican all the time, Georgia has an enormous revolutionary element, who has regularly organized to oppress the few union men sticking to their Governmt,   Hoping something may be done spedily . . . Please let no one see this for if it gets back to my County people it will cost me my life   Akerman will tell you who I am.   if I am wished for I can go to Washington. If I am written to write in Care of Col James Adkins of Rev Dept at this place. Many good citizens are now lying out at night because of voteing the Republican ticket in my County, the same in adjoining Counties, even the Representative from an adjoining County Hon E. S. Griffin shares my fears of personal harm, and neither one of us votes with the Republican party in our House." ALS, *ibid.*, RG 60, Letters from the President.

On Dec. 4, David A. Newsom, Greensboro, Ga., wrote to USG. "In complyance with the request of a large & respectable number of the members of the Republican party of this (5 Congressional Dist) I beg to address you, Enquiring what (if any thing) will be done by Your Excellency or Congress tending to the protection of loyal citizens, or their persons & property & in a free Exercise of the rights given them by the Laws of that Governmt to which they are & have ever been loyal,   To be brief I need but refer you to the report of your sub Ku Klux Committee that met in Atlanta a short time ago to prove that the persons & property of loyal Citizens in this State need protection from the strong arm of the Government & further that action is necessay by your Excellency & Congress to give such loyal Citizens a guarantee that in the future they will not be deprived of their rights of a free Exercise of the rights guaranteed them by the Laws of the United States—Especialy—the right of franchise. The fact that D. M Dubose, (a chief of the Ku Klux as has been duly proven to your sub Ku Klux Committee) holds a seat in the Congress of the United States representing 5 Cong Dist of this State, (which said Dist but for Ku Klux intimidation, would have elected Hon Isham S Fannin by a majority of least Five Thousand votes,) cleary shows that the Republican voters of this District need the interposition of the Executive & the Strong arm of the Government to the End that they may have free Exercise of the Elective franchise in the future. The spirit of Rebellion that drenched the country in blood—impoverished it, & that has ever opposed the Measures of Reconstruction is still rampant as will appear by the action of the present General Assembly of this state in ording an Election (contrary to Constitution & laws of said state) for Governor, when it is clear that His Excellcy Benjamin Conley is Entitled to Exercise the functions of Governor during the Term for which Rufus B Bullock was Elected. This rampant spirit must be subdued, Else the County will eventualy suffer again the Horrors of Civil War & those whose greatest pride it was to be loyal to their government will be victims consquent upon their devotion to the Union & the Flag of their Country." ALS, *ibid.* See *SRC*, 42-2-41, parts 6 and 7. On Nov. 24, Governor Benjamin Conley of Ga. had written to USG. "Enclosed I have the honor to hand you printed copy of a veto message in which are set forth in detail the reasons that have induced me to withhold my assent from a bill that has passed both Houses of the General Assembly of this State, entitled 'an act to provide for a special election to fill the unexpired term of Rufus B. Bullock, late Governor and for other purposes.' I respectfully and earnestly request that you will give this message your most serious consideration. Upon the maintainance of the position I have taken, depends the salvation of the republican party in Georgia. It rests with you to determine whether the enemies of the administration and of the government in this State shall be allowed by the illegal exercise of a power fraudulently obtained, to crush out the last vestige of republican government in Georgia." LS, OFH. Passed over Conley's veto, the act led to the Dec. election of Democrat James M. Smith to replace Conley.

On July 13, N. A. L. Marchant, Boone Furnace, Ky., had written to USG. "I am Informed that thare is A lodg of Kuklux Organized About five Miles from this Place Consing of About forty or fifty Members and as thare is but Verry few Union men in this Vacinity I dont See that I Can do Anything to arrest them with out Som Assistance from Som Whare els   I am Also Infarmed that in the Intearier of the State that the Kuklux ar Verry numorous and that it is unsafe for A Union Man to express his opinion Even at the Balat Box as the Principle Part of the Men who hold Offices ar Rebbles at hart them selves   A few Nights A go they left A bundle of Switches and A notice at an old mans Door Notifying him to leav the Place within ten days   he was a good Union Man and had Two Sons in the Union Army   I hope that You will giv me Instructions what to do and I asshure You that I will do all In my power to arrest every Kukluck in Kentucky" ALS, DNA, RG 94, Letters Received, 2334 1871.

On the same day, Charles Cole, "disabled Soldier who served in the 141st Penna Vols," Marble Hill, Mo., wrote to USG. "With every Consideration of respect I take the Liberty of addressing you   I am living in Dunklin Co Mo or am Trying to live there but it has come to that pass that every Union Man has to carry his life in his hand as the Ku. Klux are about (900) nine Hundred Strong and defy the Civel authoraties, and have taken it in thier own hands   I am trying to make an honest living but I will have to leave my homes and all my Crop &c   there is ten Union Men all of whome was in the Union Army who have mostly been ordered to leave for reasons unknow unless to get their crop & out of Political Spite   By the advice of a Union Sergt Dr T. C. Moody I clamed to be reble & gained thier Confidence & joined the Band of Ku Klux   we have all tried every way for to induce or Scear them to lay aside thier disguise & lawless conduct but they will not   I had the promise of the Union Mens aid in getting the appointment of Detective for that part of the State   they Sent on applications to that effect but received no answer as the Post Master is a Ku Klux We think the mail was distroyed   Hoping & Praying that you may favor me with that Appointment . . . N B there is three Distilleries in the Swamps near Millers Mill   I have the name of all the Officers & most of the men in three of the Ku Klux orders To one of which I belong" ALS, ibid., 2528 1871.

On Aug. 13, E. D. Pennington, Cherryvale, Kan., wrote to USG. "Permit me To State to you the Condition of Tennessee now under Rebel rule and authority the Federl Soldiers and officers are now in jail Some in State prison for Life having bin Indicted be fore the Grand Jurors of the Difernt Counties of Tennessee for the Killing of Bush whackers and Rebels under orders from thier Commanding officers while in the Survice of the united States and in the Line of Duty   they also have one Lady in jail at Sparta in White Co. Cuseing her of giving infirmation to Federl Soldiers in the Killing of one Bushwhacker   they also have in the Same jail one Mounterful Weaver for Killing one William Hutson a bushwhacker found in armes goverment armes at that   this man was one of the Twelve that was Chosen to Shoot this Guirrilla and the the rest of the 12 had to flee from the County and are now all indicted for this matter and the Rebels arir fixing to hunt them up Even in Kansas & M.o.   also their is Two other Soldiers in Same jail just for obeying their officers in Command   they was all good and Rialible Soldiers   the thing is just this the State of Tennessee is now under Rebel rule Entireley and Some thing must be done to Relieve those Federl Soldiers   I have also just Received a Letter from General W. B. Stokes M. C. from Tennessee Stating that they have Some of his men in jail at Smithville for the Same offence while they was under him as Col of the 5 Tennessee Cavalry   while he was Commanding Fifth Tennessee Cav he gives an awful account of the way things is going on their   I will just State to you that I was Captain of Company (B) 1. Tennessee Mounted Infantry Commanded by (Col) Garret   three of those men that is in Sparta jail belong to my Company McBroom & Orsburn Harris Mounterful Weaver which was all good and Obediant Soldiers   this is but a Small Storm to what is going on in the State of Tenn   the K. K. K going Round at midnight hours whipping and maiming Union Soldiers   this is the Case all over the State and we want you to do Some thing for those poor Soldiers that is in jail and in State Prison . . ." ALS, *ibid.*, 2931 1871.

On Nov. 6, "W. W.," Paris, Tenn., wrote to USG. "Pleas excuse me for pestering you with my letter but I mean just what I say   If you will promis to pardon & protect me from the KuKlx I will give you my evidence against the best organised band that you ever saw   I will give you the names of the leaders.   they are good democrats   I am an old rebel soldier but I consider that my party was fairly whiped on the field of battle there fore I except the situation   I will be a secret detective If you will employ & protect me from the vengence of of the KuKlx: If they Knew that I wrote you this letter I would not live a week   Hopeing to hear from you soon . . . I shal give you an assumed name untill here from you. If you will send a confidential man here I will confer with him   All he has to doe is to come to Paris and I will see him   I live in Paris" ALS, *ibid.*, RG 60, Letters from the President.

On Nov. 18, Edward M. Cheney and H. Jenkins, Jacksonville, Fla., wrote to USG. "We are instructed by the Republican State Executive Committee of this State, acting in accordance with the formally expressed wishes of leading republicans, to call Your Excellency's attention to the condition of affairs in the counties of Jackson and Calhoun in this state, as shown by the evidence given before the Sub-Congressional Ku Klux Committee, and by the affidavits herewith enclosed, and to request Your Excellency to declare martial law in said counties. The evidence given before the Ku Klux Committee was very imperfect and incomplete, as the visit of that Committee to this state was so unexpected and so hurried that many important witnesses were not summoned and others arrived so late that the Committee had not time to examine them, but the enclosed affidavit gives, as we believe, a true statement of the present condition of Jackson county,—the men who sign it being influential colored citizens of that county—one of them now a member of the Legislature and another, late tax collector of the county. . . . A special election has been called by the Governor to fill vacancies in the Legislature in these two counties, as well as several other counties, to take place on the 19th day of December next. Jackson county has a clear colored republican majority of over seven hundred votes, but, owing to the Ku Klux outrages constantly occurring, the colored people assure us that, as matters now stand, they will not dare to vote, and that to put forward a republican candidate, would simply be to insure his death and their own. It is very evident that unless they secure that protection which the Federal government alone can give, the republicans of these counties must either go into the election with the certainty of defeat and the equal certainty of useless bloodshed, or they must let the election go by default, and so renounce their dearest right as American citizens. For these two reasons, then,—first, to protect the citizens of these counties in their lives their property and their rights as citizens *now*, and, second, to secure for them, during the coming election, the political rights which the Constitution of the United States guarantees to them, we ask, in the name of the republican party of this state, that martial law may be declared in these counties; believing that course to be the only means of protecting the innocent and of punishing the guilty. Both of our senators endorse this request as does also our representative in Congress, Hon J. T Walls, who will present these papers to Your Excellency, and give you, personally, such further information as may be desired." LS, *ibid.*, Letters Received, Fla. The enclosure was an affidavit of Nov. 16 concerning murders committed by the Ku Klux Klan. On Nov. 22, U.S. Senator Abijah Gilbert of Fla., St. Augustine, wrote to USG. "I feel it my duty to call your attention to the condition of affairs existing in certain portions of this State more especceally in the Counties of Jackson Calhoun and Columbia, where organized bodies of men armed and disguised have forceably taken political control, by means of murdering Loyal Citizens, and the terrorism they have inspired by these acts. . . ." ALS, *ibid.*, Letters from the President. On Nov. 27, a correspondent reported from Washington, D. C. "Senator SCOTT and Representative MAYNARD called on the President today and laid before him the evidence taken by the Committee which recently visited Florida, and they asked of him a suspension of the writ of habeas corpus in Jackson County, which the evidence showed to be entirely in the hand of the Kuklux. . . . There are several of the witnesses from this county, who were before the Committee, that dare not return home till they are afforded the protection of the United States authorities. The President did not indicate whether he would issue the proclamation, but Messrs. SCOTT and MAYNARD are very sure that the evidence would warrant him in doing so." *New York Times*, Nov. 28, 1871. No action followed. See *SRC*, 42-2-41, part 13, especially pp. 85, 272–79, 302–5, 308–10; Jerrell H. Shofner, *Nor Is It Over Yet: Florida in the Era of Reconstruction 1863–1877* (Gainesville, 1974), pp. 231–34.

1. See Proclamation, Nov. 3, 1871.

To Columbus Delano

Washington, D. C. Oct. 23d *1871*

HON. C. DELANO;
SEC. OF THE INT.
SIR:

If it meets with your judgement you may withdraw from the Atty. Gen. the further consideration of the Claim of the Central bBranch of P. R. R. for grants of lands &c. for the purpose of giving Attys for said road the opportunity of presenting their case anew.

> Very respectfully
> your obt. svt.
> U. S. GRANT

ALS, DNA, RG 48, Lands and Railroads Div., Union Pacific Railroad, Central Branch. On March 10, 1874, the Senate Judiciary Committee, considering the Central Branch Union Pacific Railroad Co. claim, reported that on Oct. 30, 1871, Secretary of the Interior Columbus Delano had "advised the President, by letter, that he had received from the company a map showing the general direction and route of their road from its terminus to the one hundredth meridian, as also a resolution of the company adopting said route as a continuation of their road, if approved by the President. The map and resolution were transmitted with the letter, showing the request of the company of the 26th of the month, that the map and route might be approved by the President." *SRC*, 43-1-169, 9. On Oct. 31, USG signed an executive order. "The full red line shown on the accompanying map extending from the meridian of Fort Riley to a connection with the Union Pacific Railroad at the one hundredth meridian of longitude west from Greenwich. (the same having been made from 'actual survey') is hereby pursuant to the provisions of section 9 of the Act of Congress approved July 1st 1862. relating to the Union Pacific Railroad and its branches, and the 16th section of the Act amendatory of the former Act, approved July 2d 1864, approved by me as indicating and showing 'the general direction and route' of the railroad and telegraph line which the central branch U. P. R. R. Co, are authorized to construct in continuation and extension of their present completed railroad and telegraph line pursuant to and under the provisions of said 16th section of said Act. approved July 2d 1864." Copy, DNA, RG 130, Orders and Proclamations. On Nov. 2, Horace Porter wrote to Delano. "The President directs me to request the return to this office of the map showing the general direction and route of the proposed continuation of the Central Branch Union Pacific Railroad company, and the order which accompanied it" Copy, DLC-USG, II, 1. On the same day, Delano wrote to USG returning the map and the order. LS (press), Delano Letterbooks, Illinois Historical Survey, University of Illinois, Urbana, Ill. The Senate report concluded "there is no evidence that the President ever approved any such route or survey." *SRC*, 43-1-169, 12.

When Congress created the Union Pacific Railroad Co. it authorized several subsidiaries to construct branch lines, including one route through Kansas "west of the meridian of Fort Riley, to the aforesaid point, on the one hundredth meridian of longitude, to be subject to the approval of the President of the United States, and to be determined by him on actual survey." *CG*, 37–2, Appendix, 383. After one co. failed to complete the Kansas route, the Central Branch Union Pacific Railroad Co. sought federal assistance through land grants and bonds to take over the line. On June 3, 1871, Attorney Gen. Amos T. Akerman had upheld previous rulings against providing such assistance; he maintained his position despite pressure from co. attorneys. See *PUSG*, 20, 333–34, 388; *SRC*, 40-2-11, 43-1-169; Nelson Trottman, *History of the Union Pacific: A Financial and Economic Survey* (1923; reprinted, New York, 1966), pp. 117–18.

To Grenville M. Dodge

Washington, D. C. Oct. 24th *1871.*

DEAR GENERAL;

I have applied to Mr. Scott[1] for a leave of absence for Fred., to enable him to take advantage of a most favorable opportunity to visit Europe this Winter. He goes on the Flag Ship of the European Squadron and as an Aide to Gen. Sherman. Mr. Scott replied favorably, and I presume has written you to that effect. I sent Mr. Scotts letter to Fred. and directed him to apply to you for leave.

The Steamer will sail about the 15th of Nov. and I hope Fred. will be able to get here by that time.

Yours Truly

U. S. GRANT

GN. G. M. DODGE

ALS, IaHA. See letter to Frederick Dent Grant, July 30, 1871; letter to Mary Grant Cramer, Oct. 26, 1871; letter to Anthony J. Drexel, Nov. 5, 1871; letter to Adam Badeau, Nov. 19, 1871, note 2.

1. Thomas A. Scott served as president, Union Pacific Railroad Co., for one year beginning in March, 1871. Grenville M. Dodge was a director of the co.

To Alpheus S. Williams

Washington D. C.

Oct. 24. 1871.

DEAR SIR:

Your favor of the 12th inst. inviting me to attend the 5th Annual reunion of the Society of the Army of the Cumberland, to be held in Detroit on the 15th & 16th of Nov. is just before me. It would afford me the greatest pleasure to attend a meeting of that Society held anywhere, and it would be a special pleasure to visit again old neighbors and friends.

It is not probable however that I shall be able to leave Washington at the time indicated. The meeting takes place just at the time when I shall be the most busy here preparing for the meeting of Congress two weeks later.

With many regrets for not being able to attend your Society meeting, and with best wishes for a happy reunion, I subscribe myself

> Very respectfully
> Your obt svt
> U. S. GRANT

GEN. A. S. WILLIAMS
CH. EX. COM. &C—

Copy, DLC-USG, II, 1. See *PUSG*, 15, 565.

Endorsement

Respectfully refered to the Sec. of State. I̶t̶ think it advisable that the Consul Genl o̶f̶in Egypt[1] be requested to resign, in which case, should he comply, these charges need not remain on record in the Dept. of State,

> U. S. GRANT

OCT. 26TH /71

AES, DNA, RG 59, Miscellaneous Letters. Written on a letter of Oct. 25, 1871, from William W. Barr *et al.*, Philadelphia, to USG. "The Board of Foreign Missions of the United Presbyterian Church of North America, have appointed from its number the undersigned, a Committee to lay before you the following statement, and to ask your attention to it. . . . For some time past rumors have been widely abroad in Egypt, affecting the moral conduct and character of the United States Consul General in that land. His course has often spoken of to our Missionaries as a dishonor to our Country, and often as we are informed in their efforts to Evangelize and Elevate the people of Egypt, they were told to begin their work with the Consul General of their own Country. A few months since one of their members—a man who bears the marks of nearly fatal wounds received in our Union ranks during the late Rebellion, and who has the confidence of our Church at large, as a consistent christian, a devoted Missionary, and a substantial and thorough man, was led in an earnest desire we have good reason to believe, to remedy the Evils existing, to bring the matter before your Government, and also e̶x̶t̶e̶n̶d̶ afterwards through the press, in a partial degree before our Country, this act was done entirely on his own responsibility, and the Board of Missions do not undertake here to make any i̶n̶v̶e̶s̶t̶i̶g̶a̶t̶i̶o̶n̶ justification of it, or to discuss in any way the merits of the case. But it is thought to be necessary to state to you now, that since that time, this Missionary has been assaulted and beaten in a public place, that whether it be true or not the Consul General was reputed to have been cogn[i]-zant of it, and that now the whole mission feel and believe there is good reason to feel that he [is] unfriendly to them, and their work, and canno[t] in any way be looked to for protection or help in any of his personal or official relations to ~~to~~ themselves or their Missions. . . ." DS (3 signatures), *ibid.* On Nov. 15, William E. Dodge, Cairo, wrote to Secretary of State Hamilton Fish that "Consul Butlers' conduct has been such as to bring a scandal on our Country." ALS, *ibid.*, Letters of Application and Recommendation.

On Nov. 25, 1870, David Strang, Alexandria, Egypt, had written to USG. "An American citizen, who, as a volunteer, gave of his blood for our country's integrity, desires now to speak in behalf of our country's honor. Inclosed I send a slip written from Cairo by an older member of the Mission to Rev. A. Watson of Mansoora and forwarded to me by request of the writer. I have also seen a similar letter written by Mr. Watson before this was received. These, of course, are not legal evidence of corruption; but they show that the corrupt management of our consular affairs has become notorious. The action called in the slip 'our interference in consular matters' was our sending to Col. Butler last August a letter signed by all the male members of the Mission then in Egypt informing him that men asking for Agencies had been met by persons connected with the Consulate General who told them that only on payment of large bribes could such appointments be obtained. We told him that persons acting as interpreters had professed to make such demands by his authority and that regard for his reputation and the honor of our country compelled us to bring the facts to his notice. I was the bearer and one of the signers of the letter. Col. Butler thanked us for the information, and told me to assure our native friends that any bribes paid by them would be simply wasted. He also gave me a verbal promise in presence of Gen. Mott that he would appoint persons recommended by the missionaries, trusting to their experience of the people and the country as safe guides in the matter. Not long after he dismissed the person who had been foremost in demanding money, and we supposed him to be acting in earnest. It was soon found, however, that persons who presented their applications with a missionary as interpreter were put off from time to time on some frivolous pretext, while the same persons in the absence of a missionary were able to arrange matters promptly. Mr. Watson's letter, already mentioned, was occasioned by a case in Mansoora. He had written to the Consul General telling him that if an Agent was to be appointed there, he knew no one fitter than the former incumbent, but not asking the place for any person. The written answer was that for various reasons the reappointment of Mr Ibrahim Daood was 'impossible.' The man soon after came to Alexandria and quickly returned to Mansoora with the appointment in his pocket. When told by Mr. Watson that he must have used 'golden arguments' to remove the various objections he merely smiled assent. I cannot yet agree with my friends in Cairo to renounce even for a time my rights as a citizen of the Great Republic, nor can I wait while half a dozen men at different stations try to agree on one plan of action with a risk of falling into hopeless inaction. If this falls into the hands of a private secretary I earnestly intreat that it may be brought to your personal attention. I plead no personal selfish interest, but urge that it is important to American residents and travelers and to our country at large that our Consul General here should have a character above suspicion. It may also become of importance to American commercial interests if the next Congress will give American merchants the privilege of purchase so promptly refused by the present. I have no right and no wish to ask this place for any one, but do ask that we may have a good honest man. Is the request unreasonable? Such men do get abroad some times. Witness Mr. Johnson, Con. Gen. at Beyrout, Mr. Beardsley, Con. at Jerusalem, and Mr. J. B. Hay of Jaffa who acted as Consul before Mr. Beardsley's arrival. If any hoax is suspected, please ask Hon. J. A. Bingham of Ohio if his church has a missionary of my name—not a clergyman, but a secular agent—at Alexa. I do not pretend to be personally acquainted with Mr. Bingham." ALS, *ibid.* Related papers are *ibid.* In Nov., 1871, Frederick A. Starring, special agent, Treasury Dept., arrived in Egypt to investigate the conduct of George H. Butler, consul gen., Alexandria. Strang subsequently published a letter criticizing Starring's investigation as superficial. *New York Times*, March 16, 1872.

1. Born in 1840 in Mo., the nephew of Benjamin F. Butler, George H. Butler served as lt. and q. m., 10th Inf. (1861–63) and later wrote for New York City newspapers. On Dec. 6, 1869, USG nominated Butler as consul gen., Calcutta; USG withdrew this nomination. On March 4, 1870, USG nominated Butler as consul gen., Alexandria.

On July 11, 1872, a dispute between Butler and several Americans serving in the Egyptian army led to a shooting outside an Alexandria restaurant. See *ibid.*, July 14, 18, 1872; William B. Hesseltine and Hazel C. Wolf, *The Blue and the Gray on the Nile* (Chicago, 1961), pp. 116–18. On July 23, USG suspended Butler and appointed Richard Beardsley in his place. See *PUSG*, 19, 436; *New York Times*, Sept. 24, 1872. On Dec. 26, B. F. Butler, Boston, wrote to Fish. "Will you do me the personal favor to have nothing done in the matters of the Consul General at Egypt untill I see you after holidays in Washington" ALS, DNA, RG 59, Letters of Application and Recommendation. On Dec. 31, William E. Sanford, London, wrote to Butler. "You will not recollect even my name as it is about ten years since we were made acquainted by our friend Henry C. Deming at his home in Hartford, and I believe we've not met since. I'm not writing though to recall myself to your mind, but to offer my testimony in favor of your Nephew, Col. Geo. H. Butler while U. S. Consul Genl in Egypt. I spent the Winter of '71–2 in Africa and know something about the country and its inhabitants, and I think Col. Butler was the best representative that our government has had there for many years; I know not why he was suspended but if it was for thrashing some drunken exconfederate officer now in the service of the Khedive, I hope he will be restored at once that he may do it again—or a bullying Britisher—the same. I have heard that he was charged with intemperance, but if so Ive no doubt the charge is false. I was on the same dahabeeh with him, for more than a fortnight, on a voyage from Luxor to Cairo, and in all that time, he drank no ale, wine, or spirit, nor did anyone on the vessel drink any thing stronger than tea or coffee. My address for the next three or four months will be, care of Morton Rose & Co—London—E. C. England." ALS, *ibid.* On Jan. 19, 1873, B. F. Butler forwarded this letter to USG. ". . . I refer this note, now, to the President not in complaint of his action in the case of Colonel Butler, or asking that that action may be reversed because Colonel Butler's resignation was at his service at any moment at the time of his suspension, but as an evidence that I did not ask the President to appoint either an intemperate or improper officer. I know that Colonel Butler was not guilty of the charges preferred against him. I am convinced that the report of General Starring is untrue, and prompted by motives that I will not now characterize" ES, *ibid.* See *New York Times*, Nov. 16, 1875, May 10, 1877, April 2, 1883, May 12, 1886.

On Feb. 10, 1872, Beardsley, consul, Jerusalem, had written to Fish applying "for the position of Consul General at Alexandria in the event of a vacancy arising at that place." ALS, DNA, RG 59, Letters of Application and Recommendation. Related papers are *ibid.* On Dec. 3, 1873, on Beardsley's recommendation, Fish wrote to U.S.

Senator Zachariah Chandler of Mich. asking Congress to move the consul general's residence from Alexandria to Cairo. Copy, *ibid.*, Reports to the President and Congress. See *CR*, 43–1, 124.

In [July, 1872], Charles Milne, Newark, N. J., wrote to USG about personal problems and his failure to secure consular appointment from President Andrew Johnson. ". . . The President subsequently nominated me to the Senate as U. S. Consul to Bolivia S. A. and upon motion of Mr Frelinghyson the Senate unanimously confirmed my appointment. The fact was anounced in all the public prints. The State Department notified me of my appointment to the position. Subsequently the President wrote me that my Commission was regularly made out, signed by him, and put into the hands of Mr Seward. But it was about the time of his trouble with Congress commencing, and a fiery partisan of his 'policy' in this state, knowing me to be a regular Republican in sentiment, addressed a letter to the President to my prejudice, and lengthy correspondence ensued of inquiries and explanations, and my *Commission*, although never refused, nor any reasons assigned for not sending it to me, was withheld. . . . I have read to day that Consul Butler at Egypt has left that country. Would there be a prospect for me there? But I will wait to see whether my communication shall be thought worthy of your notice, before presuming to specify. Whether or not, I beg leave to inform you that I am thoroughly a *Grant* man in politics, and have been since the time that Pres. Johnson treated you so disrespectfully. And rest assured that all around where my influence extends the friends of Greely find little comfort. Scarcely a day passes that they do not read in the papers words from my pen, and they read and gnash their teeth. Hoping to see you inaugurated a second time, and that your life shall long honor the land, . . ." ALS, DNA, RG 59, Letters of Application and Recommendation. On Nov. 20, 1876, Milne, Chester, Pa., wrote to USG. "Will you allow an humble Gospel minister to address you a few words privately? My prayers have followed you ever since your first victory in the War. My affections have clustered about you all through, and a thrill of gratification inspired me when I grasped your hand in the Rink at Newark N. J, introduced by my friend Hon. John Hill, about four years ago. . . . it is now the settled conviction of all the best and wisest of my confidential Republican friends, that the Democratic Ticket has been elected, both by a powerful 'popular vote,' and a clear majority of the legal voters of the country. This is not said *aloud* among us; but you may rest assured, that this is a wide spread conviction throughout our disappointed ranks. . . . It is my solemn belief that you can now be our Deliverer a second time out of this chaos, and by some bold legal step, reverse the feelings and judgments of thousands with regard to you. Please, then, accept the opinion of a very humble citisen, which is this. That at this juncture you should,—independently and of your own motion, without consulting the Polititians on either side,— lift up your voice, and give command, with orders for the machinery set in motion to compel obedience, that *every vote* of those three states shall come to light at once, and in the presence of reliable men on *both sides*, so that there cannot be the least suspicion. Startle the Country with this, Hon. Sir, and as God is true, both parties,—*all parties*— will honor and love you and ever after say, 'Our Soldier President made some mistakes, it is true, and his good heart prompted him to promote some men who proved a vexation to him. But in the main he was all right. He, God bless him, was just and honorable to the last, and we regret every word ever spoken against him.' All men seem to think that the decision is in your hands. Decide it then, for your own sake. It will be decided any how. But if you will now decide it as advised, I can see in the act a ray of glory for your brow. If the Republicans have it, then thank Providence. If the Democrats have it, let them have it in God's name. They can do little harm. Doubtless they have good men among them. I am told you yourself was once a Democrat. They will

be watched. No fear of the Republic. Begging you will excuse this liberty, . . ." ALS,
USG 3.

To Mary Grant Cramer

———

Washington, D, C,
Oct. 26th 1871,

Dear Sister;

I have been intending to write you for some time; but the mo-
moment I get into my office in the morning it is overwhelmmed
with visitors, and continues so through the day. I now write, of a
rainy evening, after having read the New York paper.—Jennie is
with us, has been for some days. Mr. Corbin also has been with us
for a few days but left to-day. Jennie will remain until she becomes
homesick which I hope will not be soon.

I received your letter in which you gave me an extract from Mr.
Wolff's.[1] I had no recollection or knowledge of the matter whatever.
The fact is I am followed wherever I go. At Long Branch as well as
here. I some times shake off callers, not knowing their business,
who I would be delighted to see. In the case of Mr. Wolff however
I do not think that I ever knew that he had called. For the first time
in my life I had arranged to go fishing at Sea. To do so it was necessary to engage fishermen, with boat, beforehand. Gen. Porter did
not know that I had made the arrangement, and probably was not
at my house when I returned from riding the evening after Mr. W.
called. You will see the explanation. I will write it to Mr. Wolff.

Fred. after graduating at West Point accepted a position as
Asst. Civil Engineer, and gave up a good portion of his furlough to
go to work at his new profession. He has been in the Rocky Mountains since August Surveying, in pursuit of his new profession, but
with leave of absence as an Army officer. But little or nothing can
be done in the Winter by him and I have therefore got him a leave
of absence from his Eng. duties to accompany Gen. Sherman
abroad,[2] until the latter part of Apl. I expect him to sail about the
middle of next month. Gen. Sherman goes on the Flag Ship of the

European Squadr[on] which will land at some of the Atlantic ports, then proceed to the Medeteranian; tou[ching] at points during the early Winter on both sides of the sea, and in the Spring, pro[b]ably in time to attend the Carnival in Rom[e] will leave the Ship and work across the Continent, in time to be home at the time I have indicated. I will instruct Fred. to run up to Copenhagen, from a convenient point, and spend a few day[s] with you. You will find him a well grown, and much improved, boy. He is about the hight brother Simp.³ was and well developed physically. You will be pleased with him I know.

During the Harvard vacation, next year, I intend that Buck & Jessie shall go to Europe also. It may be that in the short time they will have to remain abroad they may not be able to get up to see you, but I think they will be pleased to do so, know they will be pleased to do so, and may spare time for that purpose.

I do not know but I owe Mr. Cramer an apology for not answering his letters. All have been received and I have been gratified with them. But, beside being a little negligent, I am so constantly pressed that it is almost impossible for me to get any time to devote to private correspondence.

All send our kindest regards to Mr. Cramer, and love to you and the children.

Yours Affectionately
U. S. GRANT

P. S. I shall always be delighted to receive letters from you and Mr. Cr. whether I answer them or not.

ALS, MH. On Nov. 21, 1871, Michael J. Cramer, U.S. minister, Copenhagen, wrote to Gen. William T. Sherman inviting him to join Frederick Dent Grant on a visit to Copenhagen. ALS, DLC-William T. Sherman. After touring the Mediterranean, Middle East, and Russia with the Sherman party, Frederick Dent Grant visited Copenhagen at the end of May, 1872. See letter to Frederick Dent Grant, April 28, 1872; *Memoirs of Gen. W. T. Sherman* (4th ed., New York, 1891), II, 451–52. On Nov. 24, 1871, Orville E. Babcock wrote to George Bancroft, U.S. minister, Berlin. "The President directs me to send you the enclosed letter sent to him and to say that if any person is thus representing himself a son of the President he is an imposter and he hopes he will be exposed." Copy, DLC-USG, II, 1.

1. Possibly Charles H. Wolff, whose signature headed an 1869 petition of Cincinnati businessmen recommending Michael J. Cramer as minister to Switzerland. See *PUSG*, 19, 161.

2. See letter to Grenville M. Dodge, Oct. 24, 1871.
3. Samuel Simpson Grant, brother of USG.

To Charles W. Ford

Washington D. C. Oct. 26th *1871*

DEAR FORD:

I think now I will not accept Mr. Hults[1] proposition for a compr[o]mise. I will trust now to a decission by the courts.[2]

I was gratified at the result of our exhibition at the Fair.[3] I would have been much better pleased however if young Hambletonian had taken a prize. I doubt whether there was a more promising three year old on exhibition.

It looks to me as if Mr. Schurz was not making much out of his new departure. It will be gratifying to see such disorganizers as he is defeated.[4] I hope you will be on here in the Winter to pay us a visit.

yours Truly
U. S. GRANT

ALS, DLC-USG.

1. George T. Hulse. See letter to Charles W. Ford, March 15, 1871.
2. In Dec., the U.S. Supreme Court ruled against the Dent claim upon which USG based his title to property in Carondelet, Mo. See *PUSG*, 19, 228–29.
3. See *Missouri Democrat*, Oct. 3–9, 1871.
4. See letter to Elihu B. Washburne, May 17, 1871, note 2. Beginning in Aug., 1871, U.S. Senator Carl Schurz of Mo. announced that he opposed USG's reelection; on Sept. 20, while speaking in Nashville, he called for formation of a new party. Hans L. Trefousse, *Carl Schurz: A Biography* (Knoxville, 1982), pp. 197–200. In 1871, Charles D. Drake, chief justice, court of claims, wrote to USG about "a newspaper clipping containing an account of an assassination in Springfield, Mo., of a prominent Union man by a rebel. This 'begins the verification of the results of of the Brown-Schurz movement.'" William Evarts Benjamin, Catalogue No. 42, March, 1892, p. 9.

On June 6, 1872, Schurz, Jacob D. Cox, William Cullen Bryant, David A. Wells, Oswald Ottendorfer, and Jacob Brinkerhoff, New York City, wrote an invitation. "*Confidential* ... The undersigned desire to have a conference of gentlemen who are opposed to the present administration and its continuance in office and deem it necessary that all the elements of the opposition should be united for a common effort at the coming presidential election   They respectfully invite you to meet a number of gentlemen belonging to the different branches of the opposition at the 5th Avenue

Hotel N. Y, on June 20th at 2 pm for the purpose of consultation and to take such action as the situation of things may require Your attention is respectfully drawn to the fact that this invitation is strictly personal to yourself and a prompt reply is earnestly requested addressed to Henry D. Lloyd Secretary of Committee PO Box 2209 N. Y." Copy, NN. See Caro Lloyd, *Henry Demarest Lloyd, 1847–1903: A Biography* (New York, 1912), I, 31–35; Chester McArthur Destler, *Henry Demarest Lloyd and the Empire of Reform* (Philadelphia, 1963), pp. 60–64.

Speech

[*Oct. 31, 1871*]

Mr. Perez:—I congratulate you on your promotion. It may be considered as an approval by your government of your course here, which has also been quite acceptable to us. We are especially interested in preserving the good will of the United States of Colombia, part[l]y, indeed, because they are the custodians of the only open way across the isthmus which connects North with South America. We shall omit nothing practicable on our part towards maintaining that good will, and cannot fail if your government shall meet us in that spirit of justice to which you allude, and especially if due regard be had for antecedents, realities and prospects.

Philadelphia Inquirer, Nov. 1, 1871. USG responded to remarks by Santiago Pérez, Colombian minister. On Aug. 24, 1871, Colombian President Eustorjio Salgar had written to USG. "Desiring to give to the Legation of this Republic at Washington the rank to which it is entitled by the character of the nation to which it is accredited, as well as by the importance of the business confided to it, I have thought proper to promote Doctor Santiago Perez to the rank of Envoy Extraordinary and Minister Plenipotentiary . . ." DS (in Spanish), DNA, RG 59, Notes from Foreign Legations, Colombia; translation, *ibid.* See *PUSG*, 20, 135–37, 264–65.

On April 10, Secretary of State Hamilton Fish had written to Stephen A. Hurlbut, minister to Colombia, concerning money owed by Colombia for past claims. ". . . You will mention the subject to the Colombian Minister for Foreign Affairs and may leave with him a copy of the account. You will say to him that it is desirable that the balance due by Colombia should be paid as soon as may be convenient, especially as we long ago advanced to the claimants the sums awarded to them respectively." Copy, DNA, RG 59, Diplomatic Instructions, Colombia. On Aug. 18, Pérez, New York City, wrote to Fish. "The Undersigned, Minister Resident of the U. S. of Colombia, presents his respects to the Secretary of State, and takes the liberty to ask on what day he can have the honor of being received, for the purpose of fulfilling the agreement relative to the liquidation and terms of payment of the amount which his government still owes the American Union, in pursuance of the Conventions of the 10th of September 1857 and the 10th of February, 1864. . . ." ALS (in Spanish), *ibid.*, Notes from Foreign Legations, Colombia; translation, *ibid.* See Fish diary, Oct. 5, DLC-Hamilton Fish.

On July 22, Pérez wrote to Fish. "I know that Commander Selfridge has returned from the Isthmus of Darien, after having explored the routes for an interoceanic canal, and that he has presented a report of the result of his labors. I desire to send this report, as soon as possible, to my Government, and I therefore have the honor to address you, begging you to furnish me with a copy of it, or of such part thereof as you may think proper to send me for the purpose alluded to, for which I will duly thank you. I reiterate to you the assurance of my consideration, . . ." LS (in Spanish), DNA, RG 59, Notes from Foreign Legations, Colombia; translation, *ibid.* See Proclamation, March 13, 1872.

On Oct. 3, Hurlbut, Bogotá, wrote to Fish. "In conversation to day with the Secretary for Foreign Relations the following idea was suggested. It is—That the right of way and all other privileges asked for by us in the Inter Oceanic Canal would be conceded *gratis*, by Colombia, if the Canal grantees would assume the construction and maintenance of a Rail Road from Bogotá to the lower Magdalèna somewhere in the neighborhood of the mouth of the River Caràre. Nothing more in the way of participation in the Canal enterprise would be demanded by the Colombian Government. I have no hesitation in saying that as a simply Commercial operation this proposition is highly favorable to any Company intending to build the Canal. A Rail Road from these elevated and healthy portions of Colombia to its great river at some point where navigation is uninterrupted is a matter of vital interest not only to the commercial but to the political existence of this Republic. . . . So great is felt to be the necessity of this road that by a Law of last Session, the Congress offers to guarantee 7 percent upon the Capital invested; a proposition which would ensure the building of the road if the Capitalists could see any security for the guarantee. But the revenues of this Country are loaded down to such an extent that I can see no way in which this amount can be provided for, in addition to their present pledges. Eighty five percent (85/100) of their Customs Revenue is pledged to meet existing debts, and unless some such arrangement is made as now proposed to the Foreign Bond holders to take the Salt mines in payment of their debts, and thus leave the revenue from Customs free—I can conceive of no mode of securing the proposed guarantee. This has evidently been working upon the mind of this administration, and results in the proposition to give us all the privileges we have asked for in the Canal, free, provided we will guarantee the Construction of the Rail Road asked for. . . . The only question that remains is whether Colombia will grant to the United States those Military & political rights over the Canal to wit, free passage of Ships of war &c at all times—and exclusion of all hostile vessels—This administration having opposed and struck out this clause in the original Treaty will not commit itself upon this point, but refers ~~to~~ me to Dr Murillo the incoming President, whose opinion I will obtain if possible by this mail— if not by the next. If then the United States are disposed to guarantee its construction, or say 6 percent upon $10.000.000—for 15 years I think any terms we may propose for the Canal will be accepted. I commend this proposition to the consideration of the Government, as the best solution of the problem & would take the liberty of suggesting that Senator Cameron be consulted on it, both from his position as Chairman of the Committee, & from his large acquaintance with Rail Road matters. . . . P. S. October 7th 1871 I have not yet been able to see Dr Murillo & must close for this mail. I think it would be safer to estimate the possible highest cost at $15.000.000— though I still believe it can be done with $10.000.000—" ALS, *ibid.*, Diplomatic

Despatches, Colombia. On Nov. 3, Fish endorsed this letter. "Copy of this to be sent to Senator Cameron with request for his views" AE, *ibid.*

On Oct. 17, Hurlbut again wrote to Fish. "I have had a full and explicit conversation with Dr Murillo the President Elect on the subject mentioned in my dispatch No 61 of October 3d 1871. He authorizes me to say that he has no objection to Article No Eleven of the original treaty, and in case any satisfactory arrangement can be made as suggested in that dispatch (No 61) he will use all his influence to procure the adoption by the next Administration and by the Congress, of the Treaty. It was expressly understood and declared by me in the interview, and so accepted by him, that the political & military advantages secured to the United States by said Article No (11) Eleven of the Original Treaty were in my opinion a sine quà non to any engagement in the Enterprise on our part. Dr Murillo is exceedingly anxious upon the subject of a Rail Road, and very desirous to signalize his administration by inaugurating the undertaking. I have no sort of doubt that the Treaty may be modified in almost any form desired by us, if only the construction of this Road can be assured. As the Original Treaty has failed by lapse of time, the whole affair may be considered as open. The negotiations can be resumed 'de novo,' if the Department so wish, or what in my judgment would be far better and more effective, a Treaty on the new basis, can be adopted by the Senate as an *amendment* to the Original and the Colombian Amendments. I have not lost faith in the feasibility of the Canal, notwithstanding the Report of Commander Selfridge, who seems to have gone many miles out of the way to encounter difficulties. His report on the Atrato and Napipi route, calls for 120 miles of River Navigation, 36 miles of Canal, many locks and a Tunnel of *four* miles. From San Blas to the Chèpo or Buyamè is 29½ miles—through cut on a single level, without locks and with a Tunnel not exceeding *Seven* miles & probably not more than *five*. This is undeniably, the best, most secure, and in the end most economical route. The Line of Panamà is far better than the Selfridge route. Since my conversation with Dr Murillo I have been examining the Original Treaty & the pending amendments, and at the risk of appearing officious have been engaged in drafting the propositions which have been made & putting them into form for the use of the Department. This I shall complete & forward by the next mail." ALS, *ibid.* See *PUSG*, 19, 75.

On Dec. 19, Fish wrote to Hurlbut. ". . . This Department concurs with you in the opinion that the present is a favorable juncture towards obtaining from the Colombian government a treaty for the construction of a ship Canal upon fair terms. You will consequently direct your efforts to that end. Your success may be promoted if you should intimate to that government that unless our complaint in the case of the steamer Montijo, shall be promptly and satisfactorily adjusted, it may be necessary for us to take into consideration the expediency of terminating the guaranty of the neutrality of the Isthmus of Panama, embodied in the treaty of 1846 between the United States and New Granada." Copy, DNA, RG 59, Diplomatic Instructions, Colombia. For the expedition of Commander Thomas O. Selfridge, Jr., U.S. Navy, to survey possible canal routes across Panama, see *HMD*, 42-3-113; *What Finer Tradition: The Memoirs of Thomas O. Selfridge, Jr., Rear Admiral, U.S.N.* (New York, 1924; reprinted, Columbia, S. C., 1987), pp. 155–205. See also Stephen J. Randall, *Colombia and the United States: Hegemony and Interdependence* (Athens, Ga., 1992), pp. 56–61.

On June 17, 1872, USG wrote to President Manuel Murillo of Colombia congratulating him on his election. Copy, DNA, RG 84, Colombia, Instructions. On the same day, USG wrote to Murillo praising Pérez, recalled. Copy, *ibid.* On Oct. 10,

Horace Porter wrote to Fish that USG would receive the next day Carlos Martin, the new Colombian minister. LS, *ibid.*, RG 59, Miscellaneous Letters.

Proclamation

Whereas, in my proclamation of the twelfth day of October in the year eighteen hundred and seventy-one, it was recited that certain unlawful combinations and conspiracies existed in certain counties in the State of South Carolina, for the purpose of depriving certain portions and classes of the people of that State of the rights, privileges, and immunities, and protection named in the Constitution of the United States, and secured by the act of Congress approved April the twentieth, one thousand eight hundred and seventy-one, entitled "An Act to enforce the Provisions of the Fourteenth Amendment to the Constitution of the United States", and the persons composing such combinations and conspiracies were commanded to disperse and to retire peaceably to their homes within five days from said date; and

Whereas by my proclamation of the seventeenth day of October in the year eighteen hundred and seventy-one the privileges of the writ of habeas corpus were suspended in the counties named in said proclamation; and

Whereas the county of Marion was named in said proclamations as one of the counties in which said unlawful combinations and conspiracies for the purposes aforesaid existed, and in which the privileges of the writ of habeas corpus were suspended; and

Whereas it has been ascertained that in said county of Marion, said combinations and conspiracies do not exist to the extent recited in said proclamations; and

Whereas it has been ascertained that unlawful combinations and conspiracies of the character and to the extent and for the purposes described in said proclamations do exist in the county of Union in said State:

Now, therefore, I, Ulysses S. Grant, President of the United

States of America, do hereby revoke, as to the said county of Marion, the suspension of the privileges of the writ of habeas corpus directed in my said proclamation of the seventeenth day of October, eighteen hundred and seventy-one.

And I do hereby command all persons in the said county of Union composing the unlawful combinations and conspiracies aforesaid to disperse and to retire peaceably to their homes within five days of the date hereof, and to deliver either to the marshal of the United States for the district of South Carolina, or to any of his deputies, or to any military officer of the United States within said county, all arms, ammunition, uniforms, disguises, and other means and implements used, kept, possessed or controlled by them, for carrying out the unlawful purposes for which the combinations and conspiracies are organized.[1]

In witness whereof I have hereunto set my hand and caused the seal of the United States to be affixed.

Done at the City of Washington this third day of November, in the year of our Lord one thous[an]d eight hundred [an]d seventy-one and of the independence of the United States of America the ninety-sixth

U. S. GRANT

DS, DNA, RG 130, Presidential Proclamations. On Oct. 21, 1871, Benjamin H. Bristow, solicitor gen. and act. attorney gen., telegraphed to Attorney Gen. Amos T. Akerman, Yorkville, S. C. "My dispatch of yesterday was written in the Supreme Court Room while I was engaged in the argument of a case. On reëxamination of the original draft of the first Proclamation prepared by you, I find that you doubtless intended to name Union County, but it looks more like Marion. Shall I prepare a Proclamation as to Union County?" Copy, *ibid.*, RG 60, Letters Sent to Executive Officers. On the same day, Bristow wrote to AG Edward D. Townsend requesting that this telegram be sent in cipher. Copy, *ibid.* On Oct. 31 and Nov. 24, Secretary of State Hamilton Fish wrote in his diary. "*Cabinet*—All present—. . . Akerman makes a long, long statement about the Kuklux—It appears that he made a mistake in including 'Marion' Co in South Carolina in the list of Counties named in Presidents Proclamation, instead of 'Union' Co—this mistake is to be remedied by a new Proclamation, releasing Marion, & including 'Union' He says that the Secr of State is to make returns to the Court of the names of all persons arrested & held under the suspension of the Habs Corps—by virtue of the Proclamation Prsdt directs that he furnish me the list of names—" "Akerman introduces Ku Klux—he has it 'on the brain'—he tells a number of stories—one of a fellow being castrated—with terribly minute & tedious details of each case—It has got to be a bore, to listen twice a week to this same thing" DLC-Hamilton Fish.

1. On Nov. 10, USG issued a proclamation suspending the writ of habeas corpus in Union County, S. C. DS, DNA, RG 130, Presidential Proclamations. For a similar document, see Proclamation, Oct. 17, 1871.

To William Elrod

———

Washington D. C.
Nov. 3d 1871

DEAR ELROD,

Enclosed I send you checks for $1500.00/100 which is as much as I can spare just now, and hope you will be able to get along with it. Should it be necessary however I will raise some more hereafter. I have received your letter proposing to divide expenses of the Fair between Ford, you & myself. Of course I can not think of such a thing. On the contrary I feel very much in debt to Mr. Ford for the many voluntary services he has rendered me and hope some day to be able to partially repay them. The mares that are not with foal, particularly the Ethan Allen mare I would try again this Fall. The mare that Orvil sent, if you think she will not breed, you may sell for what she will bring. The same of any other mare that will not breed and is of no use.

Yours Truly,
U. S. GRANT.

Copy, Illinois Historical Survey, University of Illinois, Urbana, Ill.

To Hamilton Fish

———

Washington D, C,
Nov. 4th 1871,

MY DEAR GOVERNOR:

~~I received~~ Your note of last night with the inclosed telegram is just received. I agree that it would be unwise to give orders from Washington closing all public offices on election day. It would give ground for charges that the object was to release all government officials & employees to enable them to interfere with the election. If however any Govt. Official chose, on his own responsibility, to close his office on that day, in response to the wishes of the citizens, I do not see that there would be harm in it. You may, if convenient, see the parties who telegraphed you, and if you then advise any other course let me know.

Very Truly yours
U. S. Grant

Hon. Hamilton Fish,
Sec. of State

ALS, DLC-Hamilton Fish. On Nov. 3, 1871, Secretary of State Hamilton Fish wrote to USG. "Late this Evening I receive the enclosed telegram—& as I leave early in the Morning, have no opportunity to consult, or to answer—As no Federal Officers are to be elected, it appears to me that a Compliance with the request would be very unwise, and might give ground to justify or defend those who may be inclined to make riot If you desire me to see the parties in NewYork & will instruct me either by letter or by telegram, I will give such answer as you may desire—" AL (initialed, press), *ibid.* On the same day, Henry G. Stebbins, New York City, had telegraphed to Fish. "The Committee of Seventy desire that the Federal Offices as well as all private places of business be closed on election day—Can such order be given—" Copy, *ibid.* Formed in Sept. to combat fraud in New York City government, the nominally bipartisan Committee of Seventy endorsed a slate of candidates for local and state office. See *New York Times*, Sept. 4, 5, Oct. 30, Nov. 3, 1871; letter to Edwards Pierrepont, Dec. 29, 1871. On Nov. 6, Fish, New York City, telegraphed to USG. "Parties who telegraphed to me are entirely satisfied that individuals in Government employ, be allowed such time tomorrow as they may desire to attend the Polls—they ~~have~~ requested me to see Collector and Post Master, which I am going at once to do" ALS (telegram sent, press), DLC-Hamilton Fish.

Note

Please acknowledge receipt of dispatch but give no order to Military, at least not further than to exercise a proper discretion in quelling disturbances should the necessity arise.

U. S. Grant

Nov. 5th /71

ANS, DNA, RG 94, Letters Received, 3858 1871. On Nov. 4, 1871, Governor Ozra A. Hadley of Ark. had telegraphed to USG. "A few disafected Republicans in Conjunction with the Democracy threaten Violent proceeding at City Election on the seventh would be pleased to have you order the post Commander by telegraph to be ready to assist in maintaining the peace if necessary—" Telegram received (at 5:30 P.M.), *ibid.* Related documents are *ibid.*

To Anthony J. Drexel

Washington D. C.
Nov. 5th 1871

MY DEAR SIR;

My son, Lieut. Fred. D. Grant, U. S. Army, sails the latter part of this week for Europe.[1] He will take but little money with him but will have a letter of credit on a London Banking House. It may be convenient for him to have also a credit in Paris. May I ask you for such a letter, say to the Amount of 5000 franks? It is probable that he will not draw all that amount, and possibly none of it. I will pay your house in Phila as he draws or will make a deposite in advance as may be most proper.

Mrs. Grant & Nellie send much love to Mrs. Drexel and the young ladies. We shall expect a visit from you this Winter. Please present my kindest regards to Mr. & Mrs. Childs.

Yours Truly
U. S. GRANT

J. A. DREXEL, ESQ,
PHILA PA

ALS, PHi. See letter to George W. Childs, April 2, 1871, notes 2 and 3.

On Nov. 29, 1872, Orville E. Babcock wrote to Secretary of State Hamilton Fish. "The President desires me to request you to be kind enough to send him, by the bearer, a special passport for Mr. Drexel and oblige." LS, DNA, RG 59, Requisitions for Special Passports.

1. For Frederick Dent Grant's departure, see letter to Adam Badeau, Nov. 19, 1871, note 2.

To John P. Newman

[*Nov. 6, 1871*]

The civil authorities in Utah need not fear but they will have ample support from here in executing all laws. I shall write Govr. Wood¹ to-day encouragingly.

In the matter of the "dream" it is a pure fiction made out of whole clothe. I never had such a dream; never told so ridiculous a story. I should shrink from the responsibility of following a dream with the lives of 40000 men, and a nation, intrusted to my keeping. . . .

J. H. Benton Sale, American Art Association, March 12, 1920. Born in 1826 in New York City, John P. Newman won acclaim as a Methodist minister in N. Y. and New Orleans. In Washington, D. C., he led the Metropolitan Methodist Church and served as U.S. Senate chaplain. In April, 1870, Newman's condemnation of polygamy prompted a written rejoinder from Mormon Orson Pratt and a debate between the two in Salt Lake City, Aug. 12–14. See B. H. Roberts, *A Comprehensive History of The Church of Jesus Christ of Latter-day Saints: Century I* (Provo, 1965), V, 287–95.

On Nov. 6, 1871, Orville E. Babcock wrote to Governor George L. Woods of Utah Territory. "The President directs me to acknowledge the receipt of your letters, and convey to you his thanks for them. They were very interesting and he hopes you will continue to keep him informed of whatever of interest transpires. He is glad to see the laws vindicated so ably in Utah and sincerely hopes your labors will be crowned with success without calling in the aid of the military." Copy, DLC-USG, II, 1. On Oct. 2, Woods had written to USG. "In my last I mentioned to you the condition of affairs and promised to write again soon. There has been much excitement in Utah since my last writing, and is now. The populace have been arming for ten days, or more, and many violent threats have been made against the Federal officials,— threats to assassinate &c These have been made in part, doubtless, to intimidate and in part with the earnestness of a wild fanaticism. Until a few days ago the Mormons did not hesitate to say, openly, that Brigham Young, if Indicted for an unbailable offense, should not be arrested. In consequence of these threats to resist the execution of the law I made Requisition upon Gen. Augur, Comdg. Dept. Platte, for more Troops and in response to my call three Companies have been sent and are now at Camp Douglas. There are now eight Companies at the Post, which will be barely enough should emergency arise But the moral effect of their presence will be great, and not only deter the Mormons from the commission of excesses, but will strengthen the hands of the civil authorities, by encouraging witnesses— apostate Mormons—to tell what they know. Brigham Young was Arrested to-day on a charge of lewd and lacivious cohabitation with Sixteen different women the Indictment being based upon a Section of the Statutes of Utah. No resistence was made. He will be arraigned to plead tomorrow. Quite a number of the prominent men of the Church have been Indicted upon the same ground. Arrests will be made as rapidly as possible. Brigham Young is also Indicted for Murder in the first Degree, as also have several of the Prophets, Bishops, and Elders; but arrests will not be made upon these Indictments, for a short time for the reason that we do not yet wish to disclose the names of certain Witnesses yet; it might prevent the Arrest of some who we very much desire. The investigation, which have been made, have disclosed deeds of horror which are unsurpassed in the history of crime. The outer World Knows nothing of the murderous infamy of Mormonism. The trials soon to be had will bring forth deeds of savage barbarity which will disgust the Nation. The testimony shall be reported in full. In the 2nd Judicial Dist in Southern Utah Judge Hawleys—Court was held recently and 8 Indictments were found. The Grand Jury left much important business unfinished, that pertaining to the Mountain Meadows Massacre particularly, and adjourned until January for the purpose of procuring witnesses. The Court convenes again at which time there will be business of great importance transacted. Only one arrest was made at Judge Hawleys last term. The Mormons are all powerful in that portion of the Territory, there being but few 'Gentile' Miners down there, and the whole power of the Church is used to secrete persons charged with crime. Kanab a remote settlement in the extreme South,— exclusively Mormon—is a place of refuge; they are prepared for resistence there, and declared that no arrests shall be made. In that Valley the most of the murderers of Mountain Meadow will take refuge and it will be useless for the Marshall, unattended with an efficient Military force, to attempt to take any of them into custody. For that reason, I suggest that we shall want at least one hundred mounted men to go to Beaver in the latter part of December to assist the civil authorities in the execution of the laws. All of the Federal Officials here, concur in its absolute necessity The same general Statement may be made of the 1st Judicial Dist—Judge Strickland—at Provo. A number of Indictments have been found against prominent Mormons, in that Dist., for Murder in the first Degree, but no arrests have been made, nor can be, without a strong Military force attending There are not Troops, sufficient, at Camp Douglas to send to these two places, I fear, with[*out*] So weakening the Post here as to render it insufficient. We feel anxious to successfully, carry out every thing which we undertake and to that end to be prepared for any emergency that may arise. I think that a three, or four Co. Post some where South of there, at Beaver, or St George, absolutely necessary until the Supremacy of the Law is thoroughly, and the leading offenders brought to Justice. I know Troops are scarce, but there is perhaps no place in the Republic where they are more needed than in Utah. The work of purification has been begun, at the right place, and in the right way and it would be ruinous to Federal Authority in Utah if we had to falter in the least. I am therefore anxious for Sufficient Military force to hold the one party in subjection and encourage others to do their duty. The present condition of affairs will not admit of delay." ALS, DNA, RG 94, Letters Received, 3314 1871. On Oct. 31, Gen. William T. Sherman endorsed this letter. "Respectfully submitted to Genl Sheridan for such action in the premises as he deems consistent with the necessities of the Frontier. I do not regard this reference as an order to comply with the request of Governor Woods of Utah, but merely for compliance—or a Report, if troops are not needed, or are unavailable" AES, *ibid.* On Nov. 6, Lt. Gen. Philip H. Sheridan, Chicago, endorsed this letter. "Respectfully returned. It has been my impression for some time past that we would be obliged to establish a Post in Southern Utah, and I have heretofore notified Judge Hawley who came to see me on the subject that I would make my recommendation as soon as I became convinced that the necessity for such Post was sufficiently great to warrant the Government in going to this additional expense. From this representation of His Excellency Governor Woods, and from representations of Judge Hawley made heretofore, I am now satisfied that the Post is necessary, but ask that its establishment may be postponed until early Spring. I do not know where to get the troops for this purpose at the present time, but in the spring I hope to have sufficient to spare. The Post should be a three or four company Post, at least one of the companies, cavalry. As soon as the proper authority for the Post is given, I will consult with the Governor of Utah as to its location, and will go to see him if necessary." ES, *ibid.* Related papers are *ibid.* See *PUSG*, 20, 120; *HED*, 42-3-1, part 2, pp. 53–54.

On Oct. 14, Saturday, Woods telegraphed to Secretary of War William W. Belknap. "Judge Stricklands court first district Utah Convenes at Provo fifty miles South tuesday october seventeenth   prominent men are indicted   the settlement is exclusively mormons   threats of resistance to arrest are made   the Judge and marshall think it impossible to arrest without troops—Colonel Detrobriand cant furnish men unless there is actual resistance in consequence of an order to that effect from Gen augur. The necessity prior to resistance is absolute   will you instruct Col Detrobriand to furnish men upon my requisition   answer by telegraph" Telegram received, DNA, RG 94, Letters Received, 3314 1871. On the same day, Belknap wrote to AG Edward D. Townsend. "This telegram has come just as I am leaving. I am not disposed to furnish troops unless there is actual resistance. . . ." ALS, *ibid.* On Oct. 15, Sherman telegraphed to Woods. "The Secretary of War & President are absent and your despatch of the 14 is referred to me. I think you are leaning a little too heavy on the Military and had better try to execute the process of the Court at Provo before appealing for military help. After actual resistance will be time for the Marshall to call for help, and that must come from the force now at Camp Douglas. I am unwilling to change Gen Augurs orders which are right and based on proper principles of Law & Military usage. The Secretary will be back next Wednesday, and your despatch and my answer will be submitted to him." ALS (telegram sent), *ibid.* Sherman's related letter of Oct. 14 is *ibid.*

On Oct. 18, Belknap, Bangor, wrote to Sherman. "The President has telegrams which lead him to apprehend trouble in Utah—& directed me to have Sheridan telegraphed that if there was much danger of trouble he could foward troops from most accessible points & they could be replaced by others—suggesting that if any were used the 8th Infy. could replace them as far as it would go.—I telegraphed all this to Townsend, for your action this morning. I think & so does the President that the information he has received is founded more on apprehension, than *real* danger & hence this telegram is merely preparatory should trouble occur." ALS, DLC-William T. Sherman. On Oct. 30, "Secretary Belknap and Gen. Sherman had a conversation with the President in relation to affairs in Utah, and whether the disturbed condition of that Territory and other difficulties in certain Southern States warrant any preparations toward making a change in the present situation of the United States troops." *New York Tribune*, Oct. 31, 1871.

In Oct., "nearly 2,500 women of Utah" petitioned Julia Dent Grant. "Honored lady, deeming it proper for woman to appeal to woman, we, Latter-day Saint ladies of Utah, take the liberty of preferring our humble and earnest petition for your kindly and generous aid;. . . We believe the institution of marriage to have been ordained of God, and therefore subject to His all-wise direction. It is a divine rite and not a civil contract, and hence no man unauthorized of God can legally administer in this holy ordinance. We believe also in the Holy Bible, and that God did anciently institute the order of plurality of wives, . . . Our Territorial laws make adultery and licentiousness penal offenses, the breach of which subjects the offender to fine and imprisonment. These laws are being basely subverted by our Federal officers; who, after unscrupulously wresting the Territorial offices from their legitimate holders, in order to carry out suicidal schemes, are substituting licentiousnes for the sacred order of marriage, and seeking by these measures to incarcerate the most moral and upright men of this Territory, and thus destroy the peace and prosperity of this entire community. . . . President BRIGHAM YOUNG and several of his associates, all noble and philanthropic gentlemen, are already under indictment, to be arraigned before a packed jury, mostly non-residents, for the crime of licentiousness, than which a more outrageous absurdity could not exist. Under these forbidding and cruel circumstances, dear Madam, our most fervent petition to you is, that through the sympathy of your womanly heart you will persuade the President to remove the malicious disturbers of the peace, or at least that he will stop the disgraceful Court proceedings, and send from Washington a committee of candid, intelligent, reliable men, who shall investigate matters which involve the right of property—perhaps of life; and more than all, the constitutional liberties of more than 100,000 citizens. By doing this you will be the honored instrument, in the hand of God, of preventing a foul disgrace to the present Administration, and an eternal blot on our national escutcheon." *New York Times*, Nov. 9, 1871.

On Oct. 31, Secretary of State Hamilton Fish wrote in his diary. "The persecutions in Utah were discussed—letter read by President from Governor Woods—Wells, the Mayor of Salt Lake City has been arrested & held to bail in $50.000. President orders George Bates to be appointed Dist. Atty." DLC-Hamilton Fish. In Feb., 1869, Governor John M. Palmer of Ill. and eight others had written to USG. "The Hon. George C. Bates, of Chicago is an applicant for the appointment as Governor of the Territory of Montana or Idaho. Mr. Bates has been a citizen of the North West for over thirty years, five of which he spent in Calafornia, and is familiar with the people and wants of that region. Believing him to be eminently qualified for such a position, as a capable and honest man, we earnestly commend him to you." DS, DNA, RG 59, Letters of Application and Recommendation. On March 25, U.S. Representative Ebon C. Ingersoll of Ill. wrote to Horace Porter. "Enclosed, I send you two communications addressed to the President of the United States, one signed by P. H. Walker, one of the Justices of the Supreme Court, of the State of Illinois, another by C. H. Ray, editor of the 'Chicago Post', Chas. S. Wilson publisher of the 'Chicago Evening Journal', Horace White of the 'Chicago Tribune' and J. B. Rice, mayor of the city of Chicago recommending the Hon. Geo. C. Bates of Chicago for appointment as Govenor of the Territory of Montana or that of Idaho. . . ." LS, *ibid.* The enclosures and related papers are *ibid.* On Dec. 6, 1871, USG nominated George C. Bates as U.S. attorney, Utah Territory.

On Nov. 13, Woods wrote to USG concerning the unauthorized departure of Brigham Young for southern Utah. Copy (typed), Brigham Young University, Provo, Utah. On Dec. 8, Woods again wrote to USG. "Brigham Young has not yet been arrested for murder but is still in Southern Utah. The case of the People vs: Brigham Young, for Lewd and lacivious cohabitation was set for trial on Monday the 4th Instant but the Deft. did not make his appearance. On that day the 3rd Ju. District Court, Judge McKean, adjourned until January 9th 1872 at which time the Criminal Calendar will be taken up and disposed of with reasonable dispatch. The adjournment of the Court was made for the reasons:—1st Judge McKean was worn out by long labor and needed rest   2nd There were many important cases, which had been submitted to him and which would require time to examine.   3rd Dist Atty Batess having but just assumed the duties of his office, and wanted time to prepare for the trial of the most important causes. Everything is very quiet here   That portion of your Message refering to Utah was recd by all 'Gentiles' here with the livliest satisfaction   The effect upon the leaders of the Church, for good, has been very great. Several of the leaders have expressed themselves, satisfied, within the last few days, that all was lost to them, so far as polygamy was concerned. I have reason to believe that the leaders of the Church are anxious for a compromise upon almost any terms looking to the admission of Utah as a State, but I have had no conference with any of them upon the subject; and will not, until I know your wishes in the premises   Standing, as I do, at the head of the Territorial Government, I could aid much in the solution of ~~this problem~~ this problem and if you will inform me of your wishes they shall be sacredly kept and faithfully executed. I am anxious that the Mormon question shall be settled during your present Administration but only upon such a basis as will be honorable to the Government, and insure safety to the people here   Hoping to hear from you soon ... A better list of officers I never saw   all are in perfect harmony. I will write you again soon and keep you posted in our progress" ALS, OFH. On Dec. 19, Fish wrote in his diary. "Akerman mentioned application of Dist. Atty Bates of Utah, for appointment of two additional Counsel to prosecute indictment for Murder against Brigham Young & says it is unusual in a Murder Case to appoint two counsel, it wd look like too strong a desire to secure a Conviction—Akerman also states that the Counsel of Young have proposed that he shall surrender himself for trial on condition that he shall be let to bail for $200.000—the President says that he must be treated like any other person under indictment for similar crimes" DLC-Hamilton Fish.

On Dec. 26, Woods wrote to USG. "Nothing spicially exciting has occured since I last wrote you. Everything is as quiet here as in New York. The firm grip with which they have been held by the Government has apparently subdued them entirely. Doubtless you know all about the assassination of Dr, Robinson in this City in 1866,—one of the meanest ever perpetrated in any Country. We now have 3, men under arrest for the murder with a strong probability of convicting them. There will also be some arrests made in two, or three days for another Assassination, here, I believe in 1867, of one Brassfield. We have a witness here who was a merchant at the time and who was in a few feet of the man when shot, who knew the assassins, and chased them from the shooting over a Block & a half—to Brigham Youngs House where they took shelter. Rich disclosures may be expected from one or both of these cases as they were both 'Church murders.' We hope to get trials in Jan. Brigham Young has not yet returned; nor do I believe he will, tho. he may. The Utah Legislature meets Jan. 8th—Exclusively Mormon. My Message is prepared. It is brief. I will send you a Copy when printed. I have absolute Veto power and can hold them in check. I hope that all will be harmony; but I shall not be cajoled, or misled. With all the light before me I think that I can assure you that every thing is in good condition here. If our lives are spared you may expect a good work here during the next six months.—a work of prudence and of good to the Government. . . . If it is desired by you or by Committees to have any one, acquainted with Utah affairs, called to Washington for consultation &c I suggest that Col Morrow be called; he is a true man" ALS, OFH. On Oct. 10, Belknap had written to Townsend. "The President desires that Lt. Col. Morrow be placed in Command at Camp Douglas. The Head Qrs. can be changed, and Col. De. Trobriand be thus relieved—leaving Morrow at Douglas" AN (initialed), DNA, RG 94, Letters Received, 3314 1871. On Oct. 17, Brig. Gen. Christopher C. Augur, Baltimore, telegraphed to Belknap conveying Lt. Col. Henry A. Morrow's protest against this order. Telegram received, *ibid.* On Jan. 12, 1874, James B. McKean, chief justice, Utah Territory, wrote to U.S. Senator John A. Logan of Ill. urging retention of Morrow as commander at Camp Douglas because he "was ordered here two years ago *by the President*, in place of an officer who fraternized intimately with the Mormon leaders and treated the civil federal officials with something like indignity. Col. Morrow has given the Mormons no just ground of complaint, but is in thorough sympathy with the President's Utah policy. . . ." ALS, *ibid.* Related papers are *ibid.*

On Jan. 11, 1872, Woods, Ogden, telegraphed to USG. "Utah affairs seriously complicated you should see Judge McKean immediately Hope he may be ordered to washington at once by telegraph necessity demands it. Answer to Salt Lake" Telegram received, *ibid.*, RG 60, Letters from the President. Attorney Gen. George H. Williams endorsed this telegram, presumably to USG. "What is your opinion of this applicatn—A leave of absence has been give to Bates" AES (undated), *ibid.* On March 11, Woods, Salt Lake City, wrote to USG. "Since Judge McKean went to Washington I have not tho't it necessary to write, knowing that he would make a faithful, and comprehensive statement of the condition of affairs, here. Nothing special has transpired since his departure; and I only write, now, for the purpose of making some suggestions. Inasmuch as 'the Church' has sent 3 Delegates to Washington with a 'Constitution' to ask the admission of the 'State of Deseret' into the Union, who will present the plausible side of the case to Congress, would it not be well to suggest to some one in either House, as soon as the Bill for admission is introduced and refered to a Committee, to send to Utah for men to come before such Committee and present the reasons *against* admission? I think it all important. If desired by Committee I will designate the persons to come. Again, Now that a Post is to be established in Southern Utah, thanks to you, it is all-important that the Dist. Judges, each be ordered to reside in his own Dist as the Organic Act requires. As it now is they all reside here, and in the remote portion of the Territory no man can appeal to the Court for protection in person & property, except when the Court convenes by law. This ought not to be. I hope the Order will be made at once   We shall try to get some money from the Territory, for Court-expenses soon—The last Territorial Appropriation Bill contained $10.000, for Court expenses, to be drawn *only* by the *Territorial* Marshal, who is a 'Mormon'. I allowed it to pass in that shape with the determination to reach it by *Mandamus.* . . . P. S. My health is poor" ALS, *ibid.* McKean conferred with USG on March 1 and 2. *Washington Evening Star*, March 1–2, 1872.

On Feb. 14, USG met a Utah delegation representing "gold, silver, copper and coal mine owners: also the owners of steamboats running from Salt Lake. This delegation believe that public opinion will soon drive away polygamy. They say that only the old Mormons have additional wives sealed to them, and that no young Mormon marries more than one woman, and that this has been substantially the case for four years past. The young Mormon women assert that they wish to live as the Gentiles do, and not have to go thinly clad, and earn not only their own living but that of their husbands as well." *Philadelphia Public Ledger*, Feb. 15, 1872. On Feb. 21, Brig. Gen. Edward O. C. Ord, Salt Lake City, wrote to Porter. "Private— . . . Tho the President & yourself have heard so much of mormon questions lately I shall bother you with my ideas for the reason that I think the influence of money among prominent officials will induce them to misrepresent—The feeling of some men after looking at this handsome city—the huge Tabernacle & the other works of art and industry of the Mormons—is that it would be hard to deprive *them* of the result of so much labor and talent—but it would have be j̶ been just as applicable to have said we wont break up Slavery for it would be a pity to deprive these southerners of the results of so much thought and industry—in other words the Mormon peasant is a Slave morally and physically—and where one knows that the church leaders have tied them up So closely that they dare or cannot sell their crops except to the Church Stores—& only for goods or tickets—that they are tithed— assessed in licences and taxed in so many shapes that the Church—which owns *all* their land nearly, or claims to—as well as themselves derives a revenue of 8 or 10 Millions of Dols from them—now Gentiles are flocking in to get a share of the mines—but if B Young & Co can get control of the State—& the laws & courts— even the mines will be controlled at least for the terms of the 1st Senatorship by them—hence they can afford to pay high ~~for retaining~~ to retain their present power—and such men as Stewart—Geo C Bates—Blair—Trumbull and every one that wants to help prevent ~~your~~ Gen Grants nomination—and are anxious to point ~~out~~ at the attempt to execute justice here as a miserable failure—will do their best to hamper the judges here and make it one—Funds—troops and the moral support of the Government to its honest officials here in proving that its laws can be executed here—are simply a necessity—Talk with Maj Powell about the necessity at once of a firm superintendt of Indian affairs for this Territory—to take the control of the Indians (who are kept hostile) from the hands of the mormons—no civil process can be executed in South Utah without a large Military force there—of course great care must be exercised to prevent the sincere mormons from having reason to believe they are to be persecuted on account of their religion but at present—they will go as their leaders go and these will obey the laws and ~~quite~~ lose gradually their hold on their simple followers *if they are compelled to do it* but now they are bribing their way through the troubles and if the state is admitted—it would be like admitting the South again with Slavery—You can ask Genl Sheridan what he knows of Geo. C. Bates—out here—well he told Gen Morrow that Mr Blair—Schurz and Trumbull were *his* friends & he would rely on them to get him through—In haste but in earnest ... my expressions to Mrs Porter & the President & family—" ALS, USG 3.

On March 1, Samuel Merrill, Des Moines, wrote to USG. "Allow me to introduce to you Col. A. J. Bell of I'll. Col. Bell spends most of his time in *Utah*. He is perhaps a familiar with the trials of the Gentile race in that country as most any other man—Col. Bell endorses Judge McKean's policy as well as that of the Governor—I have visited that Territory during the past season and as I have written you before, do most earnestly endorse their policy as right and just to the American people—" ALS, DNA, RG 60, Letters from the President. On March 20, A. J. Bell, Chicago, wrote to USG. "Permit me to hand you the enclosed letter from my intimate friend, Gov. Merrill by way of introduction. At the time it was given me I expected to go to Washington but decided it not essential, at least from present outlook. While I feel confident the Terr. of Utah will not be a state while the prospect is so full of promise of the elevation of such men as Tom. Hitch as senators, and with the certainty of the finest Mining region in the World virtually Locked up in the interest (or supposed interest) of the fanatical notions of of those infatuated people I feel that those who have carefully studied this complex question should speak out in a proper manner. While I am in favor of taking into the account the trials of those Mormons in redeeming the sage Bush plains, and also the fact that this great Gov. for Twenty years has tolerated the abomination of Polygamy, allowing families to grow up under it, it would be wicked to bastardise those innocent children; what I want and desire, is to see an enabling act by which as far as possible they may be able to fix up the past (so far as Polygamy is concerned) and the most rigid prevention of any more of the abomination. To make Utah a state at present is to shut out all hopes of peaceful & profitable mining in Utah, and will put off the time of closing out that infamous barbarous practice of Polygamy for many years to come. Brigham Young is a personal friend of mine. I have done considerable business with him, gladly would I do him a favor if in doing so would not conflict with law, and good order, but his whole *Theocracy* founded in imposition & fraud is at war with Civilization and until the developement of the mines brings Population, and general diffusion of inteligence brings better practices Utah is doomed to trials. You might as well adopt the plan attributed I believe to Govr. Pierpont of Va. in the case of the Rattlesnake '*swear him* & let *him go*' as to expet those people to abide by a promise of what they will do,—let them do it first and then no need of a promise. I have had years of experience am largely interested in Utahs permanent success, having in connection with large capitalists erected expensive works at Chicago depending on Utah for supplies of Ore & Bullion, you will pardon me for this liberty I use in this important matter, now assuming ⁿNational importance. If your policy is settled no use to make further suggestions. if however, it is still under advisement, and you desire to consult with as humble individual as myself on this subject; I will willingly at *my own expense* make the trip *at* once to Washington, of one thing you can rest assured, that any question you ask, by letter or verbally; will be as safe from the public as in your own breast, and I desire what I say the same: hoping your second term may see Polygamy wiped out . . ." ALS, *ibid.* Bell enclosed a circular advertising the "Chicago Silver Smelting and Refining Company."

On Feb. 24, Cyrus M. Hawley, associate justice, Utah Territory, Salt Lake City, wrote to USG. "Confidential . . . I desire to call your especial attention to certain interests & necessities existing in the 2d Judicial District of this Territory; and 1st This District embraces the extreme portion of this Territory, where the mountain meadow massacre was perpetrated, in which from 120 to 130 innocent emigrants were inhumanly murdered in 1857 for their property. The Court in this dist is held at Beaver City, 225 miles South of this City, and in inhabited by mormons with the exception of about 100 miners. As a matter of course, we are obliged to a greater extent than is desireable, to make up our Juries out of the friends of those who perpetrated, and caused the commission of said massacre 2d Last fall the Marshal Summond for said dist Court a good Grand Jury, who undertook the investigation of said crime with those of others; but while they found that witnesses, even among the perpetrators of such crimes are willing witnesses; yet they were unwilling to testify unless assured of the protection of the government. Another difficulty was, these witnesses were so Scattered, that they could not be summoned and brought before the Jury from distances of from fifty to 150 miles for the want of funds to pay them. Under these circumstances, I deemed it best to adjourn my Court, after disposing of the civil docket, and continue my Grand Jury until the 2d Monday in may next, thereby giving the Jury time to learn more definitely about the witnesses needed and their residences, and in the mean time to communicate the necessities of the case to the Government and military authorities and to the two Territorial Committees of Congress, which I did last fall at the opening of the present Session. 3d To carry out this purpose of the Grand Jury, and to execute the law in the premises, two things are requisite, towit, a miletary post should be established at Beaver City of at least five companies; and Piute and Severe Counties, situate within fifty miles of Beaver City, now in the 1st Judicial dist, Should be added to the 2d Judicial dist. These two counties contain probibly 200 loyal men, and these counties are 150 miles from the court in the 1st Dist, to which they are now attached. With these two counties attached to my (the Second) district Court, and we would have 300 loyal men in the district. At the begining of the present Session of Congress, I communicated to the two Territorial committees, the above facts, and asked them to introduce a bill to attach the said two counties to my district for the reasons stated, and also asked for other needed legislation: but though I have watched the proceedings of Congress, I have not observed that anything has been done in the premises. Last fall I communicated the above facts and necessities to Genl Auger, then commander of this military department, and to the Governor of this Territory, and asked for a miletary post. Both of them admitted the necessaties of the case, and promised to represent the same to you, which they inform me they have done When Genl Ord assumed command of this miletary department, I communicated the same facts and needs, with the endorsment of the Governor to him. He is now here, and he informs me, that he is now awaiting orders from the War department upon the subject. Last December I also communicated the same facts and needs in writing to the United States Dist Atty *Bates*, of this Territory, and ~~he~~ we arrainged to make a united effort to enforce the law against all violators; and we now are hopeing to have the support of Government in the undertaking. This miletary post should be located by the middle of April: for then transportation will be most easy. We have been and are doing all that is possible to do, to execute the laws and to bring criminals to Justice; but we labour under great difficulties, which cannot be fully surmounted without aid, or appreciated by persons absent from, and who are not conversant with the situation. As a Judicial officer, I must of course keep myself free from partisan feeling and action; and yet, with all my caution and endeavour, I am made the target of abuse and vilification by the powers and press of the *theocratic despotism*, which has reigned here for the last twenty four years. This I do not regard: for no such influence will or can deter me from the full discharge of my Judicial duties while on the bench—As the present Session of Congress is drawing to a close, and nothing as yet has been done for us, I felt it my duty to call your attention to the facts in the premises: for without this aid and miletary support, we are almost powerless in that part of the Territory. Congress should do something for us immediately, ~~in~~ at least in three directions, towit, 1st Provide means by appropriations or a federal means of taxation to enable us to carry on the Courts   2d Provide a Jury law by which we can secure loyal men for Jurors, and 3d Provide a Registry election law, and repeal the Territorial law for numbering ~~fo~~ votes. To these three points, together with the necessity of adding the Counties of Piute and Severe to the Second Judicial district, I called the especial attention of the chairman of the two Territorial Committees of Congress last fall at the commencement of the Session—With appropriate legislation upon these points, and with a sufficient miletary post at Beaver City, we can bring criminals to Justice, and move on and make the people respect the laws, and enforce the processes and Judgments of the Court. All of which ~~we~~ I most respectfully submit to Your Excellancies most considerate Judgment—" ALS, *ibid.*, Letters Received, Utah.

On April 18, Woods wrote to USG. "The news of the Decision of the U. S. Supreme Court in the Englebrecht Case Strikes consternation into the ranks of the Gentiles in Utah. Under the law as laid down by the Supreme Court, a Mormon Marshall will summon a Mormon Jury to try Mormon Criminals, each, and all of whom regard their duty to the Church as above all law. The Marshall and Atty. Gen. are both Polygamists, and the former is a Criminal, and under any ordinary rule would himself be under arrest for well-known crime   To say that the Decision is disastrous to us only, in part, expresses our condition   It leaves us powerless, ties us, and all the authority of the Government hand and foot, and pitches us into the Mormon Camp. Henceforward until something law will be a farce, and the Officers of the Govt. mere ninnies. I have not words to express my deep regret at the present condition of affairs here. In view of the condition of affairs I express the earnest hope that the needed legislation may be had *at once.* The Voorhies Bill is just what we need, and ought to be pushed through as soon as possible. I do hope that every exertion may be made to secure its passage. With it we can carry out your policy in Utah and make it a success; with out it we are powerless   Their triumph in the Supreme Court makes the Mormons very jubilant, arrogant—insolent. They feel, now, that all power is in their hands, and attribute their triumph to the special interposition of Divine Providence. Were it not that they want to be on their good behavior with the hope of gaining admission as a State, I would expect trouble with them; indeed it may come any way, but I will do all in my power to avoid such a calamity. There are more than twenty murderers in Salt Lake City alone, who committed some as dark and diabolical crimes as blacken the annals of human depravity who are to be turned loose upon the community; men whom every citizen knows to be murderers, and whose lives alone can atone for their crimes. If the Voorhies Bill passes, and we can have a new, and trustworthy Dist. Atty, they shall be arrested and tried and if shown to be guilty, punished. Bates has been in constant, confidential communication with your Enemies,—writing, and telegraphing of the 'situation' to Brigham Youngs Attys—with as much zeal as tho. he was Counsel for Deft. Immediately upon the rendering of the Decision he telegraphed to Depty. Dist. Atty. James L High, to assist Defts Counsel, in the immediate discharge of Prisoners.   but Mr High, who is a true man, refused to do so, knowing that the Judges could not act until they were officially informed of the Decision of the Supreme Court. I do hope he may never come to Utah again   Some time ago, as per a law of Congress I nominated one Commissioner and one Alternate to ~~prepare~~ represent Utah in the Centennial Celebration. To-day one of them, the Alternate, Mr W. H. Pitts resigned. I therefore nominate Mr. Oscar G. Sawyer of Utah, to fill the vacancy. Mr Sawyer is the Correspondent of the N. Y. Herald, and is an excellent man. Col Wickizer the Commissioner cannot attend the next meeting of the Commission to be held May 20th and as Mr Sawyer is anxious to do so I hope his Commission will be forwarded at once." ALS, *ibid.* USG endorsed this letter. "Atty. Gn.   Extract of portion refering to Com. to Int. Nat. Fair to sec. of State." AE (undated), *ibid.* See Proclamation, April 29, 1871. On July 3, 1872, Porter wrote to Charles Hale, asst. secretary of state. "The President directs me to say that he will be pleased to have you instruct Gov. Wood of Utah to come on and report in person to the President." LS, DNA, RG 59, Miscellaneous Letters.

On May 21, McKean, Washington, D. C., wrote to USG. "The House committee on the judiciary have agreed to report to-morrow the Voorhees-Bingham bill 'To aid the execution of the laws in the Territory of Utah,'   It will of course take some days to get it throug both houses of congress. My leave of absence will expire tomorrow. I would not have troubled your Excellency to ask for an extension, but Mr. Bristow, of the Department of Justice, preferred that I should make the application directly to you. I think that twenty days additional time will suffice." ALS, *ibid.*, RG 60, Letters Received, Utah. On the same day, USG endorsed this letter. "Extension approved." AES, *ibid.*

Also on May 21, Young, Salt Lake City, wrote to Belknap. "A certain congressional document reached me to-day, containing official copies of two letters,—one signed by C. M. Hawley, Associate Justice, &c.—the other by Gov. George L. Wood,

both of Utah, bearing date respectively, Jan. 12. 1872. As the subject matter contained in those letters, is calculated to create very erroneous impressions, I take this
liberty of respectfully calling your attention to a few facts in contra-distinction.
Judge Hawley alleges that at a place called 'Knob,' (meaning I suppose 'Kanab') 'the
Gibraltar of church fellows, there are one hundred and twenty men thoroughly
armed, and where the leaders of said massacre have taken refuge.' This settlement,
at the time alluded to, contained in all some twenty families,—farmers and stock-
raisers—and at no time, were there more than thirty white men there. A peaceful,
rural district, as unlike, in every respect, to a 'Gibraltar' as can well be imagined.
And the allegation that 'there, the leaders of the Mountain Meadow Massacre have
taken refuge,' is as unwarrantable and malicious, as it is unbecoming in the judicial
officer, who, expecting to try that case, officially declares, beforehand, that certain
parties there are guilty, and calls upon the highest military authority for military
power to enforce his decision. In 1858, when Alfred Cumming was Gov. of U. T. I
pledged myself to lend him and the court every assistance in my power, in men and
means to thoroughly investigate the Mountain Meadow Massacre and bring, if possible, the guilty parties to justice. That offer I have made again and again, and
although it has not yet been accepted, I have neither doubt nor fear that the perpetrators of that tragedy will meet their just reward. But, sending an armed force is not
the best means of furthering the ends of justice, although it may serve an excellent
purpose, in exciting popular clamor against the 'Mormons.' In 1859, Judge Cradlebaugh employed a military force to attempt the arrest of those alleged criminals.
He engaged in all about four hundred men, some one hundred of whom were civilians,—reputed gamblers, thieves and other camp followers, who were, doubtless,
intended for jurors; (as his associate Judge Eccles had just done in another district,)
but these, accomplished absolutely nothing, further than plundering hen roosts and
rendering themselves obnoxious to the citizens on their line of march. Had Judge
Cradlebaugh, instead of peremptorily dismissing his grand jury, and calling for that
military posse, allowed the investigation into the Mountain Meadow Massacre to
proceed, I have the authority of Mr Wilson, U. S. prosecuting attorney, for saying,
the investigation was proceeding satisfactorily, and I firmly believe, if the county
sheriffs, whose legal duty it was to make arrests, had been lawfully directed to serve
the processes, that they would have performed their duty, and the accused would
have been brought to trial. Instead of honoring the law, Judge Cradlebaugh took a
course to screen offenders, who could easily hide from such a posse under the justification of avoiding a trial by court martial. It is now 14 years since that tragedy was
enacted, and the courts have never tried to prosecute the accused; although some of
the Judges, like Judge Hawley, have used every opportunity to charge the crime upon
prominent men in Utah, and inflame public opinion against our community. I do not
wish to be understood as opposed to the erection of forts in Utah, that is the business
of the government and not mine; and all officers of the regular army who have ever
quartered here, can testify to the cordiality of their relations with our citizens, only
marred when such characters as Judges Brocchus, Drummond, Cradlebaugh, Hawley
and others, have by malicious misrepresentation sought to create disturbance, and it
is not improbable the same efforts may be made with these troops at Beaver. That
is what I am opposed to, and wish to prevent. The assertion that 'a point at Beaver
City would be the proper place to do most service to the country in preventing
Indian raids,' is well known to be incorrect, and is, obviously, a mere pretext. This
care for the Mormon settlements against Indian raids is no new thing, and, viewed
in the light of facts, it looks savagely insincere. The late Gov. Shaffer had by procla-

mation, prohibited all gatherings of militia in Utah, and when in 1871, a large, armed band of Navajo indians suddenly fell upon Kanab,—where there were not more than 10 white men, and a number of women and children—professedly to trade for horses, but in reality to steal them—a runner was dispatched to the end of our telegraph, and a message sent to Gen. Erastus Snow, commanding the militia in Southern Utah. Gen. Snow telegraphed to Gov. Wood, (Shaffer's successor, and the endorser of Judge Hawley's letter,) asking what he should do in the premises, but received no reply. The General waited some 3 hours and telegraphed again; this time requesting the operator personally to wait upon his excellency for an answer to these telegrams. The reply to the operator was 'I shall do as I like about answering it.' or words to that effect, but he made no reply whatever to Gen. Snow. As the situation was critical, some 20 men were immediately dispatched to Kanab, and others ordered out immediately afterwards. Those 20 men appearing from opposite quarters impressed the indians that they were surrounded, while they were in the very act of lassoeing the horses, heedless of remonstrance. The Governor's callousness was not calculated to win the respect of our citizens, and the call for troops to locate at Beaver for their protection, in the midst of populous settlements perfectly safe from indians, and about 140 miles from the most proper point for defense, they doubtless regard in its true light. I have taken the liberty of writing this, to give you the facts just as they are." LS, *ibid.*, RG 94, Letters Received, 3314 1871. Copies of letters from Hawley and Woods of Jan. 12 to Ord are *ibid.* See message to Congress, Feb. 14, 1873; *HED*, 42-2-285; Roberts, V, 382–419; Dean C. Jessee, ed., *Letters of Brigham Young to His Sons* (Salt Lake City, 1974), pp. 138–39, 166–67, 171–75; Stanley P. Hirshson, *The Lion of the Lord: A Biography of Brigham Young* (New York, 1969), pp. 303–8; Leonard J. Arrington, *Brigham Young: American Moses* (New York, 1985), pp. 371–73.

1. Born in 1832 in Mo., Woods emigrated to Oregon Territory (1847), worked as a carpenter and gold miner, practiced law, and then served as Republican governor of Ore. (1866–70). On Sept. 22, 1869, U.S. Senators Henry W. Corbett and George H. Williams of Ore., Portland, had written to Fish. "We respectfully recommend one of our Citizens Gov George L Woods for the position of Minister Resident in~~a~~t China. Believing our Coast to be more intimately Connected with China than any other portion of the Union, we believe this Mission should be given to a Citizen of the Pacific Coast we therfore present a distinguist Citizen of our own state and urge his appointment" LS, DNA, RG 59, Letters of Application and Recommendation. On Jan. 23, 1871, USG nominated Woods as governor, Utah Territory. See letter to John M. Thayer, Dec. 22, 1870.

On July 1, 1871, U.S. Representative Charles B. Farwell of Ill., Chicago, twice wrote to USG. "It has been intimated to me that there may soon be a vacancy in the Office of Governor of Utah Territory, and I take this early opportunity to ask you, in the event of a change being made, to appoint Philip Wadsworth Esq of this City to the place" "In a conversation with a mutual friend yesterday, I partially learned the cause of the opposition of the Chicago Tribune to your administration and to yourself personally—It is this—About a year ago, upon the advice and request of some of his friends Mr Horace White wrote you a letter to which you have never replied, and your non-reply is construed into an insult—I ~~informed~~ stated to my informant, that I did not beleive that the letter had ever reached its destination that I felt sure that if the letter was respectful in its tone, it would have been promptly answered—The support of the Tribune of yourself is to be desired by us here and of course, by yourself—and my informant said to me that if Mr White could receive an invitation to call upon you, that he would promptly respond, and that thereafter he would be your friend and yield to you his cordial and earnest support—Would it therefore not be well for you at your next visit here to have this interview? Or as white is now East, ask him to call before he returns to the West— Pardon me for offering these suggestions, but I do it, because I desire harmony here, and because I beleive that your own interests would be promoted thereby" ALS, DNA, RG 59, Letters of Application and Recommendation.

On July 23, Woods wrote to USG about an invitation to campaign in Calif. and his wish to become commissioner of Indian Affairs. ALS, *ibid.*, Utah Territorial Papers. On July 25, Woods telegraphed to USG asking permission to campaign in Calif. Telegram received, *ibid.* Fish endorsed this request: "not advisable" AE (undated), *ibid.*

To J. Russell Jones

Washington D. C
Nov. 7th 1871

DEAR JONES

Saturday of this week[1] Fred sails with Gn. Sherman for Europe. They will spend the Winter with the ship in the Mediteranean and in the Spring cross Westward through Europe and home reaching here probably about the last of June.[2] They will see you about May unless in the mean time I should find it necessary to decapitate you. Sumner, Schutz, Dana and all your admirers think it preposterous in me to give appointments to persons who I ever knew and particularly to those who feel any personal friendship for me. If I am guided by this advice your decapitation is sure.—We will send Wilson in Chetlain's place.[3]

I have not heard from Washburne recently, privately, but suppose he is well though a little uncomfortable now that they have no great excitement to keep him busy.

My family are all well and desire to be remembered to Mrs Jones.

Yours Truly
U. S. GRANT

ALS, ICHi. See *PUSG*, 20, 93–94; letter to J. Russell Jones, Feb. 8, 1871.

1. Nov. 11.

2. See letter to Mary Grant Cramer, Oct. 26, 1871.

3. On April 10, 1869, Elihu B. Washburne, Galena, telegraphed to USG. "Failure to appoint Chetlain Consul Brussells as was agreed on would embarrass me immensely ... Please answer" Telegram received (at 10:30 A.M.), DNA, RG 107, Telegrams Collected (Bound). On April 12, USG nominated Augustus L. Chetlain as consul, Brussels. On May 7, 1870, U.S. Senator John Sherman of Ohio wrote to USG. "I beg to call your attention to Dr John Wilson of Pittsburgh our late Consul at Antwerp who was suddenly recalled without notice and his successor confirmed without attracting my notice—Dr Wilson was Medical Director of the Army of the Potomac—served the Government faithfully during the War—had charge of Mr Fred Seward after his attempted assasination—is a sound Republican—and a learned and able Surgeon—To my personal knowledge he has discharged his duties as Consul at Antwerp with much satisfaction and is held in high esteem there—His removal was unexpected—is embarrassing to him—and considering his character and service seems harsh and unjust. If it is too late to repair this I respectfully ask that Dr Wilson be assigned to duty as Consul to Constantinople in place of Mr Goodenow   In behalf of Dr Wilson I will say that if this is done he will resign in one year. His entire familiarity with the duties of a Consul will make it easy for him to fill that office at Constantinople." ALS, *ibid.*, RG 59, Letters of Application and Recommendation. On the same day, USG endorsed this letter. "Respectfully refered to the Sec. of State. If the removal of the present Consul at Constantinople is proper there is no objection to the change." AES, *ibid.* On May 9, Sherman wrote to USG. "I enclose letters from Mr Washburne & Mr Jones in regard to Dr John Wilson of whom we conversed on Saturday—Please read them—Why would it not be well to send Gen. Sprague now of Minn. as Minister to Constantinople." ALS, *ibid.* On April 19, Washburne, Paris, had written to Sherman. "We were all very sorry to see your friend and our friend, Dr. Wilson, removed as Consul at Antwerp. He is a good man, a true republican and he performed great and exceptional service as a Surgeon in the Army. Why such a man should have been removed we dont know. The doctor's health is bad, and he wants some other place abroad if possible for him to obtain it. Can you not join his other friends in aiding him in getting another Consulate in Europe? I really wish you could, for it would be doing the Dr. a great favor and rendering the public a service." ALS, *ibid.* On April 20, J. Russell Jones, U.S. minister, Brussels, wrote to USG. "Col John Wilson, U. S. Consul at Antwerp is desirous of remaining a year or two longer in Europe in order to complete the education of his son,   Since my arrival here I have had occasion to see a good deal of the Col and I take great pleasure in saying that I consider him one of the best Consuls we have, besides which, he is a gentleman of fine social qualities and is just such a man as all our Consuls ought to be, Competent, honest and attentive to his duties. I shall be exceedingly gratified since you have felt compelled to give Antwerp to Mr Weaver, if you can give Col Wilson some other place." ALS, *ibid.* On Oct. 25, 1871, Orville E. Babcock wrote to Secretary of State Hamilton Fish. "The President directs me to inform you that he will be pleased to have John Wilson appointed Consul at Brussels vice Gen Chetlain resigned—The appointment to take effect Jany 1st 1872." ALS, *ibid.* Related papers are *ibid.* On the same day, Fish wrote to Babcock. "Mr Chetlains resignation does not take effect until 8th January when the Senate will be in Session—The late Attorney General held that the Presidents power of appointment could not thus anticipate a vacancy—I suppose the whole object in view will be attained by filing your note (for action when the vacancy occurs) & possibly letting

Mr Wilson know the Presidents intention" ALS (press), DLC-Hamilton Fish. On March 4, 1870, USG had nominated James R. Weaver as consul, Antwerp, to replace John Wilson; on Dec. 12, 1871, USG nominated Wilson as consul, Brussels. See *PUSG*, 19, 268–69; Augustus L. Chetlain, *Recollections of Seventy Years* (Galena, 1899), pp. 140–67.

On Dec. 8, 1871, Charles W. Kleeberg, consul, Liège, had written to USG. "In consequence of the resignation of Mr. Chetlain, the U. S. Consul at Brussels, I take the liberty of, applying to you directly for my transfer to this vacancy. The arguments, which I offer to your favorable consideration are in the first place the most extraordinary circumstances, under which I was induced to accept my present position, where I found myself exposed to unparalleled mortifications. In the second place,—and here I appeal to something stronger than to your sense of justice, and even to your generosity—it is the most intense desire for completing what I have begun under enormous difficulties, that may convince you of the expediency of the requested transfer. The prime motive for my coming here to Belgium consisted in the avowed determination, to open preliminary negotiations towards the establishment of an *American* line of steamers between Antwerp and Newyork. For two years I have devoted all my time and my little ability, and even an unproportionately large share of my miserable income to this project, until most of the prominent businessmen, and the leaders of the liberal party, including the king himself, pronounced themselves decidedly in favor of an American line, and after the most exhausting efforts I finally succeeded in finding substantial and responsible business-men, who are ready to take the matter into their hands...." ALS, DNA, RG 59, Letters of Application and Recommendation. Related papers are *ibid.* On Nov. 2, 1869, Adeline C. W. Kleeberg, Brussels, had written to Julia Dent Grant. "Ever mindful of your kindness towards me, Madam, I feel encouraged to address you these lines, otherwise it may appear bold in me to do so and if my motive is known to you I hope, my action will then be justified. Mr Kleeberg has met with a great disappointment at his arrival about his Consulate, it is proved that Verviers is not even worth 100$ and a consolidation with Liège has not taken place. Thus we are now here in Brussels on expense *without any income* and if you knew what sacrifices we made to come so far, indeed I am sure, you would sincerely sympathize with us. I appeal therefore once more to Your kind intercession for us; our position is so very embarrassing that it needs the strongest recommendation to the attention of the President...." ALS, DLC-Hamilton Fish.

To John M. Palmer

Washington, D. C. Nov. 9. 1871

Sir:

I am in receipt of your letter of the 3d inst. inquiring the nature of the orders &c. under which four companies of U. S. Troops have been ordered to the City of Chicago, and asserting your ability, as Executive officer of the State, to furnish all the protection asked in the appeal of the citizens of Chicago from these troops. In reply I enclose you copy of the appeal, of Gen. Sheridan's remarks thereon, of the orders given in sending the troops, and of all correspondence between Gen. Sheridan and authorities here since the great fire which laid so much of the wealth of of Chicago in ashes. I will only add further that no thought here ever contemplated distrust of the state authorities of the state of Illinois, or lack of ability on their part to do all that was necessary, or expected of them, for the maintenance of law of law and order within the limits of the state. The only thing thought of was how to benefit a people struck by a calamity greater than had ever befallen a community, of the same number, before in this country. The aid was of a like nature with that given in any emergency requiring immediate action. No reflections were contemplated or thought of affecting the integrity or ability of any state officer, or city official within the limits of the state of Illinois, to perform his whole duty.

I have the honor to be, with great respect,

Your obt. svt.

U. S. Grant

His Ex. Gov. J. M. Palmer.
Governor of Ills.

Copy, DLC-USG, II, 1. See telegram to Lt. Gen. Philip H. Sheridan, Oct. 9, 1871. On Nov. 3, 1871, Governor John M. Palmer of Ill. had written to USG. "I have the honor to enclose to you a printed slip cut from the Chicago Journal a highly respectable newspaper published in Chicago and respectfully ask your attention to its contents My apology for troubling your Excellency with a paper of the character of that enclosed is that it is stated therein that 'four companies of the 8th United States Infantry have been ordered from New York to Chicago and will arrive there tomorrow (today) 'subject to the call of the authorities' and that the reasons for ordering troops to Chicago are that 'The large supplies the Relief Society will have in store during the winter were not deemed safe besides threatened strikes in some quarters indicated that laborers willing to work might not be allowed to do so' and that an application stating these facts was signed by the Officers of the Relief Society and other citizens presented to Genl Sheridan and by him approved and referred to the Secretary of War &c   In addition to this—rumors in the form of telegraphic despatches from Washington and Chicago have reached me that troops were ordered to Chicago for purposes connected with the Safety of property and the preservation of order in the city but no information of the existence of the dangers alluded to have reached me from any quarter whatever   I cheerfully concede that it for the President to designate the Stations of the troops composing the army and that he is under no obligations founded upon the constitutn or the laws or upon the rules of Official Courtesy to communicate his orders or the reasons that influenced him in making them to the Governors of any of the States unless the orders in question or the presence of the troops are intended in some way to affect or influence the internal affairs of the particular state to which the troops are sent—In the latter case it will readily occur to you that the Governor of the State whose duty it is to enforce the laws is deeply concerned—for the troops—and the orders under which they are to act may operate to diminish or greatly increase the difficulties of his Official position   I am happy in the consciousness that the authorities of the State of Illinois are abundantly able to protect every interest of the people that depend upon its internal peace and good order, and am unwilling to believe that the President of the United States acting upon information of a contrary character communicated by private citizens to an Officer of the army has ordered any portion of the army into this State to be subject to the call of the authorities either to protect the store houses of the Relief Committee or to interfere with the possible though not probable 'Strikes' of laborers   I therefore deem it due to the importance of the subject to frankly inquire of your Excellency whether the troops ordered to Chicago are intended or instructed to obey the call of any authorities of the State of Illinois, or the city of Chicago, or in any way whatever to assume the protection either of property or the preservation of order in that city?" AL (incomplete), NHi; final sentence completed from *Special Message of Governor John M. Palmer, . . . Concerning the Military Occupation of Chicago* (Springfield, Ill., 1871), p. 3.

On Oct. 11, Mayor Roswell B. Mason of Chicago had issued a proclamation placing the city police under Sheridan's authority. Copy, DNA, RG 94, Letters Received, 3485 1871. On Oct. 25, after exchanging letters with Mason, Sheridan wrote to AG Edward D. Townsend that troops were no longer needed and had been redeployed. LS, *ibid.* On Oct. 31, Gen. William T. Sherman endorsed this letter to Secretary of War William W. Belknap. "The extraordinary circumstances attending the Great fire in Chicago, made it eminently proper, that General Sheridan should exercise the influence, authority and power he did on the universal appeal of a ruined & distressed people, backed by their civil agents who were powerless for good. The very moment that the civil authorities felt able to resume their functions, Genl Sheridan ceased to exercise authority and the U. S. troops returned to their respective stations. General Sheridans course is fully approved." AES, *ibid.* On Oct. 28, Wirt Dexter, Joseph Medill, *et al.*, Chicago Relief and Aid Society, wrote to Sheridan. "The undersigned respectfully & urgently request that you will cause four companies of U. S. Infantry to be stationed at or near this city until it shall appear that there is no danger of attack by disorderly persons upon the depots of the Relief & Aid Society, or other riotous proceedings, for, which the recent appalling calamity may have paved the way. We believe that the presence of a small military force in this vicinity would at the same time deter any evil-disposed persons from organizing a breach of the peace & reassure the public mind in an extraordinary degree. Thanking you for the great services you have already rendered to this stricken community, . . ." DS (11 signatures), *ibid.* On Oct. 29, Sheridan wrote to Townsend supporting this request. LS, *ibid.* On Oct. 31, Belknap, "In Cabinet," wrote to Sherman. "The President directs that four (4) Companies of the 8th Infantry be ordered to Chicago; Please telegraph Genl. Sheridan to that effect & issue the order." ALS, *ibid.*

On Nov. 20, Palmer wrote to USG. ". . . I have read your Excellencys letter and examined the papers, received, with great attention, and while I am not insensible of the kindness that promts you to disclaim all distrust of the authorities of the State of Illinois, or of their ability to do all that may be necessary or expected of them for the maintainance of law and order within the limits of the State, I have been unable to find anything in them to justify the extraordinary measure of ordering four Companies of United States troops into this State to report to Lieut Genl Sheridan to act as police under his orders It seems to me to be very well settled as a principle of American public law that the duty of protecting persons and property and the preservation of public order and peace against the efforts of disorderly persons, or from local internal disturbance, is the peculiar and exclusive duty of the States, with which the government of the United States has no concern, and in which it cannot interfere except upon the application of the legislature or the Executive of the States as contemplated by the 4th Section of the 4th article of the Constitution, and that any attempt by the Officers of the United States army to employ any part of the military forces, as proposed by the gentlemen who made the application for four Companies of Infantry to be stationed at or near Chicago for an indefinite period, and approved by Lieut Genl Philip H. Sheridan in his letter to the Adjutant Genl of the 29th October and by Genl W. T. Sherman by his telegraphic communication to Lieut. Genl Sheridan of 31st October 1871 must be improper because violative of the Constitution and the laws, I am not at all forgetful that your Excellency says that what was done in reference to ordering troops to Chicago was upon the ground of emergency to aid a people who had suffred greatly, but in this view it seems to me that the General commanding the army overlooked the fact that the disastrous fire at Chicago did not relieve the State of Illinois from any of its duties, nor transfer, any of them to the government of the United States Emergencies that demand extraordinary efforts often occur in the history of governments, but I do not remember another instance in our history where it was held that an event that created a sudden demand upon the powers and resources of a State operated to transfer any portion of the duties of the State to the United States. The great fire at Chicago ceased on the 9th of October, and the Executive of the State of Illinois under the belief that the disaster created an 'emergency' provided for by the constitution of the State, convened the General Assembly to meet in session on the 13th day of that month to make legal provision to meet all the requirements of the occasion, and on the 19th day of October, that department appropriated from the Treasury an adequate sum to maintain a sufficient police force for the protection of every interest of the people. The emergency was thus provided for by the proper department of the proper government in the only way that it could be done, or can be done. The State enlarged and strengthened, its own agencies for the enforcement of its own laws to meet the requirements of the new situation. The same calamity deprives the United States of its custom house, its post office, its court room and records, and throw upon that government the duty of adopting measures to supply the loss, but it has not yet occurred to the authorities of the State, that the losses of the United States or the interuption of its business have, so far changed the relations of the federal and state systems as to cast any portion of the duty of providing for any of the wants of the United States upon the State of Illinois, and they are as little able to understand how it is that events that cannot operate to enlarge the powers of the government of the State should operate to confer upon the Lieut General of the army the authority to interfere in matters of purely local State concern, or to authorize the General commanding the army to recognize and approve the assumption of the Lieut General, and order four Companies of United States Infantry to report to him to discharge the mere civil duties of 'police' I do not of course propose to discuss with your Excellency the question of the relative rights and powers of the United States and of the States under the Constitution, for

I will not anticipate the possibility of a difference of opinion upon the point that the duties of the Executive officers of the two systems, are defined so accurately and are kept so distinct by written Constitutions and laws, that there is no possibility of a conflict between them   The duty of the President is to see that the laws of the United States are enforced, and that of the Governor of Illinois is confined to the enforcement of the laws of the State   Neither obstructs the other, nor aids nor interferes with his duties   The Governor of a State derives none of his powers from the United States, nor are his duties subject in any respect to the consent or discretion of the President, who can in no wise enlarge, abridge, or interupt them, either by assuming them himself or by entrusting them to others. As these opinions seem to me to be incontroverible I cannot doubt that the orders to United States troops to act as Police, or to otherwise interfere in the affairs or duties of the State, or any of its officers, were made without reflection, and that the troops will be at once withdrawn from this State, or, that the orders for their government will be so modified as to prohibit their employment as Police, or in any other way to interfere with any of the duties and functions of any of the officers created under the laws of this State. The State of Illinois cannot accept their aid or permit their interference in its affairs without a sacrifice of the confidence of its citizens, nor without giving countenance to a dangerous example." ALS, *ibid.*

On Nov. 25, USG wrote to Palmer. "I have received your letter of the 20th instant and have referred it to the Secretary of War, with directions to inform Gen: Sheridan that, if the troops under his command have received any orders which in any way conflict with the provisions of the Constitution or the laws of the State of Illinois, he is instructed to rescind them." Copy, DLC-USG, II, 1. On Dec. 3, Sheridan wrote to Townsend. ". . . I beg leave to state that all documents and orders issued in relation to these companies have been heretofore forwarded to your office. It will be seen by an examination of these that no orders or directions have been given which conflict with the Constitution or Laws of the State of Illinois, and I beg leave to further state that no orders of such nature have ever been contemplated. The troops are simply occupying quarters in the vicinity of the Stock Yards near the city. I regret that his Excellency the Governor is dissatisfied and hope that the assurance herein given may allay his apprehensions." LS, DNA, RG 94, Letters Received, 3485 1871.

On Dec. 9, Palmer submitted a special message to the Illinois General Assembly. ". . . My letters to the President of the United States, of the 3d and 20th of November, will prove that I have exerted myself to induce the President to withdraw these troops from the State, or to prohibit them from interfering in its internal affairs; and those of the President to me, of date of November 9th and 25th, will show that my efforts have been fruitless, and that the President has practically referred the whole subject to the decision of the officer whose conduct is questioned. It is manifest that the order of the President, described in his letter of November 25, ends all discussion, and leaves Lieutenant-General Sheridan with four companies of infantry in Chicago with discretionary powers to intermeddle in affairs that are within the exclusive and peculiar jurisdiction of the State, and with which the President and his military subordinates have no rightful concern whatever. . . ." *Special Message of Governor John M. Palmer, . . . Concerning the Military Occupation of Chicago* (Springfield, Ill., 1871), p. 13. On Dec. 14, Horace Porter wrote to Belknap. "The President directs me to say that he will be pleased to have you call at the Executive Mansion that he may consult with you in reference to the troops stationed at Chicago." Copy, DLC-USG, II, 1. On Dec. 30, Belknap wrote to Palmer. "Referring to your message dated

Decr. 9. 1871. to the 27th General Assembly 'transmitting the official correspondence between Gen. Sheridan and his superior officers, &c.,' I deem it right, in order to remove an apparent misapprehension, to inform you distinctly what action this Dept. under instructions from the President of the U. S. took upon your letter of Nov. 20th to the President—. . . I immediately caused a copy of your letter with the President's endorsement to be sent to Genl Sheridan with instructions to him to furnish this office with copies of any orders, or documents bearing on the question, not heretofore furnished which he may have issued, or may issue—You will thus perceive that the President and Secretary of War have taken care to be fully advised upon all General Sheridan's measures, and to hold the control over them in their own hands." Copies, DNA, RG 94, Letters Received, 3485 1871; *ibid.*, RG 107, Letters Sent, Military Affairs. On Jan. 8, 1872, Palmer wrote to Belknap repeating his objections. ALS, *ibid.*, RG 94, Letters Received, 3485 1871. See John M. Palmer, *Personal Recollections of John M. Palmer: The Story of an Earnest Life* (Cincinnati, 1901), pp. 343–77; Carl Smith, *Urban Disorder and the Shape of Belief: The Great Chicago Fire, the Haymarket Bomb, and the Model Town of Pullman* (Chicago, 1995), pp. 77–80.

Order

November 14th 1871.

The Bitter Root Valley, above the Loo-lo fork, in the Territory of Montana, having been carefully surveyed and examined, in accordance with the 11th Article of the Treaty of July 16th 1855 concluded at Hell Gate in the Bitter Root Valley, between the United States and the Flathead, Hootenay and Upper Pend d'Oreille Indians, which was ratified by the Senate, March 8th 1859. has proved, in the judgment of the President, not to be better adapted to the wants of the Flathead tribe than the general reservation provided for in said treaty; it is, therefore, deemed unnecessary to set apart any portion of said Bitter Root Valley as a separate reservation for Indians referred to in said treaty:

It is, therefore ordered and directed, that all Indians residing in said Bitter Root Valley be removed as soon as practicable, to the Reservation provided for in the 2nd Article of said treaty; and that a just and impartial appraisement be made of any substantial improvements made by said Indians upon any lands of the Bitter Root Valley, such as fields enclosed and cultivated and houses erected; that such appraisement shall distinguish between improvements made before the date of the said treaty and such as have been subsequently made.

It is further ordered, that, after the removal, herein directed, shall have been made, the Bitter Root Valley aforesaid shall be open to settlement.

It is further ordered that if any of said Indians residing in the Bitter Root Valley desire to become citizens and reside on the lands which they now occupy, not exceeding in quantity what is allowed under the homestead and preemption laws to all citizens—Such persons shall be permitted to remain in said Valley upon making known to the Superintendant of Indian affairs for Montana Territory by the 1st of January 1873. their intention to comply with these conditions.

U. S. GRANT.

Copy, DNA, RG 130, Orders and Proclamations. *SED*, 48-2-95, 465; *HED*, 49-2-1, part 5, p. 554; *SD*, 57-1-452, 854–55.

In Feb., 1869, the Montana territorial legislature had addressed Congress. "We, your memorialists, the legislative assembly of the Territory of Montana, would respectfully represent that all that portion of Missoula county known as the Bitter Root valley contains several hundred of industrious white settlers, who are engaged in agriculture, manufacturing, and mining; that from year to year they have made valuable and substantial improvements, until such improvements exceed in value the property of all other portions of said county; that there are at this time about 350 of the Flathead tribe of Indians residing in said valley; that their habits and customs are so different from those of the whites, it is found to be impossible for the two races to live on amicable terms: therefore we, your memorialists, would respecfully memorialize your honorable body that a commissioner be appointed to treat with said Indians for their removal to the reservation provided for them in the Jocko valley." *HMD*, 40-3-41. See *PUSG*, 19, 550.

On Jan. 23, 1871, Charles S. Jones, agent, Montana Superintendency, Missoula, had written to Ely S. Parker, commissioner of Indian Affairs. "In the communication which I had the honor to address you on the 8th of December last, I detailed the points of a conversation held with the Chiefs of the Flat Head Nation on the occasion of my first official visit to them, during the month preceeding, in reference to their continued residence in the Bitter Root Valley; The developements on that occasion were anything but favorable to a proposition for their removal then or at any future period. Time however shows that the seed then sown is about bringing forth good fruit, for although I have not broached the subject to the Chiefs or others of the tribe since the date of the interview referred to in my communication of the 8th, yet on Tuesday last, (Jan'y 17th) Arleck or Henry, and Nine Pipes, or Joseph, two of the principal Chiefs and speaking men of the Tribe, the same who participated so actively on the first occasion, came to the Agency from their homes, 60 miles distant, and spent three days with me, during which I treated them with particular attention. In the course of a long conversation during the afternoon of the second day, they gave me a detailed account of the harassments to which they were subject in their present homes, and the demorilization which ensued consequent upon the incoming of so many whites among them, concluding by asking what I would advise them to do—I gave them to understand that it was difficult, if not impossible to apply a remedy, because of the temperament of our people, and the nature of our laws, which rather encouraged than prevented the settlement and cultivation of public lands everywhere, except upon the regular Reservations set apart for the Indians like the one on the Jocko—repeatting substantially the arguments which I had used at our first interview, together with such additional ones as subsequent reflections had inspired me, with. I then said to them in view of all these facts, and of the bitter complaints which you have this day made to me, would it not be better for you to reconsider your determination not to remove from the Bitter Root Valley, and to make up your minds to come here,   I advise you to do so; and as your friend and counsellor, having warm sympathies with you, I would not advise to a course which I did not in my heart think would bring to you many blessings and benefits. . . . They asked how their property in Bitter Root ~~Valley~~ would be valued. I told them I had no authority to say but supposed it might be done in this way—they to select one person and the Government another, who would make a valuation, which would be adopted by the President, as provided in the Treaty—After a pause Arlic the elder said, 'We see as you do, and we would like to see the Head Chief at Washington (meaning the Commissioner) in order to talk over all the matters connected with our removal and to make arrangements for it'. . ." LS, DNA, RG 75, Letters Received, Montana Superintendency.

On May 7, Charlos and six other representatives of the Flathead tribe, Stevensville, Montana Territory, wrote to USG. "The undersigned, Chiefs and Headmen of the Flathead Nation of Indians, beg leave respectfully to represent to you the importance and necessity of some final and definite action in regard to our future continuance and residence in the Bitter Root Valley. By the 11th article of the Treaty made by us with the United States at Hell Gate, in this Territory, during the year 1855, our right here was guaranteed until His Excellency the President should have ordered a survey of this Valley with a view to determine whether we should always remain here, or else remove to the regular Reservation set apart for this and other Confederated tribes on the Jocko River. Connected with this was an express provision that no part of this valley above the Loo-Loo Fork should be open to settlement or occupancy by the Whites, until the survey and decision by the President under the Treaty as before stated. Notwithstanding these solemn guarantees, no survey of the valley has as yet been made, although eleven years have elapsed since the U. S. Government ratified the Treaty; and still worse and what we most complain of is that almost our entire valley is occupied and overrun by white settlers, who impose on us in many ways, subjecting us to annoyance, inconvenience and injustice, which seem to call aloud for redress at your hands, and to you, therefore, we respectfully appeal. We are, in violation of Treaty obligations, as we conceive, encompassed on all sides by white settlers, even to the extent of villages in the midst of our settlement, and the results of the contact and association are, the drunkenness of our young men, to whom the whites will sell whiskey, as well as the demoralization of our women, which it seems impossible, with the greatest watchfulness on our part, to prevent. In view of these and other details of trouble with which we will not burden you, we ask and urge that a delegation of our tribe be allowed to visit you at Washington for the purpose of arranging and finally settling the difficulties under which we suffer, superinduced mainly as we humbly suggest, by the failure of the United States to perform its duties under the Treaty made with us. We prefer to settle these difficulties at Washington, because we believe justice will best be secured to us there; or at any rate, it will be far more satisfactory to use, as we have many grievances which we want the great Father to hear. None of our tribe, living or dead, have ever been to see you, although we hear of Chiefs of other tribes, who are always making war on you, being allowed that privilege, while we have always been the friends of the whites. We do not desire to come for amusement, but for really pressing, important, and, to us, vital business, affecting the present happiness and continued existence of our people. We ask this our Great Father, and will be thankful for such a favor." DS (all by mark), *ibid.*

On Sept. 8, Governor Benjamin F. Potts of Montana Territory wrote to Henry R. Clum, act. commissioner of Indian Affairs, recommending the removal of the Flatheads. ". . . The Flathead tribe, proper, is almost extinct: The number of the tribe and those connected with them heretofore reported to the Department, is largely in excess of the actual number. I was present in the Camp of the whole tribe, near the Village of Stephensville, about ten days ago and I am satisfied that One hundred and fifty (150) would embrace the entire tribe, Men, women and children; of which number, Forty (40) would include all the Male adults or warriors. . . . The Valley is rapidly Settling up and in a short time will be filled to its utmost Capacity. The Indians and Whites thus being brought into immediate Contact, the liability of Complications of various Kinds grows stronger daily, which will be injurious to the whites and absolutely destructive to the Indians. . . ." LS, *ibid.* Similar letters from Jasper A. Viall, superintendent, Montana Superintendency, and William H. Clagett, U.S. delegate-elect of Montana Territory, are *ibid.*

On Sept. 30, W. E. Bass *et al.*, Missoula County, signed a petition. "We the undersigned residents of Bitter Root Valley in said Territory being first duly Sworn depose and say, That we made settlement on our farms in Bitter Root Valley with the Consent of *'Victor'* Chief of the Flat Head Indians and have always maintained friendly relations with said Indians. . . ." DS (7 signatures), *ibid.*

On June 5, 1872, Congress authorized the removal of the Flatheads from the Bitter Root Valley. See *SRC*, 42-2-197. In Aug., U.S. Representative James A. Garfield of Ohio visited the Flatheads as special commissioner appointed by Secretary of the Interior Columbus Delano. See *HED*, 42-3-1, part 5, pp. 494–503; Harry James Brown and Frederick D. Williams, eds., *The Diary of James A. Garfield* (East Lansing, Mich., 1967–81), II, 66–67, 77–85; John Fahey, *The Flathead Indians* (Norman, Okla., 1974), pp. 137, 155–86.

On Dec. 1, 1872, Jones, Flathead Agency, Montana Territory, wrote to Francis A. Walker, commissioner of Indian Affairs. ". . . There is little or no disposition on the part of the Flatheads to remove here nor do the great body of them feel bound by the arrangement with Genl. Garfield inasmuch as Charloe their Head-Chief both by election and hereditory right refused to sign the agreement made with that gentleman in August last. . . . Under these circumstances I would most respectfully suggest that Charloe Head Chief together with Arlee and Adolf and an Interpreter be allowed to come with me to Washington in order to consult personally with the Hon Commissioner in regard to the matter and with a view to releive it of some of its complication. . . ." LS, DNA, RG 75, Letters Received, Montana Superintendency. On March 11, 1873, Jones, Washington, D. C., wrote to USG. "The pressure of public business rendering it difficult to see you personally I respectfully avail myself of this method of communicating to you a message from Charlos, Head Chief of the Flathead Indians among whom I have resided in an official capacity during more than two years past. He desired me to say that 'he did not wish to remove from his present home in the Bitter Root Valley, Montana, to the Reservation on the Jocko River as requested by Genl Garfield in August last; and hoped that you would not attempt to force him from the home of his fathers after so many years of kindness on their part to the whites who have settled among and finally see[m] about encompassing them.' I am sufficiently conversant with public business in Washington to know Mr President that you can give but little if any attention to such details. I however comply with my promise to the Chief in bringing the matter to *your* consideration at the earliest practicable moment after my arrival here. I congratulate you from my heart upon your accession to the Presidency for a second term, trusting that the blessings of heaven may re[st] upon the earnest efforts which you are making for the general welfare of the country." ALS, *ibid.* On Dec. 5, 1872, USG had nominated Daniel Shanahan to replace Jones; on April 23, 1874, USG nominated Peter Whaley to replace Shanahan, who had resigned.

On Nov. 1, Alley Quill quill squa, Flathead Agency, wrote to USG. "I write you to let you know how this Departement has been carrying on & how they are treating us. I want to know where is the money that is coming to us in the treaty of 1872 with general Garfield   there is $5000.00 five thousand dollar that we ought to get yearly since Agt 27th 1872   we did not get a cent yet & we must have it. Further more Peter Whaley our new Agent is not fit to hold this office   he is lead by the Jesuite priests by the nose. Such Agent that is governed by priests we do not wish to have him around here whatever. The Priests has taken enough money say to the amount of $22000,00 twenty two thousand al dollars for schooling from this agency And where is our Students   we have not got one that can read or write   is it possible that we could not get one of our natives that could not read or write after the goverment spending $22000 00 twenty two thousand dollars. It is a shame for the priests & most of the Agents except Maj. Shanahan to use us in this manner after getting so much money from us. We could send 5 Indian boys to West point or other colleges five or six years ago & spend as much as the above amount   we could be have those boys by this time fit for Senators but we have not one fit for any thing. About Peter Whaley did you send him here as a prize fighter or for the Interests of the Indians. He wanted to whip one of my chiefs on account of our threshing mechain   Whaley he wanted some of our employees to take the meachian to the Mission & threash for the priests & Michael one of my chiefs would not allow it. he wanted his Indians wheat threashe[d] first. Now you can see that the Agent is working for priests & not for us. The priests & agent are a band of speculators. We believe in the Holy Catholic Church but not in this firm that are around here. I'll will State you another affair   we had a good man here that was honest & true man by the name of Fk. Daker an Engineer   he was discharged by Whaley because he was honest & hired a man that can cheat us & harm us & Steal   we would like to have your answer in this question   if we the six Chiefs select a good man that we know is honest if you will appoint as Agent then if he does not suit you you may turn him off   if your answer is yes we will send you his name. There a boy 12 or 14 years old hired as a laborer getting $60 00 dollars a pr month doing nothing only eating   his name is David Whaley son of the agent   4 or more driving cattle for the agent & drawing goverments money   those men ought to be working for us. What kind of a goverment is this. No Doctor Interpreter no miller no wagon maker &c: I could post you more but it is to long a complaint if I was to tell you all. I wish to get the money for the Flatheads due for last two years. This letter is written by a half blood   he is one of my own tribe a native of this Reservation" LS (signature by mark, written by Duncan McDonald), *ibid.* For McDonald, see William F. Wheeler, U.S. marshal, Helena, to Attorney Gen. Amos T. Akerman, Jan. 22, 1871, copy, DNA, RG 59, Miscellaneous Letters.

On July 3, Potts wrote to USG. "I understand that charges of Some kind have been filed with the Secretary of the Interior against Col. Jasper A. Viall Superinten-

dent of Indian Affairs for Montana. I do not believe the charges have any foundation
in truth for the Superintendent is regarded here as the most efficient officer Montana
has ever had in the Indian Service—The opposition to him comes from the Democrats because they are unable to Control the patronage of his office as they have
heretofore done with Superintendents   He has caused the apprehension arrest and
conviction of certain parties for selling whiskey to Indians and their influence is
against him. . . . I regard Col V. as my most efficient aid in our present Struggle to
carry out your wishes expressed to me on my departure from Washington last
august Viz: 'Make Montana Republican'   I beg that you delay any action on said
charges until after the august election (August 7th next) and then Col V. asks for
an opportunity for Searching investigation into all his official acts—If—I thought
any of the charges true I would not ask this ~~day~~ delay but being here on the ground
I do not hesitate to say they are false and malicious—" ALS (press), Montana Historical Society, Helena, Mont. See *HED*, 42-1-15.

To Schuyler Colfax

Confidential   *Washington, D. C.* Nov. 14th *1867*1
MY DEAR MR. VICE PRESIDENT:

I have your letter of the 9th inst. and hasten to answer it merely
to set your mind at rest concerning the possible effect on me made
by such publications as those enclosed.[1] From the time of our election there has been people intent upon creating jealousy between
us. So far as I am concerned their efforts have totally failed, and I
want no evidence but my senses to tell me that their failure with
you is equally complete.

The New York Standard is largely owned, and completely controlled by Gen. Butler. He, Butler, to repeat none of our conversa-
tions except what is here pertinant, said to me that your letter published in the Independent was a bid for the Presidency, that you
were Horace Greeley's Candidate, &c. I simply replied testifying
my entire confidence in the earnestness you felt in declaring to the
contrary, but that if you should be the chose of the republican party
I did not know a better man to lead them, nor one that I could more
earnestly work in support of. My great ambition was to save all
that has been gained by so much sacrifice of blood and treasure;
that I religiously believed that that could only be done through the
triumph of the republican party until their opponents get on a National, patriotic union platform; that the choice of the republican

party was my choice; that I held no patent right to the office, and probably had the least desire for it of any one who ever held it, or was ever prominently mentioned in connection with it.

Give yourself not the least concern about the effect on me of anything the papers may say to disturb our relations.

Yours Very Truly

U. S. GRANT

HON. S. COLFAX

ALS, deCoppet Collection, NjP. On Nov. 9, 1871, Vice President Schuyler Colfax, South Bend, Ind., wrote to USG. "CONFIDENTIAL ... I send you enclosed two articles from the N. Y. Standard & Washn Republican, edited by two brothers in law, Mr Young & Mr Foley, & both of which papers *assume* to be special organs of the Administration. They are persistent repetitions of charges heretofore made by the same papers, & are of course *intended* to create suspicions & alienations on your part. Who 'inspire' these falsifications I do not know. But it is due to myself in the determination I have maintained from the time we were nominated at Chicago that there must be no ill feeling between the President & V. P as so often heretofore, to say ~~that~~ to you, that the charges, a far as they relate to me, are utterly groundless & false. If any such 'plans' were on foot, I might reasonably be expected to know *something* about them. But I declare, solemnly, that I have no knowledge or suspicion of any thing of the kind. Every where's, to friend & foe, in public & in private, in print & in correspondence, I have said to all who spoke to me on the subject of politics, that I was openly & unequivocally for your renomination & reelection—that I was a candidate & aspirant for nothing—that I preferred my present place to yours, even if it was attainable as it was not,—but that what I desired & hoped for was retiracy into private life, where I wished to live as a private citizen four years more under Your Administration. And, whenever those who were dissatisfied at any thing done by you, have come to me with their complaints, they have obtained no sympathy, nor aid & comfort; for my uniform reply ~~was~~ has been that I stood by you inflexibly & without qualifications or conditions. Even where I might have supposed something else might have been better, I have abstained from criticisms of any kind, so that no enemy could be able to use my comments in an unfriendly way. It is very rare indeed when I have had any such difference of opinion at all; & only in a very few cases where I had suggested otherwise, but where, on counsel of others better qualified perhaps to judge, you had decided differently. In a word, I can say, truthfully & conscientiously, you have had no more sincere, outspoken, unselfish supporter than the one who now writes to you. Do not suppose for an instant that I think these articles prompted by any suspicions or expressions of yours, because these papers assume to speak authoritatively for the Admn: for your friendship & confidence, which I have so much valued, have never been impaired, as I am glad to believe. They result, from backbiting, the bane of public life; & are written to create ill feeling if possible, & in the vain hope that their writers may appear to the public & to you as your special champions. If I have had any influence at all with the people, it has been to discourage & condemn the petty carping & fault finding against you & to endeavor to increase, not to diminish, the public confidence in you—Indeed I have written long letters to several Editors, old friends of mine, but who had been unjust to you, refuting in detail, one by one, their charges. Excuse me for this long letter, but these articles, under all the circumstances I have alluded to, have annoyed me. I have so often reiterated my unqualified advocacy of your renomination, & my determination not to be a candidate for any office whatever, that my frequent declinations have become a theme of jest with hostile papers. ~~In~~ But there has seemed to be a necessity for their repetition. In fact, a previous Editorial of Mr Young's last August, when I was absent from home in Minnesota, asserting what he now repeats, was met & refuted by a telegraphic report of an interviewer at St Paul, who stated that I reiterated, squarely & unevasively, what I have so often told you on this subject. It is easy to repeat it now, when the auspicious results of the elections leave no doubt as to next year's campaign, but I only ask you to remember, in justice to myself, that for two years I have said exactly what I am still saying on this point." ALS, USG 3. See *PUSG*, 19, 62–63; letter to John Russell Young, Nov. 15, 1870; letter to Schuyler Colfax, Aug. 4, 1871.

1. On Nov. 8, 1871, the *Washington National Republican* printed an editorial. "The New York *Standard* sticks to its opinion that Mr. Colfax has Presidential aspirations, and that it is the intention of Mr. Greeley and one or two other gentlemen to bring him forward in the next convention as the opponent of President Grant. On this subject that journal says: 'We are confident that Mr. Greeley has a programme for the canvass of the Presidency, which will open after our coming election, involving the nomination of Mr. Colfax. He intends to defeat President Grant if he possibly can, very much as he defeated Mr. Seward in 1860, to nurse into life as many candidates as possible, and to fall back upon Mr. Colfax as the popular and available man. . . . The policy of the opponents of General Grant in the Republican party is to defeat him in detail. They intend to build up the opinion that General Grant is not the strongest man in the Republican party, and if this opinion can gain ground, (and there are many able men in the country who are steadily fanning it into life,) the defeat of Gen. Grant will be possible, and the nomination of Colfax almost inevitable.' It cannot be denied that there are at least four leading men in the Republican party who are now opposed to the renomination of President Grant, namely, Mr. Sumner, Mr. Greeley, Mr. Schurz and Mr. Fenton. . . . It seems probable that Mr. Colfax has been selected as the 'available man' to defeat President Grant. . . . The Presidential question has been settled for the last six months, and it is not in the power of anything human to alter it. The people have resolved that President Grant shall be re-elected, and no amount of oratory and calcium lights can induce them to change their determination. Mr. Colfax is a great and worthy man. He would make a fair President, and get along very nicely with every one. But while Grant is in the field the people do not want him, and will not have him. If Mr. Greeley & Co. doubt this let them open their political circus and see how he will run." *Washington National Republican*, Nov. 8, 1871.

To Henry Wilson

Washington, D. C. Nov. 15th *18~~6~~71*

MY DEAR SENATOR:

I am just in receipt of your very kind letter of the 11th inst. I answer to set your mind at rest as to what I think duty on my part towards those *influential* men of the republican party who have, voluntarily, set themselves up aganst me. When ever I have done injustice to any man, no matter what his position, and find it out, there is no apology I am not ready to make. I have never done ought to give offence to Mr. Sumner, Mr. Schurz, the Springfield Republican people, the Cincinnati Commercial people, nor Mr. Greeley. Yet they have all attacked me without mercy. By my rule of action, before there can be peace between us, rather I should say good feeling and intimacy, the explanation *must* come from them. Mr. Sumner has been unreasonable, cowardly, slanderous, unblushing false. I should require of him an acknowledgement ~~from him~~ to this effect, from his seat in the Senate, before I would consent to meet him socially.[1] He has not the manlyness ever to admit an error. I feel a greater contempt for him than for any other man in the Senate. Schurz is an ungreatful man, a disorganize by nature and one who can render much greater service to the party he does not belong to than the one he pretends to have attachment for. The sooner he allies himself with our enemies, openly, the better for us. The Springfield Republican & Cincinnati Commercial are mere guerrilla newspapers, always finding fault with their friends, and any attempt to conciliate them would merely satisfy them of their importance. I shall endeavor to perform my duty, faithfully, and trust to the common sense of the people to select the right man to execute their will.

Mr. Greeley is simply a disappointed man at not being estimated by others at the same value he places upon himself. He is a genious without common sense. He attaches to himself, and reposes confidence only, in the fawning, deceitful and dishonest men of the party. It has been my misfortune to know personally the friends Mr. Greeley has desired to elevate. His judgement will not do to trust, and I have come to doubt his intentions.

Very Truly Yours
U. S. GRANT

HON. HENRY WILSON U. S. S.

ALS, Mrs. Paul E. Ruestow, Jacksonville, Fla. Because the original remained in USG's family, this letter was probably never sent. See following letter for a second version, presumably sent. On Nov. 11, 1871, U.S. Senator Henry Wilson of Mass., Natick, had written to USG. "I write a few words to you, and ask you to read them and then destroy this note. It is not I hope necessary that I should say to you that I am your friend or in favor of your nomination and reelection. I am anxious that all should be done to unite our friends. The great victories won this year may not after all be victories. Much depends upon our action during the next few months. We have men among us who are not for your nomination—some I fear are ready to go into any movements to defeat you even at the sacrifise of the Republican party. I wish something could be done to unite these men with us. In your position you can make advances to them. Would it not be best for you to do this at the opening of Congress? I believe if all our divisions are settled we can carry you in all the old free states and in six of the Slave States. You are strong now. See to it, I pray you, that all well disposed men are invited to act with you. I have *reason* to believe that there is a movement on foot to nominate a Republican in the hope that he will be taken up by the Democrats. Trumbull, Judge Davis, Gov. Brown, Cox, and others are thought of. It is *hinted* to me that the Tribune, the Evening Post, Chicago Tribune, Springfield Republican, Cincinnati Commercial and one or two other papers are ready to go into a movement of this kind & that several men of influence are ready to join it. Schurz thinks he has influence with the Germans. Others think they have influence with the negroes. I wish you could see Schurz as he is by all odds the most influential of any of these men. I wish too you and Mr Sumner would settle all your differences. This state is sure for you by about the old majority but it would be very pleasant to have unity and peace." ALS, USG 3. See *PUSG*, 20, 187–88.

1. On Dec. 6, Secretary of State Hamilton Fish wrote in his diary. "I call at the Presidents to introduce Miss North who has brought me a letter of introduction from Mr Moran—President says he has just had a visit from Senators Morrill of Maine & Wilson, wishing to effect a reconciliation between him & Sumner—he says he told them, that whenever S. should ~~as publicly, & openly~~ retract & apologise for the slanders he has uttered against him, in the Senate, in his own house, in street Cars, & other public Conveyances, at Dinners & other entertainments & elsewhere, as publicly, openly & in the same manner in which he has uttered these slanders he would listen to proposals for reconciliation—but even then he would have no confidence in him, or in the expectation that he would not again, do just what he has done—He says that Morrill said he was right in requiring such retraction & apology—" DLC-Hamilton Fish.

On Nov. 30, John B. Alley, Lynn, Mass., wrote to Wilson. "I feel great anxiety about the future and well-being of the Republican party. These disaffections in our ranks among our eminent men, may work our ruin. It is in your power I believe, to do much towards effecting reconciliations between the antagonisms, and I appeal to you, as one of my oldest most intimate and honored friends,—now for a quarter of a century we have worked together, sympathizing most fully with each other in sunshine and storm, in prosperity and adversity, and you know that I have no interest to serve, but for the best good of my country—and you know that no man knows better than I do your strong friendship for the President, sincere and disinterested as I know it is, and your life-long devotion to Sumner and his interests entitle you to great consideration at the hands of both, and I can never forgive you if you fail to do all in your power to effect a reconciliation these two distinguished and important characters. I had a long talk with Sumner the day he left for Washington, and he exhibited a most excellent spirit, spoke properly and kindly of the President and you know how easily he can be made exactly right, with the exercise of a little tact. You know I was quite intimate at one time with Lincoln, and we used to have considerable talk about Sumner. How fully he understood him, and how admirably he managed him! And it seems strange to me that Grant, with his admitted good sense and great judgement, should be unable to get along with this case. You know how I talked to Sumner about his course towards the President, and that too at your earnest request when I was in Washington last Spring, and he rebuked and abused me as you also remember, as he never did before; but after all he is a great and good man, with a tremendous hold upon a large and most important part of the Republican party, and if anyone acts upon any other impression, they will find themselves most wofully mistaken. Grant, I am told, thinks Sumner is of no great account; what a mistake he makes! But how natural it is for one to think things are as he wishes them to be. It makes me think of what Butler said to me of Grant, not a great while before he was nominated. In my room one evening, I was advocating and predicting the nomination of Grant; Butler was present, and he said Grant was the most unpopular soldier in the whole Army—all the soldiers nearly were opposed to him, and the talk about his being so strong with Republicans, he said was all a humbug. He was the weakest feeblest creature he said that ever was thought of for any public office of any consequences, and as soon as he was known the delusion would vanish. I told him in reply, that he had better be careful of what he said, for he would find himself obliged to swallow it all; Grant would be nominated and no man would recognize the political necessity of supporting him sooner than he, or would know how to 'stoop to conquer' better than he, and I thought he would make the first speech in his favor after he was nominated—'Never, Never, by God never.'—he exclaimed, 'If every other man in the country goes for him, By God I never will'; but it turned out as I expected, and he actually did accept the situation at once, and made, I believe, the first speech in ratification of his nomination. The great trouble is, as Mr Lincoln once said to me—Nobody tells the President just what he thinks, and he is so surrounded by flatterers and toadies that it is impossible for him to know what the outside world think. You and I have had a large experience in polictis and we know very well how uncertain every thing is in politics, and how little anyone, however strong in appearance, can afford to trifle with antagonisms. I hope therefore you will do all in your power to get Sumner put back in his old place. How easy for the President to have this done, and how strange it seems to me that he does not see the policy, and almost necessity, of doing so. With this done and Sumner reconciled the reelection of Grant would be rendered almost certain." Copy, USG 3.

On Dec. 16, Horace Porter wrote to Fish. "*Confidential* . . . The President directs me to request you to ascertain, as nearly as possible, how many recommendations for office have been sent to your department by each of the following Senators,—Trumbull, Schurz, Tipton & Fenton." LS, DLC-Hamilton Fish. On the same day, Porter wrote a similar letter to every cabinet officer. Copy, DLC-USG, II, 1. See letter to Elihu B. Washburne, May 17, 1871. On Dec. 23, U.S. Senator Roscoe Conkling of N. Y., New York City, wrote to Porter. "A list of my recommendations (I believe I have never made requests) at the various Departments would be very useful to me. May I ask you to cause it to be made." Copies, DNA, RG 56, Letters Received; *ibid.*, RG 60, Letters from the President. On Feb. 23, 1872, responding to U.S. Senator Lyman Trumbull of Ill., U.S. Senator Oliver P. Morton of Ind. spoke on the subject. ". . . I saw this afternoon a tabulated statement giving the number of recommendations made in each Department since the 4th of March, 1869, by the Senator, numbering one hundred and three. I would not have referred to this but for the fact that my motives and the motives of other friends of the Administration on this floor are impeached, that we have been substantially charged with supporting the Administration and the party for the sake of the spoils of office." *CG*, 42–2, 1181. On Feb. 24, Morton wrote to USG. "I have the honor to request that I may be furnished with a statement of the recommendations for office, on file in the various departments made by Senator Trumbull of Illinois, since the commencement of the present administration" Copies, DNA, RG 56, Letters Received; *ibid.*, RG 59, Miscellaneous Letters; *ibid.*, RG 60, Letters from the President. On Feb. 26, Conkling introduced a resolution requesting USG to "inform the Senate of the number of recommendations for appointments to or removals from office, so far as the same can be ascertained, made to the present Administration by persons now Senators from the States of New York, Missouri, Illinois, and Nebraska respectively, . . ." *CG*, 42–2, 1207. On Feb. 29, Babcock wrote to Morton. "Will you be kind enough to let me take the lists of recommendations of Mr. Trumbull, in your possession, long enough for a copy of the portion furnished by the Treasury to be made. It shall be returned to you at once, as soon as that is done." Copy, DLC-USG, II, 1. On the same day, Secretary of War William W. Belknap wrote to Trumbull. "In compliance with your request of the 27th instant, I have the honor to enclose herewith copies of your recommendations in favor of applicants for appointment, or reappointment, to office, . . ." LS, DLC-Lyman Trumbull. On March 18, the Senate passed an amended version of Conkling's resolution. *CG*, 42–2, 1759–63. On March 22, Fish wrote in his diary. "Referring to a resolution of the Senate adopted on 18 inst requesting of the President information as to recommendations for appointments, made by certain Senators, & other information of like nature, I ask what course is to be taken—whether it is intended to answer the resolution & if so how fully, & in what way part of the information called for (that of personal interviews &c) is to be dealt with—A unanimous expression of regret that the resolution has been passed, obtains—& a generally prevailing doubt as to the expediency of answering it—& a belief that even those who pressed its passage may not be very anxious to have it answered— It is however understood that each Member of the Cabinet (a copy having been sent to each) is to prepare the answer as to his own Department—It is the general remark that the extent of the inquiry, involves almost an impossibility as to some of the points, of furnishing the information, & the ascertaining of the names to which recommendations in writing have been made by the Senators indicated, will involve the examination of all the written applications which have been filed since the beginning of the present Administration" DLC-Hamilton Fish.

On April 3, Attorney Gen. George H. Williams wrote to USG. ". . . I enclose a list of the recommendations made by the Senators mentioned. . . . It has not been the custom of this Department, in making appointments or removals to credit such appointments or removals to those Senators recommending the action. I am therefore, unable to answer that part of the resolution asking for such information, or to state what verbal requests have been made to the Department by Senators or others. No appointments or removals to my knowledge have been made upon the recommendation, or at the instance of any third party acting as a go between of either of said Senators. . . ." Copy, DNA, RG 60, Letters Sent to Executive Officers. See *SMD*, 42-2-90; *ibid.*, parts 2, 3.

To Henry Wilson

————

Washington, D. C. Nov 15 *1871*

MY DEAR SENATOR:

I am in receipt of your very kind letter of the 11th inst. I abstain from expressing any views upon the subject named by you, until I see you; but acknowledge the good feeling and friendship which prompts it. It will be but a short time now before Congress meets and then there will be full opportunity of party friends discussing all questions of interest. Assuring you again of my appreciation of ~~of~~ the friendliness of your advice, I remain

Very Truly
your obt. svt.
U. S. GRANT

HON HENRY WILSON U. S. S.

Copy, USG 3. See preceding letter.

To Adolph E. Borie

————

Washington, D. C. Nov. 16th *1871*

MY DEAR MR. BORIE:

On one occasion last Summer you were kind enough to say to me that if I was in want of any means you were in a condition to aid me in getting it. At that time I did not suppose that I should require any such assistance. Now however I find myself in a condition where about $6000 00/100 would be of great service to me, and which I can repay, with interest, at about the rate of $1500 00/ 100 per quarter. My private income will do this leaving the pay which I receive from govt. to defray current expenses. I write this before enclosing note for negociation because unless it is entirely. convenient for you I do not want to send it at all.

Mrs. Grant and I will expect a visit from you and Mrs. Borie this Winter. If you have any preference as to time of coming let us know before other invitations are sent out.

My kindest regards to Mrs. Borie.

Yours Truly
U. S. GRANT

ALS, PHi. See letter to Adolph E. Borie, Nov. 18, 1871.

On Dec. 5, 1871, Horace Porter wrote to Charles Lewis, tax collector, Long Branch, N. J. "Enclosed please find a Treasury draft (No 6829.) to your order, for four hundred and sixty two dollars and forty cents, the amount of the assessment against the President and myself ($300 00 and $162 40)   I also enclose you the notices. Please return me the proper receipt." Copy, DLC-USG, II, 1. See also letter to William Elrod, Nov. 3, 1871; letter to Anthony J. Drexel, Nov. 5, 1871; *Calendar*, May 26, 1871.

To William Elrod

Washington D. C. Nov. 16th 1871

DEAR ELROD:

I will not send for the two colts until Spring. I have more horses here than I can use, and to bring more would require the purchase of feed for them where it costs more than it does in Mo.

I do not want any land cleared to get wood to burn lime with. My idea was that all the dead and down timber on the place might be cut up, and the woods thined out all over the place so as to leave the timber about the right thickness to grow. After that is gone ~~wood~~ wood might be purchased or the kiln changed so as to use coal.

In using lime on the farm I would only put it on the clover fields. At all events try the clover first.

It is not probable now that I will send any horses from here to the farm next Spring but will bring away the two colts. My old horses are rejuvinate so as to be about as good as ever, except one, and he would not be worth the transportation.

Yours Truly
U. S. GRANT

ALS, Dorothy Elrod, Marissa, Ill.

To Adolph E. Borie

———

Washington, D. C. Nov. 18th *1871*

MY DEAR MR. BORIE:

I am in receipt of your very kind letter of yesterday enclosing draft for $6.000 00/100 and thank you for the kindness manifested in the manner of sending it. It will cause me no inconvenience to repay it at the rate mentioned in my letter. You are so kind however in the manner of transmitting that I shall not worry if my ability to pay in the time specified should fail, and it should take a quarter longer. I shall though watch my balances in bank very closely until the whole amt. is paid, and ~~feeling~~ shall ever feel deeply indebted to you in addition.

Yours Truly
U. S. GRANT

ALS, PHi. See letter to Adolph E. Borie, Nov. 16, 1871.

To Adam Badeau

———

Washington, D. C. Nov. 19th *1867̶1*

DEAR BADEAU:

As I have before assured you your letters are rec'd and read with great pleasure though I may not find time to answer many of them. The information asked for by you, from the War Dept. Porter undertook to get,[1] and has obtained so far as the Clerks in the Dept. could work it out. But it does not satisfy Porter and he now intends to go to the Dept. himself and work it up. This accounts for the delay.

I have not yet written a line on my message. Will commence to-morrow and hope to make it short.—Every thing in the country looks politically well at present. The most serious apprehension is from the awards that may be made by the Commissions at Geneva and in Washington. Should they go largely in favor of the English it would at least cause much disappointment.—In speaking of political matters I do not of course allude to my own chances. It will be a happy day for me when I am out of political life. But I do feel a deep interest in the republican party keeping controll of affairs until the results of the war are acquiesced in by all political parties. When that is accomplished we can afford to quarrel about minor matters.

My family are all well and send you their kindest regards. Fred. sailed for Europe on Friday last.[2] He will be in England about May next and will stay there, I hope, long enough to do up the island pretty well.

Yours Truly
U. S. Grant

ALS, Munson-Williams-Proctor Institute, Utica, N. Y.

1. For Adam Badeau's research on a military history of USG, see letter to Hamilton Fish, March 4, 1871.

2. Nov. 17. On Nov. 18, Ellen E. Sherman had written to Julia Dent Grant. "I went over to New York Thursday night and breakfasted with the party Friday morning and at 10. a. m. I saw them off. We made a brief visit to the Vessel, remaining on board with them until the time for lifting anchor and setting sail. We then bade farewell, and after I got into the Tug Boat, Fred (your Fred) climbed down the side of the Wabash & handed me the enclosed flowers for his Mother. The sun shone brightly, the tide was out and a fine breeze was blowing as they passed from our gaze—May the dear Lord bring them safe to us again. With love to your dear Father, . . ." ALS, USG 3. On Nov. 30, Ellen Sherman, Washington, D. C., wrote to Gen. William T. Sherman. ". . . I sent Fred's flowers to his Mother, with a note telling her how Fred ran down the side of the vessel to hand them to me for her. She and the President came down the same evening & had a long talk about where Fred was to sleep &c. She was also in some concern about Fred's shirts but the President told her that when they wore a shirt awhile they thew it overboard. She was releived, for she feared he might leave his clothes lying about in some disorder, which would not be according to ship discipline, but the President had not finished his sentence, and when he added—(after throwing the shirt overboard) 'with a string to it to wash it—' she was disgusted and changed the subject, but I joined him in his laugh—. . ." ALS, InND.

On Nov. 17, Julia Dent Grant, Washington, D. C., had written to Emily (Emma) Dent Casey. ". . . We went to Boston to see Buckie & went up to New York to see dear Fred off on a tour to Europ[e.]   He goes [abroad under] most charmeing auspicies, as Aid De Camp to Genl Sherman & goes on Admirel Aldens Flag Ship—'The Wabash'—one of our finest War vessels—in fact the very finest   I am perfectly delighted that he my Fred has the opportunity just now after beeing so good as to give up his trip in the summer as he first intended   I do not think any American ever went abroad under such charmeing auspicies . . ." ALS, Ulysses S. Grant National Historic Site (White Haven), St. Louis, Mo. See letter to Grenville M. Dodge, Oct. 24, 1871.

To Thomas Murphy

Washington, D. C. Nov. 20, 1871

Hon. Thos Murphy:
Collector Port of New York
Dear Sir:

Your letter of the 18th inst tendering your resignation of the office of Collector of the Port of New York, with reasons therefor, is received. It gives me great pleasure to bear testimony to the efficiency, honesty and zeal with which you have filled the office so long as it has been entrusted to your keeping.[1]

Your own peace of mind, no doubt, will be enhanced by leaving the office of Collector, but I doubt whether such a course will, in any sense, be a benefit to the public service. Whether you remain in or out of office time will convince a just public of your entire innocense of the charges brought against you.[2]

You have had my unqualified confidence ever since you entered the office of Collector. You had that confidence before or the appointment would not have been tendered you. That confidence is still unshaken, and in accepting your resignation I want to give you the fullest assurance of this fact.

Under your management the revenues from the New York Custom house have been largely increased, and the cost of collection, in proportion to the amount collected, has been greatly diminished. This is shown by the records of the Treasury Department

With great respect
your obt. svt.
U. S. Grant

Copy, DLC-USG, II, 1. On Nov. 18, 1871, Thomas Murphy, New York City, wrote to USG. "I hereby tender my resignation of the office of Collector of the Port of New-York, to take effect upon the appointment of my successor. You are aware that during the period I have held this important trust, and because I have held it, I have been subjected to a persecution which for persistent misrepresentation and unrelenting vindictiveness, has fortunately but few parallels in the history of political strife— Throughout this somewhat trying ordeal, I have been sustained however by the consciousness of my own rectitude, and by the fact that during my official term I have enjoyed uninterruptedly, and still retain, your confidence, undiminished by the vituperation of my accusers. For the manner in which the duties of the office have been performed, I take pleasure in referring to the judgment of my official superior the Secretary of the Treasury, and to the figures of record in the Treasury Department which show how the revenue has been collected, & with what diminished percentage of cost. Unless your attention has been called to this record, I beg you will refer to it. Groundless as the aspersions cast upon me are, and fully as they have been refuted before more than one tribunal, I am conscious that my continuance in office will be made the pretext and occasion for assaults calculated to injure you and the Republican party; & rather than incur such a hazard, I would relinquish my position, even had it been coveted, which you know it was not. When appointed, I believed I could render a service by accepting the place, now I believe I can render a service by resigning it & I gladly embrace the opportunity. In severing my official relations with the Government under these circumstances, I may also properly refer to the gratifying result of the recent election in this state, which leaves the control of its affairs substantially in the hands of that great party of progress and reform, of which you are the acknowledged head, and for the success of which it will ever be my pride and duty to labor." ALS, USG 3. For Murphy's additional comments on his resignation as collector of customs, New York City, see *New York Times*, Nov. 21, Dec. 27, 1871.

On Nov. 12, George Bliss, Jr., New York City, had written to USG. "In case Hon Thomas Murphy should resign his place as Collector of the Port of NewYork I beg leave most earnestly to urge the appointment of Gen. Chester A. Arthur as his successor. . . ." ALS, DNA, RG 56, Presidential Appointments. On the same day, William Orton, George Opdyke, Alonzo B. Cornell, James W. Booth, and Addison H. Laflin, New York City, petitioned USG to appoint Chester A. Arthur if Murphy resigned. DS, *ibid*. On Nov. 14, Richard Crowley, U.S. attorney, Lockport, N. Y., wrote to USG. ". . . The New York Collectorship should be approached with dread and he is a fortunate man who can hold it and discharge its onerous duties with acceptability to the commercial interests of the Country and satisfactorily to the political interests of his party. If appointed, I have faith that Genl Arthur will do this as well as can reasonably be expected of any man, and that you will have no cause to regret that you reposed this trust and your confidence in him." ALS, *ibid*. On Nov. 15, Judge Charles J. Folger, N. Y. court of appeals, wrote to USG. "I have the honor of stating that I am informed that Honl Thos Murphy now Collector of Customs at NewYork city is about to resign his position. As of course, there will be an immediate or early appointment of a successor I venture to recommend for the position Genl Chester A. Arthur of NewYork city. I am aware that he is not of mercantile pursuits. But he is a man of nimble faculties of mind, which have been trained in the study and practice of the law; and of an extraordinary executive ability and power of organization. I do not speak this unadvisedly. His performance of executive duty while one of the staff of Gov Morgan during a very trying period of the War of the Rebellion, proved to every one who had cognizance of his work, that in a very high degree, was he endowed with the ability to take hold of, to understand and master, & to dispatch executive labor. . . ." ALS, *ibid*. On Nov. 21, Secretary of State Hamilton Fish wrote in his diary. "Cabinet—All present except Belknap & Creswell . . . The appointment of Chester A Arthur as Collector of New-York vice Murphy is spoken of—I had heard nothing of the resignation or appointment until Announced in the papers this morning—Robeson asks who Arthur is— Boutwell says a Lawyer of some prominence—President says he was a Quarter Master during the War, & has been recommended by a meeting of prominent Republicans from different parts of the State—names Conckling, Opdyke, Orton, Crowley & Folger—Some one asks me if I know him   I reply 'I know nothing about him)" DLC-Hamilton Fish. On Dec. 6, USG nominated Arthur as collector of customs, New

York City, to secure the recess appointment. In 1870, Arthur and three others, N. Y. Republican Committee, had written to USG concerning patronage. William Evarts Benjamin, Catalogue No. 27, Nov., 1889, p. 5. See Thomas C. Reeves, *Gentleman Boss: The Life of Chester Alan Arthur* (New York, 1975), pp. 51–60.

On Dec. 1, 1871, Edwin D. Morgan, New York City, wrote to USG. "Our new Collector, General Arthur, entered upon his duties this morning. I have been to pay my respects to him and now wish to offer you my congratulations upon the appointment. I desire at the same time to say, that I believe, the ability, zeal and fidelity, with which he will discharge all the duties of Collector, will vindicate most fully the wisdom of the appointment. I have known General Arthur for upwards of ten years. During the first two years of the Rebellion he was my chief reliance in the duties of equipping and transporting troops and munitions of war. In the position of Quarter Master General, he displayed not only great executive ability. and unbending integrity, but great knowledge of Army Regulations. He can say, No! (which is important) without giving offence. His position politically and socially is unexceptionable. He is a good lawyer, and would have made a wise Judge. But he is Collector and wisely so. There is no doubt but he will make as good an officer for the Government, and quite as acceptable to the public, as any one of his many predecessors in that high and responsible position." LS, DNA, RG 56, Presidential Appointments. On Nov. 29, 1875, Cornell wrote to USG. "In view of the approaching termination of the term, for which General Chester A. Arthur, was appointed Collector of the Port of New York, I beg to say that General Arthurs conduct of the duties of this great office, has given the most complete satisfaction to the Republican party in this State, and in my opinion his reappointment for another term would meet with the cordial and unanimous approval of all who have the good of the party at heart." ALS, *ibid.* On Dec. 9, U.S. Senator Roscoe Conkling of N. Y. wrote to USG with the same recommendation. ALS, *ibid.* On Dec. 17, USG renominated Arthur.

On Jan. 30, 1870, Julian Allen, "Commission Merchant and Dealer in Leaf Tobacco," New York City, had written to USG. "Allow me to add a few words in advising the appointment of Mr. Silas B. Dutcher as Collector of this port. By all means, have him appointed, if you want the party united and strengthened here. No better man than Mr. Dutcher could be selected." ALS, *ibid.*, Collector of Customs Applications. On Dec. 5, 1872, USG nominated Silas B. Dutcher as pension agent, New York City.

1. On March 10, Porter wrote to William A. Newell, Allentown, N. J. "I received your letter in regard to the application of Mr. Baker and read its contents to the President. He says he made an exception to his general rule in recommending Mr. Baker for a position in the Custom house, from the fact that he was so highly endorsed, but that he cannot well direct Mr. Murphy what course to pursue or whom not to remove in order in creating a vacancy for Mr. Baker. I think you and the Collector will be able to adjust the matter satisfactorily if you will explain all the circumstances to him." Copy, DLC-USG, II, 1.

On Oct. 30, Orville E. Babcock wrote to Murphy. "The President directs me to refer these papers to you. He does not wish this man, or any other, retained in position for the purpose mentioned in this letter.... Memorandum: The letter referred to above was addressed to the President by Edward C. Marshall, Clerk in N. Y. Custom House at salary of $1200. He tenders resignation unless raised to $2000, and claims he should have that amount as he is engaged upon a book entitled 'The Ancestry of Gen Grant', which he wishes to publish." Copy, *ibid.* See *PUSG*, 20, 269.

2. On Sept. 19, Murphy had written to Horace Greeley, *New York Tribune*, defending his political, business, and official records. *New York Times*, Sept. 20, 1871. See also *ibid.*, Sept. 23, Oct. 3, 18, 1871. On Oct. 4, USG, Chicago, "in conversation with friends while in this city, stated emphatically that to his knowledge the charges of the New York Tribune against Collector Murphy are without foundation; that he sees no reason for removing him, when from personal knowledge he regards him as fit for the place, and he will not gratify the clamors of those who have a personal or factious object in view." *Washington Chronicle*, Oct. 5, 1871. In Oct., a correspondent reported from Washington, D. C. "Judge Pierrepont of New-York is here, and had an interview with the President to-day. His business, it is said, is for the purpose of representing the absolute necessity for the removal of Collector Murphy. The President, it is said, now listens more favorably to these suggestions than he has heretofore done." *New York Tribune*, Oct. 13, 1871.

On Oct. 27, William S. Hillyer, New York City, wrote to USG. "I have repudiated my old democratic associations and come out openly for the Republican party. I found I could not trust these reformed democrats. They have simply organized against Tammany because they could not get into the ring. of course there are honorable exceptions, but it is hard to tell who are the exceptions. Ledwith, who I thought was above suspicion, has received the Tammany nomination and will undoubtedly exaccept it. Ben and Fernando Wood are now running the Reform Democracy. Of course the Republicans don't understand this. I called in to see Ben Wood the other day with another gentleman and had a talk on politics generally. I intended to tell him that I had determined to act with the Republicans hereafter. Before I had time to do this he said 'We have got these Republicans and Tammany fellows both foul now, we will have things our own way. We will beat Tammany and have control of the city until we become so rich and corrupt that some other party will get the Republicans to turn us out. That however will not be until after the Presidential election. We were about to lose the German vote, but we concluded to nominate Sigel and insure that vote against Grant's. Sigel has pledged himself that he will never vote another Republican ticket, Ottendorfer assured us of that before we would consent to nominate him. We will thus get a solid German vote against Grant. Carl Schurz has sworn that if the Republicans nominate Grant he will join us. He and Sigel understand each other'—Of course I am embarrassed about saying this publicly on account of the circumstances under which I heard it: and I think it policy to support Sigel because this thing is not known. What the party needs is consolidation—I would not counsel the removal of Murphy unless you can get some one who can consolidate. There is but one man in the country and one man out of it thaṅt can do this—Judge Robertson of Westchester and Dan Sickly. The only trouble with Dan is that his personal character is worse than Murphy's and his own ambition would make him sacrafice anybody. Murphy is true to you—true as steel—He would not do anything he thought you would disapprove, and with proper guidance would accomplish much for you. Cornell is a good man of limited abilities. The difference between him and Murphy is this—Murphy knows nobody but Grant. Cornell knows nobody but Conklin. Claflin is a clever fellow who knows nobody but Claflin Jones is a sincere and sagacious friend of yours, who feels exceedingly grateful to you because he thinks you have stood by him in spite of a tremendous pressure against him. He is utterly disgusted with Fenton and is for Conklin as long as Conklin does not make your interest subsarvient to his Darling is a very respectable gentleman but relies too much on his respectability and too little on the necessity for personal work and conciliation—The consequence is that he was badly beaten in his own district and by your strong friends. Ketchum the assessor in my district is no friend of yours and no advantage to the party. The sooner you get rid of him the better If I was you I would not remove Murphy at present. He is said to have no strength but your confidence and I would teach some of these fellows that that was enough. I think Sigel will be elected and I hope so, for two reasons. It will aid in the downfall of Tammany and it will rid you of an office holder who I have every reason to believe is not a reliable friend of yours. I think the Republicans will carry the state. *The city is doubtful.* I wish the Republicans would run a straight ticket for Legislature. The honest Democrats claim that they are in a majority in the party—The Tammany thieves claim that they have the ascendency. I would like to see them have a fair fight. If the honest democrats win they will (it is presumed) co-operate with the Republicans If the thieves win let the country know the fact that the result of an overwhelming democratic ascendency is utter and overwhelming corruption. Either Event would redound to the advantage of the Republican party in the presidential election. The success of the one would aid us to a pure election in NewYork. The success of the other would aid us to an immense increase of votes for the Rep. ticket out of NewYork. I hope to be in W. next week and will see you further on this subject" D, Hillyer Papers, ViU. In 1871, Alfred Pleasonton, commissioner of Internal Revenue, had written to USG urging removal of Patrick H. Jones as postmaster, New York City, and mentioning Franz Sigel as a desirable candidate who would have Greeley's support. William Evarts Benjamin, Catalogue No. 42, March, 1892, p. 18. See *PUSG*, 19, 286–87; Proclamation, Aug. 8, 1871.

Between March 16 and 20, 1872, Murphy, Washington, D. C., testified before the Committee on Investigation and Retrenchment. "Last fall, when I came down here on some business connected with the office, I called over at the President's. I was in General Porter and Babcock's room for a few moments. I think it was about half past 11 when I went into the President's room; this was last fall; it must have been in October or November. I think it was about the last of October; still, I am not good at remembering dates—my memory is not good. I stepped into the President's room and General Babcock told me the President would see me, and about that time the Secretary of the Treasury, Mr. Boutwell, came from the room leading from the hall. The President turned around and said, 'Mr. Murphy, there is so much noise, and talk, and scandal, about this young man Leet, who holds the general-order business in New York, on account of his being with me during the war, that I think I had better stop that, and I think that young man had better leave.' I think, as near as I can recollect, those were the words of the President.... Q. Did you comply with that hint and take the business away?—A. I replied, sir, by saying that this warfare upon Leet was all originated by the steamship companies, in my opinion, for the purpose of getting that business themselves; that, in my opinion, Leet & Stocking had done the business as well and conducted the business as well as it ever had been done, and I, for one, did not feel like giving away to such an unjustifiable clamor as had been raised against this young man. I do not know as I said so, but I felt I would rather be removed myself than do it.... Q. Have any moneys been collected from the subordinates in the custom-house, while you were collector, for political purposes?—A. Yes, sir.... There is a collection made, I believe, and always has been. I do not believe that it required any directions to have it made.... Our people—some of my subordinates—went to work and went around, and got a contribution among the office-holders. They got a contribution from the office-holders. I think they collected in my department in 1870 about $11,000.... I think, in the direct-examination on Saturday, I said that in the conversation I had with the President, in which he stated that he felt, or believed very strongly, that Leet & Stocking should be removed from the general-order business—at least that Leet should—I do not think that Stocking's name was mentioned.... I stated in my evidence that that had occurred in the early part of last fall. I was here in December, when I was not collector. The time at which I visited Washington previous to that was on the 20th of May last year ... I recollect this discussion, that the President stated to me after I became collector—almost immediately after I became collector—that he did not wish to embarrass me; that he would hold me responsible for the conduct of that office; that he would not embarrass me by asking me for any appointment; he would not allow anybody around him to do it, except one. I think he spoke of one man who was in the custom-house then, who had been formerly a classmate of his, and room-mate at West Point, and he spoke of that man very highly—being a thoroughly honest man, a good scholar, but a modest man, a man who would never push himself much forward in the world; I think that and one other man was the only person that the President ever spoke to me about, who were connected with the New York custom-house, as having any interest in.... Q. Were you one of those who recommended the appointment of General Arthur as collector of the port of New York?—A. I believe I was, sir...." *SRC*, 42-2-227, III, 349–50, 358, 371–73, 387, 432. In his testimony, Murphy admitted to a $542,500 real estate transaction involving William M. Tweed. *Ibid.*, pp. 392–93, 422. See *PUSG*, 19, 157–58; letter to John Russell Young, Nov. 15, 1870.

To Adolph E. Borie

Washington, D. C. Nov. 22d *1871*

MY DEAR MR. BORIE:

Mrs. Grant & myself will expect Mrs. Borie and yourself on the 9th of Jan.y to pay us a visit if nothing should occur in the mean time to prevent your coming at that time.[1]

I did not commence my annual Message until day before yesterday but have now got it finished with the exception of the closing scene and such alterations as may suggest themselves between this and the time of delivery. I always feel unhappy when the time comes to commence the job of writing a Message, and miserable until it is compled. I believe I am lazy and dont get credit for it. The fact is circumstances have thrown me into an occupation uncongenial to me. I tried very hard to draw you into the same vortex but you had more moral courage than I had and got out of it. I dont blame you but if I had not got as clever a fellow as I did in your place I do not know that I would have forgiven you. (Confidential) Gov.r Fish will leave me soon after the meeting of Congress. No one can regret this half so much as I do. As much as I liked the Governor before he come into my Cabinet I now like him better. The State Dept. was never better conducted than under his supervision, and never has more important measures been consumated than under his guidance. I wish he could stay with me.[2]

Mrs. Grant and Nellie send their love to Mrs. Borie and join me in kindest regards to you.

Yours Truly
U. S. GRANT

ALS, PHi.

1. On Dec. 20, 1871, USG wrote to Adolph E. Borie inviting him to include his niece in the visit, "with assurance that a young lady can find more to amuse in Washington society than old fogies like you and I. We get along pretty well but cannot conceal from our selves the fact that before the present generation of happy people were born we had our day. This is not a pleasant subject and I promise not to revive it." Robert F. Batchelder, Catalog 69 [1989], no. 48.

2. See letter to Edwards Pierrepont, Dec. 29, 1871.

To George M. Pullman

Washington, D. C. Nov. 22d 1871

MY DEAR SIR:

Mrs. Grant and myself will be pleased if we can have a weeks visit from Mrs. Pullman and yourself, commencing on the third Monday in Jan.y. I specify the third Monday because our house room admits of only a limited amount of company at a time, and we hope to have friends visit us through the Winter to fill the vacant space we have all the time. This makes it necessary to designate the time for each to come. When your new house is finished you will be much more independent.[1] You can then invite a friend to come when it is convenient, and if two or three extra should drop in they could be provided for. Public servants are not so fortunate.

I have not seen how the great calamity which befel Chicago effected you?[2] It was a terrible scourge but it is gratifying to see the response of the public, and of foreign nations, to your suffering. Mrs. Grant joins me in expressions of regard to Mrs. Pullman and yourself.

Yours Truly
U. S. Grant

Geo M. Pullman, Esq.

ALS, ICHi. In response, George M. Pullman, New York City, wrote to USG. "I need hardly assure you that it will afford Mrs Pullman and myself great pleasure to accept the hospitalities so kindly tendered in your esteemed favor of the 27th inst. which owing to my absence from home has but just reached me. I beg to thank you for the kind expressions of interest in my personal welfare during the recent great calamity, and am happy to assure you that we experienced personally comparatively little inconvenience or pecuniary loss. Mrs Pullman joins me in very kind regards to yourself Mrs Grant and Miss Nellie." ALS (undated), *ibid.* Pullman and his wife Harriet arrived in Washington on Monday, Jan. 15, 1872, and spent a week at the White House. See *Washington Evening Star*, Jan. 17, 19, 22, 1872. On Jan. 27, 1872, Horace Porter wrote to Pullman. "I fear I neglected to name to you distinctly, last night, the hour of our dinner at the Arlington. I shall expect you at *6* O'clock" ALS, ICHi.

On Dec. 9, USG wrote to ministers and consuls. "I take great pleasure in introducing Geo. M. Pullman, Esq. to Ministers and Consuls of the United States, with whom he may come in contact during his proposed visit abroad, as an esteemed personal friend of mine, and worthy of any attention that may be shown him." Copy, DLC-USG, II, 1.

1. During the early 1870s, Pullman built a mansion at Long Branch, N. J., as well as in Chicago.
2. The Pullman Co. office had burned in the fire.

To Adolph E. Borie

Washington, D. C. Nov. 23d 1871

My Dear Mr. Borie:

I am just in receipt of your letter of yesterday saying that Mr. McMichael[1] understood me to say that I should be in Phila in Dec. and wanting to know when. I did say to Mr. McM. as near as I can recollect, that I should run up to Phila some Thursday night in Dec. and remain over Sunday. It was my full expectation to stop at "Hotel Borie" though I intended to find out from the proprietor and proprietress of that well kept establishment when it would be convenient to receive me. I think it safe to say now you may fix the time any Thursday in Dec. after Thursday the 7th of the month.

Run down here and spend Saturday & Sunday with me. It will do you good. I have finished my Message since my letter to you last night, and have leisure. I do'nt want the public to know it however for I have given the *patriots* notice that forenoons I must have from now until the meeting of Congress. Our kindest regards to Mrs. Borie and yourself.

Yours Truly
U. S. GRANT

P. S. I cannot say whether Mrs. Grant and the children will accompany to Phila or not.

ALS, PHi.

1. Probably Morton McMichael. See letter to William G. Temple, Jan. 14, 1871, note 1.

To George W. Childs

Washington, D. C. Nov. 28th *1871*

MY DEAR MR. CHILDS:

Mrs. Grant and I will be please if we can have a visit of a week from Mrs. Child and you commencing on the fourth Monday in Jan.y. You know our house room is so limited that we have to invite friends in rotation, and I hope I have enough left notwithstanding the defection of Mr. Greeley & Carl Schurz,[1] to keep the the little room we have filled during the Winter.

Mrs. Grant & Nellie send their love to Mrs. Child and desire to be kindly remembered to you.

I received your note enclosing an editorial from the London Times.[2] It shows quite a change of sentiment in that leading paper towards the United States. It has always been my desire to cultivate the best of feeling between the two English speaking Nations, and, as I believe, the most enterprising as well as freest Nations of the world.

Should arbritration be successful I believe that end will be attained, and for the mutual benefit of both.

My kindest regards to Mrs Childs and yourself.

Yours Truly

U. S. GRANT

ALS, MH. On Nov. 9, 1871, USG wrote to George W. Childs thanking him "for the letters of introduction of my son to your friends in England . . . I cannot remain away long of course during the Session of Congress. But, after Congress gots to work I shall run up to Phila . . ." Renato Saggiori Catalogue [1976], no. 53. See letter to George W. Childs, April 2, 1871; letter to Anthony J. Drexel, Nov. 5, 1871.

On Feb. 28, 1872, USG wrote to Childs. "I dislike very much being absent during Legislation Days but presume the other 'end of the Avenue' can take care of matters without other harm than to distress the sore heads and democrats." Samuel T. Freeman Catalogue, Dec. 10, 1928, no. 223.

1. See letter to Charles W. Ford, Oct. 26, 1871, note 4.
2. Likely an editorial reviewing Republican prospects for the 1872 presidential election that included remarks on USG: ". . . The general opinion is that President GRANT will be nominated for re-election. In favour of this course will be the respect he has won, not only from the Republicans, but from moderate men of all parties, by his honest and conscientious discharge of duty, and the knowledge of the electors that they have in him a tried man fit for any emergency of the time. On the other side, there is only the prejudice against electing the same man twice. . . . The firmness and moderation with which order has been restored, the economical skill with which the debt has been reduced, and the good will with which international controversies have been brought to a close, make us anticipate with satisfaction the election of General GRANT to a second term of office." *The Times* (London), Oct. 31, 1871.

To John T. Hoffman

Washington, Nov: 29th 1871

SIR:

I transmit herewith a copy of a Treaty concluded in this City on the Eighth day of May last between the United States and Great Britain.

By the 27th Article the Government of Her Britannic Majesty engages to urge upon the Government of the Dominion of Canada to secure to the citizens of the United States the use of the Welland, St. Lawrence and other Canals in the Dominion on terms of equality with the inhabitants of the Dominion, and the Government of the United States engages to urge upon the State Governments to secure to the subjects of Her Britannic Majesty the use of the several State Canals connected with the navigation of the lakes or rivers traversed by or contiguous to the boundary line between the possessions of the High Contracting Parties, on terms of equality with the inhabitants of the United States.

The wisdom and the importance of these reciprocal concessions of the use of the artificial channels of water communication contemplated by the Treaty on terms of equality to the citizens or subjects of either Power are apparent. The rapid increase of population and production of the vast territory on either side of the Boundary line and on the upper lakes, demand all the channels of communication with the tide waters, which either nature or the enterprise of man has made available.

It is confidently believed that the use of the artificial water communications which the Treaty contemplates will contribute to a rapid increase of trade through those several channels and will tend to a consequent increase in the tolls and returns of profits both direct and indirect to each and all of the canals thus opened to the use of a large extent of country.

As the period is approaching when the Legislature of your State is about to convene, I desire to bring the provisions of this Article of the Treaty to its notice and to urge upon your State Government to secure to the subjects of Her Britannic Majesty the use of the several State Canals within the State of New York, connected with the navigation of the lakes or rivers traversed by or contiguous to the boundary line between the Possessions of the United States and those of Her Britannic Majesty in North America, on terms of equality with the inhabitants of the United States.

I address a similar request to other States through which are constructed Canals connected with the navigation of the Lakes.

I have the honor to be, &c. &c.

U. S. GRANT.

HIS EXCELLENCY, JOHN T. HOFFMAN
GOVERNOR OF THE STATE OF NEW YORK.

Copy, DLC-USG, II, 1. *Foreign Relations, 1871*, pp. 531–32. Copies of this letter went to six other governors. On Dec. 4, 1871, Governor John T. Hoffman of N. Y. wrote to USG. "... I have caused enquiries to be made of those charged with the administration of the Canals of this State, and learn from them that they know of no restrictions now to be found in the laws of this State upon the equal use of the Canals by British subjects and American Citizens; that there are no restrictions upon foreigners being the owners, in part or in whole, of boats entitled to navigate our Canals, nor would a boat owned wholly in Canada be forbidden the use of our Canals or be subjected to other tolls or other regulati[on] than those imposed upon boats owned in our [own] State. I shall, nevertheless, with great pleasu[re] call the attention of the Legislature to the subje[ct] and recommend them to pass such laws as they may find to be necessary to carry into eff[ect,] at once, the agreement made in the 27th Arti[cle] of the Treaty." LS, DNA, RG 59, Miscellaneous Letters. On the same day, Governor Conrad Baker of Ind. wrote to USG informing him that the Ind. legislature would not convene until Jan., 1873. ALS, *ibid.*

To William W. Smith

Washington, D. C. Dec. 3d *1871*

DEAR SMITH:

Enclosed I send you a letter from Julia to Miss Bessie Wrenshall which I wish you would do me the favor to have forwarded to her. I am not certain how to address a letter to insure its reaching her, hence trouble you.

We expect you and Emma to pay us a visit in Feb.y. The enclosed letter is an invitation to Miss Bessie to come on and spend Jan.y.

All are well and desired to be remembered to Emma, the children and yourself.

Yours Truly

U. S. GRANT

ALS, Washington County Historical Society, Washington, Pa. On Dec. 9, 1871, USG wrote to William W. Smith, Washington, Pa. "Can you not come and spend Christmas week with us yourself. Buck will be at home at that time." ALS, *ibid.* On [*Dec.*] 20, USG telegraphed to Smith. "Will you be here during Holidays   tell Miss Wrenshall to notify us when she is coming and some one will meet her at Baltimore" Telegram received, *ibid.* On Dec. 24, Julia Dent Grant wrote to Emily (Emma) Dent Casey. "I hope you are feeling right well & are enjoying the Christmass holidays   Buckie arrived last night & we shall have a house full of young people next week. Cousin Willie Smith & Bissie Wrenshall come on Tuesday as do also Fannie Drexall & Florance Juwell   You remember the Govnor dont you? Florance is his youngest daughter—Fred has arrived safely on the other side. We have not yet had letters from him—not had time   I have been very buessy geting trifels together for Christmass   I hope you will receive your box in good time & like the little cross I send you—& the other little things   Nell Sharp thought you would like the smelling bottle—All are well & send a great deal of love to you all—You ask if I did not receive *six* hundred & (75) seventy five dollars—of course I did. What did I write? I did not read my letter over after writeing & must have made a mistake which I should have corrected had I read it over—I was so often interupted which is my excuse for giving you any annoyance or uneasyness—We will all think of you & yours to morr[ow] & drink your goo[d] health   Nellie's fr[iends] & prehaps Annie & Louie will dine with us tomorrow. Hellen & Fred has the Lynn family with them. Genl Grant says he has a nice present for me. I wonder what it is—I will write & tell you—All send love to all   God bless & keep you darling sister   Write soon . . . A Happy Christmass to all" ALS, Ulysses S. Grant National Historic Site (White Haven), St. Louis, Mo.

Draft Annual Message

[*Dec. 4, 1871*]

To the Senate and House of Representatives

In addressing my third Annual Message to the Law making branch of the Government it is gratifying to be able to state that [during the past year] sucsess has generally attended, ~~during the year just passed~~, the effort to execut~~ione~~ ~~of~~ all laws found upon the statutes.

The policy has been, not to enquire into the wisdom of laws already enacted, but to ~~know the~~ [learn their] spirit and intent ~~of them~~, and to enforce them accordingly.[1]

This policy has ~~forced~~ [imposed] upon the Executive branch of the govt the execution of the Act~~s~~ of Congress, [There has been imposed upon the Executive branch of the Govermet the execution of the Act, of Congress—] approved [~~insert date~~] and commonly known as the Ku Klux law~~s~~, in a portion of the State of South Carolina. The necessity of the course pursued will be demonstrated by the report of the ~~C~~[c]ommittee to ~~I~~[i]nvestigate ~~S~~[s]outhern ~~O~~[o]utrages.

A full report of what has been done under the~~se~~is law~~s~~ will be submitted to Congress by the Atty. General.[2]

More than six years having elapsed since the last hostile gun
was fired between the Armies then arrayed against each other one
for the perpetuation, the other for the destruction of the Union, it
may well be considered whether it is not now time that all the disabilities imposed by the XIV Amendment should not be removed.
That Amendment does not exclude the ballot but only imposes disability to hold offices upon certain classes. ~~Where~~ Majorities are
sure, where the purity of the ballot is secured, to elect officers reflecting the views of the majority. I do not see the advantage or
propriety of excluding men from office merely because they were
of standing and character sufficient, before the rebellion, to be
elected to positions requiring them to take oaths the support the
constitution, and admitting to elegibility those entertertaining precisely the same views but of less standing in their communities. It
may be said that the former violated an ~~obligation~~ oath, while the
latter did not. The latter had it not in their power do so—or who
doubts but they would. If thare any great criminals, distinguished
above all others for the part they took in opposition to the government then they might be excluded from such an Amnesty.[3]
    This subject is submitted to your consideration.
    The condition of the Southern States is unhappily not what all
true patriotic citizens would like to see. ~~it.~~ Social ostracism for opinions sake, personal violence or threats towards those having political views opposed to those entertained by the old citizens prevents
emmigration and the flow of much needed capital into the states
lately in rebellion. It will be a happy condition of the country when
the old citizens of the states lately in rebellion will take an interest
in public affairs, promulgate views honestly entertained, vote for
men representing their views and tolerate the same freedom of expression and ballot ~~from~~ to those entertaining different views.
    In Utah, ~~where~~ [still] remains ~~yet~~ a remnant of barbarism re-
pugnant to civilization, decency and [to] the laws of the United
States, ~~have been found~~   Territorial officers [however have been
found who are] able and ~~disposed~~ [willing] to ~~execute~~ the same
without fear, favor, or affection [perform their duty in a spirit of
equity and with a due Sense of the necessity of sustaining the

majesty of the law].⁺ Neither Poligamy, nor any other violation
of ~~law~~ [existing statutes], will be permitted ~~in that territory nor
elsewhere~~ [within the territory of the United States]. It is not with
the religion of the self styled Saints that we are now dealing, but
with their practices. They will be protected in the ~~worship of God
"according to the dictates of their own consciences"~~ but ~~will not
be permitted to violate the laws under the cloak of religion~~.

Utah

It may be advisable for Congress to consider what in the execution
of the laws against poligamy, is to be the status of plural wives,
and their ofspring. I have nothing special to recommend in this
connection. The propriety of Congress passing an enabling act
authorizing the Territorial Legislature of Utah to legitimatize all
children born ~~before a~~ prior to a time fixed in the act might be
justified by its humanity to the innocent children and their ignorant and fanatical mothers. This is a suggestion only and not a
recommendation.

~~The year just passed~~ [The past year] has, under a wise Providence, been one of [general] prosperity to the Nation, ~~in a material
sense~~. It has however been attended with more than usual chas-
tisements in the loss of life and property by storms ~~shipwricks~~
and fire. These ~~calamities however~~ [disasters] have served to ~~bring
out~~ [call forth] the best elements of human nature in our country,
and to ~~developed~~ a friendship for us on the part of European ~~na-
tionalities~~ [nations] which goes far towards alleviating the dis-
tresses occasioned by these calamities. ~~The benevolent towards
the great sufferers by~~ [The benevolent who have so generously
shared their mean with the victims of] these calamities [misfor-
tunes] ~~alluded to, both at home and abroad, have~~ [will reap] their
reward in the conscisness of having ~~done~~ [performed] a noble act,
and in receiving the grateful thank of thousands of men, women &
children [whose sufferings they have] relieved ~~from greater suffering by them~~.

The year ~~just closed has been an~~ [The ~~foreign~~ relations of the
United States with foregn powers continus to be friendly   The
year has been an] eventful one in witnessing two great nations,
speaking one language and having one linneage, settling [by

peaceful arbitration] ~~and old~~ dispute, [of long standing and] one liable at any time to bring these nations into bloody and costly conflict, ~~by peacible arbitration~~. An example has [thus] been set which, if successful in its final issue, may be followed by other civilized nations and finally [be the means of] returning to productive industry Millions of men now ~~employed~~ [maintained] to ~~sustain Nationalities~~ [settle the disputes of nations] by the bayonet and the broad-side.

To give importance, and to add to the efficiency of our diplomatic relations with Japan and China, and to further aid in retaining the good opinion of those peoples; and to secure to the United States its share of the Commerce destined to flow between those nations and the balance of the Commercial world, I would earnestly recommend that an appropriation be made to support at least four American youths at each of their Courts, to serve as a part of the Staffs of our Ministers there.[5] Our representatives there would not be ~~on~~ [placed upon] an equality ~~footing~~ with the representaive of Great Britan, and of some other powers.

I would also recommend liberal measures ~~to~~ [for the purpose of] support[ing] ~~an increased~~ [to] the American lines of Steamers now plying betwen San Francisco & Japan & China, and ~~also~~ the Australian line (~~nearly the entire of our~~ [almost our only] remaining ~~Ocean lines~~ of [ocean] Steamers) and of increasing their services

~~A~~ [The national] debt has been reduced, and [to the] (this) [extent of]   millions of dollars durin[g] the year ~~b~~[B]y the negociation of ~~bond~~ $200.000 of National bonds, at a lower rate of interest ~~than they before bore~~, the interest on the public debt ~~reduced, so~~ [has been so far diminished] that now the sum to be raised, for [the] interest account is $13.[000000] less than on the 1st of March 1869.

~~All Indian depridations have been and wars have almost ceased.~~

~~(Foreign Relations)~~

~~The report of the See. of the Treas. made, by law, directly to Congress will show a gratifying diminution of the public debt for the last year, While it was very desirable that and a diminution~~

of expenses both for the ordinary expenses of Government and of amount to meet the interest on the public debt. It was highly desirable that this rapid diminution should take place both to strengthen the credit of the United States Country, and to convince its citizens of their entire ability to meet every dollar of liability without bankrupting them. But in view of the accomplishment of these desirable lessons [ends]; of the rapid developement of the resources of the country, its rapid increase[ing] of ability to meet large demands, and the Amount already paid by this generation, it is not desirable that the present resources [of the country] should be [over] taxed [in order] to keep up [continue] this present rapid payment. I therefore recommend a modification of both the Tarriff and Internal Tax Laws.[6] I would [recommend] suggest that all taxes, from internal sources, be relieved [abolished] except those collected from spirituous, vinous & malt liquors; tobacco in its various forms; and from stamps.

In re-adjusting the tarriff I would recommend [suggest] that a careful estimate be made of the sum that can be spared from what it is estimated can be collected under present laws, leaving surplus revenue sufficient surplus to reduce the public debt at least one pr. cent pr. annum, and then divide the relief to benefit the greatest number [of the amount of Surplus revenues collected under the present laws after providing for the current expenses of the Goverment and the interests on the public debt account and a Sinking fund of one per centum per annum, on the public debt and that this Surplus be reduced in Such a manner as to afford the greatest relief to the greatest number]. There are many articles not produced at home but which enter largely into general consumptin through articles which are manufactured at home [such as] medicines compounded, &c. [&c] which pay, each, but little [from which very little revenue is derived] but [which enter] go into general use. All such articles I would recommend should go [to be placed] on the "F[f]ree L[l]ist." I would also recommend that duty on salt be reduce to one half the present rate, and on coal[7] to F[f]ifty cents per. ton. Should a further reduction prove practicable [advisable] I would then recommend that it be taken from [made upon] those articles which can best afford it, or that the surplus be held to enable a rebate to be made upon those articles which ~~go~~ [enter] into the construction of ships. I have not entered into figures because, to do so, ~~is only~~ [would be] to recapitulate [repeat] what will be [laid] before you in report of the Sec. of the Treasury. ~~The subject of a revival of our ocean commerce, and ship building, is one which I hope will receive your earnest consideration.~~

The present laws for collecting revenues pays Collectors of Customs small salaries, but provides for moieties which, at principal ports of entry particularly, ~~brings~~ [raises] the compensation of these officials up to a ~~high figure~~ [large Sum]. It has always ~~looked~~ [Seemed] to me as if this system [~~at times~~] must [at times] work ~~at times~~ perniciously. It holds out an inducement to dishonest men, should such get possession of these offices, to be lax in their scrutiny of goods entered to enables them finally to make large seizures. Your attention is respectfully invited to this subject.

Continued fluctuations in the value of gold as compared ~~to~~ [with] the National Currency has a most damaging effect upon the increase and developement of the country in keeping up prices of every article ~~entering into~~ [necessary in] every day life. It fosters a spirit of gambling prejudicial alike to ~~N~~[n]ational Morals and [the] ~~N~~[n]ational finance[s]. If the question can be met [as to] how to give a fixed ~~and permanent~~ value to our currency: that value constantly and uniformly approrching par with specie a very desirable object will be gained. In my Message to Congress two years ago I recommended a plan by which it seemed to me this end might be accomplished without a reduction of the volume of currency except as gold come more into demand than currency but with the power of expansion, to present limits, as the latter come into demand. As the subject as presented has never been discussed I am not prepared to say that I would recommend its adoption but I again invite attention to the subject of a gradual approach to specie payment, and consideration of so much of the plan proposed as may seem to ~~have~~ [possess] merit ~~in it~~.

Army

For the operations of the Army in the past year, expense of maintaing it, estimates for the ensuing year, and for continuing

sea coast and other improvement conducted under the supervision
of the War Dept. I refer you to the report of the Sec. of War
accompanying this.

I call your attention to the provisions of the Act of Congress,
approved   which discontinues promotions in the
Staff Corps of the Army until provided for by law. I would recommend that the number of officers ~~to~~ [in] each grade in the Staff
Corps be fixed, and that when ever the number in any one grade
falls below the number so fixed that the vacancy may be filled by
promotion from the grade below. I also recommend that when the
~~head~~ [office of chief] of a Corps becomes vacant the place may be
filled by selection from the Corps [in which the vacancy exists.]

~~Your attention is particularly invited to the recommendations
of the Post Master General and, particularly to those the recommendations looking to uniting the telegraph system of the country
with the postal service~~.

The increase of the receipts of the P. O. Dept. as shown by
the [accompanying] report of the PostMaster General, ~~herewith
accompanying~~, shews a gratifying ~~growth~~ [increase] in that branch
of the public service. It is the index of [the] growth of education
and [of the] prosperity of of the people, two elements [highly]
condusive to the ~~health~~ [vigor] and stability of republics. With a
vast territory, like ours, much of it sparsely populated but all requiring the services of the Mail it is not to be expected that this
dept. can [yet] be [made] self sustaining. But ~~an~~ gradual approach
to ~~it~~ [this end] from year to year is confidently relied on, and
the day is not far distant when the postoffice department of the
government will prove a much greater blessing to the whole
people than [it is] now. The suggestions of the PostMaster General
for improvements in in the department presided over by him are
earnestly recommended to your special attention. S[Es]pecially
would I recommend favorable consideration of uniting the telegraphic system of the United States with the postal system. It is
believed that, by such a course, the cost of telegraphing could be
much reduced and the service as well if not better rendered. It
would ~~give~~ [secure] the further advantage of ~~extending~~ ~~diffusing~~

[extending] the telegraph through [portions of] the country where private enterprise will not ~~send~~ [construct] it. ~~Trade~~, e[C]ommerce, [trade] and above all the ~~tendency~~ [efforts] to bring a people widely settled into a community of interest, is [always] benefitted by a rapid intercommunication with each other. Education, the ground-work of republican institutions, is encourage by increasing the facilities to gather speedy news from all parts of the country. The desire to reap the benefit of such improvements will stimulate education. I refer you to the report of the postmaster genl for full details of the operations of last year, and for comparitive statemts of results with former years.

The policy pursued towards the indians has resulted favorably so far as can be judged from the limited [time during which] ~~that~~ it has been in opperations. Through the exertions of the various societies of Christians to whom has been entrusted the execution of the policy, and the Board of Commissioners authorized by the law of Apl. 10th 1869, many tribes of Indians have been induced to ~~cease their come onto~~ [settle upon] reservations, ~~and~~ to cultivate the soil, perform productive labor of various sorts, and to partially accept civilization. They are being cared for in [such] a way, it is hoped, [as] to induce those still pursuing their old habits of life, ~~to come in and finally and to accept the only offer which can save them from~~ [to embrace the only opportunity which is left them to avoid] extermination.

I recommend liberal appropriations to carry out the Indian Peace policy not only because it is humane, and christian like but also because is the cheapest and it is right.

I recommend to your favorable consideration also the policy of granting a territorial govt. to the Indians in the ~~Te~~Indian terri-tory west of Ark. & Mo. and south of Kansas. In doing so every right guaranteed to the Indian, by treaty, should be secured.

Such a course might, in time, be the means of collecting most of the Indians now between the Mo. and the Pacific, and south the British possessions, into one territory or one state.

The sec. of the Int. has treated upon this subject at length and I commend to you his suggestions.[8]

Public lands

I reniew again my recommendation that the public lands of
the Nation be regarded as a heritage ~~of~~ [to] our children, only to
be disposed of as required for ~~settlement~~ [occupation], and to actual settlers. Those already granted away, in great part, have been
granted in such a way as to secure access to the balance by the
hardy settler who may want to avail himself of them. But caution
should be exercised even in [a]ttaining so desirable an object.

Educational interest may well be served by the grant of the
proceeds of sale of public lands to settlers. I do not wish to be
understood as recommending in the least degree a curtailment of
what is being done by the general goverment for the encouragement of ~~so beneficial~~ education.

The report of the sec. of the Interior, submitted with this, will
give you all the information collected and prepared for publication,
by the census taken during the year 1870; of the opperation of the
Bureau of Education for the year; of the Patent Office; of the Pension office; ~~and~~ of the Land office and of the Indian Bureau.

The report of the Commissioner of Agriculture gives the operations of his department for the year. ~~and submits the necessary~~
As agriculture is the groundwork of our prosperity to much importance cannot be attached to the labors of this Dept. It is in the
hands of an able head,[9] with able assistants, all zealously devoted
to introducing into the agricultural productions of the Nation all
useful products adapted to any of the various climates and soils of
our vast territory and to giving all useful information as to the
method of cultivation, the plants, serials, and other products
adapted to particular soils, climates &c.

Quietly but surely the Agricultural beaureau is working a
great National good, and if liberally supported that good is destined to be felt in the way of protection to home industry.

The subject of compensation to the heads of bureaus, and
officials holding ~~responsible~~ positions of responsibility, and requiring ability and character to fill properly, is one to which your
attention is invited. But few of these officials receive a compensation equal to the respectable support of a family while their duties

are such as to involve Millions of interest. In private life sevices demand compensation equal to the services rendered. ~~It also~~ A wise economy would dictate the same rule in the government service.

I have not given the estimates for the support of Government for the ensuing year, nor the comparitive statement between the expenditures for the year just past and the one just preceding, because all these figures are contained in the accompanying reports or in those presented directly to Congress. Those estimates accompanyin this have my approval.

By the great fire in Chicago ~~all~~ [the most important of] the Government buildings in that city were consumed. Those burned had already become inadequate to the wants of the government in that growing city, and looking to the near future were ~~very far~~ [totally] inadequate. I recommend therefore that an appropriation be made immediately to purchase the ~~balance~~ [remainder] of the square on which the burned buildings stood, provided it can be purchased at a fare valuation, or provided that the Legislature of Ill. will pass a law authorizing its condemnation for governmental purposes; and also an appropriation of as much money as can properly be expended towards the erection of new buildings during this fiscal year. ~~Of course I do not recommend the commencement of any new building until the plan and estimate of cost has been submitted to Congress, and both approved by them.~~[10]

The number of immigrants, ignorant of our laws, habits &c. coming into our country annually, has become so great, and the impositions practiced upon [them] so numerous and flagrant that I suggest Congression[l] action for their protection. It seems to me a fair subject of legislation by Congress. I can not now state with ~~accuracy the fullness~~ [as fully as] I desire the nature of the complaints made by immigrants, of the treatment they ~~now~~ receive but will endeavor to do so during the session of Congress,[11] particularyly if the subject should receive your attention.

It has been the aim of the administration to enforce honesty and efficiency in all public offices. Every public servant who has violated the trust placed in him has been proceeded against with all the vigor of the law. If bad men ha~~d~~ve ~~got in~~ [secured] places it has been the fault of the system, ~~provided~~ [established] by law and custom, for making appointments, or the fault of those [who] recommen[d]~~ding~~ for ~~place~~ [government positions] persons not ~~personally~~ sufficiently well known to them, ~~or by so recommending without a proper regard for the responsibility of so doing~~. [personally or who give letters ~~of~~ endorsing the characters of office seekers without a proper sense of the grave responsibility which such a course devolves upon them.] A civil service [reform] which can corect this abuse is much desired. In Mercantile pursuits the business man who gives a letter of recommendation to a friend to enable him to ~~get~~ [obtain] credit from a stranger is regarded as morally responsible for the ~~responsibility~~ ability ~~and integrity of his friend, to meet his obligations~~ [integrity of his friend, and his ability to meet his obligations]. A reformitory law which would enforce this principle against all indorsers ~~for~~ [of] persons for public place would insure great caution in making recommendations.—A salutary lesson has been taught the careless and the dishonest public servant in the great number of prossecutions and convictions of the last two years.

It is gratifying to note[ice] the [favorable] change ~~that~~ [which] is taking place, ~~the country over,~~ [throughout the country] ~~to~~ [in] bring[ing] to punishment those who have proven recreant to the trust[s] ~~placed in~~ [confided to] them, and ~~for the future~~ [in elevating] to ~~elevate to place~~ [public office] none but those ~~having~~ [who possess] the confidence of the honest and [the] virtuous (~~always the majority~~) [who it will always be found compose the majority] of the community in which they live.

Civil Service

Under the authority of the 9th sec. of ~~the~~ "An Act ~~of Congress, approved March 3d 1871~~ making Appropriations for sundry civil Expenses of the Government, and other purposes, approved March 3d 1871, I convened a commission of ~~eminent~~ gentlemen most eminently fitted ~~for the~~ for the purpose to devise rules and regulations, to be adopted by the Executive, to promote the efficiency of the civil service. The commission has not yet reported, but it is earnestly hoped that their labors may result in devising regulations which can be adopted without infringing upon any constitutional right of either Congress or the Executive, and which will promote the efficiency of the civil service, relieve Congressmen from a most disagreeable task, and the Executive, and Heads of Departments from the position of appointment clerks. ~~When completed their work will be carefully and candidly reviewed, and either adopted in whole or in part, or submitted to Congress for further action, all, or so much of it as may be deemed of practicable benefit will be put into practice.~~ This law throws upon the Executive the duty and the responsibility of inaugurating a "Civil Service" reform." That duty will be met as soon as practicable after the report of the Commissioners is recd.

In my message to Congress one year ago I [urgently] recommended a reform in the civil service of the country. In conformity ~~to~~ [with] that recommendation Congress, in the 9th Sec. of "An Act making appropriations for sundry civil expenses of the government, and [for] other purposes," approved March 3d 1871, gave the necessary authority to the Executive to inaugurate a civil service reform, and placed upon him the responsibility of doing so. Under the authority of said act I convened a Board of gentlemen eminently qualified for the work, to devise rules & regulations to effect the needed reform. Their labors are not yet complete but it is believed that they will succeed in devising ~~rules~~ [a plan] which can be adopted to the great relief of the Executive, [the] heads of departments, ~~and~~ [and] members of Congress, and which will redound to the [true] interest of the public service. At all events the experiment ~~will be tried~~ shall have a fair trial.[12]

"~~To the Victors belong the spoils~~" ~~should not be a motto~~

I have thus hastily summed up the operations of the [govt during the] last year, and made such suggestions as occur to me [to be] proper for your consideration, ~~and~~ submit the[m] ~~same~~ with a confidence that your combined action will be wise, statesmanlike, and ~~for~~ [in] the best interests of the whole country.

ADf (bracketed material not in USG's hand), DLC-USG, III. See following annual
message for additional text. On Nov. 20, 1871, and subsequently, Secretary of State
Hamilton Fish wrote in his diary. "I take to the President the draft of those portions
of the Message relating to Foreign Affairs, telling him that some of them may need to
be changed, by new despatches received, up to the last moment—" "November 24 . . .
Prsdt says . . . that he recommends the abolishing of all the internal revenue taxes
except those on Spirits—Wine—Malt liquor tobacco & stamps—that he recommends a reduction of revenue from imports, by abolishing duties on those Articles not
~~entering~~ produced in the U S which enter into the Arts & Manufactures, & reducing
or abolishing duties which are not productive on other articles entering into manufac-
ture—that he thinks a more gradual reduction of the debt than hitherto is now sufficient—that he recommends reduction of duty on Salt, one half the present duty & on
Coal to fifty cents a ton—Cresswell think the reduction on Coal will be unpopular as
interfering with our own production—Prsdt says the Coal producers do not care a
particle for the duty—but Cresswell says the reduction will affect the Maryland Coal.
The question is raised whether any specification of Articles on which to reduce is
adviseable—& the opinion is in favor of omitting any recommendation as to specific
Articles   President says he has taken verbatim the Memorandum I gave him, as to
Foreign Affairs—adding something of his own with respect to Japan & omitting the
passage relating to San Domingo—I read him a letter recd this morning from Judge
Reid of Phil hoping nothing will be done to revive the San Domingo question &
express the opinion that it will be expedient to say a few words on the subject, to
forestall the objection that will be made that silence indicates an intention to revive
the subject—Creswell concurs with me—Delano dissents—refers to the quieting
effect of the Message last year, & having said what he then said the subject should
drop—I reply that that was a special Message—that this is a new Congress the
President made no opening Message to them last Spring that the Annual Message
is looked upon as a General presentation of the State of the Nation & of the general
Policy of the President, & the omission of any reference to a subject on which so
much was said a short time since, will be taken as evidence of want of steadfastness
in adhering to the policy of the special Message—Nothing definite is determined."
"November 28. Tuesday. Cabinet—meeting at 10 A M. (on special notice) the President going to attend the wedding of Justice Millers daughter   All present except
Belknap—President reads his message—some verbal alterations suggested &
adopted—I hand him a suggested draft for the part relating to Russia, & Catacazy—
and mention that the correspondence with G. B. respecting the form of the note to
the Maritime powers making known the rules in Art VI of the Treaty, has not been
closed, & that I am in hope it may be complete before the end of the week—if not
a change must be made in that respect—At the Close of the reading he asks if there
be any other subject, which ~~about~~ is thought of, not treated of in the message—I
remark that he makes no allusion to San Domingo (he having omitted to read the
passage I furnished him on that subject) & refer to the presentation of the matter
in his Message last Spring (April 5) wherein he stated in substance that he would
leave the question until the next meeting of Congress—that unless he make some
allusion to it now, it may be regarded that he intends in some way to bring it up—
and that there is much nervousness in the public mind, & among many of his best
friends, lest the question be again agitated—none of the Cabinet expressed any
opinion, but a few questions were asked & answered & the President said he would
introduce a few words in relation to it—Without calling for the ordinary routine

of business he said the time had arrived when he must go to the Wedding" "December 2. Saturday Took to the President a passage for his Message, relating to Cuba, and its relations to the U. S. He said he would adopt it, much in the form I presented, might add a few words. Also amended the part of the Message (previously given to him) refering to the ~~Joint~~ note to be presented to the Maritime Powers, bringing to their notice the rules in Article VI of Treaty with G. B, by striking out the statement that the Correspondence with reference to the note, is transmitted with the Message—inasmuch as the Correspondence is not yet closed—" DLC-Hamilton Fish.

On Nov. 15, Jay Cooke, New York City, had written to USG. "I understand from our distinguished fellow citizen Hon Cyrus W Field, that he designs applying at the next session of Congress for aid in the construction of the last remaining link of Ocean Telegraph—viz that from Puget Sound to the Southern border of Asiatic Russia, He is about to visit Russia to arrange with the Emperor such terms as will unite the efforts of the two great & friendly Nations & secure the speedy completion of the line, with its termini on our own shore, & those of Russia, I have carefully examined his plans & feel assured that he will ask nothing of either country that will involve any possible expenditure or risk—the aid asked being in the shape of a conditional guarantee of a portion each, of the interest on moneys furnished by private capitalists & under such checks & guards as will secure the guarantors from risk—In common with others who no doubt will address you on this subject I should feel gratified if you would direct the state Department to mention Mr Fields visit in its despatches to Minister Curtin & request his efforts in his behalf—or what would be more highly prized & effectual—if you would address an autograph letter to him in favor of Mr Field Further, If, in the preparation of your annual Message you would kindly refer to the importance of the completion of this link from our own shores & that such legislation be had as may seem judicious, it would no doubt ensure prompt action & favorable results." ALS, OFH.

1. On Jan. 28, 18[72], Daniel Murphy, Fort Davis, Tex., wrote to USG. "As you are the Father of the law, and you stated in your message that you enforced the law, You will see by the enclosed that your citizens are not getting the benefit of the law as it was passed by Congress. And as the appointment of Traders was placed in your hands, when you were Commanding General of the Army, and you are well aquainted with the law. I therefore ask you as I am one of the oldest Settlers of this Section of county as I have been here ever since the Mexican War, to give me that protection which the law allows me, and which I am deprived off at present" ALS, DNA, RG 94, ACP, 1038 1872. Correspondence between Murphy, a local storekeeper, and Lt. Col. William R. Shafter over the right to sell goods to soldiers is *ibid.*

2. See message to House of Representatives, April 19, 1872.

3. On Jan. 10, 1872, "prominent representatives of the colored race" requested USG "to send a message to Congress, asking for the passage of the supplementary civil rights bill as an amendment to the amnesty law. The speakers received very courteous attention, and, when they had concluded, the President remarked that he thought, although some of the rights which they had a claim to under the recent amendments to the Constitution were withheld, still the courts of law would accord all legal privileges. He considered that appending the supplementary civil rights bill to the amnesty measure would jeopardize the passage of the latter, and in that respect it would be unfortunate. The former, he thought, from his knowledge of it, would pass

on its merits as a separate and distinct measure. The delegation withdrew, seeming well pleased with their interview." *Washington Evening Star*, Jan. 10, 1872.

4. See letter to John P. Newman, Nov. 6, 1871.

5. On Dec. 11, 1871, Horace Porter wrote to James McCosh, Princeton, N. J. "The President directs me to acknowledge the receipt of your letter of the 5th inst: and thank you for your suggestion in regard to the appointment of the youths to China and Japan. He is quite pleased with it. It is his desire to spare no effort effort in creating a reform in the Civil Service of the Government, which will secure the fittest persons for Office. He will take what you say into careful consideration." Copy, DLC-USG, II, 1. See Speech, March 2, 1871.

On Dec. 18, F. W. Moore, Bloomfield, Iowa, wrote to USG. "I see by your recent message to Congress that you earnestly recomme'd that body to send at least four young men to China, and the same number to Japan, that They may acquire The languages of the people of those countries, and be fitted to perform The duties of interpretors for The Officers of our government. I hope Congress will act in accordance with your suggestion; first, because I believe it to be a good and timely one; and second, because I want to go to China as one of the number to be sent. I am a young man of Western birth, and have had but limited opportunites to aquire an education, having attended school but about eighteen months in the past fourteen years; and what schooling I had before that time did me but little good; as I was then too young to feel the advantages of learning, or to know why I should study at all. But during the last Twelve years I have employed all my odd time in various useful studies, and particularly have I devoted my attention to languages. . . ." ALS, DNA, RG 59, Letters of Application and Recommendation. On Dec. 5, James R. Kenney, Reading, Pa., had written to USG about serving in Japan or China. ALS, *ibid.*

On Jan. 20, 1872, William A. Butterfield and Frank W. Marvin, Sacramento, wrote to USG. "We are very desirous, in case several young Americans are sent to Japan, as recommended by you in your message to Congress, to learn the Language and habits of that people, for the benefit of our Government, to be included among the number. Our ages are 22 and 24 years of age." LS, *ibid.*

On June 19, U.S. Senator Daniel D. Pratt of Ind., Logansport, wrote to USG. "There is a law I believe, which Authorizes you to appoint two American Student Interpreters to visit Japan & be instructed in the language with the view of being employed as Interpreters afterwards—Mr Carlton Rice of Hamilton N. Y. desires the appointment of his son Dwight Rice and requests me to present his application which I now due, with the following testimonials . . ." ALS, *ibid.* On May 20 the House had passed a bill to train two interpreters in Japan; the Senate took no action. See *CG*, 42–2, 3661–64.

6. On Feb. 26, 1871, John A. Dix, New York City, had written to USG. "*Private &
Confidential.* . . . I do not often volunteer to make Suggestions, much less to give advice—especially where, as in this case, I have no acknowledged right to do so. But a sincere wish that your administration may be successful and that it may be continued for another term in order that the secessionists may not get possession of the Capitol, as they would be pretty sure to do under a democratic administration, induces me to speak plainly to you on two or three Subjects.—I think it would be very unfortunate for you if this Congress were to adjourn without an open and decided effort on your part to carry two or three measures. 1. The repeal of the duty on foreign coals. Along the coast & in many interior districts the price of wood places it out of the reach of the poor. Coal is their only resource, and they are at the mercy of monopolists. In this City it is from $12. to $15 pr. ton. I put in mine in Sept. at $7. The poor, who

are the great majority & who buy by the bushel & pay $20. to $30. the ton, justly demand relief. The [re]peal of the duty will not reduce the great staple of Penn. in price, for no anthricite is imported. But it will ensure to the poor a supply of fuel at a moderate price, from the coal fields of Nova Scotia when our own is inflated by selfish combinations. I assure you, General, there is a deep popular feeling on this Subject, which you cannot safely disregard—the more especially as it is founded in reason and right.—2. The repeal of the income tax. This was a war measure, and its inquisitorial character was only borne in patience as one of the necessary means of saving the Union. The necessity has ceased, and the continuance of the exaction is considered unjust and intolerable. The west, which bears scarcely any of the burden, is, I know and as I think most unreasonably, opposed to the repeal of the law; but the West has no deep feeling on the Subject, while in the East and North the dissatisfaction is universal and intense—too much so to be trifled with longer. Both Houses of Congress have on different occasions, though not by a concurrent act, expressed their opinion in favor of the [re]peal of the tax. You are known to be in favor of it. And yet, to the astonishment of the country, your chief financial officer and one of your confidential advisers is doing all in his power to defeat your wishes. Now, General, you will excuse me for saying that a house thus divided cannot possibly stand, and that a man, who has not the delicacy to withdraw from an administration, which he will not sustain in a measure of such national importance, cannot be allowed, to remain in it without compromising the moral courage and independence of its chief in the estimation of his countrymen.—I have already said more than I intended, and I will only add my earnest invocation to you to take an open and active part in the accomplishment of these two objects by the present Congress. If they are left to the Congress about to convene and carried, it will be due to the larger numerical force of the opposition & do you no credit.—I have spoken very plainly, General, but I hope not offensively. Men in Presidential chairs, like men on thrones, rarely hear the plain truth from their friends, & are apt to distrust it when it comes from their enemies. If there is any thing in this letter, which grates harshly on the sense, I beg you to commit it to the flames & forget it. Perhaps that would be the best disposition to make of it in whatever manner You may regard it; but I beg you not to treat lightly Suggestions, which are the fruit of a Sincere & disinterested regard for your political success.—" ALS, USG 3.

On Dec. 7, James W. Taylor, consul, Winnipeg, St. Paul, wrote to USG commending him on the tariff and specie remarks in his annual message and suggesting additional financial measures. ADfS (torn), Taylor Papers, Minnesota Historical Society, St. Paul, Minn.

7. On Jan. 3, 1872, Porter wrote to Henry Carey Baird. "The President directs me to acknowledge the receipt of Mr. Morris' pamphlet, 'Duty on Coal' and to convey to you his thanks for your kindness in sending it" Copy, DLC-USG, II, 1. Baird published Israel W. Morris, *The Duty on Coal* ... (Philadelphia, 1872). See "General Grant at the 'Carey Vespers,'" *USGA Newsletter*, III, 3 (April, 1966), 13–25.

8. See message to Congress, Jan. 30, 1871; *HRC*, 42-2-1, part 5, pp. 6–8.

9. See letter to Horace Capron, June 28, 1871.

10. A note here reads: "See if jurisdiction has to be [seded] also."

11. See message to Congress, May 14, 1872.

12. See message to Congress, Dec. 19, 1871. On Dec. 4, 1871, Porter wrote to Asa W. Tenney, New York City. "Your letter of the 1st. instant is duly received. The President directs me to acknowledge it, and convey to you his thanks for the kind expressions it contains. He has made the subject of Civil Service reform a prominent

portion of his message. His interest in this much desired reformation remains un-
abated." Copy, DLC-USG, II, 1.

Annual Message

To the Senate and House of Representatives: . . .

I transmit herewith a copy of the treaty alluded to,[1] which has
been concluded, since the adjournment of Congress, with Her Bri-
tanic Majesty, and a copy of the protocols of the conferences of the
commissioners by whom it was negotiated. This treaty provides
methods for adjusting the questions pending between the two nations.

Various questions are to be adjusted by arbitration. I recommend Congress at an early day to make the necessary provision for
the tribunal at Geneva, and for the several commissioners, on the
part of the United States, called for by the treaty.

His Majesty the King of Italy, the President of the Swiss Confederation, and His Majesty the Emperor of Brazil, have each consented, on the joint request of the two powers, to name an arbitrator
for the tribunal at Geneva. I have caused my thanks to be suitably
expressed for the readiness with which the joint request has been
complied with, by the appointment of gentlemen of eminence and
learning to these important positions.[2]

His Majesty the Emperor of Germany has been pleased to comply with the joint request of the two governments, and has consented to act as the arbitrator of the disputed water boundary between the United States and Great Britain.[3]

The contracting parties in the treaty have undertaken to regard
as between themselves certain principles of public law, for which
the United States have contended from the commencement of their
history. They have also agreed to bring those principles to the
knowledge of the other maritime powers and to invite them to accede to them. Negotiations are going on as to the form of the note
by which the invitation is to be extended to the other powers.

I recommend the legislation necessary on the part of the United

States to bring into operation the articles of the treaty relating to the fisheries,[4] and to the other matters touching the relations of the United States toward the British North American possessions, to become operative so soon as the proper legislation shall be had on the part of Great Britain and its possessions. It is much to be desired that this legislation may become operative before the fishermen of the United States begin to make their arrangements for the coming season.

I have addressed a communication,[5] of which a copy is transmitted herewith, to the governors of New York, Pennsylvania, Ohio, Indiana, Michigan, Illinois, and Wisconsin, urging upon the governments of those States, respectively, the necessary action on their part to carry into effect the object of the article of the treaty which contemplates the use of the canals, on either side, connected with the navigation of the lakes and rivers forming the boundary, on terms of equality by the inhabitants of both countries. It is hoped that the importance of the object and the benefits to flow therefrom will secure the speedy approval and legislative sanction of the States concerned.

I renew the recommendation for an appropriation for determining the true position of the forty-ninth parallel of latitude where it forms the boundary between the United States and the British North American possessions, between the Lake of the Woods and the summit of the Rocky Mountains.[6] The early action of Congress on this recommendation would put it in the power of the War Department to place a force in the field during the next summer.

The resumption of diplomatic relations between France and Germany have enabled me to give directions for the withdrawal of the protection extended to Germans in France by the diplomatic and consular representatives of the United States in that country. It is just to add that the delicate duty of this protection has been performed by the minister and the consul general[7] at Paris, and the various consuls in France under the supervision of the latter, with great kindness as well as with prudence and tact. Their course has received the commendation of the German government, and has wounded no susceptibility of the French.

The government of the Emperor of Germany continues to manifest a friendly feeling toward the United States, and a desire to
harmonize with the moderate and just policy which this Government maintains in its relations with Asiatic powers, as well as
with the South American republics. I have given assurances that
the friendly feelings of that government are fully shared by the
United States.[8]

The ratifications of the consular and naturalization conventions
with the Austro-Hungarian Empire have been exchanged.[9]

I have been officially informed of the annexation of the States
of the Church to the Kingdom of Italy, and the removal of the capital of that kingdom to Rome.[10] In conformity with the established
policy of the United States, I have recognized this change. The ratifications of the new treaty of commerce between the United States
and Italy have been exchanged.[11] The two powers have agreed in
this treaty that private property at sea shall be exempt from capture
in case of war between the two powers. The United States have
spared no opportunity of incorporating this rule into the obligation
of nations.

The Forty-first Congress at its third session made an appropriation for the organization of a mixed commission for adjudicating
upon the claims of citizens of the United States against Spain growing out of the insurrection in Cuba. That commission has since been
organized. I transmit herewith the correspondence relating to its
formation and its jurisdiction. It is to be hoped that this commission
will afford the claimants a complete remedy for their injuries.[12]

It has been made the agreeable duty of the United States to
preside over a conference at Washington between the plenipotentiaries of Spain and the allied South American republics, which has
resulted in an armistice, with the reasonable assurance of a permanent peace.

The intimate friendly relations which have so long existed between the United States and Russia continue undisturbed. The visit
of the third son of the Emperor is a proof that there is no desire on
the part of his government to diminish the cordiality of those relations. The hospitable reception which has been given to the Grand

Duke is a proof that on our side we share the wishes of that government. The inexcusable course of the Russian minister at Washington rendered it necessary to ask his recall, and to decline to longer receive that functionary as a diplomatic representative. It was impossible with self-respect, or with a just regard to the dignity of the country, to permit Mr. Catacazy to continue to hold intercourse with this Government after his personal abuse of Government officials, and during his persistent interference, through various means, with the relations between the United States and other powers. In accordance with my wishes, this Government has been relieved of further intercourse with Mr. Catacazy, and the management of the affairs of the imperial legation has passed into the hands of a gentleman entirely unobjectionable.[13]

With Japan we continue to maintain intimate relations. The cabinet of the Mikado has, since the close of the last session of Congress, selected citizens of the United States to serve in offices of importance in several departments of government. I have reason to think that this selection is due to an appreciation of the disinterestedness of the policy which the United States have pursued toward Japan.[14] It is our desire to continue to maintain this disinterested and just policy with China as well as Japan. The correspondence transmitted herewith shows that there is no disposition on the part of this Government to swerve from its established course.

Prompted by a desire to put an end to the barbarous treatment of our shipwrecked sailors on the Corean coast, I instructed our minister at Peking[15] to endeavor to conclude a convention with Corea for securing the safety and humane treatment of such mariners.

Admiral Rodgers[16] was instructed to accompany him, with a sufficient force to protect him in case of need.

A small surveying party sent out, on reaching the coast, was treacherously attacked at a disadvantage. Ample opportunity was given for explanation and apology for the insult. Neither came. A force was then landed. After an arduous march over a rugged and difficult country, the forts from which the outrages had been committed were reduced by a gallant assault and were destroyed. Having thus punished the criminals, and having vindicated the honor of the flag, the expedition returned, finding it impracticable, under the circumstances, to conclude the desired convention. I respectfully refer to the correspondence relating thereto, herewith submitted, and leave the subject for such action as Congress may see fit to take.

The republic of Mexico has not yet repealed the very objectionable laws establishing what is known as the "Free Zone," on the frontier of the United States. It is hoped that this may yet be done, and also that more stringent measures may be taken by that republic for restraining lawless persons on its frontiers. I hope that Mexico, by its own action, will soon relieve this Government of the difficulties experienced from these causes. Our relations with the various republics of Central and South America continue, with one exception, to be cordial and friendly.

I recommend some action by Congress regarding the overdue installments under the award of the Venezuelan claims commission of 1866. The internal dissensions of this government present no justification for the absence of effort to meet their solemn treaty obligations.[17]

The ratification of an extradition treaty with Nicaragua has been exchanged.[18]

It is a subject for congratulation that the great empire of Brazil has taken the initiatory step toward the abolition of slavery. Our relations with that empire, always cordial, will naturally be made more so by this act. It is not too much to hope that the government of Brazil may hereafter find it for its interest as well as intrinsically right to advance toward entire emancipation more rapidly than the present act contemplates.

The true prosperity and greatness of a nation is to be found in the elevation and education of its laborers.

It is a subject for regret that the reforms in this direction, which were voluntarily promised by the statesmen of Spain, have not been carried out in its West India colonies. The laws and regulations for the apparent abolition of slavery in Cuba and Porto Rico leave most of the laborers in bondage, with no hope of release until their lives become a burden to their employers.

I desire to direct your attention to the fact that citizens of the United States, or persons claiming to be citizens of the United States, are large holders, in foreign lands, of this species of property, forbidden by the fundamental law of their alleged country. I recommend to Congress to provide, by stringent legislation, a suitable remedy against the holding, owning, or dealing in slaves, or being interested in slave property in foreign lands, either as owners, hirers, or mortgagers, by citizens of the United States.

It is to be regretted that the disturbed condition of the island of Cuba continues to be a source of annoyance and of anxiety. The existence of a protracted struggle in such close proximity to our own territory, without apparent prospect of an early termination, cannot be other than an object of concern to a people who, while abstaining from interference in the affairs of other powers, naturally desire to see every country in the undisturbed enjoyment of peace, liberty, and the blessings of free institutions.

Our naval commanders in Cuban waters have been instructed, in case it should become necessary, to spare no effort to protect the lives and property of *bona-fide* American citizens, and to maintain the dignity of the flag.

It is hoped that all pending questions with Spain growing out of the affairs in Cuba[19] may be adjusted in the spirit of peace and conciliation which has hitherto guided the two powers in their treatment of such questions. . . .

The report of the Secretary of the Navy shows an improvement in the number and efficiency of the naval force, without material increase in the expense of supporting it. This is due to the policy which has been adopted, and is being extended, as fast as our material will admit, of using smaller vessels as cruisers on the several stations. By this means we have been enabled to occupy at once a larger extent of cruising-ground, to visit more frequently the ports where the presence of our flag is desirable, and generally to discharge more efficiently the appropriate duties of the Navy in time of peace, without exceeding the number of men or the expenditure authorized by law.

During the past year the Navy has, in addition to its regular service, supplied the men and officers for the vessels of the Coast

Survey, and has completed the surveys authorized by Congress of the Isthmus of Darien and Tehuantepec, and under like authority has sent out an expedition completely furnished and equipped to explore the unknown ocean of the north.[20]

The suggestions of the report as to the necessity for increasing and improving the *materiel* of the Navy, and the plan recommended for reducing the *personnel* of the service to a peace standard, by the gradual abolition of certain grades of officers, the reduction of others, and the employment of some in the service of the commercial marine, are well considered and deserve the thoughtful attention of Congress.

I also recommend that all promotions in the Navy above the rank of captain be by selection instead of by seniority. This course will secure in the higher grades greater efficiency and hold out an incentive to young officers to improve themselves in the knowledge of their profession.

The present cost of maintaining the Navy, its cost compared with that of the preceding year, and the estimates for the ensuing year, are contained in the accompanying report of the Secretary of the Navy.

. . . Under the provisions of the above act,[21] I issued a proclamation calling the attention of the people of the United States to the same, and declaring my reluctance to exercise any of the extraordinary powers thereby conferred upon me, except in case of imperative necessity, but making known my purpose to exercise such powers whenever it should become necessary to do so for the purpose of securing to all citizens of the United States the peaceful enjoyment of the rights guaranteed to them by the Constitution and the laws.

After the passage of this law, information was received from time to time that combinations of the character referred to in this law existed, and were powerful in many parts of the Southern States, particularly in certain counties in the State of South Carolina.[22]

Careful investigation was made, and it was ascertained that, in nine counties of that State, such combinations were active and powerful, embracing a sufficient portion of the citizens to control the local authority, and having, among other things, the object of depriving the emancipated class of the substantial benefits of freedom, and of preventing the free political action of those citizens who did not sympathize with their own views. Among their operations were frequent scourgings and occasional assassinations, generally perpetrated at night by disguised persons, the victims in almost all cases being citizens of different political sentiments from their own, or freed persons who had shown a disposition to claim equal rights with other citizens. Thousands of inoffensive and well-disposed citizens were the sufferers by this lawless violence.

Thereupon, on the 12th of October, 1871, a proclamation was issued, in terms of the law, calling upon the members of those combinations to disperse within five days, and to deliver to the marshal or military officers of the United States all arms, ammunition, uniforms, disguises, and other means and implements used by them for carrying out their unlawful purposes

This warning not having been heeded, on the 17th of October another proclamation was issued, suspending the privileges of the writ of *habeas corpus* in nine counties in that State.

Direction was given that, within the counties so designated, persons supposed, upon creditable information, to be members of such unlawful combinations should be arrested by the military forces of the United States, and delivered to the marshal, to be dealt with according to law. In two of said counties, York and Spartanburgh, many arrests have been made. At the last account, the number of persons thus arrested was one hundred and sixty-eight. Several hundred, whose criminality was ascertained to be of an inferior degree, were released for the present. These have generally made confessions of their guilt.

Great caution has been exercised in making these arrests, and, notwithstanding the large number, it is believed that no innocent person is now in custody. The prisoners will be held for regular trial in the judicial tribunals of the United States.

As soon as it appeared that the authorities of the United States were about to take vigorous measures to enforce the law, many persons absconded, and there is good ground for supposing that all of such persons have violated the law. . . .

Under the provisions of the act of Congress approved February 21, 1871, a territorial government was organized in the District of Columbia.[23] Its results have thus far fully realized the expectations of its advocates. Under the direction of the territorial officers, a system of improvements has been inaugurated, by means of which Washington is rapidly becoming a city worthy of the nation's capital. The citizens of the District having voluntarily taxed themselves to a large amount for the purpose of contributing to the adornment of the seat of Government, I recommend liberal appropriations on the part of Congress in order that the Government may bear its just share of the expense of carrying out a judicious system of improvements. . . .

U. S. GRANT.

EXECUTIVE MANSION,
December 4, 1871.

Copy (printed), DNA, RG 130, Messages to Congress; *Senate Journal,* 42–2, 10–20; *House Journal,* 42–2, 16–27; *HED,* 42-2-1, part 1, pp. iii–xv. Ellipses represent material covered by preceding draft.
On Dec. 6, 1871, William S. Hillyer, New York City, wrote to Robert M. Douglas. ". . . The Fenton and Greely Republicans are in a terrible quandry & they dont know what to do. They hope to control the legislature. The Presidents message was a bombshell in their camp. It is just the thing. New York is safe—The authorship to one who is as familiar as I am with the Presidents style is unmistakeable. I take great pride in assuring every one that speaks of it to me that it is Grants *own message* and no mistake. . . ." ALS, Hillyer Family Papers, ViU. In 1871, William B. Allison wrote to USG praising the annual message. William Evarts Benjamin, Catalogue No. 42, March, 1892, p. 1.

1. See reference to Treaty of Washington in preceding draft annual message; message to Senate, May 10, 1871.
2. See Nevins, *Fish,* p. 518.
3. See letter of Oct. 24, 1872, from George Bancroft, U.S. minister, Berlin, to Secretary of State Hamilton Fish reporting the result of arbitration settling the boundary off Vancouver Island. LS, DNA, RG 59, Diplomatic Despatches, Germany.
4. On Jan. 15, Sir Edward Thornton, British minister, Washington, D. C., wrote to Lord Granville. "It is generally understood that whenever the Treaty of the 8th of May last may be brought to the attention of the House of R. R. for the purpose of obtaining the passage of the laws necessary for its fulfilment, General Butler will do his utmost to prevent their being carried. He will chiefly oppose the stipulations with regard to the fisheries, wh. more nearly affect his constituents   In the consideration of these constituents he has a rival in Dr Loring, who is exerting himself to succeed

Genl Butler at the next general election. With this view Dr Loring has been endeavouring to persuade the Gloucester fishermen that Genl Butler is injuring their interests in attempting to prevent legislation to carry out the fishery stipulations of the Treaty & that their object should rather be to make no opposition to them but to urge Congress to allow to the New England fishermen a bounty upon their vessels employed in the fisheries. Dr Loring who is now here, affirms that this suggestion has found great favour with Genl Butler's Constituents. In a recent conversation with Mr Fish I alluded to the proposal wh. it is said Dr Loring has arrived here for the purpose of submitting to Congress & said that it seemed to me to be opposed to the spirit of the Treaty. It was the object of the stipulations contained in that document that the Canadian and American fishermen should be put on an equal footing; whilst the American were to be allowed to fish in Canadian waters, Canadian vessels were to be allowed to import fish into American ports on the same terms as American vessels already did so. If a bounty was to be paid to the latter by the U. S., there would be no longer any equality. Mr Fish expressed his belief that a bounty was now paid by the Govt of the Dominion to ~~the~~ Canadian fishermen, wh. I said I did not think was the case. But at any rate, he replied, the Canadians could always fit out, equip & navigate their vessels at a much cheaper rate than citizens of the U. S. Mr Fish however added that he was not sorry to hear of Dr Loring's suggestion, because it would create a division amongst the enemies of the Treaty, and would render Genl Butler's opposition much weaker than it otherwise might have been. In his opinion I am inclined to acquiesce, nor do I believe there is any danger that Congress will grant any bounty whatever to the New England fishermen." Copy, Thornton Letterbook, ICarbS. See *HMD*, 42-2-64, 42-2-69.

5. See letter to John T. Hoffman, Nov. 29, 1871.

6. On Jan. 22, 1872, Thornton wrote to Granville. "I have the honour to inclose three printed copies of a Bill wh. was passed by the House of R. R. on the 16th Inst., and subsequently sent to the Senate, authorizing the President to cooperate with Gr. Britain in appointing a joint commission to survey the N. W. Boundary between the Lake of the Woods & the Rocky Mountains. The Bill assigns $50,000 for this service, making it a condition that Engineers in the regular service of the U. S. shall be employed without additional Salary. There is little doubt that the Bill will be passed by the Senate. I likewise enclose 3 copies of the debate wh. took place on the 16th Inst. on this subject. Y. L. will observe that the original proposal was to assign $100,000 for the expenses of one year of the service; but an amendment reducing the sum to $50,000 was carried by a majority of 8 votes, the numbers being 97 to 89. Mr Fish is dis-appointed at this reduction of the amount, but consoles himself with the reflection that if the Bill be passed by the Senate the work may at least be entered upon without any further delay." Copy, Thornton Letterbook, ICarbS. See Annual Message, Dec. 5, 1870, note 3; *HMD*, 42-3-20.

7. John Meredith Read, Jr., born in 1837 in Philadelphia, graduated from Albany Law School (1859) and served as N. Y. AG (1861). See *PUSG*, 19, 175, 330. On Nov. 9, 1868, Read, president, Union Republican General Committee, Albany, had written to USG. "The result in this State was a sad disappointment to your friends. The plan which worked such singular results in the City of New York, was successfully inaugurated in the interior by the Democrats. For instance—we carried five out of the ten Wards in the city of Albany, and five of the nine country towns in the County, but the Democrats rolled up fearful majorities against us in those districts where they had *all* of the Inspectors of Election. In a single Ward in this city—the First—the Democratic majority was 1800. On the day of the election our opponents

claimed 2500 maj. in the city and 3000 in the County—They only got 1850, for Seymour, in this stronghold of Democracy. Their papers abuse and vilify my father, Judge Read, for his decisions in Pennsylvania—but if we had had a few such Judges in this State, the result would have been essentially different. I congratulate the American People—not yourself—upon your election—and desire you to present my compliments to Mrs Grant." ALS, USG 3.

8. See Speech, March 10, 1871.

9. See *Calendar*, April 5, 1871.

10. On April 11, 1871, USG transmitted "to the House of Representatives, in answer to their Resolution of March 31, 1871, a report from the Secretary of State with accompanying documents." Copies, DNA, RG 59, General Records; *ibid.*, RG 130, Messages to Congress. *HED*, 42-1-18. On the same day, Fish had written to USG transmitting correspondence concerning "the occupation of Rome by the King of Italy." Copy, DNA, RG 59, General Records.

11. See *Calendar*, June 17, 1871.

12. See Proclamation, May 3, 1871.

13. See Speech, April 30, 1872.

14. See letter to Horace Capron, June 23, 1871. On Dec. 21, W. I. Squires, Mobile, wrote to Fish. "I wish to become attached to the American Commission now organizing for Japan, and as I am uninformed as to whom I should apply, I take the libery of addressing this communication to you by way of inquiry. I am a native of Ohio—twenty-six years of age—a graduate of Oberlin College—an ex-U. S. soldier, and by profession a *Civil Engineer.* Believing that Japan offers a promising field for a competent Civil Engineer who should go under the auspices of this Commission, I wish to go. I can give *satisfactory references* and *endorsements*." ALS, DNA, RG 59, Letters of Application and Recommendation.

15. Frederick F. Low. See *PUSG*, 19, 523.

16. Promoted to rear-admiral as of Dec. 31, 1869, John Rodgers assumed command of the Asiatic Squadron in 1870. On Nov. 25, 1870, Fish had written in his diary. "Robeson, had a more recent despatch from Rodgers—he inclines to the opinion that Rodgers will act more discreetly than he will write—Prsdt 'does not entertain as high an opinion of R. as most people do' I think him eccentric & erratic, & that he may need cautioning, & restraining—" DLC-Hamilton Fish.

On Nov. 6, 1871, USG wrote to Rodgers. "I have received the very interesting and valuable photographs taken during the expedition to Corea, which you sent me. Please accept my sincere thanks for them and for your kindness." Copy, DLC-USG, II, 1. See *PUSG*, 2, 185–87; letter to Hamilton Fish, Aug. 26, 1871.

17. On Jan. 16, 1872, James A. G. Beales, New York City, wrote to USG. "Being a holder of some Venezuelan Awards I take the very great liberty of occupying your valuable time by writing you upon the subject. Notwithstanding, the remarks that you kindly made in your message concerning the tardiness with which Venezuela has taken in paying her debts to American Citizens under the Awards given us— nothing so far has been done by Congress for our benefit—the United States has no Minister in Venezuela nor have we a single man of war in Venezuelan waters— would you again recommend Congress to take at once active measures to collect the balance due upon these Awards. The amount of all these Awards is not Two Millions of dollars whereof Venezuela has paid about Seventy or Eighty thousand dollars which you kindly ordered to be divided pro rata to the holders of these Awards in July last. You of course are aware that Germany has already sent an expedition to Venezuela to enforce the Claims her subjects have against that Republic. Also you are aware that Germany and France have War vessels at Hayti for the purpose of

collecting damages done their Countrymen—While we Americans are trifled with in every way by South American Republics and by Spain without any steps being taken by our own Country to obtain redress." ALS, DNA, RG 59, Miscellaneous Letters. On May 16 and 26, Fish had written in his diary. "The Venezuelan Claims is brought up, by a question from me whether any instructions shall be given to Minister Partridge who is about to return—Prsdt remarks that he considers the Awards made as so much open to suspicion that he does not feel like pressing the demand very urgently—that he will not send a vessel of war there to make the demand—He hands me a letter from H. Woodruff to Senator Fenton dated May 13, asking his intervention to obtain ten days delay before making distribution of the money recd from Venezuela among the parties holding certificates from the Commission—He desires that delay allowed—" "Govr Morton called this morning to enquire about the distribution of the Venezuela money—has been telegraphed by Orth—is told the money will soon be distributed—& why it has been delayed (in consequence of request to Prsdt—to suspend for ten days, & his direction to that effect) I mention to him the remonstrance, & petition that has been presented to the Senate—That I find no sufficient reason in it for further delay, &c." DLC-Hamilton Fish. On June 15, Henry Woodruff, New York City, telegraphed to USG. "Will you after having referred the matter to Congress now as executive sanction the notorious corruption of that Venezuelan commission by directing the distribution of the monies advanced by the Venezuelan Gov't upon a specific understanding & thereby prejudice the rights of citizens of the U States who refused to join in the corruption & whose memorial was referred by the senate to its committee on foreign relations & is still there under consideration? Permit me to call your attention to your message of March 1st 1870 the despatch of Mr Fish to Mr Partridge Nov 20th 1869 and to the memorial copy of which I send you by this evenings mail Cannot the department of state & the senator who is urging the distribution await the definite action of Congress It is well known by that senator that the majority of the senate Committee were opposed to the action of the House they having on investigation become convinced of the thorough corruption of that commission why not let this matter rest till Congress acts definitely Senator Mortons honest friends can certainly afford to wait six months We see no necessity for your taking the responsibility of distributing the rewards of corruption" Telegram received (at 6:40 P.M.), DNA, RG 59, Miscellaneous Letters. See *PUSG*, 20, 398–99; *HRC*, 42-2-29; *SD*, 55-2-223, 3–5.

18. See message to Senate, Jan. 6, 1874.

19. On Feb. 13, 1872, USG wrote to the Senate. "In answer to the Resolution adopted by the Senate on the 19th of December last, relative to questions with Spain growing out of affairs in Cuba, and to instructions to our Naval Commanders in Cuban waters, I transmit Reports from the Secretaries of State and of the Navy." DS, DNA, RG 46, Presidential Messages. *SED*, 42-2-32. On Feb. 9, Fish wrote to USG. "The Secretary of State . . . has the honor to report that practically all the information called for by the Resolution, and not before transmitted to Congress, was communicated to the House of Representatives with your Message of December 20th 1871." LS, DNA, RD 46, Presidential Messages. On the same day, Robeson wrote to USG reporting "that the orders and instructions referred to are contained in the report of the Secretary of the Navy in answer to the resolution of the House of Representatives of the 6th of December last, a copy of which, printed by the House of Representatives in executive document No. 35, is herewith transmitted." LS, *ibid*. The enclosure is *ibid*. See message to House of Representatives, Dec. 20, 1871.

On Jan. 12, 1872, Carlos Manuel de Céspedes, president, Republic of Cuba, wrote to USG. "Encouraged by the noble words in reference to this country contained in your last message, words which have gained the gratitude of all Cubans, in arms against Spain, I do not hesitate to address you, in the absence of a recognized representative in your Republic, although I perhaps thus run the risk of seeing the high position which I occupy disregarded. Your message, honorable sir, justly states that the prolongation of the present state of things in Cuba, and the lack of a prospect of a settlement, produce uneasiness and excitement in the United States. The reserve of a statesman and your natural modesty prevented you, without any doubt, from adding that it was a source of continual trouble to the American Government, rendering its attitude towards Spain and its relations with that country at least difficult, and forcing it to keep, ~~for~~ in order to protect the interests of its citizens, an expensive squadron in Cuban waters. Even if the above reasons did not exist, you might have based your apprehensions on the inconsistencies of the Spanish Government and the demoralization of the majority of its functionaries. Thus it was that the admirable recommendation was made by you to prohibit American citizens from acquiring property in countries where slavery exists, you this condemning, although indirectly, with your di[s]approbation and displeasure, a nation which, while styling itself free, maintains and encourages this institution as far as lies in its power. A proof of the demoralization to which I have referred is found in the fact that it has been proposed, in the peninsula, to farm out the custom-houses of Cuba, for a large amount, in order to avoid the immense frauds which are committed. The present state of affairs in Cuba constitute a war ~~which~~ whose existence Spain, with unjustifiable tenacity, persists in not recognizing, carrying her presumption so far as to undertake to prevent other nations from doing so, as if they had not a right to act in accordance with their own choice in such a matter, and as if the war which is being waged by the Cubans against Spanish domination were not a war of political emancipation, marked not only by the excesses of every struggle, but by all the horrors which the Spanish character has stamped upon all the wars in which Spain has been a party. Cruelty has been carried so far, sir, that not only are men put to death who are taken prisoners with arms in their hands, but also those unfortunate persons who, indifferent to the struggle and unarmed, have remained in the rural districts where they were born or brought up; all those who, taking no part in the contest, live outside of the towns, either on account of their want of means, or because they are unaccustomed to town-life. But, like everything that is abnormal, untrue, and that is not based upon the immovable foundations of justice, this denial of the existence of a war on the part of the Peninsular Government has been found unsustainable. That Government has in vain applied the name of brigandage to the Cuban revolution, ~~which is~~ carried on by an organized army, which is daily led to battle and victory by officers of distinct grades, subject, as are the soldiers, to a law of military organization, punished, when guilty of any misdemeanor, by legislative enactments, and rewarded by the same according to their merits. The 'Diario de la Marina' may be considered as the organ of the Spanish authorities of Cuba; this journal dedicates its editorial column, in addition to the others, almost exclusively to the war in Cuba; and both in its original articles, and when it inserts decrees of the home government, allowing some play to reason and common sense, it admits the existence of this state of war, laments the losses caused thereby to fortunes, and while, true to its Spanish instincts, it honors progress and human improvement with no consideration, its tone is very loud and pompous in regard to every thing that relates to the loss of wealth. The bill introduced in the Cortes in October, 1871, for the payment of the Cuban debt, was recently printed in that journal; the product of the war subsidy is to be devoted to this end; it published, moreover, the following statements, which reveal the importance of the contest, and show what a burden it is to the Spanish treasury; the admitted expenses of the civil war up to October, 1871, were 314,500,000 pesetas; (the value of the peseta is 20 cents) the amount estimated as the expenditure for 1871–72, is 137,407,852.86 pesetas; while the deficit on account of the war amounts to 30 or 40 millions of pesetas. It is seen from the above that Havana is threatened with a commercial crisis, on account of the present illegal condition of the bank, and on account of the depreciation of the paper money with which the city is flooded; it is also evident that a civil war exists; this is plainly shown by the desire expressed by King Amadeo I. to come to Cuba and take command in person, in order to bring about the pacification of the island; such a desire would certainly never have been manifested, if, instead of the powerful forces which form our organized army, there were but a few bands of marauders who obeyed no combined and preconceived plan of war, insignificant in number, and with men of no character for their leaders. Finally, the statement published by the same journal, that volunteers and arms had been received at Havana from New York, for the army, is a further proof of the existence of a war. The frightful scenes which have recently been enacted at Havana, the political murder of several youths, and the imprisonment, with the vilest criminals, of a large number of young men, were acts of ferocity more in accordance with the character of bloodthirsty tigers than of defenders of a pretended national integrity, based on the absurd right of conquest, and maintained with the most stupid ignorance and the most sordid avarice; they were acts which, by reason of their atrocious character and the atmosphere of blood which they produced, doubtless caused you deep grief. I will not speak of them at length, Mr. President; the feeble nature of man has not the super-human self-control which would be required of me, in speaking of such a matter, by the respect which I owe to you and by my own dignity and the high office which I hold. It would not be in harmony with my character to waste many words upon the boasts constantly uttered by the Spaniards concerning the immense forces which, say they, are being levied in Spain, in order to make war upon your nation, if, acting in accordance with what it may deem its duty, it should dare to recognize the independence of Cuba; this is all the more insulting to the United States, inasmuch as I do not remember that similar language was used in relation to the English protectorate which was granted to the Venezuelans, during their war of independence, nor in relation to the British legion which took part in it, and made many a Spanish soldier bite the dust. I cannot, however, avoid adverting to the fact that, notwithstanding the infamy with which you branded the Spanish Government in the note addressed by Mr. Fish July 9th, 1870, to Mr. Lopez-Roberts, Spanish Minister at Washington, in reference to a proclamation issued by Count Valmaseda, which document threatened the extermination of an entire people, the said Count has recently issued an order, which, in spirit and tendency is only a second edition of that proclamation. I have the satisfaction of informing you, Mr. President, that very nearly at the same time, I granted a pardon, and issued orders to my officers, which were inspired by the sentiments of humanity which civilization demands. The 'Bandera Española' a paper published at Santiago de Cuba, and also a Government organ, says in an editorial that not even foreigners should be exempted from the newly created patrol-service. Thus, while it indirectly declares that a civil war exists (this being the only case in which the compulsory employment of foreigners in this capacity is authorized, and then only for the preservation of order) it creates a new source of trouble to your Government, by reason of the way in which this suggestion may affect American citizens. The detention by force, and the search on the high seas of a vessel sailing under the honored flag of the United States, by a Spanish vessel of war, is an act which the Spanish press in the island of

Cuba has undertaken to defend on the ground that it was a right recognized among belligerents, which is a tacit admission that the Cubans have such a character, as no war can exist without an adversary; the Spaniards assumed this in order to exercise the right of search on board of a neutral vessel, sailing in neutral waters, because they suspected it of carrying aid to the Cubans; now who was the other belligerent party, if not that which the vessel in question was, as they allege, seeking to aid? The principles defended by the Cubans, and the form of Government which they have established, written in the constitution promulgated by them, render it the duty of the United States, more than of any other power, to favor them. If, from motives of humanity, and in the interest of civilization, all nations are under obligations to interest themselves in behalf of Cuba, demanding a termination of the war which she is waging against Spain, the United States have a duty to perform which is imposed upon them by the political principles which they profess, proclaim and defend. To the public and official manifestation of the sympathies in our favor of that country which gave birth to Washington and Lincoln, and to so many martyrs to the social emancipation of a race, there can only be opposed motives of selfishness, fears of expense likely to arise from an imaginary war, which, should it be quixotically undertaken, would soon be terminated by the force which right and justice give. The expense which is now incurred by the United States, on account of the present abnormal state of things, will, perhaps, in the long run, be quite equal to the expense of a war. These outlays, moreover, are now productive of no benefit to the country, and, in a measure, compromise the honor and dignity of the country. You know, Mr. President, by experience, that the Cubans can expect nothing from the promises of Spain, and that it is in vain to expect that country to become convinced of the advantage which she would derive from recognizing our independence. Our struggle, like all these of its kind, will be long, but the act which justice demands of you, Mr. President, i. e. the recognition of our belligerency and independence, would shorten it very much. Excuse me, sir, if in the midst of your numerous and important occupations, I appeal to you, not as a suppliant, but in order to furnish to you the occasion of performing this act. Believe, Honorable President, that if you do so, a thousand families will bless your name, and you will gain, beside the profound gratitude of my country, the admiration of your most faithful servant," LS (in Spanish), DNA, RG 59, Notes from Foreign Legations, Cuba; translation, *ibid.* See Nevins, *Fish*, p. 637.

20. See *PUSG*, 20, 135–37, 209.

21. See reference to the "Ku Klux Law" in the previous draft annual message.

22. See Proclamations, March 24 and May 3, 1871.

23. See letter to Hannibal Hamlin, Feb. 21, 1871.

To Senate

—————

Washington, December 4. 1871.

To THE SENATE OF THE UNITED STATES.

I nominate the persons herein named for re-appointment in the Army of the United States.

Satterlee C. Plummer.[1] late Captain of the Seventh Regiment of Cavalry. (who resigned under the proceedings of the Board, convened under Section 11. of the Act of July 15, 1870, to examine officers unfit for the proper discharge of their duties, for any cause except injuries incurred, or disease contracted in the line of duty,) to be Captain in the Seventh Cavalry, to fill the vacancy created by the death of Captain Edward Myers,[2] Seventh Cavalry, on July 11. 1871.

William P. Bainbridge[3] late First Lieutenant in the Third Regiment of Cavalry, (who was mustered out under the proceedings of the Board, convened under Section 11. of the Act of July 15, 1870 to examine officers unfit for the proper discharge of their duties. for any cause except injuries incurred, or disease contracted in the line of duty.) to be First Lieutenant in the Third Cavalry, to fill the vacancy created by the death of First Lieutenant H. B. Cushing,[4] Third Cavalry, on May 5. 1871.

U. S. GRANT

DS, DNA, RG 46, Nominations. On Sept. 9, 1871, Secretary of War William W. Belknap had written to the AG. "The President directs that 1st Lt. Bainbridge formerly 3d Cavalry (dismissed thro Special Bd act 15. July 70) Capt. Wm M. Maynadier formerly 1st Artillery Capt. S. C. Plummer formerly 7th Cavalry (forced to resign under report of Hancocks Bd) be restored by re-appointment to the grades formerly occupied by them—when vacancies occur in same Regiments." AN (initialed), *ibid.*, RG 94, ACP, 5449 1871. On Sept. 12, Maj. Thomas M. Vincent, AGO, wrote a memorandum. "Under the Order of the President, letters of Appointment are herewith, in Cases of Plummer & Bainbridge, vacancies having occurred in their former regiments. But, is it not the intention of the President that Nominations to the senate, shall first be made? The Opinions of the Attornies General evidently adopt that as the Course. The views of the Senate, in regard to the restoration of an ex-officer in advance of Confirmation by that body, will appear from a Copy, herewith, of a Resolution, in Case of James W. Schamburg, an officer who had left the service by resignation. Also in the Case of Gen. Blair, who resigned in '64—see Senate Resolution herewith. As to officers who have been dismissed the service, by Sentence of Court Martial—see the act Appd. July 28. '66, Copy herewith. That the Cases of officers who were dismissed under reports of the Board (Hancock's) Convened under sec. 11 of the act appd July 15, 1870 should follow the same course, woul[d] seem from the report of the J. A. General, dated Nov. 30. 1870, relative to Certain questions arising at the organization of the Board. That Opinion pronounced the board, practically, a CourtMartial, the proceedings being 'a trial' and the authority of the board to dismiss being 'even more final than in that of a CourtMartial'" ADS, *ibid.* Related papers are *ibid.* On April 26, 1875, Belknap wrote that "The President directs that 1st Lt. Thos. L. Thornburg—2d Artillery & William M. Maynadier be appointed Paymasters in the Army" ANS, *ibid.*, 1892 1875. Related papers are *ibid.*

1. Son of Brig. Gen. Joseph B. Plummer, who died Aug. 9, 1862, at Corinth, Miss., Satterlee C. Plummer, USMA 1865, served as 1st lt., 17th Inf., transferred to the 26th Inf. in Sept., 1866, and was promoted to capt. in June, 1868. On March 5, 1869, Plummer, Washington, D. C., wrote to USG. "I have the honor to respectfully request the appointment of Paymaster in the U. S. Army, or a transfer to the commissary or Quartermasters Dept." ALS, DLC-Elihu B. Washburne. On Aug. 9, Plummer transferred to the 7th Cav.

On Jan. 13, 1871, Col. Samuel D. Sturgis, 7th Cav., Fort Leavenworth, wrote to USG. "I would respectfully beg to offer a word in behalf of Capt S. C. Plummer late of my Regiment. I have known Capt Plummer from his youth, and there is much in him that is admirable. A great deal (if not all) the trouble into which he has unfortunately fallen, has arisen, in my opinion, from mere exuberance of spirits, together with his youthfulness and his very impulsive character, from which last he too often acts without counting the cost; but he is generous to a fault; industrious and attentive to his duties; brave beyond all doubt or cavil and I beleive that with the discretion which comes with years, he would make one of the most useful, gallant and dashing officers in the service. The claim to leniency which might ~~be~~ be urged in his favor from a consideration of the Eminent service rendered to the country by his gallant Father, the late lamented Genl J. B. Plummer, is too well known to your Excellency for me to dwell upon it. Commending his case to your Excellency's favorable consideration, . . ." ALS, DNA, RG 94, ACP, P400 CB 1870. On Jan. 23, Brig. Gen. John Pope wrote a similar letter to USG. LS, *ibid.* On March 30, Frances H. Plummer, Washington, D. C., wrote to USG. "I feel so anxious about my son, and have hoped each day to see by the papers that his name had been sent in to the senate to fill the vacancy of a Captain who died some months ago belonging to the 5th Cavalry, you know you promised to appoint him to the first vacancy of his grade in the cavalry, and since the confirmation of Col. Belger by the senate I have no fear but they would confirm his appointment As you have sons of your own you can appreciate and feel for the boy who has only his Mother to aid him, Please give me an answer!" ALS, *ibid.* USG endorsed this letter. "Refered to the Sec. of War." AE (initialed and undated), *ibid.* On July 18, Frances Plummer wrote to USG. "I saw in the Paper the death of Capt. Meyer 7th U. S. Cavalry. and now hasten to remind you of your promise, that my son should have the first Vacancy of his grade in his old Regt I feel so anxious my son should be restored to the profession for which he was educated, & which he proved himself so qualified to fill, He was faithful to his duty as a soldier, & during the time he was in the Army did hard service in Texas & the West. He has been unable to obtain employment, & the little money he received after the reduction by the Goverment on the final settlement of his Accounts, is almost gone, and my heart is nearly broken with the thought of what will become of him, for the want of some kind friend to place him in a position, so that with his past experience, he may start anew, and be the comfort & support of my old age. God bless you for what you have already done for me, in getting me a *clerkship* in the *Pension Office*, which I received the 1st of July, & thank you, & words cannot express my gratitude for it. With the best wishes of my heart for you & yours . . ." ALS, *ibid.* On July 21, Horace Porter endorsed this letter. "Respectfully referred to the Sec. of War The President did promise to appoint Mrs. Plummer's son." AES, *ibid.*

On Oct. 10, Lt. Col. George A. Custer, 7th Cav., Louisville, wrote to Belknap. "Having been credibly informed from various sources that the friends of S. C. Plummer, late Captain in the 7th. Cavalry, are endeavoring to secure the reappointment, or reinstatement, of the latter to the rank of Captain in the Army I desire to submit for the consideration of the appointing power the following statement regarding the past conduct and character of a person who to escape dishonorable ejectment resigned his commission, but, who now seeks to repossess himself of it. S. C. Plummer to my certain knowledge is devoid of honor, irresponsible in character, lacking in principle and in my opinion, in which I believe the sentiment of the majority, if not of all the officers, who knew him most intimately, sustains me, is not only unfitted but wholly unworthy to hold the commission of an Officer of the Army. He has repeatedly disgraced the uniform he wore and brought discredit upon the service generally. It is widely known that if the power of the law which he is well known to have violated was fairly applied to him he would now be serving out his term of punishment at some one of the military prisons instead of being an applicant for a place for which he has proven his utter unworthiness. I have known him to be guilty of wilfull falsehood and of highly dishonorable conduct in business transactions. I was also informed, while in New York the past summer, of various acts committed by him in the City of New York, since his forced resignation from the service which I have every reason to believe were truthfully related. He was accused by citizens of good standing with having procured money from various parties upon worthless checks signed by himself and drawn upon a bank or banks in Washington, D. C., in which he had no credit nor had he ever had any. These checks were cashed upon his representation that he was still an officer of the Army. But a few months prior to his resignation he drew his pay twice for the same month and only escaped trial therefor by resigning. He disposed of a mileage account against the Government and afterwards presented the same account for payment at a different point. Upon both of these charges he would have been tried had he remained in service, should he return to the Army as a commissioned Officer they will still confront him. It can be proven that while at Fort Leavenworth, Ks. he purloined money from the drawer of the Trader's store. Numerous other charges could be sustained against him if deemed requisite. His reinstatement to his former position in this regiment (7th Cavalry) would work to the serious detriment of those officers who thereby would be deprived of the promotion to which they consider themselves justly entitled. I therefor respectfully request that if his return to the regiment or to the Army as a commissioned Officer is under consideration that this communication may be laid before his Excellency the President who from his past as well as present relations to the service will give due weight to the statements herein made." LS, *ibid.*

On June 11, 1872, Diddie L. Plummer, Washington, D. C., wrote to USG. "I wanted to see you so much this morning, but found you had left, and perhaps you may not read this, but still I write it, for who can the Fatherless go to, if not to the Saviour of our Country—our dear good President. Genl., Brother and I have no Father to speak for us, nor freind in power, but you, and let me tell your our grievances, and how terribly he has been villified and slandered. Soon after your sent in his name to the Senate, Genl Custer said he should *never be confirmed*, and wrote that here, in his letter to the Committee, and too truly has his words been fulfilled, he also wrote the most malicious letters to all the Senators, and circulated the vilest slanders all over the country. My Brother went before the Committee and refuted all the charges, and they reported him favorably, and as soon as Custer was notified of that by one of his spies here, he wrote other letters, until he had his way, and prevented my Brother from having the justice done him, which you so nobly intended him to have, and because that justice keeps Custer's brother from a file in the Regt, he has gone to any lengths, any persecution to accomplish that end, and Senator Wilson will tell you I speak the truth. Oh; Genl my heart is broken. Mother and I have been all winter waiting and hoping to have his good name vindicated by his confirmation, even if he resigned the day afterwards. Genl do still keep that place

open for him, send his name in again, for *Gods sake,* for the sake of the widow and
the fatherless girl who pleads to you, dont let our enemy be more powerful thatn
our freind, though he thinks he is,   do this Genl. and you'll receive the eternal
gratitude of a girl, who will never cease to bless you, for listening to her prayer, in
behalf of her brother, her only protector in all the world. God grant it!" ALS, *ibid.*
On Dec. 12, USG renominated Plummer, but the Senate rejected the nomination.

   On May 28, 1875, Satterlee Plummer, Washington, D. C., wrote to USG. "Will
you please reccommend me for a clerkship in the State Dept: speaking to the Secretary today. You cannot imagine how much I dislike to trouble you, and would not
do so were it not necessary. Whatever positions I have held have been merely temporary ones, and since leaving the Army, have been unfortunate in being connected
with Companies which have failed. Viz 'Samana Bay Co' & 'Texas Mining Co'. I
would like at least to be taken on trial, at the 'State Dept' Please grant my request."
ALS, *ibid.,* RG 59, Letters of Application and Recommendation. On Nov. 23, Plummer wrote to USG. "It seems that with requests I must be ever troubling you. There
is a vacancy now in the Commissary Dept. made by the death of 'Col Taylor.' Senator
Dawes and Spencer both signed my application to you, and Senator Spencer who is
a member of the Milty Comt, said that there would be no opposition, as it was not
in the line of the Army: He said you had misunderstood him in regard to what he
said about confirmation, and that it would with me, be all right. Please give *me
another chance;* and you shall have no cause to regret it. If the Commissary position
is promised, there is a vacancy of Capt & Milty. store keeper Q. M. Dept" ALS, *ibid.,*
RG 94, ACP, P400 CB 1870. On May 1, 1876, USG nominated Plummer as 2nd lt.,
4th Inf. On Aug. 18, Plummer, "Camp on Yellowstone Mouth of Tongue River,"
wrote to USG. "By the sad fate of some of my old comrades of the 7th cavalry, there
are a number of vacancies of 2nd Lt in that arm of the service. I prefer the cavalry,
will you have me transfered. I at present am serving at Gen'l Merritts request (of
Gen'l Crook) with his regiment and have been since joining this command with
recruits, and would like to be transfered to the 5th Cav there are vacancies. . . . (My
company not here, in the field at my own request)" ALS, *ibid.* On Oct. 6, USG
endorsed this letter. "Referred to the Sec. of War. I have no objection to the transfer
requested." AES, *ibid.* Following a court-martial for dereliction of duty and intoxication, Plummer was dismissed from the army on July 1, 1877. Related papers are
ibid. See *PUSG,* 15, 570; *New York Times,* Nov. 15, 1881.

   2. Edward Myers, born in Germany, joined the 1st Dragoons as a private in
1857. Continuing with the regt. (designated the 1st Cav. in 1861) through the Civil
War, he was promoted to 2nd lt. (1862) and 1st lt. (1863) and bvt. capt., maj., and
lt. col. In 1866, Myers was assigned as capt., 7th Cav.

   3. William P. Bainbridge, 2nd lt., 101st Ind., was wounded at Chickamauga, and
became capt. on the staff of Maj. Gen. Joseph J. Reynolds in 1864. In 1865, Bainbridge was assigned as 2nd lt., 3rd Cav. See *PUSG,* 18, 440–41. On March 6, 1871,
Reynolds, as col., 3rd Cav., Washington, D. C., wrote to USG. "I have the honor
respectfully to solicit the re-appointment, as a 1st Lieut. in the line of the Army, of
William P. Bainbridge late 1st Lieut 3rd Cavalry—I respectfully invite attention to
the record in Lieut B's case—There is nothing therein derogatory to his character
as an officer & a gentleman—The decision in his case was made before the receipt
of the sworn testimony of his most important witnesses—Although mustered out
for 'physical disability . . .' the complete record now shows that (while weighing only
about 120 pounds) in *eight years* service, he has not been *a day* on sick report, has
never been off duty, nor neglected any duty—His habits are unexceptionable—

Among those who applied to transfer with Lieut. Bainbridge was Lieut C. M. Edwards who has been retired leaving a vacancy in the 10th Infantry—I would respectfully request that Lieut Bainbridge be appointed to that regiment ... P. S. If a reappointment cannot be made I respy. apply for Lieut. Bainbridge to be appointed *as Second Lieutenant* (in a regiment in the Dept of Texas if practicable)" ALS, DNA, RG 94, ACP, B1358 CB 1864. On June 12, 1873, Reynolds, West Point, N. Y., wrote to USG. "I have the honor to request that *Wm P. Bainbridge late 1st Lieut 3rd Cavalry* be reappointed a *2d Lieut* in the same regiment—There are now two vacancies in this regiment—The address is Old Point Comfort Virginia—" ALS, *ibid.* Related papers are *ibid.; ibid.*, RG 46, Nominations. Bainbridge did not return to the army.

4. Howard B. Cushing, private, 1st Ill. Art. (1862–63) and 2nd lt., 4th Art., joined the 3rd Cav. in Sept., 1867. Promoted to 1st lt. in Dec., 1867, Cushing was killed in a skirmish with Apaches in Arizona Territory. See Dan L. Thrapp, *The Conquest of Apacheria* (Norman, 1967), pp. 63–78.

To John M. Brodhead

Washington. D. C. Dec: 5. 71.

SIR:

I have to state in reference to the Secret Service fund expended by me during the last quarter of 1861 and first two quarters of 1862, that, the whole amount was disbursed on account of Secret Service, but that vouchers for the balance of two hundred and ninety-nine dollars and eighty two cents ($299 82.) were either not taken, or if taken cannot now be found.

Very respectfully
Yours
U. S. GRANT.

HON: J. M. BRODHEAD
SECOND COMPT: TREASURY.

Copy, DLC-USG, II, 1. On Dec. 13, 1871, John Potts, chief clerk, War Dept., wrote to Ezra B. French, second auditor. "I hereby certify that Major General U. S. Grant, U. S. Army, has on file in this office, vouchers amounting to four thousand two hundred and twenty five dollars ($4225.) for expenditures for secret service, for the period from the 4th quarter of 1861 to April, 1863, inclusive; that the vouchers are satisfactory to, and are approved by the Secretary of War. The amount of them will therefore be passed to the credit of General Grant." Copy, DNA, RG 107, Letters Sent, Military Affairs. On Dec. 14, French wrote a similar letter to Allen Rutherford, third auditor. Copy, *ibid.*, RG 217, Second Auditor, Letters Sent. See letter to John M. Brodhead, Dec. 31, 1875.

To William Elrod

———

Washington D. C. Dec. 7th *1871*

DEAR ELROD:

Enclosed I send you a check for $500 00/100 and am glad to hear you say it is the last that will be wanted. I have no objection to clearing out the little strip of timber between me and Long that you speak of.

Has the three year old filley "Beauty" been broken? I did not intend her to be but wanted to keep her for breeding. She is fine blooded and of troting stock though a natural pacer herself. I hope she will get with foal next Spring.—Have you burned any lime yet?—I do not care to get any other breeds of cattle than those I have now. In time we will have all Alderney, if they do well, and then make butter and feed the skimed milk to the calves.

Yours Truly
U. S. GRANT

ALS, Dorothy Elrod, Marissa, Ill.

To Amos T. Akerman

———

Washington, D. C. Dec 12 *1867*1.

HON. A. T. AKERMAN ATTORNEY GENERAL.

SIR:

Circumstances convince me that a change in the office which you now hold is advisable, consulting the best interests of the government, and I therefore ask your resignation. In doing so, however, I wish to express my approbation of the zeal, integrity and industry which you have shown in the performance of all your duties, and the confidence I feel personally, by tendering to you, the Florida Judgeship[1] now vacant, or that of Texas.[2]

Should any foreign mission at my disposal, without a removal for the express purpose of making a vacancy, better suit your taste, I would gladly testify my appreciation in that way.

My personal regard for you is such that I could not bring myself to saying what I here say through the medium of a letter. Nothing but a consideration for public sentiment could induce me to indite this.

I am &c

U S GRANT

Copy, USG 3; Df, *ibid.* On Dec. 15, 1871, Attorney Gen. Amos T. Akerman wrote to USG. "Upon the subject of the appointments of which you were so kind as to tender me the choice in your letter of the 13th instant, I have concluded that I could not be useful in any of the diplomatic positions referred to, and that a due regard to the health of my family would forbid a residence in either of the districts in which there are vacant judgeships; and therefore, with many thanks for the offer, I feel bound to decline it." ALS, Free Library of Philadelphia, Philadelphia, Pa. On Dec. 12, 1871, a correspondent had reported: "The President has been semi-officially informed by members of the Supreme Court that Attorney-General Akerman was hardly competent for his high position, and that, in consequence, many most important interests of the government were being continually sacrificed. The President replied that he would have to bring about a remedy as soon as possible. . . ." *Philadelphia Inquirer*, Dec. 13, 1871. See also *New York Tribune*, Dec. 12, 1871.

1. On Nov. 17, George Opdyke, New York City, had written to USG. "I have learned that the name of Edward Fitch, Esqr of this City, will be urged for the position of Judge of the United States District Court for Southern District of Florida. From the knowledge I have of Mr Fitch, and from the assurances of mutual friends, I believe that he is well qualified for the position, and that his nomination would be satisfactory to the mercantile and commercial interests of this City, and I should be pleased to have his application meet a favorable consideration." LS, NNP. On Dec. 7, U.S. Representative William A. Wheeler of N. Y. wrote to USG. "Learning that the Hon. Edward Fitch of New York is a candidate for the office of District Judge of the Southern district of Florida, I take great pleasure in certifying to his high character and eminent fitness for the position. I do this understandingly, having known Mr. Fitch intimately for more than twenty five years. This appointment will give great satisfaction to my dist—the banner dist. of the State of New York—of which he was formerly a resident, Believing that the public interests will be subserved by the appt; of Mr. Fitch, I earnestly commend him to your favorable consideration," ALS, OFH. On May 11, 1872, Edward Fitch, New York City, wrote to USG. "Referring to the bill commonly known as 'The Goat Island Bill' now pending in the Senate of the United States and especially to the provisions therein contained relative to the appointment of three commissioners with the powers and for the purposes therein mentioned; permit me respectfully to request you, in case the said bill shall become a law, to appoint me one of the said commissioners. And as touching my qualifications and fitness for the appointment which I now ask, allow me to refer to the petitions and recommendations heretofore presented to you, wherein my appointment to the office of Judge of the United States District Court for the Southern District of Florida, then vacant, was asked." ALS, DNA, RG 59, Letters of Application and Recommendation. See *New York Times*, June 20, 1873.

On Jan. 15, 1872, USG nominated James W. Locke as judge, Southern District,

Fla. Born in 1837 in Wilmington, Vt., Locke had practiced law at Key West after service in the U.S. Navy and held positions as clerk of the U.S. court, county judge, and Fla. senator.

2. On March 8, 1871, Benjamin F. Grafton, Richard M. Corwine, and U.S. Senator James W. Flanagan of Tex., Washington, D. C., had written to USG. "We have the honor to recommend for appointment as Judge of the District Court of the United States, for the Eastern District of Texas, Judge Bird W. Gray a citizen of Jefferson Marion County Texas. Judge Gray has been on the bench a number of years in Texas, is an able lawyer—a sound republican, and in every way fitted for the position." DS, DNA, RG 60, Records Relating to Appointments. On March 10, USG endorsed this letter. "I approve this appointment." AES, *ibid.* On March 15, Akerman wrote to USG. "I have recalled from the State Department, and herewith transmit to you the resolution of the Senate, of March 10, 1871, advising and consenting to the appointment of Bird W. Gray to be District Judge of the U. S. for the Eastern District of Texas. This is the resolution which the Senate, by its resolution of March 13, instant, requests you to return to that body. I send to you also the latter resolution." Copy, *ibid.*, Letters Sent to Executive Officers. On March 17, USG wrote to the Senate. "In answer to the resolution of the Senate of the 13th instant, I have the honor to return herewith the Senate's resolution of the 10th instant, advising and consenting to the appointment of Bird W. Gray to be District Judge of the United States for the Eastern District of Texas." DS, *ibid.*, RG 46, Nominations. On May 15, USG again nominated Gray; the nomination was tabled.

On Jan. 30, 1869, Daniel Ullman, Piermont, N. Y., had written to USG. "The friends of Colonel John Appleton of Bangor, Maine, inform me that the post of Commissioner to the Sandwich Islands will soon become vacant, and request me to address you in his behalf. Colonel Appleton served under me for more than a year, and proved himself to be a good and faithful officer. His Regiment, the 81st U. S. C. Infy, was equal to any I ever had in my Command,..." ALS, *ibid.*, RG 59, Letters of Application and Recommendation. Related papers are *ibid.* On April 26, 1870, USG nominated John F. Appleton as judge, Eastern District, Tex.; Appleton declined.

On April 28, 1870, Flanagan wrote to USG. "The undersigned members of the Texas Delegation would respectfully desire to protest against the Selection of a man out their State for the position of Judge of the Eastern Dist of Texas and would respectfully request that you recall the nomination already made and in lieu thereof suggest that of C. B. Sabin of Harris County Texas a resident of that Judicial District" LS, *ibid.*, RG 60, Records Relating to Appointments. U.S. Representatives William T. Clark and George W. Whitmore of Tex. favorably endorsed this letter. AES (undated), *ibid.* On March 21 and April 22, Chauncey B. Sabin, Houston and Washington, D. C., had written to USG. "I have this day enclosed to the Attorney General reccommendatory papers for your consideration in connection with my name for the appointment of Associate Judge for the Eastern District of Texas. Judge Watrous having long since become incapacitated by paralysis from the discharge of his duties our political friends pitched upon me as his Successor whenever the law might authorize it which I believe is now being passed. I did not present the subject to you while in Washington as I regarded it as premature ..." "In accordance with the suggestions of the Attorney General I make some statements concerning myself. I am about 46 years of age a native of Otsego County New York and studied my profession in that State from '40 until '47 when I was admitted in all its highest Courts. In the latter part of 1847 I emigrated to Texas and settled in Houston where I have resided ever since. I confined my attention strictly to the practice of my profession and in 1860 and for years before was at the head of my profession in my locality as the records of the Courts will show. I was always a Union man but was compelled to remain inside of the rebellion until 1863 when I managed to escape. While there although I was compelled to appear to favor secession I was nevertheless under surveillance. On my arrival in New York via Mexico & Havanna I espoused Prest Lincoln's Emancipation Proclamation and lectured all winter through the interior of New York in its behalf and also stumped Connecticutt in 1864. In 1865 I returned to Texas and in the fall of that year deeming my residence there unsafe I sold out all my available property & came north again & in 1866 assisted in organizing the Southern Loyalists 3rd of Septr Convention at Phila the call for which was drawn by Mr Sherwood and myself. I defeated the attempt to adjourn that body *sine die* before taking action on the negro suffrage question. I stumped Long Island in the fall of 1866 and immediately after the campaign organized the Southern Republican Association which met in this city with the Hon T. J. Durant as President and led off in the move to give the 39th Congress a welcome and after the passage of the reconstruction laws I returned to Houston and in July '67 with eight other white men organized the Republican Party in that State and have labored sedulously from that day to this to demoralize the rebel element and outside of the executive aid have done more than any other man to build up the party in that State. I held the first mixed meetings of all classes and colors that ever were held there and established free speech in my locality so much so that the politicians from other localities came there to hold their meetings and deliver their addresses and the General disbanded or broke up the Post. In thus laboring for years I have exhausted all my resources and bestowed all my time and energies. I am not a *registered voter* in Texas and the new Constitution prevents any but registered voters from holding *State office.* What technical disabilities I might have had from being in the Rebellion have been removed. I always *refused* office or position from the rebels but I had paid taxes & made some contributions which I could not avoid with safety   I presume that almost every other union man (South) has done the same. Any how whatever the law is about that I am through. I have written largely for Union papers in & out of Texas but particularly for the Houston Union to the existence of which I greatly contributed. I have had a judicial experience of about 16 months and was very popular as a Judge. I have the confidence and sympathies of the Republican masses of Texas and also that of the bar and the business public. I labored very hard last year to thwart the acquisition of power by the rebels through an early election. Genl Reynolds wrote me Janry 29 '70 offering to put me on the Supreme Bench but I did not receive the letter until my return to Texas but this appointment was merely complementary & only lasts a few days and my name having been accidentally omitted on the last engrossment of a disability bill it placed me in rather an embarrassing position particularly as I had been so prominent a Republican and my bill having been delayed some *Eighteen Months* before its sudden passage. As I had laid my papers before you for Judge of the Eastern Dist of Texas after the announcement of the passage of my name & before the discovery of the mistake as soon as I learned of its accidental omission I came to Washington to explain it to you. I have no other hope now than through you and I respectfully Submit my name for your favorable consideration. Could you understand the true position of everything I should not have to solicit this office, it would be offered to me. Aside from public consideration I do not feel that with the final triumph of our cause that it is right to suffer myself to be ignored after wasting a fortune in behalf of my country and years of my time and energies. I have always stood back and given way to others in order to build up the cause and I feel now that it is but right for me to ask for a position which the community & the Party expect me to fill." ALS, *ibid.* On May 11, Flanagan and Whitmore wrote to USG. "Being very solicitous for the appointment of some person who has labored with us in the Struggle to build up Republicanism in Texas as Judge of the Eastern District of Texas we again respectfully call your attention to the propriety of reconsidering the nomination already made and again suggest the name of C B Sabin for your favorable consideration . . ." LS, *ibid.* On May 22, U.S. Senator Morgan C. Hamilton wrote to Frederick T. Dent. "In connection with the Judgeship for Texas I handed to the President a few days since, three letters with a newspaper slip for perusal, which I desire may be returned to me by the Messenger" ALS, *ibid.*, Letters from the President. On May 23, USG endorsed this letter. "Will the Atty. Gen. please send the papers called for by Senator Hamilton." AES, *ibid.* On June 21, C. C. Gillespie, Houston, wrote to USG. "Pardon the liberty I take in addressing you. I was a Confederate Colonel during the war, and an opponent of Congressional reconstruction until your election. Since then, the griefs and passions of the war having passed away, I have been a hearty supporter of your administration, and of the National Policy of the Republican party. Since the election of Gov. Davis, I have been, and am still, the writing editor of the 'Houston Union', the chief Republican organ in this State. I have the friendship and confidence of Gov. Davis, and of the leading Republicans of Texas. I have made this statement to introduce to your Excellency my earnest recommendation that you appoint Hon. C. B. Sabin to the Federal Judgeship left vacant by the retirement of Judge Watrous. I have known Judge Sabin for sixteen years, both as a political opponent and a political friend. I know him to be the original apostle of the genuine Republican party in Texas as now organized. I am as good a witness on this point as there is in the state; for, as once the journalistic leader of the opposition, he was the first and the most formidable man I had to fight. He was working for the Republican party, laying its foundations, and rendering its principles more acceptable, when the other men, however excellent, who have been elevated, were doing nothing, knew not what to do, and had no hope. He is the first man in Texas whom I ever heard set forth before the people the doctrine of 'equal rights for all.' And yet, the mass of our people, without regard to politics, had rather see him in this Judgship than any other man. He has the confidence of all, and there is no bitterness toward him. He is, just what Republicanism needs in Texas—firm in principle and gentle in spirit. As a jurist he needs no recommendation. I write this of my own motion, from my own standpoint, in opposition to nobody, in consultation with nobody, but from a sense of truth and justice." ALS, *ibid.*, Records Relating to Appointments. On Aug. 18, Sabin, Houston, wrote to USG on the same subject. ". . . Senator Flanagan has withdrawn his support but if I am nominated I am confident that Morgan Hamilton will assent to my confirmation. Senator Flanagan came out here on a grand Rail Road scheme and got defeated and wrote a very abusive letter on the administration to Govr Davis It was very demoralizing to the party in its character and I had to handle him without gloves in the Union on which I was writing   I hope it will improve the tone of his Republicanism even it it falls a little heavy on me" ALS, *ibid.* Related papers are *ibid.* On July 26, 1873, Sabin, Galveston, wrote to USG. "I desire respectfully to solicit of you the appointment of District Attorney of the United States for the Eastern District of Texas" ALS, *ibid.*

On June 21, 1870, Jefferson Falkner, Montgomery, Ala., had written to USG. "Learning that there is a vacancy in the office of Judge of the Dist. Court of the U. S. for the State of Texas I very respectfully ask the appointment. For my qualifications fitness for the position &c. I can only refer you to those of the delegation from this State who know me, viz Hon. Mr. Warner of the Senate & Messers. C. W. Buckley & R. S. Heflin of the House I state that I have made the profession of Law the business of my life am now sixty years of age and am vain enough to believe that if appointed can discharge the duties of the office to the satisfaction of the people and give you no cause of regret. I deem it proper to state that since the close of the War I have not engaged in the political strife that has prevailed in the country but have invariably advised all with whom I have associated to obey the laws and C[o]nstitution and cherfully submit to those in authority and expect to pursue the same course in the future, . . ." ALS, *ibid.*

On Sept. 11, Samuel F. Miller, U.S. Supreme Court, Keokuk, had written to USG. "I am informed that the name of General John Bruce will be presented to you for Judge of the Northern District of Texas which is supposed to be vacant or likely to be so soon. Genl Bruce studied law in my office, is a sound lawyer, an honest man, and one of good habits. He is evry way well fitted for such a position and I heartily recommend him for it." ALS, *ibid.* Related papers are *ibid.* On Feb. 14, 1871, USG nominated John Bruce as judge, Eastern District, Tex.; the nomination was tabled. On Oct. 22, 1874, Miller, Washington, D. C., wrote to USG recommending Bruce as judge, Ala. ALS, *ibid.* On Feb. 23, 1875, USG nominated Bruce for that judgeship.

On Sept. 25, 1871, Colbert Caldwell, Austin, had written to USG requesting appointment as judge, Eastern District, Tex. LS, *ibid.* On Dec. 2, Bishop Matthew Simpson wrote to USG. "Learning that Judge Caldwell of Texas is an applicant for the vacancy ion the bench in East Texas; I wd beg leave to say that when in Texas, on two different occasions in a few years past, I heard him most heartily endorsed as a true Union man. The acquaintance I formed with him personally was very pleasant, and if consistent with public interests, I shd be glad to see him appointed. I believe he wd be a true supporter of the administration" ALS, *ibid.* Related papers are *ibid.*

On Dec. 4, 1869, David J. Baldwin, U.S. attorney, Houston, had written to USG. "*Personal* . . . I have just received your notification that I am '*suspended,*' from the office of U. S. atto. for this District, but no reason or cause is assigned. I am also officially informed that Joel C. C. Winch has been appointed my successor. It is due to you, and to the cause of truth and patriotism, that you should know, that from 1 November 1860, to the close of the rebellion, I openly struggled for this nation, and suffered long and cruel imprisonment and exile therefor. That I have faithfully discharged the duties of my office, and no cause is assigned for my removal. My successor is a man of northern birth and education; voluntarily went into the rebellion; accepted a Majors Commission in the rebel armies; has applied to Congress for removal of his political disabilities, which application has been denied, and is still pending—the moral effect of all which is disastrous to you as President of this great nation, and the public morals. I am, and always have been, a thorough paced Republican . . ." ALS, *ibid.* On Dec. 6, USG nominated Joel C. C. Winch as U.S. attorney, Eastern District, Tex. On March 30, 1870, Joseph Kargé, "Profsr: Princeton College, late Col: 2d N. J. Cavalry. Bvt Brig Gl.," Washington, D. C., wrote to USG. "I venture to enclose herewith for your kind consideration, Testimonials in favor of Judge David J. Baldwin of Texas late U. S. District Attorney for Eastern Texas. Judge Baldwin is a brother in law of mine and I have known him for Twenty years. His devotion to the Union, during the darkest days of the rebellion, he demonstrated by sacrificing his property and liberty and perilling his life and when finally released after a lapse of 18 months from one of the most loathsome prisons of the confederacy, he made his escape to the North, he had to depend upon his friends for the necessaries of life. . . ." ALS, *ibid.* Enclosures recommending Baldwin as judge, Eastern District, Tex., are *ibid.* On Dec. 15, USG nominated Winch for that judgeship; on Feb. 4, 1871, the Senate rejected him. On Feb. 28, USG again nominated Baldwin as U.S. attorney, Eastern District, Tex.

On Jan. 3, John N. Camp, collector of Internal Revenue, *et al.*, Galveston, had written to USG. "The undersigned are of the opinion, from information received, that the Hon. Joel C. C. Winch may not be confirmed as Judge of the Eastern District of Texas. In case he should not be, we would respectfully, and most earnestly recommend Wm H. Goddard Esqr. to the favorable consideration of your Excellency, when an other appointment is made. . . ." LS (3 signatures), *ibid.* A petition recommending William H. Goddard is *ibid.* On Dec. 18, USG nominated Goddard as judge, Eastern District, Tex.; on Jan. 18, 1872, he withdrew the nomination and nominated Amos Morrill to that judgeship. On May 27, 1869, Col. Joseph J. Reynolds, Austin, had written to USG. "Permit me thro' this note to introduce to your personal acquaintance *Hon Amos Morrill*. Chief Justice of the Supreme Court of Texas—Judge Morrill is an old resident of Texas, is familiar with the affairs of the state and has always been a straight forward uncompromising friend and supporter of the National Government—When friends were scarce in Texas Judge Morrill was among the foremost to receive those entrusted with, National affairs and to aid them with his advice & experience—" ALS, *ibid.* On April 5, 1870, Miller, New York City, wrote to USG. "Supposing that Judge Watrous of the United States District Court for the District of Texas will resign in consequence of his infirmities I take the liberty of recommending for the place Judge Morrell, the present Chief Justice of the Supreme Court of Texas . . ." ALS, *ibid.* On Oct. 11, Morrill, Washington, D. C., wrote to USG. "Having been informed by Senator Hamilton, that I am charged with being interested or unduly prejudiced in the Galveston Railroad, as there is no other means to put myself right on the record, I beg leave to state, that neither at the present ~~or~~ nor any former time, have I been personally interested therein; that I never have and do not now feel conscious of any partialities or antipathies towards any any one man or collection of men who are litigants relative to the road—. . ." ALS, *ibid.* On Jan. 30, 1871, Thomas B. Hagais, Galveston, wrote to USG. "Your attention is respectfully called to the following Judge Amos Morrill, who has been seeking to get the appointment of Judge for the Eastern District of Texas, has removed from Austin, to Jefferson Texas and gone into the Banking business, but learning, that perhaps Judge Winch would not be confirmed, has published a Card in the Galveston Papers representing himself as a a resident practicing Attorney & Counsellor at Law of the City of Galveston, when in fact, he is not such resident practicing Attorney, but is a resident of Jefferson Texas. The aforesaid publication is made for the purpose of misleading Yourself—and others at Washington D. C. expecting that by such false pretenses to secure the appointment of Judge of the U.S. District Court for the Eastern District of Texas. It is therefore respectfully submitted to Your Excellency, whether or not a gentleman who by the use of false pretenses, seeks to secure so important a appointment is worthy of such high honors." ALS, *ibid.* On Dec. 10, Governor Edmund J. Davis of Tex. telegraphed to USG. "I especially request that Amos Morrill be not appointed Judge of Eastern Dist of Texas, Will state objection in person," Telegram received (on Dec. 11), *ibid.,* Letters from the President. On Dec. 19, Flanagan wrote to USG in support of Morrill. ALS, *ibid.*, Records Relating to Appointments. Related papers are *ibid.* On Jan. 18, 1872, Thomas C. Connolly, justice of the peace, Washington, D. C., Galveston, wrote to USG. "Permit me to state to you the following in regard to the struggle for the Office of U. S. Judge for the Eastern Dist of Texas—Gov: E. J. Davis, Judge Jas. H. Bell, U. S. Senator J. W. Flannagan & his Son Webster Flannagan State Senator & ac't'g Lieut Gov. of Texas, have mutually agreed among themselves substantially as follows—There are certain Indictments pending in the U. S. Dist Court at Tyler, Texas, against the said Webster Flannagan and certain matters in said Court affecting the interests of U. S. Senator J. W. Flannagan. These gentlemen desire to be relieved of these Court matters, and are willing to aid and assist the appointment and confirmation of any gentlemen to the U. S. Judgeship through whom they may effect said relief—Gov: E. J. Davis and Judge Jas. H. Bell are willing to relieve these gentlemen, if either of them can get the desired Office—Hence an agreement offensive & defensive entered into by these gentlemen & perhaps a few others, to secure the said Judgeship for either Davis, or Bell. If Davis gets the Judgeship Webster Flannagan becomes Gov: by virtue of his official position & Judge Bell is to be his Sec'y of State, or Atty Genl as he may prefer—. . ." ALS, *ibid.*, Letters from the President.

To Amos T. Akerman

Washington D. C. Dec: 13. 1871

Hon: A. T. Akerman:
Atty: General.
My dear Sir.

In accepting your resignation as Atty: General, to take effect on the 10th of Jany: permit me to renew the assurances of my high regard for you personally, and appreciation of the zeal and application which you have brought to the Office which you have so honorably filled. I can refer with pride to the uniform harmony which which has constantly existed, not only between us but also between yourself and Colleagues in the Cabinet, all of whom, I know, unite with me in hearty wishes for your future prosperity, health and happiness.

Your "Personal" note accompanying your letter of resignation, is gratefully received as a token of reciprocity of kind sentiments which I shall ever appreciate.

Very respectfully
U. S. Grant.

Copy, DLC-USG, II, 1. On Dec. 13, 1871, Attorney Gen. Amos T. Akerman wrote twice to USG. "I hereby resign the office of Attorney General of the United States; this resignation to take effect, (in accordance with the wish which you verbally expressed to me to-day) on the tenth day of January next." "Personal . . . In tendering the accompanying resignation of the office of Attorney General, permit me to express my grateful sense of the kindness which I have uniformly received from you during my service in the office, and my ardent wishes for the continued success of your administration." ALS, Free Library of Philadelphia, Philadelphia, Pa. On the same day, Secretary of State Hamilton Fish wrote in his diary. "In the Evening the President calls at my rooms—on leaving he asks me to accompany him—& on the way tells me that he had written to Akerman, suggesting his resignation & offering him the Judgeship in Florida—That A. had brought him two resignations—one taking effect immediately the other in (I think) ten days—He had suggested making the resignation to take effect on 15 Jany & finally A. had made it to take effect on 10 Jany—President had written to Judge Williams to meet him at his House this Evenig—he calls while I am there—presently the President sends for me in the office where he & Williams have been conversing—after a while Colfax & Boutwell come in—On leaving Williams tells me he has accepted the offer of the Atty Genlship—" DLC-Hamilton Fish.

To Amos T. Akerman

———

Washington D. C. Dec: 14. 71

HON: A. T. AKERMAN:

ATTY: GENERAL.

MY DEAR SIR:

In view of the questions that will be asked, and the Speculations that will be indulged in I think it might be advisable to send to the Senate to day the name of your successor for the Attorney Generalship. If you concur with me in this view I will send the name of Judge Williams of Oregon to take effect Jany 10th 1872.

Your obt: Svt:

U. S. GRANT.

Copy, DLC-USG, II, 1. On Dec. 12, 1871, a correspondent reported on prospective nominees for attorney gen.: ". . . The Southern Republicans are to-night urging the selection of HORACE MAYNARD. Solicitor-Gen. BRISTOW's appointment would rejoice a great many people, and would be also in the true interests of civil service reform. Ex-Senator WILLIAMS is supposed to be the gentleman decided upon in the President's mind, . . ." *New York Times,* Dec. 13, 1871. See letter to Benjamin H. Bristow, Dec. 26, 1871.

George H. Williams, born in 1823 in New Lebanon, N. Y., initially practiced law at Fort Madison, Iowa Territory. After serving as district judge in Iowa (1847–52) and chief justice, Oregon Territory (1853–57), he resumed the practice of law in Portland. A former Democrat, he served as Republican U.S. senator (1865–71). On Dec. 14, 1871, USG nominated Williams as attorney gen. On the same day, a correspondent reported: "Ex-Senator George H. Williams, . . . was confirmed within five minutes after the nomination was read, a compliment frequently paid to an ex-Senator appointed to office. Judge Williams surrenders a very large and lucrative practice before the Supreme Court to accept of this office. The appointment came to him entirely solicited and unexpected, and he was not informed of the matter until the President had settled upon his selection. The appointment is regarded here by Senators, with whom Judge Williams served for six years, as the best and strongest one that could be made. . . ." *New York Tribune*, Dec. 15, 1871. See *PUSG*, 20, 274.

On Aug. 8, 1885, Williams, Portland, Ore., stated in his eulogy of USG: "My intimate acquaintance with General Grant commenced in 1866, when in some way I became one of his advisers and counsellors in a controversy he then had with President Johnson and his Cabinet. I was exasperated at the unjustifiable attempt made to impeach his veracity, but I found him cool and undisturbed, though his honor was at stake, and undismayed by the formidable array of power and influence against him. I had frequent consultations with him after he became President and before I was connected with his administration, and I always, and under the most trying circumstances, found him the same serene, self-reliant, conscientious man and officer. I was called to his Cabinet in 1871, and for nearly four years my relations to him were of the most intimate nature, and I believe I enjoyed his unbounded confidence. . . ." George H. Williams, *Occasional Addresses* (Portland, Ore., 1895), pp. 5–6.

To Congress

[*Dec. 19, 1871*]

To the Senate And House of Representatives.

In accordance with the act of Congress approve, [March 3. 1871] I convened a Commission of emminent gentlemen to devise rules and regulations for [for the purpose of reforming the] Civil Service Reform. Their labors are now complete and I transmit herewith their report, together with the rules which they recommend for my action. These rules are [have been] adopted and will go into effect on the First day of Jan.y 1872.[1]

Under the law refered to, as I interpret it, the authority is already invested in the Executive to put [enforce] these regulations in force, with full power to abridge, alter or amend [them] at his option, when changes are [may be] deemed advisable. These vews, together with the report of the Commissioners, are submitted for your careful consideration as to whether further legislation is [may be] necessary [in order] to carry out an effective and beneficial Civil Service Reform

If left to me, without further Congression action, the ~~principles~~ [rules] ~~laid down in the rules for Civil service reform~~ [prescribed by the Commission] will be faithfully executed, but they are not binding, without further legislative action, upon my successors.

Being desirous of ~~getting~~ [bringing] this ~~matter before you~~ [subject to the attention of] Congress before the approaching recess ~~of Congress~~ I have not ~~the~~ time to sufficiently examine the accompanying report to enable me to suggest definite legislative action to insure the support which may be necessary [in order] to give a thorough trial to a policy, long needed but much neglected.

I ask for all the strength which Congress can give me to enable me to carry out the reforms in the civil service, recommended by the Commissionrs, and adopted to take effect, as before stated, on Jan.y. 1st 1872.

The law which ~~authorized~~ [provides for] the convening of a ~~Board~~ [Commission] to devise rules & regulations for [reforming the] civil service ~~reform~~, authorizes, I think, the permanent organization of a primary board under whose general direction [~~shall be held~~] all examinations ~~shall be held~~ of of applicants for public ~~place~~ [office shall be conducted].[2] There is no appropriation to continue such a board beyond ~~their~~ [the termination of its] present labors. I therefore recommend that a proper appropriation be made to continue the services of the present board for another year, and ~~that~~, in view of the fact, that three members of the board hold positions in the public service which precludes them from receiving extra compensation, under existing laws, that they be authorized to receive a fare compensation for extra services rendered by them [in the performance of this duty].

U. S. GRANT

ADfS (bracketed material not in USG's hand), Cyril Clemens, Kirkwood, Mo.; DS, DNA, RG 46, Presidential Messages. *SED*, 42-2-10, 43-1-53, 99. On Dec. 19, 1871, Secretary of State Hamilton Fish wrote in his diary. "Mr Geo. W. Curtis,—Chn of the Civil Service reform Commission, was present.—The President read a message to Congress, communicating the report of the Civil Service Commission, which he adopts to go into operation on 1st January next—Some verbal amendments were made—& the message sent to Congress—The President presented to Mr Curtis, his *MS* draft of the Message—" DLC-Hamilton Fish. On Dec. 18 and 19, correspondents reported from Washington, D. C. "The Civil Service Commission has closed its labors, and the members called in a body on the President to-day, to lay before him the report, which will make only about 50 pages of the ordinary document size. The President promised that he would give the report his early attention. . . ." *New York Tribune*, Dec. 19, 1871. "The President made the last speech on civil service reform today, and ended the debate. There was even a hearty acclaim of joy from Messrs. SUMNER and TRUMBULL when the civil service message was read, but not a word from Senator SCHURZ, who has never allowed himself to believe that anything good could come out of the White House. The message was hardly expected today, and therefore produced a decided sensation; but it was desirable to lay it before Congress before the Holiday recess, for its information. . . ." *New York Times*, Dec. 20, 1871. See letter to George William Curtis, Dec. 28, 1871; *CG*, 42–2, 210, 224; Ari Hoogenboom, *Outlawing the Spoils: A History of the Civil Service Reform Movement 1865–1883* (Urbana, 1961), pp. 90–95.

On May 16, Fish had written in his diary. "In Cabinet this morning, the Prsdt brought up the subject of the action to be taken under the law of the late Session, authorising him to establish rules & regulations looking to a reform in the Civil Service (*Sundry* Civil Service Appt, approved March 3 /71 §9) & Deficiency Bill approved Apl 20 /71   It was proposed to establish a Commission of one from each of the Departments, & one Civilian attached to the 'Civil Service Reform notion'   on discussion, thought adviseable to have a larger number of Civilians & fewer from the Departments   Concluded to have one from each of the Depts of Treasury—Post Office & Interior ~~each~~ & Geo W Curtis of Newyork—Jos Medill of Chicago D. A Walker of Georgia & A. G Cattell of New Jersey" DLC-Hamilton Fish.

On June 1, Fish wrote to George William Curtis *et al.* "The nineth section of an Act making appropriations for sundry civil expense's of the government passed March 3, 1871, provides 'That the President of the United States be, and he is hereby authorized to prescribe such rules and regulations for the admission of persons into the civil service of the United States as will best promote the efficiency thereof, and ascertain the fitness of each candidate in respect to age, health, character, knowledge and ability for the branch of service into which he seeks to enter; and for this purpose the President is authorized to employ suitable persons to conduct said inquiries, to pescribe their duties and to establish regulations for the conduct of persons who may receive appointments in the civil service.' The President has designated you as suitable persons to carry out the provisions of the act above cited. A room will be provided for your use in the Department of the Interior where you are requested to convene for the purpose of entering upon your duties at noon of Wednesday the 28th of June instant. You are also requested to communicate your acceptance or declension of this employment to me at your earliest convenience." LS, Staten Island Institute of Arts and Sciences, Staten Island, N. Y. On June 2, Fish wrote to Curtis, West New Brighton, N. Y., that USG had "designated the sum of two thousand dollars as a suitable remuneration for your services and expenses in the discharge of the duties to which he has appointed you." LS, *ibid.* See *Washington Evening Star*, June 28, 1871; *New York Times*, June 29, 1871.

On July 10, Curtis, Washington, D. C., wrote to USG. "I am instructed by the Board of Inquiry into the Reform of the Civil Service respectfully to request you to ask the opinion of the Attorney General of the United States upon two points which are herewith submitted—The Board has been considering the following resolution:

Resolved that we recommend to the President that all admissions to the civil service of the United States, with such exceptions as may be specified, shall be determined by a competitive examination open to all applicants who shall have satisfied such preliminary examination in regard to health, age, character & other qualifications, excepting political & religious opinions, as may be required.' During the debate it has been suggested that the designation of a single person for appointment by a board which is not established by the constitutional appointing power, would virtually vest the appointment in a body unknown to the Constitution: If in the opinion of the Attorney General this objection be valid, the Board respectfully asks for his opinion upon the following question: 'May the President under the act by which this Board is organized, regulate the exercise of the appointing power now vested in the Heads of Departments or in the Courts of Law so as to restrict appointments to a class of persons whose qualifications and fitness shall have been determined by an examination instituted independent of the appointing power?'" LS, DNA, RG 60, Letters from the President. In an opinion of Aug. 31 addressed to USG, Attorney Gen. Amos T. Akerman argued that Congress could not establish regulations to delegate the selection of a specific person but could restrict the choice to a pool of candidates established by examination. Copy, *ibid.*, Opinions.

On Nov. 1, a correspondent reported. "The Chairman of the Civil Service Commission had an interview with the President, to-day, lasting some time, in which he submitted a preliminary report of the results which have been reached by the commission in various branches of the proposed civil service reform. The members of the commission do not agree that there is no difference of opinion that the standard of all persons in the civil service should be raised and a better class of appointments made wherever practicable. Mr. Curtis, though a strong partisan, believes that the proper standard should be character and capacity, and that political considerations should be ignored altogether. Others of the commission fear that political considerations will never be done away with, and that they can only be offset by rigid competitive examinations. . . ." *Louisville Courier-Journal,* Nov. 2, 1871.

1. See *SED*, 42-2-10, 2–25. On Dec. 22, Fish wrote in his diary. "Nothing done except that Delano raised question as to the effect of Civil Service Rules, upon the Indian Agents &c appointed on the nomination of the various Religious Societies— President directs that an Executive order be issued re-appointing the same persons, as the Advisory Board, under the system to be inaugurated on 1st January & that Indian Agents & Superintendents, for the present be excepted from the requirement of competitive examination" DLC-Hamilton Fish.

On Dec. 23, Fish wrote to Curtis *et al.* "The President directs me to acknowledge the receipt by him from you of a report giving the result of certain inquiries made by you in part performance of your duties under the 9th section of the Act of March 3, 1871, and he asks me to state to you that he has adopted the rules recommended by you to him, and that the same will go into effect on the 1st day of January 1872. Trusting that you will consider the adoption of these rules as showing the high regard in which he holds your services he now desires that in continuance of your duties under my letter of June 1st, 1871, written by his direction and designating you as suitable persons to carry out the provisions of the act above cited, you will hereafter perform all the duties which in your report, particularly in the second rule thereof you fix as the duties of an advisory board. The President regrets that Congress has not already made adequate ~~compensation~~ provision for compensation to you." Copy,

DNA, RG 146, Civil Service Commission, Minutes. On Jan. 4, 1872, Curtis wrote to Fish accepting the appointment. LS, *ibid.*, RG 59, Miscellaneous Letters.

On Jan. 10, Curtis wrote to USG urging adoption of a rule covering temporary appointments prior to competitive examinations. Julia Sweet Newman, List No. 298 [1982], no. 45. On Jan. 11, USG wrote to Curtis. "The 14th rule submitted by you relating to temporary appointments pending the completion of the detail of examination, meets with my approval and will be carried into effect." Copy, DLC-USG, II, 1. On Jan. 20, USG and Curtis discussed congressional resistance to the Civil Service regulations. *Louisville Courier-Journal*, Jan. 21, 1872. See Hoogenboom, *Outlawing the Spoils*, pp. 105–6.

On Jan. 23, Secretary of War William W. Belknap wrote to USG designating three clerks "for appointment as a Board of Examiners for this Dept., under the 8th rule for the government of the civil service." Copy, DNA, RG 107, Miscellaneous Letters Sent. On Feb. 12, Attorney Gen. George H. Williams wrote a similar letter to USG. Copy, *ibid.*, RG 60, Letters Sent to Executive Officers. On April 18, Secretary of the Navy George M. Robeson wrote to USG suggesting three men to form the Board of Examiners in the Navy Dept. LS, *ibid.*, RG 45, Letters Received from the President.

On Jan. 23 and Feb. 2, Fish had written in his diary. "I mention that several vacancies exist in Consular Agencies, which ought to be filled, & nominations have been recd but that the Civil Service regulation prohibit the appointment without examination—that the parties reside at great distances from here—the Offices are of little value, the candidates probably wd not come here for examination & no board of examination exists—President advises that they be appointed at once, subject to such rules as may be adopted hereafter, for examination—I object,—& propose to refer the facts to the Advisory Bd wishing to oblige them to realise the impracticability of their rule, as applied to the Consular Service—much conversation ensues on the general nature, & the impracticable character of the scheme proposed by the late Commission—Among other things it is suggested that they be asked for an estimate of the expense necessary to establish their examining boards &c. with a view to laying it before Congress for an appropriation—& thus throwing upon Congress the decision whether they will carry out the proposed Scheme—I think Judge Williams made this suggestion" "I present a list of several Consular Agents whose appointments are delayed by reason of the regulation of the Civil Service Commn requiring their Examination &c before the Prsdt authorises me to make the appointments—on my objecting that the Civil Service regulations prohibit it without examination &c. he replies, 'not if I suspend them, and direct the appointment' I called attention to the fact that these appointments do not go before the Senate, & the parties would probably not accept provisional appointmts It is urged that it is not adviseable that the President revoke, or do away with the regulations which have been made—as 'that would give rise to clamor & criticism on the part of the friends of Civil Service reform—It was then decided that a Communication be made to the Civil Service Advisory Board presenting the case, & the need of early appointments, &c, &c—" DLC-Hamilton Fish. See Orders, April 16, 1872, March 14, 1873.

2. On Dec. 28, 1871, William Slade, Nice, twice wrote to USG. "Permit me to express to you my profound gratification at the efforts you are making to introduce a change in the manner of appointments to office, a change which shall recognize honesty & capacity as the necessary & only qualifications.... With the test of integrity & capacity for an appointment, I have no hesitation in respectfully soliciting at your hands a Diplomatic or Consular position in Europe & will cheerfully submit

to any examination that the rules you have laid down may require. I herewith inclose my application with more specific statements. Some weeks since I wrote my friend Hon C Delano a member of your Cabinet upon the subject of such an appointment, but it has occurred to me that perhaps the rules of the Department of State require a more formal application. . . ." "I respectfully solicit a Diplomatic or Consular appointment in Europe, where French or Italian are spoken. . . ." ALS, DNA, RG 59, Letters of Application and Recommendation. On Jan. 24, Ellen E. Sherman, Washington, D. C., wrote to USG. "I am told that the U. S. Consul at *Aix La Chapelle—Mr. Park*, will soon resign his post. I therefore make a second appeal in behalf of *Mr. Wm. Slade*. Letters from The General report all well & at Gibralter on the 28th ult." ALS, *ibid.* On Jan. 27, 1872, Elihu B. Washburne, Paris, wrote to Slade. "If I recommended any person for office I would recommend you, but since I have been abroad I have kept hands off. You may however say to the President for me that I would be very glad to see you appointed for the honor and credit of the Country. Your knowledge of both French and Italian, and your familiarity with consular duties would make your appointment a most proper and creditable one. With very best wishes for your success . . ." Copy, *ibid.* Related papers are *ibid.* No appointment followed.

On Jan. 25, Horace Porter wrote to William E. Chandler. "Pardon me for not answering your note sooner, but I had to wait for an opportunity ~~for~~ to speak to the President about the case. It seems that he has decided not to send in Smith's name. He has no objection to him, but he will probably let the office be filled according to the Civil Service rules. Many thanks for your campaign Life of Grant. . . . I do not know of any one who has opposed Smith." ALS, New Hampshire Historical Society, Concord, N. H. See Leon Burr Richardson, *William E. Chandler: Republican* (New York, 1940), pp. 122–23.

To Charles W. Ford

Washington D. C. Dec. 19th 1871

DEAR FORD:

I am in receipt of Mr. Carlin's[1] letter and feel much obliged to him for writing, beside being delighted with the account he gives of my young stock. If it would not be too much trouble for him I would like him to send for Logan and keep him in your stable this Winter, at my expense, and Mr. C. use him as a saddle horse until I call for him about Apl. or May next. If Flying Cloud can be altered I would like to have it done. Last Spring the attempt was made to castrate him but failed. I think also I shall send for the yearland that is said to be so promising and have her put in first rate hands for training.

In regard to the Carondelet property which parties wish to lease I have no objection to it on condition that if I should want to sell before the lease expires I could do so, and give possession, by a reasonable payment for improvements made. I leave the matter entirely with you.

I have got tired of inviting Mrs. Ford[2] and you to visit us, but I shall expect to see you, alone, some time this Winter.

Give my kindest regards to Benton[3] and his wife, Judge Krumm[4] and other friends.

Yours Truly
U. S. GRANT

ALS, DLC-USG.

1. Probably Nathaniel Carlin who became USG's farm manager in 1873. On July 1, 1873, Charles W. Ford, United States Express Co., St. Louis, wrote "To whom it may Concern." "The bearer N Carlin has been in the Employment of this Company for some months past and has given very good satisfaction. He quits of his own accord, as the work is heavir than he can do, I believe him to be a good man and commend him to any who may need his services" ADS, CSmH. See letter to Nathaniel Carlin, Oct. 27, 1873.

2. Ford's obituary stated that he never married. *St. Louis Democrat*, Oct. 26, 1873. See *PUSG*, 17, 137–38; *ibid.*, 20, 6.

3. On Dec. 27, 1871, William H. Benton and Ford, St. Louis, wrote to USG. "Duane M. Greene, whom we recommended to you for the Sutlership at Salt Lake, says that on finding the law had taken the appointment of Sutlers out of your hands, that he applied to you for a Commission in the Army, which you expressed your willingness to give him, and referred him to the Secretary of War to have his papers examined, and to ascertain where vacancies existed, &c., which he did, but the Secretary of War told him he thought his age would be an objection. If there is no law restricting the age of persons applying for the position of Lieutenant, We hope you will overcome the objection of the Secretary in this case." LS, DNA, RG 94, ACP, 1428 1873. Related papers are *ibid*. On Dec. 2, 1872, USG nominated Duane M. Greene as 2nd lt. See *SRC*, 44-1-282; Greene, *Ladies and Officers of the United States Army; or, American Aristocracy* . . . (Chicago, 1880).

4. John M. Krum, St. Louis attorney.

Pardon

To all to whom these Presents shall come, Greeting:

Whereas, on the 15th day of December, 1871, in the Supreme Court of the District of Columbia—holding a Criminal Term—one

James M. Davenport pleaded guilty to an indictment charging him with an assault, with intent to kill;

And whereas, his pardon is recommended by General John M. Harlan,[1] on account of his high character, his meritorious services in the Army during the war, his dependent family, the length of time he has already been imprisoned and the fact that at the time the act was committed, he was not in possession of his faculties.

And whereas, John M. Langston, brother in law of the person assaulted,[2] recommends that he be pardoned;

And whereas, U. S. Attorney Fisher, in view of the considerations before mentioned, unites in this recommendation:

Now, therefore, be it known, that I, Ulysses S. Grant, President of the United States of America, in consideration of the premises, divers other good and sufficient reasons me thereunto moving, do hereby grant to the said James M. Davenport a full and unconditional pardon.

In testimony whereof, I have hereunto signed my name and caused the Seal of the United States to be affixed.

Done at the City of Washington, this Twentieth day of December, A. D. 1871, and of the Independence of the United States the Ninety-sixth.

U. S. GRANT.

Copy, DNA, RG 59, General Records. James M. Davenport pleaded guilty to shooting at Orindatus S. B. Wall, who had been born a slave in 1826 in N. C., freed by his white father, and educated in Ohio. After prospering as a shoe merchant in Oberlin, Wall was commissioned capt., 104th Colored (1865), and worked for the Freedmen's Bureau. On April 1, 1869, USG nominated Wall as justice of the peace, Washington, D. C.

1. Born in 1833 in Boyle County, Ky., John M. Harlan graduated from Centre College (1850), studied law at Transylvania University, and joined the bar (1853). A slaveholder and Whig, he recruited the 10th Ky. and served as col. (1861–63). Davenport had lost a leg in 1864 near Atlanta while serving as capt. of that regt. See *O.R.*, I, xxxviii, part 1, 817–18. As Ky. attorney gen. (1863–67), Harlan opposed the Reconstruction amendments, but he supported USG's election in 1868 and ran unsuccessfully for governor of Ky. in 1871 as a Republican. See Tinsley E. Yarbrough, *Judicial Enigma: The First Justice Harlan* (New York and Oxford, 1995), pp. 17–20.

2. Wall's sister Caroline had married John M. Langston in 1854. See letter to John M. Langston, Dec. 15, 1870.

To House of Representatives

To THE HOUSE OF REPRESENTATIVES:

In answer to the resolution of the House of Representatives of the 6th instant requesting information in regard to certain measures with reference to the Spanish West Indies, I transmit reports from the Secretaries of State and the Navy, with the documents by which they were accompanied.

U. S. GRANT

WASHINGTON, 20TH DEC. 1871.

Copies, DNA, RG 59, General Records; *ibid.*, RG 130, Messages to Congress. *HED*, 42-2-35. On Dec. 6, 1871, the House of Representatives, "On motion of Mr Banks, Resolved, That the President be requested to transmit to this House, if not inconsistent with public interests, copies of instructions to the Naval Commanders of the United States in Cuban waters for the protection of the lives and property of American citizens, and to maintain the dignity of the American flag—And also such other information as may be in the possession of the Government, not hitherto communicated to this House, relating to the recent execution of medical students for alleged insult to the memory of a deceased Spaniard—And also with relation to the failure of the Spanish government to carry out in its West Indian colonies the reforms voluntarily promised by the statesmen of Spain." D, DNA, RG 59, Miscellaneous Letters. Secretary of the Navy George M. Robeson on Dec. 19 and Secretary of State Hamilton Fish on Dec. 20 sent USG the information. Copies, *ibid.*, RG 45, Letters Sent to the President; *ibid.*, RG 59, General Records. *HED*, 42-2-35. On Nov. 27, Fish had written to USG. "I enclose for your information a translation of a cipher telegram just received from the Vice Consul General at Havana, relating to threatened violence there. I have recommended to the Secretary of the Navy that a vessel of war be sent there at once for the protection of Americans." Copy, DNA, RG 59, Domestic Letters. In Nov., eight medical students had been executed and others sentenced to chain gangs for allegedly desecrating the grave of Col. Gonzalo Castañón. Philip S. Foner, *A History of Cuba and Its Relations with the United States* (New York, 1963), II, 225. See Annual Message, Dec. 4, 1871, note 19; *HED*, 42-2-35.

On Dec. 1, the League of the Daughters of Cuba, New York City, had petitioned USG to assist Cuban refugees. DS, DNA, RG 59, Miscellaneous Letters. On Dec. 19, Fish wrote in his diary. "The President hands me a petition addressed to him in the name of the Ladies & officers of the 'League of the Daughters of Cuba' praying the Government of the U. S. to furnish & equip a suitable vessel to convey to Laguayra a number of destitute Cubans now in N. Y—Phila & NOrleans—Submitting the petition to the Secr of the Navy, he says that he has no vessel: that a transport vessel wd be required—. . . In the Evening Madm Villaverde, sent me her card at the Arlington. I called upon her in the Parlor—she spoke of the petition that had been handed to the Prsdt by the League of the Daughters of Cuba—was told it was impossible for the Govt to send persons out of the Country—that the policy is to encourage immigration not to send emigrants away—that frequent applications are made by individuals to be returned to the Country whence they came—but are invariably refused—She says Adml Porter told her they could be sent on the vessels of the Navy—is told in answer that no War vessels are going to Venezuela—if any should go they will not have accommodation for passengers, as they are calculated to accommodate only their necessary crews—that a special transport will be necessary, & that there is no appropriation for that even if it would be proper to send people out of this Country   She then speaks of the Murder of Eight Medical Students in Havana, & of the condemnation of some 30 or more others to the Chain gang, & hopes this Govt will interpose—In reply is told that we regard the sentence & execution of these young men as an inhuman, barbarous & utterly indefensible Act—but it is, like the condemnation & execution of Rossel, & other communists in France, & like other cruel sentences & executions in other parts of the World, a matter between the Govt & its own Citizens, with which as a Government another Power has no right to interfere, but that informally, & unofficialy the good offices of this Govt have already been used, & will continue to be used to endeavor to secure the discharge of those of the Students still subject to sentence—. . ." DLC-Hamilton Fish.

On Jan. 22, 1872, Carlos G. de Garmendia, Baltimore, wrote to USG. "I went to Washington last week for the purpose of paying my respects to your Excellency and to see whether your Excellency, prompted by a natural impulse of humanity could obtain from the authorities in Cuba the favor of a reconsideration of the severe sentence passed by a court martial upon thirty one medical students, all mere boys, among whom is included the only son of my eldest sister, Mrs. Lopez Lage, my second mother on earth, and which boys, as your Excellency is well aware are now dragging a heavy chain and breaking stones in Havana under the merciless rod of an old convict, called *'capataz'* or overseer, who thinks, is doing his duty whenever he breaks a limb of any of said boys as I understand it happened a few days since, thus causing *another death* and increasing to *nine* the number of victims who have paid with their lives for what was merely a student's frolic, and by no means such a crime as was imputed to them. It is a feeling of horror, Mr. President which impels me to trouble your already sufficiently well tasked attention. It is because I believe your voice will be heeded by the numberless humane and respectable Spaniards, in and out of Spain, to which Nation I have always belonged, although a resident in this country since May 1852 (twenty years ago) that I take the liberty of addressing your Excellency this communication.—Nearly seven years had elapsed since the spring of 1865 when I had the honor of travelling with your Excellency in the same car from Atlanta to Washington—had not seen your Excellency before nor since until last Thursday when I had the pleasure of shaking your hand at your Excellency's Reception and passingly I mentioned the above fact—Your kind reply 'very glad to meet you again' encouraged me for my poor sister's sake for my young nephew's sake, for all the student's sake, . . . My poor sister has been struck down by the blow—her letters show almost a derrangement of her own mind—She thinks that perhaps my social position and numerous connections in this country will bring her some consolation—I had also intended to ask the Most Reverend Archbishop Spalding of this city, who is a relation of my wife, to write a christian and supplicating appeal on behalf of those poor students but His Grace continues very dangerously ill and can see no one. I do therefore Mr. President turn my eyes to Your Excellency alone with the conviction that your generous and humane heart will not allow this appeal to go unnoticed and that your Excellency, availing yourself of your high and exalted position, will do all in your power consistent with dignity, propiety and state policy, to carry comfort and perhaps life itself to the afflicted *Mothers* of the thirty one medical students of the Havana University!" LS, DNA, RG 59, Miscellaneous Letters.

Endorsement

Refered to the Atty. Gn. with the request that the first Territorial Judgeship becoming vacant be tendered to Judge Lewis.[1]

U. S. GRANT

DEC. 21ST /71

AES, DNA, RG 60, Records Relating to Territorial Appointments. Written on a letter of Dec., 1871, from U.S. Representative George W. McCrary and U.S. Senator James Harlan of Iowa to USG. "We would both recommend, and urge, the appointment of Hon. J, R, Lewis of Iowa as U, S, District Judge for Washington Territory, in case of a vacancy. Jude Lewis was lately District Judge in Idaho, and was wrongfully ousted from that position *by the forgery of his resignation*, his successor having been appointed before the forgery was discovered. We know Judge Lewis to be a first class lawyer and judge, and a man of great integrity, and we believe that justice to him and the best interest of the public service require his appointment." LS, *ibid.* U.S. Delegate Norton P. Chipman of D. C. endorsed this letter. "I unite most heartily in this request. I have known Judge Lewis many years: he is an excellent lawyer and an honest man. As an old friend and law partner I followed somewhat his record as Judge on the bench in Idaho: and I believe no one of our U. S. Judges in the Territories has performed his duties more impartially or with greater ability. But aside from the question of Judge Lewis' ability the fact that he was tricked out of his position by a forged resignation would seem to make it eminently proper to reinstate him at the earliest opportunity & I trust it will be done" AES (undated), *ibid.* On May 10, USG nominated Joseph R. Lewis as associate justice, New Mexico Territory; he declined the nomination. On July 12, Horace Porter, Long Branch, N. J., wrote to Attorney Gen. Amos T. Akerman. "The President directs me to acknowledge the receipt of your letter and to request you to appoint Daniel B. Johnson Jr of Minnesota Judge of New Mexico." ALS, *ibid.*, Letters from the President.

On Nov. 15, 1870, J. R. Morris *et al.*, Walla Walla, Washington Territory, petitioned USG. "It having Just come to the knowledge of the Undersigned citizens of Walla Walla County Washington Territory, that a petition is being secretly circulated and signed by a few of our citizens praying for the removal of the Honorable James K Kenedy associate Justice of the Supreme Court of said Territory and Judge of this District, that said petition contains no specific charges against His Honor but makes general charges of the most false and malicious character such as, 'that he is totally unfit by nature and wholly disqualified by education for the position which he holds.' His Honor Judge Kenedy is absent, having gone to Olympia to attend a term of the Supreme Court, but we, the Undersigned, knowing His Honor as well as we do, and the upright, able and impartial manner in which he discharges his official duties, and know[ing] said charges to be unwarranted and without any foundation whatever in fact, and believing that his removal would not only be an injustice to a deserving and faithful officer but an injury to the public, deem it our duty, in the absence of hiHis Honor and without an opportunity of consulting him, to Respectfully but earnestly *remonstrate* and *protest* against his removal We would further say that we have had no Judge of this District whose decisions and offical acts have been more generally approved and concured in, than have His Honor Judge Kenedy's, And we do most esincerely believe that said petition was gotten up and is being circulated by a few discontented persons for their own interested purposes And not for the public good, or the better administration of law and Justice, And we further believe, and do most unhesitatingly represent, that the great body of our most inteligent and responsible fellow citizens concur with us in this Remonstrance" DS (58 signatures), *ibid.*, Records Relating to Territorial Appointments. On April 12, 1869, USG had nominated James K. Kennedy as associate justice, Washington Territory. Kennedy resigned in Oct., 1871. On March 12, 1872, USG nominated Lewis to replace Kennedy.

In Feb., 1875, Nathan T. Caton and Benjamin L. Sharpstein, Walla Walla, wrote to USG. "A most extraordinary effort is being made by a member of this bar to secure the removal of Hon Joseph R. Lewis associate Justice of the Supreme Court of this Territory and Judge of the First Judicial District To secure that end a large number of petitions were in October last secretly printed and forwarded to different points in this District, to Eastern Oregon and Idaho Territory for signatures. So secretly have these petitions been circulated that it has not been possible for the bar here to secure a copy until a short time since. These petitions have been much circulated and signed here by transient persons from the mines who are here for the winter only and spend their time in gambling and other disreputable practices. The Sporting men generally have signed these petitions probably for the reason that twenty or more of them were indicted and fined for a violation of the Statute in relation to gaming. These petitions were also signed as we are credibly informed by soldiers from the post, as also in Idaho and Oregon A. very small number of our worthy citizens have signed them and those who did—so done upon a mistake of facts or from private malice Resolutions of this bar signed by all the members thereof save two beside the party engaged in the move were presented to the court at its November term, best expressive of the views of this bar on the subject a a certified copy whereof is herewith attached and a printed copy is in the margin hereof We also append hereto a statement from many of the officers and leading citizens of our city on the subject as well as all of the officers of Yakima County in this District In relation to this matter we further have to say that we believe that Judge Lewis has given more general satisfaction to the members of the bar and to all others having business before him, who were competent to judge than has been given in this District during its past history We also say that we are assured that our people generally endorse his ability and integrity both as a Judge and as a private citizen For these reasons and feeling that it would be a great loss to the profession and an unmerited thrust at honor and integrity on the bench and an unhallowed triumph of wrong to suffer the removal of Judge Lewis, we earnestly pray that he be retained" LS, *ibid.* The enclosure is *ibid.* This letter drew in reply an undated broadside headed "Hamlet's Ghost." ". . . The above letter was first published in *Puget Sound Dispatch*, March 18th, 1875. The paper stated that Caton and Sharpstein were appointed at a meeting of the Walla Walla bar held in February of that year, a committee to write an address to the President expressive of their views. All the other members of the bar disavowed any knowledge of, or participation in, such meeting. When Mr. Caton was nominated for Congress he immediately, and apparently by preconcerted arrangement, telegraphed JUDGE LEWIS. Judge Lewis' term of office expires about the time our next Delegate in Congress will have to be at Washington. Caton sustained him as far as lay in his power before, even by the grossest slander on the character of 800 of the best citizens of Walla Walla and Yakima counties, and by the most unblushing misrepresentation as the above quoted document bears witness. Will those who signed the petition referred to show their appreciation of these compliments by voting for the author of them? Will they vote for the man who, if elected, will surely do all in his power to secure the re appoint-ment of Judge Lewis? Will those so-called 'gamblers' *who were fined* show their gratitude to Mr. Caton for his part in the matter, by supporting him now at the polls? Will any man who is opposed to *double-dealing* vote for Mr. Caton for Delegate to Congress? There is no disputing the fact that if Judge Lewis was sent to Washing-ton as delegate from this Territory the vast east side of the Cascade Mountains would be as poorly represented as heretofore. Our in interests would be neglected, our wants disregarded. and our demands taken no notice of, unless by giving them attention it would subserve Judge Lewis' own sordid ends. If this be true of Judge Lewis it is doubly true of a tool of his. For the man who becomes the tool of another is without force of character, and is made of such stuff that you can mould and shape in any form you wish. A person in the clutches of a man like Lewis dare not call his name his own. His senses are confused, his ideas limited, his judgment warped, and he is afraid to act without first consulting his liege lord and master. Now then the question: Is Judge Lewis a suitable person to represent the true interests of the people on this side of the dividing line? If he is, then vote for Hon. N. T. Caton, for Mr. Caton is 'Hamlet's Ghost' stalking the land; he is the Hon. Joseph R. Lewis in disguise." D (printed), *ibid.* In several undated printed petitions, "citizens of the 1st Judicial District of Washington Territory" represented to USG and the U.S. Senate "that they regard Joseph R. Lewis, Associate Justice of the Supreme Court of said Territory and Judge of said District, as a partial, dogmatical, supercilious, unscrupu-lous and corrupt man, wholly unfit for said position. They therefore pray for his speedy removal therefrom, . . ." DS, *ibid.*

In Dec., 1872, and on Jan. 30, 1873, Alexander Ross, Cape Girardeau, wrote to USG. "I, hereby make application for the Office of Associate Justice, or Attorney of Washington Territory, or Such other district as you may deem proper, if I am deemed worthy. I, have no Special Claim to advance, unless it be an unwavering adherence to my Country in her day of need: and a faithful discharge of every duty intrusted to me. Having been appointed by you to a responsible position in the Q. M. Dpt Western Dist of La, in the Summer of 1863. under, and by the recommendation of Genl Isaac F Sheppard then in Command. In 1867, on the recommendation of the Hon Charles D Drake the Hon Chief Justice, S P Chase nominated me one of the Registers in Bankruptcy, which nomination was Confirmed by the Hon Samuel Treat Judge of the U. S. Dist' Court, Eastern District of Missouri, which position I now hold. My Docket being now clear of all cases refered to me, and no further business. The duties of Said office has in a great measure prepared, and qualified me for advancement. My age is thirty eight, have been in practise fourteen years. . . ." "I herewith send application for Office of Associate Justice of Washington Territory. In making this application I depend on my own merits alone; having nothing to offer but the record I have made, together with the opinions of the leading men of this City. If intrusted with the position I will strive to fill it with Credit to myself and the Government, as I have always done heretofore in places of trust that I have filled

As we have no senators in Washington that belong to our party, I take the liberty of sending this direct to your excellency, knowing it will receive that courties attention from you, that I have received in person heretofore." ALS, *ibid.*

On Oct. 13, 1874, John C. Churchill, Oswego, N. Y., wrote to USG. "I learn that the Hon Orange Jacobs, Chief Justice of Washington Territory, has resigned his office on the occasion of his nomination by the Republican Party for delegate to Congress from that Territory. The Hon Samuel C. Wingard, now United States District Attorney for that Territory, is a candidate for the vacancy and I write on his behalf to ask for him the appointment. Mr Wingard has won an enviable reputation for himself as a lawyer, and public officer, and man, while performing the duties of his present office, and I do not doubt will succeed equally well upon the bench should you think favorably of his appointment. He is a staunch friend of the Administration & of the Republican Party, and his appointment I think will be of service to both. Mr Wingard is my brother in law for which reason I ~~felt~~ feel more interest in the matter, and I shall be very much obliged if he shall receive the appointment." ALS, *ibid.* On Dec. 21, Hazard Stevens, Olympia, Washington Territory, wrote to USG. "Having been unable from temporary absence to join the members of the bar of this place in recommending S. C. Wingard Esq, for the position of Chief Justice of the Territory, I respectfully add my tribute to the many which have already been tendered him, and which he so well deserves, in just recognition of his personal integrity and independence of character, of his entire freedom from the many partizan cliques which have so often proved an injury to our Territory, and of his talents, learning and experience in every way fitting him for the position in question. As an old resident, as a practising member of the Bar for Several years, as formerly Attorney for the N. P. R. R. Co, I have had constant intercourse with Mr. Wingard both unofficial[ly] and in his position as U. S. District Attorney, and I believe him to be the best qualified man for the place, in Washington Territory, with perhaps the sole exception of Hon. R. S. Green, Associate Justice now presiding in this Judicial District, and that his appointment would be highly acceptible to the people generally." ALS, *ibid.* Related papers are *ibid.*

On Dec. 18, Abraham J. Seay, St. Louis, wrote to USG. "Herewith I send you letters of some of my Republican friends in this state who desire that I shall be appointed to the office of Judge of U S District Court for Washington Territory— Having been Constantly at the front with the first Division 15th Army Corps from the time of its organization at Helena Ark. Dec 1862 until the last gun was fired near Raleigh N. C. I have frequently seen, and several times conversed with you, but you doubtless, have forgotten me—I do not ask the appointment on account of any acquaintance, but hope you will reject my application unless you are satisfied that I would fill the office with integrity and ability." ALS, *ibid.* On the same day, George W. Fishback *et al.*, St. Louis, petitioned USG. "The undersigned would respectfully ask you to appoint Col. Abraham J. Seay of Franklin County Mo. to the position of District Judge for Washington Territory, and in support of this request beg leave to state, that Col. Seay is a lawyer of respectability and good standing at the bar of the 9th & 18th Judicial Circuits of this state. He has had a fair practice also in the Supreme Court of Missouri and in the United States Courts. During the late war Col. Seay was a brave and gallant soldier; enlisting as a private and leaving the service at the close of the war with the Commission of Colonel of the 32d Mo. Infantry. His political record briefly stated is as follows: He supported Mr. Lincoln's Administration—strongly opposed Mr. Johnson's and has warmly supported and defended the present administration throughout. Has made two vigorous campaigns in his (5th) District for Congress at his own expense (though a man in moderate circumstances), and owed his last defeat more perhaps to his unflinching opposition to inflation and his fearless advocacy of the payment of the national Debt according to concract, than to any other cause. Col. Seay has the confidence of the Republicans of this State who though regretting his removal from them would be glad of his appointment to a position he is so well qualified to fill." DS (8 signatures—including John F. Long, William H. Benton, and John McDonald), *ibid.* Also on Dec. 18, Chauncey I. Filley, postmaster, St. Louis, wrote on the same subject. ALS, *ibid.* On Dec. 21, Henry T. Blow, Washington, D. C., wrote to USG. "The enclosed letter will explain Col Seays request of me in regard to his appointment.—I have known Col Seay for several years and have regarded him as an excellent man and a good Lawyer, and will be gratified if you can consistently confer on him the office which his friends solicit for him" ALS, *ibid.* Related papers are *ibid.* On Jan. 16, 1875, USG nominated Lewis as chief justice, Washington Territory, to replace Orange Jacobs, and Samuel C. Wingard as associate justice in place of Lewis.

1. Lewis, born in 1829 in London, Ohio, attended local schools, studied law while teaching, and was admitted to the bar (1854). Moving to Iowa (1855), he joined the Republican Party and held minor offices. On April 13, 1869, USG nominated Lewis as associate justice, Idaho Territory. See letter to Amos T. Akerman, March 15, 1871; H. K. Hines, *An Illustrated History of the State of Washington* ... (Chicago, 1893), pp. 548–59.

To Benjamin H. Bristow

Washington, D. C. Dec. 26th *18~~66~~71*

DEAR SIR:

Your communication of the 20th inst. tendering your resignation as Solicitor General, was duly received, but has not been acted up. I now return it to you feeling highly gratified that you have consented, at my request, to reconsider the matter, and to continue in an office which you have so ably filled from its creation under our government.[1]

With great respect,
your obt. svt.
U. S. GRANT

HON. B. H. BRISTOW
SOLICITOR GN.

ALS (facsimile), DLC-Benjamin H. Bristow. On Dec. 20, 1871, Benjamin H. Bristow wrote to USG. "I have the honor to tender my resignation of the office of Solicitor General. It is due to you as well as myself to say that I am moved to this course by considerations of private and professional interests, which have pressed upon me for some months and which now seem to admit of no further delay. In thus severing my official relations with your Administration I beg leave to express my gratitude for the honor you did me in my appointment and for the kindness which you have uniformly extended to me." LS (facsimile), *ibid.* On Dec. 26, Bristow departed for Louisville after promising USG that he would continue as solicitor gen. *New York Times*, Dec. 27, 1871. Born in 1832 in Elkton, Ky., Bristow graduated from Jefferson College in Pa. (1851) and practiced law in Ky. An ardent Unionist, he fought at Fort Donelson and Shiloh as lt. col., 25th Ky., and resigned as col., 8th Ky. Cav., to serve in the Ky. Senate (1863–65). On April 25, 1866, President Andrew Johnson nominated Bristow as U.S. attorney, Ky. See *PUSG*, 20, 95; *New York Times*, Dec. 25, 1871; Ross A. Webb, *Benjamin Helm Bristow: Border State Politician* (Lexington, Ky., 1969), pp. 104–5.

On Sept. 17, 1870, Walter Q. Gresham, New Albany, Ind., had written to USG. "Some time since Col B. H. Bristow declined the office of Asst Atty Genl. mainly, I think, because the salary did not justify him in abandoning his private practice—I am reliably informed that Mr Delano is anxious that Col B shall be appointed Solicitor General, an office recently created by Congress—The Commr of Internal Rev doubtless knows of the Colonel's intimate acquaintance with all the revenue laws—I write this without Bristow's knowledge; but I know that, while he is not an applicant for any office, and likely never will be, still, if the position of Solicitor of General is tendered him, and he has reason to believe that his appointment will be agreeable to you, he will not decline—I am intimately acquainted with the Colonel, and I know of no man of more promise—He is incorruptible—he has sense, will and courage, and he is true as steel to his friends—He is already in the front rank of his profession in Kentucky—He would be a most valuable man to the govermt in that office: and knowing him as I do, I would like to see him at Washington and near you—He was an early friend of yours, & I know you could rely on his friendship & judgment—If it should be thought that in thus addressing the President, I have done something indelicate or improper, I can only ask you to remember that it is the act of an old personal friend, who is trying to do you a favor" ALS, DNA, RG 60, Applications and Recommendations. On Sept. 21, Judge Bland Ballard, U.S. District Court, Louisville, wrote to USG. "I most earnestly recommend to your Excellency Col B H Bristow as eminently qualified for the office of Solicitor General of the United States. I know Col Bristow well and I know him to be a gentleman of rare natural abilities of fine scholarship and of the highest order of legal attainments. Moreover he possesses true courage, unflinching integrity untiring industry and, in fact, every quality which is required for the position to which his friends would assign him. I need not, I am sure, allude to the Colonels military or political record—This—is known to your Excellency—Pardon me for saying, that valuable as were his services to the Union during the days of the Rebellion they have been hardly less valuable since. He has, at all times been a true Republican and a faithful public servant." ALS, *ibid.* On Sept. 24, William Dennison, Columbus, Ohio, wrote to USG. "I am informed that Col Bristow of Kentucky may be reccommended to you for the office of Solicitor General of the United States, in which case, I desire to heartily join in the reccommendation. I am quite sure you cannot make a better appointment nor one that will give more satisfaction to the Country—The Col is an excellent lawyer, a gentleman of the highest personal character & an earnest friend of your Administration—His appointment could not but be exceedingly gratifying to the Republicans of Kentucky & the South." ALS, *ibid.* Related papers are *ibid.* On Oct. 11, USG appointed Benjamin H. Bristow as solicitor gen. and subsequently nominated him to the post on Dec. 7.

On July 5, John W. Forney, *Washington Chronicle*, had written to USG. "The name

of Hon. Joseph Casey, of Pennsylvania, has been presented to you for the position of
Solicitor General under the new bill for the organization of the Department of Justice;
and it gives me especial pleasure to bear testimony to his marked and peculiar qualifications for that office. His signal ability for as Chief Justice of the Court of Claims,
while confirming the high hopes that induced his appointment by Mr Lincoln, has
been recognised by the whole profession and by the U. S. supreme Court in affirming
his decisions. Courteous, dignified, and full of energy, knowing the public men of the
Country by his service in Congress, and his long residence at this Capital, he is of all
men the best, in my opinion, to be your new Solicitor General. I would have Called to
say all this and more in his behalf, if you had been in town, or if I had not to leave
Washington myself." ALS, *ibid.*

On July 11, U.S. Senator Daniel D. Pratt of Ind. wrote to USG. "I am asked to
speak to you of the qualifications of Abram W. Hendricks for the position of Solicitor
General. I cheerfully bear testimony to his high qualifications as a man and lawyer.
He has had large and varied experience at the Bar of Indiana in the State and Federal
Courts   He has one of the very best legal minds of in the State and it is well stored
with legal lore. His private life is singularly pure. I have joined my Colleague in
recommending H. C. Newcomb for Assistant Atty Genl. I withdraw nothing said in
that letter. But in case Mr N. should not be nominated for that place, I respectfully
request the nomination of Mr Hendricks for the Office of Solicitor General." ALS,
ibid. Related papers are *ibid.* On Aug. 30, 1869, Asst. Judge Advocate Gen. William
M. Dunn, Washington, D. C., had written to USG. "Permit me to earnestly recommend the appointment of Col. A. W. Hendricks, of Indianapolis, to fill the office of
U. S. District Judge for the District of Indiana, recently made vacant by the death
of Judge McDonald. Col. Hendricks formerly resided in Madison Indiana and was my
law partner about twelve years. He is a lawyer of first class ability and a gentleman of
the highest character. At present, he is practicing law as the partner of his Cousin
Ex Senator Hendricks. They have never been members of the same political party.
Col. Hendricks has never devoted himself to politics but there is no more reliable
Republican in the State of Indiana. He was one of the Republican candidates for
Judge of the Supreme Court on the first Republican ticket in the state." ALS, *ibid.*,
Records Relating to Appointments. Related papers are *ibid.*

On Aug. 23, 1870, Morton McMichael, Philadelphia, wrote to USG. "I am
informed that the name of Isaac Hazlehurst, Esqr, of this city, has been presented
to you in connection with the office of Solicitor General, created at the recent Session
of Congress. Having known Mr H. during all his mature life I feel well qualified to
speak of his merits, & I am bold to say that he has eminent qualifications for the
position. . . ." ALS, *ibid.*, Applications and Recommendations. A related recommendation is *ibid.*

On Oct. 10, Aubrey H. Smith, Philadelphia, wrote to USG. "I have learned from
the note of Mr Wallace, the Reporter of the Supreme Court of the United States,
which I take the liberty of enclosing to you, that the name of Mr J. Hubley Ashton
is before you in connection with the Office of Solicitor General. I have known Mr
Ashton professionally and socially for many years, first as Assistant District Attorney for this District and Afterwards as Assistant Attorney General of the United
States; And now have much pleasure in adding my testimony to that of Mr Wallace
as to his learning, character and especial fitness for the honorable office to which he
aspires. I am sure that his Appointment would be acceptable to the Bar of the Eastern
District of Pennsylvania And particularly so to that of Philadelphia where he is best
known." ALS, *ibid.* The enclosure is *ibid.* On April 29, 1869, J. Hubley Ashton,

Washington, D. C., had written to USG resigning as asst. attorney gen. ALS, *ibid.*, Letters from the President.

1. On June 22, 1870, USG signed a bill establishing the Dept. of Justice as of July 1. This act consolidated legal officers in other depts. under the attorney gen. and created the position of solicitor gen., "an officer learned in the law, to assist the Attorney-General in the performance of his duties, . . . and who, in case of a vacancy in the office of Attorney-General, or in his absence or disability, shall have power to exercise all the duties of that office." *U.S. Statutes at Large*, XVI, 162. See *CG*, 41–2, 1568, 3034–39, 3065–67, 4490, 4692; *HED*, 41-3-90.

Endorsement

Refered to the Sec. of State.[1] I hope the Spanish Govt. will give Dr. Howard his immediate release   Atrocities already inflicted upon American Citizens has turned the whole country against Spanish rule in Cuba to such a degree that t[he] people are scarsely longer capable of judging impartially in matters between Spain and American citizens.[2] Mr. Roberts must see this himself, and the danger to his Govt. unless more moderation is shown.

U. S. GRANT

DEC. 27TH /71

AES, DNA, RG 59, Miscellaneous Letters. Written on a letter of Dec. 25, 1871, from Emilie Dutton, Philadelphia, to USG. "Early in July last at Long Branch, you were solicited by several persons (some of them friends of mine, others previously unknown to me) in the name of humanity to use your powerful influence with the Spanish Government in favor of my son, Genl [F]rederico F. Cavada, of the Cuban Patriot army, whose capture by the Spaniards was announced by telegraph from Havana on July 4th—As I had been assured, you kindly took personal interest in the case, and caused despatches to be sent to Havana and elsewhere, to initiate measures for my son's benefit. Your action in this case, created in me a sentiment of gratitude, which only a mother's heart can know—But alas! all efforts were of no avail; not only because my unfortunate son was in the [h]ands of those who were determined on vengeance [o]nly, and would not listen to the pleadings either of justice or mercy, but also because those efforts were [t]oo late—My son was captured on June 30th and [al]though ill, and too weak to walk without assistance was executed on July 1st. With a heart already lacerated, I now a[gain] approach you as a suppliant, not only in the name o[f] mercy but also in the name of justice. My brother, Dr John E. Houard, an American citizen, a native of th[is] City (Philadelphia) but for many years a resident of Cienf[uegos] (Cuba) was arrested and thrown into prison there, over [—] year ago, for reasons which were not made known to him and which to justify his imprisonment, he knew ther[e] were none. He repeatedly demanded an examination of his case, which demand I am informed, was als[o] recently made by the American Consul at Havana in obedience to instructions from the State Departmen[t] of this country. Thus imperatively called upon to ac[t] the Spanish Authorities in Cienfuegos organised a court-martial; not to try, but to condemn; and t[he] result was that they did condemn my brother to eig[ht] years hard labor in the chain gang, and confiscati[on] of all his property; to work under a cruel task m[aster] on the public roads, coupled with criminals of t[he] vilest sort. . . ." ALS, *ibid.* See telegram to Hamilton Fish, July 5, 1871; *HED,* 42-2-223.

On Jan. 3, 1872, M. E. Eldred, Camden, N. J., wrote to USG. "As I have never before written to a President I may now commit some great blunder, but should not the President be the father of his people? so I will think of you so and write to you as a man, with a loving heart as well as a great one, and then I shall not go so far wrong. There are many who are clamoring for what they call the 'rights of women'—among them the elective franchise, I want none of it, but there is one right that does belong to us, and that is the right to plead the cause of the suffering and oppressed. So would I plead the cause of Dr. Houard of Cienfuegos. He is the brother of an old friend of mine and in deep sorrow of heart I beg of you to consider his case and exercise your great influence for him. . . ." ALS, DNA, RG 59, Miscellaneous Letters.

On Jan. 11, Secretary of State Hamilton Fish wrote in his diary. "Mr Roberts— 'nothing special to say'—I refer to the case of Dr Howard mention that there hasve been sent to me a certificate of the naturalization of his Father, & of his baptism in Philadelphia—Roberts is expecting information from Havana by Steamer due tomor- row—" DLC-Hamilton Fish.

On March 28, USG wrote to the House of Representatives. "I transmit to the House of Representatives, in answer to their Resolution of the 19th inst. a report from the Secty of State & the papers which accompany it:" Copies, OFH; DNA, RG 59, Reports to the President and Congress. *HED,* 42-2-223. On the same day, Fish had written to USG concerning ". . . the case of Dr Jean Emilie Houard, who signs himself Emilio Houard—The Secretary of State has accordingly the honor to lay before the President copies of the papers mentioned in the subjoined list, such papers containing the information relating to the case of the said Houard" Copy, DNA, RG 59, Reports to the President and Congress. *HED,* 42-2-223. See *HMD,* 42-2-174, 42-2-185, 42-2- 188; *CG,* 42-2, 2741-44, 2783-95, 2817-18.

On May 9 and June 7, after discussions with the Spanish minister, Fish wrote in his diary. "Admiral Polo (Spain) has enquired of Mr Podestad respecting the slow prog- ress of business before the Claims Commrs he says it proceeds from the neglect of the parties to make out their cases—that only one case has been prepared—He asks what can be done with the claims of Spanish Subjects on this Govt that there are several for property destroyed, & injuries sustained during our war—He is told that the present is not a propitious time for considring them—that until the case of Dr Houard, & the claims now before the Commission are settled, it would not be proba- ble that Congress would entertain the question of settling these claims—" "The subject of Dr Houard is discussed—he professes a strong anxiety to have his re- leased—says his Govt has informed him that if the question of citizenship is raised they must insist on his being a Spaniard—that by their law he is such, that the father became a Spaniard by accepting a concession, & the son being then a minor, & resident of the Island became a Spaniard But if the question of citizenship is not raised, they are disposed to lay papers for his pardon before the King—. . . Adl Polo has recd the papers in his case from Havana Says the proceedings before the Court were entirely regular but *intimates* that the evidence was not strong of any complicity on his own part—but that various of his relatives were in the rebellion." DLC- Hamilton Fish.

On June 13, at Long Branch, a *New York Herald* reporter asked USG what would happen if Spain refused to release Houard. Julia Dent Grant interjected. "Then you'll take him, won't you?... It is for you to protect American citizens abroad." USG responded. "There's no better way to do it, ... than to demand their protection at the hands of any nation where they may be threatened with abuse. As to what we shall do in case Spain refuses to give Dr. Houard up, that is a matter that the Cabinet has not discussed at all, and both of you ought to see plainly that it is not for me to discuss it here." *New York Herald*, June 14, 1872. Released at Cadiz in July, John E. Houard arrived in N. Y. in Aug. *New York Times*, July 9, Aug. 21, 1872. On Oct. 7, Houard, Philadelphia, wrote to USG. "Impelled by a sense of duty and a warm sentiment of gratitude, I beg to convey to you my acknowledgement for the kindly interest that personally and in your highly official capacity you gave to my sufferings during my late imprisonment in Cuba and Spain, and until my final release was accomplished. I can but feel prouder of my country that my claim to it for justice and protection, was so nobly responded to, by the action of Government in my behalf." ALS, DNA, RG 59, Miscellaneous Letters.

1. USG's endorsement was later published in an effort to discredit U.S. policy toward Cuba. *New York Herald*, Oct. 22, 24, 1872. See Fish diary, Oct. 25, 1872.

2. On Jan. 11, J. Rumsey Dabney, Cadiz, Ky., wrote to USG. "There is some probability of a war with Spain, at least to judge from the papers. For God sake let us go in and Cuba, voluptuous Cuba, will be the reward. People every where wish something to stir them up, times are dull. A war with Spain would be very popular in this State. Count on me when the time comes,   I know something of Gen., Uptons approved tactics, and like you can leave the more inviting vocation of peace for that of war." ALS, DLC-Benjamin H. Bristow. Dabney added a note to Benjamin H. Bristow, solicitor gen. "Will you be so kind as to place this in the hands of his Excellency U. S. Grant, President of the United States, or place where he can get same. Do not fear for it is only a communication, and is addressed in very respectable language, I mean not intended to insult the Presidential ear. Nor is this an infernal machine, nor an *useless* appeal for Executive Patronage. You are acquainted with my father T. C. D." ANS, *ibid.*

To George William Curtis

[*Dec. 28, 1871*]

... Had I seen your letter in time your suggestion to call the first meeting of the Board on the 4th of Jany, '72 would have been accepted. It makes no difference however because no appointments which have to go to the Senate for confirmation can be made before the reassembling of Congress ...

Carnegie Book Shop, Catalogue 269 [1963], no. 176. In Dec., 1871, George William Curtis, Washington, D. C., wrote to USG. "I hoped to have had the pleasure of seeing you for a moment at Senator Chandler's on the evening before I left Washington but

I learned with sympathy & regret the reason of your early departure. If I had ~~had so been fortunate~~ seen you I should have ventured to remind you that new letters of designation to the old Board are necessary, and that we had thought the 4th of January was as early as we could conveniently meet again. And I should have asked you if it would not be advisable in any executive order upon the subject which you may issue on the 1st of January to state that ~~while~~ the rules were now in force, ~~yet~~ and that pending the completion of all details by the advisory Board, vacancies as they occurred would be filled in accordance with the general spirit and intention of the rules. I am sure that my interest in the subject will excuse to you this apparent intrusion; and I beg to be allowed to say how deeply touched & gratified I was by your ~~kind presentation~~ thoughtful gift of the ~~autograph~~ autograph ~~copy~~ of a message which will be [—] ~~a valuable not only~~ most highly prized by me, ~~but~~ by the country as the mesage itself."

ADf (initialed), Staten Island Institute of Arts and Sciences, Staten Island, N. Y. An author and orator, Curtis, born in 1824 in Providence, R. I., lived at Brook Farm (1842–43), served on the editorial staffs of the *New York Tribune* (1850) and *Putnam's Magazine* (1853–57), and after 1863 was political editor of *Harper's Weekly*. Curtis supported the impeachment of President Andrew Johnson and advocated USG for the Republican presidential nomination. He later opposed the annexation of Santo Domingo and the removal of Ebenezer R. Hoar and Jacob D. Cox from the cabinet but refused to join the Liberal Republican opposition to USG's reelection. For USG's rejection of Curtis as a cabinet member, see following letter. See also message to Congress, Dec. 19, 1871; letter to George William Curtis, March 26, 1873; Charles Eliot Norton, ed., *Orations and Addresses of George William Curtis* (New York, 1894). In 1872, Curtis wrote to USG accepting a dinner invitation. William Evarts Benjamin, Catalogue No. 27, Nov., 1889, p. 6.

To Edwards Pierrepont

Washington D. C. December 29, 1871

I am just in receipt of your letter of yesterday enclosing a slip from the New York World containing an infamous falsehood and slander directly against you, and indirectly against me. In the first place, "leading republicans were not busy at the White House explaining something about Pierrepont's record as one of the law officers of the War Dept. during the war." You did not make me a present of $20,000. You know whether you paid any sum that you may have subscribed for election purposes or not. I do not doubt but you did. People were not busy disparaging you to me when it was supposed that Govr. Fish was determined to leave the Cabinet, nor would I have permitted them to do so. The fact is I was very anxious to have Govr. Fish remain . . . I like him very much personally and in view of important unfinished business commenced under his administration of the State Dept. I thought and still think the country will feel easier if he remains there until all such business is closed.

... I should state that ... I did talk to the other members about his successor, and all of them concurred with me that you were the person to take his place ... This part I state to you confidentially ...

Charles Hamilton Auction No. 5, Oct. 8, 1964, no. 81. On Dec. 29, 1871, the *New York World* had published a report. "December 26.—It is asserted by men high in authority in Washington that inasmuch as Secretary Fish had expressed a sincere desire to retire from the Cabinet, that his friends in the Senate and House had determined to quietly concede to him that privilege, until they learned that the President had actually offered the place to Edwards Pierrepont, a man, in their judgment, unworthy of it. Then it was that the Senatorial written request was made to Secretary Fish to withdraw his resignation. He complied. Seconding this Senatorial action, the House Committee on Foreign Affairs called upon Secretary Fish, and, through General Banks, congratulated him upon his determination to remain. The truth is that the Secretary was overwhelmed with appeals of an extraordinary character to remain before he complied. As a matter of delicacy it was deemed best by the officials acting in this matter not to express the real cause of their sudden anxiety to the Secretary. While this action was being taken at the Capitol leading Republicans of New York City were busy at the White House explaining something about Pierrepont's record as one of the law officers of the War Department during the war, which was not very creditable to that gentleman. The fact that he made Grant a present of $20,000, and another statement that he subscribed $20,000 for election purposes in 1868 and did not pay it, were made to act against him with the Senate,   Another argument used against him was that he was a member and candidate of the 'Committee of Seventy,' of New York City; that that committee was getting to extend its dictatorial powers slightly beyond its municipal limits, and that their nominee was not unexceptionable. The President got a little wrathy over the Senatorial interference at first, but, notwithstanding some little indignation since expressed by a few of the Committee of Seventy, because the President would not carry out his programme and send Mr. Pierrepont's name to the Senate, he is now satisfied that Pierrepont could not be confirmed by that body, and, on the whole, that he (the President) would prefer that Mr. Fish should remain. Accordingly, I learn from high Republican authority, it is finally settled on both sides that there is to be no change in the State Department during the present administration." *New York World*, Dec. 29, 1871. On Jan. 10, 1872, Edwards Pierrepont, New York City, wrote to USG. "I have waited for your return to Washington before sending my deepest thanks for your recent letter so full of frank & noble manliness—It will not be forgotten—As I have never said or written any thing but in earnest favor of Gov. Fish, and of the wisdom of his being retained;—I hope no envious slanderer will tell him otherwise. I *seek* no man's place, and only wish what may fairly come with honor and propriety. ... Mrs Pierrepont seeing the address of this letter, bids me send her best love to Mrs Grant & Miss Nellie in which I would be allowed to join" ALS, USG 3.

On Oct. 13, 1868, Secretary of the Navy Gideon Welles wrote in his diary that Pierrepont had written to Alexander T. Stewart and donated $20,000 to assist in USG's election. "Pierrepont has been paid enormous fees by Stanton and Seward.

He is a cunning and adroit lawyer, but not a true and trusty man." *Diary of Gideon Welles* (New York, 1960), III, 452.

On Nov. 17, 1871, Secretary of State Hamilton Fish wrote in his diary. "Belknap & Atty Genl read letters of Edwards Pierrepont, advising that Govt discontinue criminal proceedings against Polhemus & Jackson, the Broker through whom Paymaster Hodge, is said to have made speculations with Government Money, they knowing it to be Government Money—Pierrepont intimates that the prosecution will involve other parties & names Jay Cooke & Co—Much criticism is made upon the letter & the advice it gives—& it is decided that the prosecution be proceeded with vigorously—There is no dissenting or hesitating voice.—Pierrepont has done himself no credit by his action in this matter" DLC-Hamilton Fish. See letter to George H. Stuary, Sept. 11, 1872.

On Nov. 21 and Dec. 4, Fish wrote in his diary. "After the Cabinet adjourned the President requested me to remain—& spoke of my leaving the Cabinet, & of my successor—important that he come from NewYork or Pennsylvania—knows no one in Pennsl that would answer,   In NY only three names occur to him—Andrew White, Geo W Curtis & Edwards Pierrepont—Reasons why he can't take White—does not like Curtis—'would rather even have John Forney—& would not think of that' & knows no one unless it be Pierrepont—I tell him frankly, that while I like Pierrepont, & would be very glad that he have some recognition from this Administration, he will not be suitable for the State Department—that he is a Fillibuster—& was not faithful either to the administration or to the discharge of the duties of his office while Dist-Atty, in the Cuban matters—that he Continually presented to the newspapers, immediately on their receipt, the substance of the confidential instructions conveyed to him from the Atty Genls Dept & from the State Dept by the Presidents directions, & then omitted to carry them out—That his appointment would not give confidence, or satisfaction to the Public, & that I knew it would not be agreeable to some of his Cabinet—He says Boutwell is the only one to whom he has spoken on the subject, & he said it would be agreeable to him. (I would expect that from B—to me he has deprecated the appointment)—I ask if he has given up thoughts of Senator Edmunds   he says E. would make a good Sect & he should like him for the place—has not spoken to him about it, but is convinced he would not give up his place in the Senate & his professional business, which (as Senator) he can conduct, but Could not as Secretary—He introduces Morgan's name, saying that he is not equal to the place—I ask if he has thought of Judge Hunt in connection with it—He has not—but says it strikes him more favorably than any name he has thought of—" "In the Evening Conkling (Senator) comes to my room, and urgently remonstrates against my quitting the Cabinet—He deprecates any change, is especially fearful of Pierreponts being appointed—thinks he will be selfish, & self willed—says he has no following in NY—that he is always engaged in some side schemes—& does not command confidence—People think he made a large amount of money, under Stanton, & under Seward 'for doing very little & doing it very badly'—that if appointed the Story of the twenty thousand dollar cheque will be revived—He says the money on that cheque was never paid—that there is a long story about it—that part was paid, & a large part of that was spent in a 'glorification of Pierrepont'" DLC-Hamilton Fish.

On Dec. 4, Fish wrote to USG. "When last I explained to you the reasons which impel me to seek relief from the duties of my official position, you requested me to withhold my resignation until the meeting of Congress—Congress having convened, and the reasons which make my resignation a matter of duty to myself, &

to my family, continuing, I now beg leave to place in your hands my resignation of the office of Secretary of State of the United States, to take effect so soon as my successor shall be prepared to enter upon the duties of the office—In thus severing the official relations between us, and retiring from the high position to which you had called me, I beg to express my very grateful appreciation of the extreme friendship which both in public & in private relations, I have ever experienced at your hands, and of the support which you have extended to me in my efforts to discharge the public duties which you committed to me—I shall ever cherish the most earnest wishes for all that may contribute to your happiness, and to the success of your Administration, in which success are involved the best present interests, and the future welfare of the nation—With assurances of enduring regard & esteem . . ." ALS, USG 3. On Dec. 5 and subsequently, Fish wrote in his diary. "Senator Cameron remonstrates against my resignation—urges the ill effect it will have on the party & on the Country—& refers to the danger from the choice that may be made of a successor   Senator Frelinghuysen calls at the Department & does the same   Cabinet—All present—. . . At the close of the meeting I handed the President my resignation of the office of Secr of State—taking it, he said he supposed he knew what it was—was very sorry, but could say no more than he had said—I spoke with him about Succession to know how long I may have to remain—he had not said any thing to any person whom he had thought of for the place—Pierreponts name was mentioned   he said he had spoken to three members of the Cabinet about him—I told him that I was sure the appointment would not give satisfaction—that P. was leagued in with M. O. Roberts & others, & would be full of schemes, &c that I regretted the necessity of saying these things, as P. was personally my friend, but I was too much his (the President's) friend, to allow such a thing to be done & not advise him—He requested the other members of the Cabinet to remain and I left— As I was going out Robeson following me to the door, asked 'are you going to leave us' replying in the affirmative, he said 'well, all I can say is that it is a crime—I repeat it, it is a crime'—" "Decr 6 . . . I took to the President the 'Catacazy correspondence' in answer to a call from the Senate—While there he referred to my resignation—saying that he had promised not to urge my continuing longer &c & he meant to adhere to his promise—but he was very sorry, &c   did not know what he should do—referred to the good feeling existing through the Country, & the confidence of the public & of the Republican Senators, & Congressmen in me—spoke most flatteringly of my administration of the office   while he did not in terms, urge my withdrawal of my resignation, he did ~~not~~ most earnestly present his wish that I should do so—I told him that I had made all my arrangements, (family arrangements) &c looking to my retirement, & I could not see any way now of changing them—He said that several Senators had spoken to him on the subject, & that understanding that I had expressed the wish for additional force in the Dept they had said that any thing I might wish in the way of organization or otherwise in the Dept could & would be carried without delay if I would remain—The question was then left, . . ." "Decr 20 . . . PRESIDENT   I tell him that in view of the urgent requests made to remain in office, & his own warmly expressed wish that I do so, I have determined to continue in the Dept of State—He replies with great warmth thanking me, & says 'I cannot express to you what a great gratification it affords me. I could not fill your place—& the Country has as I have the greatest confidence in your Administration of the Foreign Policy of the Govt   you have not only avoided serious complications from questions arising at the time, but have inaugurated a policy in our relations with other Powers, which gives promise of the avoidance of embarrassing questions in the future, as well as having disposed of some of the most difficult & threatening questions of the past'—He added 'you have afforded me a great relief & I am sure every member of the Cabinet, & of our friends in Congress, & the country will be delighted with your decision'—" DLC-Hamilton Fish. See Proclamation, July 4, 1871; letter to Schuyler Colfax, Aug. 4, 1871; Nevins, *Fish*, pp. 494–97, 513–17.

On Feb. 6, 1872, Pierrepont wrote to USG. "I have just recd a letter from our friend Ingalls. Whenever you deem it important I shall always go to you; but my judgment tells me that at this time it were better to keep away. I try to keep all petty vanities and jealous spite subordinate to greater designs. I have been so much behind ~~the~~ the scenes of official place, within the past ten years, that I am not blinded by the glare of the foot-lights. Placed as you are, no man's advice is so good as your own, and you can follow no man but yourself. Suggestions and facts from others are very valuable, but when they are digested your own brain must evolve the true course of action. Whenever the time comes that you need my aid, you will have it with a single earnestness, as you well know. But I sincerely trust that no number of men will ever induce you to act a single hour in advance of your own good judgmnt. *Time* solves many things which are perplexing and when it is not perfectly clear what to do, the wisdom is, to do nothing. I well know that to a man of your stamp, the wise thing to do will present itself in due time. I know that the men best fitted to assist you, at a crisis which may come, will somehow appear to your mind as best fitted, and until they do so appear to you, they are not wanted and would not be useful. I have an earnest desire for your re-election; it would secure the national prosperity and vindicate my own repeated prophecy and perfect the renown whose base was so deeply laid in the record of the war. I have unbounded faith in your inspirations, and common sense. I cannot know the varied embarrassments which beset you, but I believe that you will act as wisely as circumstances will permit— no man can do better. Whatever men's jealousies may do else, they will not prevent me from being your true devoted friend" ALS, USG 3. See *PUSG*, 19, 105–6, 210–12; *ibid.*, 20, 183–84, 316–17.

To J. Rodman West

———

Phil Pa
Jan 4th 72

HN J R WEST[1] USS
WASHINGTON DC

Gov. Warmouths[2] dispatch of this date to you received. His His report of proceedings of US. Marshal is of such an Extraordinary character that I will have the matter investigated at once   Please show this dispatch to the Atty Gen'l

U. S. GRANT

Copy, DNA, RG 60, Letters Received, La. *HED*, 42-2-268, 50; *HMD*, 42-2-211, 313.
When USG visited Philadelphia, Jan. 4–8, 1872, he stayed with Adolph E. Borie. On
Jan. 4, U.S. Senator J. Rodman West of La. telegraphed to USG, care of Borie. "The
following just received from Governor Warmoth: 'NEW ORLEANS, *January* 4. J. R.
WEST, *United States Senate:* The United States marshal arrested myself, the lieutenant
governor, a number of State senators, a large number of the members of the house,
and took us to the custom-house. We were, after some delay, released on our personal
bonds. While we were absent the speaker of the house, without a quorum, put to
vote and expelled six members, Carr, Dewees, Gover [*Souer?*], Wheyland, Lasaliviere,
McFarland. There are four companies of United States troops now in city. This revolutionary movement will involve the *destruction* of the State government, unless the
President takes immediate action and stops his officials. The democrats and custom-
house republicans of the senate are now on the Wilderness, breaking a quorum of the
senate until the arrival of four democrats, when they intend to turn out the lieutenant
governor, and then effect an entire revolution of the government. I wish you to go and
see the President, and lay the matter before him. H. C. WARMOTH, *Governor.*' If not
improper, I would be glad to know by telegraph if you take any action." *HED*, 42-2-
268, 49–50. On the same day, Governor Henry C. Warmoth of La. telegraphed to
USG. "Six state senators employed in the New Orleans Custom house have formed a
Conspiracy with the Democrat senators to prevent a quorum of the state senate &
have succeed throughout this entire week in this plot   They have the support of the
Collector of customs the U. S. Marshal & several of Your appointees here and the
revenue Cutter Wilderness has been & still is employed to take these Conspirators
beyond the reach & jurisdiction of the Sergeant at arms empowered to arrest them
in order that a quorum may be secured & public business transacted   at the moment
of assembling of the House of Rep's today a number of U. S. deputy marshals armed
with warrants from a U. S. Commissioner based upon a frivolous affidavit of members of the Conspiracy suddenly arrested eighteen 18 representatives four 4 senators
and the Governor & Lieut Gov   The effect of this was break the republican majority
in the House of Rep's   during the Confusion Consequent upon this outrageous proceeding the Conspirators Claiming to be the house but not numbering a quorum of
that body illegally rejected six 6 republican members & seated in their places democratic Contestants   threats of violence backed by U. S. troops to carry out this plot
are freely made   I respectfully request to be informed if as claimed you sustain the
Collector. the Marshal & other federal officials in theis revolutionary attempt to
overthrow the state gov't an attempt which if not discontinued by your appointees &
their Democrat allies must result in anarchy and bloodshed." Telegram received (at
2:30 A.M.), DNA, RG 94, Letters Received, 37 1872; *HED*, 42-2-268, 51; *HMD*,
42-2-211, 312–13. On Jan. 5, Warmoth telegraphed to West. "The custom-house
republicans and the twenty democrats have organized a house in the Gem Coffee-
House, on Royal street, having forty-two members present. They are arresting the
members found on the street and carrying them there by force. They intend to force
a quorum and try to suspend me with articles of impeachment. They have seventeen
senators and we have seventeen—a tie. I wish you to go to the Attorney General
and stop this arresting of members. It is an outrage that the constitutional rights
of the members of the legislature and the officers of the government should be
subject to such ridiculous treatment. It is necessary you should see the Attorney
General at once. I have no reply to any of my dispatches to the President. We had
fifty-eight members voluntarily present to-day. Tell the Attorney General to stop
these proceedings until he can receive a report from the district attorney, which

should be requested. The President can stop these outrageous proceedings by telling his appointees to desist from their efforts to overturn the government. I addressed a communication to Commissioner Woolfley requesting a copy of the affidavit made against me, but he refused to furnish the same." *Ibid.*, 314. On Jan. 6, West twice telegraphed to USG. "The following telegram received from Governor Warmoth: 'NEW ORLEANS, *January 5.* Hon. J. R. WEST, *Washington:* Tell President Grant at once that the pretended house of representatives, organized to-day by Carter, is composed of twenty republicans and twenty-four democrats. In the regular session of the house there were fifty-four republicans and five democrats. I desire to know from the President direct whether he wishes his civil appointees here to continue their support to Carter's treasonable combination, the object of which is to overthrow the State government, and the effect of which will be riot and bloodshed. This unholy conspiracy derives importance and strength alone through the countenance given it by Collector Casey and other Federal appointees, and the necessary inference that the President favors the movement. The city is excited and a riot threatened. I wish to know whether the President desires his name and patronage to be employed in accomplishing the object and producing the effect before mentioned. The condition of affairs is that of insurrection, and I want President Grant to instruct General Emory to use his whole force to assist me in suppressing it, and to answer me whether he will do so—either yes or no. H. C. WARMOTH.' I respectfully request an answer at your earliest pleasure." "I sent the following dispatch this morning to Governor Warmoth: 'Dispatch for President received this morning and forwarded. It occurs to me that you assume a false position in asking United States troops to suppress any insurrectionary or riotous movement until you have exhausted the power of the State; meanwhile the Federal troops should not molest you.'" *HED*, 42-2-268, 51–52. On the same day, Warmoth telegraphed to USG. "United States marshals have again attempted to arrest me and members of the general assembly and the officers of the peace. Having once been arrested myself upon the same charge, and having submitted myself to the judicial authority of the United States, I cannot but regard the attempt to re-arrest me, together with the members of the general assembly, as an effort to subvert the government of the State. I have, therefore, neglected to obey the writs. The laws of the United States have not been violated." *HMD*, 42-2-211, 313. On Jan. 5, John J. Williamson, New Orleans, had telegraphed to Secretary of the Interior Columbus Delano. "The custom house republicans & the democrats in the house have organized a bogus house of representatives in a drinking Saloon & the old leadingers of the Ku Klux of 1868 with mob of Drunken followers are defying the local govt & are doing duty as sergeants at arms & deputy U S marshals   another attempt has been made on a writ of U S Commissioner Weller to arrest the Governor Lieut Governor members of the federal assembly & the peace officers to give these men an opportunity to take possession of the Capitol. Will not the President express his disapproval of this attempt to subvert the local government we shall surely have riot & bloodshed before tomorrow night unless the president acts." Telegram received, DNA, RG 94, Letters Received, 37 1872. See *HMD*, 42-2-211, 462–74.

On Jan. 4, James F. Casey, collector of customs, New Orleans, had telegraphed to USG. "Yesterday Senate met   no quorum—House met had a stormy time   Carry offered Resolution that the speakers seat be declared vacant & that Waters declared speaker   Carey put the motion & declared it Carried   A Rush was made to the Chair   when Carter warned them not to advance on the platform they fell back & after some other skirmishing the House adjourned   Warmouth having bought five votes the night before hoped to Carry out his plans but the Courage of Carter prevented—last night Warmouth had the side entrance boarded up & this morning the speakers Room & Hall of Representatives filled with police some in uniform but most in citizens dress—When the hour for meeting of the House arrived Carter found his room filled with police also the House He ordered them out they refused some party unknown to me swore out [w]arrant & Warmouth & many of his friends were arrested & brought before a United States Commissioner were released on bail—Senate met no quorum Intense excitement in the City—Gen Emery very Careful will not be drawn into false position—I mailed an important letter to you last night—Three Senators to arrive when they reach here the thing will be settled if not before House still in session—six of Warmouths men were unseated & anti Warmouth contestants seated—Think todays work will settle it— House adjourned—The Democrats voted with us not as a bargain to save the State from the ruin" Telegram received, DNA, RG 94, Letters Received, 37 1872. On the same day, John M. G. Parker, New Orleans, telegraphed to USG. "Warmouth is defeated in attempt to remove speaker Carter and fast losing strength. Carter sustained by best citizens who are jubilant over prospects of reform" Telegram received, *ibid.* On Jan. 5, U.S. Senator William P. Kellogg of La., New York City, telegraphed to USG. "I respectfully ask that you be not influenced by any exparta statement from New Orleans but await the facts. Am Confident that the federal officers are fully justified in whatever they have done." Telegram received, *ibid.* On Jan. 5 and 6, Casey telegraphed to Secretary of the Treasury George S. Boutwell. "Do not form hasty opinions regarding proceedings in this city. Suspend judgment until you hear both sides of the question. False reports will probably be sent to Washington as to the situation." "Telegram of yesterday just received by me, having left office on account of serious illness of my wife. In view of the extraordinary state of affairs, and the illegal interference by armed police with the legislature, certain senators called upon me to afford temporary refuge till arrival of their colleagues places them in position to resist any forcible attack upon their rights. I afforded them such temporary asylum on board Wilderness. The vessel has not left the limits of the city, and no expense has accrued to the Government in consequence of my action. A further, and I think satisfactory, explanation will be made personally or by letter. They have left the vessel." *HMD*, 42-2-211, 421, 423.

On Jan. 31, Casey, New Orleans, testified before the Select Committee to Investigate the Condition of Affairs in the State of Louisiana. "Q. State anything you may know in regard to certain senators of Louisiana going on board the revenue-cutter Wilderness early in January of the present year.—A. The cutter was placed at their disposal by my order; I am not sure whether the order was written or verbal. I sent a message to the captain of the cutter some time during the day on which they embarked—somewhere about the middle of the day—perhaps at 1 o'clock. Q. Had you consulted with these gentlemen beforehand?—A. No; they asked me if they could take a trip on the cutter; I told them yes; it was a request made and granted. Q. How many senators went aboard?—A. I believe fourteen or fifteen; I am not positive as to the number. . . . They wanted to be away until other senators arrived, whom they expected to act with them. Q. If they should come into the senate they would make a quorum for the transaction of business, and they wished to prevent a quorum until other senators arrived?—A. One would naturally suppose that was the reason. . . . I had not the impression that their purpose was merely to take a pleasure trip. . . . they kept below most of the time to avoid being seen; they expected to return the next day, at furthest; they supposed there would be no effort to arrest them, because it would not be known where they had gone; they supposed that would be a safe place to prevent discovery.... Q. Do you know how long these senators were aboard the cutter?—A. I think they went on board Monday afternoon, and it must have been Friday or Saturday before they left the cutter.... Messrs. Bowman, Blackman, Thompson, and Daigle, were democrats; the others were republicans. Q. Were some of them colored senators?—A. Yes; two. Q. By whose order was the cutter brought back to New Orleans, and the senators landed?—A. By my order. Q. Had you any orders from any higher authority upon the subject?—A. Yes; I had a telegraph from Assistant Secretary of the Treasury Hartley, but the cutter had been ordered back before I received the telegraph.... The supplies furnished were paid for by myself personally. The bills have been made out against me, and, I think, most of them paid. I have always paid the bills whenever an excursion has gone with the revenue-cutter.... Q. You are collector of this port and brother-in-law of President Grant?—A. Yes, sir.... Q. Before the senators went on board the cutter, had they not been secreted in the custom-house?—A. They came here to caucus sometimes; they were in the habit of visiting the custom-house. Q. Were they not concealed in the custom-house the night before they went on board the cutter?—A. Not to my knowledge.... Q. Did you not know that you were abusing your position, as a Federal officer, in attempting to control the local affairs of the State?—A. No. I thought the affairs of the State were such that almost any means taken to remedy them would be a benefit to the country. Q. You thought the property of the General Government could be used here in favor of one party or faction here, and against the other, without any dereliction of duty on your part?—A. I thought, under the circumstances, it could.... Q. You think, now, you did make a mistake in the course you pursued?—A. If it had not had the effect of bringing this committee down here, to investigate the condition of affairs here, it would not have accomplished the good results it has.... Q. Have you sent any written explanation to Washington of your course here?—A. I have written a great many private letters to the President.... I write to him every few days.... Q. Has he asked any explanation of you?—A. No, sir.... Q. Has the administration approved your course here?—A. I do not know. Q. Has it disapproved it?—A. I suppose the Secretary did, by ordering the cutter to be returned to New Orleans.... Q. Do you know whether the administration at Washington is acquainted with the purpose of those senators in going on board?—A. I do not know. I should think they would, from the notoriety that has been given to the fact. Q. In writing to the President or to any member of the administration, did you state for what purpose they went on board the cutter?—A. Not that I recollect. Q. Were you ever asked by any member of the administration to state why they went on board the cutter and why they remained on board?—A. I think not...." *Ibid.*, pp. 97–100.

On Jan. 4, 6:30 P.M., Secretary of War William W. Belknap had written to AG Edward D. Townsend. "*Personal & Immediate*—... Senator West has just been to see me with a telegram from Gov. Warmoth of Lousiana stating that he & several officials have been arrested by the U. S. Marshal &c—that the State Government will be broken up—that there are four Companies of U. S. troops in the City &c. In order that we may be informed as to the part the troops are taking, please telegraph at once to the Comdg. Officer there & ascertain what part, if any, the troops have taken & if any under what circumstances—I simply wish to know the facts." ALS, DNA, RG 94, Letters Received, 37 1872. On Jan. 5, Belknap telegraphed twice to USG. "The following telegram for you has just been received from Governor Warmoth:—'Danger of a riot and tumult is imminent. There is no quorum in the Senate and hence the legislature cannot call on you for assistance. The absent Senators are on the U. S. Revenue Cutter "Wilderness," I respectfully ask that General Emory be instructed to co-operate with me in preserving the peace and protecting the Government from attack and overthrow.' (Signed) H. C. Warmoth My own impression is that at present it is best to let General Emory act in accordance with his own judgment." "In reply to telegram from me General Emory says that the U. S. Troops have taken no part whatever in any arrests recently made ~~by~~ of State Officers in New Orleans" Copy and ALS (telegrams sent), *ibid.*, RG 107, Telegrams Collected (Bound). On Jan. 6, Attorney Gen. Amos T. Akerman telegraphed to USG. "The reports directed in your telegram of Thursday night have been ordered. Have seen Secretary of War, who hands me the following just received addressed to you. New Orleans January 6th By order of the House of Representatives and in their behalf I respectfully request under article four and section four of the Constitution of the United States that the general commanding be directed to furnish such military force as will be sufficient to protect them as the legislative branch of the government from the revolutionary, illegal and violent course of the executive of the State (Signed) Geo. W. Carter Speaker of the House of Representatives.' I think this request should not be complied with. The House alone is not the Legislature. Last night hearing that attempts were to be made to re-arrest the State officials under United States process, and that resistance was possible, I thus dispatched to the District Attorney and Marshal. 'Keep the legal process of the United States from being abused for political purposes. Collision with the State Government must be avoided if possible.'" Copy, *ibid.*, RG 60, Letters Sent to Executive Officers. On the same day, Belknap twice telegraphed to USG. "I have seen all New-Orleans telegrams directed to you. My opinion is that no action beyond an investigation as to the facts—should be taken, until the matter is clearly understood" "The following telegrams have been received—dated last night, fifth instant. *First*—From John M. G. Parker to you. 'Failing to depose Speaker Carter, Warmouth prevents him from acting. State House guarded by Police and Thugs—Great excitement among citizens irrespective of party who approve Carter's course and sustain marshal Packard.' *second*—From General Emory to Adjutant General. 'Nothing but the free display of the U. S. forces at hand and the acquiescence which each of the contending factions and the citizens generally yield to the U. S. authorities, has prevented a serious fight here to-day. The contending parties have pledged themselves to submit their grievances to the arbitrament of the law. If it should prove that they have done so in good faith, order can be maintained. If not a very bloody riot must ensue, for the citizens are greatly exasperated. It might be well to send me another regiment at once, though I do not demand it as necessary to preserve peace. There is already a misunderstanding of the terms on which it was agreed to maintain peace and tomorrow may bring a repetition of the disturbances of to-day. After your telegram of this morning I thought it would be proper to state the condition of things at the close of the day.' (Signed) W. H. Emory. I have conferred with the Attorney General and am of opinion no more troops should be sent unless farther demanded by Emory." ALS and LS (telegrams sent), *ibid.*, RG 107, Telegrams Collected (Bound). See letter to William W. Belknap, Jan. 15, 1872.

1. Born in New Orleans in 1822, West attended the University of Pa. (1836–37), served in the army during the Mexican War, and settled in San Francisco, where he published the *San Francisco Price Current.* As col., 1st Calif., and brig. gen., he commanded in the Dept. of New Mexico, Dept. of Ark., and Ala. Returning to New Or-

leans, he held office as auditor for customs (1867–71) and was elected Republican U.S. senator. See *PUSG*, 19, 444.

    2. Warmoth served as lt. col., 32nd Mo.; staff officer for Maj. Gen. John A. McClernand; and judge, provost court, Dept. of the Gulf. He was elected governor in 1868. See *PUSG*, 8, 480–82; *ibid.*, 18, 300; telegram to James F. Casey, March 27, 1871; Warmoth, *War, Politics and Reconstruction: Stormy Days in Louisiana* (New York, 1930); *HMD*, 42-2-211, 298–99, 334, 349–51, 374–75.

To James F. Casey

Troops cannot be used Except under provisions of law

JANY. 10TH 72

Copy, DNA, RG 60, Letters Received, La. On Jan. 6, 1872, James F. Casey, collector of customs, New Orleans, telegraphed four times to USG. "Warmouth has issued proclamation for House of Representatives of which George W Carter is Speaker to disperse this House assembled yesterday with Speaker Carter in chair at twelve 12 oclock in compliance with previous adjournment but not at Mechanics Institute as the entrance was barred by police force—Governor after adjournment of the House day before yesterday surreptitiously notified his friends to meet in Extra Session same day with closed doors without a quorum. It is believed they are said to have expelled the Speaker at eleven half oclock, yesterday said extra session adjourned sine die at 12 oclock—Gov Warmouths socalled House met in session soon after adjournment of the House—Governor thus revolutionizes it before its regular session the following day Gov Warmouth House Continues the same Members were unseated by Contest day before yesterday thus claiming a quorum Speaker Carters House is regarded as the only legal House by nine tenths of the citizens & excitement runs high this House will impeach Warmouth if protected today It is believed the Citizens seem to be resolved to protect Carter & his House Even with force" "All Judges Except Dibble Will Sign protest against legality of Warmouths House the most influential Papers and Citizens En masse Endorse action of House If Control of troops when Needed is assured to legitimate House of Representatives None will be required for the Moral Effect will lose Govr all his adherents most prominent democrats Say they will cheerfully aid Your reelection to Secure Warmoths defeat defeat Several impromptu meetings on Canal Street tonight Endorsing action of House" "Genl Emory has withdrawn all troops & refused to aid Warmoth in coercing House. Police armed with rifles *specer* I believe in company with a few militia marched to the House occupied by legislature to oust them the militia refuse to use force & have retired with the police intense excitement & determination of citizens en masse to support the House which fully pledged to reform speeches are being made by Carter & most prominent citizens white & colored without distinction of party to fully five thousand people" "Extract from New Orleans times this evening reform & repeal the necessary combination the interest we feel in common with the great body of our honest citizens in the struggle of the factions now going on in this city springs entirely from our desire to see the long promised reforms in our government carried out and from our estimates of the sincerity of the Professions, of the two factions in regard there to   we have always favored any combination in the legislature to effect this end   such an end and such a combination should be pursued without any reference to other political results   no national or political issue ought to deter the good citizens of Louisiana from a coalition with any party to release this people from the degrading bondage in which they are held through the operation of these infamous acts known as the Election & registration bills the Constabulatary & militia bills the School funding & metropolitan bills   there can therefore be no doubt or hesitation as to the course in regard to these bills of all who unite or act with that party or act to keep it in power   they thereby place themselves clearly & unequivocally on the side of the most shameful & corrupting despotism & against the people who will be certain to hold them to a serious reckoning for their treason   but the democrats are sought to be deceived or intimidated from their duty in the obvious course indicated by the appeal to their partisan prejudices through the suggestion that they are giving aid to the grant administration Separating themselves from their party in the nation & contributing to secure the renomination of the prest   if these were inevitable effects of a combination against the state administration & there should be any just grounds for the Pretense that the adherents of Gov Warmoth were opposed to grant there will no hesitation throughout this State among all classes of honest citizens in uniting in the declaration that the repeal of the vile bills of which this State has been made the object slave & Pitiful victim of the most rapacious round of political knaves & adventurers that ever desolated a Country far outweighs in interest & importance any measures which could be involved in the presidential Contest" Telegrams received (the third and fourth at 10:12 P.M. and 11:30 P.M.), *ibid.*, RG 94, Letters Received, 37 1872. On Jan. 8, Orville E. Babcock wrote to USG, recently returned from Philadelphia. "I hand you herewith all the telegrams from NewOrleans received during your absence—All were sent on receipt to the Secty of War. I send also copies of Gen Emory's despatches, which the Secty of War sent for your information—No other despatches of importance received during your absence ... P. S. I enclose a note from Dr Parker—to which he is anxious to receive an answer this evening—in order to have it published—" ALS, *ibid.* Enclosures are *ibid.*

On Jan. 9, Col. William H. Emory telegraphed three times to AG Edward D. Townsend. "Confidential—For the last three 3 days peace has been maintained solely by the display of the U. S. troops and a contest for the State House is at this moment only avoided by my placing troops near that point with definite orders to prevent riot—The difficulties between the contending parties are as far from a solution as ever and the members representing the factions in both Houses are so nearly equal & so bitter that the collission if it be allowed to come on must be a very disastrous one—The facts are not sufficiently apparent to justify me in committing the Government to either side—... No result is obtained & the contending parties are getting farther apart & more desperate than ever—I therefore respectfully suggest that I should be instructed to declare Martial law ..." "I learn my telegram of last night did not leave this City until this morning, The troops are in hand and I can keep the peace probably without the proclamation of martial law, but it will be claimed that they have done so, in the interest of the Governor's faction of the legislature it may be as well to suspend action on that part of my telegram requesting martial law to be proclaimed until today has passed" "I think it due to the right understanding of the uses being made of the troops here to state the fact that the building occupied by the warmoth legislature is the same as that occupied by the Governor for his office,   the Call for troops to go to its protection has been made twice and the Call in each Case especially set forth that an armed Mob was approaching. The troops are not stationed in proximity to that building as has been represented in telegrams from here they are in fact stationed near my headquarters and are about equidistant from both legislative buildings and any protection apparently afforded one faction of the legislature is incidental to the fact that it occupies the same building as the Governor's," Telegrams received (the first at 11:35 A.M., the second at 1:35 P.M., and the third on Jan. 10), *ibid.*

On Jan. 9, Casey twice telegraphed to USG. "Governor Warmoth is asking General Emory for more troops, and this morning published a proclamation, from which I make the following extract: 'The civil authority of the State has ample power to enforce the law and preserve order. Within its limits the temper and disposition of the people of all classes and political opinions are to sustain the authorities in the discharge of their duties. There is no need, in Louisiana, of any extraneous power or military force to assist the State authorities in maintaining order and enforcing law.' If he can keep the peace, the people ask that troops be withdrawn from the city. If not, that martial law be proclaimed. You will understand, from my former dispatches, the effect troops protecting Mechanics' Institute has on the anti-Warmothites. Warmoth's friends flooding the city and North with false statements; he also controls the agent of Associated Press. Warmoth's friends have also so assiduously circulated the report that authorities at Washington are in favor of his wing of the party that many are deterred from acting. A large majority of the citizens respect the Federal Government, even should it oppress them by continuing Warmoth's usurpation over them; but if it gives them relief they will as one man testify their gratitude." "Warmoth, with police and militia to guard the Mechanics' Institute and prevent, by force, his own men from leaving and his opponents from entering, and the presence of Federal troops to answer his requisition in case of collision between police and sergeant-at-arms of house, give great advantage to Warmoth and intimidate anti-Warmoth members, and if continued will have a most disastrous effect. I agree with the dispatch just sent to Kellogg by Packard as the only solution." *HED,* 42-2-268, 56. On the same day, J. Henry Burch and thirteen others, New Orleans, petitioned USG. "We, the undersigned, colored members of the house of representatives, (Carter, speaker,) desire to state that we have been deprived of our rights, as members of said house, by the police under control of Governor Warmoth; that we are earnest adherents of reform measures, and curtailment of the enormous [—] of the governor, and for that reason are obnoxious to him; that, after a regular adjournment of the house on Thursday to meet on Friday, at 12 m., Governor Warmoth, in a surreptitious manner, without authority of law, and in violation of the constitution, convened a so-called extra session, which pretended to adjourn *sine die* at 11.30 a. m., on Friday; that, by the action of this revolutionary so-called house of representatives, it was pretended that the speaker was deposed, though there was not a quorum present; that on Friday, at 12 m., the regular hour of meeting, Governor Warmoth had the hall of the house of representatives guarded by the police and the few military that could be induced to respond to the call, and the speaker's room barricaded, with intent and purpose to continue as speaker, by force, if necessary, a man named Brewster—said to have been elected by said house during extra session; that the house, save the minority controlled by the governor, was compelled by reason of the presence of armed police, and from fear of violence of death at their hands, to retire to another hall, there to hold their sessions until such time as competent authority can replace them in possession of the hall legitimately belonging to them; that we are now beset by the executive and some part of the judicial depart-

ment of the State government, in the interest of Warmoth, with unwarranted interference with the legislative department of the government; that we ask the protection
due as representatives of the people and our race, and we therefore claim the protection of the United States Government for our house of representatives, and that,
finally, in conjunction with the State central republican committee, and with the
masses of the people, irrespective of color or party, we request that you declare
martial law, and thus give us our rights." *Ibid.* (bracketed word omitted in source),
pp. 54–55.

On Jan. 10, Casey telegraphed three times to USG. "Police has now occupied
all approaches to temporary hall of house of representatives, to prevent meeting of
house at regular hour to-day. Cannot General Emory be directed to furnish troops
to protect and clear the approaches to the hall? The regular hall where Warmoth
has been sitting is also guarded by police and militia, so that Warmoth controls
both buildings." "Received for transmission to you a communication from fifteen
State senators, too long for telegraphing. It alleges that governor has taken forcible
possession of the State-house, police, militia, and armed thugs, and has excluded
therefrom all citizens not in his interest, together with speaker and majority of legal
members of the house; and he has by force maintained an illegal house of representatives. It gives a synopsis of proceedings of the legislature this session, and declares
that the subscribers cannot attend the session of the senate for fear of threatened
and illegal imprisonment. In order that they may discharge their duties to the State,
they beg you to declare martial law. Will forward by mail." "The original of dispatch
to you by democratic committee of this morning asking for martial law is in my
possession. They have also telegraphed to Kerr, to urge martial law. The killing of
Whyland last night is said by police to have been done by McCormick, a sergeant
of the house appointed by Carter. Citizens who witnessed the row say the shooting
was done by police. Some bankers and brokers, holding securities based upon the
action of Warmoth and his legislature, are opposed to martial law, and are giving
him secret support. Warmoth controls the police, militia, and some courts, and can
do any unlawful act which the citizens can only resist by force. This being riot, the
regular troops step in and suppress it. The sentiment of nine-tenths of the citizens
are exceedingly friendly to the administration, and say they cannot fight the troops,
and hail the Government as their deliverer, if Warmoth usurpation could be checked."
Ibid., pp. 57–58. On the same day, H. D. Ogden and F. Fusilier, Democratic State
Committee, New Orleans, telegraphed to USG. "The executive committee of the
State central committee of the democratic party of this State have resolved to request
your Excellency to immediately declare martial law in the parish of Orleans. The
governor has subverted by armed violence the government of the State, and the
committee resort to the recommendation of this extreme remedy, in the interest of
public order and public peace and the preservation of the community, against the
state of anarchy precipitated upon the people by the revolutionary proceedings of
the governor." *HMD*, 42-2-211, 372.

Also on Jan. 10, U.S. Senator William P. Kellogg of La. wrote to USG. "I have
just received the enclosed dispatches from Judge Cotton & Mr Packard. I hope
Something can be done for the *Citizens* in this matter   will you please read dispatches & oblige" ALS, OFH. On Jan. 9, Stephen B. Packard, U.S. marshal, New
Orleans, had telegraphed to Kellogg. "After consultation, have concluded martial law
for parish of Orleans best solution, and mayor has just telegraphed President to
declare it. I think under martial law General Emory can settle State-house question.
Warmoth has an illegal assemblage in the institute, and house cannot get possession

without fight, when troops will have to interfere as executive department in same building. House meets in hall over Gem Saloon; best halls refused; afraid of assault by police. Immense mass meeting will be held to-morrow night Lafayette Square. Can't help associated press, whom Warmoth owns, lying. Warmoth will attempt to compel obedience to injunction of Dibbley court, and punish members for contempt. Citizens determined to sustain Carter's house. Warmoth determined to break up. Must be collision soon. Executive or judicial no right to extinguish legislative department. Get better news agent here if want facts. Dispatches sent Blair by democrats. Public opinion is fully with us, and must judge yourself whether to present matter in Senate." *HED*, 42-2-268, 53. The telegram from J. B. Cotton, New Orleans, to Kellogg is *ibid.*

On Jan. 11, Casey telegraphed to USG. "The following is the editorial of the Bee of this morning. After reading give to press: '*The situation.* The seizure by Governor Warmoth's police, yesterday morning, of the building at No. 17 Royal street, where the house of representatives, under Mr. Carter's speakership, had held its session, created considerable excitement in this city, and the general opinion that the difficulty between Governor Warmoth and his adversaries could be settled in no other way than by President Grant establishing military in this parish. Accordingly, a number of telegrams were forwarded to Washington by citizens, representing the necessity that existed for martial law, but at a late hour last night the President had not seen fit to direct General Emory to declare it. There is however, reason to hope that, when the President and his advisers come to comprehend the true condition of affairs here they will feel themselves justified in granting the request that has been so urgently addressed to them. We see no *other* possible solution of the difficulty than by the interference of the Federal Government.... We again appeal to the President of the United States, and ask him to come to the relief of our downtrodden people.'" *Ibid.*, pp. 63–64.

On Dec. 18, 1871, U.S. Representative J. Hale Sypher of La. had written to Governor Henry C. Warmoth of La. "*Confidential* ... Will you delegate Senator West or myself to assure the President *for you,* that the vote of Louisiana in the National Convention and in the Electoral College will be cast for his re-elect[ion] to the presidency? *On Conditio*[n] that all the federal officials i[n] [—] shall cease their opposition [— —] Administration and work [—] harmony with you to carry the State for the Republican Party. I have seen the President several times recently in relation to our local matters, and I am lead to hope for amicable settlement of the local differences in our State— Let me hear from you at your earliest Convenience   I hope you are very well" ALS, Warmoth Papers, Southern Historical Collection, University of North Carolina, Chapel Hill, N. C. On March 25, 1872, a correspondent reported from Washington, D. C.: "A large delegation of Louisiana politicians arrived here today. Lieut. Gov. PINCHBECK is among them, and is very earnest in advocating the renomination of Gen. GRANT. As many of the remainder of the delegation as alluded to the Presidential topic were equally pronounced in favor of the Administration. They represent that, in spite of the sensational stories to the contrary, the Louisiana Republicans, of whatever local political stripe, are almost a unit for Gen. GRANT." *New York Times*, March 26, 1872. On March 27, Horace Porter wrote to Lt. Governor Pinckney B. S. Pinchback of La., Washington, D. C. "The President has just received your note, and desires me to say that his engagements will not permit him to have an interview with you this evening. If any other time will suit your convenience he will be pleased to accord you an interview." Copy, DLC-USG, II, 1. About this date, "Lieutenant Governor Pinchback had another interview, in which it was again urged that the

President interfere in the condition politics assume in the State of Louisiana. The President replied that he thought he would be initiating a bad policy to meddle with the politics of any State; that it would be setting a questionable precedent for the future. The people resident in that State understood the situation there better than he, and he would prefer that they would harmonize by settling their difficulties among themselves." *Washington Chronicle*, March 29, 1872. See *PUSG*, 19, 126–27; letter to William W. Belknap, Jan. 15, 1872.

To Hamilton Fish

Washington, D. C. Jan.y 11th *1872.*

HON. HAMILTON FISH,
SEC. OF STATE;
DEAR SIR:

Enclosed I send you a letter from Governor Parsons,[1] of Ala. with draft payable to Minister Partridge.[2] The letter explains the object of the draft, and gives all the information that Gov. Parsons has of the whereabouts of the parties for whom it is intended. Will you be kind enough to send Mr. P. the letter and draft with instructions to have the parties found, if possible, and sent home and notify Gov. P. of the action taken. Should the parties not be found the draft should, of course, be returned.

Very Truly Yours,
U. S. GRANT

ALS, DNA, RG 59, Miscellaneous Letters. On Jan. 4, 1872, Lewis E. Parsons, Mobile, wrote to USG. "The enclosed draft for four hundred & ten dollars, by Jay Cooke &Co. of Washn D. C. on Jay Cooke &Co. of New York, numbered 4342 payable to & endorsed by me, as suggested by your Excellency, to the order of Genl. James R. Partridge, American Minister at Rio Janeiro Brazil, is herewith transmitted to aid Mrs Samuel D. Watson & her children to return to this, their native land. The amount has been contributed for this purpose by her friends in this state. The last letter they have from her bears date Sept. 3. 1871 at Linhares, Rio Doces, Province of Espirito Santo Brazil—Mr Watson was then dead & she mentions her intention to leave that place, where there were no Americans & go to San Paulo, where she says there are many. This for the sake of her children. Since that letter was written her friends in Alabama have learned though a Mr. William Norris, whose father resides somewhere between Rio Doces & Rio Janeiro, that a widow & her children, formerly of Talladega Co. Ala. had come on foot from Rio Doces to his his fathers—subsisting on the way on roots & that one of the children died before they reached there from having eaten of a poisonous root—Her friends suppose this must be Mrs Watson & her children, as they know of no other family from our county in Brazil—Trusting that Genl. Partridge may be able to find them at an early day & tendering you the hearty thanks of Mrs Watsons friends—. . . P. S. Please direct that the safe arrival of this letter & draft may be communicated to me, at Talladega Ala." ALS, *ibid.* On March 18, Parsons, Talladega, wrote to USG. "I have the honor to inform you that the friends of Mrs Samuel D. Watson have recd a letter from her dated 'Linhares Brazil January 2nd 1872', in which she says, that she and her children are on their way to Rio—Mrs W—has probably reached Rio by this time, and, if you will cause this information to be transmitted to Genl Partridge, you will confer a lasting favor upon the lady herself and upon her friends in Alabama—I have not recd an acknowledgement from the State Department of the draft by Jay Cook and Co for $410 00, which I endorsed, as suggested by your Excellency to the order of Genl Partridge for the purpose of defraying the expenses of Mrs Watson and children to the United States—" LS, *ibid.*

On Jan. 22, James R. Partridge, U.S. minister, Rio de Janeiro, had written to Secretary of State Hamilton Fish. "In connexion with the interest expressed by the President, in his last annual mMessage, in the condition of the population in the Southern States, and the measures he recommends for their relief, I have thought it would not be unacceptable if I recurred to the condition of those (women and children) who came from those States to Brazil after 1865, and still remain—chiefly in the province of San Paulo—simply because they have lost everything and are without employment or the means of returning. Our Government has very generously offered free passage home to such on board any U. S. vessel returning from this Station; and all who *could* go, in that way, have already gladly availed themselves of this liberality. But those who suffer most hardship here, are those who, personally, deserve it least. I refer to those families of women and children, who have lost here those relatives on whom they depended for support; who cannot be accommodated on board of a man of war; and who are without the means of paying passage home. . . ." LS, *ibid.*, Diplomatic Despatches, Brazil. On Feb. 20, Partridge acknowledged the receipt of Parsons's Jan. 4 letter to USG and the draft. LS, *ibid.* On Feb. 28, Partridge wrote to Fish. "In further reply to your No 28 in relation to the case of Mrs. Saml D. Watson (see my No 37), I beg to say that Mrs. Watson and her children arrived in Rio about three weeks ago; that some gentlemen there raised a subscription and secured a passage for them on board the 'Campanero,' which left for Baltimore, on the 18th. instant. I therefore re-enclose the draft on Jay Cooke &Co. of New York (No 4342) for $410. to be returned to Governor Parsons together with the letter addressed by him to the President enclosed in your No 28 to me. The departure of Mrs. Watson became known to me just one day too late to report this to you by the last packet." LS, *ibid.* See *PUSG*, 20, 444–45.

1. Born in 1817 in Lisle, N. Y., Parsons, an Ala. lawyer and state legislator (1859–65), was successively a Whig, Know Nothing, Douglas Democrat (1860), and Unionist. Appointed provisional governor of Ala. (June 21-Dec. 20, 1865), he opposed black suffrage, was elected to the U.S. Senate on Nov. 28, 1865, but was precluded from taking his seat by the Dec. 4 congressional resolution creating a joint committee to study conditions in the Southern states. After supporting Horatio Seymour for president (1868), Parsons became Republican speaker of the Ala. legislature (1872). See *SRC*, 42-2-41, part 8, p. 95; Sarah Van V. Woolfolk, "Five Men Called Scalawags," *Alabama Review*, 17 (1964), 45–55.

On Oct. 15, 1874, U.S. Representative Alexander White of Ala., Florence, telegraphed to USG. "I recommend Lewis E. Parsons for District Court Judge." Telegram received (at 12:55 P.M.), DNA, RG 60, Records Relating to Appointments. On Dec. 8, U.S. Representative Charles Pelham of Ala. wrote to USG. "In recommending Ex Gov Lewis E Parsons for the position of Judge of the District Court of the United States

for the State of Alabama to fill the vacancy made by the resignation of Judge Richard
Busteed, I desire to call your Excellencys attention to the following facts—Mr Parsons has been a citizen of Alabama since 1839. was admitted to practice law in the
Supreme Court of Alabama in 1842 since which time he has been a regular practitioner in that court and is justly regarded one of the ablest Attorneys in the state—
My acquaintance personally with Mr Parsons began in Jany 1857. and I dont think
that he had taken an active part in politics before that time—since then I have known
him intimately having practiced in the same courts with him all the time except from
1868 to 73 during which years I was presiding as Circuit Judge in the State Court &
during that time he was an active practitioner and I had equally as good opportunities
to know his status as an attorney and a citizen   In 1859 he was elected to the Legislature of the State of Alabama as a *Union man*—In 1860 he canvassed the state as an
Elector for the state at large on the *Union democratic ticket.* He opposed the secession
of the state in 1861 and was known throughout the state to be opposed to the
Rebellion ~~through~~ during its continuance—In the year 1863 he was elected to the
Legislature mainly by the votes & influence of the 'Union Constitutional men' when
he introduced what were known as the 'Peace' or 'Reconstruction Resolutions.' In
65 he was appointed Provisional Govenor of Alabama and afterwards elected to the
United States Senater under the Constitution of 1865. In 1869 Mr Parsons supported
and voted for Hon R S Heflin the Republican candidate for Congress and since that
time has uniformly acted with and supported the Republican party—In the campaign of 72 he canvassed the state of Alabama as Elector for the State at Large on
the Republican ticket—At the same time he was elected as Republican nominee to
the Legislature of Alabama and was unanimously elected Speaker of the House in
the 'Court House Assembly'. . ." ALS, *ibid.* No appointment followed. See letter to
Charles W. Buckley, Nov. 21, 1870.
    2. See letter to Hamilton Fish, Dec. 21, 1870.

Endorsement

————

A similar dispatch was rec'd from Gn. Granger[1] this evening and
refered to the Atty. Gen   It probably will be well to give Gen.
Granger orders to preserve the peace until further information
is rec'd.

                                                    U. S. GRANT

JAN. 11TH /72

AES, DNA, RG 94, Letters Received, 90 1872. Written on a telegram of Jan. 11, 1872,
from Governor Marsh Giddings of New Mexico Territory to USG. "Disorder and
domestic Violence Exists in our Legislature   Civil authority is insufficient   will you
order General Granger with such Little force as may be Practicable to aid me in
Prudently preserving order and maintaining the authority of Law" Telegram received (at 11:00 P.M.), *ibid.* On the same day, Col. Gordon Granger, Santa Fé, had
telegraphed to USG. "The scenes which took place in the legislature of Louisiana
on the third and fourth are being duplicated here—upon requisition of the Governor

I have furnished troops to prevent Violence   please give me instructions" Telegram received (at 4:45 P.M.), *ibid.* On Jan. 12, AG Edward D. Townsend telegraphed to Brig. Gen. John Pope, Dept. of the Mo., Fort Leavenworth. ". . . The President directs that Granger be instructed to use U. S. troops to maintain peace, but carefully to avoid taking sides with either party—. . ." Copy, *ibid.*, Letters Sent.

On Jan. 15, Secretary of State Hamilton Fish wrote in his diary about a discussion with USG. "I shew him telegram rec' from Wetter (Secy of New Mexico) asking advice respecting the organization of the Territorial Legislature—& mention that Senator Ferry of Mich. had shewn me this morng a telegram from the Govr (Giddings) which suggests that Wetter is aiding certain parties in N. M. to change the political complexion of the Legislature & is working in with Democrats—Prsdt directs that answer be sent to Wetter to take no steps until full report be made of all the facts" DLC-Hamilton Fish. On Jan. 24, an investigative committee reported that "the action of His Excellency, Marsh Giddings, Governor of said Territory, in making requisition for United States troops, to be stationed in and about the halls of legislation, and the action of Milnor Rudolph, late Speaker of the House of Representatives of this Legislative Assembly, in advising and procuring such requisition for troops, was hasty and ill-considered in the extreme and entirely unwarranted by the state of public feeling existing at the time such requisition was made. Resolved, That the present division in the House of Representatives, is owing to the obnoxious character of Joseph G. Palen, present Chief Justice of this Territory—added to the fact, that Governor Giddings, by the abuse of his veto power, has sought to defeat the evident will of the people, as expressed in the bill assigning the said Chief Justice to the most remote district of the Territory. Resolved, That the conduct of the said Chief Justice, and his associate, Hezekiah S. Johnson, in assuming, as Judges of the Supreme Court of this Territory, to pass upon the action of the House of Representatives of this Legislative Assembly, by which said House declared that certain contestants were entitled to seats in that body, and in assuming to decide, under a proceeding upon *Habeas Corpus*, that said action of the House was revolutionary and void, were guilty of a gross abuse of their judicial powers; and that by their conduct in this instance, they have shown themselves to be utterly unworthy of the high positions in which chance has placed them." *Report of the Committee of Investigation of the Council of the Legislative Assembly of the Territory of New Mexico, Appointed to Examine into the Stationing of U. S. Troops in and about the Legislative Halls of said Territory* (Santa Fe, 1872). Related documents are in DNA, RG 59, New Mexico Territorial Papers. See *PUSG*, 20, 375–78.

On March 17, 1873, U.S. Delegate José M. Gallegos of New Mexico Territory wrote to USG. "In regard to the matter of Chief Justice of New Mexico, The Attorney General refers me to you. Out of a bar numbering twenty-four (24) lawyers (a list of which I enclose) only eight (8) recommend Judge Palen. Were his claims to reappointment very strong, he surely would have a larger proportion of the members of the legal profession in his favor. I have filed statement, *on oath*, from gentlemen well informed in the premises, showing that it would be an injustice to the people of New Mexico to re-appoint Judge Palen. . . ." LS, DNA, RG 60, Records Relating to Appointments. A related letter is *ibid.* On March 13, USG nominated Joseph G. Palen to continue as chief justice, New Mexico Territory.

On June 5, 1871, U.S. Senator Thomas W. Ferry of Mich., Grand Haven, had written to Fish. "Upon consultation with our friend & worthy Citizen, Mr Chandler & I find that the secretaryship of one of the Territories will not be so acceptable to him. May we then renew our personal request that upon the happening of the first vacancy Marsh Giddings Esq. may be appointed a Governor of one of the Territories of the Union? Your compliance will exceedingly oblige us both." ALS, *ibid.*, RG 59, Letters of Application and Recommendation. On June 13, Ferry, Chicago, telegraphed to Fish. "Give Marsh Giddings, Warners place New Mexico—" Copy, *ibid.* On July 16, U.S. Senator Zachariah Chandler of Mich., Detroit, wrote to Fish. "Mr Ferry informs me that Ex Senator Warner has declined the Governorship of New Mexico. If so I hope you will be able to give it to Judge Marsh Giddings of this State Senator Ferry & I are exceedingly anxious to do this thing & Michigan is almost without representation in Territorial appointments while Kansas is *well taken care of* Ferry informs me that the appointment lies between Michigan and Kansas. If this be so! it ought not to lie there long. Michigan never wavers *anywhere* She is Sound at the ballot box, at conventions in the Senate, House of Representatives *everywhere* & 1.250.000 such People are not excelled even by Kansas. I hope you can do it on Ferrys a/c if for no other" ALS, *ibid.* On July 27, Fish wrote to Chandler. "*Private* . . . All right—I send a Commission as Govr of New Mexico, for Mr Giddings to the President for his signature to day." ALS, DLC-Zachariah Chandler. On July 8, 1870, USG had nominated Giddings as consul gen., Calcutta. On May 22, 1871, Ferry, Washington, D. C., wrote to Fish. "We respectfully recommend the appointment of Genl. Allyne C. Litchfield Consul General at Calcutta in place of Marsh Giddings Esq who has resigned" ALS, DNA, RG 59, Letters of Application and Recommendation. On the same day, USG nominated Allyne C. Litchfield as consul gen., Calcutta. On Dec. 6, USG nominated Giddings as governor, New Mexico Territory. See Endorsement, May 19, 1873; Calvin Horn, *New Mexico's Troubled Years: The Story of the Early Territorial Governors* (Albuquerque, 1963), pp. 152–64.

On May 18, 1871, Thomas Murphy, collector of customs, New York City, had written to USG. "The many friends of Col. Alfred M. Wood of the City of Brooklyn are anxious that he should receive the appointment of Governor of New Mexico. . . ." LS, DNA, RG 59, Letters of Application and Recommendation. On the same day, Sigismund Kaufmann, New York City, wrote to USG. "I understand that Col. Alfred M. Wood of Brooklyn, late Mayor of that City, has been named by his friends as a fit Gentleman for the office of Governor of New Mexico, if a vacancy should occur. It would give me great pleasure to see Col. Wood appointed . . ." ALS, *ibid.* Related papers are *ibid.* No appointment followed.

1. Former maj. gen. of vols., often subjected to USG's criticism, Col. Gordon Granger assumed command of the District of New Mexico on April 29, 1871. See *PUSG*, 5, 307; *ibid.*, 17, 140–42.

To Henry L. Dawes

Washington D. C. Jan.y 12th *1872*

HON. H. L. DAWES: M. C.

DEAR SIR:

I hope you will be able to pass to-day the resolution offered by you yesterday to send a Congressional committe to New Orleans to investigate affairs there.[1] I made the request of the Speaker of the House[2] the evening of the 10th inst. to obtain such a committee.

The condition of affairs there is as bad as possible no doubt but I have not been able to see any justification for Executive interference.[3]

> Very respectfully
> Your obt. svt.
> U. S. GRANT

ALS, DLC-Henry L. Dawes. Born in 1816 in Cummington, Mass., Henry L. Dawes graduated from Yale (1839), became a lawyer active in Mass. politics, entered the U.S. House of Representatives in 1857 as a Republican, and served as chairman of the Ways and Means Committee (1871–75). On Jan. 12, 1872, Governor Henry C. Warmoth of La., New Orleans, telegraphed to U.S. Senator J. Rodman West of La. "I see by the papers that you proposed yesterday the appointment of a committee to investigate Louisiana affairs. I thank you for it. We will show a most *damnable* conspiracy between democrats, custom-house officials, and the United States marshal to overthrow the State government. A United States commissioner, until lately a clerk in the United States marshal's office, issued writs, arrested the governor, lieutenant governor, members of the senate, and twenty members of the house, at the moment of assembling, and during the absence of the members seven were turned out and six conspirators seated in their places. The house was intimidated by an armed secret society called the Seventy-six, which was assembled near the capitol by a proclamation in the papers of Thursday morning. Democrats, with Herwig and Coupland, deputy collectors; Ingraham, keeper of the bonded warehouse; O'Hara, an inspector; and Sypher, an assistant on custom-house work, all senators, have succeeded in breaking a quorum of the senate, by being absent on the revenue-cutter Wilderness for a week, and are now in the State of Mississippi. The bolters consist of twenty democrats and twenty republicans, several of the latter employés in the custom-house. They hold informal meetings in the building now. The marshal, collector, and other officials, having failed to overthrow the government by fraud and mob violence, are now inducing people to request martial law. Many people have requested it, among others six democratic district judges. The only two republican judges refused to sign. The citizens' committee, representing property-holders' association, passed a resolution requesting martial law by a vote of twenty-one to nineteen. The avowed object of this movement is to use United States troops to put expelled conspirators back into the house of representatives, where they can renew their efforts to overturn the government. . . . This is for Mr. Dawes, of the House." HED, 42-2-268, 73–74. On March 20, Secretary of State Hamilton Fish wrote in his diary. "Boutwell says he has had an interview with Warmouth of Louisiana, that W. professes an entire willingness to reconcile & unite the party— that he has (as B. thinks) just grounds of complaint—that Casey & Packard have behaved badly to him   Says that a fund of $50.000 was raised of which $18.000 was appropriated for the Senate ($1.000 for each Member) & the remainder for the lower House of Louisiana—to secure the passage of what was Called the 'Levee Bill'— that this money (which he calls a 'Corruption fund') was held by Casey, & actually locked up in the Government Safe in the Custom House—He thinks Casey ought to resign, & Packard to be removed—in which case Louisiana will be ensured for the Republican ticket" DLC-Hamilton Fish. See telegram to James F. Casey, March 27, 1871, note 1.

On May 12, 1872, Horace Porter wrote to James F. Casey, collector of customs, New Orleans. "The President has for the first time read over the testimony recently taken by the Congressional Committee in regard to affairs in New Orleans. His conviction is that both you and your deputy Mr. Herwig have proved efficient and honest officers so far as the interests of the goverment are concerned and that a fair and impartial examination into your official conduct would exonerate you of every charge brought against you in that capacity, yet the suspicions that will fill the mind of the public in reading the testimony and the loss of confidence on the part of the people who have no opportunity ~~to~~ ~~to~~of investigating and weighing all the facts in the case, induces him to request that both you and Mr Herwig will ~~tend~~ upon receipt of this letter tender your resignations. His confidence is you both is unshaken in regard to the manner in which you have administered the offices intrusted to you, but he feels that public opinion must have its weight when its judgment rests upon sworn testimony" ADf, USG 3; copy, *ibid.* On May 17, Casey wrote to USG. "Enclosed I send you my resignation   I enclose two so you can use the one you think best   I know you would have not asked for it if it had not been necessary and although feeling some what mortified that it was necessary and knowing how my enemies would chuckle over it still I accept it as one of the accidents that may occur and havent a word of complaint but feel that I have been sustained by you as kindly and generously as ever man was and I only hope you will think I take it as I really do   I feel confident some of the influences brought to bear ~~was~~ere not of a proper caracter as I am satesfied some of the Committee were working in the interest of of Warmoth, but you could not act on supposition therefore I can well see how you were compelled to take the course you did   Many persons are anxious I should remain in office   while this would be pleasant for me still I am more than willing to act as you think best   Persons are protesting by private letters petitions and the various political organization are passing resolutions sustaining me and asking my retention in office   While I am not doing any thing to accomplish this still it is very pleasant to me as it will show you that I deserved the confidence and trust you placed in me at least in the opinion of the people here   I am intterupted so often I can not write as I want to but will write again tomorrow   I would request you to read the letters sent on to you by different parties about me as it will show you how many friends I have   Emma and the children are very well and sends much love to you all   Remember General I appreciate your kindness and because it becomes necessary to remove me will make me just as true to you as if I am retained" ALS, *ibid.* The enclosures are dated May 17 from Casey to USG. "I have the honor to tender my resignation as Collector of the Port of New Orleans to take effect from the date of the qualification of my successor. I desire to convey to you the deep sense of gratitude I feel for the consideration and kindness extended to me in the discharge of my official duties. I shall labor to secure the continued success of your administration and whether in public or private life my whole energies will be directed to that end." "I have the honor to tender my resignation as Collector of the Port of New Orleans, to take effect at your pleasure. . . ." LS, *ibid.* On May 16, Stephen B. Packard, U.S. marshal and president, Republican State Central Executive Committee, New Orleans, promulgated a resolution. "At a meeting of this Committee held this day, the following resolutions were offered by Hon. George W. Carter, and unanimously adopted: Resolved, That after a full consideration of all the facts of the case, and with due reference to the interest of the public service, and the success of the Republican Party, in our judgement each class of interest specified requires the retention of: Col. James F. Casey and Depty. Coll. P. F. Herwig in their present official positions, and we earnestly request the President to suspend any action looking either to their resignation or removal. Resolved, That a copy of this resolution be forwarded to the President by mail." DS, *ibid.* On May 17, Edward C. Billings, New Orleans, wrote to USG. "With reference to the action of the administration as to Messrs Casey and Herwig, I beg leave to say—I think the view of the party here is almost unanimously as follows: that Col Casey and Mr Herwig have with great fidelity discharged their official duties, and labored for the interests of the party; and if consistent with the interests of the National Party, they would strongly desire to see them retained. My own opinion, is decidedly, that so far as our interests in Louisiana are concerned, nothing would be gained for us, by their being displaced. I would further respectfully request that your Excellency would take no final action as to the resignations and none as to successors until our Philadelphia delegation (of which I am a member) can have an interview with you. We are in perfect harmony with Col Casey and will present to your Excellency his and our views on the subject. We will come to Washington at the earliest practical moment and I respectfully suggest that no matter what action is to be taken, no harm can be done by leaving matters in their present state till then." LS, *ibid.* On the same day, J. M. Hoyle, New Orleans, wrote to USG. "I take the liberty of addressing you upon a Subject of serious consequences to this City and State, that is the resignations of our Collector of the Port, Col Casey and his Chief Deputy Mr Herwig. Let me beg of you not to accept of them, for by so doing, you will deprive us of the only chance we have left to carry this State for the Republican Party, against the corrupting influences of the Governor of this State, for any new appointment that you might make, would be open to the new influences that the Position would give him, and in no way, better our position, or give us any more Strenght. Hoping you will take this letter in the Spirit that it is writen by one of your Staunch Supporters, ... My references are Senators, Kellogg, Sypher and Sheldon." ALS, DNA, RG 56, Collector of Customs Applications. On May 21, Fabius McK. Dunn, appraiser of merchandise and president, Orleans Parish Republican Executive Committee, New Orleans, promulgated a resolution. "At a regular meeting of this Club held on the above date the following communication was received and on motion unanimously adopted. ... Whereas Rumors have been circulated that Col James. F. Casey, Collector of the Port of New Orleans and Special Deputy Collector P. F. Herwig, have for some reasons unaccountable to the Republicans of this parish, been induced to tender their resignations. and. Whereas, The Republicans of the parish of Orleans have invairably found in Col James F Casey and Hon P. F. Herwig friends as well as true Republicans therefore be it Resolved That we the Parish Committee, parish of Orleans, representatives of the Republicans of this parish do hereby endorse the actions the actions of Col James F. Casey and Hon P. F. Herwig as leaders in the Republican party, as well as Collector and Sp'l Deputy Collector of the Port of New Orleans. Be it further Resolved That if the rumors aflot have any foundation whatever, we the duly accredited representatives of the Republican party in this parish, request our Senators and Representatives in Congress to use their utmost influence to have Col. James F Casey and Hon. P. F. Herwig, retained as Collector and Deputy Collector of the Port of New Orleans. Be it further Resolved That, a copy of these Resolutions, be forwarded to President U. S. Grant and to our representatives in Congress, and to each ward club in this Parish for endorsement, and to the State Central Ex Committee, with the request that they approve the same and that a copy to each Parish Committee in the State, and that said committees be instructed to furnish a copy to each Ward Club in their respective parishes, requesting Concurrence." Copy, USG 3. Related clippings are *ibid.* In [*May*], Harlow J. Phelps *et al.* petitioned USG. "The undersigned representing the business interests of this city urge the retention of James F. Casey as Collector of the port of New Orleans. His management of the business is very satisfactory and a change at present will seriously affect the interests of business men." DS (24 signatures), *ibid.* On June 4, the La. delegation visited USG "to protest against the removal of Collector Casey, speaking kind words in his favor, and saying that it was the wish and for the interest of the Republican party that he be retained." *Louisville Courier-Journal*, June 5, 1872. USG retained Casey as collector of customs, New Orleans.

    1. On Jan. 11, Dawes asked unanimous consent for a resolution: "That a select committee of five be appointed by the Speaker of the House of Representatives, whose duty it shall be to inquire into the condition of the government of Louisiana, so far as regards the administration and execution of the laws of the United States and the safety of the lives and property of citizens thereof, and to report the same to this House with such recommendations as they may deem expedient;. . ." *CG*, 42–2, 372. On Jan. 15, the House passed a revised resolution. *Ibid.*, pp. 396–97. U.S. Representatives Glenni W. Scofield of Pa., George W. McCrary of Iowa, H. Boardman Smith of N. Y., Stevenson Archer of Md., and R. Milton Speer of Pa., three Republicans and two Democrats, constituted the Select Committee to Investigate the Condition of Affairs in the State of Louisiana. On Jan. 24, this committee met USG before leaving for New Orleans. *Washington Evening Star*, Jan. 24, 1872. See *HMD*, 42-2-211.
    2. James G. Blaine.
    3. On Jan. 10, Porter had written to Secretary of the Treasury George S. Boutwell. "The President has read your letter and thinks it well to send a reliable person to New Orleans to make a thorough investigation of affairs in your department." Copy, DLC-USG, II, 1.

To Benjamin F. Flanders

[*Jan. 12, 1872*]

BENJ F. FLANDERS[1]
MAYOR N. O. LA
Martial law will not be proclaimed in New Orleans under existing circumstances, and no assistance will be given by Federal authorities to persons or parties unlawfully resisting the constituted authorities of the State.

U S GRANT

Copies, DNA, RG 94, Letters Received, 37 1872; *ibid.*, Letters Sent. On Jan. 8 and 9, 1872, Mayor Benjamin F. Flanders of New Orleans telegraphed to USG. "I earnestly recommend and request that you declare Martial law in the Parish of Orleans—I beleive that such action is necessary to prevent a scene of bloodshed and I doubt if it

can in any other way be avoided forty Eight hours" Telegram received, *ibid.*, Letters
Received, 37 1872. "The meeting to-night effected no good, but demonstrated intense
exasperation. I renew former request for martial law, as the only solution of the difficulty. Without martial law the troops cannot act further without compromising the
administration." *HED*, 42-2-268, 60. On Jan. 9, George W. Carter, New Orleans, telegraphed to USG. "The executive is holding the hall of the house of representatives by
the police, and excluding citizens and members therefrom, and attempting, by violence
and intimidation, to control the action of the members. Over half the senate are absent
from the State, and afraid to return, lest violence and arrest should be practiced upon
them. The excitement and indignation against the government is so great among the
people of both parties that an outbreak is imminent and cannot be avoided without a
declaration of martial law. But for the proximity of United States troops to aid the
police, a collision would have taken place ere this between the police and the citizens.
For the protection of the house of representatives, over which I preside, and to prevent
bloodshed, I respectfully suggest a declaration of martial law, and the community,
without distinction of party, will justify the same." *Ibid.*, p. 61. On Jan. 10, Flanders
telegraphed to Attorney Gen. George H. Williams. "I have to-day a petition signed
by a thousand citizens, without regard to party, asking me to swear in citizens for
volunteer police to protect persons and property, in the absence of the regular police,
withdrawn for political purposes; but I cannot comply, because a late law forbids the
mayor to organize or use a police for any purpose. Let us have martial law at once.
The people generally, of all parties and classes, desire martial law. The democrats have
committed themselves, and are the most earnest in favor of it." *Ibid.*, p. 60. On Jan. 12,
Flanders telegraphed to USG. "I must again renew and urge my request for declaration of martial law in the parish of Orleans. The public mind is in a state of great
excitement, suspense, and alarm. Any hour may bring a collision which would only
end in a scene of bloodshed. The desire for martial law is nearly universal with good
citizens of all classes." *Washington Chronicle*, Jan. 13, 1872.

On Jan. 9, Col. William H. Emory, New Orleans, had telegraphed twice to AG
Edward D. Townsend. "A number of the prominent Bankers and property holders are
to be at my Headquarters at four (4) P. M—this evening—I strongly advise no action
be taken on the proposition about martial law, until I communicate what they have to
say—" "The committee referred to in my despatch, of which Mr J. H. Oglesby is the
head, propose first to confer with the two factions and threaten martial law before
asking for it, and I fully concur with Mr Oglesby in that proposition. In the meantime
there is another negotiation going on between the factions themselves which I think
very likely to lead to peace—The U. S. Troops are in position near my Headquarters
to quell any riot or disturbance, and there is not the least disposition in any quarter
to come in contact with them or to disobey any mandate that I have a right to give—
Under these circumstances, though I am greatly in want of additional troops for the
routine business of the Department under the Enforcement Act, I shall not call on
Gen'l Terry for reinforcements in the present phase of affairs—" Copies (the first
sent at 1:45 P.M.), DNA, RG 94, Letters Received, 37 1872. On Jan. 10, Emory twice
telegraphed to Townsend. "The committee which I have designated as the committee
of bankers and capitalists, is in fact the committee of fifty one, of which Mr Marks is
president, composed of the citizens, representing the property and substance of the
city, and appointed by the people to redress grievances,   It has not completed its
labors to settle the war between the factions, and through a sub committee now at
my head quarters, suggests that th[e] consideration of the subject of declaring martial
law, should be postponed to enable them to make further efforts. There is nothing

in the military situation to demand immediate action and I therefore concur in the request of this committee," Telegram received (on Jan. 11), *ibid.* "Early last evening a member of the Legislature was killed in the Streets of the city,   the killing is charged upon the Carter faction and a Coroners Jury has so determined   a Sergeant at Arms and several others have been arrested and a warrant has been sued out for the arrest of Mr Carter himself   The armed Police have seized the hall in which Carters faction were lately in session   I have been ~~applied~~ appealed to by Mr Carter to aid him in regaining ~~the~~ his hall but have positively refused to lend the aid of the troops as requested. I was appealed to by the Governor to aid him in making the arrest of Mr Carter as an accessary to the killing but have declined to use the troops for that purpose—The troops are still at their temporary barracks near these headquarters   so far as the ~~acts~~ action of the Legislat~~ors~~ure and their personal movements are concerned all the effects of Martial Law now exist with the power of ~~the~~ effecting results in the hands of the Governor. The opponents of the Governor claim that the legitimate ~~reason~~ resource is to redress their evils (which is to go into armed resistance) is only restrained by the presence of the U. S. forces. They ~~presume~~ admit that the troops are bound to prevent riot and against them they have apparently no wish or inclination at present to operate   ~~as~~ As I am aware that applications have been sent to the President to declare martial Law and as I may at any moment think proper to recommend it myself I have thought it my duty to communicate the situation. There is great excitement.—I have asked General Terry to send me a squadron of Cavalry at once   a force of that kind is absolutely necessary outside of the present emergency. The Committee of Bankers and capitalists are to meet me at seven O'clock P. M. this evening." Copy, *ibid.* On Jan. 11, Emory twice telegraphed to Townsend. "The committee of fifty one failed to make any compromise between the two factions and in place of bringing me their conclusion at seven o'clock as promised invited me to attend their meeting at hour which I did not deem it advisable to do. Their is nothing more in the military situation to require any military action on the question of martial law, and as the civil authority has officially informed me it does not longer apprehend a riot and that being my own judgment I have sent part of the troops to the barracks and will return the remainder tomorrow   The legislative question is as far from settlement as ever but my part being ended if the committee have anything further to communicate I shall suggest it to be done by the committee," "The following resolutions were handed me ~~by~~ after my telegram of ten thirty had been forwarded,   The citizens association which has passed these resolutions is beyond all doubt the representation of wealth and business capabilities of the city and their means of information of the condition of affairs are more to be depended on than mine,   I therefore recommend these resolutions to the earnest consideration of the Government   These resolutions were handed me in person by Mr Clinton U. S. Treasurer, one of the committee of fifty one ... in view of the facts as stated by the committee to wait upon the Commanding Genl and the committee on conference that they have been unable to effect any arrangement with the two factions and it being extremely important that the difficulty should be brought to an end and that very promptly be it therefore resolved, 'that in the opinion of this committee the only way to solve the problem and to bring our heretofore peaceful city back to a healthy condition is to request Genl Emory to apply to the President of the U. S. for authority to proclaim martial law. . . ." Telegrams received (on Jan. 12), *ibid.* On Jan. 12, USG received a copy of the second telegram. *Ibid.* On the same day, Secretary of State Hamilton Fish wrote in his diary. "CABINET—All present Judge Williams taking his seat as Aty Gnl   The New Orleans difficulties are the subject of considerable discussion—No difference of opinion as to the absence of any justification of granting the request of the Mayor & other prominent Citizens that Martial Law be proclaimed—Considerable discussion as to the form of a reply to be sent—Williams draws a reply which was eventually adopted, almost in the words proposed by him." DLC-Hamilton Fish. A related clipping is *ibid.* During the cabinet meeting, Secretary of War William W. Belknap wrote to Townsend. "Telegraph Genl. Emory as follows: 'Your course is approved. The President has sent the following telegram to the Mayor of New Orleans . . .'" AN (initialed), DNA, RG 94, Letters Received, 37 1872. See letter to James F. Casey, Jan. 10, 1872; letter to William W. Belknap, Jan. 15, 1872.

    1. See *PUSG*, 4, 88–89. Briefly capt., 5th La., Flanders became a special agent of the Treasury Dept. (1863), lost an election for governor of La. (1864), resumed as special Treasury agent (1866), acted as military governor of La. (1867–68), and had served as mayor of New Orleans since 1870.

    On Feb. 9, 1872, Flanders testified before the Select Committee to Investigate the Condition of Affairs in the State of Louisiana. "I am mayor of the city of New Orleans, and was in August last. I have been a resident of the city since December, 1842. . . . I own property worth about $18,000. . . . Q. Did you watch carefully the indications of disturbance in the city in the days preceding the 9th of August convention?—A. Tolerably so. . . . Q. Will you state whether in your judgment the holding of that convention in the United States court-room, and the presence of the United States troops, were proper and necessary as precautionary measures?—A. It was my opinion then, and is now, that the holding of a convention was proper, under the circumstances, and expedient for the party who held it here. . . . Q. Governor Warmoth requests me to ask you if you have not been the counselor and adviser of the customhouse party?—A. I have not. I have several times been asked my opinion, but have not been their adviser, as a general thing, no more than I have of the other side. I have given advice to the other side. . . ." *HMD*, 42-2-211, 519–20. See Endorsement, Aug. 3, 1871.

To William W. Belknap

————

Washington, D. C. Jan.y 15th *1872*

HON. W. W. BELKNAP,
SEC. OF WAR:
DEAR SIR:

    Enclosed I send you a dispatch just received from New Orleans signed, as you will see, by the Gov.r,[1] Lt. Gov.r[2] and Speaker of the House of Rep.s of La. It is my recollection that the claim of the Lt. Gov.r to his place has been doubted on the ground that he was elected by the Senate on a special call for that branch of the legislature alone, and that the Gov.r himself has admitted that he was not constitutionally elected. The place of the Speaker is also contested and it looks to me that a compliance to this call for the use of troops would be for the Govt. to recognize one of two bodies calling themselves the Legislature of La.[3] This I want to avoid, if possible, until the question is settled in a manner more consistent with our institutions. Of course if there is danger of bloodshed and riot I should like to prevent it. But I prefer the testimony of others interested in peace and quiet rather than those interested in establishing the claims of either of two factions to be the legitimate legislature of the state before taking action.—Please call on the Atty. Gn. and obtain his views, and if any action is deemed advisable see me this evening.

Very respectfully
your obt. svt.
U. S. GRANT

ALS, DNA, RG 94, Letters Received, 37 1872. *HED*, 42-2-209, 15, 42-2-268, 77–78. On Jan. 15, 1872, Orlando H. Brewster, Lt. Governor Pinckney B. S. Pinchback, and Governor Henry C. Warmoth of La., New Orleans, telegraphed to USG. "I have the honor to communicate the following concurrent resolution of the General assembly of this state & unite with it in the request made 'wheras certain evil disposed persons under the pretense of authority are exciting the public mind disturbing the peace defying the lawful authorities & otherwise attempting to revolutionize the constitutional Govt of the state of Louisiana & whereas, the Governor of the state of Louisiana has thus far maintained the constitution & laws of the state & prevented riot & bloodshed & otherwise upheld the authority of the state as well as the right of its representatives of the people in General assembly convened by the Judicious of use of the militia & police forces of the state & wheras the fundamental law of the U. S guarantees to each state of the federal union a republican form of Govt which it is the sworn duty of the President of the U S to maintain, Therefore be it resolved by the senate & house of Representatives of the state of La in general assembly convened that the President of the united states be & is hereby respectfully requested by the General assembly of the state of La to furnish & place at the disposal of the Governor of this state such military forces of the united states as may be necessary to enable the Governor to preserve the public peace & enforce & maintain the constitution & laws of the state of Louisiana against any unlawful combinations assemblages or persons in said state & that the Governor be and he is hereby requested to forward to the president of the united states a copy hereof for his action'" Telegram received (at 6:35 P.M.), DNA, RG 94, Letters Received, 37 1872. *HED*, 42-2-209, 14, 42-2-268, 78. On the same day, U.S. Senator J. Rodman West of La. twice telegraphed to Warmoth. "Cannot start Williams, as he is asleep. Have seen General Townsend, who says that General Emory's orders have not been changed and he relies upon his keeping the peace. Townsend will see Belknap and President the first thing in the morning. Keep me advised." "President tells me Emory shall not take his troops to New Orleans again without orders from him. You must rely upon God and the right." *HMD*, 42-2-211, 74, 314.

Also on Jan. 15, Attorney Gen. George H. Williams telegraphed to Warmoth. "The President has referred to me your dispatch of this date, representing that the Legislature of the State has asked to have the military forces of the United States placed at your disposal to preserve the public peace, etc. There is a contest as to the legality of the election of the Lieutenant Governor, and also as to the existence of the lower branch of the Legislature, dispatches having been received here from two persons, each claiming to be Speaker thereof, and the President does not feel that he would be justified in deciding those questions at this time and under existing circumstances; and is unwilling to interfere in State matters with the military power of the Government, except in a clear case of legal right and overruling necessity." LS (telegram sent), DNA, RG 94, Letters Received, 37 1872. On Jan. 16, Warmoth telegraphed to Williams. "The President misapprehends the nature of the request of the general assembly. It does not ask him to decide whether the lieutenant governor was legally elected, or which of the two houses is the legal house of representatives. This is a question which the general assembly can and will settle itself, unless it is overpowered by the mob. . . ." *HED,* 42-2-268, 81.

On Jan. 14, Warmoth had telegraphed to USG. "A dispatch in this morning's papers announces that the Attorney General has expressed the opinion that United States troops should not be brought to this city unless martial law is declared. General Emory is impressed by this announcement, and has given notice to that effect. Under section four, article four of the Constitution, I think we are entitled to the presence of the United States troops to prevent riot in this city. I respectfully ask that General Emory be authorized to have his troops in the city under arms, as we are in imminent danger of riot and mobs that may possibly be as fatal to New Orleans as was the late disaster in Chicago. The simple presence of troops will prevent domestic violence." *Ibid.,* p. 76. On the same day, Col. William H. Emory twice telegraphed to AG Edward D. Townsend. "Colonel Geo. W. Carter who claims to be speaker of the legislature & is recognized as such by the retiring members has taken advantage of the facts contained in my letter addressed to the governor this morning & one addressed to him to issue an extra which has this moment come into my hands prefaced by inflamatory remarks which must be calculated to excite a mob to morrow which must greatly disturb the peace & Prosperity of this great city & I have been compelled to warn him that I shall recall the troops & place them in position on canal st to avert this impending riot until I can get an answer from Washn. In the meantime I have informed the mayor of the city what I have done & notified him that if he calls upon me for aid to suppress the riot he can have it. I therefore urgently request that you will immediately instruct me if my course is approved in withdrawing the troops & what my further action shall be I do this in view of the fact of a telegram received here to the effect that the attorney Genl has given it as his opinion that my course in bringing troops in to the city is illegal." "I wish to add to my telegram of this morning that the line of action pursued by me in the last ten days having resulted in no approximate Settlement of the quarrel between the legislative factions & the executive of the State . . . I fully request to be instructed under this new phase of affairs how to act in the matter I shall have the troops in readiness & bring them to a point where they can act on any telegram You may send me" Telegrams received (at 8:00 and 11:30 P.M.), DNA, RG 94, Letters Received, 37 1872. *HED,* 42-2-209, 11, 42-2-268, 75–76. On Jan. 15, 10:00 A.M., Secretary of War William W. Belknap telegraphed to Emory. "The Attorney General has given no opinion whatever. Your action as indicated in your telegrams received last night is approved. Exercise your own discretion as to the general course to be pursued, but do not bring the U. S. troops to the City without orders from here. Report from time to time by telegraph the changes in the situation." ADf, DNA, RG 94, Letters Received, 37 1872. On the same day, Emory telegraphed to Townsend. "The excitement in this city is hourly increasing and if something decisive is not done to signify the wish of the President one way or another the force of the opponents of the Warmoth party will become so overwhelming that the small U. S. force stationed here will become insignificant and utterly powerless to subdue the impending riot to offset the telegram approving my course there are freely circulated throughout the city and I have in my possession Extracts from telegrams from men high in position in Washington purporting to be written by authority of the President to the effect that if I have brought the troops back to this city I have made a great mistake when in fact the troops have never been further out of the city than ~~the~~ barracks on the edge of the city. Under these circumstances these telegrams being directed to responsible parties here it becomes essential that I be more positively instructed with authority to show my instructions An authentic word from the President indicated to me whether I am wholly to withdraw the troops or take a decisive step in the other direction and hold the capitol of the state is necessary to settle the difficulty . . ." Telegram received (at 10:00 A.M.), *ibid. HED,* 42-2-209, 12, 42-2-268, 79. A copy was sent to USG. DNA, RG 94, Letters Received, 37 1872. Also on Jan. 15, Emory telegraphed three more times to Townsend. "Telegram rec'ed orders will be complied with not to bring United States troops to the City unless by orders from Washington." "Your telegram received, instructions covered the case, and I hope for the best results, the Governor's party is in strong force at the Capitol the Carter party holding a meeting at the Cosmopolitan Hall and the u. S. troops all at Jackson Barracks." "The Carter legislature adjourned until ten a m tomorrow. Their firmness and numerical strength both probably overestimated The Warmoth legislature has hurriedly repealed the laws most obnoxious to the citizens & the Governor signs the bills tonight. A joint resolution passed Constituting Committee to frame new laws. Subsidence of excitement attained by this action Future tranquility depends upon the nature of laws adopted" Telegrams received (the third at 5:20 P.M.), *ibid. HED,* 42-2-209, 13–14, 42-2-268, 80.

On Jan. 19, Warmoth telegraphed to USG. "There is every reason to believe that we shall have turbulence in this city to-morrow. It is reported that a messenger has arrived from Washington with the information that your Excellency approves and sustains the attitude of the combination of democrats and employés in the custom-house here, and encouraged by this, it is asserted they will employ the mob, made up by the secret political societies here, and take the state-house and usurp the government. I regret that your Excellency does not see proper to respond to the call made by the general assembly, and also by the executive, for the use of the military forces of the United States to prevent riot by a timely disposition of troops where there is reason to apprehend a necessity for their use, and, by their passive interposition between the hostile parties, danger of collision may be averted, as your Excellency ordered on the 25th of August, 1868, when General of the Army. The condition of affairs is such that I deem it my duty to inform you again of the danger of domestic violence, and renew the request for aid to preserve the city from riot and bloodshed." HMD, 42-2-211, 317. See *ibid.,* p. 321; HED, 42-2-268, 81–83. On Jan. 21, Emory telegraphed to Townsend. "The expectations expressed in the four pm telegram of yesterday are not likely to be fulfilled. Colonel Carter publishes an address to the people of Louisiana in the morning papers saying that he shall tomorrow at Eleven thirty a m through the Sergeant at Arms of the House ~~of~~ over which he presides proceed to remove from the hall of the House of Representatives and the approaches thereto the police and armed men etc etc and concludes a long address reciting grievances by inviting the people to meet him at rampart street near Canal which is near the State Capitol at ten am tomorrow . . ." Telegram received (at 2:00 P.M.), DNA, RG 94, Letters Received, 37 1872. *HED,* 42-2-209, 18.

On Jan. 22, Orville E. Babcock wrote to Belknap. "The President directs that you hold your troops in readiness to suppress a conflict of armed bodies of men, should such occur, and to guard public property from pillage or distruction. Keep this Dept. informed of your action, . . . The President wants a despatch in like the above in substance sent to Gen Emory—" ALS (first two sentences in USG's hand), DNA, RG 94, Letters Received, 37 1872. On the same day, Mayor Benjamin F. Flanders of New Orleans telegraphed to USG. ". . . the demonstration to-day in aid of Carter was very large, and it is believed would have effected its object without bloodshed, but for the telegraphic order to General Emory, which was read to the crowd, and was understood as sustaining Warmoth. . . ." *HED,* 42-2-268, 83. Also on Jan. 22, Emory twice telegraphed to Townsend. "Your telegram received, and the troops are ordered to hold themselves in readiness. In the meantime I have deemed it proper to furnish each of the contending parties, with a copy of the telegram directing me to interfere and prevent any conflict between armed bodies" "The troops being at their barracks good faith required I should Communicate to each of the Contending parties my orders to hold the troops in readiness to suppress a Conflict of armed bodies of men & to guard public Property. Upon this announcement by Col. Carter the Crowd dispersed and the troops will not be required . . ." Telegrams received (the second at 2:30 P.M.), DNA, RG 94, Letters Received, 37 1872. *HED,* 42-2-209, 19–20. On Jan. 23, a correspondent reported that Emory's telegram conveying news about New Orleans had been read during a cabinet "session of considerable length to-day, . . ." *Philadelphia Public Ledger,* Jan. 24, 1872. On the same day, U.S. Senator William P. Kellogg of La. wrote to Stephen B. Packard, U.S. marshal, New Orleans. "*Personal* . . . Saw President last night . . . He is very much insensed with the Course of Warmouth & he very reluctantly gave the order he did yesterday tho Sect of War it was not intended to be used as Emory used it. The Troops were not moved & were not intended to be moved—and they will not be moved. . . . Grant is awful down on Warmouth he will give him fits when he gets a chance—for his tricks—he undstands that they have been trying to put him in a false position West recd a long dispatch Sunday from Warmouth Containg Carters *Proc* &c with a request signed by Warmoth asking him to lay them before President &c West wanted delegation to go to Prs but I refused & so did rest concluded not to go—he went alone—& beggig begged for troops in Warmoths name and with his telegram—. . ." ALS, Warmoth Papers, Southern Historical Collection, University of North Carolina, Chapel Hill, N. C.

On Jan. 31, Emory, New Orleans, testified before the Select Committee to Investigate the Condition of Affairs in the State of Louisiana. ". . . Q. Which one of the factions was benefited by the presence of the troops?—A. That I cannot say. That is a very knotty point to determine. . . . it was my studious desire to avoid taking part with either. . . . Q. Had you any private communication with parties in Washington during these troubles here?—A. None whatever. Q. Did you have any advices from parties in Washington other than those you have given the committee?—A. None whatever. . . ." *HMD,* 42-2-211, 64–65. On Oct. 4, Emory reported to Townsend on the La. conflict. LS, DNA, RG 94, Letters Received, 3777 1872. On March 20, Belknap had written to USG. "I have the honor to return to you copy of a Resolution of the House of Representatives requesting a copy of all correspondence between the Executive Department and Colonel Emory, commanding the military forces in Louisiana, from the 20th December, 1871, to February 1st 1872, & to say that the War Dep't. possesses no record of any direct correspondence between yourself and that officer for the period in question;—all your orders to him in regard to his command having been transmitted through the Adjutant General of the Army. In compliance with a similar Resol'n of the House, addressed to the War Dep't., I had copyies of all correspondence between it and Colonel Emory—with the exception of such as had no bearing upon the political affairs of his Department prepared & the same has this day been transmitted to the House of Representatives." Df, *ibid.*, 846 1872; copy, *ibid.*, RG 107, Letters Sent, Military Affairs. See *HED*, 42-2-209, 42-3-1, part 2, pp. 92–100; Joseph G. Dawson III, *Army Generals and Reconstruction: Louisiana, 1862–1877* (Baton Rouge, 1982), pp. 113–28.

1. On Feb. 6, Warmoth testified before the Select Committee. "Q. Do you not believe that the course of the President in refusing to disavow the acts of his officials here has caused a division of the republican party in the State?—A. I think that if the President had removed these gentlemen we would have had none of the trouble we have had during the last few months. Q. You believe they were supported by the President; would the custom-house party be strong enough without it to make any fight against you?—A. The belief being prevalent that the President will support these officials in their assault upon myself and the State government; and I don't believe that without it their attacks would amount to the dignity of a tempest in a teapot. Q. What reason can you give for President Grant's want of interest in the affairs of this State?— A. I have not any means of knowing the reasons that actuated him in his course, if he has pursued any course at all, in relation to the matter. . . . Q. In your judgment could President Grant have prevented these troubles by what you regard as a proper exercise of his appointing power?—A. I have no doubt about it. . . . I think that the President might have stopped the whole thing if he hadn't lent his ear to these people, who, from their own interested motives, have misrepresented the facts. . . . Q. Has any antagonism which has sprung up grown out of the action of men holding office and claiming to represent him?—A. I think that any antagonism that has grown up against President Grant here has sprung up in the manner in which I believe, and we believe, he has been misrepresented by his employés. . . . I think the republicans have a right to expect that General Grant will remove these men who have brought disgrace upon his administration, and have brought ruin—not ruin, but confusion—on the republican party of this State. . . ." *HMD*, 42-2-211, 357–58, 361, 395, 398.

On Dec. 4, U.S. Representative Frank Morey of La. wrote to Warmoth. "Yours of 27th is at hand. Bourman was sworn in yesterday. Grant is very open in his opinion of you—to this effect, the shrewdest, sharpest, boldest, ablest and most conscienceless young man that he ever knew—Williams says little, but there is a hope and desire in official circles that the matter may be settled by the Courts—at the same time there is a strong disposition to 'get at the bottom of things—' I do not think there will be any more Committees—the Prest has said that 'we wouldn't know any more than we do now' I think too it is suspected that as usual you might come a little ahead before such a tribunal—" ALS, Warmoth Papers, Southern Historical Collection. See letter to James F. Casey, March 27, 1871; letter to William W. Belknap, Jan. 5, 1873.

2. Born a free mulatto in 1837 near Macon, Ga., Pinchback gained notoriety as a riverboat gambler, served as capt., 2nd La. Native Guards and 74th U.S. Colored Inf. (1862–63), entered politics in New Orleans, and promoted black suffrage and education in Ala. (1865–67). Returning to La., he was elected state senator in 1868.

On April 7, 1869, USG nominated Pinchback as register, New Orleans Land Office. See James Haskins, *Pinckney Benton Stewart Pinchback* (New York, 1973).

Warmoth testified before the committee. "Q. You say you called an extra session in December last for the purpose of electing a lieutenant governor?—A. Yes, sir. . . . Q. What was the cause of your anxiety to secure the election of Pinchback?—A. I wanted him elected because he was a representative man of the colored people of the State, and the office had been, by the traditions of our party, conceded to that race; and I wanted him elected for another reason: He belonged to the political party acting with me, and I did not want the gentleman running against him elected. Q. What interest had you in the office of lieutenant governor?—A. No interest other than the general interest a political partisan has in the success of his party. Q. Both candidates were republicans?—A. Yes, sir; both claimed to be. . . . Coupland was a custom-house republican; Pinchback was not. . . . The difference between a custom-house republican and a republican is that a custom-house republican in almost every case holds office in the custom-house, and is under the control of the custom-house and custom-house chiefs, who are inimical to me and to the party acting with me. . . . I think they would vote for a democrat and use their influence for the success of the democratic ticket in preference to the success of the ticket I might be at the head of, or my friends. Q. Would you not prefer the success of the democratic ticket to that of the custom-house republican ticket?—A. It would depend upon who was at the head of the ticket. . . ." *HMD*, 42-2-211, 353–55. See *ibid.*, pp. 540–41.

On Feb. 10, Pinchback, New Orleans, wrote to committee chairman U.S. Representative Glenni W. Scofield of Pa. ". . . With reference to the detractions and vilifications of Messrs. Flanders, Walker, and others, who have severally maligned me and endeavored to impress your committee with the belief that I am an unworthy republican, not a representative colored man, and do not enjoy the respect and confidence of the colored people, it may not be inappropriate for me to invite your attention to the facts that from the period of the organization of the republican party in this State, when I commenced my political career here as the organizer of a ward club in this city, to the present time, when I occupy the second office in the Commonwealth, having satisfactorily passed through all the intervening stages of promotion which the free suffrages of my party could bestow, and the recipient even of Federal recognition by being appointed register of lands by President Grant, it has remained for these gentlemen to discover and to declare now and not till now that I am not a representative man of my race or of my party. . . ." *Ibid.*, pp. 489–90.

3. On Jan. 15, Brewster, New Orleans, had written to Emory. "I have the honor, on this part of this branch of the legislative department of the State, to inform you officially that the house of representatives, composed of sixty-five members sitting in the constitutional place of meeting, of which I am the duly elected speaker, has, by resolution, a copy of which I herewith inclose, requested the governor to protect the hall of the house of representatives and the avenues thereto from a mob; that in response to this request the governor has employed the militia and police to keep the halls of the house and the streets in front clear of unauthorized persons. I am also in receipt of information that G. W. Carter, unlawfully assuming to act as speaker of the house of representatives, has proceeded to swear in a large number of persons as assistant sergeants-at-arms with the object of using them to attack the police and militia and force their entrance with an armed mob into the hall of the house. All legal claims of Mr. Carter and others, claiming seats in the house, will be peacefully and legally adjudicated by the house itself if its deliberations are protected. . . ." *Ibid.*, p. 73.

On Jan. 30, George W. Carter, New Orleans, testified before the committee. "Q. How long have you been in Louisiana?—A. Four years about. I came from Texas, though I was originally a Virginian.... Q. You and the governor were political friends at one time, were you not?—A. Yes; personal and political. Q. You separated during the summer of 1871?—A. Yes; the separation grew out of that election.... My last communication from Washington was Judge Williams's response to Governor Warmoth, asking for troops. I have never had any communication with the Federal authorities except General Emory, and never advised with them. I have never consulted with anybody in the custom-houses, and never advised with the officials there.... Q. Do you believe that without the aid of the Federal troops Governor Warmoth would have been able to maintain his position here?—A. I know he would not...." *Ibid.*, pp. 27, 35. For related testimony on the competing legislative houses and speakers, see *ibid.*, pp. 212–25.

To Roscoe Conkling

———

Washington, D. C. Jan.y 17th *1872.*

HON. ROSCOE CONKLING: U. S. S.

DEAR SIR;

To restore harmony in the political situation it looks to me that a point would be gained by getting Warner out of a position where he will necessarily keep up the existing feud between himself and the republican Senator from his state.[1] The Mission to the Argentine Republic[2] is now vacant and I would gladly give it to Warner if he would accept it, being fully confidant that he would fill the position advantageously to the country.

I would telegraph this to Warner myself but think it better that he should receive the suggestion from some one of his old collegues in the Senate, and therefore write to you, not to ask you to telegraph against your judgement, but to ask you to do so if you agree with me as to the propriety of such a course, and you feel no delicacy about it. ~~doing so~~

Yours Truly

U. S. GRANT

ALS, DLC-Roscoe Conkling. On Dec. 6, 1871, USG nominated Willard Warner as collector of customs, Mobile; on Jan. 22, 1872, USG withdrew the nomination. On Jan. 30, USG wrote to Warner. "Upon the presentation of Executive order of January. 30th 1872. you are hereby directed to turn over to William Miller the office of Collector of

Customs for the District of Mobile, in the State of Alabama, and all the publice property connected therewith. Your nomination as Collector for said office having been withdrawn from the Senate, your commission dated June 29th 1871 is hereby revoked." Copy, DNA, RG 130, Orders and Proclamations. On the same day, USG wrote to William Miller restoring him to office. Copy, *ibid.*

On Jan. 24, U.S. Senator John Sherman of Ohio had written to Warner. "I am disgusted beyond expression at the withdrawal of your nomination by the President. I came upon us without notice and after all doubt of your confirmation—if indeed there ever was any—had disappeared. It was well understood that the committee would report you after Spencer had exhausted all pretences for delay and your confirmation was absolutely assured. In this condition of affairs the action of the President was a surprise and mortification I went to Chandler & he told me it was without notice to him and that he was in your favor and I believe him. I scarcely know what to do. I could not talk with Grant about this without showing a feeling that may do you injury—but in a day or two I probably will. My advice is that you ask a leave of absence and come directly here and fight this thing out. It is humiliating and annoying that such men as Spencer & Busteed should control all the patronage of a State, and that such men as you should be made the victims of a plainly malicious opposition. I dont know what to make of it and rarely allow myself to talk much less write of the tendency of events." ALS, Warner Papers, Tennessee State Library and Archives, Nashville, Tenn. On Jan. 30, Jacob D. Cox, Cincinnati, wrote to Warner. "Yours of 26th is just received, & while I sincerely sympathize with your just indignation, I cannot say that I am surprised. I long since made up my mind that professions of friendship made by Grant were of no real meaning or value, & that the slightest supposed interest on his part is sufficient to make him sacrifice the friends to whom he has avowed the warmest attachment. He perfectly knows you & he know[s] Spencer, & he cannot but respect you & despise him; but he thinks Spencer can be of use to him, & does not hesitate to throw you over in behalf of a man of no character or principle. He did the same in regard to Judge Hoar and at the same instance & demand substantially. That was the turning point in his political career. He then determined to sell his best friends for the sake of support for a second nomination, or for support in the San Domingo or any other scheme in which he might set his heart. That the people do not yet see & comprehend this is a matter of amazement to me. The humbug of Grant's good purposes is still repeated & harped upon, when those of us who have been behind the scenes know that a low & unscrupulous cunning is the ruling motive of his public life, and that his professions are merely the counters with which he plays his game on public opinion. His dishonesty in this is weak, for he might just as well have had a greater popularity on a higher platform of principle & character. In your own case I am sure that good faith to you & firm adherence to your friendship would have been the wise policy for him even with reference to Georgia & Alabama politics; but his mind is not large or generous enough to ~~establish~~ appreciate the advantages of honest adherence to principle or to friends. The country will learn this some day, but whether in time to prevent his reëlection is not certain. I *hope* it will...." ALS, *ibid.* On Feb. 9, Warner, Mobile, wrote to Gen. William T. Sherman, Nice. "... I have *not* been confirmed because Grant would not let me. His special Champions Conkling and Chandler kept my nomination for over six weeks in Committee of Commerce, and then just as the pressure of public opinion was about to compel the Committee to report Grant withdrew my nomination. My confirmation was beyond doubt had Committee reported. I turned over this office to my successor yesterday. He is a childish old man worth $250.000. and was a slave trader before the war. There is no excuse for The Presidents conduct towards me. Justice, friendship and sound political policy alike required that he should sustain me. He deliberately sacrificed me to propitiate Spencer—a friend for a foe—a soldier for a sutler—a life long Republican for a spoils hunter—an honest man for a debauched scoundrel. He has hurt himself, not me, by this act of blundering treachery. Horace Porter and Cameron aided Spencer. Porters class mate at West Point, D. C. Rugg, who was found on demerit, becomes Deputy Collector by my removal, superceding Col. Buck an Ex. M. C. and Grant Elector from this district. I was supported by entire state Rep. Com. all Republican Editors but one whose paper Spencer owns, by all the best men of the state and by all the people of this city of all parties. The importers *all* telegraphed Thurman for my confirmation. But all did no good. Without a word of notice to any of my friends I was removed and no explanation has been made to me. General, Grant has fallen, or rather put himself in bad hands, and is going onto the breakers unless he quickly changes his course and crew. He will be beaten at the election, if nominated at Philadelphia unless he cuts loose from his weak and corrupt associations. If John will speak his mind, he will say the same thing. . . . Before my removal, I was asked by telegram from Senator Sawyer, if I would accept Mission to Argentine Republic. The offer, it is now said, came from Grant. I answered promptly 'With thanks, No.' I am planting and shall return to my plantation for the present and shall not stave. . . ." ALS, DLC-William T. Sherman. See letter to Charles W. Buckley, Nov. 21, 1870.

1. George E. Spencer.
2. On April 1, 1872, Speaker of the House James G. Blaine and six others petitioned USG. "The undersigned, learning that the name of Hon. Benj. W. Norris of Alabama is presented to you for the post of Minister Resident at the Argentine Republic respectfully join in the recommendation—Mr. Norris is a native of Maine and has in years past held honorable positions in our State Government—He is a man of industry, energy and probity and has always been a most zealous member of the Republican party—whose principles he has always consistently supported—" DS, DNA, RG 59, Letters of Application and Recommendation. Related papers are *ibid.* No appointment followed.

In an undated petition, U.S. Representatives Charles Hays and Benjamin S. Turner of Ala. recommended to USG "Joseph H. Speed, from Perry County, Alabama, as Minister to the Argentine Republic—. . ." DS (docketed "April 1872"), *ibid.* Spencer added an undated endorsement. AES, *ibid.* On April 3, 1871, USG had nominated Joseph H. Speed as postmaster, Marion, Ala.

On June 24, 1872, U.S. Senator Oliver P. Morton of Ind., Indianapolis, wrote to USG. "Personal . . . Colonel Gilbert A. Pierce of Valparaiso, Indiana, who has for two or three years been connected with the office of the Secretary of the U. S. Senate upon the recommendation of Mr Colfax, desires to be appointed Minister Resident to the Argentine Republic. Col. Pierce is a lawyer by profession, a man of considerable literary ability, was a good soldier, is undoubtedly qualified for the position, and, I have no doubt, will be recommended by Mr Colfax. It is very probable that this appointment might have the effect of reconciling an unfortunate difficulty that has sprung up in Mr Packard's district and which now threatens serious injury to the Republican party. Mr Colfax, living in that district, will be able to give you much fuller details than I can; and if you have not already made an appointment to Buenos Ayres, I would be glad to have you hold it up until you can understand the character of the trouble in Mr Pack-ard's district, and the probable propriety of appointing Col. Pierce." LS, *ibid.* On Dec. 8, 1871, U.S. Representatives Jasper Packard, John Coburn, Jeremiah M. Wilson, William Williams, and James N. Tyner of Ind. had written to USG recommending Gilbert A. Pierce as 5th Auditor of the Treasury. DS, *ibid.* Vice President Schuyler Colfax, U.S. Senator Daniel D. Pratt of Ind., and Morton favorably endorsed this letter. AES (undated), *ibid.* An undated letter from Packard to USG urging Pierce's appointment as auditor, with supporting endorsements, is *ibid.*, RG 56, Appointment Div., Treasury Offices, Letters Received. No appointments followed.

On Oct. 26, 1872, Rutherford B. Hayes, Cincinnati, wrote to USG. "Dr W. F. Tibbals of this City is a gentleman of upright and honorable character whose reputation talents and experience qualify him to perform creditably the duties of any position in the public service which he is likely to seek. . . ." ALS, *ibid.*, RG 59, Letters of Application and Recommendation. Related papers recommending William F. Tibbals as minister to Argentina are *ibid.* No appointment followed. On Dec. 3, USG nominated Julius White as minister to Argentina. See letter to Hamilton Fish, July 16, 1872.

Endorsement

Refered to the Sec. of War who will please examine the report upon which Mr. Buckley was dismissed and reinstate him if the facts warrant such a course. If however the Superintendent, and instructors oppose the reinstatement on other grounds than that of exceeding the limit of demerit for the half year Mr. Buckley need not be restored to his place at West Point.

U. S. Grant

Jan.y 18th 1872

AES, DNA, RG 94, Correspondence, USMA. Written on an undated letter from Horatio L. Buckley, Freeport, Pa., to USG. "The petition of the undersigned, Horatio L. Buckley of Freeport Armstrong Co. Penna, respectfully represents, that; I entered the Union Army in Oct. 1868, and was honorably discharged in Feb. 1870; and also that one of my brothers died in the service, and my only remaining one was killed at the Second battle of Bull Run, leaving me the only male member, of my family. I was appointed a Cadet at West Point, on the recommendation of the Honorable Darwin Phelps, of my district; and entered the Academy about the 1st of Sept. 1870, and remained there until the 18th of Dec. 1871. when I was discharged for having one demerit over the allowed number. During the sixteen months that I was there, I was never under arrest, and was never reported for any serious offence. At the annual examination in June 1871, I stood thirtysix in a class of fiftytwo members, During the six months ending Nov. 30th 1871. I was unfortunate enough to receive 101. demerits, all of which were received for ordinary little offences, and many of which would have been found unjust if examined into. For several weeks while in the hospital, I was unable to see the report books, and could not write explanations for two or three offences for which I was reported; and although I did not deserve these reports, yet when I .went the proper authority to have them removed, no attention was paid to my request. My standing in mathematics at the time of my discharge was 32 in a class of 49 members. In consideration of my having been dismissed on one demerit, I have the honor to petition that I be reinstated, I like to see stringency and severity in the rules of the Academy, but to be dismissed on 101 demerits, while many of them were absolutely undeserved is, to me, an injustice which I pray you may see fit to rectify." ALS (docketed Jan. 2), *ibid.* On Jan. 27, 1872, Secretary of War William W. Belknap wrote to USG. "Upon your reference to me of the application of Horatio L. Buckley, a Cadet at the Military Academy, for reinstatement, I referred the whole matter to the Superintendent with a view to ascertaining whether any insuperable objections existed to his return. I have now the honor to state that the Superintendent and Academic Board of the Academy oppose his restoration on other grounds than that of deficiency in discipline. The Superintendent also reports that the best interests of the Academy require the rigid enforcement of the Academy Regulations, which were violated by Cadets Buckley and Colby." Copy, *ibid.*, Letters Sent, USMA. On Dec. 28, 1871, and subsequently, Rebecca Buckley, Freeport, wrote to USG seeking her son's reinstatement. ALS, *ibid.*, Correspondence, USMA. On July 8, 1872, Orville E. Babcock endorsed one such letter. "Similar applications to this have been so often & repeatedly negatived, that it is useless to reply further." AES, *ibid.* Related papers are *ibid.*

On Aug. 1, 1870, Buckley had written to USG. "It has been my earnest desire; from early boyhood up, to obtain a Cadetship at West Point. and I hope my anxiety to obtain this will be sufficient reason to pardon my presumption in thus addressing you. I made application for this two years ago, through Hon. Thos. Williams of Pittsburgh, Pa.; but for some reason did not succeed, I have since served Sixteen months in the Regular Army, I was discharged last February from Co M. 5 U. S. Cav. on application of my mother, my only remaining parent. She having already lost two sons in defence of their country though[t] that sufficient, She would now give her full consent for me to go to West Point. I now most respectfully solicit your notice in this case. and hopeing that in you kindness you will not neglect this, . . ." ALS, *ibid.*, Unsuccessful Cadet Applications.

To Enoch C. Wines

——————

Washington D. C. Jan 25th *1872*

Dear Sir:

I am in receipt of your letter inviting me to attend the public meeting to be held in New York City on the 26th inst, under the auspices of the National Prison Association. My engagements will not permit me to be present but I beg to assure you of the interest

I feel in your efforts in behalf of penitentiary reform. The cause in which you are laboring has my warmest sympathy with its objects and my best wishes for its success.

Very respectfully
Yours
U. S. Grant

Mr E. C. Wines
New York City.

LS, InHi. On Jan. 26, 1872, Enoch C. Wines reported on prison reform to a public meeting at Steinway Hall. *New York Times*, Jan. 27, 1872. Born in 1806 in Hanover, N. J., Wines was raised in Shoreham, Vt., graduated from Middlebury College (1827), taught school, and entered the Congregational ministry (1849). A prominent writer on educational and theological subjects, he became secretary of the Prison Association of New York (1862), prepared with Theodore W. Dwight a *Report on the Prisons and Reformatories of the United States and Canada,* ... (Albany, 1867), and founded the National Prison Association (1870).

In [*March*], 1871, Wines had written to USG. "The undersigned respectfully represents: That, in October last, a National Congress on Penitentiary and Reformatory Discipline was held in Cincinnati, Ohio, in which representatives from twenty-five States were present, including several Governors of States; and that the said Congress passed a vote to the effect that the time had come when an International Prison Congress might be held with promise of good results. The undersigned was invited to become the Commissioner of the said National Congress to undertake the work of organizing the proposed International Congress. Among the duties assigned to the Commissioner was that of visiting the several States of Europe and conferring with their Governments, with a view to securing their coöperation. A National Committee was appointed to take charge of this movement, and instructed to 'endeavor to endeavor to procure from the General Government an honorary appointment for their Commissioner, as being likely to secure consideration and facilities abroad, not otherwise attainable.' The undersigned might go into an extended detail of the considerations which prompted this enterprise, and of the benefits expected from it. But he forbears such a recital, from an unwillingness to trespass upon the time of the President, and contents himself with the statement that the movement thus inaugurated is believed, by those engaged in it, on both sides of the Atlantic, to be one in which the interests of civilization and humanity are vitally concerned. In behalf of the National Prison Congress and the Committee appointed by it, . . ." LS (undated), DNA, RG 59, Letters of Application and Recommendation. On March 7, USG endorsed this letter. "Respectfully refered to the Sec. of State with approval. Mr. Wines asks only a commission with out any compensation." AES, *ibid.* Wines again wrote to USG. "I had the honor, some days ago, to present to you an application, endorsed by prominent members of Congress, for recognition, by the Government, of an important movement in the interest of humanity, viz. an International Congress on Penitentiary and Reformatory Discipline, which you kindly referred, with your approval, to the Secretary of State. On conferring further with the gentlemen who signed that paper, and others, it was thought that the President would himself prefer the express authority of Congress to grant the commission asked; and, accordingly, a joint resolution was introduced into the Senate by Senator Morton, and passed unanimously by both Houses, authorizing the President to appoint a Commissioner to the proposed International Congress, with a proviso to the effect that the said mission should be without cost to the Government in the way of either salary or expenses. I have the honor to transmit to you the application referred to, through Mr. Speaker Blaine, and to request that you will favor me with the commission desired." ALS, *ibid.* On March 24, USG appointed Wines.

On Dec. 7, Horace Porter wrote to Wines, New York City. "The President received your letter dated Nov: 28th and desires me to say that he feels a deep interest in the cause of which you write, and hopes that the labors of the International Congress may result in great good. He also wishes me to inform you that, at the date of the receipt of your letter his message was virtually finished." Copy, DLC-USG, II, 1.

On Feb. 23, 1872, USG wrote to the Senate transmitting Wines's preliminary report. DS, DNA, RG 46, Presidential Messages, Domestic Affairs. *SED,* 42-2-39. See Endorsements, Dec. 12, 1872, June 29, 1876.

To Gen. William T. Sherman

Washington, D. C. Jan.y 26th *1872*

DEAR GENERAL:

I received your very welcome letter from Madeiri in due time. No doubt since that you have had a very enjoyable time. My advice is that, now you are away, if it should require a month or two more time to see all that you want to see, take it. You cannot be sure of an other opportunity. Mrs Sherman may not thank me for this advice, but I shall inform her that I have given it the next time I call. If wrong she may blow me up and inform you that I have no concern about matters which interest her more.

There is no special news here. Politicians are at their usual tricks in presidential election years. The democratic policy was tried in Ohio to defeat your brother's reelection to the Senate.[1] The plan was to unite sufficient of the disaffected republicans in the legislature upon Cox,[2] or any other reform republican, to elect him with the entire democratic vote. They failed. The same plan will be tried in the selection of president if there is the least hope of success. I have only called on Mrs. Sherman twice since you left but shall call occasionally to see that all are well. No doubt you will receive letters by the same mail that takes this informing you that all are well.

I have no doubt but you will have a grand time, and receive attentions that would be irksome if it were not for the good feeling and kindness expressed. I hope you will see Washburne, Jones, Schenck Curtain[3] and Badeau before you return. Present my kindest regards to each of them.

Faithfully yours

U. S. Grant

ALS, DLC-William T. Sherman. On Feb. 21, 1872, Gen. William T. Sherman, Rome, wrote to USG. "I received here your friendly letter of Jan 26, and Fred got all of his of same date. He has also written you fully, so that I need not bother you further than to say, that he has been perfectly well ever since we landed at Gibralter, with the exception of the first three days after reaching Rome, where our good hostess Mrs Marsh called a physician, who soon disposed of his temporary ailmt. He is now in perfect condition and we are on the point of starting for Naples, to stay a week & then for Malta, Alexandria & the East. Were it not for the social labor, imposed on us by the kind attentions of our Country men abroad, of which Italy & all Europe is full, we would have abundance of time to see all that is interesting in this Classic Land—I hope as we progress we will pass beyond the usual field of travel and of tourists so that we will be less diverted from the real object of our journey. I am not yet certain that Admiral Alden can meet us according to appointmt to convey us to Malta & Alexandria.—If he do, it will be the most interesting portion of our journey, but on parting with him, I enjoined on him not to let our personal wishes lead him to neglect his official duties. We can find passenger steamers to carry us to all the points in the programme, but it would be much more agreable, to reach such places as Syracuse, Malta and Alexandria in a National ship, which could await our pleasure, rather than the regular steamers, which carry mails, and run to a Regular schedule of time. I will bear in mind your kind hint, not to hurry, or neglect this opportunity which I feel will be the last, and shall go as far East as the Caspian sea, and the Caucasus if possible. The trip up the Volga, ought to bring us to Nishni and Moscow in all april, so that we can turn back towards Prussia, & France in Early summer. If there be then, no hurry, I propose to delay in France and England. All nations and all people seem friendly to the Americans, and I am extremely gratified at their interest in our public and private affairs.—I am glad to perceive that spite of rumors of difficulty with Spain & England you preserve the attitude of calmness & peace.—We can triumph over our Enemies, if any we have by peace & prosperity better than by war. Give the United States absolute peace & tranquility the balance of this century, and we shall have an hundred millions of people, with corresponding resources, and can laugh at any foreign foe. Our only dangers are from within, and these will call for the exercise of patience & wisdom. Excuse my touching on these points, but they will arise in daily observations here in Rome, where nations have been born reared & died, again & again, just as one City is built here on other destroyed cities. I am sure this trip will be of infinite service to Fred, and I will encourage him all I can do, to profit by it, and you may assure Mrs Grant, that I will watch his health, with a parents Eye. He sees many pretty girls here, who are enough to tempt any boy—but I will try to prevent his making any serious attachmts. He promises me on this score, that he will confide absolutely in his mother. Thank you for attentions to my family, and I believe Mrs Sherman will appreciate them very highly—. . . Mr Marsh, with whom we are staying is a scholar & gentleman—universally esteemed by our people & the Italians. He is disturbed by rumors that he is to be changed, which he cannot afford, as changes involve heavy expense" ALS, USG 3. See letter to Adam Badeau, Nov. 19, 1871, note 2; letter to Frederick Dent Grant, April 28, 1872.

On March 9, Sherman, Valetta, Malta, wrote to USG. "I have felt so sadly, so deeply disappointed at not receiving any advantage from our fleet, but quite the contrary, that I must in justice to you let you know my construction of the facts. I was always very careful to tell Alden that on no event would I ask him to divert a ship from her legitimate course for my convenience or pleasure, but as he would undoubtedly have occasion to send a vessel to the East I wanted to avail myself of it to see Malta with its famous harbors and Fortifications—the Isles of Greece, and Straits of the Dardanelles. We therefore agreed to meet at Naples March 1.—We were there punctually but the fleet did not come; and I telegraphed to our Consul to know when the fleet *had* sailed, and got answer that the Fleet had not sailed at all, and would not come at all—A day or two after I got a despatch from Alden, that he had just heard from *home* & he could not keep his appointmt. We had to abandon our trip & turn back or go ahead trusting to chances.—On arrival here I got another despatch from Alden repeating that he was prevented by orders from home, and that his disappointmt exceeded my own—This is a clincher, and I am at a loss to imagine the cause of these orders. If war is imminet it seems to me timid & bad policy for our Great fleet to be shut up in a neutral port,—but I see no signs of war here, or elsewhere and wherever we go, under every flag—we, especially your son is received with a warmth & fervor that would increase your natural pride. Here in Malta the Fleet would be in the highway of Nations whereas at Villa Franca, it is unseen unfelt, and I may almost say ridiculo[us] for good. Of course this is none of my business, but now we are compelled to grope our way, taking chance vessels, and we cannot visit, Athens, the Isles of Greece, and other points of great interest, but must take through lines. Fred is now strong, vigorous and well. And I feel assured you & Mrs Grant will be satisfied that his journey has been of infinite service to him. The Governor General here is a Grant who claims to be a relative of yours, & he seems a fine old soldier. We will work our way Eastward scuffling with Jew & gentile—with Turk and Greek for staterooms & berths, thankful that at all events Uncle Sam has not wasted any thing on us—In due time we will emerge at St Petersburg, some time in the Month of May. Thence, Our Journey home, will be more or less rapid according to news from home: but I bear in mind your kind offer of more time and shall take advantage of it in Germany, France and England during the Summer—" ALS, USG 3.

1. See letters to John Sherman, May 17, June 14, 1871. On Jan. 26, 1872, U.S. Senator John Sherman of Ohio wrote to Gen. Sherman. ". . . I think Gen Grant has found out that my strength in Ohio was equal to his own & that Mr Delano is not the Representative of the Republicans of Ohio. . . . Ellen sometimes in private comments too severely on Capt Grant being with you but the general expression is that his going with you was a natural desire of the President in favor of his son—& that Capt Grant was as proper an 'Aid' as any other officer. I never heard any criticism of it except by Ellen and I have expressed the hope to her that she will not mention the subject to

others   Grant will be renominated and reelected—I do not see any basis for a coalition of the elements opposed to him—My election was considered a fair test of such an attempted coalition and it failed. . . ." ALS, DLC-William T. Sherman. See Rachel Sherman Thorndike, ed., *The Sherman Letters* . . . (New York, 1894), pp. *333–35*. See also *John Sherman's Recollections of Forty Years* . . . (Chicago and New York, 1895), I, 478–80.

2. On Jan. 16, U.S. Representative James A. Garfield of Ohio wrote to Jacob D. Cox, Cincinnati. ". . . I have felt totally unwilling to fight, with weapons such as Sherman used, in this contest, though I have no doubt, that either of us could have taken the Senatorship, and that too, without conditions, if we had really said the word. I am glad, that our names were talked of thus in companionship, it befits our past and may decorate our future   It is not yet possible to see the outcome of our involvements here. I think there are explosive elements, collecting under the foundation of the present Administration, which, while they may be harmless, still may explode at the wrong time. The great body of Grants superserviceable friends, are furious against the Civil Service Report, and the indications are that Grant must back down or offend his defenders. If he backs down, he offends a large body of people. In the meantime the Civil service attitude of the Administration, is made most absurd by the disgraceful revealments being made every day by the Committee, which is investigating the *Custom House New York*. It is the talk now on the street to day, that Grant will make a clean ~~sp~~ sweep of *Porter and Babcock* and Leet and Co., et id &c. This may be very good or very bad news, as you choose to take it. . . ." ALS, Cox Papers, Oberlin College, Oberlin, Ohio.

On Jan. 31, Cox wrote to La. senator John Lynch. ". . . From the President & Congress nothing can be hoped. Grant is thinking only how to be renominated & reëlected, and the men who control the organization of the Repub. party are devoted to means & selfish purposes, conscious that the end of their power is fast approaching, & determined to prolong their political existence by all the dishonest & low tricks which the mere politician can invent. My only real hope is in a new organization of parties, for though it is possible, it is quite improbable that Grant, Morton, Cameron, Chandler & Co. can be unhorsed, & the Republican organization purified. I continue to mind only my private business, keeping up my thinking about all this. I suppose I might have been U. S. Senator by saying the word, but my prudence as to private affairs makes me shrink from any form of public life. . . . I suppose you have seen that Grant has sacrificed Willard Warner to the demands of such a scamp as Spencer of Alabama. G's conduct in this is only a fair sample of the infamous system he has adopted, of seeking the support of the vilest tools at the expense of cutting loose from the only friends who could give character to his administration. I told Warner long ago that he must expect this; that from the day Judge Hoar was asked to resign the Atty Generalship there was nobody who could rely upon Grant's pretende[d] friendship, still less upon his preten[ded] honesty. You have had your share in this experience, & know that honest performance of duty has been for two years past the surest way to lose favor with the administration. I hope the Liberal Republican organization of Missouri may prove the nucleus of a movement that will defeat Grant, & shall do whatever I may to help it. . . ." ALS (press), *ibid.* See letter to Charles W. Buckley, Nov. 21, 1870.

3. On Feb. 3, 1872, Andrew G. Curtin, minister to Russia, Nice, wrote to Gen. Sherman. ". . . Notwithstanding that there is a coolness in the Russian Cabinet towards our Govermt in consequence of the recall of Catacazy I am quite sure you will be received and treated in Russia very kindly—. . ." ALS, DLC-William T. Sherman.

To William W. Belknap

Washington D. C. [Jan. 30] 18[72]

Direct Gn. Terry to ~~to~~ assign to Maj. Merrill[1] ~~to~~ command of ~~Sub Dist. embracing all the Counties in S. C. where the writ of H. C. has been suspended.~~ all the troops in S. C & N. C.[2] so far as to controll them in the discharge of their duties in executing the laws against Ku Klux.

AN, DNA, RG 94, Letters Received, 364 1872. On Jan. 31, 1872, AG Edward D. Townsend endorsed this note. "As Major Morgan who commands in North Carolina is senior to Major Merrill, the Secretary of war says Let Merrill be assigned to command of a District embracing all military stations in the State of ~~North~~ South Carolina." AES, *ibid.* On Jan. 31 and Feb. 1 (originally dated Jan. 31), Townsend wrote and telegraphed to Brig. Gen. Alfred H. Terry, Louisville. "The President directs that you assign Major Lewis Merrill, 7th Cavalry, to command a District embracing all Military stations in the State of South Carolina so far as to control them in the discharge of their duties in executing the laws against Ku Klux." "The President directs that ~~as Major C. H. Morgan, 4th Arty who commands in North Carolina~~ you ~~assign~~ place under the orders of Major Lewis Merrill, 7th Cavalry ~~to command a District embracing all military~~ such troops stationed in the States of North and South Carolina as may be necessary, so far as to enable him to control them in the discharge of their duties in executing the laws against Ku Klux." L (initialed), *ibid.* On Feb. 1, Townsend telegraphed to Terry. "Suspend action on letter of thirty first (31st) ultimo regarding assignment of Major Merrill, modified by letter mailed to you this date. Acknowledge receipt" Telegram sent (initialed), *ibid.* On Feb. 5, Terry wrote to Townsend. "I have the honor to acknowledge the receipt of your letters of the 31st ult. and 1st. inst. relative to placing additional troops under the command of Major Lewis Merrill, 7th Cavalry. For some time past I have intended to make an inspection of the posts in North Carolina and South Carolina, but circumstances have prevented me from carrying my intention into effect. I expect now to leave here in a few days for those posts of this department, and after examining into the present state of affairs there I will give such orders as will best carry into effect your instructions." LS, *ibid.*

1. Lewis Merrill, born in 1834 in New Berlin, Pa., USMA 1855, held Civil War commands chiefly in Mo. and Ark. and became bvt. brig. gen. of vols. Inspector-gen., Dept. of the Platte (1866–68), he was promoted to maj., 7th Cav., as of Nov. 27, 1868, and assigned to garrison duty at Yorkville, S. C., in March, 1871. See *PUSG*, 18, 521; Proclamation, March 24, 1871.

On Jan. 8, 1872, Attorney Gen. Amos T. Akerman wrote to Secretary of War William W. Belknap. "It is deemed important that Major Lewis Merrill U. S. A. commander of the Post at Yorkville South Carolina who is now I believe at Columbia South Carolina under orders from the War Department should be present in person at Washington for communication with the officers of the Department of Justice in reference to the execution of the Enforcement Laws in South Carolina. I therefore will esteem it a favor if you will order him to report to Army Head quarters at Washington. Mr. Williams my successor as Attorney General concurs in this request." Copy, DNA,

RG 60, Letters Sent to Executive Officers. On Jan. 17, Merrill, Yorkville, wrote to AG, Dept. of the South. ". . . In my previous reports I have repeatedly expressed the opinion that the local civil authorities were powerless to cope with the strength of the Ku Klux Conspiracy even if willing to make the attempt, and I have been compelled to believe that the desire to make the attempt was entirely wanting—It was impossible to believe that such numerous crimes should be repeated almost daily for month after month with no instance of punishment and hardly the commonest formality of investigation, and at the same time to credit the assertion of the civil functionaries that they were sincerely zealous in their duties and desirous of bringing the offenders to justice. The pretence that it was impossible to detect the criminals was transparent as I have been able with the very limited means at my command to trace numbers of these crimes far enough to make it certain that an honest, fearless and vigorous discharge of duty by the civil officers would have brought to light all the facts needed to bring the offenders to trial. . . . Whatever doubts I have entertained of the wilful connivance of the civil authorities at these crimes were entirely dissipated by the facts of the session of the civil court in September—These completely demonstrated the truth of my assertion that the Courts were not only unable to prevent these outrages but were unwilling to try to do so. . . . Immediately subsequent to the adjournment of the Court, I went to Columbia to confer with the District Attorney and endeavor to concert some means of bringing better things about in this section—It was very evident that the means at my command (which were limited to moral influence and to giving aid to the victims in advising the legal methods of seeking redress) were utterly inadequate to meet the secret power of the Ku Klux, rightly called by themselves the 'Invisible Empire' for a more absolute and tyrannical control than they held over the whole people where they existed has never been exercised by human power—I was hopeless of the possibility of ordinary means being made equal to the destruction of the conspiracy but I was so impressed with the danger not only to this section, but to the whole country of permitting it to go on unchecked that I was unwilling to spare any effort to break it up or even to check it. I here received your notice that the Hon. the Attorney General would shortly come to Yorkville to investigate the facts and to endeavor to devise some means for the repression of the organization, I met him in Columbia and after some conference with him then returned to Yorkville accompanied also by US. District Attorney Hon D. T. Corbin. A comparison of the evidence in the possession of the Attorney General with the facts which I had long been collecting convinced him that the worst reports which had been heretofore made of the power and of the infernal purpose and conduct of the order fell far short of the facts. It has since become evident that what at that time would even by those persons most familiar with the facts have been deemed the wildest exaggerations falls short of the truth. The facts as now found are astounding and it is impossible to make even the most temperate statement of them without risk of being suspected of exaggeration The warning proclamation, and the proclamation suspending the writ of Habeas Corpus followed close upon the report of the Attorney General of the facts, but even before this and indeed on the very day of his arrival many of the KuKlux leaders suspected that means were being devised to bring them to justice, and with the cowardice which has characterized all their infamous crimes, fled, leaving their poorer followers and ignorant dupes to stand sponsors for the crimes of which they had been the chief authors and instigators Two days after the telegraphic notification of the suspension of the writ of Habeas Corpus, by direction of the Attorney General I began effecting the arrests of such persons as he had evidence to show were guilty of crimes, and whose arrest he directed. The troops were so disposed that a large number of arrests were effected simultaneously over the County. The effect of this, coupled with the fact that it was instantly apparent to the KuKlux that no blow was struck in the dark, and no arrests made at random or on mere suspicion, was surprising. The rank and file were bewildered and demoralized. Looking about for their Chiefs and Councillors and finding that to get orders or advice they must go to them in jail or follow their flight, they recognized the fact that the game was up, that the organization was broken, and all over the County they betook themselves to flight or came in and surrendered.... Whatever opinion may be entertained of the propriety of the methods prescribed by the Law, there has been no instance in which these have not been rigidly adhered to, and the event has at least demonstrated that those or similar measures were the only ones adequate to meet the facts of crime here.... While earnestly recommending that the Civil power alone be returned to at the earliest period that may be possible, I must also invite careful attention to the necessity for being sure that respect for law is firmly established and its just administration certain and unmolested before the aid of the military arm of the Government is withdrawn...." Copy, *ibid.*, RG 94, Letters Received, 2586 1871. For related reports and papers, see *ibid.*; *SRC*, 42-2-41, part 5, pp. 1599–1614. See also Louis F. Post, "A 'Carpetbagger' in South Carolina," *Journal of Negro History*, X, 1 (Jan., 1925), 40–50; Allen W. Trelease, *White Terror: The Ku Klux Klan Conspiracy and Southern Reconstruction* (New York, 1971), pp. 369–76; Everette Swinney, *Suppressing the Ku Klux Klan: The Enforcement of the Reconstruction Amendments 1870–1877* (New York, 1987), pp. 205–44.

On March 1, 1873, U.S. Senator Thomas F. Bayard of Del. introduced a resolution asking USG to inform the Senate "whether any commissioned officer of the United States Army, while on duty in the State of South Carolina, has received or attempted to procure payment of any money or other valuable consideration from the Legislature of said State, or endeavored to procure legislation to that effect, as a compensation or reward to him for services performed in the line of his duty as an officer of the Army or otherwise ..." *CG*, 42–3, 2017. On Feb. 10, 1874, Bayard reintroduced the resolution. *CR*, 43–1, 1349. A subsequent debate centered on allegations that Merrill had collected $21,400 in rewards for convictions of Ku Klux Klan conspirators. *Ibid.*, pp. 1378–81, 1465–71. See Trelease, *White Terror*, p. 417.

2. On Jan. 23, 1872, Townsend forwarded reports of renewed Ku Klux Klan activities in N. C. counties bordering S. C. to "the congressional Committee for the Investigation of Alleged Outrages in the Southern States." *SRC*, 42-2-41, part 2, pp. 591–92. See message to Senate, Jan. 17, 1871.

On April 20, 1871, Governor Tod R. Caldwell of N. C. wrote to USG. "I have the honor to transmit herewith a letter from the Hon. G. W. Logan, Judge of the 9th Judicial District of North Carolina, asking protection for the people of Cleaveland and Rutherford counties against outrages threatened by lawless bands of disguised men which infest those counties. From information received from good and responsible Union men residing in Rutherford county I am satisfied that a number of loyal men and women of both colors have been most cruelly treated by scourging and otherwise at the hands of a disguised band who come mostly from Cleaveland county, N. C. and from an adjoining District in South Carolina. My information is that some of the desperadoes are known to the victims, but those who have been punished fear to expose those whom they know lest they may be more severely visited in the future. It is the opinion of good citizens that a full exposure would be made if the sufferers had some assurance of being protected in case they testify against their assailants. I am sorry to say, that from the best lights before me, I am compelled to believe that in certain localities in North Carolina it is an utter impossibility to convict any of the members of this murderous Klan in our State Courts—perjured witnesses and suborned jurors are ever ready at hand to shield and protect their guilty accomplices. I have known of no single instance of any disguised person being brought to punishment for crime committed, except the single instance of some colored men in Alamance county, who, following the evil example of their white neighbors, undertook to set up a law for themselves in their neighborhood. They came to grief and are now properly expiating their crime in the State's prison. If, however, they had belonged to the Ku Klux organization, I have no idea that they would have been convicted of any offence. I can offer the people of Rutherford and Cleaveland no protection except such as is afforded by the civil law. If I were to call out the militia of the State and quarter one or more companies in this disaffected region, it is likely that a large portion of the soldiers would be members of the organization that had perpetrated the outrages complained of. Under the circumstances, therefore, I deem it my duty to submit the matter to your consideration, and in behalf of those who are oppressed and threatened, to ask your Excellency if compatible with your sense of expediency and justice to order a company of cavalry or such other force as you may deem advisable to be quartered either in Cleaveland or Rutherford County for the protection of the loyal people thereof, and to assist the civil authorities in executing the law and preserving the peace." LS, DNA, RG 94, Letters Received, 1414 1871. The enclosure is *ibid.* On April 11, J. B. Carpenter, Raleigh, had written to Caldwell. "Mr Neathery will enclose to you a letter from Judge Logan containing a request for Military aid, and as Judge Logan expected me to give you a detailed account of some of the various outrages committed in our County, I will say that within the last month not less than fifty persons have been whiped and otherwise maltreated by dsguised men as I am creditably informed and honestly believe, and these outrages have been on the increase for the last two weeks I have a hastily drawn memorandum of some of the latest cases.... In every case that I have heard of these men have denounced the Radicals and made threats against the lives and persons of of the leading Republicans of our County, this there is no chance to make all these outrages from personal feuds in the different neighborhoods as the whole working shows it to be a well organised movement. The republicans of Rutherfordton have slept on their arms for near three weeks expecting almost every night a raid, if we do not get help we are gone, I shall go to Washington City from this place, and if you think that you can consistently ask for troops for our protection from the letter of Judge Logan. please do so at once, by Telegram from Salisbury.—I will be at the Ebbit House tomorrow night and remain until I hear from you I carry with me a certified copy of Judge Logans letter, and if you wish could lay it before the President, with your approval, and perhaps get troops sooner." ALS, *ibid.* On May 10, Carpenter, Rutherfordton, wrote to USG. "Some weeks since Gov Caldwell forwarded to you a letter from Judge G W Logan 9th Dist North Carolina detailing outrages committed in Rutherford County North Carolina, and requesting that troops be sent to this County We have anciously waited to hear from you. as our County is in a deplorable condition Murder, arson & midnight outrages on peaceable citizens is rampant. There is scarcely a night, but that some person is whiped or scourged by Ku Klux, and we do most respectfully ask that you will give us protection, Numbers of republicans lie out from home of nights, as they fear for their lives. The civil authorities give what protection they can, but it amounts to almost nothing. as the Ku Klux can always prove themselves clear, out of not less than Seventy cases in this County and Cleveland which adjoins this County, not a single case has been tried and the parties convicted and punished, and unless we get protection from the Governent, we must either give up our principles or flee the Country. This letter is written at the request of many of the republicans of this County, and that you may know is genuine. I hereunto set my hand and affix the seal of the County Clerk of the Superior Court for Rutherford County" ALS, *ibid.*, 1748 1871. On June 9, Maj. Charles H. Morgan, 4th Art., Raleigh, wrote to AG, Dept. of the East. "I have the honor to acknowledge the receipt of instructions to investigate and report upon the subject matter of the letter of Mr J. B. Carpenter to the President U. S. asking that troops may be stationed in Rutherford & Cleveland Counties to protect the people from Ku-Klux raids—Under the discretionary power granted to me by the Dept. Commander under date of May 5th 1871 I transferred Battery "A" 4th Art'y, Capt E Thomas Comdg. to the county seat of Cleveland County on the 25th May—I have not yet received any report from Capt Thomas. I am satisfied however that it is not advisable to station any more troops in that neighborhood at present, Capt Thomas being able to effect all that a larger number could accomplish—. . . I saw Mr Carpenter yesterday, and he distinctly stated that they did not require any troops in Rutherford—being able to take care of themselves— The Republicans have, or had, a majority of about 800 votes in that County—Mr Carpenter thought the troops now at Shelby should go to Mooresboro—. . ." ALS, *ibid.*

On April 27, Judge J. L. Henry, N. C. Superior Court, Asheville, had written to Victor C. Barringer, Washington, D. C. "I will be glad to hear from you & know what is going on in the Federal Capital. The K. K. bill is regarded as a *failure* among the Conservatives down here, and dont amount to much. I dont think it will suppress the K K unless vigorous measures are used by the Prest to enforce it thoroughly. I had some persons arrested on Bench Warrants a few days ago for outrages in Madison County, & have ordered others arrested, God only knows where this thing is to end. I have not much hopes of the election this summer because our strong Republicans in the Tobacco region will be overrun by K. K. & the negroes & white Republicans wont vote,. . ." ALS, *ibid.*, RG 60, Letters Received, Senate. Barringer endorsed this letter, evidently to U.S. Senator John Pool of N. C. "I enclose the within. It would be well perhaps to lay its substance before the President." AE (undated and initialed), *ibid.* On May 3, Samuel S. Ashley, Raleigh, wrote to Pool. "Many thanks for your speeches which I have this day recieved. They contain matters of great importance to the Country, but alas, which I am afraid that the Country will never understand. These Ku Klux ~~organizations~~ outrages are the result of a wide-spread and perfected organization. I͟t see it stated in the papers that the outrages have ceased. This is far from the truth. Every day we receive here intelligence of the activity and murderous lawlessness of the Klans—and this from different parts of the State. Yesterday news came from Harnet County, that armed and disguised men attacked a colored man's house—scourged his wife, and shot the man himself. In the affray one of the villians was killed and another badly wounded. Of course the vengeance of the brotherhood will now be aroused in that section—. . . I understand that U. S. troops are to be sent to Rutherford & Cleveland Counties. I hope that with them will be sent faithful officers and skilful detectives. It is to be feared that too many United States soldiers sympathise with these Ku Klux. Many of the soldiers are Irish and bitterly hostile to the negro. I am satisfied that no Irish soldiers should be sent south at the present juncture. If Genl Grant does not address him self vigorously to the work of suppressing these Klans, the Country will soon have a bloody rebellion on hand. To tamper now is to fan the flame. You will excuse me for thus troubling you. I thought the information might not be altogether unacceptable to you." ALS, *ibid.* On May 8, Pool wrote to Akerman. "Mr. Ashley is the Superintendent of Public Schools in North Carolina. I receive letters, by almost every mail, from different parts of the State, detailing outrages & threats. I hope to be able to see you in a few days." ALS, *ibid.*

On June 12, Judge Albion W. Tourgee, N. C. Superior Court, Washington, D. C., wrote to USG. "Mr Ashley and myself, called this morning to pay our respects and with the hope that we might have a few moments of conversation in regard to affairs in our State (North Carolina). We do not wish to intrude upon your time unnecessarily, nor have we any *axe* to grind, but we would like, if it meet your pleasure a few minutes conversation upon this subject, the importance of which, in a national point of view, we think to be fully appreciated by very few except yourself—Our principal object in coming here was to see you upon this matter. If consistent will you appoint a short time for an interview? If it be presuming upon your time and attention too much, of course, we would not ask it—" ALS, Duke University, Durham, N. C.

On June 16, Pool wrote to USG. "I have just received information of a serious character from North Carolina. A witness summoned before the Committee of Investigation, (Mr. J. B. Carpenter), of Rutherford Co. while here before the Committee, had his newspaper presses [&] fixtures distroyed by disguised men—The other witness summoned, but not yet in attendance, Mr J. M. Justice, a member of the N. C. Legislature, has been taken from his house & whipped. Both these gentlemen are of high character, standing, family connection & inteligence. Great excitement prevails—I hardly know what to advise, but hoped to consult with you on the subject. I learn that the Judge of the Circuit has been compelled to leave, in order to save his life. There being an election now pending, & these disturbances being on the increase, I have great apprehension of most wide spread disorder, & of most serious results." ALS, DNA, RG 94, Letters Received, 1612 1871. On June 22, Morgan endorsed the letter. "Respectfully returned. The instructions of the Department Commander have been anticipated, by my circumstantial report of June 17th 71 which furnishes all the information within my reach on the subject. I saw Mr Justice yesterday and he informed me that an attempt was made to shoot him last Saturday night but the facts are not very satisfactorily established to my mind as yet. Mr Justice's statement was, in effect, that some man presented a pistol & snapped a cap at a man sitting in Mr Justice's window (supposing the man to be Mr Justice) and fled on the failure of his pistol. This occurred at Rutherfordton" AES, *ibid.* On July 3 and 5, James M. Justice testified concerning the Ku Klux Klan in N. C. *SRC,* 42-2-41, part 2, pp. 102-64.

On June 17 and 18, Morgan had written to AG, Dept. of the East. "I have the honor to state for the information of the Department Commander that I deemed it necessary, during my recent visit to Shelby & Rutherfordton to direct Capt Thomas to transfer his Battery to the latter place. 2d Lt. Greene, with a sergeant and ten men was directed to move forthwith, and arrived there, doubtless, this morning—the remainder of the Company will follow as soon as the stores can be transferred. I recommend also that an additional Company be sent to the same neighborhood. It would be well if Cavalry could be sent—There are two or more companies within two days march at points in So. Carolina, I believe, at Spartanburg & Yorkville—from which localities one of the Camps of Ku Klux came to participate in the raid

upon the town of Rutherfordton—I consider it advisable to keep a company at
Rutherford continually until all cases now pending or which may come up under
the Enforcement Act, and the Act commonly known as the Ku Klux bill are disposed
of—I advise also the stationing of a detachment temporarily at Mooresboro, about
half way between Shelby and Rutherfordton—If the people now under bonds are
brought before the coming session of the Federal Court at Marion guards will have
to be furnished there—I have also an application for troops to assist the Revenue
officers in breaking up illicit distilling in Rutherford Co. . . ." "In making my special
reports, as called upon from time to time, of affairs in different sections of this state
it has often seemed proper for me to submit some general comments on the organization known as the Ku Klux Klan. By embodying these comments in a single report
I will be able in future to confine my special reports to mere statements of facts—
I trust therefore that the Department Commander will not think I am going outside
of my duty in presenting the following report when it has not been specially called
for—For convenience I give my views first as to the extent of the organization; then
as to how far prominent men are connected with it; and finally its object—I have
information concerning the operations of the Klan in but about a half dozen Counties,
viz: Rutherford Cleveland Harnet, Chatham, Moore and Sampson—Since I have
been stationed here the Counties which were the scenes of disorder last year have
been perfectly quiet so far as I know. I do not by any means suppose that the Klan
is in existence only in the Counties named. The order in this state I believe to be
part & parcel with the one disturbing the peace of So. Carolina, and other Southern
States and connected by a common system of oaths signs &c. It is emphatically
denied by the conservative press in this State that the order has the support or
sympathy of any prominent and leading citizens—It has certainly a great many
apologists among this class, but it is no doubt true that intelligent and thinking men
understand that the operations of the Klan are injurious to the interests of the
conservative party at large—There are however many men of local prominence,
whose political vision is limited to townships and counties, who are active supporters
of or sympathisers with the order—There are others taking little part in politics
who favor the order because it seems calculated to preserve 'the supremacy of the
white man' and relieve them from the apprehension of negro rule. I feel satisfied
that the order has its strongest supporters among the women of the country, who
are notoriously bitter beyond description in their feelings towards northern people
and southern Republicans—It can hardly be doubted that these women manafacture
the disguises worn by the Klan, which are in some instances quite fancifully trimmed.
The women are also knowing in many instances to the places of concealment of
disguises   Horses and mules are not so plenty that fifty or sixty of them can be
assembled for a raid, without the fact becoming known to others than the riders. A
considerable proportion of the parties arrested for going in disguise heretofore have
been mere boys of 16 and 17 years of age—To sum up on this point it may be stated
that vigorous denunciation of the Klan is rarely heard in this State except from
Republicans—Every one has ready the language of apology; 'they are only administering a sort of rude justice'; 'they never whip any one to that stays at home to mind
his own business'; 'if it wasn't for them there wouldnt be a chicken in the Country';
these are the kind of remarks one hears in travelling—In my opinion the attention
of the civil authorities should be drawn to the fact that the U. S Commissioners
themselves belittle the crime very much by either discharging arrested parties on
their own recognizances or on insignificant bail. This fact shows the state of public

opinion here—for it is owing to the weakness of Commissioners in yielding to the sentiment of the Community in which they hold office, that such insignificant bail is exacted—It is perhaps true on the other hand that parties are often bound over on imperfect testimony. These night-raiders are guilty usually of burglary, punishable by the laws of N. C with death; of robbery; and of an assault with deadly weapons. A common tramp charged with these crimes would be committed without bail—but when a dozen or more combine, and in addition to the offences named are guilty of violation of the Acts of Congress against going upon the highways in disguise, they are released upon bail bonds of from $100 to $1000—and the Commissioners office is made the scene of merrymaking & levity during the making out of bail bonds— There remains the question whether the object of this organization is political—I am firmly convinced that it is, and thought so long before the raid on Rutherfordton which should satisfy an impartial mind—The conservatives in Rutherfordton bore testimony to the fact that there was no ground of complaint against Mr Justice except in his political course—Whether the order was originally designed as a political engine I can not say—but that it was soon discovered that its effect was to establish such a terrorism over the blacks as to keep many of them from the polls is certain. It was only necessary then to select victims from among those men obnoxious to charges of immorality of some kind to effect a double purpose; first to make it appear that the morals of the community were being regulated and afford ground for apology and explanation; and still effect the political purpose of frightening some one from the polls. I have seen men who have been cruelly beaten, and warned during the whipping that they ought to turn conservative, yet it is loudly asserted by the apologists for the Klan that politics had nothing to do with these cases, and the victims are charged with being nuisances of one kind or another against whom the neighbors have arisen because the law didnt reach the case exactly—I am of opinion that in some instances parties not members of the Klan have assumed their disguise and perpetrated outrages which have gone to the credit of the Klan. I have only to add, in conclusion that I have arrived at these opinions by a gradual setting aside of preconceived notions of an entirely opposite character—" ALS, DNA, RG 94, Letters Received, 1612 1871. On July 8, Morgan again wrote to AG, Dept. of the East. "I have the honor to enclose herewith a communication from Capt V. K. Hart Comdg. 7th U. S. Cavy, verifying the report forwarded by me yesterday concerning the surrender of members of the Ku Klux organization—. . . The Governor does not appear to have formed any definite opinion as to the cause of these surrenders—I see no reason to change my opinion already expressed that the secret of the movement is in the desire to avoid the jurisdiction of the U. S. Courts—It is to be regretted that the U. S. Civil authority is not represented at Rutherfordton just now by some person of very considerable legal ability and intelligence—The Governor stated to me that he had written to the Judge now conducting the examinations that persons guilty of violations of the 'Ku Klux Bill' should be bound over to appear before the Federal Courts—but I do not see that this is in the power of a State Judge—I suggested that the judge could not do this but that the preliminary examination would have to repeated before the U. S. Commissioner—I represent these facts—though somewhat foreign to my duties perhaps—because I do not know of any other way by which they are likely to reach the proper authorities" ALS, *ibid.* The enclosures are *ibid.*

On July 21, Orville E. Babcock wrote to Horace Porter. "Senator Pool, and Col Hinton called to see me to day and reported the progress in N. C. They say that the Sheriffs with the assistance of the troops have arrested a large number of those people indicted. There are some 300 indictements and no one but the officials know who they are. That they gave it out, that all those people belongling to Ku Klux who would come in own up &c would ~~be~~ not be arrested. They say that a great many have come in, owned up and given very valuable information. In one case the head of the *Klan* came in with his men. masks and all. They think that if a company of cavalry could be sent to Aberdeen Miss—to be used by the Marshal, and the same course pursued, as in N. C. they would stop the K K and would probably get much valuable information—They report that there are now over two hundred people indicted in the vicinity and the people do not know who are indicted,   They say that the K K intend to make a ride as they term it just before the election in N. C. and thus awe the people—They think two companies of infantry at Raleigh— would prevent it—and they want also a Co of Cav at Rutherford as I telegraphed today—They think that with this raid in Miss. they will get sufficient information to demonstrate positively the connection of the opposition with the KuKlux, and their intention to crowd out all loyal people. This should be attended to at once if done at all—Had the Secty of War, been here I should in all probability not have telegraphed you to day, but the Secty is away, Gen Townsend is away (for one day) and Gen Whipple did not think he had any authority to act unless I gave a positive order. He did not say so to me but I saw how he was situated. The record against the KuKlux is said to be very damaging to the democrats.—No news—all well here . . . P. S. I shall be away for one week so any orders for troops should be sent direct to the D of W—." ALS, *ibid.*, 2671 1871. On the same day, Porter, Long Branch, telegraphed to Babcock. "DIRECT THEM TO BE SENT AT ONCE.. FROM FORT MONROE OR WHEREVER MOST AVAILABLE" Telegram received, *ibid.*, 1612 1871. Related telegrams are *ibid.*

On July 17, Caldwell wrote to USG. "I have the honor to transmit for your Excellency's consideration a communication this day received from the Sheriff of Robeson County with the endorsement of three of the leading citizens of said County—. Messrs McDiarmid & Howell who brought the communication to me, represent that there are not more than *eight* desperadoes, most of whom have been outlawed, who are committing the outrages complained of & who have caused the whole County of Robeson to become panic-stricken. I have furnished the arms & ammunition they ask for, & it does seem to me that by proper exertion they have it in their own power to suppress this lawless band, as they are known to the County authorities and as the Sheriff is authorized by law to call out the whole power of the County as a posse to assist him in arresting them—. Having made this statement I forward you the communication with the hope that it may receive such consideration as its merits entitle it to—." LS, *ibid.* On July 15, R. M. Millan, Lumberton, N. C., had written to Caldwell. ". . . At the earnest request of the citizens I would further request Your Excellency to represent our condition to the federal government at Washington, and, if possible, to secure for our protection the immediate presence and cooperation of a strong detachment from the U. S. Army. Cavalry, I think, ~~w~~could render us most effective service. The recent threat of the outlaws in regard to the abduction of our women and the burning of the property of citizens indiscriminately has naturall excited great terror and alarm, and demand immediate action. ~~I~~We therefore beg Your Excellency to act as speedily as possible" ALS, *ibid.* On Aug. 5, Morgan endorsed these papers. "Respectfully returned—I see no reason to change the opinion heretofore given, that troops ought *not* to be sent to Robeson

Co for the purpose indicated. To send Cavalry there would be absurd—The truth is, not that the people can not capture these outlaws, but that they will not undertake the work earnestly and persist in it—There is danger in it—and they have persuaded themselves that it is the duty of the Government to relieve them from their troubles, . . ." AES, *ibid.* Related papers are *ibid.* See *SRC,* 42-2-41, part 2, pp. 283–304.

On Aug. 2, Robert M. Douglas, Washington, D. C., wrote to Judge George W. Logan, N. C. Superior Court, Rutherfordton. "Your letter of July 28 to Senator Pool was yesterday referred to me. I am informed by Adjutant General Townsend that all the Troops in the state are subject to the order of the Commanding Officer, Col Morgan, I think it is. One, or even both if necessary, of the Companys stationed at Raleigh might readily be moved to Rutherfordton, as they are not needed at Raleigh. Your proper course would be to apply to Col Morgan   If you experience any difficulty in the matter, if you will write either to Sen Pool or myself, I will arrange it." Copy, DNA, RG 94, Letters Received, 1612 1871. On Feb. 14, Logan had testified in Washington, D. C., concerning Ku Klux Klan activities in N. C. *SRC,* 42-1-1, 185–90. On Aug. 7, Nathan Scoggin, U.S. commissioner, Rutherfordton, wrote to Morgan. "At this time there are a number of K. K. prisoners in our Jail, & we are almost daily having more arrests made,   among the prisoners are some leading K. K. which among their friends has created much feeling, & I have been informed from what I believe to be a reliable source that an attempt will be made this week to release them from prison, therefore I respectfully ask & request that you send us at once another Company of Troops" ALS, DNA, RG 94, Letters Received, 1612 1871. On Aug. 9, Morgan wrote to AG, Dept. of the East. ". . . On the 8th ultimo I forwarded a petition (in Judge Logan's handwriting) for more troops and informed the Dept. Commander that I had declined the request. On the 14th ult. I made a report of my last visit to Rutherfordton, in which I stated that I saw no reason to change my decision of the 8th   After my visit Judge Logan seems to have attempted to procure an additional Company through Hon. Senator Pool. It is for this reason that I lay the correspondence before the Department Commander that he may be familiar with the case should it come to him through another channel—I have consulted His Excellency the Governor on this matter, and my views appear to accord with his— He is of opinion that the U. S. Commissioner possesses the requisite authority to remove the prisoners—but in order that there may be no mistake in the matter has to day telegraphed to his Honor Judge Bond for advice—As for the projected raid on the jail, I believe the apprehension is without any foundation—. . ." ALS, *ibid.* On Aug. 11, Logan wrote to Pool. "Yours of the 7th recd & I hasten to reply by return mail—After receiving the Letter from Mr Douglas, I sent an *Express* to Raleigh to Col Morgan for a company of Troops. I have to day recd an answer from him declinging to send them. *I must have another Company here,* if the Government relys on me to succeed—I hope you will see the authoritys at once, & have Col Morgan telegraphed, to send a company here without delay—This is a very busy day with me. I will write you fully by next mail—I am getting on well—I shall not look *back, dont fear*—Tell Genl Townsend to try & have a *true* man put over the Troops here." ALS, *ibid.* On Aug. 17, Belknap endorsed these and related papers to Townsend. "Have these troops furnished if they can be spared" AE (initialed), *ibid.* On Aug. 18, Gen. William T. Sherman, Washington, D. C., endorsed these papers. "All the dispositions of the troops in the South have been made without my being consulted by the Dept. Commanders. Therefore I can only say that Gen McDowell has subject to his orders, plenty of troops to supply this demand or any other. The whole of the 8th Infantry is doing nothing in NewYork harbor,—As to Cavalry it is well known there is none to be spared unless taken from Gen Terry, who need them quite as much as the Marshal does in North Carolina." AES, *ibid.*

On Sept. 7, Arnold Galloway, Wilmington, N. C., wrote to USG. "Wishing to be excused for the liberty I am taking, I wish to informe your Hon that I have been Poisend by some Parties in Onslow County N. C. by some of the Rebels. and I never expect to Get over it. I would like to know as I am a Poor Colerd Man if I Could not have the Case Investigated. and If they Guilty Parties Cant be brought to justice, I have not dobt but what Some of them made some Complains to the Dept before this. if they did I would kindly thank you for the information." ALS, *ibid.*, 3156 1871. On Nov. 3, Alferd Rogel *et al.*, Wilmington, wrote to USG. "We the undersigned Citizens from Sampson County, Are here to Attend the US Dist Court, of the Cape Fear Dist. whereas our lives are in danger if we return. as we attend in the Case of Minnes Harring the witness who was killed for testifying against the sampson Klu Klux. We Pray Your Hon to give us some protaction to return to sampson Co. for our property which we left behind us. as it would not be safe for us alone to return and we Cant do with our Necessarys of life, which we left behind us. as our meanes ar very poor. hoping you will take the metter in Consideration and lend the donetroten Colord Men a Chance to reclaime which belongs to him, . . . P. S. They have sworn to kill us if we return" DS (4 signatures—signed by mark), *ibid.*, RG 60, Letters from the President.

On Dec. 28, Tourgee, Greensboro, N. C., wrote to USG. "Permit me to call your attention to a fact which, more than any other which has come to my knowledge, illustrates the wisdom and beneficence of ~~the course which~~ your administration ~~has adopted~~ at the South.—~~Last week~~ ₐAt the Superior court of the county of Alamance, at which I had the honor to preside last week, a grand jury composed of a large majority of members of KuKlux organization, including one chief of a camp, ~~indicted~~ presented bills of indictment sixty-three members of the Klan for felony and eighteen for the murder of Wyatt Outlaw, who was hung as you may recollect ~~in sight of the the yard~~ on a tree in the Court House Square Feb 26th 1870—~~Most~~ Many of those indicted are of the most respectable families of the county—The confessions now in my hands also reveal the perpetrators of similar crimes in other counties—I do not doubt, within a month I shall hold ample evidence as to every K. K. crime in this District—Nothing, Mr. President, but the ~~firm and~~ prompt and unflinching firmness of your course in relation to this vexatious question could have rendered such a thing possible—To the State government the KuKlux was an impregnable fortress. Sixty-four times I had tried in vain to break into its walls and secure testimony sufficient to enable me to demand from juries indictment and conviction—The former had a few times been secured by a predominance of Republican jurors—the latter never. And so it would have remained until the end of time, ~~but that~~ had not your wise and patriotic course so frightened the adherents of the Invisible Empire that they began to deserts in squads. ₐAnd this is the result—a *KuKlux* Grand jury *indicts for KuKluxing* I believe, Mr. President, that I have the honor to present to you the first flag of truce, the first act of submission, upon the part of foes more bitter and dangerous than those which yielded at Appomattox, and I beg leave to offer you the sincere thanks and congratulations of every peace loving citizen of this much KuKluxed District, for the victory which gives us safety and vindicates the law, even in the mouths of our enemies—. . . ~~I doubt, sir, if even you can fully~~

appreciate the debt which we who have watched the ravages of this foe from our own potals, owe to you, or the gratitude and reverence we feel." ADfS, Chautauqua County Historical Society, Westfield, N. Y.

To Charles W. Ford

Washington D. C. Jan.y 30st *1872*

DEAR FORD:

I have your letter of the 26th inst. All the lands remaining to Burnes & Carlin within the Cerre & Bolé tracts, at the date of my compromise with them, is now mine without an adverse claimant. That obtained from Carlin, 47 arpents is mine in whole. That got from Burnes Holliday has an interest in, but not large except in one lot. In all the lots except one, where H. has any interest, if my memory serves me right, Holliday's his interest is one fifth. I can not find the plat of these lands so as to give you the numbers accurately but they will be found on record. I think no one will attempt to interfere with any arrangement you make in regard to it. I shall be very glad when my land near Carondelet acquires such a value as to justify me in selling it. I have too much unproductive property. Elrod thinks he will make the farm pay but I hardly credit it. If some of the colts should turn out Dexters it might, but not otherwise.

I shall be glad to see you here.

yours Truly

U. S. GRANT

ALS, DLC-USG. On Jan. 26, 1872, Charles W. Ford, St. Louis, had written to USG. "I have agreed to lease lots 70 & 71 in section 39—in the Bolay tract. for four years. with the condition. that if sold in the mean time. that he should give up quiet possession—on payments for such crops as he may have in the ground—This ground lays on the north side of the creek. I learn from young Goodson—that a man named Sangford. claims to have a lease of the Seigerson Tract, from some lawyers or land agents in St Louis—he could not learn who they were, and that this lease includes the whole of the Bolay tract. How can this bee? I thought all the lands—discribed by the yellow lines—(on the map) was lands which had been compromised with Carlin & Burns—and absolutely yours? It appears also. that there is another fellow named Zeiglemyer, living in Carondelet—who in has posesion of lot 78—containing 8 630/ arpents.

This is in Sec 5—I have told my tenant to go on and fence in this ground if any one offered to interfere—to prevent it to let me know This land is covered by Sangfords Lease if in reality he has any lease at all,   I think it desirable to have all this land in possession of parties who will take leases from you—That would give you constructive possession any way. I should be glad to hear from you on this subject. before I go East as it may be necessary to go down and see the parties before I leave, which will be betwen the 5th & 10th of Feby" ALS, DLC-USG. In Feb., Ford stayed in the White House as a guest. See *Louisville Courier-Journal*, Feb. 16, 1872. See *PUSG*, 19, 228–29; *ibid.*, 20, 138–39, 144–47, 149, 165, 177–78, 278; letter to Charles W. Ford, Feb. 2, 1871; letter to William S. Hillyer, [Jan., 1873].

To William S. Hillyer

Washington D. C. Jan.y 31st *1872.*

DEAR GENERAL:

I am very much surprised at the contents of the letter which you enclose to me from Mrs. Rawlins. Like you however I do not find fault with her course nor consider it remarkable. I have only this moment received, and read, your letter and Mrs. R's and therefore am not prepared to decide beyond the possibility of a change of views as to the best course to pursue. It is to be presumed that the gentleman to whom Mrs. Rawlins is married will not want the charge of the children but even if he does I think it would be better to have them go with their relations in Orange Co. New York, who I know will be glad to take them.

The house where Mrs. Rawlins now lives may be sold if the same can be got for it that was paid; if not it should be rented. Will you inform me of a good Agt. in Danbury to look after this matter? All the furniture of course Mrs. R. should keep as her own private property. In the first payment on the Danbury house I used the salary voted to Gen. R. by Congress.[1] One fourth of this is due to Mrs. Rawlins. It strikes me that I had better purchase for the benefit of the heirs of Mrs. R's share of the Washington house, and pay her in addition her share of the purchase money for the Danbury house. You are authorized at all events to communicate these views.—I am very much obliged to you for the offer to take the children until arrangements can be made for them. If Mrs. Rawlins desires I wish

you would and let me know so that I may write to their relations
on the subject.

Yours Truly

U. S. Grant

Gn. W. S. Hillyer

ALS, Hillyer Papers, ViU. On Jan. 29, 1872, Mary E. Rawlins, Danbury, Conn., wrote
to William S. Hillyer. "I am going to be married this evening, and being aware that in
accordance with the instructions governing the use of the Fund, my portion of the
income derived therefrom will cease, and knowing that you are equally well informed
upon the subject I take the liberty to ask you to inform President Grant of my intention, and to ascertain, if possible, what different arrangements—if any—he wishes to
make with regard to the care of the children, and the disposition of this place. I desire
to mention in this connection that Mr. Daniels is fully cognizant of the peculiarly
involved circumstances of the case, and will in *no* event reside here, but will pursue his
business in New York as heretofore   I desire to be informed through you of the
President's action in the matter." ALS, *ibid.* Hillyer had met USG about Mrs. Rawlins
in Jan. *SRC,* 42-2-227, II, 449. See letter to C. F. Daniels, March 20, 1872.

1. On May 11, 1870, USG had signed legislation paying the remaining portion
of John A. Rawlins's annual salary to the executors of his estate. *U.S. Statutes at Large,*
XVI, 666. After purchasing the Danbury house, USG wrote to Mrs. Rawlins with
news regarding her finances as well as furniture sent from Washington, D. C., adding
wishes for happiness in her new home. Paul F. Hoag, May, 1959, no. 28. See letter to
Mary E. Rawlins, Feb. 13, 1871; letter to William D. Rawlins, July 19, 1872.

Calendar

1871, JUNE 1.   Attorney Gen. Amos T. Akerman to USG. "I have reëxamined the case of Richard J. Shoener, in which Mr Killinger takes an interest, according to my promise of yesterday. . . . He was not a regular employee, but was occasionally engaged to take charge of, and distribute the mail, in the postal car between Washington and New Jersey. Letters were missed, and he was watched and caught in the act of opening them, and abstracting the contents. Mr Keasby, the District Attorney, reports that there was no doubt whatever as to his guilt, that there is nothing in the character or circumstances of the crime to make it just or expedient to exercise clemency by any diminution of the term of his imprisonment; but Mr Keasby adds that, as he had borne a good character previous to the offence, and has conducted himself well in confinement, it may be well to pardon him just before the end of his term, in order to restore him to citizenship. He was sentenced for two years to expire next October. Allowing the reduction for good behavior, the term will expire in August, and it occurs to m that all that his friends can reasonably ask of you is to grant a pardon then."—Copy, DNA, RG 60, Letters Sent to Executive Officers. On July 12, USG pardoned Richard J. Schoener upon the recommendations of U.S. Senator Simon Cameron of Pa., seven U.S. representatives from Pa., and others.—Copy, *ibid.*, RG 130, Pardon Records.

1871, JUNE 1.   Secretary of the Treasury George S. Boutwell to USG, Long Branch. "Reduction of debt for May four million four hundred thousand, (4,400,000.)"—Copy, DNA, RG 56, Telegrams Sent.

1871, JUNE 4.   John W. Case, Auburn, N. Y., to USG. "Have respect for a prisoners letter. I am pleading for mercy. On the 28th of January. 1869—the Post Office ofat Phelps, Ontario Co. N. Y. was robbed of two letters, some postage stamps, a mail key and five dollars in money. A short time after the robbery, I was arrested for the Crime, it was my first offence and I thank God that I did not deny the charge. . . . At the age of sixteen I entered the army for the war. I joined and served three years as a member of the Eighth (8) N. Y. Cavalry, "D." company, was wounded twice at the battles of Auldie and Beverly Ford—At the surrender of Harpers Ferry, Our brigade cut our way through the enemy's line, my horse was shot from under me and I was made a prisoner of war, about ten miles from the Ferry. . . ."—ALS, DNA, RG 48, Miscellaneous Div., Letters Received.

1871, JUNE 4.   Ann M. Scott, Phoenixville, Pa., to USG. "I write thes few lines to yo   I did not Know how to go tow   My sister was sold from the state of Mariland seventeen years a go   she wrot to her friends since she got free say that she would come home but she could not get her Monney to come   She di[e]d ᵗᵒ two mounth ago and has left a little boy and the say that she give him to them and do not want her friends to have him   she live in attlanta georgian   wil you plase to make them give him up   I can take Care of my sister child   plase sir let me Know if you will do any thing fore me   plase sir to exces me fore trouble yo   I do want my sister Child

Mis Clark has got Child   Direct you letter in Cae of Miss Boyle"—ALS, DNA, RG 105, Letters Received. On June 14, Eliphalet Whittlesey, Bureau of Refugees, Freedmen and Abandoned Lands, wrote to Scott that Ga. courts offered her only recourse.—Copy, *ibid.*

[1871], JUNE 9.   To Secretary of the Navy George M. Robeson. "PLEASE RELIEVE CLARK FISHER. CHIEF ENG. OF TICONDEROGA PORTS-MOUTH ME.   VESSELL SAILS ON TUESDAY NEXT."—Telegram received (from West Point, N. Y.), DNA, RG 45, Letters from the President. On Jan. 9, USG had nominated Clark Fisher as chief engineer, U.S. Navy.

1871, JUNE 10.   Secretary of the Treasury George S. Boutwell to USG recommending an increase to $100,000 of the penalty bond for the collector of customs, Chicago.—Copy, DNA, RG 56, Letters Sent to the President.

1871, JUNE 10.   E. B. Lookins, Portsmouth, Va., to USG. "Immediately on the papers implicating Mr. Lyons in Smuggling Sigars, being sent back to Commissioner Foster at Norfolk for my affidavit, He (Lyons) was informed of the fact by some person (to me unknown). He and his friends a[s] I learn, are already at work with money and [im]portunities, to influence United States Officers; I am ready to have this case tried on its merits, and I would most respectfully suggest that some U. S. Attorney be selected to try it who has not been connected with it heretofore, unless it be Mr. Beach who gave it fair Consideration,   I would not be understood as casting any reflections on the U. S. Officers, but it is probable the trial will bring out evidence of bribery, and I hope that no suspicion will rest on any man who may represent the Government. However if the Government will not accede to this request I hope I will be allowed to employ prosecuting counsel to aid the U. S. Attorney, although my means are limited—The incubus of unfaithful officers must be gotten rid of if the Republican Party would succeed, and a fair trial will rid them of Mr. Lyons. I think justice demands that, Lyons be suspended until after the investigation; his retention in office implies the confidence of the Government in his innocence, which the information in its posession does not warrant"—ALS, DNA, RG 56, Letters from Executive Officers. See *PUSG*, 20, 357.

On Nov. 14, 1872, William H. Lyons, Portsmouth, transmitted to USG resolutions unanimously adopted by "The Grant Republican Club No 1. of the City of Portsmouth," congratulating USG on his reelection.—LS and copy, USG 3.

1871, JUNE 16.   Elihu B. Washburne, Paris, to USG. "This letter will introduce you to Mr. Bayard Clarke, Junior, the son of my old friend and former associate in Congress from N. Y., the Hon. Bayard Clarke. The young man is highly educated, speaking both French and German equally as well as his own language, of excellent character and good principles. On his return

home he may wish to visit Washington and pay his respects to you. I beg
to Commend him to your usual courtesey."—ALS (press), DLC-Elihu B.
Washburne.

1871, JUNE 17. USG proclamation authorizing Secretary of State Hamilton
Fish to exchange ratifications of a commercial treaty with Italy.—DS, DLC-
Hamilton Fish. On March 30, 1871, USG had transmitted the treaty to the
Senate.—DS, DNA, RG 46, Presidential Messages. On April 15, the Senate
ratified this treaty.

1871, JUNE 19. Nippawa and three others, Americus, Lyon County, Kan.,
to USG. "We have got a friend to write for us what we wish for you to
know—Since our yearly payments have been withdrawn we have but few
friends—but when we had money comeing every year we could get what
we wanted—what we wish is to get into a better way of farming—we have
never had land enough broken to raise enough to last us one year—we wish
to raise corn to sell and enough to keep our Ponies in order so that we can
work them in the spring—haveing no grain to feed them in the spring we
cannot get our crops in without help from white men—and since our money
is run out and the Farmer has sold all the down wood on the reserve we
have nothing to pay with—therefore some of our land lies idle that ought
to have been in crops   we have lost a great manny of our ponies from the
cold last winter which put us back—the Farmer we have over us takes no
interest in learning our boys to farm—and we wish you to give us a one
that will live in one of our houses and be with us every day—to see that
our boys do their work right   the Farmer that is at the mission has all he
can do to attend to that farm—we do not see him at the Caholy camp once
a week   we wish you to give the situation to William Pettyjohn for he is
our friend and not for money alone   we wish to know before haying—. . .
as wee have made ready for A hunt pleas direct to W Pettijohn if we can
have him for our farmer"—D (signed by mark), DNA, RG 75, Letters Received, Kansas Agency. Pipawa and eight members of the Kaw council also
petitioned USG. "Wee the counsell of the Kaw tribe of indians wish to State
our case to you and Wish you to aid us for we know, you can do so   first
then what is the reason that our Men that have money coming cannot have
it paid to them   they could do better if it was so   they could get evry thing
cheaper   by being bound to trad at the store of one man he makes us pay
twenty five cents for bacon when we could get it for fourteen other places,
Wee never get any money   if they sell timber we gen no money   We the
coun sell Know that their is a remidy for this if we can get you to take it
in hand   wee, wish to farm but wee have not the means to farm with and
if any person offers to help us they are for bidden   Wee are placed like
children and cannot make One step without help   evry thing we get we
have to get it from the trader and pay his prices   is it just to keep us in
this cituation   it seems as if their is Know person that cares for us   their

is a great many of our tribe now that has not brede to eat   some say they
are lasy   well whos fault is it if some are   when We had plenty money
coming white man want it   they not care if injun have now money   all
gone let injun starve or sell out and go   wee wis to stay here and become
Citizens work lik and live like white man   this is their words through go
wolf who served in the ninth Kansas   they wis you to send Some one of
your men that is good and see for you   they wish you to write to isawaa
he is the speaker of their couns   he sais you can help them   they got one
white man to write and yes send it to study   makes him mad at white man
no let whit[e] man make hay on shares for isawa So isawa poney have no
hay   this is their trouble   do as you like but I believe if you would wite
isawa a letter it would do him good for they believe tha you are the best
man living   he sais you must send him a letter to america . . . Wee your
humble servants pray you to look in to our cituation"—AD (docketed as
received on Sept. 8), *ibid.*

1871, JUNE 20. William Johnston, Washington, D. C., to USG. "I have been
at the Executive Mansion several times to see you, but it never was convenient, and so I take this method of saying a few words in regard to the
business of my old friend George T. Jones. Near thirty years ago, when we
were both young, Mr. Jones and I had our offices in adjoining rooms of the
same building in Cincinnati, and I was quite conversant with his affairs. He
was then esteemed an accomplished bank-note engraver and printer, and
executed the state bonds and such for the states of Ohio and Indiana, &c.,
&c. The distinction he had acquired in his profession brought him into the
Criminal Courts as an expert in the trial of indictments for counterfeiting;
and this led him, to whether he would or no, into the dangerous and thank-
less business of ferreting out, detecting and bringing counterfeiters to punishment. By a natural sequence of thought, Mr. Jones began to study out
and devise means to prevent counterfeiting. This brought him to the conclusion that the engraving art was exhausted, and that something must be done
in the preparation of bank-note paper, and in the chemical compound and
application of colors. Several years of hard study and expensive experiments
resulted in several discoveries and inventions for which he took out patents.
These devices have been so highly recommended by chemists, photographers
and bankers that I cannot doubt their importance to the business community
at large, but more especially to the Treasury Department; and by advice of
men whose opinions are entitled to consideration, Mr. Jones has offered
them in various ways to the Department. When proposals were invited, by
Commissioner Delano, for Revenue stamps to prevent frauds on the revenue,
Mr. Jones was an applicant, had the highest recommendation of the chemist
appointed by the Revenue Department, and was the lowest bidder, and by
every consideration of justice was th entitled to the contract. But the Secretary of the Treasury resolved to advertise for bidders in the public press.
At this nick of time, I called on the Secretary to tell him who and what Mr.
Jones was, and to assure him of his ability to execute his contract, having

first seen Governor Cooke, ~~She~~ Messrs. Sheppard, Huntington Kelley, Blake and others, who stood ready to be his sureties, and stated that all the means necessary were at his command for fulfilling the contract. But the Secretary of the Treasury cut the conversation short by the declaration that this was not a question—that he would advertise, and the lowest bidder should have the contract, and, if Mr. Jones was the lowest bidder, he should ~~have the contract~~ take it for granted he ~~He did advertise~~ was able to execute his contract. He did advertise, and Mr. Jones was again the lowest bidder.— Instead of giving him the contract, the Secretary appointed a commission, consisting of Senator Edmunds, R. W. Taylor and W. P. Sherman, Esquires, to inquire into what I had been informed was not a question in the case. Whether this commission was appointed to divide the responsibility of breaking a promise or from real doubts as to Mr. Jones' ability, I will not undertake to say; but they ascertained at least that others were able to execute the contract, and reported against Mr. Jones, at the same time recommending that one denomination of the national currency should be given to him, to test the value of his inventions on bank-notes, bonds, &c. The contract for the Revenue stamps was given to Mr. Carpenter, of Philadelphia, not to be executed in the usual way, but in accordance with Mr. Jones' patent. Against this attempt at piracy, as ~~legal~~ Mr. Jones' legal adviser, I entered a solemn protest, and notified Mr. Carpenter, Secretary Boutwell, and all others whom it might concern, that I should prosecute, in the Federal courts, any one who might infringe Mr. Jones' patent-rights. This resulted in a compromise, by which Mr. Carpenter agreed to pay Mr. Jones a royalty for the use of one of his patents, during the continuance of his contract. Now, I am well informed that, instead of giving Mr. Jones one denomination of the National currency to execute (as recommended by the commission), in order to test the value of his inventions, *preparations are being made in the Department* to *appropriate another of his inventions* appertaining to bank-notes and bonds, without saying 'by your leave' to the inventor. Now, in my poor judgment, both as a lawyer and a man, discoveries and inventions, which have cost a man years of thought and thousands of money to work them out, are as much his property and as worthy of protection as his wardrobe, his library, or the tools of his trade; and the infringement of his rights is not the less unjust because it is done by a high official of the Government. The right of eminent domain, as exercised in time of war, cannot be made a pretext for taking a citizen's property for nothing. What I respectfully suggest is that you should so far interfere in this matter as to prevent the infringement now going on in the Department, in the finishing of bonds, &c., and carry out the recommendation of the commission appointed by the Secretary, and give the improvements of Mr. Jones a fair trial. If they are as good as the chemists, photographers and bankers represent them to be, the ~~g~~Government ought to have the benefit of them, and the inventor ought not to ~~have~~ be driven to expensive law[suits] to protect his rights. Desiring to see your Administration, in all its departments, free from reproach, . . ."— ALS, OFH.

1871, JUNE 22. Pinckney Ross, collector of customs, Pearl River, Miss., Shieldsborough, to USG. "I was informed by the hon Secretary of the Treasury a few days ago that, it had been decided that there would be a change made in the office that I now hold, and that my resignation would be received if rendered. I have in no case over stepped the pale of the law, or knowingly violated any Regulation nor neglected any part of my duty. Now, I am at a loss to know what has given rise to the dissatisfaction there seems to exist. I have many enimies here who have been trying for six months past to have me removed for no cause only that I am a true Republican will ever fight the Republican's cause, and will take no sides with Rebels. There is but one true Republican here, that is competent and trustworthy to receive the appiontment if the Department is really desirous of my resignation. I will beg to have the privilage of naming my successor as I know those that live here by their action, though President I am desireable of holding it myself, during your term only. by granting me this request, you will confer a lasting favor on your humble servant hoping to hear from your honor soon"—Copy, DNA, RG 56, Collector of Customs Applications. On Dec. 6, USG nominated H. W. Wilkinson to replace Ross.

On June 12, 1872, Ross wrote to USG. "It really seems singular if not in consistency, to see the man that I was removed to make room for, as collector of customs in and for the district of Pearl River, whose commission is fresh from your hand, and he now acting and sympathising, with the Greeley, sorehead movement, yet such is actually the case. now on the other hand as regards myself, I have and still intend to regard my party success, paramount to individual interest & will stand by and support the Philadelphia nominations . . . P. S. I regard the some of the men representing mississippi in congress as responsible for this gross abuse of Federal patronage, as you are of course not supposed to know the character or disposition of the men recommended to you for appointment. now hoping you will act in the interest of your & my party in future . . ."—ALS, *ibid.*

1871, JUNE 23. Horace Porter, Long Branch, N. J., to B. Waller Taylor. "The President directs me to acknowledge the receipt of your letter of the 8th inst. and to say that he read with no little surprise your application for his approval of a patent life preserver coupled with a proposition to give one of his children a pecuniary interest in your invention. It is scarcely necessary to say that both your request and proposal are declined."—Copy, DLC-USG, II, 1.

1871, JUNE 29. USG endorsement. "Apt. may be made to one of the places suggested."—AES, DNA, RG 59, Letters of Application and Recommendation. Written on a letter of June 24 from Governor Henry D. Cooke of D. C. to USG. "Mr. J. H. Hawes of this city was recommended by myself, Genl Chipman and others, in May last, for a Consulship, Mr Hawes' failing health makes an urgent necessity for a speedy change of climate, and I respectfully request his appointment as Consul to Geneva, Switzerland

Reference is respectfully made to the papers filed in May relating to Mr. Hawes' appointment."—LS, *ibid.* In April, John H. Hawes, Washington, D. C., had written to USG. *"Personal* ... This paper will be presented by Governor H. D. Cooke, who will add some oral explanations. I laid down a commission from President Lincoln on Mr. Johnson's accession to the presidency, and have devoted all my time and energies since to the republican cause. I have suffered a loss, thereby, of nearly $5000, *in cash,* besides my time, and my health is seriously impaired. I now need a slight return from the party I have always faithfully and sometimes, at least, effectively served. I require a change of climate for a limited period...."—ALS, *ibid.* On March 23, James Harlan *et al.,* Washington, D. C., had petitioned USG. "Mr. J. H. Hawes was appointed to the position of Principal Clerk of Surveys in the General Land Office by President Lincoln. Upon Mr Johnsons accession to the Presidency he resigned and engaged with Judge J. M. Edmunds in the work of organizing the loyal element in the unreconstructed States, through the instrumentality of the Union League of America, and the printing of the Great Republic newspaper as the official organ of the organization. He gave his time and services to the cause *for two years,* and aided by personal appeals in Philadelphia, New York, Boston and Providence, in raising large sums of money to carry on this work, *without any compensation whatever,* and is a personal looser by reason of these services to the amount of *$4600 in cash* besides his time. He also edited a small campaign paper, called the *National Radical* during the last Presidential campaign which was conducted with vigor and obtained quite a wide circulation in nearly all the western and southern states...."—DS (8 signatures), *ibid.* On April 17, James M. Edmunds, postmaster, Washington, D. C., wrote to USG. "Understanding that Mr. J. H. Hawes may become an applicant for Some Consulship I have to say in his behalf, that he is a thorough Republican, has been a warm supporter of the administration, and that he made considerable Sacrifices in the Campaign for the reconstruction of the Southern States. He was also prominently instrumental in the establishment of the New National Era in this City, now conducted by Mr Fred, Douglass. Mr, H. is a gentleman ability and cultivation & will, I believe, fill with credit to himself and fidelity to the Country, any place which may be assigned to him."—ALS, *ibid.*

On July 3, Orville E. Babcock wrote to William Hunter, asst. secretary of state. "I intend to leave here for Long Branch on Thursday, to see the President. If you have any matter to send please let me know. Judges Poland, and Edmunds called to see me in the case of Mr Hawes and the endorsement of the President. If you will be so kind as to send me the record of the incumbent of the office at Geneva, Malaga and Osaca, I will submit them to the President, and let him decide, if he wish, to which place to appoint Mr Hawes."—Copy, DLC-USG, II, 1. On Aug. 3, Horace Porter, Long Branch, N. J., wrote to J. C. Bancroft Davis, asst. secretary of state. "The President directs me to request you to write to our Consul at Geneva, and ask him whether he would like to go to Osacca Japan in case Scott Stewart resigns informing him of the salary of that office. Should he desire to make

such a change it will enable the President to make an appointment which he
has wanted to make for some time to Geneva. Should there be no prospect of
Stewart's resigning, then name to Mr. Upton, at Geneva, any consulship
which may be vacant and which you think he might select in preference to
Geneva."—ALS, DLC-J. C. Bancroft Davis. On Aug. 18, Hawes wrote to
Cooke. "Mr. C. B. Young, proprietor of Emerson Institute, on 14th street,
and a friend of mine, has had an interview with the President for the purpose
of endeavoring to secure my appoint as Consul to Geneva or some place on
the Continent where his family might also be located. I should be most
happy if it could be so, but I notice there is a vacancy at *Chin Kiang, in
China* and will accept that if it will expedite matters, as I am exceedingly
anxious now to have the appointment at the earliest practicable day."—ALS,
DNA, RG 59, Letters of Application and Recommendation. On Aug. 23,
Porter endorsed this letter. "Respectfully referred to the Sec. of State   If
there is a vacancy here the President has no objection to Mr. Hawes' appointment"—AES, *ibid.* On Aug. 26, Secretary of State Hamilton Fish endorsed Hawes's letter. "There is no vacancy in Geneva—G W Flint, recently
Appointed to Chin Kiang by the Prsdt direction, does not accept—appoint
this applicant to the place"—AE, *ibid.* On Sept. 11, Chipman wrote to USG.
"I desire respectfully to ask the appointment of Mr J. H. Hawes of this city
to be Consul at Osaca Japan or some equivalent consulship. I believe this
request is not now for the first time made altho' I have never till now asked
the appointment from you. Recently in conversation with the Secretary of
State I was informed that he knew of no objection to Mr Hawe's appointmt
to Osaca should Mr Stewart, present incumbent, now on leave of absence,
not return. . . ."—ALS, *ibid.* Related papers are *ibid.* On Dec. 6, USG nominated Hawes as consul, Hakodadi (Hakodate), in place of Elisha E. Rice.

On Feb. 24, Speaker of the House James G. Blaine had written to USG.
"The bearer of this note E. E. Rice Esq late US. Consul at Hakadade, Japan
would like to return as Consul at Yeddo—I should be exceedingly glad, if
you could find it consistent to give him the appointment—Mr. Rice's long
residence in Japan, his familiarity with the language & general acquaintance
with American interests there render him a valuable representative of our
country"—ALS, *ibid.* On March 9, USG nominated Rice as consul, Hakodadi, in place of Ambrose C. Dunn.

On April 7, 1870, Dunn, Dublin, Va., had written to USG. "I have the
honor most respectfully to ask the appointment of Consul to Honolula Ha-
waiian Islands. I am a defeated Republican candidate for Congress in my
state, and on account of my Republican principles I am ostracized and cannot
make a living at my profession there. I refer to the accompanying testimonials as to my character and qualifications."—ALS, *ibid.* Related papers are
ibid. On July 13, USG nominated Dunn as consul, Hakodadi, in place of
Rice, whom President Abraham Lincoln had nominated for the office on Jan.
5, 1865. On Dec. 18, 1870, James Longstreet, surveyor of customs, New
Orleans, wrote to USG. "My friend A. C. Dunn Consul at Hakodadi, writes
me of his wife's bad health and asks for a transfer, to Yokohama, Kanajawa,

Honolula, or Hong-Kong. He suggests these places, as he is under the impression that there will be vacancies at each of them soon. We have no claim for such great kindness from you: but I feel that you will excuse the liberty that I take in preferring the application, leaving to your better judgment the proper action in the premises."—ALS, *ibid.* For charges against Dunn, see Fish diary, Feb. 17, 25, 1871, DLC-Hamilton Fish. For Dunn's C.S. Army service, see *O.R.,* I, xxv, part 2, 712, 763; *ibid.,* xxix, part 1, 55–56; *ibid.,* IV, ii, 583.

1871, JUNE 29. Secretary of the Navy George M. Robeson to USG. "The Hon. Henry D. Cooke, Governor of the District of Columbia, has made application to this Department for one hundred and thirty-five stand of arms for the use of the 1st Col'd Regiment of District Militia. I have the honor to refer the Governor's request to you for such order as you may desire to give concerning it. The arms are at the Navy Yard in this city, and are not required for use of the Navy."—Copy, DNA, RG 45, Letters Sent to the President.

1871, JULY 2. Sarah Hamilton, Lexington, Va., to USG. "I seat my self to drop you afew lines to let you know how I bean treated . . . I em old now i em going on forty six and i em in the famely way again and i ant abel to doo inny thing   wee well parish if thare ante somthing done for us   tha took my home and it wos wothe too hondred dollars to me and more to . . . rite soon for i dont now how i will live"—AL, DNA, RG 48, Letters Received, Miscellaneous Div.

1871, JULY 6. USG endorsement. "Refered to the Hon. Sec. of State   Please send ~~G~~general letter."—AES, DNA, RG 59, Miscellaneous Letters. Written on a letter of July 4 from Birdsey G. Northrop, secretary, Conn. Board of Education, New Haven, to USG. "I am commissioned to inspect schools abroad & especially in Germany sailing 15th inst. Gov. Jewell, Pres. McCosh of Princeton, & Yale & Harvard Professors give me numerous letters. But in getting access to Educational Men & Institutions, none would serve so well as a general letter from you to our Ministers in Europe. . . ."—ALS, *ibid.* See Northrop, *Education Abroad, and Other Papers* (New York and Chicago, 1873). On May 31, 1873, Orville E. Babcock wrote to Northrop. "The President directs me to acknowledge the receipt of your very cordial invitation to be present at the Thirteenth Annual Meeting of the National Educational Association in August, and in reply to assure you that he feels great interest in the cause of education believing that in education of the people lies the safety of the Republic. At this date he is unable to promise that he will be present, and is of the opinion that he will not be able to accept. . . ."—Copy, DLC-USG, II, 2.

1871, JULY 7. Ira W. Raymond, Arizona City, to USG. "Can you not send on an officer that will look out for Government Affairs here in this Territory

Goods are sent in here from Sonora Mexico every day worth thousands of Dollars—and no duty or Revenue Collected   Hoping you will see to it . . ."—ALS, DNA, RG 56, Letters Received. On Dec. 20, Secretary of War William W. Belknap wrote to USG reporting Raymond's arrest and imprisonment "for imposture—pretending to be a Govt detective. . . ."— Copy, *ibid.*, RG 107, Letters Sent, Military Affairs. See *New York Times*, Oct. 24, 1871.

1871, JULY 8.   Charles W. Petherbridge, Richmond, to USG. "As you will perceive by the accompanying documents, I am an applicant for a chaplaincy either in the Army or Navy of the U. S. A. Should you confer this honor on me, it will be my pleasure to give a cordial support to your administration and also to secure to your administration the support of my friends,   It is due to myself, as well to you to state, that, *no political disabilities* rest *on me, nor have any political disabilities ever rested on me, that I am aware of,* . . ." —ALS, DNA, RG 94, ACP, 4203 1873. On June 10, Leroy M. Lee, Richmond, had written to USG. "The Rev Charles Wesley Petherbridge, a regularly ordained Minister of the Methodist Episcopal Church, South, applies for the position of Chaplain, either in the Army or Navy of the United States of America. Army prefered. . . ."—ALS, *ibid.* On July 11, Elizabeth Van Lew, postmaster, Richmond, wrote to USG. "Permit me to say that I do not know a minister here so able to make application for the position he desires—as the Rev. C. W. Petherbridge   Mr. Petherbridge is beloved and respected & very highly-commended by his friends—Mr. Petherbridge can furnish excellent testimonials as to character and ability—. . . Looking over the above I see that I have omitted to say that the appointment of this gentleman would give me much pleasure—accept and pardon my postscript—"—ALS, *ibid.* Related papers are *ibid.* On Dec. 1, 1873, USG nominated Petherbridge as post chaplain.

1871, JULY 9.   Amanda M. Fenno, Big Suamico, Wis., to USG. "At the begining of the late war my three sons volenteered in the army   The eldest came home all right. The second died of typhoid pneumonia soon after his discharge and the third recd. commision in the 17th Infantry. but the temptations incident to the army proved to much for him and while on leave of absence in Chicago last spring he became intoxicated and gambled away goverment funds. and is now held at Fort Snelling awaiting trial   His name is D. G. Fenno   he has a wife and little girl entirley dependent for support and for their sakes I pray you will do all you can to remit his punishment. He is truly penitent and pledges himself never to touch the cup again" —ALS, DNA, RG 94, ACP, F95 CB 1868. On July 12, Lusa J. Fenno, New London, Wis., Darwin G. Fenno's wife, wrote to USG requesting leniency.— ALS, *ibid.* On Sept. 15, Fenno was cashiered, sentenced to five years in prison, and fined $1500 for embezzlement, gambling with government funds, breach of arrest, and desertion.—D (printed), *ibid.* On Dec. 28, Brig. Gen. Oliver O. Howard wrote to USG. "D. G. Fenno formerly an of[ficer] of the

Army, was for some time on duty [in] New Orleans in this Bureau. While on duty with me I notice that his record was good. While recently in Minnesota, I had from a Volunteer Officer of high standing' in Stillwater the best accounts of this Young man's conduct since his imprisonment, and it is generally believed that liquor was the cause, and the *only* cause of his committing the crime. While this is nothing to relieve the heinousness of his offence, yet it does not appear that he was ever a thief before, and under the assurances of future good conduct taken in connection with past record, I recommend that his punishment be mitigated."—LS (press), Howard Papers, MeB. On Jan. 10, 1872, Secretary of War William W. Belknap wrote to USG. "I have the honor to return to you the recommendation of the commissioner of the Freedman's Bureau for the pardon of D. G. Fenno, late 2nd Lieut. 17th Infantry, cashiered and imprisoned for embezzlement and its enclosures, & to report that in my opinion, the demands of justice have not been sufficiently met by the punishment he has already receivd."—Copy, DNA, RG 107, Letters Sent to the President. On Dec. 5, USG remitted the remainder of Fenno's sentence.—D (printed), *ibid.*, RG 94, ACP, F95 CB 1868. See *PUSG*, 17, 607–8.

1871, JULY 11.   Charles McCarty, Chapmans Creek, Kan., to USG. "after My regards too you Plees alow Me too remind you off the 15 Day off June 1863 when I fell throu the birg one ¼ off a Mile South Midelburgh Tennesee oun the Mississippi centril R R   I wass runen the Engin for the us gover and badley inger Sou ash I wass noat abel too work for about 4 Four years at aney thing and I Mit Say that I have noat worked Moore than 18 Monts Since it hapened an till too Day I noat abl too work one ¼ off the time and cant doo that Saim at My traid   Sow you will See I am in a verey bad fix I wrot you a letter a bout 5 years a go in regards too thiss and you Said you woud See what you cood doo for Me when congress wood Seet   My papers have been inn the hands off the Members off congress From the 6 districk off Indiana for 5 years without aney Moove what Ever   I wrot a letter too a frend off Mine and He laid it before one off the clerks offa the house last March and the clerk Sais thiss has not been at aney time before the committee off claimes nor was it to the last congriss before aney committee   thiss iss the clerks ansor   Mr grant I hoap you will doo Some thing for Me at thiss next Setten off congress ash your the onley Man that iss at Washington that I know how iss a quinted with thiss axedeent   I hoap too whear from you Soon"—ALS, DNA, RG 48, Miscellaneous Div., Letters Received. In 1868, USG had endorsed papers relating to McCarty's application for a pension.—Copies, *ibid.*, RG 107, Register of Letters Received; *ibid.*, RG 108, Register of Letters Received. On June 22, 1874, USG signed a bill granting McCarty a pension of $8 per month. See *HRC*, 43-1-173; *CR*, 43–1, 1685, 2041, 5069, 5388.

1871, JULY 12.   To AG Edward D. Townsend, from Long Branch. "On receipt of Lieut Church's resignation accept it, and grant one year's leave."—

Telegram received, DNA, RG 94, ACP, 2400 1871. Filed with papers concerning 1st Lt. Richard C. Churchill, asst. professor of drawing, USMA, who resigned as of Sept. 1, 1872.

1871, JULY 14. Brig. Gen. Oliver O. Howard to USG. "I have known Mr A. F. Boyle for several years. During my prosecution he was clerk of the Congressional Committee & enjoyed the confidence of all my friends on that committee. I have ever found him an ardent republican & an active man with a great variety of ability & attainment—I take pleasure in uniting with Mr Arnell & others in commending him to you—"—ALS (press), Howard Papers, MeB. See *HRC*, 41-2-121.

1871, JULY 19. Enoch Hoag, superintendent, Indian Affairs, Central Superintendency, Lawrence, Kan., to USG. "Having learned with sorrow of the judgement of a Texas Court, condemning to death—the two Kiowa Chiefs—'Satanta and Big Bow' convicted of depredation and Murder, in that State—and anticipating, the fearful consequence to the *Border inhabitants* of that and contiguous Settlements, likely to result from these executions, I am led to intercede in behalf of the unfortunate Chiefs, for Executive clemency, that their Sentence be commuted to *Imprisonment for life*—and that they be removed to some quiet and safe place of confinement further North—that the excitement prevailing amongst the Indians, affected, be allayed, and they *assured*, that these criminals will receive kind treatment under the govt of the U. States where they will be permitted to do no more harm. It will be observed, that no raiding has been done, since the imprisonment of these chiefs—and their consignment to a hostage life will have a restraining influence against a continuence of raiding on the frontier Settlements."—ALS, DNA, RG 60, Letters from the President. Related papers are *ibid.* On May 24 and 28, Gen. William T. Sherman, Fort Sill, Indian Territory, had written to AG Edward D. Townsend. "Our party reached here yesterday four days from Fort Richardson. I find the Post admirably located, and far advanced towards completion for six Companies of Cavalry. The buildings are all of stone with shingle roofs made near the Post. Gen Grierson commands with four Companies present and two absent on picket at the mouth of Cache Creek. The Indian agent Mr Tatum has his agency close by, and I have had a long conversation with him and am satisfied he is a good honest man   He admits frankly that the Indians of his agency, the Kioways and Comanches are beyond his control, that they come and go as they please, and he was not at all surprised to hear that they were a hundred miles off, killing citizens engaged in their usual business, and stealing horses, and mules. . . ." "Yesterday quite a large party of the Indians came in for their usual Rations, and Satanta not only admitted to the Agent Mr Tatum, but boasted of it—that he had headed the raid into Texas, wherein the seven men were Killed, and the corn train plundered of its mules & Contents. Mr Tatum and the Interpreter Mr Jones brought him up to me at the Quarters of the Comdg Officer Gen. Grierson, where Satanta again admitted ~~to me~~ that he was there, only varying the details somewhat, as he saw it was not an object to be proud of. I told Mr Tatum the Indian Agent, to say whether he should be arrested on the spot—and he answered that he not only desired it, but requested it to be done. We manoeuvred a little till we could get all who were concerned in that particular affair. The result is that we have arrested, and hold in close confinement—Satanta, Satank, and Big Tree—If Gen McKenzie comes in to this Post Gen Grierson will deliver these prisoners to him to be carried back to Texas for trial and punishment...."—ALS, *ibid.,* RG 94, Letters Received, 1305 1871. On June 8, Sherman, Fort Gibson, Indian Territory, wrote to Col. Benjamin H. Grierson, Fort Sill. "We reached this place at 9 Am yesterday, having spent one day viz Monday at the Indian Council. I find nothing new here from Texas or Fort Sill, and therefore must await results before I can do anything more about the Kioways—but Every body—Mr Hoag, and the Grand Council were pleased that we had taken Satanta &c in the manner we did, and they all express a hope that they will meet their deserts.... I am writing at the Agts office before breakfast, and since beginning the letter I have received yours of May 31, and June 3—Now that you are in communication with Genl McKenzie it is all right. He can take Satanta &c back to Richardson with him, and it will I *know* do the Kioways a heep of good. If you and McKenzie can lay a trap to catch some party of horse thieves in Texas, near the line, and hang Every one of them it will stop this raiding. Insist on the surrender to Mr Warren of *41.* Good mules, and tell Kicking Bird—when he comes in, which he will be sure to do, sooner or later, that if another raiding party goes from the Reservation to Texas, we will have to search his Camps for Stolen Stock, and if that wont do, we must abrogate the Treaty, declare them outlaws, and open their Reservation to Settlement ..."—ALS, ICN.

On Aug. 4, Attorney Gen. Amos T. Akerman wrote to Benjamin R. Cowen, act. secretary of the interior, concerning Hoag's letter. "... It does not appear that these Indian Chiefs were sentenced by any U. S. court. Indeed, I infer from the papers, which are not very distinct upon this point, that the conviction was in a State court of Texas. If such was the case, the government of the United States has no control over the matter ..."—Copy, DNA, RG 60, Letters Sent to Executive Officers. On Aug. 2, Governor Edmund J. Davis of Tex. commuted the sentences of Satanta and Big Tree to life imprisonment. See letter to George H. Stuart, July 22, 1871; William H. Leckie, *The Military Conquest of the Southern Plains* (Norman, Okla., 1963), pp. 146–55.

On Aug. 12, Lawrie Tatum, agent, Kiowa Agency, Fort Sill, wrote to Hoag. "Yesterday the Kiowa Indians brought here and delivered to me Thirty eight mules and one horse, which with the two previously delivered, makes forty mules and one horse, to pay for the forty one mules that Satanta and his company lately Killed and drove off from the train near Fort Richardson Texas. They are a very good lot of mules, some of them superior. The following is what I said to them, after the mules were delivered, as I wished no misunderstanding between us.... After I read the foregoing to them Kicking Bird on behalf of the Kiowas said 'We intend to cease raiding and depradating on the white people and hereafter follow the example of the Caddo Indians, who have long been on the White mans road. As evidence of our good intentions we have brought in the mules as required of us. And now we want you to write a strong appeal to the officers at Washington for the release of Satanta & Big Tree, who we think have now suffered enough; and then every thing will be right'"—Copy, DNA, RG 94, Letters Received, 1305 1871. On Sept. 2, Sherman endorsed this letter to Secretary of War William W. Belknap. "Now that the Kiowas have surrendered the stolen stock, and have come back to their Reservation I am satisfied they will behave themselves, and should have rations according to their Treaty. Kicking Bird can control these Indians provided Satanta never returns, and I hope he will be hung according to his Ritcheous Sentence"—AES, *ibid.*

On Aug. 13, William Lang, Weatherford, Tex., had written to USG. "I have written an a a letter to Prsadent Johnson and one to congress and I havent had any answer and I concludeed that I would write one to you and let you know the great suffering of the people on the frontier by the out Rages of the Indians   hundreds of famelies are scalped anuly and thousands of mules and horses are killed and stolen   General Sherman was hear this Spring and Summer and knowed of one man beeing chaind and burned to death   when general Sherman was leaving hear he was asked about the out Rages of the Indians and he Replyed that the out Rages they commited was not worth notice   it is Reported in the Eastern Stats that it is white people I have lived hear 10 year past and I kno the Indians and white men come in to gether   they have bin Seene and Some times they have no white me with them   what I have put on this paper is trew   Direct your letter to Wm Lang Weatherford Parker County Texas and I will Send you 1000 Sirtificats"—ALS, *ibid.* On Aug. 31, Sherman endorsed this letter. "This paper is returned to the Secretary of War. There have been no raids abut Weatherford since I passed, and if Satanta & Big Tree be hung, according to their sentence, that part of the Frontier of Texas will b[e] comparativly safe"—AES, *ibid.*

1871, JULY 20.   T. Spicer Curlett, Litwalton, Va., to USG. "I am the Candidate of the Republican Party in Lancaster Co Va, and am certain of election to the Legislature as we have, & hold a large majority—My intention in writing to you as the Head of our Party is, I want an opinion on a subject which bothers me a good deal—After having stood insult on insult and having been forced into sending a challenge to a former Rebel Officer, the Rebs here declare my vote, & right to hold office null & void—If a good & true Republican must stand insult without the chance of defending himself I would like to know what to do—Can my vote be taken from me for defending myself—I am well aware you have thousand of such letters as mine, but I certainly shall expect the Head, & Leader of our Party to Pprotect me in case this comes into Court—I was grossly insulted, I had no friends, so I acknowledge sending the challenge, but what I desire to know can this deprive me of the right to run for & hold the office of Delegate in State Legislature   Hoping you will notice this . . ."—ALS, DNA, RG 60, Letters from the President.

On Sept. 23, 1872, Curlett wrote to USG. "Formerly when a resident of Baltimore I applied to the President for an appointment as Lieutenant in the Army, my application being endorsed by Gen'l G K Warren & others— I was promised a favorable consideration but up to this time have heard nothing from it—I now make this second application directly to you, and claim that as the Leader of *our* Party in Lancaster, and as a strong friend of the administration I am entitled to a favorable consideration of my application. Trusting that when a vacancy does occur you will remember . . . I am 24 years of age."—ALS, *ibid.*, RG 94, Applications for Positions in War Dept. On May 25, 1876, Curlett wrote to USG. "I apply to *you* directly, for an appointment in the consular service of the U. S. I have served *you*, and the Party faithfully since my first vote in 1868,—and since that time I have been most useful to the Party of which I am a member—I am at present a Member of the Va—Legislature—, and assistant Presidential Elector for the 1st District in next campaign. . . ."—ALS, *ibid.*, RG 59, Letters of Application and Recommendation. Related papers are *ibid.* No appointment followed.

1871, JULY 21.   U.S. Senator Roscoe Conkling of N. Y., Utica, to USG. "The consulship at Dundee Scotland has I learn become vacant by the death of Dr Smith, and I beg to present the name of Matthew McDougall for the succession. . . ."—ALS, DNA, RG 59, Letters of Application and Recommendation. On July 26, Horace Porter endorsed this letter. "Respectfully referred to the Sec. of State with the request that Mr. McDougall be appointed Consul at Dundee"—AES, *ibid.* Related papers are *ibid.* On Dec. 6, USG nominated Matthew McDougall as consul, Dundee.

On July 22, James Barnet, "at one time a shoeless Printer's Devil," Chicago, wrote to USG. "The liberty is taken of presenting you, by mail, with a copy of the 'Martyrs & Heroes of Illinois,' issued a few years ago. As the matter speaks for itself, we will refrain from quoting the praise of the Press—even from the Chicago *Times.* Two years' time was spent in collecting the Sketches, and hundreds of letters written in trying to reach the relatives of the fallen, so that truthful Biographies might be given. The book was not got up as a speculation, nor as a matter of profit, but from a desire to do something to perpetuate the memory of unselfish men who went and met death for their Country. In the dark hours of the Rebellion, our ward full of Copperheads, a few of us got drilled as a Home Guard, that treason in our midst might not succeed. Not being an Office-seeker nor a praise-hunter,—a Republican of age with the party,—I would still advert to the vacancy of the Consulship of Dundee, Scotland, (the place of my nativity) by the demise of Dr Smith. I am slightly known to a few in Chicago such as the Hon. Joseph Medill and Isaac N. Arnold. With good wishes for the head of the Republic, . . ."—ALS, *ibid.*

1871, JULY 24.   John W. Forney, collector of customs, Philadelphia, to USG.
"I venture to present to your kind acquaintance the bearer, C. M. Levy Esq
of New York, who will explain his business. He is a very leading and influential member of the Hebrew persuasion, and is intimately connected with
some of the prominent Republicans of that denomination in this city. I have
known him for a long time and have perfect confidence in his integrity and
patriotism. If you can give him the benefit of a short private interview I
think you will find him useful and worthy of consideration."—LS, OFH. See
PUSG, 18, 356–57; Lincoln, *Works,* VII, 4–5.

1871, JULY 24.   A. Wellington Hart, New York City, to USG. "I had the
honor to transmit a Memorial signed by the leading and influential Israelites
of New York who irrespective of political influences sought in my behalf an
appointment from your administration. As I had not sought for office, I was
not aware of any vacancy, nor did I think it a matter of delicacy even to
request a particular office. I have since learned that I should define what I
wished. In view that the present incumbent has enjoyed the office since *1861*
I very respectfully solicit the position of *Consul at Liverpool,* where I resided
as Merchant Banker for sixteen years"—ALS, DNA, RG 59, Letters of Application and Recommendation. On July 29, Hart wrote to Secretary of State
Hamilton Fish. "I was rather surprized this morning at receiving an official
circular with your signature to the same, and the Envelope, informing me
that there was no vacancy in the Consulate at Liverpool (although the incumbent has Enjoyed it since 1861) & intimating that you declined to receive
applicants and that papers must be filed &c. . . . I wrote the President that
my coreligionists numbered 450 to 500 000 in the States that their vote is
nearly 70 000 (19/20th DEMOCRATIC)   I pointed out to the President that
in addition to a deep rooted prejudice against him for his Paducah 'General
Order' the Israelites *for their numbers,* had been ignored! the negro elevated
to a Mission & the Jew discarded.—I went to Washington by invitation of
Mr Cameron—then Secy of War in 1861—from War to Ordinance & thence
to Int Rev. office   I was the only Israelite of 4500 Clerks & was forced to
resign after 8½ years service to make way for a negro neophyte! in latter
office.—The President very kindly responded that 'he had carefully considered my letter & would give it his serious attention' has led to my receiving
your circular. Either a mistake or a meaning which I would rather not attempt to infer—I happened to show this letter to some Jewish friends &
the reply & at once on their own volition a Memorial was drawn up setting
forth facts as I have stated & asking the President to confer on me an appt
I forwarded the paper to Long Branch with 3 Extracts from Hebrew Papers & heard that unless I asked for something the result would be 'pidgeon
holeing'   I asked for the Consulate to Liverpool   I simply fulfilled a duty
I owed myself & the President to Enlighten him on that which I imagine
few Politicians are aware of—that in the next Presidential contest—if
close—this 70 000 vote divided between NY, Penn, Ill, & Ohio, where ⅘ of
the Jews reside—THEY HOLD THE BALANCE OF POWER   My kinsman Emanuel

B. Hart has ever been the favorite child of Tammany possessing influence, patronage & weight. Why? because he has received honor from the Democracy & controls to some extent the vote here—& the Republican party ignore the Jew unless they are pressed & what have they done for them? Nothing! I refer to Halgarten & Co Bankers, Moses Taylor, Wm Orton who endorsed the Memorial strongly J & J Stuart & Co. J S. Nixon, Chief Justice Moses of S. C. & even Mr Boutwell.—I suggested to the President *to Elevate* the Jew higher than former administrations as a stroke of Political policy *the* filing *of my papers* is a some what curious acknowledgment of an act of kindness. I yet think it is a mistake—I knew of no Vacant positions in any of the Departments I was selected on behalf of my race as a fit person for the President to recognize & if the President thinks his party is strong enough to sting my Coreligionists with neglect I must act Content & time will prove he is wrong I owe it to myself to give you this Explanation"—ALS, *ibid.* Related clippings are *ibid.* No appointment followed. See *PUSG,* 19, 424–26.

1871, JULY 25. Secretary of the Treasury George S. Boutwell to USG. "A small quantity of distilled spirits has been seized in the District of Alaska for a violation of the 4th section of the Act of July 27th 1868, and of the Executive Order of February 4th, 1870, made in pursuance thereof. The liquors have been advertised under the 11th and 12th sections of the Act of July 18. 1866, (chap. 201), and no claimant having appeared, the property would be sold according to the usual course of procedure in such cases, were it not doubtful whether such sale would be consistent with the existing Executive order. It is therefore respectfully suggested that the order be so modified as to allow sales of spirits seized as aforesaid, of which the value does not exceed $500, under such regulations as may be prescribed in each case by the Secretary of the Treasury. A copy of the report of the Collector of customs at Sitka upon the subject, is herewith enclosed, together with a draft of such an order as is supposed would meet the exigencies of the case."—Copy, DNA, RG 56, Letters Sent to the President. A draft executive order authorizing such sales, dated July 1871, is *ibid.* See *PUSG,* 20, 99; *SED,* 43-2-24, 43-2-27.

1871, JULY 25. U.S. Senator Oliver P. Morton of Ind., Indianapolis, to USG. "I have been informed by a gentleman in whom I have implicit confidence that a vacancy lately occurring by the resignation of the U. S. Vice-Consul at the port of Chefoo China has been filled by the appointment of a British subject, contrary to the wishes of the American residents of that place. The Americans residing there have united in a petition to Mr Low, U. S. Minister to China asking that one of their number be appointed to the position and have recommended Mr M. G. Holmes for the same...."—LS, DNA, RG 59, Letters of Application and Recommendation. On Aug. 1, U.S. Representative James C. McGrew of West Va., Kingwood, wrote to USG recommending Matthew G. Holmes because of his connection with West Va.—ALS, *ibid.*

Related papers are *ibid.* On Dec. 6, USG nominated Holmes as consul, Chefoo.

1871, JULY 26. Anna M. Dobbins, Vincentown, N. J., to USG. "I have of late thought much and seriously About the Indian Race. The Ideah that because *they were born here and lived here America belong'd to them, (although there was no other Race beside themselves) appears very unreasonable to me I was born here more than sixty years ago and yet I have never thought that any part of America that was not held nor occupi'd by another belonged to me. I think only the part that they occupied and cultivated beloned to them, if they think otherwise it it is high time they were better inform'd.* and can it be possible that they think that because they were here first that nobody else has A rigth to come, if so their hostility is not to be wondered at. . . . it would be better for Them to cultivate the land and have Comfortable Houses to live in. I hope they may learn wisdom from what they Suffer."—ALS, DNA, RG 75, Letters Received, Miscellaneous.

1871, JULY 26. Rabbi Max Lilienthal, Cincinnati, to USG. "The Israelites of our beloved country are under lasting obligations to you for the fairness and impartiality, with which you treat their race. May now one of their Rabbis ask you the favor, of appointing his son to a cadetship in the West-point-Academy? My son Jesse has graduated at Woodward High-School with the best percentage in all his studies; has then visited our Law-School, and would have been admitted to the bar, if he had attained the proper age. But he is only seventeen years of age. If your Excellency wishes, I can have him recommended by the two representatives of our city; by the Board of Trustees and the Faculty of Woodward High-School; by the Judges of our Superior Court, by the Bar, and the most prominent citizens of Cincinnati. But your Excellency values more the ambition of an aspiring American, who thirsts for the knowledge, to be acquired at our efficient national Academy, and is then willing to serve his country. By granting my humble petition, you will forever oblige . . ."—ALS, DNA, RG 94, Correspondence, USMA. Jesse Lilienthal did not attend USMA.

1871, JULY 27. To Secretary of State Hamilton Fish. "I hereby authorize and direct the Secretary of State to affix the seal of the United States to a warrant to Samuel Brown, to receive into custody, A Henry Elliott a fugitive from the justice of the United States."—Copy, DNA, RG 130, Orders and Proclamations. On July 25, John M. Davy, district attorney, Monroe County, Rochester, N. Y., had written to USG requesting the extradition from Ontario of A. Henry Elliott, indicted "for forging certain Monroe County Bonds, . . ."—DS, *ibid.*, RG 59, Miscellaneous Letters.

1871, JULY 28. Horace Porter, Long Branch, N. J., to Secretary of War William W. Belknap. "Appoint Forsythe, Chaplain By direction of the President,"—Telegram received, DNA, RG 94, ACP, 3407 1871. On the same day, Belknap transmitted an order appointing "Revd John Forsyth D. D. of Newburgh N. Y. Chaplain and Professor of Ethics & Law at the Military Academy"—ADS, *ibid.* John Forsyth replaced John W. French, who had died on July 8.

On March 31, U.S. Senator Matthew H. Carpenter of Wis. had written to USG. "I am told that the Revd Dr. Hugh Miller Thompson, of Nashota, Wisconsin has been recommended to you to be appointed Chaplin at West Point, in case of vacancy. I know him well. (1) He is the ablest preacher in the West. (2) He is one of the best scholars in the land. (3) He is the best man that ever lived, inside the church or out side of it. If genius, eloquence, ripe learning and 'good FELLOWship' be desired, no better selection could be made. I have loved him for years. I should regret to have him leave Wisconsin, more than I can express; but at the same time, as he might be benefited by the change, I most cordially recommend him; *and earnestly beseech you* to appoint him, if a vacancy exists or shall occur."—ALS, *ibid.*, 5451 1871. In Jan., 1872, Hugh M. Thompson was installed as rector, Christ Church, New York City.

On April 28, 1871, Charles H. Van Wyck, Washington, D. C., wrote to USG. "I would be much gratified if my Brother Geo P. Van Wyck could be appointed or detailed as chaplain at West Point He entered the service as chaplain in 1862 and served during the war. In 1867, he was appointed chaplain in the Regular Army. He would doubtless be competent to discharge the duties of professor connected with the office of Chaplain He graduated at Rutgers College Newbrunswick also at the Theological seminary at the same place I enclose recommendations from a few friends in the House & Senate I feel exceedingly Anxious that my brother should recieve this appointment The President could do me no greater favor"— ALS, *ibid.*, Correspondence, USMA. The enclosures are *ibid.* See *PUSG*, 18, 533.

On May 19, William T. Sprole, Newburgh, N. Y., wrote to USG. "I respectfully solicit your favorable consideration, of this, my application for a reappointment to the Chaplaincy of the Military Academy, at West Point. The circumstances of my removal, as well as its injustice, I presume you know. Without any intimation, and I may confidently add, without the shadow of a reason, in justification of the act, I was suddenly thrust out. I ask my return as a matter of justice. A great wrong has been done me, and I flatter myself, that you will regard it, as entitling my request to some consideration. My qualifications for the office, are known, to all who are familiar with the history of the academy, during the ten years, of my connection with it. I can refer in this behalf to every army officer, now living and loyal to his country, who graduated during my period of service. Every member of the Academic Board, as then constituted, and who still survives, can bear witness to my fidelity; and, to no one do I more readily refer, your Excellency, than my friend General Porter, your private Sec'y. Though somewhat advanced in life, I am as able phisically & mentally to perform the duties of the office, as when I was honored with that position;—while in point of experience, I am certainly in advance, of what I then was.... P S. This application is made in the belief that my successor (Mr French) has declared his purpose to demit his office."—ALS, DNA, RG 94, Correspondence, USMA. Sprole had served as chaplain, USMA (1847–56).

On June 17, 1871, Francis Vinton, Trinity Church, New York City, wrote to USG. "I commend the Rev. Malcolm Douglass, as a Candidate for the Office of Chaplain & Professor at the US-Mily Academy WestPoint. He is the Son of the late Major Douglass, sometime Professor of Engineering at the Academy. He is a Clergyman of high standing & reputation in the Prot Episcopal Church & would honor the station to which he aspires. His appointment would promote the welfare of the Cadets & Professors & people & would gratify the Public"—ALS, *ibid.*

On July 14, Alfred Nevin, Philadelphia, wrote to USG. "It is publicly announced that the Chaplaincy & Professorship of Ethics and Law, in the Military Academy at West-Point, is vacant by reason of the decease of the Rev: J. W. French, D. D. This position would suit my taste and training (as I was a member of the Bar before entering the Ministry), and if you shall see your way clear to give me the appointment, you will bring me, as well as my numerous friends in this city and State, under enduring obligation. The enclosed testimonials for the Professorship of English Literature, at Princeton College, (though they did not prevail, because the successful candidate was a graduate of the Institution,), will serve to show my qualifications for any such post. They are from the most eminent Clergymen of this city, and could be doubled in number, if necessary. My friend—Senator Scott, (now in S. Carolina) will address you in relation to the appointment I now solicit, and I would be gratified if no action was taken in relation to filling the position, until he is heard from, and I have the pleasure of seeing you next week."—ALS, *ibid.* On July 15, Senator John Scott of Pa., Spartanburg, S. C., wrote to USG. "The death of Rev John W. French Chaplain and Prof of Ethics at West Point has create a vacancy, for which I am requested by a very strong influence from Philada to present the name of Rev. Alfred Nevin D. D. a Presbyterian Minster of that City. I do this the more willingly because of my own personal knowledge of Dr Nevin, and my belief of his eminent qualifications in every respect for the combined duties of Chaplain and Professor. I will not weary you by detailing them but express the hope that the application which will be made to you may result in his appointment.... P. S. The sub committee has been engaged at this place for past ten days. There has been a terrible state of persecution in this county; over two hundred people have been whipped since last October, and I have deemed it proper to say to some of the leading citizens here that if any of the witnesses called before the Committee are visited by violence, or if the whippings continue after this exposure of them, we shall certainly call the Presidents attention to the necessity of placing the county under Martial law."—ALS, *ibid.* On July 21, Nevin, "Metropolitan Hotel," Long Branch, wrote to Belknap. "I came to this place on Wednesday, with a Committee of distinguished Presbyterian Clergymen, to have an interview with President Grant in reference to the Chaplaincy and Professorship of Law, in the Military Academy at West-Point. The President has informed me that he ordered through you the selection of a Presbyterian minister for this position. But not feeling certain whether the *selection has yet been made,* he asked me to leave my testimonials, that he might forward them to you, in connection with others, from many eminent Presbyterian Ministers of Pennsylvania, forwarded last week. . . ."—ALS, *ibid.* Related papers are *ibid.*

On July 18, Edward B. M. Browne, Milwaukee, had written to USG. "I figure upon the full amount of your charity in allowing myself this importunity, emanating wholly from motives selfish in their nature.—Having learnt of the vacancy, created in the 'West Point Military Academy' by the resignation of Prof. French, I ventured my application to the Secretary of War for the position of Chaplain to West Point.—The press, throughout the land, dwells largely on 'the claims of the Episcopaliens and Methodists to that office, so much so that president Grant is at a loss to make a choice between them . . .' Now I fail to see, (I am convinced your Excellency will side with my views) what claims any *particular denomination* can have upon that office. It appears to me that we, the Jews have equal rights with them, hence I applied and lay my prayer before your Excellency.—In fact it seems to me that, the Jews have perhaps more just claims as the Christian clergy, because no Jewish Minister has yet been given a single office while the Christian Clergy is very well represented in the offices of the U. S.—I am the Rabbi of 'Emanuel Temple' in this city, duly graduated Rev. A. M., M D., LLB, 26 years of age, and am willing to fill besides the chair of any branch in the academy, falling in the line of my professions, ready to undergo the necessary examination.—My references are the Revs: Isaac M Wise and Max Lilienthal of Cincinnati Ohio, James K Gutheim of N. Y., Robert Collier of Chicago, J N. Dudley and D. Graham of Milwaukee.—In conclusion I would state that I was Chaplain to our State-Senate during the last session.—"—ALS (ellipses in original), *ibid.* See Endorsement, Aug. 27, 1875.

1871, JULY 30. To Secretary of War William W. Belknap. "You may transfer F. W. Roe from the 24th to the 1st Inf.y, if there is a vacancy in that regiment."—ALS, DNA, RG 94, ACP, 3336 1871. On Aug. 2, Belknap favorably endorsed papers granting transfers to 2nd lts. Fayette W. Roe, Julius H. Pardee, and Thomas S. Mumford, recent USMA graduates.—AE (initialed), *ibid.,* 3337 1871. On July 12, AG Edward D. Townsend had telegraphed to USG, Long Branch. "Application of Cadet Mumford for fifth Cavalry, with your approval tenth (10) inst: received this date. General Orders making assignments has been already issued, and he was put in ninth Cavalry. Two above him were assigned to 5th and twenty more above him applied for same regiment—He graduated thirty six. There is one vacancy in fifth, but should he now be transferred to it he would lose one file in rank. Do you desire him ~~him~~ transferred?"—Copy, *ibid.,* ACP Branch, Letters Sent. Mumford remained as 2nd lt., 9th Cav.—E, *ibid.,* ACP, 3337 1871.

1871, AUG. 1. USG order. "In view of the facts contained in the foregoing report, and upon the recommendations in the case, the Executive Order of February 23rd 1871, directing the setting apart of certain lands, therein described, at *Fort Rawlins*, Utah Territory, for military purposes, is recalled, no reservation having been made under said order."—Copies, DNA, RG 130, Orders and Proclamations; *ibid.*, RG 107, Letters Sent, Military Affairs.

1871, AUG. 1. Brig. Gen. Oliver O. Howard to USG. "I recommend without qualification Mr Edward S. Fowler for Asst Paymaster U. S. A. He is thoroughly competent, quick & accurate in figures, prompt & attentive in the performance of duty & of strict integrity. His father was one of our finest officers It will be very gratifying to me to hear of his appointment"—ALS (press), Howard Papers, MeB. For Edward B. Fowler, former col., 84th N. Y., and Edward S. Fowler, see *New York Times*, Jan. 17, 1896, April 26, 1915.

1871, AUG. 10. To Earl of Dalkeith, Edinburgh, from Long Branch. "Owing to absence from home I did not receive your congratulations and expressions of friendship for the American people in time to send a reply to be read at the Centennial Celebration of that eminent scholar and historian whose birth you commemorate. The American people, who have been instructed and edified by Sir Walter Scott's works of history, poetry and fiction, will highly appreciate your cordial expressions of friendship and reciprocate them in all sincerity."—*New York Herald*, Aug. 11, 1871. On Aug. 9, the Earl of Dalkeith had telegraphed to USG. "The proceedings of the national celebration of the centenary of Sir Walter Scott in this city of his birth are on the eve of beginning. Many distinguished Americans have accepted our invitations. We offer congratulations to the American people through their President, General Grant, himself of Scotch descent. May a lasting friendship subsist between them and us. An answer by return to be read at the National Festival is earnestly requested."—*Philadelphia Public Ledger*, Aug. 11, 1871. In an undated cable, probably written in July, Cyrus W. Field, London, wrote to USG. "I was in Edinburgh yesterday and was informed by the Committee of the National Celebration of the centenary of Sir Walter Scott that it was their intention to send you on the 19th instant a telegram in substance as follows: ... I found that the Committee were very anxious to get a reply from you which they could read at the Banquet, which will undoubtedly be on a very magnificent sale. Any answer you may make will be forwarded free."—Copy, DLC-Hamilton Fish. On Aug. 9, J. C. Bancroft Davis, asst. secretary of state, wrote to USG enclosing Field's cable.—Copy, DNA, RG 59, Domestic Letters. On the same day, Field spoke at the banquet in Edinburgh celebrating Sir Walter Scott's centenary.—*The Times* (London), Aug. 10, 1871.

1871, AUG. 10. Maj. Gen. John M. Schofield, San Francisco, to USG. "I beg leave to solicit your most favorable consideration of the application of Mr Selim Woodworth for an appointment to the Naval Academy. He is the eldest son of the late Captain Woodworth who died here last Winter and whose services are well known to the Navy Department. The Young man is a bright promising youth of fourteen years, of good character and well prepared to enter the Academy. He has a taste for sea life and an honorable ambition. I am confident he would do credit to his honorable name in the Naval Service of the country."—Copy, DLC-John M. Schofield. Selim E. Woodworth, who entered U.S. Naval Academy in 1872, graduated in 1879.

1871, Aug. 11.   George W. Gibbons, editor, *Workingmen's Journal*, New York City, to USG, Long Branch. "I wrote to Mr Fish in regards to the appointment of my son Geo W. Gibbons Jr as a commercial agent or consul. I need not remind you of the policy of my paper in regards to your administration, and of the Hopes I Entertain of your reelection   I Expect you will do me this Favor as It is the only one I Have asked, and I Expect you will do it"—ALS, DNA, RG 59, Letters of Application and Recommendation. On the same day, Gibbons wrote to Secretary of State Hamilton Fish. ". . . I Have advocated the policy of this administration and will support it to the Best of ability now and in the Coming Campaign. not However, unless I See my Services appreciated"—ALS, *ibid.* On Dec. 21, 1869 and Jan. 8, 1870, George W. Gibbons, Jr., had written to Fish on the same subject.—ALS, *ibid.*

On June 2, 1875, George W. Gibbons wrote to USG. "There will be a Conference of the Leaders of the Workingmen throughout the United States in Oct next in this city. Your name will be mentioned for renomination, as an necessity for the Public Weal. If you have no objection would like to consult with you before we proceed further in the matter"—ALS, USG 3.

1871, Aug. 15.   Attorney Gen. Amos T. Akerman to USG. "On the 26th of January last, you referred to me the petition of Mrs. Anne R. Elliott, widow and executrix of William Elliott, late of Beaufort, South Carolina. She prays for the restoration of certain lands in South Carolina, the property of her testator, which were seized by the United States forces during the late rebellion, and were afterwards, while in possession of said forces and in the absence of the owner, sold for the payment of the United States land tax, and bought in for the Government. The Government is represented now to hold the lands under the title acquired by this purchase. It is alleged that the deceased Mr. Elliott and his family have always been loyal to the United States. The counsel for Mrs. Elliott urges upon me the consideration that, as the lands in question were in the occupancy of the forces of the United States at the time the tax was imposed, the Government should not have exacted the tax from the absent owner, and, therefore, that the sale for taxes was inequitable. If this be all true, I am not aware of any law which authorizes you to give the desired relief. Nakedly stated, the case, according to his presentation of it, is this: The United States has, according to law, acquired property under circumstances which make the acquisition oppressive and unjust to the late owner. While an act of Congress restoring the property might be a piece of most righteous legislation, the executive cannot restore it, unless authorized by law. No such law existing at present, I regret that you are powerless to aid this lady in the premises. My delay in considering the matter has been at the instance of the counsel for Mrs. Elliott, who wished to submit his views upon it."—Copy, DNA, RG 60, Opinions. See *CG*, 41–2, 3256; *U.S. Statutes at Large*, XVII, 330–32; Willie Lee Rose, *Rehearsal for Reconstruction: The Port Royal Experiment* (Indianapolis and New York, 1964), pp. 118–20, 242, 358–60.

1871, AUG. 18.   Attorney Gen. Amos T. Akerman to USG. "In pursuance of the wishes expressed in Gen. Porter's letters of the 10th and 15th insts, the sum of $5000 has been turned over to Col. Whitely, for use in the detection and prosecution of crimes against the United States, in New York."—Copy, DNA, RG 60, Letters Sent to Executive Officers. On Feb. 7, 1872, Hiram C. Whiteley testified before the Committee on Investigation and Retrenchment probing criminal activity in N. Y. in his capacity as "chief of the secret-service division of the United States Treasury."—*SRC*, 42-2-227, II, 687–736. See also *PUSG*, 18, 228–32; *New York Times*, Jan. 11, 1872, Sept. 9, 1874.

1871, AUG. 29.   USG endorsement. "Respectfully refered to the Sec. of State. If no objection exists to granting the leave requested please [a]uthorize it."—AES, DNA, RG 59, Miscellaneous Letters. Written on a letter of Aug. 26 from U.S. Senator Oliver P. Morton of Ind., Indianapolis, to USG. "Confidential . . . Col Thomas J. Brady Consul at St Thomas is now at home on leave of absence but will return in September. He desires leave to come home again in October to remain several months. He will leave the office in good hands, so that its duties will be well performed, and there will be no detriment to the public service. I am anxious to have the leave granted to him as he is in position to render important political service during the coming winter which he is anxious to do, but does not wish to give up his place. I would not make the application for him if I did not think it important. If the leave is granted he wishes to know it before he returns. I shall be obliged if you will favor me with an answer."—ALS, *ibid.* On Aug. 13, 1870, Morton had written to Fish. "Col Gray has as yet been unable to determine whether he can accept the Consulship to St Thomas, but will in a few days. Should he decline I shall be glad to recommend for the place Col Thomas J. Brady of Muncie of Indiana, a gallant soldier, an editor and well qualified for the position. I shall be glad to have Col Brady get the place if Col Gray declines"—ALS, *ibid.*, Letters of Application and Recommendation. On Dec. 6, USG nominated Thomas J. Brady as consul, St. Thomas, Danish West Indies. See *PUSG*, 10, 222; *ibid.*, 20, 435.

1871, AUG. 30.   John M. Harlan, Louisville, to USG. "I beg leave to commend to your most favorable consideration the bearer hereof, Mr G. W. Griffin, of this city. Mr G. is the author of a book recently published, with the title '*Studies in* Literature,' and is a gentleman of excellent literary attainments. He desires to visit Europe, and would be gratified if he could receive an appointment as Consul, or some like position, to the end that he may maintain himself while pursuing his studies in Europe. For any such position as that indicated Mr Griffin possesses every requisite qualification of mind and character. He is a self-made man and deserves the consideration of the Government. . . ."—ALS, DNA, RG 59, Letters of Application and Recommendation. On Sept. 4, John W. Forney, collector of customs, Philadelphia, wrote to USG. "The bearer, George W. Griffin Esq., of Louisville Ky. author of a capital life of George D. Prentice, late lamented editor of the Louisville Journal, calls upon you with some strong recommendations from your personal friends and I beg to add my own wish that he may be received with your characteristic civilities."—LS, *ibid.* On Nov. 1, Solicitor Gen. Benjamin H. Bristow wrote to Secretary of State Hamilton Fish. "Mr. G. W. Griffin, of Louisville, Ky., whom I had the honor to present to you in person some weeks ago, says to me, in a letter received a few days since, that, if the appointment of consul at Copenhagen has not been made, he would be glad to have it. . . ."—LS, *ibid.* Related papers are *ibid.* On Dec. 6, USG nominated Gilderoy W. Griffin as consul, Copenhagen. On Dec. 9, William B. Belknap, Louisville, wrote to USG. "My attention has recently been called to the appointment of Mr. Griffin, of this city, to the office of consul at Copenhagen. My impression is that his position, during & since the war, does not entitle him to any consideration from your administration. I hope to have the facts in a few days and will communicate them. I do not know that this is a matter of any consequence, but if he managed to obtain letters of our best men under false representations, I will, if this be established, make it known. I would not write now but I see his name is before the Senate"—ALS, *ibid.* On March 31, 1874, USG nominated Henry B. Ryder to replace Griffin, who had resigned.

On Aug. 9, 1875, Michael J. Cramer, U.S. minister, Copenhagen, wrote to Griffin. ". . . With regard to the President's mind having not yet been relieved of your supposed connection with the attacks upon my character during the last Presidential Campaign, let me say with all cando[r] & sincerety that I never for a moment supposed that he knew anything about the sources of those attacks; and even if he did, the strong letter you published in the Washington National Republican in my defense, would most certainly have relieved his mind as to your supposed connection with them. My wife has been in Washington during the last inauguration; & at Long Branch the following Summer, but she never heard the President speak a word about that affair; nor did she mention it to him. . . ."—ALS, *ibid.* On May 31, 1876, USG nominated Griffin as consul, Apia, Friendly and Navigators' Islands.

1871, AUG. 31.   USG endorsement. "The Opinion of the Retiring Board in the case of Paymaster Rodney is concurred in. Let him be retired on furlough pay, for misdemeanors."—Copy, DNA, RG 94, Letters Received, 2189½ 1871. On Aug. 21, Secretary of the Navy George M. Robeson had written to USG. "I have the honor to submit for your decision the record of the proceedings of a 'Retiring Board' in the case of Paymaster, Robert B. Rodney of the Navy. The Board report it as their opinion that 'the peculiar mental temperament' of Paymaster Rodney incapacitates him from active service in the navy of the United States, and that his incapacity does not result from any incident of service. I respectfully recommend that the opinion of the Board be concurred in, and that Paymaster Rodney be retired upon furlough pay."—Copy, *ibid.*, RG 45, Letters Sent to the President. On June 24, a navy retiring board had ruled that ". . . said temperament of Paymr Rodney, according to the evidence laid before the board, developes itself in an entire disregard to the laws, regulations, customs and proprieties of the service, and has been manifested persistently while said Rodney was attached to the North Atlantic fleet, in language and conduct to the subversion of good order and discipline, and proceeds, in the opinion of the board, in part from fanaticism and in part from the groundless belief that he is a victim of persecution."—Copy, *ibid.*, RG 94, Letters Received, 2189½ 1871. Paymaster Robert B. Rodney had been court-martialed for insubordination and detached from his post on May 8, after he allegedly distributed religious pamphlets aboard ship and published a letter in the *New York Sun*. On May 26, Rodney, Washington, D. C., wrote to Robeson. "I went to your house this evening, not on any business of my own, but in behalf of another—my yeoman Saml Ford, now, and for *five months* past, a close prisoner on the monitor 'Terror,' near the tropics—a victim to Roman Catholic persecution, from which the flag of his adopted country has been no protection. For being a teacher in the Protestant church ashore, he was denied shore liberty; and then as soon as the N. Y. 'Sun' of Feb 24 arrived, he was, on presumption, flung into irons. I entreat your attention to my official request dated and handed in today at the Department; and ask the telegram for his transfer north, not only for the reasons given therein, but in the name of common humanity. I am about to leave the city, and must therefore write this."— Copy, *ibid.* Related papers are *ibid.* See *SRC*, 45-2-350; *SD*, 57-2-55.

1871, AUG. 31.   J. Wright, Chicago, to USG. "Having written to Genl Pleasonton two letters requesting the return of the four papers, relative to Secretary Boutwell's adoption of the material part of Mr Galvin's financial plans for selling Treasury gold and buying Bonds with the proceeds since the fourteenth of Septr 1869, he informs me by letter that these papers were, immediately after their receipt by him, forwarded to you only for your perusal as requested by my letter accompanying them. On apprising Mr Galvin of the contents of the General's letter, he instructed me to write to you requesting the return of the papers. I shall, therefore, feel obliged by your ordering them to be returned to me as previously requested by my letter to Genl Pleasonton, which accompanied them."—ALS, OHi. See George S. Boutwell, *Reminiscences of Sixty Years in Public Affairs* (New York, 1902), II, 206; *New York Times*, Jan. 16, 1873.

1871, AUG.   Charles White *et al.*, Hopkinsville, Ky., to USG protesting the removal of Samuel Feland as postmaster, Hopkinsville, "to make room for

Mrs. S. H. Burbridge, the present incumbent—. . ."—DS (49 signatures), DLC-Benjamin H. Bristow. On May 13, 1870, USG had nominated Susan H. Burbridge as postmaster, Hopkinsville; in 1874, USG renominated Burbridge.

1871, SEPT. 1.   W. G. Stewart, Lancaster, S. C., to USG. "I trust that you will recieve with indulgence, the following inkling, penned for the benefit of a great many men, women & children in our Section of Country. The subject is in regard to Notes given for Negroes, during and prior to the late War, Our State Constitution expressly says, such debts are 'Null and Void', the General Government accepted the Constitution as it is expressed. Efforts are being made, to enforce the collection of this class of debts, that has been suspended, so long by the General Government, You being the Executive head of State, Can the strong arm of the Government stand still, and see so many of its Citizens broke up, root & Branch, by this pressure, will the poor private individual have to pay for this kind of, (or what was once) propperty, after it is taken away, from him, by the Government. Do hope, you will bring this matter to the attention of the propper authorities, so as to be beneficial to a large class of good Citizens among us. If I understand, the Supreme Court has not decided finally yet. The U. S. Government, has suspended the collection of these debts for a number of years, can it not do the same for all time to come, and even prevent, the cost of litigation, which will be *exceedingly heavy* to the *parties concerned in the Suits.* In some cases, where a single purchase had been made for $1100 or $1200, prinçiple & interest will amount to, or near to, $3.000, for even one Negro, it was as common in former days to buy, as to sell. It is depriving many citizens of equality before the Law. It is no more for the Seller to lose, than the purchaser, of this former Species of propperty; for the buyer to lose, & then pay another man, the amount of loss; can, this be called equality,— Justice will Answer the echo. Do hope, the right tribunal will take the Subject in charge, for the relief, of the oppressed & unfortunate purchaser, . . . P. S. Since writing the above, have been requested to ask, if ever, or when was, Gen. Canby's order recinded, in regard to the Suspension of Notes given for Negro Claims."—ALS, DNA, RG 60, Letters from the President.

1871, SEPT. 2.   George Stoneman, Wilmington, Calif., to USG. "I beg leave most respectfully to represent that I am today in reciept of Special Orders N 322 War Department Adjt Generals Office Washington August 19th 1871, revoking so much of Special Orders No 317 as places me, by direction of the President, upon the Retired List, with the full rank of Major General; and this revocation, is based upon the ground of 'a misconception of the law' by the Board of Examination. . . . Now it is respectfully submitted, that the Board was called upon simply to ascertain and report to the President for his information, certain *facts,* and upon these facts to base a recommendation, upon which recommendation the law authorizes and enables the President to act— The Order (No 322) goes on to recite, that the law requires, 'in explicit terms, that an officer shall be disabled by "wounds"—not by disease—to enable the

President to retire him on the rank of the command held by him when so wounded'. . . With the view of having this misunderstanding corrected, and to the end that justice may be done to all concerned, this appeal is made to the President of the United States, claiming that, if it shall be found, that Special Orders No 322 are based upon a misunderstanding of the views entertained by the Board, as is evidently the fact, then am I *entitled* to all the rights, privileges, and benefits, arising and resulting therefrom—My case is a peculiar one, and very probably without a precedent, and in justice to myself and to my family, I cannot rest content until I feel satisfied that it is thoroughly understood by the President, and until I have exhausted all proper means, to obtain that which, the findings and recommendations of the Board, and a usually liberal interpretation of the laws of Congress, will warrant me in Expecting. Hoping for a gracious reception of this communication, and asking for a patient and careful consideration of the points indicated therein . . ."— ALS, DNA, RG 94, ACP, 3414 1871. Related papers are *ibid.* On Nov. 11, AG Edward D. Townsend wrote to Maj. Gen. John M. Schofield, San Francisco. "I am directed by the Secretary of War to return the report of Colonel George Stoneman, dated September 31. 1871, and to say that the Secretary having read the report finds in it repeated expressions of criticism—to use the mildest term applicable—upon the acts and policy not only of the War Department but of the President of the United States. The language and tone of the report are deemed so disrespectful and improper that it cannot be received. The Secretary expects that the report will be amended in accordance with the better judgment of Colonel Stoneman and returned with as little delay as practicable—"—Copy, *ibid.*, Letters Sent. On Nov. 18, Townsend wrote to Stoneman. ". . . I am directed to inform you that the President having examined the arguments contained in all the papers relating to the case, adheres to his ~~decision~~ order ~~in regard~~ retiring you with rank of Colonel."—ADf, *ibid.*, ACP, 3414 1871; copy, DLC-John M. Schofield.

1871, SEPT. 4.   Horace Porter, Long Branch, to Secretary of the Navy George M. Robeson. "Please send by express the President's light overcoat left at your house"—Telegram received, DNA, RG 107, Telegrams Collected (Bound). USG had stayed at Robeson's house in Washington, D. C., when attending a cabinet meeting on Sept. 1.—*New York Times*, Sept. 1, 1871.

1871, SEPT. 5.   Secretary of State Hamilton Fish to USG. "Mr Mac Veagh has filed his resignation of the mission to Turkey, to take effect on 16th inst. & intimates a wish that an immediate appointment of a Successor be made. I think however that if no publicity be given to the fact of the resignation being presented, there need be no haste to fill the place before your return, unless you desire to do it immediately. I write to Mr Mac Veagh requesting him to say nothing on the subject, for the present, until your wishes be known. I enclose a letter from Mr Blanton Duncan, referred to me by the order endorsed on the envelope which requests the Secretary to give certain information asked for in the letter, which appears to be a private letter from Mr

Duncan addressed to Genl Dent. Of course, I will comply with the request if the reference was intended to embrace such request—but it would involve the Department in delicate & embarrassing difficulties, & cause much additional labor, if required to give account of its official correspondence, or of its conduct with reference to questions with other Powers, to parties interested, or professing (as does Mr Duncan) to representing those interested, & who apply through informal & unofficial channels. A letter was addressed to Mr Duncan in May last (in answer to one addressed by him to you) informing him, that the Government could not ask compensation in cases such as that presented by him—Supposing that the reference, or at least the request for information, may have been inadvertent & observing the absence of your own mark of reference, I delay compliance with the order, to learn whether it was intended in its full purport—"—ALS (press), DLC-Hamilton Fish. On Sept. 6, Horace Porter, Long Branch, wrote to Fish. "The President directs me to say, in reply to your letter of the 5th inst. that the endorsement was made upon the enclosed letter from Blanton Duncan without his knowledge, and he is of opinion that the request for this information should not be granted"— ALS, DNA, RG 59, Miscellaneous Letters. On March 19, Blanton Duncan, Menton, France, had written to USG. "I desire, that you should know some facts, in order that you may enforce redress for an insult to the Government, more than any indemnification for wanton injury done. My father Hon Garnett Duncan, 71 years of age, an American citizen formerly a member of Congress, & the intimate friend & associate of many of our leading Statesmen of the past 50 years, has resided for some years in France near Bougaval, 15 miles north of Paris. At my solicitation he left his residence in September, leaving the effects under the charge of his gardener, but first fastening the U. S flag to the house to denote that the entire property, real [&] personal was owned by an American citizen. Fully conscious, that, under international law, an invading Army could requisition the premises & make use of them, but under the mistaken impression, that the Prussian officers were *all* gentlemen, who would respect private property, & especially that of an American citizen, his instructions to the Servants *Explicitly commanded, that every facility should be offered, & every politeness shown to the troops,* who demanded the use thereof. How this was appreciated your Excellency can perceive from the narrative below. 'I arrived on the 26th February & found the house very dirty, with straw on every floor for soldiers to sleep on. The furniture was all carried off or broken—They seemed to destroy from mere wickedness. A handsome secretary that cost 80 f. & a rose wood set of drawers they broke up to kindle fires. Marble tops of furniture they smashed—One wardrobe they carried off & they broke the rich plate glass of another into a hundred pieces & otherwise injured it. The 4 beds, mattrasses, bed & table linen, 8 tables, knives & forks—all gone. Not a chair or a knife, or a table or a mattrass left—Clocks gone too & the books. From my telescope they took the lenses, & left only the legs & barrel. *They paid little respect to my flag—still a little, for they went past it 300 or 400 yards in the village, & found one of the villagers* WHOM THEY FORCED, SWORD IN HAND DRAWN, TO CLIMB UP & TAKE IT DOWN, THEN THEY CAREFULLY

WRAPPED IT UP & TOOK IT OFF AS SPOILS OF WAR. [I] do not know what our Government will say to such treatment of our [c]herished emblem—I had the authority of the Mayor to raise it over the gate. The devastation at Villiers le Bel & Gounasse is terrible to look upon. The Germans are the most expert pillagers you can imagine. As a rule they found almost everything that was hidden away or buried. My papers were scattered all over the house. The Prussians still occupy it' The U. S. Government is [r]espected throughout the world, because of its prompt & vigorous action in demanding & enforcing reparation for any insult to its National honor, & proper respect for the rights & privileges of its citizens. The wanton [d]estruction & pillage of private property, belonging to a neutral, is an outrage, utterly unjustifiable, but comparatively unimportant, in consideration of the gross & [gra]tuitous insult committed. The com[m]anding officer, who occupied that position can easily be traced out, for their records will show what troops were there at various periods. These facts can all be established, & your Excellency can determine whether to exact an apology for the offense & punishment of the offender. If the U. S flag in any quarter of the Globe is to be pulled down, by orders of an armed force, without ample satisfaction for the insult, it is neither in accordance with the sentiments of the American [n]ation, nor with the known, Expressed views of your Excellency, [w]hose past vigorous course in pro[c]uring proper respect for our Country in its international relations [c]an leave no doubt of future action"—ALS, *ibid.* On June 2 and 12, Elihu B. Washburne, Paris, wrote to Fish concerning Garnett Duncan's complaint against the Prussian army.—LS, *ibid.*, Diplomatic Despatches, France. Related papers are *ibid.* On Aug. 28, Blanton Duncan, Louisville, wrote to Frederick T. Dent. "I wrote from Europe, about the commencement of March, a letter to the President, calling his attention to the outrage committed by the Prussian troops in taking down & stealing the American flag nailed fast on my fathers' house near Paris, & afterwards stealing all his effects, worth $10.000. And our Representatives at same time were protecting German subjects in France!! Hon J G Benet sent my letter on receipt to the President—My father afterwards established all the facts by copious affidavits & forwarded his demand for indemnity through Mr Washburne to the President, to be urged at Berlin—Will you do me the favor, if it is not too much trouble, to say what disposition was made of my letter & whether Mr Fish has done anything with the demand? My father, whom I left in Europe 3rd August requested me to obtain this information & send it to him."—ALS, *ibid.*, Miscellaneous Letters.

On April 27, Edward F. Beale, San Francisco, had written to U.S. Senator Simon Cameron of Pa. "I saw with great regret the slip I send from a Newspaper in relation to the Mission to Constantinople. Gen Grant certainly did not say [he w]ould give me the appointment, but he [said] there was no one he would personally prefer, and while he would not commit himself by a positive promise concerning an event so far in advance, he assured me that I would be Every way most a[g]reeab[le] to him as McVeaghs successor. I hope you will be good enough to see him on the subject, and ask also the cooperation of my other friends of the Senate if, as I suspect, the slip I send you is [no]t merely newspaper nonsense. I have made considerable haste with my business here because I felt sure after my interview with Gen. Grant, and your assistance and exact knowledge of the time of McVeaghs return, I might reasonably expect the appointment, and I wish you would be candid with me as to your views of the matter. . . ."— ALS, DLC-Simon Cameron. On May 29, George H. Boker, Philadelphia, wrote to Fish. "Please to convey to the President, and accept for yourself, my thanks for the confidence which you have shown in me by tendering to me the position of arbitrator in the boundry question between Great Britain and Liberia. . . ."—ALS, DNA, RG 59, Miscellaneous Letters. On Nov. 3, Fish recorded in his diary that USG had named Boker as minister to Turkey to replace Wayne MacVeagh.—DLC-Hamilton Fish. On Jan. 2, 1872, Porter wrote to Charles R. Ide, Philadelphia. "The Presidents me to say that he owes you an apology for not answering your kind note enclosing an invitation to be present at the reception tendered to the Hon: Geo: H. Boker by the Union League of Philadelphia. Your note was mislaid and not found till to day and though he bore the matter in mind mind he could not recollect the day of the reception. It would have been impossible however for him to have left the capital at that time."—Copy, DLC-USG, II, 1. See *PUSG*, 19, 254–55, 437; *ibid.*, 20, 282–83.

1871, SEPT. 5. Elias W. Fox, surveyor and act. collector of customs, St. Louis, to USG. "In the latter part of the month of July last an Inspector of Customs belonging to the District and port of Detroit mich was successful in tracing two small lots of merchandise which had been smuggled into the states (from Canada) to this city, and seized the articles (a coat in one case, and 1000-cigars in the other) as well as accomplished the arrest of the consignees. It became my duty as the Chief officer of the Customs to report the cases to the District Attorney, who in the vacation of court had the defendants bound over to answer before the Grand Jury in November next. The names of the parties are as follows. *A. G. Richardson*—Clerk Violation of Act July 18 /66—incurs the penalty named in Section 4. Received a frock coat value $25. *J. L. Sanderson*—Stage Proprietor Violation same law. Received a lot of 1000 Cigars. The penalty prescribed for these offenses being *alternative*, (fine or imprisonment) I was precluded from compromising them or accepting any satisfaction of them and as before stated was compelled to give them to the Dist' Atty for action. I am however well satisfied that the ends of justice will be fully served if I am authorized to accept payment of a fine and have the cases dismissed—the parties are very respectable citizens (in name and reputation at least) and did not I am sure realize the enormity of their error in these instances—they confess the wrong and beg me to intercede with you in their behalf to order a suspension of proceedings. I therefore respectfully ask that you cause the necessary order to issue directing me to receive from Mr A. G. Richardson—a fine of $50—and from Mr. J. L. Sanderson a fine of $100—both to pay all costs

incurred and on payment of said fines and costs proceedings against them
to be quashed."—LS, DNA, RG 60, Letters Received, Mo. On Oct. 5, J. L.
Sanderson, St. Louis, wrote to USG. "in the Month of august Last there
Was Sent Me from Vermont A box of Cigars which came from Canada and
No Duties having been paid upon them—I was Arrested at the time of the
Dilevey of the Cigars. It Was but a Single box Sent to Me for My own
use—and the Question of Duties Never once Entered My Mind until My
arrest—I am A Member of the firm of Barlow Sanderson & *Co* for Many
years past and am Now Engaged as Mail Contracting and staging on the—
plains & I Never purchased goods of any kind With a View to Sell and
Make a profit uppon them—and Not being acqu[i]nted With Matters of
that Sort—I never thought of the Duties until So reminded by the officer
. . ."—LS, *ibid.* Charles W. Ford endorsed this letter. "I take the liberty to
say—that I know Mr Sanderson very well. Have had busines transactions
with him for fifteen years past. He has always sustained a character beyond
[reproach.] He became involved in this matter though shere thoughtlessness—It was, no doubt, as he stated, that he never thought of it. Mr
Sanderson is a man of property—which he has made himself—with a character & reputation, I belive, unblemished. He feels Keenly the disgrace that
naturally attaches to an indictment In view of the facts in the case & the
absence of any wilful intent to violate the law, it seems to me your Excellency would be justifiable in making such order in the case, as would save
Mr Sanderson and his family frm the mortification of an indictment, which
I pray will be done."—AES (undated), *ibid.* On Oct. 26, Horace Porter endorsed this letter. *"Respectfully referred to* the Honorable the Attorney General, who will cause this suit to be discontinued."—ES, *ibid.* Related papers
are *ibid.*

1871, SEPT. 6. Secretary of War William W. Belknap to USG. *"Personal . . .*
I have the honor to forward to you a copy of a letter just received from
Hon: Benj: F Butler, requesting copy of your letter to the President asking
his relief from the command of the Army of the James, and, in connection therewith, copies of a letter addressed by you to the Secretary of War and of a
telegram to the President on the subject of General Butler's removal, which
have been carefully copied from your own letter book in this Department;
No *letter* to the President on this subject has been found, and it is believed
the telegram and letter to the Secretary of War are referred to. General
Butler has been advised of this reference for your decision whether the
copies shall be furnished."—Copy, DNA, RG 107, Letters Sent. See *PUSG*,
13, 223.

1871, SEPT. 6. Brig. Gen. Oliver O. Howard to USG. "A young man has
presented himself here to join our Preparatory Department, by the name of
Wm M. Lynch. He is I understand the son of a gentleman who was once
your teacher in Georgetown, Ohio, Mr Isaac Lynch. The young man is
between 16 and seventeen years of age, bright and active and eager for an
education. Now if I can secure a scholarship for him at the rate of $130 a

year this will be all his expenses at the institution, covering board. I think his father could easily pay the rest. Now could you not, Considering the circumstances aid me with some wealthy friend to procure a scholarship for this worthy lad? I have advised him to write you a letter himself that you may judge of him better than by my representations. If you can do this without discommoding yourself I shall be most deeply thankful."—Copies (2), Howard Papers, MeB.

1871, SEPT. 8. Horace Porter, Long Branch, to Secretary of War William W. Belknap. "The President directs me to say that a Mr. Stevens, of Hoboken is about to make some experiments in testing the strength of boilers, and represents that the only convenient and safe place in the vicinity of New York is Sandy Hook. He requests that if the Engineer in charge should report favorably upon the application that you will approve it."—ALS, DNA, RG 77, Fortifications, Letters Received. On Sept. 18, Francis B. Stevens, Hoboken, wrote to Belknap. "I applied to the President, some ten days ago for permission, to try some experiments, on exploding steamboat boilers, at Sandy Hook. Genl Grant said that the matter would have to be referred to you, and that he would write to you. As I cannot make these experiments after the cold weather sets in, I would respectfully request your decision at your earliest convenience"—LS, *ibid.* On the next day, Belknap wrote to Stevens authorizing the experiments.—Copies, *ibid.; ibid.,* RG 107, Letters Sent.

1871, SEPT. [8]. U.S. Senator Cornelius Cole of Calif., San Francisco, to USG. "California is fully righted up and is in line for next year, with all sails set."—*Washington Evening Star,* Sept. 8, 1871. On the same day, William G. Morris, U.S. marshal, San Francisco, telegraphed to USG. "We have elected our Governor and whole State ticket. Two congressmen sure; and probably the third. Present advices also indicate we shall have the Legislature by a decided majority."—*Ibid.*

On Sept. 13, Governor Edward M. McCook and U.S. Delegate Jerome B. Chaffee of Colorado Territory telegraphed to USG. "Colorado has gone republican by an increased majority. The legislature is almost unanimously republican."—*Ibid.,* Sept. 13, 1871.

1871, SEPT. 8. Morris Pinshaw, Virginia City, Nev., to "United States Grant." "I write to inform you I will be in Washington during the session of Congress and desire your decission in regard to my title to the Water Privellage of Lake Bigler granted me by the state of Nevada   One Von Smith of Sanfrancisco and Wm Sherron of the California Bank are trying to swindle me out of my title guaranteed me by the state of Nevada. If your honor will consult with Genl Foster Genl Wright and Maj King the Sutro Tunnell Commissioners, they will give you information in regard to the steam Swindlers   My Dear Gel if you will be so kind as to let me know by return mail if you will sustain the title guaranteed me by the state of Nevada should the subject be brought before Congress by the Sam steam swindlers

I will be ever grateful . . ."—ALS, DNA, RG 48, Lands and Railroads Div., Letters Received. For William Sharon's role in water rights and mining the Comstock Lode, see *HRC*, 42-2-94.

On Nov. 24, Orville E. Babcock wrote to Brig. Gen. Andrew A. Humphreys. "The President directs me to inquire whether you have received the report of the Commissioners ordered to 'examine and report upon the Sutro tunnel in the State of Nevada.' If you have not, he directs that you procure it if possible in time to be transmitted with his annual message upon the assembling of Congress."—LS, DNA, RG 77, Letters Received. See *SED*, 42-2-15; *PUSG*, 19, 549.

1871, SEPT. 11. Christopher C. Andrews, U.S. minister, Stockholm, to USG. "There being in my Congressional district in Minnesota from 5000 to 8000 Indians whose condition I have heretofore made a subject of some study, I feel that I may ask your indulgence while I submit a few observations on Indian matters. Acknowledging the reforms that have already been instituted during your administration I think still further improvements can and ought to be made. And it is because of the attention you have paid to this branch of the public service that I am led to hope for further improvements therein. I have received information from time to time as to the Indians in Minnesota and it is to the effect that their condition is not materially improving. They now and for years have received from the United States under treaties about $140,000 annually in goods and money, which is exclusive of course of large appropriations that have been made on their account at the conclusion of new treaties. They are thus living upon and exhausting their capital. These payments will expire in a few ye[a]rs, and as their reservations are comparatively small it will not be a great many years before, under the present system, their supplies from the government will terminate. I visited these Indians (merely as a traveller) first in 1856. Through the *personal exertions* of the then Commissioner of Indian Affairs—Mr. Manypenny, and one of the most zealous ones we have ever had—the principal Chief Hole-in-the-day was cultivating a farm. I had the pleasure to find him at work in his corn field, though he was still wearing broad cloth breeches. The good Commissioner, Congress and the Government having failed to *establish* any *system* whereby the efforts of such indians would continue to be encouraged and directed the consequence was this indian fell back into his old ways and finally degenerated, I almost might say, into a vagabond. I mention the fact to illustrate that we ought to have an Indian system established by law and regulations, which will not be dependent mainly on the philanthropic personal interest of the President and his immediate subordinates; and so that the good done by one administration shall not be undone by a succeeding one. As to some improvements looking to the establishment of a system that will render the Indians self supporting and that will promote their civilization I would state. I. The Indian Office has never procured through its subordinates such full and particular information concerning the Indians as to enable Congress properly to judge of their needs. Reports of Superinten-

dents and agents have commonly consisted of general statements, conclusions, and observations instead of facts. In years past at any rate, agents and
superintendents who have been engaged in embezzling annually say $25.000
out of the Government and the Indians, have in their reports palmed off on
the Indian bureau an old sterreotyped disquisition on Indian Civilization,
instead of being rigidly required to report facts; while no little that has been
reported as facts has been absolutely false. (I need not tell you of course,
that such dishonest officials have generally had at least one or two members
of Congress to back them)   The Indian Office ought to collect annually full
and exact information as to how many Indians till the soil and to what
extent, what number engage in other and what industries and to what extent, their habits of living, statistics of thier sanitary condition, their education what number if any are saving of their earnings what number intemperate what offences they commit, their desire and fitness for civil and political
rights, the obstacles that immediately stand in the way of their engaging in
industrial pursuits, and all such facts as will enable Congress to judge of
the real state or progress of their civilization. Until Congress acquire more
information than the published reports of the Indian Office afford (I have
not seen those from the past two years) it is difficult to see how they can
legislate intelligently on the subject. II. It should be the policy of the law
to *take away* from superintendents or agents the *temptations* to peculation.—
One step though comparatively trifling in this direction would be to immediately abolish the allowance for travelling expenses of agents. This provision
heretofore has led agents to find an excuse for almost constantly travelling
about instead of remaining at their post of duty. III. It is important that
Indian Agents be first class business men,—men of organizing and administrative ability. And to obtain such it would seem that their compensation
should exceed $1,800 a year the amount beside quarters and allowance for
a clerk now generally paid. IV. That ther[e] should be a corps of *Inspectors*
in the Indian service, composed of the very best men for the position without
regard to politics, who should frequently visit the different tribes and report
as to the fidelity and capacity of those employed in the Indian service and
upon matters relating to the improvement of the condition of the Indians.
Inspectors were of great advantage, so far as my observation extended in
our late war. We now have them in the army to see that the regulations are
adhered to. If it is necessary where we have two commissioned officers to
one hundred men how much more necessary there should be inspectors to
overlook Indian agents who have under their charge on an average about
five thousand indians a number of employees, and considerable public money
to disburse.   V. The question how to cause all the Indian *children to be instructed*, at least in reading and writing English, is worthy of much study.
In 1854 I visited 'Friends Mission' west of the Missouri River where a
number of Indian boys and girls were gratuitously fed and clothed at the
mission as an inducement for their parents to send them to be instructed.
The plan operated only tolerably well. It seems to me ~~there should be~~ authority should go hand in hand with bounty and kindness. Where possible

I would have compulsory education enforced; and would submit that there should be some legislation providing for compulsory instruction. Suppose it be indirectly compulsory, as for example, that families who neglected to send their children to school, where a school was provided, should receive no share of the goods and money annually distributed by the United States. VI. The following appear to be some of the obstacles that have heretofore prevented the Indians from adopting industrial or civilized habits: 1. Petty wars between different trib[es] which have kept them living together in camps and always armed, for protection. 2. The practice of having everything in common so that what one produced others expected to share and consume. 3. The dishonesty and incapacity of agents and other white men employed over them which has lessened their influence when they have attempted to get the indians to work 4. Frequent changes of their 'permanent' reservations. 5. The meagre returns for their agricultural efforts under all the circumstances have promised little more than the products of hunting and fishing. 6. Dependence on what is paid them by the Government, under their treaties 7. The selling of spirituous liquors to them. 8. Love of adventure and of a wandering life, a fascination for martial exploits, a superstitious prejudice against manual labor, the result of excessive ignorance and vanity. VII. It is doubtless too much to expect that any symmetrical and sufficient plan whereby the Indians can be converted into property holders, producers, tax payers and law abiding citizens can be at once devised or that any one plan or system will be adapted to every tribe. I should rather expect we could better *grow into a system by practi*[*ce*] so to speak than immediately establish one in theory. My ideas would be, having first secured competent men for agents, with inspectors to follow them up to require each agent to set in motion such reasonable proceedings as he deemed advisable to get as many a[s] possible of his tribe actually engaged in industrial pursuits. I would require him to report fully and in detail as often as quarterly, on the results and progress. In this way it could be ascertained what measures are and what are not practicable and from time to time such general enactments and regulations could be adopted as would gradually form a complete system. VIII. Meantime I would recommend as further immediate measures in respect to annuity or treaty indians, that a homesteads, say of eighty acres, each be surveyed off and a patents therefor issued to heads of families, with condition that the land should be inailenable and exempt from attachment and execution. That the selling of spirituous liquor to the Indians be made punishable by imprisonment in the peniteneary. That provision be made for giving premiums for the first and second best farms cultivated by each tribe, on condition that the crops should exceed a certain fixed value. Again asking your indulgence for occupying your attention on a subject which may seem out of my province and assuring you of my hearty sympathy in your efforts thus far to ameliorate the condition of the Indians . . ."—ALS (press), Andrews Papers, Minnesota Historical Society, St. Paul, Minn.

1871, SEPT. 12.   L. Bethune, Montrose, N. C., to USG. "The object of addressing you at this time is to call your attention to the injustice done to the citizens of cumberland co[u]nty no ca[rolina.] The injustice took place as follows. The year after the unfortunate civil War ceased, which had the effect to lower the the morar standard of a vast number of our fellow citizens all over our country, as your honor cannot help observing. The federal government sent down revenue officers to collect a direct tax from the people of cumberlaland. Those officers advertized that if the people did not promptly atten and pay the tax their land houses & lots would be sold to raise the tax   now the people of cumberland had suffered more than the surrounding counties from the fact that the army was southward from 40 to 50 miles wide until it approach cumberland   it was then closed up, and all the army thus pass[ed] through cumberland. You may guess therefrom that [the ci]tizens were in poor fix to meet the tax—Take my case as an example,   Kilpatricks corps left me nothing in the house or on the farm worth picking up, which obliged me to make a larg debt on credit to prevent the family, which consisted all most entirely of colored women and children from perishing. I had not a dollar to pay the tax, nor had my neighbors money to lend me. I was therefore compelled to go to the Brokers and submit to a usurious interest to get money to pay that tax—and to this day the people of the surrounding counties have not been call'd on to pay that tax—Now Sir the government should treat its citizens with unpartial justice, not make fish of some and flesh of others—If the government has relinquis[hed] the idea of collecting that tax from all the Southern people alike it shold return the money to the citizens of cumberland which they were copell'd to pay when they were they were in a poor situation to have done so—I had part and but part of the loss and damage which Kilpatricks corps inflicted on m[e] in the two days and one half was around me, and if your honor would add a word to the board in my favor, you will place an old man, now 86 years old under many obligations to you. as to my loyalty, I may be pardoned for saying that it would not suffer materially by being compared with the loyalty of any citizen in the country I was so decidedly oposed to Secession that had I been in the meridian of life I would have sold my farm even at a sacrifice and have moved beyond the limits of the Seceedd States—But I was too old & frail to do that. When the army left me I was forced to mak[e] a large debt on credit which I have not been able as yet able to liquidate, and I am exceeding anxous to get able to pay all my just debts before I am call'd hence—. . . P. S. Excuse my writing my sight is dim and my hand trembly—as above"—ALS, DNA, RG 56, Letters Received.

1871, SEPT. 13.   Henry W. Oliver, Jr., Pittsburgh, to USG. "Capt Geo S Gallup, 1st Infantry, USA, an old resident of this City, has been Sentenced by Court Martial, to loss of rank and pay, and confinement to ~~of~~the limits of camp for one year. Hot blood and thoughtlessness—during a dispute about alleged persecution of Capt Gallup by the Officers making the charges—appear to have caused the trouble. Capt Gallup enlisted early in 61, Served well and faithfully thro the War, he has a family depending on him for Support,   His friends here are a legion, all who know him respect and honor him. I think you will find on examamination of the papers relating to the Case, that the punishment is too Severe, and if you can, and will Set aside the finding of the Court, you will please and delight your friends here. I request your action in this matter; not only as a citizen and friend of yours, but particularly as Chairman; and on behalf of the Republican Co Ex Com, of which, years ago, before the War, in the early and weak days of our Party, Capt Gallup was a hard-working reliable member."—ALS, DNA, RG 94, ACP, G451 CB 1866. Found guilty of conduct unbecoming an officer for drinking with enlisted men and quarreling with another officer, Capt. George S. Gallupe, 1st Inf., had been sentenced on Aug. 14.—*Ibid.*, Letters Received, 2415 1871. Related papers are *ibid.*

1871, SEPT. 16. To Secretary of War William W. Belknap. "Please order the discharge of Geo. L. Taylor, Co. C. 3rd U. S. Cavalry, now in Arazona. Taylor had two brothers killed in the war and his mother is now low and will scarsely live to see him."— *The Collector,* No. 767 (1958), m257.

1871, SEPT. 16. To Secretary of War William W. Belknap. "You may extend the leave of absence of Lt. Jno. McA. Webster, 22d U. S. Inf.y. Sixty days to enable him to finish the settlement of his ~~father's~~ mother's estate."—ALS, DNA, RG 94, ACP, 1173 1875. 2nd Lt. John M. Webster, USMA 1871, was the son of Col. George Webster, killed at Perryville, Ky., on Oct. 8, 1862.

1871, SEPT. 18. John H. Tighe to USG. "I have the honor to submit my application for an appointment in the Pay or Subsistence Departments of the United States Army. I trust a brief narrative of my services in connection with the Quartermasters Department during the late war will not be deemed ~~of~~ out of place, . . ."—ALS, DNA, RG 94, Applications for Positions in the War Dept. No appointment followed.

On Jan. 23, 1863, Lt. Col. Charles A. Reynolds, Memphis, had written to Brig. Gen. Montgomery C. Meigs. "I beg to recommend to you Capt— John H. Tighe Asst Qr Master, Volunteers for appointment or transfer (if possible) to the Qr. Master Dpt. of the Regular Sevice. Capt. Tighe has been associated on duty with me in the Dpt. of the Tennessee, for several months, and I take great pleasure in bearing unqualified testimony to the zeal energy and honesty with which he has discharged the manifold and arduous duties committed to his charge."—ALS, *ibid.*, ACP, T688 CB 1865. On the same day, USG endorsed this letter. "I heartily endorse the within recommendation. Capt. Tighe is one of our most active and efficient Quartermasters, and already has experienc[e] to make his services valuable."—AES, *ibid.* Related papers are *ibid.* See *PUSG,* 6, 260–61.

1871, SEPT. 22. Elihu B. Washburne, Paris, to USG. "I do not suppose there is now, or is likely to be any complaint in regard to Judge Barron, the 5th Auditor, for I am assured that he discharges his duties with great ability and unimpeached integrity. As a faith public officer, an honest man and a staunch republican I should be very sorry to see him disturbed."—ALS (press), DLC-Elihu B. Washburne. In *1869*, U.S. Senators Timothy O. Howe and Matthew H. Carpenter of Wis. *et al.* had written to USG. "The undersigned beg to request the appointment of Hon: Henry D. Barrown of Wisconsin as Chief Justice of the Territory of Dakota, to fill the vacancy in that office. Judge Barrown is a distinguished citizen of Wisconsin, and will fill the place with ability and honor."—LS (6 signatures, undated), DNA, RG 60, Records Relating to Appointments. On April 15, 1869, USG nominated Henry D. Barron as 5th auditor, Treasury Dept. On Dec. 14, 1871, USG nominated Jacob H. Ela to replace Barron, who had resigned.

1871, SEPT. 23.   T. H. Hatch & Co., U.S. Representative Aaron A. Sargent of Calif., and fifteen others, San Francisco, to USG *et al.* recommending James F. Stuart.—Copy, DNA, RG 48, Lands and Railroads Div., Letters Received. On June 10, 1876, James F. Stuart, San Francisco, wrote to Secretary of the Interior Zachariah Chandler. "... In 1871 & 1872 I spent 8 months at Washington contesting fraudulent surveys of Mexican Grant claims before the Commissioner and Secretary. Before I left here for Washington, one of the judges of the Supreme Court knowing what business I was going to Washington on proposed to draw up a letter to the President and Secretary reccommending me and soliciting their aid in forwarding my business—That letter I presented to the President who indorsed it over to the Secretary, and I delivered it to the Secretary ..."—ALS, *ibid.*

1871, SEPT. 25.   U.S. Senator Alexander Ramsey of Minn., St. Paul, to USG. "I desire to address you in behalf of Lieut. Douglass Pope 13th. Infantry at Camp Douglass Utah, recently tried by Court Martial for drunkeness and disgraceful conduct while in that condition;... Lieut Pope was on staff duty at Dept. Hd. quarters in this city for nearly two years, during all of which time the officers associated with him testify that he did not indulge in liquor at all and that his conduct as an officer & a gentleman was creditable to himself and the service   Lt. Pope served thrgh the war of the rebellion & thrgh the Indian war on this frontier creditably. But were he alone involved in the consequencs of his youthful folly, I would not thus appeal to you Mr President, annoyed as you are with your multitudinous cares—but Lieut Pope married about three years since into one of the oldest and most respectable families of Minnesota—he married the oldest daughter of Gnl. H. H. Sibly the Commder of the expedition against the Sioux Indians in 1862 & 1863 & formrly Governor of this State—Genl. Sibly has the Sincerst Sympathies of all our people, without distinction of politics or nationality & for his sake & for the sake of his my connections here I beg you Mr President to modify the sentence of the court, should it be of the extreme character, ..."—ALS, DNA, RG 94, ACP, 4347 1871. On Oct. 24, Henry H. Sibley, St. Paul, wrote to Orville E. Babcock. "*Personal & private* ... I learn that Lieut Pope has forwarded his resignation through the military channels, but if his sentence can be remitted by the President, or mitigated without a publication in general orders of the specifications, but simply of the charges, as has been frequently done in similar cases, I, and his other friends, would

much prefer that he should remain in the service.... I take the liberty to
enclose herewith Mr. Campbell's letter to me, also Senator Ramsey's strong
appeal to the President for clemency to the delinquent. I know you will do
what you can consistently, to aid me in my trouble, for the sake of my friend,
your father in law, with whom my relations for more than twenty five years,
have been of a friendly, and indeed intimate character...."—ALS, *ibid.* On
Sept. 28, Brig. Gen. John Pope, Fort Leavenworth, Kan., had telegraphed to
AG Edward D. Townsend concerning his nephew, 1st Lt. Douglass Pope.
"Please withhold the proceedings in the Case of Lieut D Popp, thirteenth
Infantry until his resignation forwarded on the twenty fourth reaches Washington   I have asked the president by letter to accept and not promulgate
the Sentence"—Telegram received (at 4:07 P.M.), *ibid.* On Oct. 10, Secretary
of War William W. Belknap wrote to Townsend. "The President directs that
the resignation of 2d. Lt. Douglas Pope be accepted"—AE (initialed), *ibid.*
See *PUSG*, 15, 505.

1871, SEPT. 26.   Maj. Cyrus B. Comstock, Detroit, to USG. "Some time
since I wrote mentioning Maj. J. B. Wheeler, Engineers as a candidate,
should Prof Mahan's place become vacant. I enclose an extract of a letter
from Prof. Church, showing his estimate of Maj. Wheeler. I think the appointment should be made from the Majors of Engineers—Craighill would
be a good appointment; Abbot I am told would not accept it:"—ALS, DNA,
RG 94, Correspondence, USMA. On Sept. 27, U.S. Senator Matthew H.
Carpenter of Wis., Milwaukee, wrote to USG. "I have heard that Prof. Mahan of Military Academy is dead. Of course the vacancy in that professorship
will soon be filled. I take the liberty to recommend Col J B. Wheeler of the
Engr Corps for the place,   I know him well, and believe no better selection
could be made."—ALS, *ibid.* On Dec. 4, USG nominated Maj. Junius B.
Wheeler as professor of civil and military engineering, USMA, to replace
Dennis Hart Mahan. For Mahan's suicide, see *New York Times*, Sept. 17,
1871.

1871, SEPT. 27.   To William B. Allison, Dubuque, from De Kalb, Ill. "Arrangements have been made to send my party by Dixon. Much obliged for
the tender of train from Cedar Rapids."—ALS (telegram sent), Carol S.
Skaggs, St. Petersburg, Fla. On Sept. 25, Brig. Gen. John Pope, Leavenworth,
Kan., had telegraphed to USG. "Is it your intention to accompany excursion
train over Chicago & S Western Road tomorrow for Leavenworth"—Copy,
DNA, RG 393, Dept. of the Mo., Telegrams Sent. On Sept. 26, USG joined
a party marking the opening of the Chicago and Southwestern Railroad,
from Chicago to Leavenworth.—*Missouri Democrat*, Sept. 27, 1871.

1871, SEPT. 27.   Governor John M. Palmer of Ill. to USG. "At the request
of Mrs Mary White I have listened to her accounts of the wrongs she has
suffered and have also read her petition to you   I do not know that her

statemts are correct, but it does seem to me that they merit investigation"—
ALS, DNA, RG 60, Letters from the President. On Sept. 26, Mary White, St.
Louis, had written to USG. "Your petitioner Mary White would respectfully
represent to your excellency that heretofore during the year 1864 and for
two years subsequent thereto she was a resident of Daviess County in the
State of Missouri That while a resident there and since that period she has
been denied the priviledges of a citizen and the protection of the civil laws:
That from the treatment received from the people and administrators of the
laws in Daviess County Mo. she has suffered greatly in body and mind; and
now appeals to you as the custodian of the rights of the people, and the
friend of the humble and poor to examine, or cause to be examined into,
and investigated, the matters and things hereinafter set forth. Your petitioner says that in Augusst AD 1861 her husband enlisted in the State
Militia of the State of Missouri as a volunteer cavalryman of said state
militia under Col. McFerrin and continued in said Service until he was taken
sick in the month of December AD 1863 when he was discharged on account
of illness, and returned home and died Oct 7th 1864. That shortly after the
death of my husband I became blind by reason of neuralgia induced by my
trouble & the extra exertion I had to make for a livelihood   After becoming
blind I was taken to St Joseph Mo. and placed under the care of Dr. Octtas
and while absent my children (all being small) were left at home by them-
seleves. During my absence the house in which my children were left was
burned and with the burning of my house I lost all there was in it except
the clothes the children had on and a few bed clothes. My house was burned
January 16 /65. Shortly after my house was burned I returned home still
blind and unable to provide for my family—A neighbor repaired a Smoke
house that was still standing on my farm and we moved into that. I had to
beg for the provisions we used and carry them from the neighbors in our
wagon.—Shortly after we moved into the Smoke house our harness was
stolen and we were reduced to the lowest extremity of poverty and hunger
I remained blind until June 1865 when I went to St Louis to be placed
under the care of a physician and remained there until March 1866. In order
to prohibit me from getting relief from the City of St Louis the Rebels of
Daviess County wrote to St Louis that I owned 400 acres of land and was
able to care for myself And the aid sent me by the Union Aid Society was
stolen from the Post Office In March 1866 I returned home and commenced putting out my spring crop when a disloyal or (Klu Klux) mob came
and destroyed all that was left on my farm and drove me away. After the
mob went away I returned and commenced rebuilding when they again
returned and again destroyed what I had done hung my little boy and bound
me and carried me Eighty miles from home without a warrant of arrest or
cause for such proceedings   I then had the mob arrested and tried—at the
trial they were permitted one to testify for the other and they swore I had
stolen a horse and upon this false charge I was imprisoned where I remained
four days without trial. While I was imprisoned they sent their agents to
me and said if I would sell them my farm they would let me go free. On

my refusal to do so they took me out of jail without an examination and gave a pretended bail bond for my further appearance When my case againt the mob came on for trial they then swore I was not a resident of the State of Missouri and could not prosecute a case in their courts without first giving bond for the costs and finally upon some fraudulent pleas or by some ledger-demain I was non-suited Again I presented my petition for a hearing and an examination was again refused, and the same the fourth effort I made, with the further remark on the part of the Judge that my case was not fit to come before the Court. For these reasons I was unable to get a hearing at any of the Courts in the State. I then sent a petition to Governor Fletcher but never received any answer or communication from him I subsequently got up a petition signed by the surrounding citizens who were acquanted with the facts and presented it to Governor Brown—(under the direction of Gov. Merrill of Iowa) but Gov. Brown said upon examination that he would not investigate the matter. I then made a personal appeal to the Judge of the District Court of United States at Jefferson City Mo. but Judge Gregal [*Krekel*] refused to grant me a hearing. And now having exhausedted all my means of redress within the State of Missouri And having my property forcibly taken from me and the possession of it refused to me, and driven a begar from my own home—And refused admittances to the Courts because they are a part and parcel of the same 'Klu Klux Klan' that robbed, burned and plundered me, And instead of doing justice, are sworn to defend each other in their murder Arson and robbery I appeal to you to have the matter investigated and if the facts as I have herein stated be found to be true that I have my property restored to me and these villians who plunder a soldiers widow—and hunt her to the death for the single reason that she is loyal to her country and her God be properly punished for their crimes. And that the fact may be vindicated that in this land of ours all citizens are entitled to protection in life and property and that it is no crime to be loyal to the Government for which I have sacrificed the support of my life."—DS, *ibid.* On March 28, 1872, Governor Cyrus C. Carpenter of Iowa wrote to USG. "From the Statement made to me by Mrs Mary White in reference to her troubles I am of opinion that the matters of which she complains demand at least an impartial investigation—"—ALS, *ibid.* On Aug. 8, White, Des Moines, wrote to USG requesting an investigation.—ALS, *ibid.* Related papers are *ibid.* On Aug. 24, Secretary of War William W. Belknap wrote to White. "Your letter of the 6th ultimo to the President, asking for redress of injuries sustained at the hands of traitors during the late war, a full statement of which it is alleged was previously forwarded, having been referred to this Department, I beg to inform you, after a thorough search, that no record of such claim can be found."—Copy, *ibid.*, RG 107, Letters Sent.

1871, SEPT. 28. U.S. Senator Cornelius Cole of Calif., San Francisco, to USG "& the Secty of the Navy." "*R, C, Spaulding* must not be detached from service as paymaster at san Francisco, reasons for it by letter,"—Telegram received, DNA, RG 45, ZB, Rufus C. Spalding. On Sept. 29, Cole wrote "To the President *or* Secretary of the Navy." "Refering to my despatch of yesterday I have to say that Pay Inspector, R. C. Spalding was assigned to duty as US Naval Paymaster at this place about July last, and by the rules of the service, I understand, is entitled to 'shore duty' for three years—He has maried a San Francisco lady of high social standing and has come to be regarded as a citizen of our State & City. By his promptness, courtesy & fair dealing since he entered upon the duties of the position he has made many friends among our best business men, and by a prudent disposition of the patronage of his office has strengthened the good feeling entertained towards the Administration in this community. . . ."—ALS, *ibid.* On June 12, 1876, Rufus P. Spalding, Cleveland, wrote to USG. "I have a nephew in the Navy who has for many years acted as Pay Master. He has always been regarded as an honest man. Within the last year he has been subjected to a trial by court martial in consequence of the dishonest practices of a disbursing clerk who has fled from the United States. The Naval Court Martial has recently closed its investigation, at San Francisco, and the finding has been transmitted to the Hon. the Secretary of the Navy. I wish to say to you, Sir, that if the officer alluded to (Pay Inspector R. C. Spalding) has been guilty of any fraud or embezzlement, or any other intentional dereliction of duty I have no desire to shield him from punishment: but if he has only yielded to outside influence and kept an improper person in his office as clerk by whom he (as well as the public) has been deceived I hope and trust he may be regarded as a proper object of executive clemency. As I have not the honor of a personal acquaintance with the Secretary of the Navy, I take the liberty to address you, Sir, directly, and to ask at your hands a favor which any chief magistrate may, with propriety accord to the humblest citizen."—ALS, *ibid.*, Letters Received from the President. On Aug. 14, Daniel Ammen, act. secretary of the navy, wrote to USG. "I have the honor to submit for your decision the Record of proceedings of a General Court Martia[l] in the case of Pay Inspector Rufus C. Spalding U. S. Navy who has been found guilty of the charges preferred against him, and sentenced to be dismisse[d] from the Naval service of the United States. I respectfully recommend approval of the sentenc[e.]"—Copy, *ibid.*, Letters Sent to the President. Rufus C. Spalding, pay inspector, U.S. Navy, was dismissed from the service on Aug. 18.

1871, Sept. 28.   S. C. Montjoy, consul, Lambayeque, Peru, to USG. "I have the honor to make application to Your Excellency for an appointment to a cadetship in the National Military Academy at West Point, for my son, *Charles Arthur St Agueda Montjoy*—in the coming class of 1873. In support of this application I can only say that, I have been in the Consular service of the United States for some years, in a Consulate where no salary was annexed; and where, I hope, I have been the means of eaverting some difficulties between my country and the Republic of Peru where I am located; and to have been of some considerable service in the protection of my countrymen, in proof of which, I have the honor to refer Your Excellency to the adjoined report of those services, from the Honorable, the Secretary of State. I can only further say that my long residence at my post of duty, places me in that list of officers of the United States, who, having no Congressional District, are constrained to invoke directly, the benevolence of Your Excellency."—LS, DNA, RG 94, Correspondence, USMA. No appointment followed. An undated memorandum of Secretary of State Hamilton Fish states that "Mr. Montjoy is a native of the State of New York and was appointed Consul at Lambayeque, on the 18th of March 1867. He has been assiduous in the performance of his duties and punctual in sending his returns and accounts. He reported to the Department on the 15th of September, 1866, the departure of one Millan a native of Chile and resident of Lima, for the United States, for the purpose of *contracting* for two thousand families of blacks to go to Peru. He stated, that, it was 'the intention of the parties "interested to give the *speculation* the coloring of free colonization in that country," but when they arrived there they were to be *sold* in the same manner as the Chinese Coolies for the term of eight years for the sum of three hundred and seventy five dollars each under the pretext of remunerating the speculator, passage and advance money, each one to receive during the eight years twenty five cents in Bolivian currency, daily, equal to 33½ per cent: less on hand money. He stated, that there was no necessity for him to depict the horrid cruelties inflicted upon the Coolies, which would be the fate of the deluded people who might be brought there under that Contract, if permitted to be carried out by the U. S. Government.'. . .'"— D, *ibid.*

1871, SEPT. 28. S. W. Thomas, Philadelphia, to USG. "A Presiding Elder from Northampton & Accomac Co Eastern Shore Virginia has been on that District four years. He is not an ardent Republican, yet he wishes and will work for your Election because he believes that your Election will secure peace and forever silence the opposition to our church. He says that in those counties the *Union* men have no organization and make no regular ticket, that the colored people are overawed and if they dont vote square for Democrats then they are arrested and Kept in Jail until the Election is over. He says as Each man gives his vote his name is announced and also the persons named on his ticket. He thinks someone ought to be sent into those counties at once and organize the party for local Elections and ~~that~~ thus they will be drilled for the General Election. He also states the colored people are in the majority but the whites tell them such fearful lies that they are mislead or abused. I felt it my duty to call your attention to these matters. I suppose I ought to write to Some Committee, but being wholly uninformed as to political matters I forward the facts and leave you to act as you deem best."—ALS, DNA, RG 60, Letters from the President.

1871, SEPT. 29. USG endorsement. "Refered to the Chief of Engr."—AES (facsimile), Historical Documents International Inc., Aug. 18, 1995, no. 131. Written on a circular advertising "The Moody Floating Fort." On Oct. 26,

Secretary of War William W. Belknap wrote to USG. "I have the honor to present to you the accompanying report of the Board of Engrs. upon Fortifications expressing their views upon the floating battery designed by Mr. John Moody for the defense of harbors, and the remark of the Chief of Engrs. upon the efficacy of his floating Electrict Telegraph Station and Light Ship for Mid Ocean, in response to your reference of the subject to that officer on the 29th. ultimo—"—Copy, DNA, RG 107, Letters Sent, Military Affairs.

1871, OCT. 2. Stephen Thomas, pension agent, Montpelier, to USG. "It is with great pleasure that I recommend to your favorable consideration Mr Scott Montgomery for an appointment as Cadet at the West Point Academy. he is a colored Boy of not over, I think, one fourth African desent, is a native of La. he with a brother about two years older than himself came to my Regt, the 8th Vt. in the Spring of 1863, near Opelousa La. and followed it during all the hard marches until he left it in the fall of 1864 at Winchester Va & came to Vermont—When he left the Regt he did not know the alphabet. he is now a fair writer as is Shown by his application reads well, has been through Greenleaf's Arithmatic and Elementary Algebra, Greens English Grammer & his Analysis—Quackinbos History of the United States—Geography—Latin Grammer and read the first Oration Cicero and has proceed as far as the Verb in Greek. he has accomplished thus much & worked during the Summers to obtain funds to pay his expenses during the remainder of the year He is of good Size—fine form—healthy, & remarkable good habits & good disposition For intilectual ability he is not often Surpassed or Seldom equaled—I think he is not as old as the petition States. when he came to the Regt in 1863 we then Supposed him to be not over eight years of age but neither himself or brother knew his age I believe it will be a benifit to the Country and especially to the African race to have him educated at the West Point Academy Trusting it will be consistant to give him the Appointment asked for—"—ALS, DNA, RG 94, Correspondence, USMA. On Aug. 10, Scott Montgomery, Townshend, Vt., had written to USG asking for a cadetship.—ALS, *ibid.* Thomas and others endorsed this letter. "The undersigned respectfully represent that the above petitioner, Scott Montgomery, is a mulatto man of the age of nineteen years, that he sustains a good moral character,—has health and physical developements suited to military service and is a good scholar. We, therefore, recommend him for the appointment prayed for in his petition."—ES (13 signatures), *ibid.* U.S. Senator Justin S. Morrill of Vt. added a separate endorsement. "I beg leave to present the petition of Scott Mongomery for a Cadetship at Westpoint and say that the applicant, as he has been represented to me, possesses extraordinary merits."—AES (undated), *ibid.* Montgomery did not attend USMA.

1871, OCT. 4. William Spence, Murfreesboro, Tenn., to USG. "I have the honour to apply to you for the appointment of Marshall for the district of

Middle Tennessee. For my fitness for the Office I refer you to Senator Wm G Brownlow Hon Horace Maynard Judge Milligan of the Court of Claims in Washington. I am well known to every Republican in Tennessee   I feel confident that I can fill the Office with credit to the State & Government and do our party as much good as any man in Middle Tennessee. I hope you will consider my application to have this appointment."—ALS, DNA, RG 60, Records Relating to Appointments. On Oct. 1, U.S. Representative Roderick R. Butler of Tenn., Taylorsville, had written to USG. "After compliments the death of Genl Harrison creates a vacancy in the office of marshall for the middle District of our State   Genl Stokes wants the position and I want him to have it . . ."—ALS, *ibid.* On Oct. 9, M. T. Sanders, Nashville, wrote to USG. "I have the honor to ask of you the appointment, as United States Marshal for the middle District of Tennessee in the place made vacant by the death of General T. J. Harrison   I was the regular deputy Marshal, and am now attending to all of the business   I am and have ever been a Republican have taken an active part in the politcs of this district, gave liberally both of my time and means to secure your Election and that of every Republican who have been before the people. . . ."—ALS, *ibid.* On Dec. 6, USG nominated Spence as marshal, Middle District, Tenn., to replace Thomas J. Harrison, who had died on Sept. 28. See *PUSG*, 20, 311, 355–56.

1871, Oct. 9.   To William R. Smith. "I have to acknowledge the receipt of a very fine bunch of banannas raised in the open air at the Botanical Gardens, and for which I am indebted to your kind thoughtfulness. They proved very sweet and luscious fruit and were highly appreciated. Please accept my thanks."—Copy, DLC-USG, II, 1.

1871, Oct. 12.   Orville E. Babcock to R. C. Smith, South Hancock, Maine. "The President desires me to acknowledge the receipt of your letter of the 6th of Sept. and return you his thanks for your very kind offer, but he could not keep the eagles if he had them."—Copy, DLC-USG, II, 1.

1871, Oct. 13.   USG order. "In pursuance of the Authority conferred upon me by the 16th section of the Act entitled 'an Act to regulate the diplomatic and consular systems of the United States' Approved August 18, 1856. I do hereby prescribe in addition to the fees heretofore prescribed, that the sum of five dollars shall be charged for the granting or issuing of each passport granted or issued in any foreign country by any Diplomatic or Consular Officer of the United States."—DS, DNA, RG 59, Miscellaneous Letters. *Foreign Relations, 1872,* p. 4.

1871, Oct. 13.   Charles M. Lynch, Erie, Pa., to USG. "I cannot forbear presenting for your consideration the case of Private Edward Carter Co B. 29 U. S. Colored Troops who has manifestly been treated unjustly by the decisions in his case, and appeal to you as the last and highest resort. I

appealed to the Hon. The Secretary of War, and the matter again fell into
the hands of the Assistant Adjutant Genl, only for him to affirm his former
decision Edward Carter was a slave and when our Army passed over or
near the plantation of his master he joined our Army and was mustered into
the service of U. S. In the 'Mine Explosion' at Petersburg he was taken
prisoner and was not released until the fall of Richmond—The facts of his
case verified by affidavits establishing his identity &c are all on file in the
war department He applied for an honorable discharge and it was granted
but to *date* the *day after capture* while a *prisoner* of *war.* He was either entitled
to a discharge to date with the close of the war, the muster out of his
regiment, or not entitled to one at all. The affidavits on file sets forth his
whole claim. Hoping this may meet your distinguished consideration . . ."—
ALS, DNA, RG 94, Colored Troops Div., Letters Received. On Nov. 11,
Secretary of War William W. Belknap endorsed this letter. "In consideration
of the facts in this case—that the soldier was a slave up to the time of his
enlistment, and served but about two months before being captured—it is
believed that he could not have been aware of his duty to report upon being
released, and an honorable discharge, as of the date of the muster-out of his
regiment, is hereby ordered to be substituted for the one given him by the
Comdg. Genl. Dept. of the East."—ES, *ibid.*

1871, OCT. 16. "Republican," Austin, to USG. "Republicans wishing for
your success, and believing in your administration, and ability, as Com-
mander in chief of the United States Army, respectfully inform you, that the
Democratic Post Commander, at Austin Texas, (Capt. Sellers.) permits one
A. N. Shipley, and family, to occupy a Government building, inside the
United States Garrison. Said Shipley is not in *any way* connected with the
Government, but is *universally* known as an *inveterate drunkard,* and *gambler.*
Upon inquiry, I learn that at one time during the War, he was stationed in
New-Orleans as Quarter Master—and frequent assertions in *Bar Rooms* at
Austin, *confirm* the *belief* that his returns have *not* been rendered. The facts
above stated, I glean by inquiry, and *personal* observation, and therefore feel
no hesitation in bringing the same to your notice. You will readily understand the *influence* he sways, from the fact of his being protected by a *Government Officer,* which he would not have, under *other* circumstances. For several
months past, this man Shipley, has been engaged in soliciting subscriptions
to aid the Democracy, Democratic Barbecue, &c. &c. I understand he occupies a *great portion* of his time vilifying the State Administration, and the
Government at Washington. Trusting that what I have stated herein, is
sufficient at *least,* to cause an *investigation. . . ."*—AL, DNA, RG 94, Letters
Received, 3895 1871. On Nov. 29, Capt. Edwin E. Sellers, 10th Inf., wrote
to AG Edward D. Townsend. ". . . Mr Shipley was appointed trader at the
Post of Austin in 1868 by General J. J. Reynolds which appointment has
never been revoked, although he discontinued the business of Trader after
the Garrison became reduced to a one Company Post; he has however kept
the Officers Mess from the time of his appointment as Trader untill the

present   Mr Shipleys' Character as a gentleman is well known to all of the Officers who have been Stationed here, and to many of the old army Officers ..."—LS, *ibid.* Related papers are *ibid.* Alexander N. Shipley enlisted as a private in 1848, was commissioned 2nd lt. in 1857, and served as lt. col. and q. m. before resigning in July, 1865.

1871, OCT. 17.   John P. S. Gobin, Lebanon, Pa., to USG. "I beg leave respectfully to *urge* the appointment of Rev W. D. C. Rodrock of Duncannon Pa to a Chaplaincy in the U. S. Army. As Chaplain of the 47th Regt. Penna Vols during the Rebellion he served during the entire war, faithfully and creditably, in *all respects....*"—ALS, DNA, RG 94, ACP, 961 1873. On Jan. 18, 1869, Gobin had written to USG on the same subject.—ALS, *ibid.,* R34 CB 1869. On Jan. 10, 1873, William D. C. Rodrock, Eureka, Pa., wrote to USG. "... All the *claim* I have on you, is, that I *served* with and under you through the *whole* war, voted for you twice & *influenced* my friends, as far as a Clergyman can consistantly do so, to do the same. I am serving a small Parish, with a small salary, my wife, five children, and Mother to provide for. In our Campaign, under, Sheridan, in '64 and '65, I contracted an affection in my, throat, from which, I *continually* suffer, in my official labors.—Hence it occurred to me, that, perhaps, *through you,* I might secure *some* appointment. If not a Chaplaincy?—a clerkship in the Custom House at Philada or some *similiar* position...."—ALS, *ibid.,* 961 1873. No appointment followed.

On Nov. 18, 1871, Hermann Bokum, Atlanta, wrote to USG. "I beg leave to state that from the year 1862 to the year 1865 I held the position of Chaplain of the United States Army, being stationed at the Turners' Lane Hospital in the city of Philadelphia. In the fall of 1865 I was honorably discharged. I have lately had charge of a congregation in this city, but my connection with that congregation has terminated. I now beg to apply for a chaplaincy in the United States Army whenever a vacancy may occur, With expressions of gratitude for the kindness with which you always have treated me ..."—ALS, *ibid.,* Applications for Positions in War Dept. No appointment followed.

On Nov. 22, Charles O. Cook, Boonsboro, Md., "Pastor of M. E. Church," wrote to USG requesting a chaplaincy "at the Soldier's home or one of the points in Washington, Balto. Philadelphia or New York."—ALS, *ibid.* No appointment followed.

1871, OCT. 18.   James Bird, Winnipeg, to USG. "Personally appeared James Bird of the Parish of St Paul, in the Province of Manitoba, who being duly sworn deposes and says: That about the year 1854, deponent was Indian interpreter at the trading post of the Missouri Fur Company, called Fort Benton, in what is now Montana Territory: that Col Cummins, United States Commissioner and Governor Stevens, in behalf of the United States, held a treaty with the Blackfeet nation and other tribes East of the Mountains, and the Flathead and Shoshone tribes from the West side of the Rocky Mountains, at a place about ten or twelve miles below Fort Benton: that at said treaty, this deponent acted as Indian Interpreter for the period of seven days while the conference was held, and during a period of three months in collecting the Indians together: that for said services, deponent was paid by Governor Stevens for interpreting for th Indians on West of the Mountains: but nothing was ever paid for interpreting and negotiating with the Blackfeet and other Indians East of the Mountains. Col Cummins promised to make such payment, but it was never made. Deponent asks and prays, that the Government of the United States will allow him five hundred dollars, with interest from date of said treaty and for the purpose submits this affidavit as a petition to the President of the United States."—D ("signed by mark on account of blindness"), DNA, RG 75, Letters Received, Montana Superintendency. See Charles J. Kappler, ed., *Indian Treaties 1778–1883* (Washington, 1904; reprinted, New York, 1972), pp. 736–40.

1871, OCT. 23.   William Slatter, Monrovia, Liberia, to USG. "Thou whom is the first President i ever voted for in my life, (and also, the first man. i am about 55 years of age, or, was born, march 16th 18,16, Montgomery county Tennessee And was enrolled a pri Souldier, on the (28. day of September One thousand eight hundred Sixty three, to Serve three years, or, during the war. i was discharge out of Service of The, U. Ss. army. on 31st, day of May, 1865, Nashville Tenn collerd troops, captin, S, D, Frast of Company, G, 12 Regiment,)   And after i was discharge out of the, U., Ss. army, i bought me Some Black Smith tools and carpenters tools, And, on monday the 1st day of November 18,69, i left the, U. Ss. For Liberia, And the 23rd day of December. 1869, i landed on the african Soaal,   But the remarkable Sean hapened with me, i never had a pasage through me in 46, days, after that i had the fever. And it lasted me about (12) months. And the Rashings the Society gives me lasted. 6, months; And i am a beging of you, for 12 months rashing, to give me a chance to clear out my farm, and plant it. . . ."— ALS, DNA, RG 59, Miscellaneous Letters. Slatter, a Methodist minister, commented on Liberia's politics and economy and complained that established settlers mistreated new arrivals.

1871, OCT. 23.   Jacob Thompson, Memphis, to USG. "I have the honor to enclose for your information, copies of Commodore Maury's resolutions and the address in explanation of them, delivered before the Memphis Agricultural Society on the 17th Instant—. . . I add my earnest desire to the wishes of the society, that your Excellency will deem it wise & good to take the lead in this matter, and to get the influence of this Government with other nations, in order to induce them to send their leading Meteorologists and Physicists to meet in conference such persons as your Excellency may designate, for the purpose of devising and setting on foot an international systematic, and uniform plan of meteorological observation, co-operation, and research, together with a widespread system of crop reports & forecasts, such as those to which these resolutions point—"—ALS, DNA, RG 59, Miscellaneous Letters. See *PUSG*, 6, 397–98; *ibid.*, 15, 33–34; *ibid.*, 17, 201–2.

1871, OCT. 26.   U.S. Senator George E. Spencer of Ala., Decatur, to USG.
"General Coon deserves the appointment of Consul to Rio de Janeiro above
all other aAlabamians   Wickersham not entitled to it"—Telegram received
(at 10:41 P.M.), DNA, RG 59, Letters of Application and Recommendation.
Related papers are *ibid.* On Dec. 6, USG nominated Datus E. Coon as consul,
Rio de Janeiro. On March 5, 1872, USG nominated Joseph M. Hinds to
replace Coon, who had declined the position. See *PUSG*, 19, 382. On March
1, 1873, USG nominated Morris D. Wickersham as postmaster, Mobile.

On Nov. 6, 1871, Renwick Z. Willson, New York City, had written to
USG. "The acting consul of the United States at Rio Janiero, Francis M.
Cordeiro, refused to take charge of and forward home M. B. Willson, boy
on ship 'Queen of the East'. My son, the said M. B. Willson, had become
deranged, and the Capt, of the Queen of the East,' sought to have him
returned by the Consul on the Steamer South America which left Rio Janiero
on Sept. 24th, two days after Capt. Stoddard put into Rio, & reached this
port Oct. 19th. Our poor boy has been put on board the British bark Aleyone
and will not reach home until sometime in Dec. Knowing your humane
feeling and convinced of your interest in our poor seamen, I appeal to you
for their sake to take measures to bring this Consul to a sense of his duty,
and convince others that they cannot with impunity prove derelict to their
duty and to humanity. . . . Judge Davis U. S. District Attorney advises to
represent this case to you—"—ALS, DNA, RG 59, Miscellaneous Letters.

1871, OCT. 27.   To Governor Rutherford B. Hayes of Ohio. "It has been
Decided to Designate the Thirtieth Proximo as Thanksgiving   Proclamation Issued today"—Telegram received (at 3:00 P.M.), OFH. On Oct. 11,
Horace Porter had written to Mary P. Taber, New York City. "The President
desires me to acknowledge the receipt of your letter of yesterday and say
that the date of Thanksgiving day has not been determined, but in all probability it will be appointed for Thursday, November 23d when he hopes you
will have a very happy reunion with your children."—Copy, DLC-USG, II,
1. See *PUSG*, 19, 251.

1871, OCT. 27.   To Sinclair Tousey, New York City. "I have the honor to
acknowledge the receipt of your 'Indices of Public Opinion', a copy of which
you were kind enough to send me. I shall avail myself of an early opportunity
to read it, and must beg you to accept my sincere thanks for your remembrance, and for the volume which is a valuable addition to my library."—
Copy, DLC-USG, II, 1. Tousey, born in 1818, president, American News Co.,
a prominent member of the Union League Club, printed privately *Indices
of Public Opinion, 1860–1870* (New York, 1871), a collection of his letters
and essays.

1871, Nov. 1.   M. During, Barton, Md., to USG. "Not understanding the
English language perfectly, I take the liberty to apply to you in german
language for protection of my own person, my sick wife and children, and

property. Yesterday evening a company of twenty to twenty five men surrounded my house and commenced to bombard it with stones. Witnesses: My neighbor Mr. Davis, his wife and daughter. On the ground, that I and all my folks disturb nobody, not even a child, I believe they are KuKlux who have the intention to murder me and my folks, and destroy my property, because I am a republican, and a lutheran minister of the gospel. My late son Paul, who died as a soldier in General Hospital on Davids Island, served four years during the war in the 1st Ohio Vol. Cavy. Regt.) As the local authorities, who are all Democrats, dont give me any protection, I most respectfully ask Your Excellency to take such action, in accordance with the KuKlux law, that I, my folks and my property will be protected. . . ."—ALS (in German), DNA, RG 94, Letters Received, 3940 1871; translation, *ibid.* On Dec. 15, James F. Wagner, special agent, Baltimore, wrote to Postmaster Gen. John A. J. Creswell. ". . . The complaint of the Revd During is entirely unfounded in fact—there are no *unlawful* organisations whatever at Barton, Md. . . . It is true that on the night of referred to in his letter of complaint, he did with the other citizens of the town experience much annoyance, it being 'Hallow Eve'—night—Oct 31. . . ."—ALS, *ibid.*

1871, Nov. 1.   Gen. William T. Sherman to Lt. Gen. Philip H. Sheridan, Chicago. "Indian agent Wham has been Relieved   the President dirrects that Genl John E Smith act as the Indian agent at Laramie in place of Wham until a new agt appointed & arrives"—Telegram received, DNA, RG 393, Military Div. of the Mo., Letters Received; copy, *ibid.* See *PUSG*, 18, 590; Carol A. Ripich, "Joseph W. Wham and the Red Cloud Agency, 1871," *Arizona and the West*, 12, 4 (Winter, 1970), 325–38. Jared W. Daniels replaced Wham, a veteran of the 21st Ill. and former 2nd lt. On March 3, 1877, USG nominated Wham as paymaster.

1871, Nov. 3.   Eldad C. Camp, Washington, D. C., to USG. "On 24th ultimo you directed my suspension from office U. S. Dist Atty Eastern Dist Tenn— I am informed this action is based on joint petition of Senator Brownlow and Congressmen Maynard & Butler in which they state substantially 'that there is an opinion prevails that the office has not been properly conducted— that they neither own or disown the truth of such report but recomend my removal'   This is in my opinion an implied charge made against my official conduct—I have applied to the Hon Atty Genl for an investigation of any charges thus insinuated against me but he declines to take any action for the reason that the action taken was taken by you and without his knowledge— However after consultation I deemed best to and have telegraphed Mr Brownlow & Maynard as follows 'Are you willing I should have an investigation of *charges insinuated* against me before further action taken'—Brownlow answers 'he makes no recomendations bas on basis of any charges' &c— Maynard answers 'If Brownlow & Butler wish it certainly'   Thus matters stand—I want an investigation by the Atty Genl if any charges are preferred—if none I desire to be reinstated—after which if in your judgt tis believed best for the best interests of the Republican party I should resign I will do so. . . ."—ALS, DNA, RG 60, Records Relating to Appointments. On March 13, 1869, U.S. Representative Horace Maynard of Tenn. had written to USG recommending Camp.—ALS, *ibid.* On Nov. 4, 1871, Horace Porter wrote to Attorney Gen. Amos T. Akerman. "The President directs me to request you to withdraw the suspension of U. S. Attorney E. C. Camp, E. Dist. of Tenn., and direct him to resume his duties."—Copy, DLC-USG, II, 1. On Dec. 6, USG nominated George Andrews to replace Camp.

1871, Nov. 4.   To Secretary of State Hamilton Fish. "Will you please extend the leave of absence granted to Gov. Ed. M. McCook, of Col.—thirty days."—Copy, DLC-USG, II, 1. On Jan. 23, 1872, Governor Edward M. McCook of Colorado Territory wrote to Orville E. Babcock. "I recd yours of the 14th a day or two since, and had already, in thought, concurred with you as to the propriety of not using your name publicly for fear of bring some attack on the President through this—I shall telegraph to Longbottom to-day not to use any American names until he hears from me by mail, when I will enclose him a copy of part of your letter and of Course he will see the propriety of following your suggestion; but I think it will be necessary to have two or three good American names that are known in London—for instance Henry Clews, and Huntington of the First National Washington—Cant you induce them to permit their names to be used as Trustees or Directors—It involves no responsibility whatever pecuniary or otherwise, and the project is not one which any person may fear to have their name associated with. If these names do not happen to come within your influence, Secure two others and simply telegraph their names to me without comment and I will understand what you mean. You will have to act promptly as I have recently recd a letter from Mr Longbottom hurrying me up. He is going in for Earnest. If I were in the East I could arrange matters without trouble, as it is I must leave this part of the programme in a great measure with you. I presume namers of the Banking fraternity would be the best, as they are the beloved of all money grubbing Englishmen— and being engaged in ~~their~~ an enterprize within their legitimate sphere no reflections could be cast upon yourself the President or any person Else. I presume you saw the Saulsbury resolution asking how long I had been Governor, and how long in Europe. It was instigated by an anonymous coward who signs himself 'Raymond North' Banker, Denver, and mails his letter at Medea Penn. He says 'McCook ~~I~~ ha~~ve~~s been more than a year in England not on any public business, but bulling the stock of the now famous little Emma mine.' Also 'McCook is a *rabid abolitionist,* and if my appeal to you to present this resolution is in vain, please send it back to me and I will try to get some other Democratic member to present it.' How is that? Those sentences are extracts from a letter addressed to Conner of Texas enclosing the same resolution presented by Saulsbury, and accompanied I presume by the same character of letter. Mr North appears to be 'pinched' by the fact that I am a 'rabid abolitionist,' and I presume is actuated by personal malice, probably I have declined to pardon some brother or other friend of his who is in the Penitentiary—The papers here came out unsolicited by me and gave the thing a thorough raking over and said all sorts of complimentary things about my efficient administration. I never had anything to do with the Emma mine, and even if I had I claim the same right with other officials both civil and military to visit Europe or any place Else should the President see proper to grant me leave. Army, Navy, & civil officers of all kinds have visited Europe unofficially during their terms, and though Europe frequently swarms with members of Congress I have not yet heard of any of them declining to accept their pay for the time they were absent. I have only had two leaves of absence since appointed, and I think if the *animus* of this anonymous fellow was known to republican Senators they would unanimously forgive me for being absent with leave, and being a rabid abolitionist both. No such man as North has ever lived in Denver or in Colorado—We will elect two delegates here for the Phila convention, I dont know whether I had better go or not. If desirable the Delegates will be instructed—Write to me and tell me what you think about this and also about my friend 'Raymond North.' Remember me to Genl Porter"—ALS, Babcock Papers, ICN. On Feb. 5 and 12, March 19, and May 3, McCook wrote to Babcock on the same subject—a potential British-led mining venture in Colorado.—ALS, *ibid.* On Feb. 26, Fish wrote to Babcock. "The U. S. Despatch agent at New York has informed the Department of the arrival there by the steamer 'City of London,' of a case for Governor McCook addressed to your care. . . ."—Copy, DNA, RG 59, Domestic Letters. On Jan. 16, U.S. Senator Eli Saulsbury of Del. had offered a resolution requesting USG to inform the Senate "how much of the time the said McCook has been absent from the Territory in Europe or elsewhere since his appointment, and whether by permission or not, and whether on public duties or not, and whether his salary has been paid to him during his absence or not, and how much has been paid to him as salary for the time he has been absent from the Territory."—*CG,* 42–2, 406.

On Feb. 15, McCook wrote to USG to report on territorial legislation. ". . . Your attention is also called to the fact that when you appointed me Governor of this Territory, it was largely in debt, without money in the Treasury, without credit, and overburdened with taxes. Now the Territory is entirely free from debt, there is enough money in the Treasury to meet all current expenses for the coming year, *and no taxes whatever levied for the year 1872.* I believe no other body politic on the Continent can say that they are entirely free from taxation; and I congratulate myself upon the fact that these marked financial changes have taken place during my administration, and after the Legislative power of the Territory had passed from Democratic into Republican hands."—ALS, OFH. On Feb. 29, Babcock wrote to McCook. "The President directs me to acknowledge the receipt of your letter of the 15th inst: and in reply communicate his congratulation on the general State of the Territory under your charge—but more especially its financial condition."—Copy, DLC-USG, II, 1.

1871, Nov. 5.   J. H. Clendening, Fort Smith, Ark., to USG. "Having learned
accidentally that strenuous efforts are being made to remove Col. Roots.
U. S. Marshal. Western Dist of Arkansas. In the interest of your Administration and the party I desire to intrude a few facts on your attention. The
enclosed editorial clipped from the Patriot of yesterday marked. 1, is a tissue
of falshood from first to last. which can be refuted here *in toto.* I presume
this article shaddows forth the charges made against Col Roots. So far as his
fealty to the National Administration is concerned, (I speak from personal
knowledge) when I say you have no warmer or more valuable friend in this
state. The other charges made are as devoid of truth as this. In part proof.
I also enclose a copy of proceedings of a large meeting of colored citizens
relating to article appearing in 'the Patriot' against them. . . . I assure you
Mr President, the interests of the party in this state require that removals
should be made with great caution. I wrote a few days since to Genl. Babcock at length of affairs in the state and presuming he has shown you the
letter I will not go into any further statements but will close, by urging
upon you, patient investigation in *every* case presented from this state, . . ."—
ALS, DNA, RG 60, Letters Received. Enclosed newspaper clippings are *ibid.*
At about this time, William L. Taylor *et al.*, grand jurors, wrote to USG
commending William Story, judge, and Logan H. Roots, marshal, Western
District, Ark.—DS (21 signatures, docketed Nov. 1, 1871), *ibid.*, Letters
Received, Ark. On June 19, 1872, USG suspended Roots.

1871, Nov. 7.   USG endorsement. "Refered to the State Dept. I see no
objection to the apt. of Mr. Turner when the resignation of Mr. Stewart is
tendered."—AES, DNA, RG 59, Letters of Application and Recommendation. Written on a letter of Nov. 6 from Thomas A. Scott, Philadelphia, to
USG. "Some years ago, as a special favor to me, my nephew T. Scott Stewart
was appointed to a consulship in Japan. I have reason to believe that he will
resign his position shortly: and the object of this application is to ask that
his successor may be Mr. Daniel Turner of Philadelphia. He is the son of
Commodore Peter Turner, formerly of the U. S. Navy, and a nephew of
Commodore Daniel Turner: is a young gentleman of perhaps thirty years
of age, and of fine education and ability. His family is now so situated that
this appointment will be of great service and value to him I hope, therefore,
that on the receipt of the resignation of Mr. Stewart, you will request the
Secretary of State to give this appointment to Mr. Turner. I am sure he
will make a competent and faithful officer for the Government."—LS, *ibid.*
Commodore Peter Turner had died on Feb. 19. On Dec. 19, USG nominated
his son Daniel as consul, Osaka and Hiogo.

On May 25, Sarah S. Turner, Washington, D. C., had written to USG.
"In an interview which you were kind enough to give me a few weeks since,
you were pleased to say that you would like the Hon. Secretary of the Navy
to nominate my son, Wm J. Turner, for a future vacancy in the Marine
Corps. I regret to learn that the occurrence of a vacancy in that corps, which
he might fill, is not probable, and would therefore most respectfully beg of
you an appointment for him as 2d Lieutenant of Infantry to fill one of the

vacancies expected to occur during the coming month of June. He is now in the 5th Cavalry having entered the army with the understanding that he should receive a commission in the course of a short time. I beg leave to remind you that he is a son of the late Commodore Turner of the Navy, and of a family which has done service to the State in many generations during and since the Revolution."—LS, *ibid.*, RG 94, ACP, 3725 1873. USG appointed William J. Turner as 2nd lt. as of Oct. 1, 1873.

1871, Nov. 8. To Henry A. Ward, Rochester, N. Y. "I am in receipt of the beautifully executed raised map of the island of Santo Domingo, you so kindly forwarded to me by Express. Your personal observations added to your thorough investigation enable you to execute this map with great accuracy. Please accept my sincere thanks for the map and for the kind sentiments expressed in your letter of transmittal"—Copy, DLC-USG, II, 1. Born in 1834 in Rochester, Ward assisted Louis Agassiz at Harvard and became professor of natural sciences at the University of Rochester in 1861. He traveled widely to collect fossils.

1871, Nov. 8. Almira Lincoln Phelps, Baltimore, to USG. "A Cuban gentleman, eminent in his profession of the law, having been obliged to leave his country on account of republican principles is desirous of finding employment as a translater of Spanish, or an assistant in matters relating to international laws. At this time when the affairs of some of the West India Islands have become complicated with our government, the services of such a man might be valuable—He was appointed as one of the Commissioners to go to Madrid to treat with the Cortes on Cuban affairs; the disregard of the remonstrances of the Commissioners was followed by the revolution. Senor Camejo having had his large estates confiscated now seeks employment for the support of his family. This application on his behalf is made without his solicitation, or knowledge;—I believe that he would prove a valuable assistant in the State department and that the favour to him would be the *gain* to the Country. You may possibly remember recieving from me (when the guest of Mr Albert of our city) a copy of the National Book '*Our Country*', edited and presented by me for the benefit of Hospitals during the war:— and you may recollect my son General Charles E. Phelps who unites with me in recommending Senor Camejo to your notice."—ALS, DNA, RG 59, Letters of Application and Recommendation.

1871, Nov. 8. Thomas Buchanan Read, Rome, to USG. "I have just heard from Mr R. N. Savage, whom I have the pleasure of knowing, that you have paid me the compliment of placing my picture of 'Sheridan's Ride,' in an honorable position in your cottage at Long Branch. I cannot forget the compliment you once paid me, when we were riding together in the Walnut Street cars in Philadelphia, when you asked me for an autograph copy of my poem of 'Sheridan's Ride,' for your son. Therefore, as one of your most ardent friends, I request as a favor, that you will allow me to replace the

picture by one a great deal better; one for which the General sat while he
was here. I desire to leave in your hands the best picture I have painted,
inasmuch as you have paid both the General and myself the compliment of
being our friend. As the picture I replace will be of no further use to you,
may I ask ~~to~~ you to allow Mr Savage to accept it from me, as a proof of my
regard for him A friend of mine, Mr Connellan has offered to be the bearer
of the picture to you. Any kindness you can shew either to him or to Mr
Savage will be gratefully appreciated . . ."—LS, MiU-C. On Feb. 5, 1872,
USG endorsed this letter. "Acknowledge receipt and acceptance of exchange
of pictures"—AES, *ibid.* On Nov. 17, 1871, Read had sent to USG "a copy
of my painting of 'Sheridan's Ride' the same to be exchanged for the copy
now in possession of said Ulysses S. Grant . . ."—DS, USG 3. Related papers
are *ibid.* In 1872, Chester A. Arthur, collector of customs, New York City,
wrote to USG forwarding "a picture of 'Sheridan's Ride.'"—William Evarts
Benjamin, Catalogue No. 27, Nov., 1889, p. 4.

In Dec., 1871, Read wrote to USG. "As you have a boy who has recited
my poems and I have none of my own to tell of your deeds, will you assist
me in a matter which lies near my heart at this present time. Can you inform
me whether my adoption of a young Scotch boy over here, with all due
formalities in presence of the U. S. Minister, giving him my own name,
thereby renders him an American citizen? My boy is distantly connected
with our late General Macpherson & bears the same name. I should be
greatly obliged to You my dear General if you would reply to this at your
earliest convenience as your answer is of considerable importance to me"—
LS, DNA, RG 59, Miscellaneous Letters.

1871, Nov. 9.   Governor William Claflin of Mass. to USG. "I shall esteem
it a favor if you will give your personal attention to the petition signed by
Oliver Cutts & Co, Isaac Rich & Co, & others in regard to claims against
the Haytien Government, which will be presented to you by Capt Oliver
Cutts. Mr. Isaac Rich (of Isaac Rich & Co) is a personal friend of mine & I
know him to be a man of strict integrity & his firm to be one that would
make no unjust claim or sign any petition that was not right in every respect. Upon looking the matter over, I am satisfied that our Government
should take active measures for the protection of the interests of the petitioners, as the course intended to be pursued by the Haytien Government
is repudiation to a great extent, & certainly very unjust to them. . . . Sincere
thanks for all passed favors"—ALS, DNA, RG 59, Miscellaneous Letters.
See message to Congress, April 5, 1871 (2), note 2.

1871, Nov. 11.   Christopher C. Andrews, U.S. minister, Stockholm, to USG.
"I have taken the liberty to send to you personally a copy of a document
recently issued from the British Foreign Office containing some interesting
reports on the condition of the Industrial Classes &c. in different countries."—ALS (press), Andrews Papers, Minnesota Historical Society, St.
Paul, Minn.

1871, Nov. 13.   To Thomas Sampson, detective, New York City Police, authorizing the extradition of William E. Gray, London, a former Wall Street investment broker wanted for forgery.—Copy, DNA, RG 59, General Records. See *New York Times*, Feb. 4, 1872, July 10, 11, 1878, May 23, 1879.

1871, Nov. 15.   USG endorsement. "Refered to the Sec. of War. Please name Mr. Hodge as a member of the Board of Visitors for West Point next year."—AES, DNA, RG 94, USMA, Board of Visitors. Written on a letter of Nov. 14 from David Hunter, Washington, D. C., to USG. "*Private....* The name of the gentleman you were so kind as to say you would send to West Point, next June, as a Visitor, is the Revd Charles Hodge, D.D. LL.D. for more than forty years a Professor in the Theological Seminary, in Princeton, New Jersey. I take the liberty of sending for your acceptance, the first, and only volume out, of Dr Hodge's new work on Theology, now being published in Europe and in this country. From it, you will be able to obtain some first rate theology, when your mind is running in that direction; and also to judge of the man you honor with the appointment,   With many thanks for your kindness,..."—ALS, *ibid.* On Jan. 11, 1872, Charles S. Hamilton, U.S. marshal, Milwaukee, wrote to USG. "It will be exceedingly gratifying to me, to be appointed one of the Board of Visitors at West Point, this coming summer. I can then accompany my son when he reports at the Academy. With sincere regards to yourself & Mrs Grant ..."—ALS, *ibid.* On Jan. 15, U.S. Senator John Sherman of Ohio wrote to USG. "Allow me to express the hope that you will designate Henry B. Curtis Esq of Mt. Vernon Ohio as one of the Examiners at West Point Academy—His papers are among those submitted by the Secy of War—Mr Curtis is an old & leading lawyer—the head of a Republican Family of influence   He has never sought an office and the courtesy of this appointment will I know be gratefully appreciated"—ALS, *ibid.* On Jan. 17, U.S. Senators Zachariah Chandler and Thomas W. Ferry of Mich. wrote to USG. "We respectfully recommend the appointment of Hon Louis S. Lovell District Judge at Ionia Michigan, upon the current years Board of Examiners of the Military Academy at West Point"—LS, *ibid.* On the same day, U.S. Senator John A. Logan and U.S. Representatives John L. Beveridge, Charles B. Farwell, John B. Hay, and Henry Snapp of Ill. wrote to USG. "The undersigned respectfully recommends the appointment of Dr Joshua Rhoads to be a visitor at the West Point Military School. Dr Rhoads has been for many years principal of the 'Institution for the Education of the Blind' at Jacksonville, in the state of Illinois. He is a man of learning, and holds a very high position in the educational institutions of the country."—LS, *ibid.* On Feb. 5, Henry A. Thompson, president, National Bank of Baltimore, wrote to USG. "I have the honor to present this as my application for the appointment of 'Visitor' to the Military Academy at the ensuing June examination—I graduated no 6 in the Class of 1819, and refer to the records of the Adjutant Gen'l's Office for the manner in which I performed my duties during the twenty years I served in the Artillery, Topographical & Engineer Corps, when domestic troubles compelled me to

retire from service A residence in this my native place, for thirty years,
has made me acquainted with most of our Business Persons, amongst whom
are many of your personal & political Friends. Should this favor be granted
to an old *Graduate*, it will be a pleasant Souvenir in my declining years, that
I have made a visit to our Alma Mater, under such favorable circumstances."—ALS, *ibid.* Related papers are *ibid.* On Feb. 19, U.S. Representative
Mark H. Dunnell of Minn. wrote to USG. "I would very respectfully recommend the selection of Prof. E. J. Thompson. Prof. of Mathematics in the State
University of Minnesota. at St. Anthony. Minn, as one of the Examiners at
the next annual examination at West Point—He is a gentleman of ability &
I would be exceedingly glad to have him appointed—"—ALS, *ibid.* On April
8, U.S. Representative William A. Handley of Ala. wrote to USG. "I have
the honor to respectfully refer the letter of Wm. B. McLellan of Talladega
Talladega County Alabama, Soliciting the appointment of visitor to the West
Point Military Academy the present year, Genl McLellan is about seventy
five years of age, a Farmer by occupation Politically a Democrat besides he
is a worthy honorable gentleman and I shall be pleased if agreeable with
your wishes to have him appointed one of the visitors to the West Point
Military Academy the present year from the State of Alabama."—ALS, *ibid.*
On April 9, U.S. Senator John Scott of Pa. wrote to USG. "I have been
solicited, and I cheerfully comply with the request, to recommend the appointment of Gen. D. B. McCreary, of the City of Erie, Penna, as one of the
Board of Visitors to the United States Military Academy at West Point.
Gen. McCreary was an officer of Penna Volunteers during the late war, and,
as a recognition of meritorious service, was subsequently appointed to the
Office of Adjutant-General of Pennsylvania. It will afford me special pleasure, if you can gratify Gen. McCreary, by conferring upon him the appointment desired."—LS, *ibid.* A related paper is *ibid.* USG appointed Charles
Hodge, Louis S. Lovell, Hugh T. Reid, James L. Scudder, Charles W. Eliot,
George A. Thruston, and Henry R. Pierson to the board of visitors, USMA,
for June 1872. See *HED*, 42-3-1, part 2, pp. 793–804.

1871, Nov. 15.   U.S. Senator Oliver P. Morton of Ind., Indianapolis, to USG.
"If there is any position you could give Major I. S. Stewart by which he
could support his family and himself you would confer a great favor upon
~~him~~ his family and friends. You know his capacity and energy, and I commend his case to your special and kind consideration."—ALS, OFH. See
PUSG, 7, 351; *ibid.*, 16, 266; *ibid.*, 18, 344. On Aug. 13, 1863, Maj. Isaac S.
Stewart, paymaster, Vicksburg, had written to USG requesting a leave of
absence.—ALS, DNA, RG 94, ACP, S142 CB 1870. On Aug. 14, USG, Vicksburg, endorsed this letter. "I would respectfully ask that Gn. Thomas grant
the leave of Absence asked for within. The loss of the funds belonging to
the Pay Dept. on board the Steamer 'Ruth' will prevent payments being
made here for some time so that I think Maj. Stewart can be spared without
detriment to the service."—AES, *ibid.* Stewart resigned as of July 31, 1870.
On Sept. 9, Frederick T. Dent wrote to AG Edward D. Townsend. "The

President desires me to say that it is his wish that Major Stewart Pay Dept should come under that provision of the law giving one year's pay to officers resigning"—AES, *ibid.*

On Oct. 23, 1872, Stewart, Chicago, wrote to "General," presumably Dent. "I enclose herewith the letter which the Greely leaders were after I wish you to give it to the President who can judge for himself as to my friendship for him, and the extent of my ungratefulness to him for past Kindness. please give him the enclosed letter my enemies may try to distroy me with him and even though they should succeed I cannot forget his past friendship to me. I shall return to Indiana about the 2d day of Nov and after the election I will be in Washington, We expect to give Grant 10.000 majority but it may only be 5000 however we are shure of the state, Hendricks has been giving me H___ Thing look much better in Chicago and generally over the Country."—ALS, Dent Papers, ICarbS. On Sept. 4, Joseph D. Webster, Chicago, had written to Stewart. ". . . you are authorized on my behalf to deny in the most emphatic manner all statements of Gen. Grant having been drunk or in any degree under the influence of liquor at the battle of Shiloh. I was at this time his chief of staff and chief of artillery. I breakfasted with the General at Savannah on Sunday, the first day of the battle. I went on board the boat with him and rode into the field with him at about 8½ o'clock, in person, and was necessarily with him, except at intervals of absence on duty, during the whole day. I lay down with him long after dark that night, on a small parcel of hay which the Quartermaster put down to keep us out of the mud, in the rear of the artillery line on the left, and I never heard till long afterward of any idea entertained by anybody that he was drunk, nor did I see him drink during the day, and I am sure he was perfectly sober, as he was self-possessed and collected during the varying fortunes of that celebrated battle. If there are any words in which I can deny the miserable charge more fully and distinctly, I am ready to adopt them."—*New York Times*, Sept. 12, 1872. On Jan. 18, 1873, USG nominated Stewart as collector of customs, Alaska Territory; on Jan. 28, USG withdrew the nomination at Stewart's request.

1871, Nov. 16.   William H. Conkle, Washington, D. C., to USG. "I have the honor to respectfully submit for your personal consideration the framing of an 'International Code', based on International Law, and made acceptable, with reference to disputed points, to the European Powers, by correspondence thro' the State Dept. The Hon. Attorney General could have the work prepared: and the object of this letter is that I may be assigned to its preparation, under him, with authority to secure, with his approval, the assistance of certain eminent lawyers of the Philadelphia Bar, of which I am a member. The importance, necessity and binding force of this great work is universally admitted. The 'Code Grant' is actually demanded by the civilization of the age, and will far overshadow in superiority, by reason of its international character, the celebrated 'Code Napoleon.' It is respectfully requested that an answer may be accorded this communication, in order that I may furnish endorsing testimonials, should the matter receive your approbation."—ALS, DNA, RG 60, Letters from the President.

1871, Nov. 18.   Horace Porter to Duke W. Anderson, pastor, 19th Street Baptist Church, Washington, D. C. "The President directs me to say that your note of the 8th inst., inviting him to be present at the dedication of your church, was mislaid during his absence from the city, and was not brought to his notice till to-day. He regrets that his engagements will not admit of his attendance at the time you mention. He congratulates your congregation upon the completion of so handsome a place of worship, and hopes that its dedication may prove an occasion of deep interest to all who share in a desire to promote the spread of the Christian religion."—George W. Williams, *History of the Negro Race in America* ... (1883; reprinted, New York, 1968), II, 498. See *PUSG,* 19, 389.

1871, Nov. 20.   Francis M. Scala, Washington, D. C., to USG. "Justice to me and my family compels me to lay before your honore the gravances of an old Soldier of 31. years Servece into the marine corps of the United States; Spotless of any charges what ever. Therefore having Seen into the national ripublican that one one Mr: F. Frease had been apointed to be the Leader of the U. S. marine Band in my place before my time expired; I ~~called~~ whent to see the Secritary of the Navy, there I meet Mr: R: Wallach which he had Seen the Secritary in my bealf; and the answer that he got was that the Secritary would not be warred and that he had made the apointment and would not alter it any more; So Mr: R. W. asked what were the charges against me to which he was told that a musical commity had made complain that the music made by the marine Band under me was not good &c: &c: and last charge was from the masons of Washington for not assisting them in a concert in Baltimore at night after one day of hard marching and playing all over Baltimore and next day we had to do the Same thing in Washington graties   now in rigard to last charge, my order from the General was as Soon as the Band got true with the procesion to come direct to Washington which I did accordingly and as for this Mr: Freas which as bean apointed to my place: hime and his wife have bean for long time and are this very day imployed into the Treasury Department at a Salary of $100. each per month and he never was into the Service but two or three years; and I an old enlisted Soldier of 31. years United States Servece got to be turned out me and my family into the Street without even the Benefit of a court marshal as every poor Soldier is enteneled by law: therefore hoping that your Eccellenzy will See me righted ... the Rank of Leader of the Band, always as being costumary 'like the Rank of Corporal, and Sargint,' taken and given by the Genl: Comdt"—ALS, DNA, RG 45, Letters Sent to the President. Born about 1820 in Naples, Scala enlisted when the U.S.S. *Brandywine* visited Naples in 1841, then transferred to the Marine Corps and joined the band, which he led after 1855. See Stuart E. Jones and William W. Campbell III, "The President's Music Men," *National Geographic,* CXVI, 6 (Dec., 1959),

752–66; David M. Ingalls, "Francis Scala: Leader of the Marine Band from 1855 to 1871," M.A. Thesis, Catholic University of America, 1957; *New York Times,* April 20, 1903. Henry Fries, a German-born clerk in the 2nd Auditor's office, replaced Scala as of Dec. 14, 1871.

1871, Nov. 21.   To Wells W. Leggett. "I take pleasure in stating that I have known Mr Wells W. Leggett for several years as a man of ability and integrity   I knew him in the Army as a very meritorious officer, and as a cadet at the Military Academy where he graduated with honor."—Copy, DLC-USG, II, 1. See *PUSG,* 10, 333. On March 7, 1869, Manning F. Force, Cincinnati, had written to U.S. Senator John Sherman of Ohio. "Wells W. Leggett, son of Gen. Leggett of Zanesville, now about to graduate at West Point, desires me to write to you in the matter of his intended application for the post of Secretary of Legation. When he was appointed to the Academy, the president endorsed upon the appointment that it was given for services rendered during the war, and would not require him to enter the army after graduating . . ."—ALS, DNA, RG 59, Letters of Application and Recommendation. On March 11, Gen. William T. Sherman endorsed this letter. "Respectfully submitted to the President through the Sec of State with a recommendation that it would help the Army much in the reduction required by Law, if some of our officers could have civil appointments"—AES, *ibid.* Appointed 2nd lt. after graduating USMA on June 15, Leggett resigned as of Jan. 10, 1870, and practiced real estate and patent law. Possibly when visiting USMA in June 1869, USG wrote an undated note to Col. Thomas G. Pitcher, superintendent. "W. W. Leggett ~~R. Q. Shirley~~ U. G. White J A. Rucker J. A. Augur . . . Please send the above named Cadets to the hotel this p. m. immediately after the boat race, and oblige, . . ."—ANS (facsimile), Alexander Autographs, Inc., Feb. 4, 1997, no. 828.

1871, Nov. 21.   Zachariah Wheat, Shelbyville, Ky., to USG. "Please find herewith enclosed a petition for the pardon of Simeon Cook, charged with making an assault on Gibson, the US Mail agent, at North Benson Station, on the Rail Road near Frankfort Ky, some time ago. The petition is signed by sundry citizens, myself among the number. This paper had its origin under the following circumstances—One Addison Cook, a brother of the petitioner Simeon Cook, was said to be the leader of the Ku Klux Klan in Shelby County Ky, & had a falling out with one Hiram Bohannon & threatened his Bs life—Bohannon met with Cook once, who assaulted & chased him into a cornfield where he hid from Cook, who was then heavily armed—in a day or two thereafter, Bohannon who had meanwhile armed himself, met Cook & shot him down fatally. Bohannon was Indicted & tried for Killing Addison Cook & found guilty of Murder in killing Cook. The petitioner Simeon Cook, through friends proposed to petition the Govr of Kentucky for a pardon of Bohannon, if Bohannon & his friends would petition your Excellency for a pardon of Simeon Cook, & this was mutually agreed to, & an attempt is now made to have both pardoned. Since Bohannon killed Cook, we have had no more Ku

Klux operations, the ring leader being killed. I am persuaded, that if both those persons were pardoned, it would heal up the wounds in that part of the Country & pacify the Community & restore order in that part of the Country. But for this conviction on my part, I would not be willing to see Sim Cook pardoned,—I know him; he is a young man, the son of a widow, & has been away from home ever since the commission of the offence by assaulting Gibson, & that matter being laid on him—and is afraid to return for fear of a prosecution for the assault on Gibson the mail agent on the rail road. I have no doubt, that Cook is sorry for his conduct, & is cured of such foolish notions, by his sufferings away from his home, his mother & his friends, & the loss of his elder brother Addison, before spoken of. I am a law and order man, & yet solicit a paden for Sim Cook, believing I should do a good act, if I succeed in procuring him a pardon, by bringing about peace in that disquieted & distracted neighborhood—Please act on this application & let me know the result—I hope it may be favorable—As we are strangers to each other, I refer you to Genl B H Bristow, who knows me, as one of those who is in favor of Universal Justice & Humanity, & called Radical Republicans. Yours in the bonds of the Union."—ALS, DNA, RG 60, Letters Received, Ky. The enclosed petition is *ibid.* USG did not pardon Simeon Cook.

On Feb. 24 and subsequently, Secretary of State Hamilton Fish had written in his diary. "Prsdt mentions the violence which has been perpetratd on the Mail Route between Louisville & Lexington Ky which passes through Frankfort, (State Capital) The Route Agent is a Colored man, who has been subjected to repeated violence—attempts to drag him from the Cars &c— for some time it has been necessary to send a ~~squad~~ guard of soldiers (10) on every train to protect it. He determines no longer to continue this protection—& gives instructions to Mr Marshall (representing the P M-G) to discontinue the route under the provisions of the Act of Feb 28 1861" "March 24 /71 ... The Kentucky mails, which were discontinued between Louisville & Lexington, by reason of alleged insecurity of the Agent, & the necessity of sending a military guard, were considered—they are not to be restored without further assurance of security" "April 4 ... Creswell reads a draft order, restoring the mail route in Kentucky, between Louisville & Lexington, on the ground that there is a large military force now there— He says that _____ Gibson the Colored route agent has resigned, because they will not send a military guard on the train & that the P. O. agent has recommended the appointmt of another route agent—a white man—This will afford the claim of a triumph over the Govt to those in Kentucky who objected to the employment of a negro in the mail service of the Govt"— DLC-Hamilton Fish. William H. Gibson had been assaulted on Jan. 26. See *CG*, 42–1, 237–39; *Louisville Courier-Journal*, Feb. 1, April 5, 1871; *New York Times*, March 25, 1871.

1871, Nov. 23.   U.S. Senator Adelbert Ames of Miss. to USG. "I have the honor to recommend for appointment as an officer of the army *Jacob R. Pierce* of Mississippi. He is a very intelligent young man—a graduate of a

college. He was recently appointed on the recommendation of the M. C. of
his District as Postmaster of the town of Oxford Miss."—ALS, DNA, RG
94, Applications for Positions in War Dept. On Sept. 28, Ames, Sardis, Miss.,
had written to Horace Porter recommending Jacob R. Pierce.—ALS,
ibid. On Dec. 6, USG nominated Pierce as postmaster, Oxford, Miss.; this
nomination was withdrawn. On Dec. 18, USG nominated Pierce as 2nd lt.,
24th Inf.

1871, Nov. 25. To George B. Loring, Salem, Mass. "Your favor of the 20th,
with enclosure reached me in due time. Please accept my sincere thanks for
the kind expressions towards the administration contained in the article and
letter."—Copy, DLC-USG, II, 1. On Oct. 25, Loring had written to USG. "I
enclose a slip of an address issued by the Republican State Central Committee of Massachusetts—reference to which as forthcoming, I had the honor
to make to you, when I had the pleasure of meeting you in New England.
I am confident that the allusions to your Administration, express the sentiments of the Republican party of this Commonwealth; and I am sure they
will give expression to these sentiments when they elect their delegates for
the National Convention."—ALS, OFH. On Oct. 27, on the back of this
letter, Horace Porter drafted a reply to Loring.—ADf (initialed), *ibid.*; copy,
DLC-USG, II, 1. On Dec. 29, Porter wrote to Loring. "The President directs
me to convey to you his thanks for your kindness in sending him a copy of
your article in the Traveller on 'One term principle.' It is the best argument
on the subject he has yet seen, and cannot help but attract great attention."—Copy, *ibid.* In 1872, Loring wrote to USG supporting his renomination.—William Evarts Benjamin, Catalogue No. 27, Nov., 1889, p. 8.

1871, Nov. 25. Orville E. Babcock to Alexander R. Shepherd, D. C. Board
of Public Works. *"Personal . . .* I hate to worry you but you will be doing the
'Chief Magistrate of our great Republic' and his good lady a great favor if
you will have 17th St. curbed & paved down to 'D.' St. as it is now it will
be almost impossible to get a carriage to the Presidents Stable, and perfectly
impossible to do so without getting it covered with mud. The stable will be
ready for use by the 15th of Dec. I am prepared to have the road properly
paved ~~out as far as~~ from the stable to 17th St. Can you have this done? Of
course the President has not mentioned this subject. I use his name without
any authority,—but I know he will hate to see his carriage come from the
stable all mud as it must if that street is not paved. The curbing is on the
spot. . . . P. S. I make this a personal note as I do not wish it to go on file,
for the N. Y. Sun. and the Capitol would be abusing the President for having
a road to his stable."—ALS, DLC-Alexander R. Shepherd.

1871, Nov. 27. Horace Porter to John L. Thomas, Jr., collector of customs,
Baltimore. "The President directs me to write you and state that, if not
incompatible with the good of the public service, he would be pleased to
have you appoint Mr. E. G. Fast of Washington, to some position in the

Custom House at Baltimore, with a salary of not less than $1800. a year. Upon the receipt of your reply, Mr Fast will be instructed to report to you."—Copy, DLC-USG, II, 1. On Oct. 17, 1872, Edward G. Fast, Baltimore, wrote to Secretary of the Treasury George S. Boutwell requesting that his salary as clerk and interpreter be increased from $1,500 to $1,800 per year.—ALS, DNA, RG 56, Letters from the President.

On Sept. 27, 1866, Bernardin F. Wiget, president, Gonzaga College, Washington, D. C., had written a letter of introduction. "Mr. Gustavus Fast is known to me, having been employed as Professor at this College for some time; & from my personal observation I judge him to be an eminent scholar, especially in Mathematics, Natural Philosophy etc, a gentleman highly educated."—ALS, *ibid.*, RG 94, ACP, F64 CB 1869. See *PUSG*, 17, 499. Born in Germany, Fast was appointed 2nd lt. as of Aug. 17, 1867, and resigned as of Aug. 18, 1868. On Aug. 10, 1869, William H. Brisbane, Horace Greeley, and others, New York City, wrote to USG. "The undersigned respectfully represent: That we regard the services of Lieut Edward G. Fast, late Engineer and Ordnance Officer of the Staff of Maj. Gen. Jeff. C. Davis, Alaska, as having been of great value to the cause of Science and antiquarian research, as well as to the development of the natural resources of our new Territory; That having met with so great success in collecting images, relics vocabularies and other materials for elucidating the history of the Aborigines, and having become familiar with the people and to some extent with their language, we think it very desirable that his services should still be retained in the same department, in order to complete what he has begun— We therefore respectfully solicit for him a reinstatement in his former position, which he was obliged from ill health to resign; and would express our hope that the acceptance of his resignation may be revoked, restoring him to his position, and permitting him, in addition to his official duties, to complete the explorations and researches which his zeal for the honor and advantage of his adopted country has prompted him to undertake."—DS (13 signatures), DNA, RG 94, ACP, F64 CB 1869.

1871, DEC. 1.   To I. Bulson, San Francisco, giving a recipe for whitewash.— *Machinery*, Nov. 1, 1906, no. 51. Probably spurious.

1871, DEC. 1.   To Luther P. Hubbard, secretary, New-England Society, New York City. "I am in receipt of your very kind letter of the 27th ult: and have to thank you for the very cordial invitation extended to me to be present at the dinner of the New England Society on the 22nd inst: I regret exceedingly that I have not yet been able to attend any of the annual dinners of the N: E. Society from the fact that the day selected occurs during the opening of the Session of Congress, at which time my public duties prevent me from leaving the Capital."—Copy, DLC-USG, II, 1. See *New York Times*, Dec. 23, 1871, Sept. 19, 1894.

1871, DEC. 1.   Thomas Bonner, Jr., Ashland, Ala., to USG. "you will Pardon me for the Liberty I'v Thus taken in addressing this note to you. But on the night of the 28th of Nov last their was a collard Boy taken out & floged severly by two men in Disquize, for no known reason, Except he was talking of leaving his employer, when his time Exspired. Sir cannot this be stoped if it is not it will soon be that we cant get hands to cultivate our farmes. This is no Idle tale to make Political Capital off—I am a Democrat never voted a Republican ticket in my Life nor have no inclination to do so, I have but little doubt but what this thing could be stoped or Brought to Light, if some person living here was clothed with the propper authority— if you think Propper you can direct some one to corrisspond with me & I will give my Idia how some off them might be cought, Hoping you will Pardon me for the Liberty I have taking ... P. S. I can give you as good Refference as their is in the State, as to my Being of a Gentleman. Private"— ALS, DNA, RG 60, Letters from the President.

1871, DEC. 1. Jay Cooke, Philadelphia, to USG. "L. M. Johnson, Consul General of Syria, has returned to this country, and has either resigned, or is about to resign his office. The business is in charge of J. Baldwin Hay, a gentleman of the very highest character, who has lately married a step daughter of my brother-in-law, Mr. Moorhead. He has long resided in Syria, at Beyrout with his mother and aunts, and is one of the thirteen life members of the diplomatic corps. He is now in charge of the office, and is in every way qualified for entering upon its active duties having acted as Vice Consul for some years past. He has also been Consul to Jerusalem. American visitors and residents speak in the highest terms of him. He understands Arabic, Greek, French and all the Oriental languages. He is an earnest Christian man, & will do much good in the position he asks for. His appointment as Consul General would give great satisfaction not only to Americans in that country, who sojourn or who may be travelling there, but also to numerous friends here, . . ."—LS, DNA, RG 59, Letters of Application and Recommendation. On the same day, Anthony J. Drexel, Philadelphia, wrote to USG. "It has been a rule with me not to trouble you in regard to appointments of any kind, but I make an exception in the case of Mr J Baldwin Hay who is now vice Consul General of Syria and whom I would like to see raised to be Consul General in place of Mr L. M. Johnson resigned. I know all about Mr Hay and feel assured his appointment would be right and proper on every ground."—ALS, *ibid.* On Dec. 6, Wilbur F. Paddock, Philadelphia, wrote to Adolph E. Borie. ". . . Mr. Hay has lived in the East for many years—speaks Arabic & Greek & the French language fluently—is on good terms with the Turkish Gov. & has served as U. S. Consul in Jaffa & Jerusalem. . . . I write to ask your influence with the President for his promotion to the full Consul Generalship—I am satisfied from all I can learn that he would be an excellent man for the post. Beside this, I am anxious for his Elevation as he is my brother in law having married the sister of my wife the daughter of Mrs Wm G. Moorhead of this city. . . ."—ALS, *ibid.* On Dec. 8, Borie endorsed this letter to USG. "No doubt *patriots* are scarce and I send this for what it may be worth to you, the writer being our Pastor and a very nice man & was *always* very patriotically Republican."—AES, *ibid.* In

[*Dec.*], Bishop Matthew Simpson, Philadelphia, wrote to USG. "Permit me to commend to your attention the application of the friends of Mr Hay, now Vice Consul at Beirut, for the position of Consul General of Syria. . . ."— ALS, *ibid.* Related papers are *ibid.* On Dec. 19, 1871, USG nominated John Baldwin Hay as consul, Beirut. See Hamilton Fish diary, Jan. 13, 1872, DLC-Hamilton Fish.

1871, Dec. 4. To Congress. "I transmit herewith to Congress a report dated, November 8th 1871 received from the Secretary of State, in compliance with the requirement of the Act of March 3d 1871 making appropriations among other things, for the increase of expenses and compensation of certain diplomatic and consular officers of the United States on account of the late war between France and Prussia. The expenditures therein mentioned have been made on my approval."—Copies, DNA, RG 130, Messages to Congress; *ibid.*, RG 59, General Records. *HED*, 42-2-10. On Nov. 8, Secretary of State Hamilton Fish had written to USG providing "the amounts expended on his approval, for the purposes mentioned in the appropriations at the Legations at Madrid, Paris, Berlin and London, and the accompanying correspondence. A further report will hereafter be submitted to you embracing the amount of increased expenses and allowances for extraordinary services to the several consular officers of the United States in France and Algeria."—Copy, DNA, RG 59, General Records. On Dec. 2, 1872, USG transmitted to Congress the supplemental report from Fish, received the same day.—Copies, *ibid.*, Reports to the President and Congress; *ibid.*, RG 130, Messages to Congress. *HED*, 42-3-24.

1871, Dec. 4. To Congress. "I hereby transmit to Congress a report dated the 4th instant, with the accompanying papers received from the Secretary of State in compliance with the requirements of the 18th section of the Act entitled 'An Act to regulate the diplomatic and consular systems of the United States' approved August 18, 1856."—Copies, DNA, RG 130, Messages to Congress; *ibid.*, RG 59, General Records. *HED*, 42-2-9. On the same day, Secretary of State Hamilton Fish had transmitted to USG reports on fees collected by consuls and commercial agents.—Copy, DNA, RG 59, General Records.

1871, Dec. 4. John B. Royce, Berkshire, N. Y., to USG. "You may be a little surprised to receive such a Letter,—from a stranger too,—But I have the utmost confidence in our Chief Executive, & would be happy to do some '*chores*' for him & the people over whome he presides—(if I can be permitted) And the thought strikes me, that I can be of service to my country, as well as Beneficial to an ignorant & Barbarous people, dwelling within the borders of our Country; Say the Indians, within the bounds, & contiguous to the Northwestern Paciffic R. Road   If commissioned & fitted out, say to go to Puget sound & Eastward from there—to obtain an Interpreter & hold council with the Chiefs of the tribes   All the weapons of Defence I would carry would be some very Beautiful little Books of the 1st Rudiments of Learning—nicely Bound & attractive in appearance Especially to the young.— then would try to convince them that I was a very good friend to them.— that I would advise them to make a *lasting* Peace with our Govt—and agree with the Govt for a certain tract of Land to be set off to them,—perhaps between the Line of the N. P. R. Road & the British posessions—or some other place.... Since writing on the 4th have seen of the Success of Comr Vincent Colyer among the S. W. Indians—I don't know but they will have to be Exterminated as some of the tribes were before the *March* of the Israelites to the Land of canaan: have sometimes thought the Govt. ought to '*Lassoo*' them (Figuratively) as the Indians do the wild horses & hold them so they could not hurt themselves or any body & tame, subdue & make them useful,... If you do not want me for the service named—is there any other way I can serve you without going among the Klu Klux—(I think should like Indians better—for safty   Please ans. or Let some one do it for you if you have too much other business to allow you to do so—...."—ALS (completed Dec. 7), DNA, RG 75, Letters Received, Miscellaneous.

1871, Dec. 5.   To Congress reporting "that William Heine, a consular clerk was, on the 30th of August last, removed from the office for the following cause, viz:—insubordination, disobedience of orders, and disrespectful conduct towards his superiors."—DS, DNA, RG 46, Presidential Messages. *HED,* 42-2-8. On Oct. 6, William Heine, Washington, D. C., had written to USG insisting that his removal as consular clerk, Liverpool, arose from reporting "certain illegal ways the Consul used to increase his income." —ALS, DNA, RG 59, Letters of Application and Recommendation. Related papers are *ibid.* See also *ibid.,* RG 94, ACP, H1203 CB 1867; *HRC,* 35-1-25.

1871, Dec. 5.   U.S. Representatives William D. Kelley, Leonard Myers, Alfred C. Harmer, and John V. Creely of Pa. to USG. "Whereas Mr George Gerard of Pennsylvania, lately U. S. Consul at Cape Town, Cape of Good Hope, having informed us, the undersigned, that on the 23d ultimo he sent to the President, through the Department of State a petition praying for a new appointment to a Consulate of Schedule B. This is to recommend the said George Gerard for a continuance in office, believing him fully qualified for the post he now solicits, having rendered himself in his past official transactions worthy of the confidence of the Government"—DS, DNA, RG 59, Letters of Application and Recommendation. On Nov. 5, 1872, George Gerard, Philadelphia, wrote to USG. "Permit me the privilege to congratulate Your Excellency for your reëlection as the Chief Magistrate of the Nation—Having, as citizen, contributed, in Philadelphia, in the work of yesterday, I now heartily rejoice at the *splendid result*; and I pray the Supreme Ruler to bless Your Excellency with perfect health and continued happiness—...."—ALS, USG 3. On Nov. 28, J. Gillingham Fell, Philadelphia, wrote to USG. "There is an old gentleman of Philada well known to many of our best people, Mr George Gerard, Ex Consul at the Cape of Good Hope who is willing to go to Demerara or to Port Stanley both of which he says, are vacant and not desireable, one being sickly and the other out of the world—I promised to write to you and say that he is worthy and that it would be a charity if you could appoint him—"—ALS, DNA, RG 59, Letters of Application and Recommendation. On March 5, 1873, Gerard wrote to USG. *"Personal* . . . With all my heart I congratulate Your Excellency on your second inauguration as our Chief Magistrate—I take this auspicious occasion to remind Your Excellency that I am yet without a Consular appointment—I am mortified to see that I am thus forgotten when the posts at *Jerusalem* and *Demerara* are vacant either of which I would be gratified to fill—Pardon me, Mr President if I presume again to approach Your Excellency in this *free manner*—your own heart invites me to open you mine with candor—you are the source of the Executive gifts—a word to Mr Fish, and I will be happy"—ALS, *ibid.* Related papers are *ibid.* On June 16, 1874, USG nominated Gerard as consul, Port Stanley.

1871, DEC. 6. USG endorsement. "Refered to the Sec. of War. If there are no charges accompanying the recommendation of the Col. of the 1st Art. for musterout of Lieut. Humphreys and if there is a vacancy of 1st Lt. in the Reg.t, he may be nominated for his old position."—AES, DNA, RG 94, ACP, H1141 CB 1864. Written on a recommendation of Feb. 1 from Maj. Godfrey Weitzel. "Mr. B. S. Humphreys who has recently been mustered out of the U S Army upon the recommendation of the Colonel of his regiment served under me more than a year during the late war as Lieutenant in the 1st U-S. Artillery. He was one of the very best duty officers in my command, and he was inferior to none in gallantry and good conduct on the battle field. I write this testimonial with the greatest pleasure as an act of justice to an officer who was once carried past me on the battle-field in a blanket bleeding from several severe wounds received in the honest discharge of his duty."—ALS, *ibid.* On Dec. 12, 1872, USG nominated Ballard S. Humphrey as 2nd lt., 9th Cav. See *ibid.*, 206V CB 1866. On April 24, 1873, George M. Robeson, act. secretary of war, wrote to Attorney Gen. George H. Williams inquiring whether Humphrey was required to refund the one year's pay he received when mustered out in 1870.—Copy, *ibid.*, RG 107, Letters Sent, Military Affairs. See Endorsement, [*Dec. 31, 1870*].

1871, DEC. 6. USG endorsement. "Refered to the Sec. of the Treas."— AES, DNA, RG 56, Appointments Div., Treasury Offices, Letters Received. Written on a letter of Dec. 5, probably from John W. Forney, collector of customs, Philadelphia, to USG. "I have the honor earnestly and sincerely to recommend David W. Mahon Esq., for the last fifteen years chief clerk in the office of the First Auditor of the Treasury for that position, recently vacated by the death of the lamented Major Thomas L. Smith. Mr. Mahon is a native of Pennsylvania, and although . . ."—L (incomplete), *ibid.* On Dec. 14, USG nominated David W. Mahon as first auditor, Treasury Dept.

1871, Dec. 6. Secretary of War William W. Belknap to USG. "I have the honor to present to you a memorial from General Schuyler Hamilton, late an Additional Aide-de-Camp to Lieut-Gen'l Scott, who claims to be an officer of the Regular Army, and asks to be placed on the retired list of the Army with the rank of a Major-General, with such pay and emoluments as he may be by law entitled to, to date from his resignation as 'an officer of the Volunteer service of the United States.'... I think he has no valid claim."—LS, DNA, RG 94, ACP, 4635 1871. On Jan. 4, 1872, Belknap wrote to Schuyler Hamilton, New York City. "The draft of a proposed J[oin]t Resolution of Congress for your relief, has been submitted to the President as requested in your letter of the 23d ultimo transmitting it, and I am directed to inform you that he is disinclined to express an opinion on a private bill in advance of its passage. The draft of the bill is herewith returned."—Copies, *ibid.*; *ibid.*, RG 107, Letters Sent, Military Affairs. On Feb. 12, U.S. Representative Benjamin F. Butler of Mass. introduced a bill for Hamilton's relief; no action followed.—*CG*, 42–2, 973.

In late 1869, when Hamilton sought nomination as minister to Denmark, Butler, Gen. William T. Sherman, and Brig. Gen. John Pope had supported his application.—DNA, RG 59, Letters of Application and Recommendation. On Oct. 15, Hamilton wrote to Sherman. "... I served Genl Grant once— He does not know it—When Halleck was in Command at St. Louis—He seemed to think he must select the Commander for the movement on Donaldson &c from three Genls Curtis—Grant—Pope—My Official opinion was asked as to these three—I said if there were no other reasons to be considered than Military fitness there was no room for a moments hesitation—Grant was the man—giving my reasons—If there were other reasons—He could telegraph & Grant could come up to St. Louis in a few hours—He could then judge by a personal interview of his fitness in other respects—This was done—Grant came up   I was present at the interview—Grant recd. his orders the next day or very shortly—He took Donaldson—Without my suggestion it might have been Pope or Curtis instead of Grant. It was something to secure the opportunity—"—Copy, *ibid.* See *PUSG*, 3, 264; *ibid.*, 19, 160–63.

1871, Dec. 8.   USG endorsement. "Accepted"—AES, DNA, RG 60, Letters Received, Del. Written on a letter of Dec. 6, 1871, from Willard Hall, Wilmington, Del., to USG. "My age, the twenty third day of this month December will, if my life shall be continued, complete my ninety first year, and unusual sickness this last year lead me to present to you and ask you to accept this my resignation of my office of Judge of the District Court of the United States for Delaware District, to which I was appointed by President Monroe May 6th 1823 in vacation of the Senate, and afterward December 9th 1823 by and with the advice and consent of the Senate, I having held it forty eight years and six months...."—ALS, *ibid.*

In Dec., U.S. Senator Simon Cameron of Pa. wrote to USG. "I take the liberty of urging upon your fovorable attention the name of Edwd G Bradford of Wilmington Delaware for Judge. He is a gentleman of fine social and professional standing, while his political leadership in the Republican party is not less promonnent and able. I am impelled to this act by the conviction that his appointment would be both popular and right."—ALS, NNP. USG endorsed this letter. "Atty. Gn."—AE (undated), *ibid.* On Dec. 11, Horace Porter wrote to Attorney Gen. Amos T. Akerman. "The President directs me to request that the nomination of Mr Bradley as U. S. Judge, Delaware Dist be sent to him by 12 o'clock to-day"—LS, DNA, RG 60, Letters from the President. On Dec. 23, Edward G. Bradford, Wilmington, wrote to USG thanking him for the appointment.—ALS, *ibid.*, Letters Received, Del.

1871, DEC. 8. John Fitch, New York City, to USG. "Mr. John D. Cromwell of the City of NewYork applies for the position of Commercial agent at Port au Prince, Hayti. He is a colored man. Was born in Philadelphia emigrated to, and resided in Port au Prince quite a number of years. He is well educated and speaks the Spanish and French languages fluently. He is about fifty years of age; in good health; and every way qualified to fill such a position at that place. His accompanying Petition is correct as to the facts therein stated. He is well known and much respected in NewYork among the colored people as well as others. His appointment would be a good one."—LS, DNA, RG 59, Letters of Application and Recommendation. Related papers are *ibid.*

1871, DEC. 8. Jay Cooke, Philadelphia, to USG. "In common with others interested in the National Banks, we have been greatly pleased with the manner in which Mr. Hulburd has discharged the arduous duties of the Comptroller of the Currency. He has been prompt and efficient and watchful over the interests of his Department. I think he is universally popular with the Banks, or at least as much so as it is possible for one to be who exercises so strict a supervision over them. His recent prompt action at Chicago was an evidence of what a skilful and practical management can do in restoring public confidence. I earnestly urge his re-appointment, and shall feel personally gratified if he is continued in the position which he now so nobly fills."— LS, DNA, RG 56, Appointments Div., Treasury Offices, Letters Received. Petitions to USG recommending Hiland R. Hulburd's reappointment are *ibid.*; an unsigned copy (press) of one is in DLC-James A. Garfield. On Feb. 6, 1872, USG renominated Hulburd as comptroller of the currency. See *Washington Chronicle*, Feb. 6, 1872.

1871, DEC. 9. To Brig. Gen. Joseph K. Barnes, surgeon gen. "Will Surgeon Gen. Barnes please see the bearer, a blind Winnebaga Indian, and advise him if any thing can likely be done to restore his sight."—Swann Auction Galleries, Sale No. 243, Nov. 3, 1949, no. 51.

1871, DEC. 9. USG endorsement. "Refered to the Sec. of War. Let mr Weber be put down as next supernumerary to those already appointed so as

to be notified to enter in Sept. should there then be a vacancy for him."—
AES, DNA, RG 94, Correspondence, USMA. Written on an undated petition
from James Lindsay, pension agent, St. Louis, *et al.* to USG.—DS (23 signatures), *ibid.* On April 24, 1872, John A. Weber, Farmington, Mo., wrote to
USG. "You will doubtless remember, that, upon my calling upon you, in
December last, to see if I could not prevail upon you, to appoint my son
Kossuth W. A. Weber a cadet at large to the military academy at West Point,
you kindly gave me an order, to the Hon. Secretary of War, who informed
me, that, in case three of the ten gentlemen, selected already by you, as
cadets, failed to appear, or were unable to pass the requisite examination—
my son should be the fourth appointed, after the number of ten then appointed by you.... The memorial which I had the honor to present to you,
and on which you endorsed the order above refered to, fully set forth, how,
from the situation of affairs in this District—it being overwhelmingly democratic, and the appointment of cadets, by Democratic Representative in Congress, from this District, being altogether made from among the party
friends of such Representatives—I was compelled to look *only* to *you*, for
aid in behalf of my son; and the indulgent and gracious manner, in which
you listened to my claim, induces me to address you personally now...."
—ALS, *ibid.* Related papers are *ibid.* Kossuth W. A. Weber did not attend
USMA.

1871, DEC. 9.   S. A. Morse, Yorktown, Va., to USG. "I write to ask if you
would appoint to have me appointed for Custom house officer or rather
Collector, at this place, as it need one very much   E. W. Massey, was Collector here some time since, but ~~has~~ is now elected for another office, and by
that we hasve no Collector here. I am a poor Colored man, and honors your
ability and hoping you may or have me appointed for the office I has aforesaid. Trusting my request be granted. Please give me an answer to this
soon."—ALS, DNA, RG 56, Collector of Customs Applications. On Feb. 1,
1873, Edmund W. Massey, collector of customs, Yorktown, wrote to USG
resigning and "recommending my very efficient special Deputy James J Mc-
Donald for the position thus made vacant...."—ALS, *ibid.* On Feb. 28, James
J. McDonald, Yorktown, wrote to USG recommending Thomas E. Milstead
as collector of customs, Yorktown.—ALS, *ibid.* On March 21, USG nominated Milstead; on March 23, the Senate tabled this nomination; on Dec. 1,
USG renominated Milstead; on Dec. 18, the Senate confirmed this nomination.

1871, DEC. 11.   U.S. Senator Oliver P. Morton of Ind. to USG. "I enclose
to you a letter addressed to me by E. D. Mansfield of Morrow, Ohio. Mr
Mansfield is an able political writer and has long been connected with the
Cincinnati Gazette; in fact, I do not know any man connected with the newspaper press of the Northwest who has rendered greater services to the Republican party than E. D. Mansfield. He has been a steady and consistent
Republican and a warm and active friend of yourself, having vindicated your

course in regard to Santo Domingo and Mr Sumner with ability from the start. He is a man of great labor, and has been distinguished for his knowledge of statistics and for the industry with which he has collected facts for the preparation of important articles. He is in very moderate circumstances and needs employment, and I take pleasure in commending him to your consideration. This letter will state the kind of labor for which he is particularly fitted; and I should be gratified if something could be found for him to do which would afford him a reasonable compensation"—LS, OFH. On Dec. 14, Orville E. Babcock wrote to Secretary of the Interior Columbus Delano. "The President will be pleased to have you read these letters and return them to him. If you desire the services of Mr: Mansfield the President will be pleased to have him employed."—Copy, DLC-USG, II, 1. On Dec. 27, Delano endorsed papers to USG. "I have addressed a letter to Mr Mansfield enclosing a copy of the report of the Commissioner of Education, (within.) and advising Mr M. to place himself in correspondence with the Commissioner in order to arrange matters as suggested by Gen Eaton."—AES, OFH. Edward D. Mansfield, USMA 1819, wrote several books, including *A Popular and Authentic Life of Ulysses S. Grant* (Cincinnati, 1868).

1871, DEC. 13. USG endorsement. "I have no objection to the Apt. of Gn. Wessell's son. to an Inf. Regt."—AES, DNA, RG 94, ACP, 531 1872. Written on a letter of the same day from Henry W. Wessells, Washington, D. C., to USG. "I have the honor to make application for the appointment of my son Morris C Wessells. as a 2d Lieutenant in the Army, when it can be done in the interests of the Service—If necessary, I can procure testimonials from reliable Officers of the Army . . . Age.18.6 mos"—ALS, *ibid.* USG appointed Morris C. Wessells 2nd lt. as of Dec. 18. On Feb. 14, 1872, Henry Wessells, New York City, wrote to Frederick T. Dent. "The boy got his commission and is already en route to join his Regt. in Texas—We are under infinite obligations to you for your courtesy and influence in this matter, and I trust the youngster will do credit to himself and the Service—Although from a democratic locality in Connecticut, his relatives are all warm supporters of the Administration, and being the Son of an old Officer of the Army, I feel as if the President is justified in making the appointment—Wishing you all kinds of prosperity, . . . That 'cuss' Greeley, dont care for the one term—it is all malignant spite—"—ALS, ICarbS. See *PUSG,* 19, 287.

1871, DEC. 14. John M. Gordon to USG ridiculing his administration. —Pamphlet, Gordon, *Tableau, No. 15, Containing a Letter to General U. S. Grant,* . . . (1871).

1871, DEC. 17. Ann Nash, Morris, Minn., to USG. "I take the pen to send you a few lines   you Must not take it bad up for riting to you a stranger My husband Albert Nash when he was in the armey he sent me your pictur he sad you was the best Man in the armey and that is what Made me Dare rite to you   I was living in Democrat setlement and after he went to the armey they ruend me in—Evry way they could so that was I frade for my life   so I heard that the Soldrs should get land, then Sold out went Round looking for land   I found a good peace of land   when I came to the land-office and wanted the land for the Dead Soulder Albert Nash the Nothary said ther is no land for the Dead Soulder . . ."—ALS, DNA, RG 48, Miscellaneous Div., Letters Received.

1871, DEC. 17.   John F. Neville, St. Louis, to USG. "I most respectfully call your attention to the following facts, relating to my services, and detention of my pay for said service, with request that you will please give the same a consideration. . . . I have been deprived of my pay for services of one half month in the 7th Mo, Vol,—And four months pay in the 40th Mo, Vol, and 3 month pay proper, allowed to Officers who were in Service betwen March 9th, and April 9th, 1865,   I have filed a claim with Congress, which is now in the hands of the Committe on claims. I am in needy circumstances, and the little pittance due me would at this time releive myself and family from great want. I trust your Excellency will render me such aid as may be in your power towards getting Justice done me   Trusting you will favorably consider my petition . . ."—ALS, DNA, RG 233, 43A–D1. See *PUSG*, 7, 514; *ibid.*, 9, 600; *House Journal*, 41–2, p. 554.

1871, DEC. 18:   Elias W. Fox, surveyor of customs, St. Louis, to USG. "The real-estate firms of '*Lanham* & *Long*', and '*H. W. Leffingwell & Co*'—both of this city, are desirous of being placed in charge of the sale of the Arsenal property whenever the Gov't is prepared to put it in the market. I take pleasure in recommending the services of these gentlemen and beg that you will so far interest yourselves in their behalf as to name them to the proper bureau officer having the matter in charge. I feel sure no better selections of Agents could be made, the old time residence and well known probity of both firms being sufficient guaranty that they will well discharge the trust. I will simply add that it will be agreeable to both firms to act in conjunction in the management of the sale."—LS, DNA, RG 156, Letters Received. See *U.S. Statutes at Large*, XV, 187–88; J. Thomas Scharf, *History of Saint Louis City and County*, . . . (Philadelphia, 1883), I, 534–36.

1871, DEC. 18.   Mary C. Grant, Altoona, Pa., to USG. "you no doubt, will Be surprised on recipt of a letter, from a stranger, pardon the presumption I take in addressing you. I some time past Learned of your whair abouts, and Learned, of your kindness, to soaldiers widdows. . . . if I Could procure some means, or other, to get a sewing machine, I Could then get a long, . . ."—ALS, DNA, RG 48, Miscellaneous Div., Letters Received.

1871, DEC. 21.   Secretary of War William W. Belknap to USG. "The enclosed letter from a correspondent of Hon. F. P. Blair, which you referred to the Hon. Atty. General for his recomdn in the premises, having reference to the case of John Pryor late of the 6th Indiana Vols., who was tried and convicted by a General Court Martial, and is now undergoing sentence, has been forwarded to this Department, and I therefore beg to state, briefly, for your information the facts of the case.—John Pryor late of Co. "I", 6th Inda Vols., and one James L. Stilf[e]x, a private of Co. "B", 9th Mass. Vols., Infy, were a part of the guard of a train of wagons on the way from Fort Ridgeley to Fort Snelling. On the morning of July 29. 1865, the former told the comdg officer of the guard that Stilfex had stolen his pocket book, & that 'he was after him.' Although forbidden to interfere with Stilfex, he proceeded to the wagon in which his victim was sitting, and after demanding his pocket book, raised his gun, which he held in his hand during the conversation with the officer, & deliberately shot him through body, killing him almost instantly, and wounding another man. The records show that his trial was perfectly fair and impartial, & that he failed to establish his defense, which was 'intoxication', when the crime was committed. He was convicted of murder and sentenced to be hung—which sentence was approved by General Pope, in Sept 1865, but after repeated and urgent solicitation the President commuted his sentence to imprisonment for life—Many petitions have been presented and different statements made with a view to his pardon, and five different reports have been made on the case by the J. A. G., who has thoroughly examined it, but the Dept. still holds, as heretofore, in the absence of satisfactory proof to the contrary, that the homicide was a deliberate murder, perpetrated in pursuance of a threat and prompted by a malice, openly avowed; and the assault was so unprovoked that the punishment already suffered is not regarded as sufficient atonement for the crime."— Copy, DNA, RG 107, Letters Sent, Military Affairs. On Feb. 10, 1872, Belknap wrote to U.S. Senator Francis P. Blair, Jr., of Mo. on this subject.— Copy, *ibid.* See Johnson, *Papers,* 9, 225, 227.

1871, DEC. 23. William M. Evarts, New York City, to USG. "I venture to ask your favorable attention in behalf of an application which will be made to you for the appointment of Mr. J. De F. Richards to some office which will furnish a respectable support for his family, for which Mrs. Evarts & myself feel a very strong interest. Senator Spencer, of Alabama, and Mrs. Richards have already brought the circumstances of the case to your notice. They seem to appeal very forcibly to the favor of the Government in Mr. Richards' behalf. His efforts, as a pioneer in the movement which was to carry the wealth and industry and intelligence of the Northern people to supply the wastes at the South, maintain the new order of society produced by emancipation, and rebuild the ruined loyalty of the community there, have resulted in the proscription of himself, and the loss of the very considerable property which he embarked in the undertaking. . . ."—ALS, DNA, RG 59, Letters of Application and Recommendation. J. DeForest Richards, Congregational minister, moved to Ala. (1865). Professor at the University of Alabama (1869–71), he died at Mobile in 1872.

1871, DEC. 24. George Deshon, New York City, to USG. "I write this letter at the request of Mr Joseph Marrin a particular friend of mine and guardian of Cadet Francis Marrin, to ask a special favor. I understand an application will be made to you for a leave of absence for Cadet Marrin. Genl Sickles will present the application and he will inform you of the particulars of the case, which are also known to me. Now my old friend do strain a point, if you can, to bring about the success of this application There ought to be a dispensing power somewhere, when regulations become oppressive. I hope this young man who is talented and well behaved, will have an opportunity afforded him to recover his health and go on with his studies. I am already in debted to you for several favors, although the last one in Mccarthy's case proved abortive in consequence of the Senate not acting upon your nomination made so kindly at my request. I hope better success this time. Now, my old friend, what is the use of having your old classmate & roommate the President of the United States if he does not grant a favor now & then to his oldest & most familiar friends. I rely entirely on your good will in this case and wishing every prosperity & happiness . . ."—ALS, DNA, RG 94, Correspondence, USMA. On Dec. 26, John Morrissey, New York City, wrote to USG. "Cadet Francis J. Marrin, now at West Point, was appointed on my nomination, whilst I was a representative in Congress. He is an orphan, whose eldest brother was killed at the first battle of Bull Run and whose mother, a widow, became insane and died in consequence. Cadet Marrin was carefully educated by his relatives and is a young gentleman of fine talents and of engaging and soldiery qualities. A youthful indiscretion, for which I do not apologize but which may nevertheless be pardoned, and the effect of which was not known to himself or apparent when he entered the Academy, produced some time ago a soreness of throat which compelled him to abstain from class and leaves him, now that he is well, unduly prepared for his examination. His guardian, Mr. Joseph J. Marrin, a member of the New York bar and a valued friend of mine, requests for him a leave of absence for seven months, in order that he may continue with the class of 1872, being assured by eminent physicians of this city that, by special treatment during that time, the disturbing cause referred to may be eradicated. I cordially endorse the application for leave of absence and hope it may be favorably considered and granted."—LS, *ibid.* On Jan. 9, 1872, Daniel E. Sickles, minister to Spain, New York City, wrote to Orville E. Babcock on the same subject.—LS, *ibid.* Francis J. Marrin entered USMA in 1871 but did not graduate. For Deshon, see *PUSG*, 9, 478–79.

1871, DEC. 27. To Fr. Dahm, Sandusky County, Ohio. "I am in receipt of your very kind letter, and also the Keg of wine, Please accept many thanks for both, but especially for the very kind sentiment contained in the letter."—Copy, DLC-USG, II, 1.

1871, DEC. 27. To Samuel F. Miller, U.S. Supreme Court, introducing Benjamin F. Tracy, U.S. attorney, Eastern District, N. Y.—Parke-Bernet Sale, Oct. 13, 1964. See *PUSG*, 19, 374.

1871, DEC. 28. David Klein, New York City, to USG demanding compensation for patented pontoon bridges allegedly used by the U.S. Army.—ALS, DNA, RG 77, Accounts, Property Returns, and Claims, Letters Received.

Related papers, including a letter of Dec. 15, 1873, from Klein to USG, are
ibid. See *HRC*, 43-1-318.

[*1871*]. USG note. "I have no objection to the name of M. L. Woolsey
being placed as supernumerary next below those already named for West
Point in the class of /73."—ANS, DNA, RG 94, Correspondence, USMA.
On Dec. 14, 1871, Commodore Melancthon B. Woolsey, Washington, D. C.,
wrote to USG. "I take the liberty of trespassing upon your valuable time
for a few minutes, for the purpose of making an appeal to your Excellency
in behalf of my son, *Melancthon Lloyd Woolsey,* who is now in his 17th year,
and is studying at the Polytechnic Institute at Brooklyn, N. Y., with the
hope, that he may receive by your authority, an appointment at large, as the
son of an Officer, to enter the Military Academy at West Point. I would
respectfully urge, in his behalf, the long military service of his family: for,
should he be so fortunate as to receive this appointment, he will continue
to the fifth generation, in direct succession, the devotion of his family to the
Army and Navy of our Country. I respectfully append hereto, a synopsis of
historical record of the above named facts."—LS, *ibid.* The enclosure is *ibid.*
Melancthon L. Woolsey did not attend USMA.

1871. Benjamin H. Brewster to USG concerning political support for USG
in Pa.—*The Collector,* April, 1909, p. 104. See *PUSG,* 19, 223–25.

1871. U.S. Senator William P. Kellogg of La. to USG concerning patronage.—William Evarts Benjamin, Catalogue No. 27, Nov., 1889, p. 7.

1871. Brig. Gen. Montgomery C. Meigs to USG commending an appointment to the Naval Academy.—William Evarts Benjamin, Catalogue No. 27,
Nov., 1889, p. 8.

1871. Samuel Ward to USG about "a fee which will be pronounced reasonable by any one familiar with the constant struggle of red tape and circumlo-
cution against any money claim, however just and equitable."—William
Evarts Benjamin, Catalogue No. 27, Nov., 1889, p. 10. Also in 1871, Ward
wrote to Orville E. Babcock concerning a mutual acquaintance: "He is little
better than a swindler, and is an unfit person to have anything to do with
the Executive."—*Ibid.,* Catalogue No. 42, March, 1892, p. 22.

1872, JAN. 3. Horace Porter to U.S. Senator Henry B. Anthony of R. I.
"The President directs me to acknowledge the receipt of your note of the
31st ult:, and the safe arrival of the Naragansett turkey which you were
kind enough to send him, He wishes me to convey to you his sincere thanks
for your thoughtfulness and say that the turkey proved a very fine one
indeed and any State might be proud to raise it."—Copy, DLC-USG, II, 1.

1872, JAN. 3. Horace Porter to Mrs. N. M. Fellhousen, Albany, N. Y. "The
President directs me to acknowledge the receipt of your letter and the safe

arrival of the fowls. He wishes me to give you many thanks for them and more especially for the kind sentiments which prompted the gift. They are very handsome and he will have good care taken of them."—Copy, DLC-USG, II, 1.

1872, JAN. 3.   Horace Porter to John W. Forney, collector of customs, Philadelphia. "The President desires me to acknowledge the receipt of your letter of the 30th ult: and thank you for the enclosed article. The facts are new to most readers and their publication will serve a good purpose."—Copy, DLC-USG, II, 1. Forney wrote weekly articles for the *Washington Sunday Chronicle* and *Philadelphia Press*, collected in his *Anecdotes of Public Men* (New York, 1873).

1872, JAN. 3.   Patrick Donnelly, Buffalo, to USG. "I hope you will excuse me for taking the liberty of writing you this letter which I would not dare to do only I think I have some small claim on the Government and is at present in poor circumstances. The object of me writing is to try and obtain some Government Employment so as I could earn a comfortable living for myself and Famly. I have tried hard to find employment here in Buffalo and having no means of going elswhare I have to remain. It is hard to get work in Buffalo without a man have friends to put him in. I enlisted in the U. S Army the first day of march 1860 at Boston Mass Lieut Van Vost being then Recruiting officer. . . . My second enlistment expired on the 18th day of July 1867 at Fort Porter Buffalo N. Y. Failing in my expectations after being Discharged only some 21 days I enlisted for the 3rd time in the 4th U. S Arty at Fort Delaware Del. and finely was Discharged at Fort Macon N. C. on the 13th of August 1870 after a continued service of 10 years 5 months & 12 days. If long and faithful service is recognized as a merit I hope to obtain one of the thousand situations in the gift of the Government. After being Discharged last time I had a little money saved and started a small business here in Buffalo But failed owing to ignorance of the Business a man after serving so long seems out of his element and to compete with Veteran dealers he have a small chance of success. And every situation is controled by some clique of Politians or socities. So that a stranger have no chance without Friends to get in to any of them   the Employment I wish to get here is letter Carring, or anything Else they chose to put me to being thank ful for any kind of work   I would have no objection to leave Buffalo whereever they chose to send me   When I left they army if I had went to Kansas or Nebaraska and took up a claim I would have been better off to day and have a home of my own   But I did not understand the law that time & now when I do understand it I have not the means of doing so. . . ." —ALS, DNA, RG 59, Letters of Application and Recommendation.

1872, JAN. 7.   William H. Haskell, president, Republican General Committee *et al.*, Albany, N. Y., to USG. "We the undersigned Republicans of the City of Albany, most respectfully present to you the name of P H White, late Captain of the Chicago Mercantile Battery, for consideration. . . ."—DS

(5 signatures), DNA, RG 59, Letters of Application and Recommendation. On Feb. 1, Isaac F. Quinby, Rochester, wrote to USG. "The bearer of this letter Captain P. H. White formerly of Chicago Mercantile Battery really needs no introduction to you for without doubt you well remember him as being under your command during the first two or three years of the late War. . . ."—ALS, *ibid.* On Feb. 8, Patrick H. White, Albany, wrote to USG. "I have the honor to ask for the appointment of Consul to St Johns N. B. as regards my qualifications Services to my country during the late rebellion &c I would respectfully refer you to the letters and petition herewith Enclosed. and to Page 319 Badeau life of Grant. if I would be thankfull for any place in your gift."—ALS, *ibid.* No appointment followed.

1872, JAN. 8. To House of Representatives. "In answer to a resolution of the House of Representatives of the 6th of December, requesting to be informed if any further action is necessary by Congress to secure the immediate temporary preservation of the archives or public records now in the State Department, I transmit a report and accompanying papers from the Secretary of State"—Copies, DNA, RG 59, General Records; *ibid.*, RG 130, Messages to Congress. *HED*, 42-2-42. On the same day, Secretary of State Hamilton Fish had written to USG. "The Secretary of State, . . . respectfully refers to the report of Theodore W. Dimon, the Disbursing Clerk and Superintendent of the building occupied by the Department of State, for the particulars of a fire which broke out in the building on the evening of December 5, . . ."—Copy, DNA, RG 59, General Records. On Dec. 6, 1871, Fish had recorded in his diary a conversation with USG. "I mentioned to him the fire that had happened, & my solicitude for the preservation of the Archives &c, & that I should ask the Secr of the Treasury to give me the use of a fire proof room or two, for the deposit of the Rolls Archives &c—which he approved—"—DLC-Hamilton Fish.

1872, JAN. 8. Field W. Thompson, Newport, R. I., to USG. "I have the honor to apply to youre Exclency by advice of My friends in the City of Newport for A Cituation in the Goverment employ as Fort Keeper at Fort Taper Newbedford Mass or Some other Cituation which I would be Capable of atending to as I am prety well worn out after twenty nine years Servise in the united States army twenty years in the 4th Infantry Co B. as bugler Known to youre Exclency by the name of Tabe. Nine years in Batery B. 3rd Arty Seven of Which I was first Sergant   I have Very good recomdation from My Company Commanders   I have A young famly Calling on Me for Suport and I am not able to do hard work   youre Exclence will please remember an old Solde[r] Who Served throw the Mexican War an the rebelan   With respect youre Exclency I wait the results of this reques[t]"— ALS, DNA, RG 107, Appointment Papers.

1872, JAN. 9. Governor James M. Harvey of Kan. *et al.* to USG. "The undersigned believing that Kansas should be recognized in the selection of officers for the new Territories in consequence of her early history, identifying her citizens with border life in all its phases. They gave the first vital existence to a real party whose purposes were to restrain the spread of slavery, and they were successful. Kansas is the birth place of the Republican party. Her people have never avoided the discharge of any duty that would give strength to those principles, or security to the government. Yet with such a history, she has never had a Govenor of any one of the new Territories appointed from any of her citizens, save one, and that one was a Democrat. In seeking that recognition we would respectfully request the appointment of the Hon James F Legate to be Govenor of Washington Territory, believing him eminently fit for the position by his culture, experience in public life and his integrity of character, and sound Republicanism."—DS (100 signatures), DNA, RG 59, Letters of Application and Recommendation. On Oct. 13, 1871, and Jan. 9, 1872, Secretary of State Hamilton Fish wrote in his diary. "President directs me to write to Govr Solomon of Washington territory, to the effect that the charges against him are such that his resignation will be accepted—He says that Garfield (the delegate from the Territory) represents a very strong feeling adverse to his continuance in office— It is stated that Solomon attempted to *bribe* the Treasury Agent—" "President hands me resignation of Ed. S. Salomon as Governor of Washington territory to take effect 6th Apl—I ask if he intends to allow him to remain in office until that time—he says yes—I regret for he has misbehaved & ought to be removed at once, not allowed to resign—still less to defer the date of his resignation   President directs nomination of James F. Legatt of Kansas, in his place"—DLC-Hamilton Fish. See *PUSG,* 20, 350–52.

On May 18, 1871, U.S. Senators Samuel C. Pomeroy and Alexander Caldwell of Kan. had written to Fish recommending that James F. Legate "be appointed Governor or Secretary of a Territory."—LS, DNA, RG 59, Letters of Application and Recommendation. Related papers are *ibid.* On Jan. 10, 1872, USG nominated Legate as governor, Washington Territory. On Jan. 23, U.S. Delegate Selucius Garfielde of Washington Territory wrote to USG. "I respectfully but earnestly request the withdrawal of the name of James F. Legatt as Governor of Washington Territory, and the appointment of Col. Elijah P. Ferry, of Olympia in said territory, to that position. By reference to 'Reports of Committees' No. 47 to 84, 2nd Session 40th Congress, from page 4 to 12, it will be seen that Mr Legatt, to say the least, was engaged in most disreputable and dishonorable actions in connection with the impeachment trial of Andrew Johnson, then President. The man who has admitted that he was engaged, for pay, in an attempt to bribe U. S. Senators, is not a suitable person to hold high position under a just and patriotic administration. Aside from the record above cited, many persons now in this city, both resident and non-resident, unite in bearing testimony to his moral unfitness for the position to which he has been nominated. The signatures to the enclosed letter bear testimony to Col. Ferry's good character, integrity and ability, to which I cheerfully subscribe. He is now residing in the territory where he has won the confidence of the people and acquired

a high character for public usefulness. At the time Col. Ferry was appointed
Surveyor General by your Excellency, he was an applicant for the position
of Governor which he did not receive for the assigned reason that he was
not a citizen of the territory. That objection is now removed. His appointment would promote the interests of the territory and of the party. In any
event and under all circumstances I desire to enter my earnest protest
against sending a man to my territory to fill this high position whose character and record are clouded as darkly as that of James F. Legatt."—ALS, *ibid.*
The enclosed letter of Jan. 15 from U.S. Representative John F. Farnsworth
of Ill. to USG, endorsed by U.S. Senators Lyman Trumbull and John A.
Logan of Ill., U.S. Representatives John L. Beveridge, John B. Hay, Jesse H.
Moore, and Horatio C. Burchard of Ill., U.S. Representative Horace Maynard
of Tenn., and U.S. Senator Thomas W. Ferry of Mich., is *ibid.* On Jan. 26,
the Senate confirmed Legate. On Feb. 1, U.S. Senator Charles Sumner of
Mass. moved reconsideration of this confirmation. On Feb. 6, Orville E.
Babcock wrote to Legate. "I enclose the papers, and the President desires
that you return them to him after you have made the use of them you
wish"—LS, *ibid.* On April 9, USG wrote to the Senate. "I hereby withdraw,
at his own request, the nomination of James F. Legatt, sent to the Senate
January 10th 1872, to be Governor of the Territory of Washington."—DS,
ibid., RG 46, Nominations. See *HRC*, 40-2-75.

On Oct. 11, 1871, Farnsworth, St. Charles, Ill., had written to USG.
"I earnestly recommend the appointment of Col E. P. Ferry, Governor of
Washington Territory—in case there is to be a *change*. Colonel Ferry is at
present the Surveyor General of that Territory, tho formerly a citizen of my
district—. . ."—ALS, DNA, RG 59, Letters of Application and Recommendation. On April 24, 1872, USG nominated Elisha P. Ferry as governor, Washington Territory. See *PUSG*, 19, 373.

On Sept. 14, 1871, U.S. Senator John Scott of Pa. wrote to USG. "I
forward with this the letter of Gen. Morehead endorsing as a proper person
to be appointed Govenor of Washington Territory, Gen Charles Albright of
Mauch Chunk, Carbon Co. Penna. I cordially concur in all that Gen Morehead has said, having personal knowledge of Gen Albright and knowing
that he deserves all that is said of him. He has moreover, recently been a
traveler and careful observer through that region, and I am satisfied would
make a popular and efficient administrative officer"—ALS, DNA, RG 59,
Letters of Application and Recommendation. The enclosure is *ibid.* In an
undated letter, Bishop Matthew Simpson wrote to USG. "Learning that a
change may occur in the Governorship of Washington Territory, and that
the friends of Genl. Albright have presented his name, it gives me pleasure
to say that I am acquainted with the Genl and believe him to be in every
way, worthy of such a position. He is a gentleman of fine attainments, of
business habits and ability, of strict integrity and of firm devotion to the
interests of his country. He was associated with Gov ~~Geary~~ Reeder in Kansas, and you know his record in the recent war. The District in which he
lives has a large opposition majority, but he has been and is an unflinching

supporter of the Administration. I doubt whether a more judicious appoint-ment cd be made, if there is a vacancy, and it can be filled from Pennsylva-nia."—ALS, *ibid.* On Sept. 18, Charles Albright, Mauch Chunk, wrote to U.S. Senator Simon Cameron of Pa. "I enclose a letter from Bishop Simpson to the President, which I trust you will use in my behalf in securing me the Governorship of Washington Try. I assure you Genl, ~~that~~ you will please many of your friends in giving me a helping hand."—ALS, *ibid.* On Sept. 29, U.S. Representative Lazarus D. Shoemaker of Pa., Wilkes-Barre, wrote to Cameron recommending Albright.—ALS, *ibid.* Cameron endorsed this letter to USG.—AES, *ibid.*

On Feb. 23, 1872, William E. Dodge *et al.*, New York City, petitioned USG. "The undersigned Citizens of New York City take great pleasure in recommending to your favourable Consideration for the Appointment to the Office of Governor of Washington Territory Richard D Lathrop Esq late of this city now resident of Kansas. Mr L. for a great number of years was the head of one of our largest mercantile Houses of this city and during the War of the Rebellion this House was among the first to offer bounties to volunteers for enlistment besides contributing largely and nobly for the Support of those principels for which So much blood and treasure were expended. Mr L has always been a consistent Republican and during the many years of his mercantile life in our midst has borne an irreproachable character for honesty and integrity and we would regard his appointment to this honourable office as adding another testimony to the disposition of our honoured Chief Magistrate to place none but honest and Competent men in places of public trust and high position."—DS (43 signatures), *ibid.* On March 2, Richard D. Lathrop, "Late of New York City now of Ottawa Franklin County Kansas," Washington, D. C., wrote to USG. "I am very sorry to learn through our mutual friend Honl George Opdyke of New York, that your Excellency cannot consistently grant my petition for the appointment to the Governorship of Washington Territory, which I had much desired, please allow me to hand your Excellency with this note, my application for that office, and personal letters regarding it, that you may see the character of my endorsement. Many of the names are known to your Excellency, . . . May I not ask ~~your~~ the favorable remembrance of your Excellency should any thing hereafter offer in your gift which you may think may be of advantage to me either in this or any country. Wishing your Excellency most triumphant success as I assuredly believe you will have, in the approaching campaign . . ."—ALS, *ibid.* Related papers are *ibid.* No appointment followed.

In Feb., U.S. Senator Cornelius Cole of Calif., *et al.*, had written to USG. "The undersigned cordially recommend R. Guy McClellan of San Francisco for Governor of Washington Territory."—LS (5 signatures), *ibid.*

1872, JAN. 10. USG endorsement. "Refered to the Sec. of War. I have no objection ~~the~~ to the apt."—AES, DNA, RG 94, ACP, V27 CB 1870. Written on a letter of Nov. 28, 1871, from Col. Rufus Ingalls, New York City, to

USG. "Permit me to ask your favorable consideration of the application of Capt G. von Blücher for the position of Lieutenant in our Regular Army, I remember Capt von Blücher as an Officer who served during the War on the Staff of Maj. General R. O. Tyler and in other capacities with great credit to himself. He is a gentleman of superior Culture and intelligence, and I consider that his reappointment would be of advantage to the service. For the Cavalry he would make a skillful, brave and dashing officer."—Copy, *ibid.* On Dec. 1, von Blücher wrote to USG. "I have the honor most respectfully to apply for an appointment as 2nd Lieutenant in the Regular Army. I resigned my position as 1st Lieut in October 1870 for the purpose of taking up arms in the Franco-Prussian War, which I could not have done as an Officer of the U. S. Army. The War there being over, and having previously settled in the United States, I have returned to this my adopted Country. I respectfully call your Excellency's attention to enclosed recommendations and to records now on file in the War Department, as to my conduct during and since the war, which will show that I have always performed my duty, to the utmost extent of my ability, and as a true Officer and Soldier of the Republic.—Hoping that your Excellency will favorably consider my Application."—ALS, *ibid.* Related papers are *ibid.* On Aug. 17, 1872, Secretary of War William W. Belknap wrote to AG Edward D. Townsend. "Gustav Von Blucher, by direction of the President, to be appointed 2nd Lieutenant. Before appointment is issued, however, he should be notified that he will be required to refund the years pay drawn by him—"—AN (initialed), *ibid.* On Aug. 19, von Blücher wrote to Townsend agreeing to refund the year's pay drawn by him in Oct., 1870.—ALS, *ibid.* On Oct. 8, 1872, A. F. Higgs, Philadelphia, wrote to Belknap. "IMPORTANT ... I see published this A M the appointment of Gustav Von Blucher of West Va to be 2nd Liut—At this time when evry supporter of the Administration has his hands full beating down calumnies against it and the Executive, to see the *re* appointment of this scallawag, known to so many people as such, causes one to reflect if there is any limit to mistakes—Blucher resigned to go to Prussia to fight against the French, a pretty business to begin with— While stationed at Governors Island he lived openly with a woman whom he passed off for his Wife. His legal wife whom he married in Harpers Ferry came on to New York and requested Capt D. J. Young M S K of Ord to get from the officers a certificate to that fact, in order that she might claim a divorce   however, they made up some way, he bringing up a contra case against her for a little bit of business with Lt Miller of the old 16th Infy at Atlanta, which Blucher formerly belonged to, & which was found out by intercepted letters sent from Miller to Mrs B through a negro girl employed by Blucher & who accesuses him of being a good *friend also to her* (the negro girl)   While in business Cor Broad & Exchange Place I often saw Blucher visiting an office for the purpose of getting his pay acts cashed three & four months ahead, . . ."—ALS, *ibid.* On Dec. 6, USG nominated von Blücher as 2nd lt., 22nd Inf.

On June 10, 1875, Col. David S. Stanley, Fort Wayne, Mich., wrote to

asst. AG, Div. of the Atlantic. "Enclosed please find the resignation of 2d
Lieut Gustav Von Blücher 22d Infantry accompanied by Charge & specifications preferred against him. Notwithstanding the serious nature of the
charge, I recommend that his resignation be accepted and that the charges
be filed with his resignation. I make this recommendation because so far as
is now known, the government has not suffered loss, and there is no remedy
for the persons defrauded, as Lieut Von Blücher has but little property, and
his debts here are large, and he has debts wherever he has been, for the
time, he has been in the service, since his reappointment in the Army   I
am reliably informed that he resigned from the 9th Infty under charges, but
I had no intimation of the bad character of this officer until my attention
was called to his case, by his brutal abandonment of his sick family, leaving
them without any means for their subsistence last winter. I am now convinced that the man is simply a rascally profligate. Another reason for permitting him to resign is that the witnesses are widely scattered and to Court
Martial him will be tedious and expensive . . ."—LS, *ibid.* Von Blücher was
charged with simultaneously pledging his May, June, and July, 1875, pay to
satisfy four separate debts.—D, *ibid.* On June 25, Belknap accepted von Blücher's resignation.—AES, *ibid.*

1872, JAN. 10. A. P. Bickmore, Hyde Park, Mass., to USG. "There is about
to be a Company of fifty members orgniesed in this vacnaty to locate one
one of the Islands in the Southern Pasiffic And wish your honor to point
out the largest and most furtile one. that belongs to the United States oOne
in the most direct line of ocean steamers so at anytime it could be used as
a coal station. And also please state what aid you think Goverment would
lend in protecting said colony from the Natives untill said colony could
provide measures to protect themselves   Said company will be organized at
once and will compise men of the Grand Army mostly all smart industerous
and mostely temperate.   will all will be actual cetlers If your honor sees fit
to answer the above, . . ."—ALS, DNA, RG 59, Miscellaneous Letters.

1872, JAN. 13. Archbishop of Oregon City Francis N. Blanchet, Portland,
to USG. "Being perfectly convinced that it is of the utmost importance for
the Head of the Executive to be kept well posted with the matters individuals may have to heat with his Ministers, I had the honor to forward for your
excellency's information, in the beginning of November 1871, a letter and a
pamphlet containing my correspondances with Gen. Parker and Hon. C
Delano, Secretary of Interior, on the Subject of the rights of our Church
to certain Catholic Indian reservations, and the unjust distribution of the
assignments. Your polite acknowledgment of the receipt of my communication with a return of thanks was duly appreciated. I have also sent to your
excellency, not long ago, a copy of my letter of December 28, in answer to
that of Hon. Delano of December 6th, concerning the offer of the Klamath
agency. And because my last of the 11th instant to Hon. C Delano contains
my thanks for the Klamath agency and the restoration of the grand Ronde

reservation to its owners, I consider it to be for me a very pleasant duty, not only to transmit to you a copy of the same, but also to offer to your excellency, by the present, my best acknowledgments and thanks for this noble act of justice, in which you have had the greatest share. I beg of Almighty God to bless you and reward you for your good dispositions to render equal justice to all."—LS, InNd. Enclosed in a Jan. 18 letter from Blanchet to Archbishop of Cincinnati John B. Purcell, also enclosing Blanchet's letters of Dec. 28, 1871 and Jan. 11, 1872 to Secretary of the Interior Columbus Delano.—*Ibid.* See Annual Message, Dec. 5, 1870; Peter J. Rahill, *The Catholic Indian Missions and Grant's Peace Policy: 1870–1884* (Washington, D. C., 1953); Robert H. Keller, Jr., *American Protestantism and United States Indian Policy, 1869–82* (Lincoln, Neb., and London, 1983), pp. 176–80; Charles Ewing, *Circular of the Catholic Commissioner for Indian Missions, to The Catholics of the United States* (Baltimore, 1874); *HED*, 42-3-1, part 5, pp. 460–62.

On Oct. 13, 1870, Donato M. Gasparri, S. J., Albuquerque, had written to USG. "We the undersigned Members of the Society of Jesus, Albuquerque, Territory of New Mexico, respectfully and earnestly recommend the appointment of Captain Santiago L. Hubbell for appointment as U. S. Indian Agent for the Navajoe Indians. Capt. Hubbell has all the necessary qualifications being honest, capable, and an energetic business man. He has lived in the Territory for about twenty three years, and is connected by marriage with one of the best and most prominent families of the Territory. If it could be said of a citizen of the Republic, that he was entitled to an office on account of services rendered his Government this would be true in this Case, Capt. Hubbell having honorably served the Government of the United States both during the Mexican War, and the War of the Rebellion. The Captain would be in our humble opinion an acquisition to the Indian Bureau as an Indian Agent for these Indians, being perfectly conversant with the Spanish language which the majority of these Indians speak, and acquainted with their habits, customs, mode of life, and the country over which they roam. Without doubt his appointment will be satisfactory to the Indians, and to the people and a great auxiliary to the Government in the successful prosecution of its humane policy towards the wild tribes."—LS, DNA, RG 48, Appointment Papers, New Mexico Territory. Forwarded with an undated letter from Pierre J. De Smet, S. J., St. Louis, to Ely S. Parker, commissioner of Indian Affairs.—ALS, *ibid.* No appointment followed.

On Dec. 2, 1872, USG nominated Toussaint Mesplié as post chaplain, to date from Aug. 17. On Oct. 15, Mesplié, Washington, D. C., wrote to USG. "On behalf of the Catholic Church I have the honor to invite your excellency's attention to the fact that the Said Church is not represented on the Board of Indian Commissioners, the members of which are appointed by you to exercise a general Supervision over Indian affairs in accordance with the enactments of Congress   The Church which I have the honor to represent on this occasion has always taken a deep interest in the Christianization and civilization of the Indian tribes, as attested by her missionary labours on this continent since the year 1573, nearly one hundred years before any of the Sects had began to labour for the elevation of the aborigines. It is therefore with mortification that she finds herself ignored in the Board of Indian Commissions, composed of representatives of the various denominations, and respectfully asks that her claims be recognized   I am requested to present for your favorable Consideration the name of G. A. Vermarsch, a reverend Father of the church, who has devoted many years of his [l]ife as an Indian missionary in the far west and to [res]pectfully solicit his appointment as a member of said [Bo]ard, to fill the first vacancy occurring therin,   Be pleased to inform me of your action in the prem[ise]s at an early date"—LS, *ibid.*, Appointment Div., Letters Received. See *HED*, 42-2-1, part 5, pp. 730–31. For Mesplié, see letter to John M. Thayer, Dec. 22, 1870 (2); Cyril Van der Donckt, "The Founders of the Church in Idaho," *American Ecclesiastical Review*, XXXII, 1 (Jan., 1905), 1–19; *ibid.*, 2 (Feb., 1905), pp. 123–34; *ibid.*, 3 (March, 1905), pp. 280–91.

On [*May 13, 1873*], George Deshon wrote to USG concerning a decision not to redistribute some Indian agencies to Catholic missions. "I must frankly say to you that all my hopes of any justice in regard to our Catholic missions rest entirely on your good sense and determination to do right in spite of the opposition of your inferiors.... I cannot for a moment believe that you can concur in this, for you are not the man to deceive an old friend, and amuse him by false hopes when you intend to do nothing. No, you would rather tell me frankly to dismiss all hopes in the matter, if you meant to do nothing, rather than allow me to waste my time and worry myself with much anxiety and trouble, and finally be discredited as a credulous enthusiast, who expected much and realized nothing.... This will be the case unless you stand up for me and see that I get what is right and just. Every time I have seen you since your elevation to the Presidency, I have been impressed by your candor, friendliness and honesty of purpose, and I have only feared that in the multiplicity of business, my affairs might be crowded out and overlooked. As you have several times declared you would attend to them, I leave them in your hands with the utmost confidence and with a warm esteem and affection for you,..."—Copy (second ellipses in original), printed in Vincent F. Holden, "Was President Grant Really Anti-Catholic?" *Information: The Catholic Church in American Life*, 74 (Jan., 1960), 51; Rahill, pp. 93–94. See *PUSG*, 9, 478–79.

1872, JAN. 15.   USG endorsement. "Respectfully refered to the Atty. Gen. for his opinion upon the question asked by the Gov.r of this territory."— AES, DNA, RG 60, Letters from the President. On the same day, Governor Henry D. Cooke of D. C. had written to USG. "In order that the legislation of the Legislative Assembly of the District of Columbia may be valid, I desire the opinion of the Attorney General on the following point. to wit:— Whether the term of any session of that body, regular or called, except the 1st session as provided for in the concluding paragraph of section 5 of the organic act, can be legally continued beyond the term of sixty days. exclud-

ing holidays and sundays"—LS, *ibid.* On the same day, Attorney Gen.
George H. Williams wrote to USG that "no session of the legislative assem-
bly of the District can legally continue beyond the term of sixty days."—
Copy, *ibid.,* Opinions.

1872, JAN. 15. To Senate. "I transmit for the consideration of the Senate
with a view to ratification, a Convention between the United States and His
Majesty the Emperor of Germany relative to the rights, privileges and duties
of Consuls and to the protection of trade marks signed at Berlin, on the
eleventh ultimo. A copy of the despatch of the 11th ultimo, from Mr Bancroft, which accompanied the Convention is also transmitted for the information of the Senate."—DS, DNA, RG 46, Presidential Messages. Related
papers are *ibid.* On the same day USG transmitted a similar convention with
Austria-Hungary.—DS, *ibid.*

1872, JAN. 15. Lindsay Murdoch, collector of Internal Revenue, 2nd District, Mo., Marble Hill, to USG. "In the belief that your Excellency will not
consider this communication intrusive, I address you for the purpose of
making a statement relative to certain matters personal to myself and some
other Republicans in this locality   In regard to any difference there is between Col C. A. Newcomb U. S. Marshal and my self, it has arrisen on my
part, from a belief that he has failed to perform his whole duty in the arrest
of offenders against the law Revenue laws, and failure to do anything to
enforse the Ku Klux act, altho I have appealed to him frequently in person
and by letter, and requested others to do the same, he fully and completely
knows the miserable condition of affairs in South East Mo but from some
unexplained cause has wholly failed to give an intelligent co-operation with
my office in the suppression of irregularities tho frequently invited to do
so—... In regard to Assessor B. Smith, of my District, I accepted him just
as he is, and got along with him as I best could and made no complaints as
to his official conduct, until forced to do so in self defence—I have been the
receipiant on several occasions of the spiteful attentions of Col James Lindsay of the Pension office and I understand that he and Col Newcomb are
instigators of certain charges they intend to preferr against me ... I have
good reason to believe I have been the object of the unceasing hostility of
Assessor Smith, without any retaliation on my part, and that Gen McDonald
(Supervisor) drew the hostility of the assessor and that of his friend Newcomb on himself by taking my part and requesting him to mind his own
business—I believe he relies on his influence with Col Newcomb to be retained in position more than on any merits he posesses as an assessor and
is resorting to the cheap resource of petition to establish his reputation for
efficiensy and popularity very much under par in this district—I believe I
can successfully refute all charges made against me, andif there are any made
of sufficient gravity to demand an investigation—In the hope that your
Excellency will overlook any impropriety I may be guilty of in addressing
you on this subject ..."—ALS, DNA, RG 56, General Records. On March

30, A. M. Casebolt, editor, *Marble City Weekly News*, Cape Girardeau, wrote to USG. "I drop you this note simply to inform you of the gross insults practised upon the Republican party in this revenue district.—I learn that a man by the name of Richard Parker is making endeavors to secure the collectorship now filled by Lindsay Murdoch, who I understand is about to be removed. Under Murdoch's administration we have been controled by democrats appointed by Murdoch in our locality, and such men are doing us a vast amount of injury politically. This man Parker will carry out the same programme.—They do this in order to get the leading democrats to go as securities on their official bonds.—This matter we have had to contend with until it has become a difficult task to carry on successfully the present political struggle. Should the present incumbent, Murdoch be removed, we would suggest to your excellency the name of Judge Henry Bruihl of this county as a suitable person to fill the duties of the office. Mr. Bruihl is a man of age and experience, a true republican in every sense of the word, and should he be appointed, would not have to go outside of the Republican party to fill his offial bond.—Parker is a mere boy, about 22 years of age, inexperienced and would be compelled to resort to democrats to fill his bond.—I commenced the publication of the 'News' immediately after the surrender, and have fought against odds; yet if had not been for the negro, it would have been impossible to have succeeded.—With five sons I entered the army in 1861, and adhered faithfully to the cause during the entire rebellion,—Two of my sons bit the dust fighting under Sherman, and I grieve to see democrats and boys (as is the case here) holding office under the federal government. I would be highly pleased to have you take this matter under consideration, and give us men who are true in this trying hour, men who will help to sustain the party and not give their assistance to its enemies. We are determined to defeat the democratic party at all hazards."—ALS, *ibid.* Related papers are *ibid.* On March 25, 1873, USG nominated Alonzo B. Carroll to replace Murdoch.

1872, JAN. 15. Capt. Robert Nugent, 13th Inf., Camp Douglas, Utah Territory, to USG. "I have the honor to ask for the appointment at large of my Son Frederick F. Nugent, who is 16 years of age, to a Cadetship at West Point or the Naval Academy as it may please the President . . ."—ALS, DNA, RG 94, Correspondence, USMA. On Feb. 23, Lt. Gen. Philip H. Sheridan, Chicago, endorsed this letter. "Respectfully forwarded approved and recommended."—ES, *ibid.* On March 4, Maj. Gen. George G. Meade, Philadelphia, wrote to USG. "Capt. Robt Nugent 13th Infy Bvt Col. U. S. Army, advises me that he has made application for an appointment at large for his son to the Military or Naval Academy, and asks that I will certify to his professional record.—Capt Nugent's military history is given in 'Henry's History of of civilian appointments'—page 406;—and I take great pleasure in stating that whilst the Army of the Potomac, was in front of Petersburgh & during the operations terminating at Appomatox C. H—Capt Nugent comd as col of the 69th N. Y vols—commanded the 2d Brigade 1st Divn 2d Army corps (known as the Irish Brigade) with credit and distinction, and that in my judgment his military record during the war justifies his asking the favor from the Goverment which he seeks."—ALS, *ibid.* On Oct. 27, 1873, Nugent again requested from USG an at-large appointment to USMA for his son.— ALS, *ibid.* On Nov. 12, Sheridan endorsed this letter. "Captain Nugent is a good officer & nice gentleman—would like to see his son get an appointmt."—AES, *ibid.* Frederick Dent Grant also endorsed this letter. "I have placed this before the President of the united States & he directs me to forward it to the Adjutant General of the Army to be placed on file"— AES (undated), *ibid.* Related papers are *ibid.* No appointment followed.

1872, JAN. 16.   To Senate. "In answer to the Resolution of the Senate of the 16th of May last, calling for papers, correspondence and information relating to the case of the Ship 'Hudson' and 'Schooner 'Washington' I transmit reports from the Secretaries of State and of the Navy, and the papers by which they were accompanied"—DS, DNA, RG 46, Presidential Messages. *SED*, 42-2-19. On May 17, 1871, Secretary of the Navy George M. Robeson had written to USG. "I have the honor to acknowledge your reference to this Department of a copy of a Resolution, adopted by the Senate of the United States on the 16th instant, calling for information on the subject of the seizure of the American ships 'Hudson' and 'Washington' at the Falkland Islands, by the British Authorities, in the year 1854; and to transmit herewith a copy of a despatch dated April 1, 1854, from Commo. W. D. Salter, at that time commanding the Brazil Squadron, together with the report and correspondence therein mentioned, from Commander W. F. Lynch, regarding the subject of the Senate's inquiry."—LS, DNA, RG 46, Presidential Messages. On Jan. 16, 1872, Secretary of State Hamilton Fish wrote a similar letter to USG.—LS, *ibid.* Related papers are *ibid.*

1872, JAN. 16.   Commodore William Reynolds, Washington, D. C., to USG. "I beg leave respectfully to make application for an appointment for a Cadetship at West point for the class of 1874 for John Fulton Reynolds Landis, a nephew of the late Gen. John F Reynolds, and the son of H. D. Landis of Chestnut hill Philadelphia"—ALS, DNA, RG 94, Correspondence, USMA. Landis graduated USMA in 1878.

1872, JAN. 16.   Charles Butterfield, Yellow Springs, Ohio, to USG. "I trust you will pardon the liberty I have taken in adressing you a line, the nature of which I will be brief in stating   I am an Indian belonging to the Chippewa of Lake Superior having been away from my people for a year or more, but instructed Richard Smith our agent to retain the anuity money that I anually drew in his possession & subject to my order   I rec.d a letter from him in reply which He stated He would do so. But unfortunately the agent was last on the Steamer R. G. Coburn foundered on Saginaw Bay Lake Huron on his way home   I sent his letter also my own affidavt to the Commison of Indian affairs nearly two moncts ago but no notice has been taken of my

papers   I therefore Would most respectfuly ask that you will have the matter referrd   I am very poor with a family and find it very difficult to get
along away from my people among Strangers   I have submited this as all
our people say the Great Chief at Washington does not allow the agents to
Cheat us any more"—ALS, DNA, RG 75, Letters Received, Mackinac
Agency. On March 12, Butterfield, Cincinnati, wrote to Francis A. Walker,
commissioner of Indian Affairs, concerning this matter.—ALS, *ibid.*

1872, JAN. 17.   Capt. Ephraim D. Ellsworth, Mechanicville, N. Y., to USG.
"In April last through my Friend Mr. Dunn I forward my request to be
placed upon the retired List   That not beinge done then I had one year
Leave of absence granted me.   the Same reason I then gave for asking to
be placed upon the retired list Still exist and I am anxious for such disposition of my Case   will you pleas informe me of any thing further is nessaray
on my part and if so what course should be taken to accomplish the object
My age I was Sixty two years old Last May the 22."—ALS, DNA, RG 94,
ACP, 1900 1871. On June 8, 1870, Ellsworth, Vergennes, Vt., had written
to USG. "after my son Col Ellsworth was assassinated, I went on to Washington after his Horse and while thare President Lincoln said that his friends
wanted he should give me a position in the army. he asked me what I wanted
I tolde him that I was not capatable of filling any responcable position so
he gave me the position as Military Store Keeper in the ordnance department, and he wrote a line to Gen. Ripply to asign me an easy position &
he asign me to Champlain arsnal, V.t. an now I see by the papers that this
post is to be Solde, and I am geting old & feeble by having the newralaga &
rheumatism very bad, and got hurt two years ago by being thrown out of
my wagon . . ."—ALS, *ibid.* Related papers are *ibid.* See Lincoln, *Works,* IV,
385–86; *ibid.,* V, 192.

1872, JAN. 18.   USG endorsement. "Respectfully refered to the Sec. of State,
Dr Cameron prefering a Consulship to other appointment."—AES, DNA,
RG 59, Letters of Application and Recommendation. Written on a letter of
Jan. 10 from Anthony Higgins, U.S. attorney, Wilmington, Del., to USG. "I
take great pleasure in recommending to your favorable notice Dr John Cameron of this City and State who desires to obtain an official position under
the Federal Government. Dr Cameron is well known here as a gentleman
of high integrity, great worth of character, and ofor a most unflinching
support of advanced radicalism. Any appointment given him would aid a
most deserving republican, and secure to the Government a faithful and
capable public servant"—ALS, *ibid.* Related papers are *ibid.* No appointment followed.

1872, JAN. 20.   U.S. Senator John Sherman of Ohio to USG. "I have carefully
read all the papers on file in regard to the Postmaster at Chillicothe Ohio,
and am clearly of the opinion that *George P. Holcomb* ought to be appointed.
The weight of recommendation is with him and his fitness, merits and supe-

rior qualifications are fully established. Next to Holcomb in merit and qualifications stands Frank J. Esker, and he has the additional merit of having
been a soldier, and has had experience as a Deputy Postmaster. Wm W. Bond
is an excellent young man but his *recommenders* are mainly non resident. The
applications by the three Ladies named are not sufficiently supported by
evidence of qualification and local support. I therefore advise that Mr. Holcomb be appointed. As Gen Browne will not vacate the office for a month
or two you may be able to refer the case to an examining Board but it is a
question whether it is not better at once to close the matter before undue
controversy is excited—"—Copy, DLC-John Sherman. On Jan. 24, USG
nominated George P. Holcomb as postmaster, Chillicothe.

1872, JAN. 22. Secretary of War William W. Belknap to Lydia Slocum,
Clyde, Ohio. "The President has handed me your letter of the 2d inst., with
a request that I would inform you that he is utterly powerless to render you
any pecuniary assistance from the public treasury, in any way save by a
pension, if you are entitled to one; and your letter has accordingly been
referred to the Secretary of the Interior—who will inform you upon that
point—"—Copy, DNA, RG 107, Letters Sent. See *PUSG*, 11, 397–98.

1872, JAN. 22. U.S. Senator John Pool of N. C. to USG. "It would be very
gratifying to many of our friends in North Carolina, if William Lassiter
should be appointed to a Second Lieutenantcy in the Army. He is a very
steady & worthy young gentleman, of good education & excellent family
connections. His father is a prominent lawyer, & an unflinching friend of
the government, in North Carolina. He was true to the Union during the
War, & has suffered for it as much as anyone in the State. This appointment
of his son would be very gratifying to him & to all his friends throughout
the State"—ALS, DNA, RG 94, ACP, 3826 1873. On June 21, William W.
Holden, former governor, of N. C., and four N. C. supreme court justices,
Raleigh, wrote to USG urging Lassiter's appointment.—DS, *ibid.* Related
papers are *ibid.* On Oct. 1, 1873, USG appointed William Lassiter as 2nd
lt., 16th Inf.; Lassiter had attended USMA (1868–71).

1872, JAN. 23. Horace Porter to Jay Gould, New York City. "I have to
acknowledge the receipt of your letter of the 17th inst: and to request you
to accept the thanks of the President and myself for your politenes in extending the courtises of your rail road and Steamboat lines."—Copy, DLC-
USG, II, 1. On Jan. 3 and twice on Jan. 4, Porter had acknowledged similar
favors from railroad and freight officials.—Copies, *ibid.*

1872, JAN. 26. USG order. "The within recommendation of the Secretary
of the Interior is approved and certificates of allotment in the form proposed
will be issued by the Comr of Indian Affairs to the Santee Sioux Indians
entitled to allotments of land under the provisions of the Act of Congress
approved Mch 3d 1868"—Copy, DNA, RG 48, Indian Div., Letters Sent. On

the same day, Secretary of the Interior Columbus Delano had written to USG. "I have the honor to invite your attention to the accompanying report of the Commissioner of Indian Affairs, dated the 18th instant referring to the Act of Congress of the 3d March 1863, and the authority given by it to the President to set apart lands for certain Sioux Indians, and to assign 80 eighty acres each, to such as would adopt the pursuit of agriculture. The Indians known as the Santee Sioux desire to avail themselves of the benefit of said Act, and I enclose herewith a form of Certificate of allotment which the Commissioner suggests be issued to said Indians. I approve the suggestions of the Commissioner of Indian affairs and recommend that an order be issued by the Executive to carry the same into effect."—Copy, *ibid.* See *PUSG,* 19, 515–16; *HED,* 42-3-1, part 5, p. 596, 601–2; Roy W. Meyer, *History of the Santee Sioux: United States Indian Policy on Trial* (Lincoln, Neb., 1967), pp. 140–41, 162–63.

1872, JAN. 28. G. J. Skipwith, Dallas, to USG. "You may think it Strang my wrighting to you but nothing asked for nothing had & Prapes you may have forgoton me I was with you at Cairo a Steam Boatt Capt under Washinton Graham I was at Bellmont fort Donillson Run the Bolockade at Island no Ten with the Steamer Terray was at Pitsburg Landing Run the dispatch Boat Boath days of fight Run the Blockade at Vixbug all of witch I neaver drew anny Pay for as I neaver asked for it I Have Bin in Texis Sinse the Whar moast of the Time on the Rio Grand & I wold Like Soam Sithatation in the imployment of the Goaverment if you feele as I am deeserving of it & if So it Will thankfuly Received . . ."—ALS, DNA, RG 107, Appointment Papers.

1872, JAN. 29. USG endorsement. "Refered to the Sec. of War. If, after the apt. of the graduating class next June, there should be a vacancy of 2d Lt. in any Inf.y or Cavalry regt. Mr. Hogan may be aptd."—AES, DNA, RG 94, ACP, 4649 1873. Patrick H. Hogan was appointed 2nd lt., 1st Cav., as of July 27, 1872.

On Dec. 17, 1867, U.S. Representative Luke P. Poland of Vt. had written to USG. "Enclosed I hand you an application for the appointment of P. H. Hogan to a Lieutancy in the regular army—signed by all the Vt delegation who are now in the City. Mr. Hogan after what you said to us the other day does not expect an appt until after the 1st of July next. If then there shall remain a vacancy there, I very sincerely hope that Mr Hogan may be favorably considered. . . ."—ALS, *ibid.* Related papers are *ibid.* On March 17, 1869, Hogan, Washington, D. C., wrote to USG. "I have the honor respectfully to apply for the Appointment of 'Presidents Secretary to Sign Land Patents.' The enclosed Certificates from the Officers of the General Land Office in which I am employed as Clerk, show that I have discharged my duties well and faithfully. I served in the Army, in the First Vermont Vol Cav Regt during the late war, was twice wounded, and honorably discharged by reason of expiration of term of Service. I sincerely trust your Excellency will find it compatible with the interests of the public Service to nominate me for the above mentioned position."—ALS, *ibid.*, RG 48, Appointment Div., Letters Received.

1872, JAN. 30.   To Senate. "I nominate the following named Officers of the Quartermasters Department, for promotion in the Army of the United States, under the Act of July 28, 1866, and the Opinion of the Attorney General of the United States, dated January 22, 1872, copy herewith. . . ."— DS, DNA, RG 46, Nominations. Attorney Gen. George H. Williams ruled that vacancies in the q. m. dept. "above Assistant Quartermaster to the rank of Colonel, created by said act of July 28, 1866, are to be filled by promotion according to seniority, and not at the option of the President and Senate."— Copy, *ibid.* See *PUSG*, 16, 13–14. On Feb. 15, U.S. Senator Lyman Trumbull of Ill. submitted the judiciary committee's report on the nominations, which cited a March 3, 1869, act forbidding appointments and promotions in the q. m. and other depts. ". . . If it be deemed advisable to re-arrange the grade of officers in the Quartermaster and other Staff departments of the army your committee are of opinion that the appropriate manner of doing it would be by the enactment of a law for that purpose."—Copy, DNA, RG 46, Nominations. On March 6, U.S. Senator John A. Logan of Ill. introduced a bill authorizing the President to nominate "certain officers of the quartermaster's department to the positions they would have held in the department had the law of promotions by seniority been carried out under the act of July 28, 1866, to March 3, 1869 . . ."—*CG*, 42–2, 1449.
    On March 5, Secretary of War William W. Belknap wrote to USG. "I have the honor to transmit to you the enclosed request of several officers of the Quartermaster's Department for reconsideration of your action in the matter of recent nominations to the Senate of certain parties for appointment in the Quartermaster's Department of the Army."—Copies, DNA, RG 94, ACP, Letters Sent; *ibid.*, RG 107, Letters Sent, Military Affairs. On March 11, Maj. Gen. John M. Schofield, San Francisco, wrote to USG. "I am informed a Bill has passed the Senate and is now before the House, the purpose of which is a readjustment of grades of some some of the officers of the Quarter Masters Department, among whom is Lieut. Col. R. O. Tyler, now Chief Q. M. of this Division. Without entering upon the merits of the general question involved in this legislation, I beg leave to invite your attention to the fact that Col. Tylers appointment to his present rank was designed as a reward for distinguished and gallant services *in command of troops in the field,* where he was severely wounded, so much so as to unfit him for other than staff duty. It would be a very great hardship for an officer of Col. Tylers War record, upon which he received the well earned Brevet of Major General and rank of Lieut. Colonel in his Corps, to be degraded from a position so nobly earned, and which he has filled so long in an able and entirely satisfactory manner. Permit me, my dear General, to express the hope that Col. Tyler may not be subjected to this great humiliation."—Copy, DLC-John M. Schofield. See *PUSG*, 10, 458–59. USG had nominated Lt.

Col. Robert O. Tyler as maj., q. m.; on March 19, he withdrew this nomination along with the others made on Jan. 30, and explained this action to the Senate. "... This course is pursued in consequence of the question which has arisen as to the legality of the promotions proposed, and for the purpose of referring the case to the Attorney General for his opinion."—DS, DNA, RG 46, Nominations.

On June 3, Culver C. Sniffen wrote to Belknap. "The President has just approved (2 P. M.) S. 757—'An Act to authorize the appointment of certain officers in the Quartermasters Department,' and it geoe to the Secretary of State within 15 minutes."—ALS, *ibid.*, RG 94, ACP, 611 1872. Related papers are *ibid.* On June 4, USG renominated some officers previously nominated.

Index

All letters written by USG of which the text was available for use in this volume are indexed under the names of the recipients. The dates of these letters are included in the index as an indication of the existence of text. Abbreviations used in the index are explained on pp. xv–xx. Individual regts. are indexed under the names of the states in which they originated.